A History of Balance, 1250–

The ideal of balance and its association with what is ordered, just, and healthful remained unchanged throughout the medieval period. The central place allotted to balance in the workings of nature and society also remained unchanged. What changed within the culture of scholasticism, between approximately 1280 and 1360, was the emergence of a greatly expanded sense of what balance is and can be. In this groundbreaking history of balance, Joel Kaye reveals that this new sense of balance and its potentialities became the basis of a new model of equilibrium, shaped and shared by the most acute and innovative thinkers of the period. Through a focus on four disciplines – scholastic economic thought, political thought, medical thought, and natural philosophy – Kaye's book reveals that this new model of equilibrium opened up striking new vistas of imaginative and speculative possibility, making possible a profound rethinking of the world and its workings.

JOEL KAYE is Professor in the Department of History at Barnard College, Columbia University. His previous publications include *Economy and Nature in the Fourteenth Century: Money, Market Exchange, and the Emergence of Scientific Thought* (Cambridge, 1998).

A History of Balance, 1250–1375

The Emergence of a New Model of Equilibrium and its Impact on Thought

Joel Kaye

Barnard College, Columbia University

CAMBRIDGE
UNIVERSITY PRESS

University Printing House, Cambridge CB2 8BS, United Kingdom

Cambridge University Press is part of the University of Cambridge.

It furthers the University's mission by disseminating knowledge in the pursuit of
education, learning and research at the highest international levels of excellence.

www.cambridge.org
Information on this title: www.cambridge.org/9781316620281

© Joel Kaye 2014

First published 2014
First paperback edition 2016

A catalogue record for this publication is available from the British Library

ISBN 978-1-107-02845-6 Hardback
ISBN 978-1-316-62028-1 Paperback

Contents

Illustrations

Acknowledgments

In the dozen years that I have been working on this book, I have relied on the help and support of many people and institutions, and I have accumulated many large debts of gratitude. I realize that by listing their names I can provide them only a very partial requital and an equally partial sense of what I owe them, but at the least it is a start. To begin with, I could not have brought this project to conclusion without the help of those colleagues who read and offered insightful comments on one or more chapters over the years: Caroline Bynum (whose wisdom I have relied on from beginning to end), Paul Freedman, Joanne Freeman, Martha Howell, Adam Kosto, Michael McVaugh, Edward Peters, David Reisman, Neslihan Senocak, Nancy Siraisi, Pamela Smith, Heinrich von Staden, Paul Strohm, Edith Sylla, Simon Teuscher, Lisa Tiersten, Giacomo Todeschini, Peter Travis, Carl Wennerlind, and my anonymous readers at Cambridge University Press.

I offer my thanks and my gratitude as well to those scholars who showed a generous interest in my project over the years and who shared their thoughts on particular aspects of it. Even a partial list must include Brigitte Bedos-Rezak, Ann-Marie Bouché, Carolyn Collette, Giles Constable, Emma Dillon, Susan Einbinder, Carmela Franklin, Barbara Hanawalt, Robert Hanning, Lisa Kiser, Lester Little, Maaike van der Lugt, Robert Somerville, and my trusted colleagues in History at Barnard. I add here Sophie Forrester, for her excellent editorial advice on the whole manuscript, and Deborah Shulevitz for her assistance in its preparation.

Finally, there are those, outside the circle of academe, who have literally lived this project with me, plying me with questions over years of dinners, patiently inquiring about my progress, and silently willing me to finish. Of these, I must mention Christine Doudna, Steve Fraser, Serge and Anne-Marie Gavronsky, Wendy Gimbel, Bart Gulley, Rick Grand-Jean, Sally Helgesen, Bailey and Susan Kuklin, Doug Liebhafsky, Jane Lurie, Chuck, Gabriel, and Benjamin Reich, Alexi and Remy-Bess Steinfink, and Jean Strouse.

As important as my friends, family, and colleagues have been, I could never have completed a project of this size without the generous support of research institutions and funding agencies, along with the people who serve and direct them. My project began with a National Endowment for the Humanities (NEH) fellowship in 2000, during which I sketched a research plan for my project on the history of balance and began to look in the direction of medieval medicine. Holding, as I did, the vague notion that Galenic medicine was associated with "the balance of the humors," I thought I would investigate further. At the end of this semester's leave, after having spent six weeks as a visitor at the American Academy at Rome (at the invitation of its director, Lester Little) researching medical manuscripts at the Biblioteca Vaticana, I began to realize how vast and bountiful was the intellectual landscape I had wandered into. On the basis of this first foray into medicine, I applied for and was awarded a year-long National Science Foundation (NSF) book-project grant for 2001−2 to continue my studies of this subject. I spent much of the NSF year reading early printed editions of Galenic writings and their scholastic commentaries in the Rare Book Room of the New York Academy of Medicine, where I relied on the kind assistance of its librarians, Miriam Mandelbaum and Arlene Shaner.

To the extent that my teaching allowed, I continued my study of medicine until 2003−4, when I was admitted as a scholar in residence to the Institute for Advanced Studies, School of Historical Studies. That year I wrote the book's first chapter (the current Chapter 3) on the legacy of Galenic balance and I made a start on the scholastic reception of Galenic balance. I cannot thank everyone who made my stay at the Institute so rewarding, but I must mention two who helped me more than I can say: Caroline Bynum, in her key role as the faculty member in European medieval history, and Marian Zelazny, the indispensable administrative officer of the School of Historical Studies.

In 2007−8, I had the great good fortune to spend a year as a fellow at the Dorothy and Lewis B. Cullman Center for Scholars and Writers at the New York Public Library. During my residence there, in the presence of wonderful colleagues, and under the leadership of its excellent director, Jean Strouse, I wrote most of the three chapters devoted to the question of balance in medieval political thought.

My work on the two chapters on scholastic economic thought was greatly aided by a resident fellowship at the Liguria Study Center in Bogliasco, Italy, in the spring of 2010. The staff, physical setting, and congenial group of fellows at Bogliasco provided an idyllic environment for study and contemplation. I completed the writing of these two chapters that same summer in Princeton as a visitor at the Institute for Advanced Study, School of Historical Studies.

Over the last two years, I wrote the concluding chapter on balance in scholastic natural philosophy, and I composed the book's Introduction and Conclusion. To do so, I relied on the library of Smith College in the summers and on Columbia's Butler Library and the library of the General Theological Seminary in Chelsea during the school year (aided by several course releases from Barnard College). I am deeply grateful to each of these fine libraries and institutions.

In a time when historians and even whole departments of history have begun to be assessed in terms of quantitative production, judged in terms of the number of articles (or even pages) published yearly: when as a result scholars (particularly young scholars) are increasingly urged to publish often, and consequently early; and when academic presses are ever more intent on enforcing shrinking word limits on manuscripts they will accept, I offer my sincere thanks to Barnard College for its unhesitating support over the many years of this project, and to Cambridge University Press for accepting a manuscript that greatly exceeds the length dictated by current norms.

There are, finally, three people in my life to whom I am most profoundly indebted. Two are my sisters, Julie and Carole, who have loved and supported me for so long that they have become, quite simply, a part of me and will always live in my heart. The third is my wife Thea, my true love, my inspiration, and my source of strength. Over these past years she has given more to me and to the writing of this book than I can possibly express in words. I dedicate this book to her with all my heart.

Introduction

A concern with balance and the requirement for balance was central to virtually every intellectual discipline in the medieval period. The ideal of *aequitas*, represented by the scales of justice, lay at the heart of the discipline of law; the vast scholastic literature on ethics came to be centered on the Aristotelian concept of the equalizing mean or *medium*; the balancing of sin against penance and grace was central to the economy of salvation in penitential theory; in mathematics the equation received increased attention after the mid twelfth century with the Latin translation and diffusion of Al-Khwarizmi's *Algebra*, or *Compendious Book on Calculation by Completion and Balancing*. In the discipline of medicine, concern with balance and equalization was, quite simply, everywhere, with the central aim of medical practice universally held to be the restoration of systematic balance (*aequalitas* or *temperamentum*, in their terms) to the body that was losing or had lost it. In literature one can point to the continuing centrality of the ideal of "mesure," which signified the maintenance of personal balance in the face of life's trials, and above all to Dante's *Commedia*, which opens with the author lost in the woods at the mid-point (*nel mezzo*) of his life, and ends with a paradisiacal vision of perfect balance, "la forma universale," the cosmic antidote to the personal, social, political, and religious imbalance that preoccupied the author.

In the chapters that follow, I show that preoccupations with balance lay at the core of medieval economic thought (Chapters 1 and 2), medical theory (Chapters 3 and 4), political thought (Chapters 5 to 7), and natural philosophy (Chapter 8), and I argue that an analysis of the forms of balance that are assumed and applied within these disciplines are crucial both to their formation and to their scholarly comprehension. The preponderance and sheer weight of this concern raises the question: is balance a universal and unchanging state or ideal, or can it assume different forms from culture to culture and even within the same culture? Can the sense of what constitutes balance change over time?

My book provides evidence for a series of claims: that balance has a history; that between approximately 1280 and 1360 a radically new sense of balance and its potentialities emerged and evolved within the upper levels of university speculation; that this new sense of balance served as the ground of speculation in multiple and widely varying disciplines; and that, consequently, changes in the sense and imagination of what might constitute balance had the effect of opening up striking new vistas of imaginative and speculative possibility. I will argue that, from the late thirteenth through the mid fourteenth century, this new sense of balance came to underlie the most innovative and forward-looking speculations within scholastic thought. Within these speculations, whose boldness, scope, and brilliance can still be appreciated today, we can see evidence of a profound re-visioning of the image of the world and its workings.

Countless words and concepts have changed over time and thus can be said to have a history. But balance, I want to suggest, is different. Even in our common understanding today, balance is tied to a generalized and mostly unconscious *sense* – our physical awareness of our bodies and selves within our environment(s). It finds expression as an unworded *feeling* for how objects and spaces are or ought to be arranged; as an *apprehension* of how things properly fit together and work together in the world. The sense we have of its presence or absence in large measure determines our judgment of what is right or wrong, ordered or disordered, healthful or dangerous. Judgments grounded in the sense of balance extend to an exceedingly wide range of subjects, from profound speculations on social, economic, aesthetic, political, and cosmic order down to our unease when we see a picture hanging unevenly on a wall.

Recognition of the wide range of subjects within which the sense of balance comes into play allows us to appreciate its great importance to our psychological, intellectual, and social life, but it also tends to encourage a biological and hence essentialist understanding of it. Since we recognize that balance as an interior sense is natural to ourselves and to all humans, it is hard for us to imagine it as developing within specific cultural contexts and as changing in form over historical time. Balance is balance: we all know what we mean by it; we all trust our sense of it; we never imagine that it is changing or even can change, and we certainly never think of ourselves as agents of its change. This is not only true today: it was the case with every thinker I consider in this book, even as I assign them an active role in the project of reshaping balance and reimagining its potentialities.

Despite the central place that the concern for balance held in virtually every intellectual sphere within medieval thought (or, perhaps, *because* of its inescapable centrality), it was almost never brought to the fore as a subject of discussion in itself. It acted as the pervasive *ground* of thought rather than as a recognizable subject of thought, and as such it exercised its great influence beneath the surface of verbal expression and conscious recognition. For this reason, modern historians, too, have so far failed to recognize balance in the medieval period (or in any period, for that matter) as a subject in itself or to imagine it as changing in form over historical time, shaped within specific cultural contexts. My project is to bring balance from the periphery to the center of historical inquiry. With all the difficulties involved in historicizing a subject that was never itself a subject of explicit scrutiny and discussion, there are, I hope to show, great advantages to be gained by doing so.

Having made these preliminary claims about balance, I quickly add that the word "balance" (*bilancia*) itself, and its close relative "equilibrium" (*aequilibrium*), only rarely appeared in medieval writings. When they did, their use and meaning rarely transcended their original ties to the common mechanical scale (*bilanx*) and the simple equality of two equally balanced weights (*aequi-librium*) that the scale was designed to find and measure. In the medieval period neither term had gained the metaphorical and mathematical breadth they enjoy today when we routinely speak of fields, systems, or multiple forces "in balance" or "in equilibrium."[1] In the absence of the *words* "balance" and "equilibrium," Latin thinkers used a cluster of related terms to convey many of the meanings we attach to these words today. At the center of this cluster was the word "equality" (*aequalitas*) and its cognates: *aequalis, aequus, aequare, aequabilis, aequivalentia, adaequatio, aequitas*, and others. In addition to these words, other weighty concepts were harnessed to the near-universal concern for attaining and maintaining balance/*aequalitas*. Among these were *justitia, temperantia, symmetria, medium, medietas*, and *proportionalitas*.[2] The frequency and plasticity with which these terms were used indicates that the absence in the medieval period of the words equivalent to our "balance" and "equilibrium" in no way speaks to the parallel absence of many of the meanings now conveyed by these words.

While the words and terms expressing the ideal of balance/*aequalitas* held fairly firm throughout the medieval period, the spoken and unspoken meanings attached to these words changed profoundly, with a dramatic

---

[1] From the evidence of the *Oxford English Dictionary*, it is only in the later seventeenth century that these words come to be applied to a dynamic state in which multiple objects and forces are systematically ordered and integrated within a relational field.

[2] In ancient Greek, *meson* (middle), *mesotês* (medium), *isonomia* (equality), and *symmetria* perform the same function. The situation in Latin is reflected in Charles Du Cange, *Glossarium mediae et infimae Latinitas*, 10 vols. (Graz: Akademische Druck- u. Verlaganstalt, 1954), where the meanings allotted to *aequilibrium* and all of its cognates (*aequilibratio, aequilibritas*, etc.) occupy less that one-quarter of a column (vol. I, col. 1008), while for comparison, the meanings attached to *aequalis* occupy six columns, *aequitas* receives eight columns, and *aequus* eighteen columns. *Bilanx* is allotted a mere six lines (vol. II, col. 1985), with no expansion of meaning beyond the mechanical scale.

shift occurring over the period 1280–1360. The ideal of balance and its association with what is ordered, just, fitting, and healthful remained unchanged. The central place allotted to it in the structure and activity of the cosmos remained unchanged. What changed within the culture of scholasticism was the range of possibility and potentiality attached to the sense of what balance is and can be. In order, therefore, to convey the story of this transformation and to appreciate its effects, it is necessary to go past the words themselves in search of the evolving apprehension or unworded *sense* that lay beneath them – the sense of what constituted the desired state of *aequalitas* (in their terms) or balance (in ours), and the sense of how this state might be achieved and maintained.

The problem is how to talk about and describe the changes in this unworded sense. Although my intent is to link the history of balance to the history of ideas, it is clear that balance in the medieval period cannot be thought of or treated as an "idea" in the normal understanding, since it was never verbalized or communicated directly and intentionally from thinker to thinker. Even the word "concept" carries too many connotations of conscious definition to be applied to it. But although the complex sense of what actually constituted *aequalitas* remained unworded across the medieval period (as it does in almost all pre-modern periods and cultures), it was far from unstructured. Indeed, I want to argue that this compound and complex sense, although open to change and variation, nevertheless possesses a degree of internal cohesion and coherence sufficient to allow it to be recognized and identified as a particular and definable "model," with the understanding that under certain circumstances, new "models of balance" can take shape and come to supplant (or complement) earlier models.

Just as balance has both a passive meaning (i.e., the equalized end or goal of a process) and an active meaning (i.e., the process of attaining that end), so it can be modeled in two ways. In what follows I designate the desired *state* of balance, "the model of equality," and the conjoined sense of the *process(es)* through which this state might be achieved and maintained, "the model of equalization." By using the word "model" I intentionally foreground the *sensible* attributes of shape, working order, and patterned motion that give weight and generative intellectual power to the underlying sense of balance/*aequalitas*. By attaching words like "shape," "weight," and "working order" to my understanding and application of the term "model," words that emphasize the sensible and the particular, I hope to underscore the fundamental differences between my use of the term and the way it is commonly understood and applied in the social sciences today. "Models," in my application of the term, are not abstractions, not generalizations, and not idealized representations.

As I have come to imagine and apply them, models of equality and equalization are composed of a cluster of interlocking assumptions, both implicit and explicit, both conscious and unconscious, which together form a coherent and cohesive *unity*, characterized by a high degree of internal logic and interior reflectivity. They are highly distinctive and individualized structures, which have a real existence and presence within the mind.[3] Indeed, in the period I study, where the expectation and requirement of balance provided the ground of speculation in discipline after discipline, I have found that models of equality and equalization possessed remarkable power – nothing short of the power to determine both the limits and the possibilities of what could be imagined, envisioned, and comprehended.

Although models are open to profound changes in their elements and in their effects on thought and imagination, they possess sufficient similarities from one to the other to permit comparison and to make possible the recognition of a pattern to their evolution. The way I have come to see it, there was one dominant model that had been shaped and shared by the most innovative and influential scholastic thinkers over the period *c.* 1225–75.[4] Then, in the last decades of the thirteenth century, a new way of modeling equality and equalization began to emerge within university culture that was strikingly different in form and effect from the earlier one it (partially) displaced. For reasons that I discuss throughout the book, this "new model of equalization" is the first of the medieval period that merits being characterized at the same time a "model of equilibrium." The emergence of this "new" model of equilibrium and the intellectual effects that flowed from it form the central themes of this book.

What, then, are the major distinguishing elements of the new model of equilibrium that emerged and evolved between 1280 and 1360, and how do these elements differ from those that comprised the previously dominant model? For the sake of clarity, I have assigned a separate paragraph to each of the new model's primary elements. I want to stress, however, that models are active and *working* entities, whose interior logic binds the totality of their elements into a functional unity. Since all the elements work together and reinforce each other, none can be neatly detached and considered in isolation. Thus, the order in which I list the elements can offer only an approximation of the prominence and importance of each to the functioning whole. I limit myself to naming only those elements that are integral to

---

[3] Given current debates and uncertainties concerning the characterization of "deep mental structures," I have chosen not to apply the term, as evocative as it is, either to the sense of balance or to models of equality and equalization.
[4] I describe the features of this earlier model in Chapter 5.

the logic that binds the new model of equilibrium. In my description of these elements here, my goal is to be as concise as possible, since they are considered in detail at various points in the body of the text. I note that many of the elements I list here differ profoundly, whether in degree or kind, from those that constituted all previous medieval models of equalization.

- **The potentialities of systematic self-ordering and self-equalizing are recognized and explored**.
  The new model is characterized by the striking imagination that the working system is capable of ordering itself and equalizing (balancing) itself simply through the dynamic interaction of its working parts. This apprehension of what might in modern terms be called "dynamic equilibrium" or "systematic equilibrium" sets the "new" model apart from all others that preceded it.
- **Balance comes to be viewed as an aggregate product of systematic activity**.
  Where formerly balance had been viewed as a precondition of existence, built into Nature in the Aristotelian scheme, or instilled into creation by a creating God, now the focus shifted to the visualization and exploration of complex functioning systems in which balance (*aequalitas*) came to be seen as an *aggregate product* of the systematic interaction of multiple moving parts within the whole.
- **Focus shifts from the individual part to the systematic whole**.
  The new model is marked by a shift in analytical focus from the individual, its individual nature, and its place within a fixed hierarchy or ontology, to the working system of which it is a functioning part. The meaning of the part comes to be subsumed within the meaning of the whole.
- **Within the working whole, faith in the systematic process of interior self-ordering replaces the need for an exterior orderer or overarching ordering intelligence**.
  Where the existence of an overarching unitary mind or divine intelligence was the virtual precondition for the establishment of order and equality in older medieval models of balance, in the new model the dynamic intersection of diverse parts within the working whole is sufficient in itself to achieve and maintain *aequalitas*. The imagination of systematic self-ordering and self-equalizing is thus linked to the potentially subversive recognition that the interior logic of the working whole (e.g., the physical body, the body politic, the city, the marketplace, or nature itself) is capable of replacing overarching mind or intelligence as the basis of its order and equalization.[5]

---

[5] I say "potentially subversive" because for the most part those thinkers who took this recognition furthest (e.g., Peter of John Olivi, Arnau de Villanova, William of Ockham,

- **Aggregation, externalization, and depersonalization come to characterize systematic analysis.**
  With the shift in focus from the individual to the aggregate "unity" comes a parallel shift in intellectual interest away from inherent interior qualities and natures and toward the details of motion, activity, and change.
- **The knowledge sought and valued is public in contrast to private knowledge; open in contrast to hidden or secret knowledge.**
  The strong partiality toward knowledge that is public, open, and arrived at through universalized forms of reasoning and logic, which characterizes the new model, distinguishes it not only from certain models that preceded it in time, but notably from models that immediately succeeded it in time, in which the personal, the private, and the secret were once again identified with true knowledge.
- **Relational thinking replaces hierarchical thinking.**
  Relativity replaces hierarchy as the basis of order and identity within the moving system. The value and identity of individual parts, rather than being fixed by nature, are assumed to be fluid and relational, determined with respect to their ever-shifting position and function within the systematic whole now conceived as a relational field. Order and equalization are seen to come from the interacting parts within the system itself, rather than from the top down. Indeed, the working system possesses no fixed top, bottom, or center.
- **Relational thinking proves to be transformational.**
  The focus of analysis shifts from the consideration of fixed and normative values to an ever more sophisticated understanding of the implications of relativist determinations. As thinkers come to recognize that varying points of reference result in widely varying determinations, relativity enters and transforms the realm of perception. Relativistic thinking comes to permeate the understanding of the structure and working principles of all systematic activity, including that of the cosmos itself.

Nicole Oresme) show no signs that they associated it with a limitation of divine power. Indeed, each of these thinkers also contributed to the theological current that asserted the absolute power of God (*potentia dei absoluta*) in the strongest terms. But while they assumed and asserted that God had the power to intervene in every realm of order at any time, they also envisioned and speculated on the workings of self-ordering and self-equalizing systems in naturalistic terms, without reference to this intervention. The distinction between God's absolute power to intervene and the power that God actually exercised (*potentia dei ordinata*) became one of the great themes of the fourteenth century. On the other hand, speculations grounded in the new model of equilibrium turned, at times, toward explicit critiques of both royal and papal assertions of their authority to impose order from above.

- **Proportionality is redefined and reapplied as the language of proportion and ratio comes to predominate.**
  Since proportions and ratios are themselves relations, the language of proportion and ratio comes to dominate mathematical analysis in all disciplines. Ratios and proportions, rather than being taken (as previously) as fixed markers of identity, are now imagined to shift continually in relation to the shifting position and function of parts within the whole. The systematic goal of *aequalitas* is consistently understood in proportional terms that shift with respect to shifting contexts and functions (*aequalitas ad iustitiam*) rather than as an absolute determination fixed precisely at 1:1 (*aequalitas ad pondus*).
- **Lines replace points, fluidity replaces fixity, and concern with the details of motion and change replaces the search for essences and perfections.**
  In the ongoing analysis of the self-equalizing system, the ideal of fixity gives way to the acceptance of fluidity; the philosophical search for essences and perfections gives way to the passion to apply quantification and schemes of measurement to change and motion. Measurement by the discrete and numbered point gives way to measurement by means of the graded line or continuous "latitude" (*latitudo*), capable of fluid expansion and contraction and thus applicable to the newly dynamic and complex process of systematic equalization.
- **The conceptual creation of a "world of lines" opens the way to measurement by continuous "latitudes."**
  The image of the world and the working systems that comprise it is transformed from one composed of discrete points and perfections to one composed of ever-expanding, contracting, and intersecting lines – what I call "a world of lines." The recognition that the continuum was fundamental both to the structure of the cosmos and to its comprehension was a dominant feature of scholastic thought from the beginning of the thirteenth century. But thinkers associated with the new model of equilibrium expand the conceptualization and employment of the line as a medium of measurement and relation to another level entirely. This expansion was signaled by the greatly expanded role and elaboration of the measuring *latitudo* in their speculations.
- **The underlying mathematics moves from arithmetic to geometry.**
  Within the new setting of a world of lines, a fluid geometry replaces arithmetic as the basis of both mathematical and philosophical analysis and understanding.
- **The underlying mathematics moves from addition and subtraction to multiplication, while at the same time it moves beyond integers into the realm of exponential powers.**
  The mathematics of the new model expands from its ground in addition

and subtraction to comprehend the reality of rapid, even exponential, multiplication. Scholars move beyond working with integers in their analysis and explanation of systematic activity, to work and speculate with exponential powers. Multiplication moves from being feared and shunned as an inherently destabilizing factor (in all but the spiritual realm) and becomes a factor capable of being integrated into the reimagined ideal of *aequalitas*.

- **Estimation and approximation are accepted as legitimate and necessary ways of knowing**.

  Given the complexity, fluidity, and relativity built into the modeling of the working system, thinkers began to accept estimation and approximation as legitimate ways of knowing and measuring. Indeed, those who shared in the new model often noted that estimation and approximation were the *only* ways that humans can know and measure entities undergoing constant motion and change. The abandonment of the possibility of full and perfect knowledge accompanied the abandonment of absolutes and individual perfections as the primary objects of philosophical investigation.

- **Probability and probabilistic reasoning are accepted and employed**.

  Where in earlier models of equalization the "merely probable" had no ontological status, it attains such status within the new model. No true mathematics of probability developed in this period, but what did develop was the understanding that probabilities represent a real (if discounted) "appreciable value" (*valor appreciabilis*) that can be estimated and employed in the process of analysis. The inescapable indeterminism attached to systematic activity within the new model opened the way for the acceptance and integration of probabilistic thinking.

- **Good function becomes a primary consideration**.

  The capacity of the system simply to work and work well (i.e., to maintain itself in balance/*aequalitas*) is taken *in itself* as a sign of its value, without reference to its capacity to work toward ends that conform to traditional or hierarchical ideals. Indeed, the recognition that a system works well compels, in certain cases, the revaluation of traditional beliefs and ideals that the system either ignores or transgresses. Questions posed increasingly center on the problematic "how does it work," not on why it works, or to what ideal ends it works, or whether its workings conform to normative expectations. This element activates some of the model's most transformative effects.

- **"Fittingness" appears as a prime value in itself**.

  As parts are judged in terms of their capacity to contribute to the proper working of the whole (rather than with respect to their inherent individual natures), the determination of what qualifies as "fitting" (*decens, compe-tens, conveniens*) becomes a primary concern, as do questions regarding the specific fit of parts to parts and parts to whole. Good fit in terms of function (*conveniens ad opus*) comes to be recognized as essential to the systematic attainment and maintenance of *aequalitas*.

- **Positive value is granted to difference and diversity**.
  This element accompanies many of the conjectures that most clearly reflect the new model of equilibrium. In a number of cases, the proper working of systematic activity is specifically said to depend on the existence of a diversity of parts and powers, with the tension produced by difference and opposition acting as a critical engine of the process.
- **The new modeling of balance is invested with transformative power**.
  Within the dynamic of the working system, individual parts that are *un*equal or *im*balanced or *ir*rational or *dis*ordered in themselves and their natures can nevertheless find balance and equalization in the natural play of objects, functions, and forces that comprise the func-tioning whole. Scholars begin to speculate that unbalanced, unequal, and even antagonistic parts can actually facilitate the balancing of the whole. This represents a sharp departure from all previous medieval models.
- **Examples of the model's transformative effects**.
  Entities which had formerly been shunned as destabilizing and inimical to the process of equalization, such as doubt, risk, indeterminance, rampant multiplication, the unbounded, the infinite, the mathematically incommensurable and "irrational," even willed inequalities, were now, within the new model of equilibrium, open to being integrated into the process of producing and maintaining systematic *aequalitas*. Within the new modeling of balance, the individual thing or nature was "freed" in a sense from the necessity of carrying balance within itself, even from carrying meaning within itself. This "freeing" within the new model of equilibrium dovetails with the evolution in this period of philosophical nominalism and the movement toward a minimalist ontology associated with William of Ockham.
- **The new model of balance is differentiated from harmony**.
  This final element is distinguished by its absence rather than its pres-ence. Although the ancient ideal of harmony can match up well with certain models of equalization, including all previous medieval models, it does *not* map onto the new model of equilibrium and differs from it in essential ways. The most astute recognition of their differ-ences appears in the writings of the philosopher/theologian Nicole Oresme (*c.* 1320–82), in his speculations on the structure and order

of the heavens.[6] I will let Oresme, whose speculations represent some of the purest instantiations of the new model of equilibrium, outline the differences in his own words, but I add a few words here. Harmony is an unchanging ideal that is built upon the fixed, precise, and knowable ratios of whole numbers. On the contrary, the proportions that constitute *aequalitas* within the new modeling of balance are understood to be fluid and in flux, varying continuously with respect to position within the relational field and the requirements of function. Indeed, the perfect 1:1 equality of two precisely equal and numerable quantities that the mechanical balance achieves (*aequalitas ad pondus*) is recognized again and again to be either absent from or actually inimical to life. One of the striking implications of the new model, and one of the factors that makes its emergence so historically significant, is that those who shared in it and speculated on its terms renounced many of the most intellectually comforting aspects associated with the ancient ideal of harmony: fixity, purity, precision, perfect numerability, perfect knowability, and the reassuring assumption that natural activity conformed to the human mind and made sense in human terms.

I have introduced the elements of the new model of equilibrium here in their most general form. In the chapters that follow, I present the particular forms that these elements take and the particular way they cluster in varied disciplines. What is clear, I hope, is how complex and many-faceted models of balance can be, and how utterly intertwined their elements are: each supports each; each comes back to each. When a cluster of concepts link to form a meaning-web of such complexity and reflectivity, its weight and impact is multiplied far beyond the sum of its parts. It becomes more than a collection – it becomes, in their terms, a "unity" (*unitas*), a cohesive working whole. It possesses a characteristic feel, a characteristic motion, a characteristic rhythm, which can be sensed and experienced. As the cluster takes on these quasi-sensible qualities of weight, motion, and rhythm, it becomes, in my definition, a "model." Models, in turn, due to their inner cohesion and high degree of interior reflectivity, possess sufficient weight and force to alter and redirect perceptions and thoughts. Moreover, the continuation of models (including the new model of equilibrium) over decades leads me to surmise that the weight they accumulate also gives them the capacity to persist – to maintain their status and structure in the face of all but the most profound perturbations to their formative environments.

---

[6] Oresme's speculations in this area appear in Chapter 8.

In every case, I hope to show that each of the elements listed above, taken both singly and as parts of an interconnected and integrated model of balance/*aequalitas*, underlay – indeed, actively directed – the most innovative speculations that appeared across widely varying intellectual disciplines over the period 1280–1360. The phenomenon of the model's appearance across these widely divergent fields, along with its power to organize and redirect essential insights when it does appear, points to the highly significant role that the history of balance plays in the history of ideas in this period and, I suspect, in all periods. That many of the elements that constitute the "new" model differ markedly from those that had constituted all previous medieval models of equalization, adds further to the importance of pursuing a *history* of balance, rather than merely considering it in terms of its basis in biology or brain function. At the same time it raises the question: how does a change of this magnitude occur? What might lie behind the transformation of balance, given that the subject itself was never raised, never explicitly recognized, and certainly never debated within the intellectual culture of scholasticism? And given that models of equalization lie beneath the level of consciousness and are rarely if ever communicated directly or subjected to criticism, how do they come to be shared by thinkers across disciplines? How can we explain the direction they take and the forms they assume?

I have already suggested that models of balance/*aequalitas* have a real presence and exert a real force within the human mind. At the same time, I want to argue that even though they are never explicitly recognized or verbalized, these models are both shared and shaped within particular intellectual cultures. The construction of the model is to a large degree a common, if unconscious, project. To the extent that individual thinkers share with others an intellectual inheritance, a socioeconomic and political environment, and an institutional setting with particular institutional goals, values, and training, they are open to communally sharing (and shaping) a model of equalization. At the same time, it is highly unlikely that every member of such a community will come to possess the same model or to possess it in the same degree. The fully realized form and effects of the "new model of equilibrium" are present in only a portion of scholastic writings from the late thirteenth to the mid fourteenth century. It is significant, however, that the scholastic writings in which the model does appear are those that are commonly recognized today as being particularly acute, astute, and forward-looking. Indeed, I want to argue that there is a direct connection between the capacity to sense the new potentialities of balance inherent in the new model of equilibrium and the capacity to move to the forefront of this very competitive intellectual culture. Those who had fully intuited and could apply the new model could see things, imagine things, and speculate on things that those who had not could not.

As I have come to see and apply them, models are generated in three distinct yet mutually reinforcing ways. One way is through the scholar's intellectual apprehension and internalization of forms of equalization embedded within authoritative texts. In this work I focus on two major examples of this sort: (1) the reception and reworking by scholastic *medici* of the detailed and sophisticated modeling of bodily *aequalitas* found in the medical writings of Galen of Pergamum (d. *c.* 216 CE), which by the end of the thirteenth century became available to thinkers in fields far afield from medicine; and (2) the reception of the writings of Aristotle, particularly concerning his analysis of the forms of equalization underlying justice in the *Nicomachean Ethics*, and his analysis of equalization in the *Politics* as it pertains to the formation of law and the process of election.

A second way the model is shaped is through the scholar's participation in an intellectual culture. Within such cultures, the assumptions that underlie the model of balance/*aequalitas* may never be the subject of conscious analysis or debate in themselves. Nevertheless, they are open to being "sensed" or intuited by the deepest and most sensitive readers and thinkers as they are passed back and forth through the mutual exchange of texts and insights. The universities of Bologna, Padua, Montpellier, Oxford, and Paris in the later thirteenth and fourteenth centuries provide excellent examples of intellectual cultures in which models of equalization were communally shared and shaped to a considerable degree. The triumphant ideal of the Common Good (*bonum commune*), which I discuss at many points in the chapters that follow, provides an example of a powerful set of ideas, actually shared within these textual communities, that carried and conveyed a complex sense of balance/*aequalitas* as applied to the aggregation of interacting individuals within the *civitas*. To share in thinking about the implications and potentialities of the Common Good (as many scholars did) was to share in thinking about the implications and potentialities of systematic equalization, whether or not it was ever consciously recognized in these terms.

A third way the model is shaped is through the scholar's daily interactions with those environments that functioned, in effect, as concrete social forms of equilibrium. Important among these are the economic structures of the marketplace, which scholars were often required to navigate and to which they devoted considerable attention; the institutional structures of the university community in which they came to physical and intellectual maturity; the political structures of the *civitas* with which they interacted as students, masters, and officials; and the social, physical, and technological environment of the living city itself, in which they were immersed, whether at Bologna, Padua, Montpellier, Oxford, or Paris. Within these environments (all of which, as we will see, were described at the time as sites of equalization organized around the core ideal of balance/*aequalitas*), scholars were required to establish their own *personal* equilibrium as they made their way in the world. Success, then as now, was tied to the scholar's capacity to comprehend the logic of his environments, to sense and intuit their rhythms, and to adjust to their ever-evolving structures and demands.

The construction of models of equality and equalization out of these three distinct shaping influences – one textual, one intuitive, and one experiential – underlies their crucial mediating function between unconscious sense and conscious science. Since these models possess both shape and weight, they can carry meaning, and they can convey meaning. As they were shared, they were continually open to change and refinement. But this refinement occurred not through open debate, since they were never the subject of debate. Rather, refinement took place through a process in which thinkers brought the equilibrium they projected onto the subjects of their inquiry (e.g., the workings of the body, or the body politic, or the marketplace, or of nature itself) ever more closely into line with the equilibrium they experienced and intuited in their own physical, social, and technological environments. In short, models of balance/*aequalitas* were (and, I believe, still are) refined in the direction of establishing "satisfying" solutions; solutions that along with fulfilling intellectual requirements also made intuitive sense; solutions that "fit" (*convenit*) and were "fitting" (*conveniens*), to use words of great currency in philosophical discourse in this period; solutions that were believed to "work" because they were congruent with the group's sense and perception of how things actually worked in the world they experienced.

In a previous book, I argued that the perceptual shifts which were essential to the emergence of scientific speculation in the fourteenth century – quantification, relativistic determinations, probabilistic reasoning, the focus on motion and change rather than on essences and perfections, and more – were grounded in the experience and comprehension of the monetized urban marketplace of the thirteenth and fourteenth centuries, as filtered through the remarkable intellectual culture of the medieval university.[7] Overall, I endeavored to show that even the most

---

[7] Joel Kaye, *Economy and Nature in the Fourteenth Century: Money, Market Exchange, and the Emergence of Scientific Thought* (Cambridge University Press, 1998).

abstract and seemingly "detached" scholastic speculations were shaped by the material and socioeconomic contexts in which they were produced. In the years since, I have seen no reason to retreat from these earlier arguments. On the contrary, I continue to find further reasons and examples to support them. The questions I want to pursue further in this study relate more to the "how" than to the "what." How are changing socioeconomic environments and experiences translated into new apprehensions and abstract speculations of the highest intellectual order? Does the scholar's evident comprehension of and sensitivity to his environment(s) provide a sufficient explanation for this translation, as I argued earlier? Or might there be more particular and specialized mediating structures facilitating and underlying this translation? I now think that models of balance/*aequalitas* are those mediating structures.

These models – cohesive and self-reflective unities that weave together the experiential, the intuitive, and the ideational, and that are shaped by the "sense" of how things actually work and find order in the world – are, I suggest, uniquely suited to mediate between environment and intellectual invention, between sensation and science. As I now see it – and hope to convey – models of equality and equalization serve as the primary medium through which social, economic, and technological environments affect and activate the production of new perceptions, new imaginations, new insights and ideas, and even radically new images of the world and its workings.

Given my sense of the crucial role that models of equalization play in the history of ideas, and my finding that up to now this role has gone virtually unnoticed, I focus my analysis and arguments in this present work less on their causes than on the models themselves. In particular, I focus on the new model of balance/*aequalitas* that emerged in scholastic culture in the later thirteenth century, which I designate (for reasons to be made clear) "the new model of equilibrium." On the one hand I investigate its particular elements, its structures, its interior logic, its binding forces, and the evidence of its appearance in various scholastic discourses. On the other hand, I trace its profound effects on thought – the forward-looking speculations and imaginations that the shift to this new model suddenly made possible in discipline after scholastic discipline.

The causal arguments that I do make in the following chapters are for the most part indirect, conveyed through the ordering of the chapters themselves. Chapters 1 and 2 center on the evolving definition of *aequalitas* within economic life and thought between 1150 and 1300, as evidenced in both legal writings and dedicated treatises. These chapters point to the conclusion that a continual interchange between economic actualities, experiences, apprehensions, and rationalizations, channeled within a textual tradition in which *aequalitas* remained the *sine qua non* of justice in exchange, played a crucial role in the emergence of the new model of equilibrium. While my focus in this volume remains entirely in the medieval period, I suspect that dominant forms of economic exchange in every period and every society shape the sense and cultural modeling of balance on the deepest level. This would apply to the circular exchange of yams in the Trobriand Islands; the reciprocal patterns of gift exchange in the early medieval period; the monetized exchange of goods and services in the urban marketplace of the thirteenth and fourteenth centuries; the explosion of credit and speculation in the seventeenth and eighteenth centuries; and the credit-card economy of the present day.[8]

Chapter 3 is devoted to Galen of Pergamum's rich and sophisticated modeling of the multiple processes of systematic equalization that take place naturally within the human body. Chapter 4 traces the scholastic reception and diffusion of the Galenic model of equalization from the thirteenth through the first quarter of the fourteenth century. While the writings of Aristotle are generally taken as the textual point of departure for scholastic speculation, I have found that the most dynamic and productive texts behind the construction of the new model of equilibrium came not from Aristotle but from Galen and his continuators, both Arabic and Latin. By joining my analysis of textual influences on the evolution of medical thought in Chapters 3 and 4 to my analysis of influences on the modeling of *aequalitas* coming from the experience and comprehension of economic life in Chapters 1 and 2, I hope to do some justice to the complex interplay of texts and contexts that contributed to the history of balance in this period.

Chapter 5 examines the intellectual, social, physical, and technological setting in which the transformation of balance occurred. Its focus is both on the University of Paris and on the great commercial city that surrounded it. It presents a view of the city of Paris as representing, in itself, a working system of equalization, immense in its size, complexity, and ordering capacity. Chapters 6 and 7 focus on the political environment(s) of the fourteenth century and on the solutions that two great thinkers, Marsilius of Padua and Nicole Oresme, put forward to resolve perceived failures of *aequalitas* in the political realm. Where Chapter 6 focuses on

---

[8] In this respect, see, for example, Lorraine Daston, "Attention and the Values of Nature in the Enlightenment," in *The Moral Authority of Nature,* ed. Lorraine Daston and Fernando Vidal (University of Chicago Press, 2003), 100–26, at 120: "The [Enlightenment naturalist's] choice of the word 'economy,' used here in its eighteenth-century sense of an intricate system of interrelated, functional parts, was not accidental ... The patterns of observing and describing in Enlightenment natural history and political economy resembled one another strongly."

Marsilius' monumental political treatise, *Defensor pacis*, Chapter 7 focuses first on Oresme's *De moneta* (*c.* 1355), his treatise on the politics of money and minting, and then turns to consider his vernacular translation and commentary to Aristotle's *Politics (Le livre de politiques d'Aristote)*, written almost twenty years later (1374). When I first read the *Politiques* years ago, I saw no disjunction between the attitudes and positions Oresme upheld in this later work and those he had held earlier in the *De moneta*. But on re-reading the *Politiques* through the lens of balance, I have come to a very different position. Indeed, where I saw and still see the *De moneta* as one of the clearest and furthest expressions of the new model of equilibrium as applied to the political sphere, I now read the *Politiques* as a sign that the model as a whole is well on its way to collapse by the 1370s. Gone is Oresme's earlier faith in the capacity of the political community as a working unity to order and equalize its affairs through the "natural" interaction of its component parts – the essence of the new equilibrium. At the conclusion to Chapter 7, I speculate on the possible causes of this collapse and on its implications.

The final Chapter 8 on the impact of the new model of equilibrium in the area of natural philosophy offers some of the clearest examples of the process of its shaping as it was passed from thinker to thinker and generation to generation within the university over the first half of the fourteenth century. Here we see the elements of the model in sharp detail: the focus on systematic function; the prominence of relational thinking; the language of proportion and ratio; the replacement of the discrete by the continuous; measurement by "latitudes" within a conceptual "world of lines"; the replacement of arithmetic by geometry; the acceptance of multiplication in a nature marked by the dynamism of exponential powers; the acceptance of estimation and approximation; the employment of probabilistic thinking; even the new value allowed to difference and diversity.

I regret not having found a more fitting and descriptive name for this "new" model of balance. The word "new" makes sense only in terms of the model(s) that had immediately preceded it in scholastic culture. It fails as a marker outside of this narrow perspective and certainly so with respect to models that come after it or are active in cultures outside Europe. One solution to finding a proper and fitting name would be to establish a taxonomy of models within which this one could be placed and named. This, of course, would require extending the history of balance to other periods and other cultures. My hope is that it will be. Such a taxonomy of models, were it to be constructed, could then serve as a near universally applicable conceptual frame, capable of permitting the finding and drawing of relationships between cultures and speculations that at present often lack a meaningful basis for comparison. It could be applied, for example, to crucial questions, such as how the "new" model of the Latin schools relates and maps onto earlier models of equalization realized within medieval Islamic culture in such areas as medicine, optics, geology, and physics. Equally importantly, such a taxonomy might also make possible the comparison of the modeling of equilibrium of the late thirteenth and fourteenth century with that found reoccurring in the seventeenth century in the works of such thinkers as Galileo and Spinoza, or even (dare I suggest?) in the later writings of Darwin and Einstein.

I recognize that I am far from the first historian to think that his particular lens has claims to universality. There are, without doubt, other questions and categories that can be applied across cultural and temporal boundaries. But balance, I want to argue, is different. To begin with, it is a form rather than a content. It is less a thought than a generalized sense or apprehension that provides both the ground within which thoughts and questions are ordered and the boundaries that determine what questions can be asked, what thoughts are thinkable, and what imaginations are possible. My sense is that models of equality and equalization are as universal as they are (and as commensurable as I think they can be) *because* they transcend content and work beneath words. Their lack of verbal expression does not diminish their directive force. On the contrary, the judgment that balance is healthful and productive and imbalance unhealthy and destructive is nearly universal, as is the association of balance with justice and righteousness and imbalance with the illicit and sinful. I would argue that whether explicitly verbalized or not, the presence or absence of balance tests entire fields of thought, belief, and imagination. If the presence of balance/*aequalitas* (however imagined within the particular culture) is either apparent or the likely end result of a way of thinking or seeing, the thought and vision are good. If not, not. In this, models of equality and equalization can be seen to function in pre-modern cultures in much the same way that conservation laws function in the present.

But how is one to define the model's structure when it is never explicitly discussed or described; when, in all probability, it was never consciously grasped by the subjects who employed it? Granted the difficulties involved in this project, I believe this task is manageable, and I have sought to provide a template to help make it so. I want to suggest, moreover, that the very unconsciousness of models of equality and equalization may well render them a more fruitful subject for historical inquiry than intellectual contents that are fully conscious and made explicit in texts. The fact that the model is not consciously shaped and presented, not colored and tailored to fit a set of normative expectations and ideals, allows it

considerable advantages as a marker of thought. By avoiding the controversies that often accompany the presentation of explicit thoughts and
propositions, models avoid the kind of intellectual ruts and distortions
that controversies encourage.

Difficulties of recognition, for both scholars in the past and scholars
in the present, may also help to explain the sheer scope of change represented by the emergence of the new model of equilibrium in the later
thirteenth century. The thinkers I consider who played a major role in
reshaping balance and reimagining its potentialities were certainly not
fully conscious of the implications of what they were doing – nor were
their potential critics. If they or their critics had been, I think it unlikely
that they would have or could have been as bold in their speculations as
indeed they were. Then again, the model's grounding in physical sense
and feeling – the reason for its existence beneath the level of words – is just
what facilitates its function as the medium between experience and intellection, and this, in turn, is just what renders it such a fruitful ground for
historical study. And finally, the existence of models of equality and
equalization beneath the level of verbal expression and conscious content
is what makes possible both their presence in every culture and their
comparability across cultures. One of the great advantages I see to bringing these models to the center of the history of ideas is the potential it
creates for comparative studies of historical development between and
across different disciplines, periods, and cultures.

1 Equality and equalization in the economic sphere, part 1: The scholastic discourse on usury to 1300

> Usury is where anything more is required in return than was given. For example, if you lend 10 solidi and you seek anything more in return (*et amplius quesieris*), or if you lend one measure of wheat and you demand more in return.　　　Gratian, *Decretum* II, 14, 3, c. 4 (*c.* 1145)

> It is not possible to demand anything more in return (than the sum lent) without violating both equity and equality (*absque aperta lesura equitatis et equalitatis*).
>
> Peter of John Olivi, *Tractatus de emptionibus et venditionibus, de usuris, de restitutionibus* (*c.* 1295)

> The reason why [money of a certain kind] can be bought or exchanged for a price [more than itself] is because ... money which in the firm intent of its owner is directed toward the production of probable profit (*ad aliquod probabile lucrum*) possesses not only the qualities of money in its simple sense but beyond this a kind of seminal cause of profit within itself, which we commonly call "capital" (*communiter capitale vocamus*). And therefore it possesses not only its simple numerical value as money/measure but it possesses in addition a superadded value (*valor superadiunctus*).
>
> Peter of John Olivi, *Tractatus de emptionibus et venditionibus, de usuris, de restitutionibus* (*c.* 1295)

Throughout its history, scholastic economic thinking centered on the proposition that equality (*aequalitas*) is the proper and required end of all exchange. In line with this proposition, both in the scholastic discourse on usury (the subject of this chapter) and in the discourse on price and value (the subject of the next), writers universally identified the process of economic exchange as a process of equalization, which is to say, a process of achieving a just *balance* between exchangers. This position is stated and restated from the time of Gratian's early analysis and discussion of usury in the *Decretum* (*c.* 1145), to Thomas Aquinas' questions on usury and just price in the *De malo* and the *Summa theologica* (*c.* 1268–72), to Peter of John Olivi's path-breaking questions on usury and price in the 1290s, to Jean Buridan's discussion of price and value in the 1340s and 50s – to name but a few of the major writers in this tradition.

Between the mid twelfth and the mid fourteenth century, the ideal of exchange equality remained constant, as did the words that scholastics used to designate it: *aequalitas, aequitas, aequivalentia, medium, medietas, mediocritas, temperantia,* and *justitia,* among others. The word most frequently used, *aequalitas,* was routinely identified with the exalted ideal of justice *(iustitia),* symbolized by the balancing scale. This further solidified *aequalitas* as an unchallengeable requirement in exchange. At the same time, it contributed to the associative link between the stated goal of *aequalitas* and the idea and image of balance – an association that had many contributing sources. Just as balance has a passive meaning (i.e., the equalized end or goal of a process) and an active meaning (i.e., the process itself of attaining that end), so over the whole of the medieval period the concept of *aequalitas* applied to both the passive goal of equality and the active process of equalization.

While the ideal of exchange *aequalitas* held firm over these two centuries of rapid commercialization and urbanization, and while the words designating this ideal held fairly firm as well, the spoken and unspoken meanings attached to this ideal changed profoundly. Gratian's assumptions about what constituted equality and equalization differed greatly from Thomas', Thomas' from Olivi's, Olivi's from Buridan's, even as each continued to use the same words and terms in reference to it. For this reason, if one is to grasp what scholastic writers meant, or understood, or assumed by the words they used, it is necessary to go past the words themselves in search of the evolving apprehension or unworded *sense* that lay beneath them – a sense of what constituted the desired state of *aequalitas* (in their terms) or balance (in ours), a sense of how this state could be achieved and maintained in the economic sphere, whether in agreements between individuals or as a product of transactions taking place across communities of exchangers.

Since the scholastic logic of exchange was so carefully constructed around the requirement for *aequalitas,* as assumptions and understandings concerning its possible forms changed, so too did judgments concerning which contracts could be defined as licit (i.e., working in the direction of equalization) and which illicit. Evidence for this changing judgment is particularly notable in the writings of clerics, both canon lawyers and theologians, with cardinals and popes among their ranks. The responsibilities attached to their positions required them to decide whether and in what ways new social and contractual forms could (or could not) be brought within the bounds of rationality and legality, i.e., could or could not be imagined as congruent with the requirement of *aequalitas.*

The persistence of the usury prohibition in scholastic economic thought over centuries is often taken as a sign that medieval churchmen were ignorant, even willfully ignorant, of the details of economic life in their society. The truth is more interesting. As we will see below, the early solidification of the Church's condemnation of usury, and the ever-increasing sense of danger and sin that attached to usurious acts, had the effect of forcing scholastic moralists, legal scholars, and theologians to become expert in the ways of the marketplace. Only this way could they hope to recognize usurious transactions and root them out. The stakes were believed to be very high: the fate of souls hung in the balance. Those clerics who undertook this task were gradually brought to recognize (and often to accept) that economic life functions according to its own rules and principles – principles that demanded attention and comprehension even if they were often distinct from, if not at odds with, often-stated principles governing the Christian life. They came to see that economic truths are provisional and approximate rather than absolute; that economic value is shifting and relativized rather than ordered to any recognizable hierarchy; and that economic judgment functions around risks and probabilities rather than certainties.

Despite their recognition of these dichotomies, theologians and canon lawyers remained confident that they could carry their exalted ideal of *aequalitas* into the marketplace as the essential test of licit exchange. As we will see, however, the *aequalitas* that emerged from its immersion in the marketplace in the second half of the thirteenth century was far, far different from the one that had entered it a century and a half earlier. The goal of the judges remained consistent over this period: to align economic rules and behavior with the ideal of equality/justice. At the same time, however, the ever-multiplying speed, volume, and complexity of commercial and market exchange over these inflationary years had the effect of pressuring and continually reshaping the definitional bounds of *aequalitas* in the minds of these same judges, as they sought to reconcile, insofar as possible, their constantly restated ideal with the constant appearance of new contractual and transactional forms of exchange.

The goal of these first two chapters is to outline the changes that occurred in sense, assumption, and intellectual definition pertaining to the requirements for balance/*aequalitas* in economic exchange over the twelfth and thirteenth centuries, as legists and theologians responded to rapid developments in the economic sphere. Both chapters will show that by the end of the thirteenth century, these changes eventuated in the emergence of a new model of equality and equalization that differed profoundly from all models that had preceded it. I will argue that to this new model of equalization the word "equilibrium," with its rich modern connotations of *systematic* self-ordering and self-equalizing, can for the first time be applied. The following two chapters trace the continual interchange between intellection and economic actuality that underlay the process through which earlier models of equalization evolved into a model of systematic equilibrium.

Part 1: Equality and equalization in the medieval discourse on usury

There were two major spheres of speculation within scholastic economic thought: questions relating to usury and contracts of loan (*mutuum*), and questions relating to the determination of price and value in exchange (*emptio/venditio*).[1] The establishment of equality and equalization between exchangers remained an unquestioned and frequently asserted ideal in both, and there were many places where the assumptions and requirements worked out in one sphere corresponded with those in the other. There were also, however, differences sufficiently great to warrant treating each of the two spheres separately.

Historians of medieval economic thought have previously noted the extent to which usury theory was constructed around the requirement for equality in the loan contract or *mutuum*. They have recognized that the presence of *aequalitas* or a willed *adaequatio* signified the required presence of *iustitia* in the exchange, while inequality signified injustice and hence the sin of usury.[2] But even those modern scholars who have been most sensitive to the centrality of equality in usury theory have generally failed to recognize it as a concept in evolution, or even as a concept capable of evolution. When it is mentioned, equality is represented as an essentialized ideal, a conception without a history, the same in the twelfth century as it was in the fourteenth. In contrast, I have found that conceptions of both equality and equalization have a history, and that changes in the definitions they carried and conveyed had a profound impact on the structure and content of writings on usury from the twelfth century onward.

---

[1] I introduced this subject in my *Economy and Nature in the Fourteenth Century*, and I considered it again in "Changing Definitions of Money, Nature, and Equality, c. 1140–1270, Reflected in Thomas Aquinas' Questions on Usury," in *Credito e usura fra teologia, diritto, e amministrazione*, ed. Diego Quaglioni, Giacomo Todeschini, and Gian Maria Varanini (École Française de Rome, 2005), 25–55. In what follows, I make selective use of my earlier findings, supplementing them to suit the changed focus of my discussion here.

[2] Gabriel Le Bras, "L'usure," in *Dictionnaire de théologie catholique*, vol. XV (Paris: Letouzey et Ane, 1950), cols. 2333–7 at 2333. See also the "Introduction" to the treatise on usury by Alexander Lombard, *Un traité de morale économique au XIVe siècle: le "Tractatus de usuris" de maître Alexandre d'Alexandrie*, ed. A. M. Hamelin (Louvain: Nauwelaerts, 1962), 79: "Le premier élément accepté et indiscutable est celui de l'égalité."

Aequalitas as defined in Gratian's question on usury in the *Decretum*

I begin my study of usury with the question Gratian devoted to the subject in his *Decretum* (*c.* 1145), the first time in the history of canon law that a question had been dedicated exclusively to this subject. While I use the definitions Gratian offers as a starting point for the history of balance/*aequalitas*, I also recognize that taking his treatment of usury as characteristic of mid-twelfth-century attitudes presents certain problems. The opinions he cites in the process of establishing his own position are chosen from the writings of the Church Fathers, dating mostly from the fourth to the sixth centuries, with the most recent canons cited dating to the early ninth century. Moreover, early glosses on the *Decretum*, particularly those from the first decades of the thirteenth century, indicate a level of economic knowledge and sophistication considerably in advance of that found in Gratian's text. Nevertheless, Gratian leaves no doubt that the authoritative opinions he selected possessed *for him* an intellectual coherence sufficient to provide both an adequate definition of usury and a defendable position opposing it.

His first citation is to St. Augustine, who defines the usurer simply as one who in a loan contract (*mutuum*) expects to receive back more than the precise amount he lent.[3] The implication is that the slightest difference in quantity between sum lent and sum returned – even the lender's *expectation* of the slightest difference – creates an inequality which constitutes the essential injustice of usury. In this opinion, Augustine extends the scope of usury to cover the loan of all manner of fungible goods: wheat, wine, and oil in addition to money, under the same strict requirements for a perfect numerical equality between amount lent and amount returned.[4] Gratian's second citation is to St. Jerome, through whom he introduces the concept of "superabundance" (*superhabundantia*) to express the idea that any excess whatsoever beyond the arithmetically equal in the loan

---

[3] St. Augustine cited in Gratian, *Decretum*, II, 14, 3, c. 1, in *Corpus iuris canonici*, ed. A. Friedberg (Graz: Akademische Druck- u. Verlaganstalt, 1959), vol. I, col. 735: "id est si tu mutuum dederis pecuniam tuam, a quo plus quam dedisti expectes."

[4] *Ibid.* (continuing): "non pecuniam solam, sed aliquid plus quam dedisti, sive illud triticum sit, sive vinum, sive oleum, sive quodlibet aliud, si plus quam dedisti expectes accipere, fenerator est, et in hoc improbandus, non laudandus." Although Augustine does not use the technical term "fungible" in this citation, his debt to Roman law is clear. In Roman law, fungible goods have two qualities that set them apart from other goods: (1) they can be freely replaced by another of like kind and identical quantity in the satisfaction of an obligation, and (2) such substitution is necessary because the fungible (whether wheat, wine, oil, or in this case money) is consumed in its use, so the original cannot be returned.

contract is to be condemned as usurious.[5] Where in the Christian spiritual realm "superhabundantia" is a benefit promised to believers, Jerome insists that its production in the economic sphere is an unnatural deformation. Over succeeding centuries this word appears frequently in discussions of usury to signify the production of an unnatural excess that violates the requirement for arithmetical equality in the loan contract and in other forms of economic exchange. In the third opinion cited by Gratian, St. Ambrose supplied a simple rule that was repeated in writings on usury countless times thereafter: "usury is anything whatsoever that exceeds the sum lent (*quodcumque sorti accidit usura est*)."[6]

In all, there is a striking simplicity and uniformity to the model of equality assumed to be proper to the *mutuum* in Gratian's citations. The model assumes an arithmetical equation of 1:1, with each side of the equation numerable, perfectly knowable, and perfectly fixed once known. Similarly striking in its simplicity is the model of equalization governing how this equality is to be achieved. It is a model based on the literal and original meaning of the word "equilibrium," the balancing of perfectly equal weights.[7] In this, it precisely mirrors the workings of the mechanical scale, which, not coincidentally, was the standard iconographic representation of *iustitia* throughout the medieval period. Contractual equality and contractual justice in each of the canons cited by Gratian is represented by the perfect balancing of two numerically equal values at a single knowable and achievable point. The slightest arithmetical inequality represents an imbalance (*superhabundantia*) which is at the same time a violation of justice, a violation of the natural order, and a sin against divine and divinely mandated order.

Here as elsewhere, the model of equality and equalization that Gratian's text assumes tells us a great deal about how he views the details of economic life. In each of the canons cited, money is identified as a numerable physical coin of specified and unchanging weight and value. This identification is underscored through the linking of the coin to fixed and quantifiable measures of wheat, wine, and oil. Since the measures of all these commodities were, in the universe of Gratian's canons, fixed

---

[5] *Ibid.*, c. 2: "Quod prouidens diuina scriptura omnis rei superhabundantiam aufert, ut plus non recipias quam dedisti. Item: §. 1. Alii pro pecunia fenerata solent munuscula diuersi generis accipere, et non intelligunt scripturam usuram appellare et superhabundantiam quicquid illud est, si ab eo, quod dederint, plus acceperint."

[6] *Ibid.*, c. 3. This represents, indeed, Gratian's final *sententia* or judgment at the conclusion of his question on usury, *ibid.*, c. 4: "Ecce euidenter ostenditur, quod quicquid ultra sortem exigitur usura est."

[7] In the Galenic medical tradition, the form of balance represented by the mechanical scale measuring (and equating) weights was designated by the term "aequalitas ad pondus."

and knowable, it would be possible to recognize immediately the slightest addition to the principal (*ultra sortem*) in the return of the loan, and to condemn that production of inequality as the unjust excess of usury. Ten *solidi* lent requires precisely ten in return, with the absence of any sense that the value of these coins might be subject to change over time or place or circumstance.[8] In the texts cited by Gratian, the usurious contract takes place in a static social space composed of discrete entities and actions that remain separate and can be considered in isolation. There is no sense in any of the canons that the loan contract is embedded in personal, social, spatial, or temporal contexts that could affect its outcome or definition in any way. There is no consideration of the circumstance or position or status or relation of the participants in the exchange that might justify the lender asking for or even expecting one penny more in return than the sum he has lent. And not only the participants to the exchange are imagined as innocent of context and relation; in each of the cited canons, economic value itself, along with the numerable coin, is assumed to be similarly isolated: perfectly measurable, knowable, absolute, and unchanging. We will see that all of these "economic" assumptions change considerably in the century following Gratian's *Decretum* (i.e., 1150–1250) and then change dramatically again in the century between 1250 and 1350. Changing right alongside them are assumptions concerning what actually constitutes equality and proper equalization in the loan contract.

Pressures on the redefinition of economic *aequalitas* after Gratian

By the end of the twelfth century, the authority of the anti-usury prohibition was fully established through Gratian's text and myriad legal and theological texts that followed from it. At the same time, rapid monetization, commercialization, and market development over this half century had opened the door to ever more lending opportunities and ever greater need for loans. As a result, merchants and others involved in credit operations were caught in a bind. One way they responded was to invent a variety of accounting techniques and contractual forms surrounding the *mutuum*, some of which, no doubt, had the purpose of disguising usurious (i.e., arithmetically unequal) loans and credit operations. This strategy of evasion was well known to the

---

[8] *Decretum*, II, 14, 3, c. 4: "Usura est, ubi amplius requiritur quam quod datur. Verbi gratia, si solidos decem dederis, et amplius quesieris, vel dederis frumenti modium unum, et super aliquid exegeris."

Roman and canon lawyers of the time.[9] The decretal *Consuluit* issued
by Pope Urban III (1185–7) recognized the problem and responded
to it by adding Christ's command from Luke 6:35, "Lend, hoping
for nothing again," to the Old Testament texts previously cited in the
condemnation of usury. From this point on, moralists equated the mere
hope of gaining an unequal return with mortal sin. Given the difficulties
that judges had in penetrating the thicket of new contractual forms,
their strategy was to internalize the test of usury so that the economic
actors themselves would share responsibility for its determination.[10]

The expanded emphasis on intention in credit transactions that followed allowed canon lawyers and theologians to continue to assert the
absolute ideal of arithmetical equality, even as the increasing complexity
of commercial credit transactions (and changing assumptions concerning
the fixity of economic values) made such an equality increasingly difficult
either to define or enforce. Moreover, as the primary question for
Christians engaged in all forms of credit became "did I or did I not intend
inequality in the transaction," and as the responsibility for maintaining
equality was personalized and interiorized, many were required to become
knowledgeable in the ways of economic practice as never before. This
group included individuals who engaged in credit transactions, their
confessors, the clergy responsible for ordering the Christian life, and the
legal scholars who were increasingly called on to provide judgments on
these questions. One unintended consequence flowing from the logic of
the usury prohibition was that those who would judge and enforce it,
even those clerics most suspicious of the corrupting effects of commerce
and the pursuit of monetary gain, had no choice but to pay ever closer
attention to the details of economic life.

Aequalitas and the law

The century following the publication of Gratian's *Decretum* was a forma-
tive period for the study and teaching of both canon (Church) law and civil
(Roman) law. Both laws developed side by side in the setting of the
University of Bologna, which was at the same time the first university in
Europe and its first law school. Where the science of canon law developed

---

[9] T.P. McLaughlin, "The Teaching of the Canonists on Usury (XII, XIII and XIV
Centuries)," *Mediaeval Studies* 1 (1939), 81–147, esp. 97, 112–25.

[10] Instructions to confessors on how to sensitize their charges to the sin of usury appear for
the first time in the *Summae confessorum* of Thomas of Chobham (1215–16) and Raymond
of Penafort (1225–7). On the project of interiorization, see Giacomo Todeschini, "La
riflessione etica sulle attività economiche," in *Economie urbane ed etica economica nell'Italia
medievale*, ed. Roberto Greci (Rome: Laterza, 2005), 151–228.

around the text of Gratian, the science of civil law developed in this same period around the texts constituting the *Corpus iuris civilis*. These texts, *Digest*, *Codex*, *Institutes* (and later *Novellae*), first compiled and published in the time of the Emperor Justinian (*c*. 534 CE), and first recovered for study at Bologna in the first half of the twelfth century, contained the distilled legal wisdom and judgments of six centuries of Roman jurisprudence.

From its earliest days, the medieval profession of law placed an extra-ordinary value on the ideal of *aequitas*. The historian Paolo Grossi has called the concern with *aequitas* "the golden key" to medieval legal thought, noting that the ideal is spoken of "obsessively" by the greatest legists of the medieval period.[11] Already in the twelfth century, the followers of the jurist Martinus associated *aequitas* directly with the divine. In their words, "*aequitas* is nothing other than God" (*aequitas est nihil aliud quam Deus*).[12] It was in good part because lawyers had such confidence in this ideal that they could project it so forcefully into their analysis of forms of economic life. For this reason, too, both Roman and canon lawyers could accept it, without question, as the ultimate test of liceity in economic contracts.[13] Since in Roman law and canon law the scope of usury was explicitly limited to loans involving "those things which are dealt in by weight, number, or measure," including, of course, weighable, numerable, and measurable coin, the lawyer's *aequitas* mapped nearly perfectly onto *aequalitas*, with its physical and mathematical overtones.[14]

For all the implications of numerability and knowability that the word "equality" still carries today when used in its mathematical sense, it also carries significant abstract associations, particularly when applied, as it most commonly is, in the political and social sphere. It is important to note, therefore, that the *aequalitas* championed by medieval canon lawyers and theologians, and applied by them to economic contracts, had nothing to do with the abstract ideals of political or social equality enunciated in the seventeenth and eighteenth

---

[11] Paolo Grossi, *L'ordine giuridico medievale* (Rome: Laterza, 1995), 211: "E di *aequitas* si parlerà ossessivamente in tutte le grandi decretali dell'età classica."

[12] André Gouron, "Some Aspects of the Medieval Teaching of Roman Law," in *Learning Institutionalized: Teaching in the Medieval University*, ed. John Van Engen (University of Notre Dame Press, 2000), 161–76, at 164.

[13] Grossi, *L'ordine giuridico*, 181–2: "[*L'Aequitas*] sarà il campo della rappresentanza, del contratto a favore di terzi, dei titoli al portatore, della lettera di cambio, cioè il campo tutto nuovo dei nuovi traffici commerciali."

[14] *Digest*, 12.1.2.1., ed. Theodore Mommsen, in *Corpus iuris civilis*, vol. I (Berlin: Weidmanns, 1954). Also, T. P. McLaughlin, "Teaching of the Canonists," 99–101. McLaughlin here cites Huguccio, *Summa*, in c. 14, q. 3: "Mutuum enim consistit in his rebus quae pondere, numero vel mensura constant veluti vino, oleo, frumento, pecunia numerata, aere, argento, auro etc." The limitation of the usury prohibition to the quantifiable and numerable is clearly apparent in the canons cited by Gratian above.

centuries and still current today. The medieval ideal of *aequalitas* could be measured and applied with some sense of certainty.[15] As such, it was thought to have a real presence in both nature and the human condition, deriving from the central place it was thought to occupy in the divine order of creation.[16] In the often-repeated phrase taken from the biblical Book of Wisdom, God has "ordered all things in measure, and number, and weight."[17] *Aequalitas*, as the quantifiable aspect of *aequitas*, had a concrete reality that could be judged and applied by legists toward the production and restoration of just balance in the world.

At the same time, as the thirteenth century progressed, it was becoming ever clearer to legists that the ideal numerical equality demanded by Gratian's canons was difficult, if not impossible, to impose upon credit contracts when they were embedded in the real world of economic exchange. Everyone after Gratian who wrote on the problem of usury from the practical and legal side recognized that establishing an equation between benefit and loss in the loan contract was extraordinarily difficult, and more difficult still were the many questions connected to the matter of restoring what were determined to be illicit gains. Solutions offered by lawyers to questions touching on usury and restitution from the thirteenth century onward became increasingly latitudinarian in order to do justice to the actual complexities attached to exchange and to provide equitable solutions to real problems. For the most part, the position espoused by theologians remained that a loan should be made out of charity and without any hope of return beyond the sum lent. But within the disciplines of Roman and canon law, which required the observation and analysis of actual cases and existing conditions, the realization grew that if the lender was to be denied the expectation of reward, he must at the same time be protected from damages associated with the act of lending.

To ensure this protection, canon lawyers began to apply the Roman law concept of *interesse* to the loan contract. In Roman law, *interesse* was a monetary penalty applied to damages resulting from the breaking of a contract. From the last decades of the twelfth to the early decades of the thirteenth century, lawyers began to see the logic of extending *interesse* to the loan contract as an indemnity to the lender for the failure of the borrower to meet his contractual obligations.[18] In the most commonly

---

[15] Grossi, *L'ordine giuridico*, 180.   [16] *Ibid.*, 213.

[17] Wisdom, 11:21: "sed omnia mensura et numero et pondere disposuisti."

[18] John Baldwin, *Masters, Princes, and Merchants: The Social Views of Peter the Chanter and his Circle*, 2 vols. (Princeton University Press, 1970), 1: 282; McLaughlin, "Teaching of the Canonists," 140.

cited case, the lender was permitted to charge a penalty if the borrower failed to repay his loan within the agreed time period.[19] Since justifying *interesse* (as a monetary penalty incurred by the borrower) from the beginning of a loan would mean the virtual dismantling of usury theory, medieval legists who acknowledged legitimate *interesse* in specific cases, were careful to define it as an "extrinsic title," outside the form of the contract itself, awarded only as the result of loss resulting from contractual failure (*damnum emergens*). In this way, they argued, a payment made to the lender *ultra sortem*, could still be just and legitimate, i.e., could still be integrated into the requirement for *aequalitas*, if it was made not as a reward for the act of lending, but solely as compensation for contractual damages incurred by the lender (*non lucrum sed vitatio damni*).[20]

Introducing proportion into the equation

Whether intrinsic or extrinsic, the recognition that *interesse* could apply to credit contracts meant that the violation of a strict arithmetical equality between sum lent and sum returned no longer infallibly constituted usury. In Roman law through the time of Justinian, where moderate usury was accepted and not condemned, the difference in the relative position of lender and borrower, and the difference in what each stood to gain or lose from the loan contract, was allowed to express itself as a legal interest rate – a fixed proportional difference between the amount lent and the greater amount received back in return.[21] Even though medieval canon lawyers and other observers after Gratian became increasingly sensitive to the differing positions of lender and borrower in the *mutuum*, and even

---

[19] McLaughlin, "Teaching of the Canonists," 140–3; see also, John Noonan, *The Scholastic Analysis of Usury* (Cambridge, MA: Harvard University Press, 1957), 109–12. The analysis of usury has evolved considerably in the three-quarters of a century since the publication of McLaughlin's important study ("Teaching of the Canonists") and the half-century since the publication of Noonan's book. Both have been criticized in recent decades, most often for reading too great a unity and homogeneity into the tradition of writings against usury, both in law and in theology. Moreover, neither was aware of the crucial writings on usury by Peter Olivi (see below in this chapter) and the tradition of economic thought based on these writings. Nevertheless, both works have earned their place in the historiography of usury, and for the most part both can still be relied upon for details relating to its textual history before Olivi. Where their judgments have not been superseded, I continue to cite them.

[20] Noonan, *Usury*, 106; McLaughlin, "Teaching of the Canonists," 125–47, esp. 141–2; Jean Ibanès, *La doctrine de l'Église et les réalités économiques au XIIIe siècle* (Paris: Presses Universitaires de France, 1967), 25–7.

[21] On the differences between the Roman law of the *Corpus iuris civilis* (issued 534 CE, during the reign of Justinian) and canon or Church law on the subject of usury, as well as differences between medieval Romanists and canonists on this subject, see McLaughlin, "Teaching of the Canonists," 83–95.

though they were acutely sensitive to the requirement of equality in exchange, they were unable to follow the example of Roman law by simply integrating proportionality into the loan contract.

There was much more at stake here than the overturning of a purely economic position. Abandoning usury theory would, by the thirteenth century, entail overturning a string of papal decisions and authoritative canons, beginning with those cited by Gratian. And, further, it would mean overthrowing the theological edifice of sin, restitution, and penance that had been built upon these canons since the twelfth century. At its furthest, it would mean overturning divine laws against usury, with their source in the Hebrew and Christian Bible. As the social effects of monetization and commercialization became ever more pervasive, however, those lawyers who confronted questions surrounding credit were pushed to recognize the obvious: that borrowers benefited from the money made available to them, while lenders often suffered economic damages from losing the use of their money.

Over the course of the thirteenth century, canon lawyers devised a solution to this problem: they continued to insist that a loan should be made without hope of receiving back more than the sum lent, but at the same time they recognized specific cases in which the lender could licitly demand indemnification for economic loss, even in cases where the borrower had fulfilled the contract to the letter. One of the most liberal interpretations of this position was offered by the great canon lawyer, Hostiensis (Henry of Susa/Henricus de Segusia), in his magisterial *Summa super titulis decretalium*, commonly known as the *Summa aurea*, which he completed in 1253.[22] Every aspect of Hostiensis' discussion indicates that he was paying very close attention to the actualities of economic exchange in his society.[23] In allowing the lender to demand an increase beyond the sum lent in compensation for actual damages

---

[22] For a study of his *Summa aurea* and an appreciation of his place in medieval canon law, see Clarence Gallagher, S.J., *Canon Law and the Christian Community: The Role of Law in the Church According to the* Summa aurea *of Cardinal Hostiensis* (Rome: Università Gregoriana, 1978).

[23] The verse which begins Hostiensis' discussion of usury in the *Summa aurea* cites twelve legitimate exceptions to the rule that "nothing may be received beyond the sum lent." For an analysis of this verse, see McLaughlin, "Teaching of the Canonists," 125–45. For a penetrating discussion of the scope and implications of Hostiensis' exceptions, see Giacomo Todeschini, "Eccezioni e usura nel Duecento: osservazioni sulla cultura economica medievale come realtà non dottrinaria," *Quaderni storici* 131 (2009), 443–60. Todeschini argues that these exceptions were intended to apply only to certain segments of the population, namely professional merchants of good reputation and clerical agents representing the economic interests of ecclesiastical institutions. The full weight of the usury prohibition, therefore, fell, and was intended to fall, primarily on the marginalized in society.

suffered (*damnum emergens*), Cardinal Hostiensis (he was raised to the cardinalate in 1262 and served in that office until his death in 1271) remained on well-trodden legal ground.[24] Much more singular and notable was his acceptance of an increase beyond the principal (*ultra sortem*) to indemnify a lender for the gain he merely *might* have made with his money had he not lent it. He wrote:

> if some merchant, who is accustomed to pursue trade and the commerce of the fairs and there profit much, has, out of charity to me, who needs it badly, lent money with which he would have done business, I remain obliged from this to his *interesse*, provided that nothing is done in fraud of usury ... and provided that said merchant will not have been accustomed to give his money in such a way to usury.[25]

Such indemnification *ultra sortem* came to be known under the title *lucrum cessans* (i.e., "lost profit").[26] Hostiensis insisted on classifying *lucrum cessans* as an external title rather than as a legitimization of usury. This was true even though in cases where the lender was a merchant "accustomed to pursue trade and the commerce of the fairs and there profit much," *interesse* could conceivably be calculated from the beginning of the loan as part of the loan contract itself. Hostiensis did not see a problem here. Despite his acceptance of *lucrum cessans* in the cases above, which not only justified returns *ultra sortem* but actually required them to maintain equality between lender and borrower, he continued to insist that the very idea of "legitimate" or "moderate" usury involved a contradiction in terms, since usury was, in itself, evil and unnatural.[27]

In Hostiensis' thought we see the tension that arose from the desire (or pressure) to maintain old ideals in a new and charged economic environment. This tension was reflected in conflicting models of equalization. The old model of a simple arithmetical equality, on the pattern of the mechanical scale balancing two perfectly equal weights at a single point, remained in force, attractive for its simplicity and its clarity, even while it was being severely pressured by the growing recognition that credit transactions occur in weighted social contexts rather than in a static abstract space. The growing recognition that the participants in

---

[24] McLaughlin, "Teaching of the Canonists," 145; Baldwin, *Masters, Princes and Merchants*, 279–84; Ibanès, *La doctrine*, 25–7.

[25] Hostiensis, *Commentaria super quinque libros decretalium* (Venice, 1581), book V, *De usuris*, 16, cited and translated by Noonan, *Usury*, 118.

[26] McLaughlin, "Teaching of the Canonists," 145; Noonan, *Usury*, 118; Barry Gordon, *Economic Analysis before Adam Smith* (New York: Barnes and Noble, 1975), 149–53.

[27] Hostiensis, *Summa aurea* (Venice 1574; reprint Turin: Bottega d'Erasmo, 1963), book V, *De usuris*, col. 1630: "Quia omnis usura immoderata est, et ideo hodie omnis usurarius infamis est."

credit exchanges were, in economic terms, often *un*equal, with the borrower gaining and the merchant lender losing, lay behind the rising acceptance of *interesse* as a legitimate monetary indemnification in loan contracts. The growing recognition over the thirteenth century that the relation of inequality between borrower and lender was in some sense a *proportional relation*, one whose numerical value was open to representation and equalization through the numbered scale of money, lay behind the far more adventurous intellectual arguments in support of *lucrum cessans* to indemnify *potential* or *probable* lost profit. The existence of unchallengeable scriptural and legal canons led medieval lawyers and moralists to continue to excoriate usury as unnatural and sinful *in se* and to insist on older rigorist ideals of strict arithmetical equality (*quodcumque sorti accedit*), while at the same time admitting "external titles" to added values (*damnum emergens, lucrum cessans*) and thus moving in practice toward a modified conception of proportional equalization – toward a just balance defined in proportional terms, rather than fixed at 1:1.[28]

Adding doubt and risk to the exchange equation

The examination of particular economic contracts that came under the watchful eyes of the canonists over the course of the thirteenth century presents yet another view of the transformation of *aequalitas* in economic thinking. Two of the most complex and problematic of these contracts were time sales (*venditio ad tempus*) connected primarily to commercial goods, and annuities (*census, redditus*) connected primarily to real property. In modern terms, both contractual forms fall squarely under the heading of "aleatory contracts," a name derived from the Latin for a game of dice (*alea*) and hence a player of dice or gambler (*aleator*).[29] Both forms rendered judgments concerning economic justice and equality immensely difficult due to the varying amounts and kinds of doubt and risk that were built into them. Both forms were inescapably situated in the shadow realm of the possible and the probable; their outcomes rested on unknowable events that lay in the future. Knowledge concerning their outcomes thus lacked all certainty and fixity. For this reason both contractual forms presented the same question: how, some centuries before the invention

---

[28] McLaughlin, "Teaching of the Canonists," 125, n. 357. On developments in usury theory taking place beneath the continued restatement of traditional and often abstract ideals, see Ovidio Capitani, "Sulla questione dell'usura nel Medio Evo," in *L'etica economica*, ed. O. Capitani (Bologna: Il Mulino, 1974), 23–46.

[29] Under this category fall all forms of contracts involving profit and loss resulting from chance or contingent events and outcomes, including, importantly, wagers and gaming "contracts" of all kinds.

of a mathematics of probability (before it was even imagined that such a mathematics was possible) to establish an equality between contracting parties, given outcomes that are merely possible or probable and, moreover, possible or probable in differing degrees and as a result of differing factors.[30] Since justice and *aequitas* required the maintenance of *aequalitas* in all credit contracts, and since the parties to these contracts themselves had been made responsible for such conformance, with the fate of souls lying in the balance, the question was far from merely academic. But that does not mean that all could agree on how to contain the uncertainty of doubt and risk within the bounds of *aequalitas*. There was no set position on the question that satisfied lawyers, theologians, and confessors of any generation, much less from one generation to the next, as commercial exchange continued to multiply in degree and complexity over the thirteenth century.[31] Meanwhile, merchants continued to invent new contractual forms of credit, in part because the dynamic of commercial

---

[30] The last half-century has seen a series of important studies on the theological, philosophical, and mathematical problems posed by aleatory contracts. One point that intellectual historians have clearly established is that the class of problems posed by the presence of risk and doubt in economic contracts proved to be a great impetus to the development of a mathematics of probability in the early modern period. Notably, in early modern sources on aleatory contracts, historians have found the same focus on questions relating to the establishment of equality/equity as in medieval sources. The writings of Lorraine Daston are exemplary in this matter. See, in particular, her *Classical Probability in the Enlightenment* (Princeton University Press, 1988), esp. 15–48; Lorraine Daston, "The Domestication of Risk: Mathematical Probability and Insurance 1650–1830," in *Ideas in History: The Probabilistic Revolution*, vol. I, ed. Lorenz Krüger, Lorraine Daston, and Michael Heidelberger (Cambridge, MA: MIT Press, 1987), 237–60; Lorraine Daston, "Fitting Numbers to the World: The Case of Probability Theory," in *History and Philosophy of Modern Mathematics*, ed. William Aspray and Philip Kitcher (Minneapolis: University of Minnesota Press, 1988), 221–37. A similar sensitivity to the confluence of economic concerns, the search for equality, and the invention of a mathematics of probability appears in Edith Sylla, "Business Ethics, Commercial Mathematics, and the Origins of Mathematical Probability," in *Oeconomies in the Age of Newton*, ed. Margaret Schabas and Neil de Marchi (Durham, NC: Duke University Press, 2003), 309–37.

[31] For studies that take the question of aleatory contracts and commercial risk back to the medieval period, see James Franklin, "The Ancient Legal Sources of Seventeenth-Century Probability," in *The Use of Antiquity: The Scientific Revolution and the Classical Tradition*, ed. Stephen Gaukroger (Dordrecht: Springer, 1991), 123–44; James Franklin, *The Science of Conjecture: Evidence and Probability before Pascal* (Baltimore, MD: Johns Hopkins University Press, 2001); Giovanni Ceccarelli, *Il gioco e il peccato: economia e rischio nel tardo medioevo* (Bologna: Il Mulino, 2003); Giovanni Ceccarelli, "Risky Business: Theological and Canonical Thought on Insurance from the Thirteenth to the Seventeenth Century," *Journal of Medieval and Early Modern Studies* 31 (2001), 607–58; Giovanni Ceccarelli, "The Price for Risk-Taking: Marine Insurance and Probability Calculus in the Late Middle Ages," *Journ@l Electronique d'Histoire des Probabilités et de la Statistique* 3.1 (2007), article 3; Sylvain Piron, "Le traitement de l'incertitude commerciale dans la scolastique médiévale," *Journ@l Electronique d'Histoire des Probabilités et de la Statistique* 3.1 (2007), article 2.

expansion called them into being, and in part, no doubt, to disguise interest-bearing loans (*in fraudem usurarum*).[32]

One such form, in common use by the last quarter of the twelfth century, was the "time sale" (*venditio ad tempus*). Here a buyer would receive goods from a seller (on credit, as it were) in exchange for a future payment at a price higher than the goods were valued in the present. Was this a legitimate sale or a disguised loan? The difference between the current and higher future price could be interpreted as a return on a loan *ultra sortem*, beyond the principal lent, and thus beyond the bounds of equality. The archbishop of Genoa wrote to Pope Alexander III (1159–81), asking whether such a contract should be judged licit or usurious. Alexander responded with the decretal, *In civitate*, in which he held that insofar as the increase was due solely to the intervention of time, such contracts were clearly usurious.[33] While Alexander's intent was to close a contractual loophole and to enforce a rigorist position on usury, he unwittingly opened the door to a large field of potential equivocation by adding an exception. If, he wrote, rather than certainty, there was a legitimate *doubt* as to whether the goods would be worth more or less in the future, then the future payment could be greater than the current price without there being disguised usury in the contract.[34]

Some forty years later, in the decretal *Naviganti* (1237), Pope Gregory IX, a leading canonist in his own right, considered the legality of two more contracts. His first decision was in regard to a very common contract of the time, the "sea loan" (*foenus nauticum*), in which a sedentary party acting as a creditor lends a sum of money to a travelling merchant to trade with, while retaining all the risk involved in the future transaction. If, for example, the ship were to sink or the merchandise were to be ruined, the sedentary merchant would absorb the loss of the entire sum he had invested. In return for assuming all the risk of the venture (*periculum sortis*), the sedentary merchant contracts to receive a certain portion of

---

[32] Historians have credited the invention of such contractual forms, whose purpose and effect was to divide and distribute the ever-present risk and dangers associated with commerce, with fueling the commercial expansion of the thirteenth century. See, for example, Yves Renouard, "Le rôle des hommes d'affaires italiens dans la Méditerranée au Moyen Âge," in *Études d'histoire médiévale*, 2 vols. (Paris: SEVPEN, 1968), 1: 405–18. For examples of loans disguised by the sheer complexity of medieval business dealings, see Étienne Fournial, *Les villes et l'économie d'échange en Forez aux XIIIe et XIVe siècles* (Paris: Les Presses du Palais Royal, 1967), 214–17.

[33] *Decretales Gregorii IX*, V.19.6, *In civitate*, in *Corpus iuris canonici*, ed. A. Friedberg (Graz: Akademische Druck- u. Verlaganstalt, 1959), vol. II, col. 813.

[34] *Ibid.*: "Licet autem contractus huiusmodi ex tali forma non possit censeri nomine usurarum, nihilominus tamen venditores peccatum incurrunt nisi dubium sit, merces illas plus minusve solutionis tempore valituras." See also Noonan, *Usury*, 90–1.

the profit made from the trade, in addition to the original sum he lent. Here we have a case where the uncertainty of risk, borne solely by the lender, would seem to expand the mathematical equality required in loan contracts, rendering licit the lender's acceptance of a sum *ultra sortem*. But Pope Gregory disagrees, or so the wording of *Naviganti* would have it, and he charges the sedentary merchant in such cases with usury. In doing so he deemed this form of contract illicit and usurious, despite its commonness and its having gained general acceptance up to this time.[35]

In Gregory's response we seem to have a reaction against loosening the bounds of *aequalitas* in the name of risk alone. But in the very next sentence within *Naviganti*, Gregory returns to the general case of time sales, and he confirms Pope Alexander's earlier decision justifying a numerically unequal return where doubt exists. He writes: if there exists true doubt (*verisimiliter dubitatur*) concerning the future price of the goods, then the contract is licit, despite the manifest quantitative inequality between the two sums separated by future time.[36] Once again, with this judgment, the inescapable uncertainty built into contracts involving an unknowable future is understood to confound any simple definition of just equality based on a purely equal numerical return. Moreover, in support of his decision regarding contracts *venditio ad tempus*, Pope Gregory offered what appears to be a general rule: "By reason of such doubt, usury is excused" (*Ratione hiuius dubii etiam excusatur*). If there is not outright confusion and contradiction within the decretal *Naviganti*, there is certainly a wobbly understanding and application of the requirement of *aequalitas* – perhaps a wobble that simply befits the intractability of the problem of equalization when applied to credit contracts that extend to an unknowable future – as so many commercial contracts do.[37]

Despite the unquestioned and unquestionable authority attached to papal decretals, Gregory's judgment in *Naviganti* did not close the book on the question of risk and doubt – very far from it. Indeed, as it turned out, the mixed message that it contained served as a spur to economic

---

[35] *Decretales Gregorii IX*, V.19.19, *Naviganti*, col. 816: "Naviganti vel eunti ad nundinas certam mutuans pecuniae quantitatem pro eo quod susciti inde periculum recepturus aliquod ultra sortem, usurarius est censendus." The ruling was later interpreted as holding that the original lender cannot be guaranteed the return of his full capital solely for assuming the risk of his complete loss; he must also assume the risks associated with losses deriving from the commercial activity undertaken by the borrower.

[36] *Ibid.*: "Ratione hujus dubii etiam excusatur qui pannos, granum, vinum, oleum, vel alias merces vendit ut amplius quam tunc valeant in certo termino recipiat pro eisdem; si tamen ea tempore contractus non fuerat venditurus."

[37] For a defense of the logic behind the distinction between risk (*periculum sortis*) and doubt (*ratione dubii/ratione incertitudinis*) in the decretal *Naviganti*, see Le Bras, "L'usure," cols. 2336–72.

analysis and speculation and, no doubt, to intellectual hair-splitting as well, for generations and centuries following.[38] One thing is clear: the evolving discussion within canon law and theology moved in the direction of expanding the definition and understanding of equality in credit contracts far beyond the one-to-one test of Gratian's canons. By the mid thirteenth century, the modeling of *aequalitas* no longer reflected the form of the mechanical scale, where two perfectly equal weights find a single point of balance, and where the slightest imbalance is clearly known and immediately revealed. A generation after the promulgation of *Naviganti*, Hostiensis could write in the *Summa aurea*: "and thus, by reason of probable doubt, many things [contracts and contractual forms] are licit which otherwise would be deemed illicit."[39]

Stretching the bounds of *aequalitas* yet further: the census contract

A second set of cases through which doubt entered the economic equation concerned the *census* contract. In this agreement, one party, A, transfers ownership rights of a piece of land to B, and in return B contracts to return to A an annual payment, representing a fixed proportion of the land's total value at the time of the agreement. This annual payment is specified to continue either for as long as A or his specified heirs live, i.e., a "return for life" (*redditus ad vitam*), or in perpetuity (*redditus perpetuus*), in which case the annual payment was set at a reduced proportion of the original value. If, for example, the value of the land that A transfers to B is 20 solidi, B contracts to return 2 solidi annually to A, or one tenth of the land's original value.[40] The census contract was of particular importance to

---

[38] See for example, the solution arrived at by Thomas Aquinas, which if it does not explicitly contradict *Naviganti*, manages to find a way, by altering the definition of such contracts (i.e., by considering them as partnerships rather than as loans), to reward risk with a required percentage of the profits, in *Summa theologica*, II.2.78.2. Others took other tacks. More than two centuries later, Domingo Soto (1495–1560) was still working over the question, still working out a way to justify profit from risk as he moved in the direction of what we would today recognize as an insurance contract. On this subject, see Franklin, "Ancient Legal Sources of Seventeenth-Century Probability," 129–30; Ceccarelli, "Risky Business," 610–14.

[39] Hostiensis, *Summa aurea*, col. 1623:"et sic ratione probabilis incertitudinis multa sunt licita quae alias non licerent."

[40] A classic work on the early history of the census contract is Fabiano Veraja, *Le origini della controversia teologica sul contratto di censo nel XIII secolo* (Rome: Edizioni di storia e letteratura, 1960). See also John Munro, "The Medieval Origins of the Financial Revolution: Usury, Rentes, and Negotiability," *International History Review* 25 (2003), 505–62; McLaughlin, "Teaching of the Canonists," 120–2; Alexander Lombard, *Tractatus de usuris*, 93–97.

canon lawyers because it was widely and profitably used by ecclesiastical institutions in this period, and its continuance was considered by many in the Church to be essential to institutional economic health.[41] Such reliance underscores the reality that the dynamic interplay between contracting parties in the marketplace, which was of such concern to canon lawyers, was not the exclusive field of lay economic actors, but that Church institutions of every kind and size were deeply involved in these transactions.[42]

The question the lawyers asked of the census was a simple one: if land valued at a certain sum of money has been transferred by one party to another in exchange for smaller annual monetary payments (by the thirteenth century, most census contracts were stipulated in terms of a numbered price [pecunia numerata] due annually), and those annual payments eventually total more than the original monetary value advanced, is this not a usurious loan in its clearest definition: "where more is received in return than was given"?[43] If, for example, a contract redditus ad vitam stipulates that the annual payment will be 10 percent of the original value advanced, the return would be precisely equal only in the unlikely event that the recipient dies after precisely ten years have passed.[44] If the recipient lives for fifteen, twenty, or more years, then the total repayment could be double or more the original sum. And if, as became increasingly common, the agreement stipulated a perpetual annual return, then the possibility of an "equal" return, in any sense that Gratian would have understood the term, is completely and necessarily destroyed.[45] How is this not usurious?

Raymond of Penafort, the same legal scholar who collected and published Pope Gregory IX's decretal Naviganti in the collection known as the Liber Extra (1234), was the first lawyer to offer an opinion on the liceity of the census contract. Not surprisingly given the tradition before him, Raymond established as his guiding principle that liceity is linked to a

---

[41] Veraja, Contratto di censo, 7, 23–4.

[42] Giacomo Todeschini has repeatedly argued that we cannot understand the development of medieval economic definitions, distinctions, and doctrines without keeping this firmly in mind. See, in particular, Il prezzo della salvezza: lessici medievali del pensiero economico (Rome: La Nuova Italia Scientifica, 1994), esp. 163–228; Giacomo Todeschini, I mercanti e il tempio: la società cristiana e il circolo virtuoso della ricchezza fra Medioevo ed Età Moderna (Bologna: Il Mulino, 2002).

[43] E.g., Gratian, Decretum, II, 14, 3, c. 1.

[44] A 10 percent annual payment is common in the contracts that Veraja examined, though he found evidence of returns ranging from 5 to 12.5 percent.

[45] Tellingly, Veraja has found that the terms for a perpetual return were generally the same as those for a life return (Contratto di censo, 20–3), indicating that there was simply no expectation of (or concern for) numerical equality over the life of the contract.

fixed and knowable numerical equality: the annual payment stipulated in contracts *redditus ad vitam* must be pegged to the age, health, and probable number of years remaining to the party receiving the annual payment. The total sum of the return must be approximated, insofar as possible, to the original value of the transferred land. If the original value was intentionally lower than the sum most likely to be returned, then the contract was *in fraudem usurarum*.[46] Raymond attempted here to fit the census contract, which was very favorable to the economic health of ecclesiastical institutions, to the old model of commutative equality, even though it had doubt and approximation built into it. It was not an easy or comfortable fit. At this point, however, he was still holding firm to the traditional requirement of a numerically quantifiable equality in the exchange.[47]

The liceity of the census contract continued to be the subject of debate in the decades following Raymond's decision. In 1251 Pope Innocent IV (1243–54), a renowned legal scholar and former professor of law at Bologna, took up the question in his great work on the *Decretals*, written over decades of his life, as part of his commentary on the decretal *In civitate*.[48] His argument – the most elaborate by a canonist of the thirteenth century – contained a number of parts, each of great interest and importance to the history of equality. Pope Innocent was clearly not satisfied with the previous decisions concerning the liceity of the census contract, and he took a decidedly different tack. He argued that the census contract is not formally usurious because it is not properly a loan (*mutuum*) but is rather a contract of sale (*venditio*). Therefore, the canons from Gratian governing the determination of equality in the *mutuum* do not apply to it.[49] If, he wrote, the census contract is indeed a sale, one is no longer bound by the perfect equality required by usury theory. By viewing the *census* contract in strictly formal terms as a sale, Innocent transferred the judging point of commutative equality from the eventual outcome over the life of the contract to the moment at which the agreement was made. All that is required, he writes, is that the price agreed to *at the time of the sale agreement* by both parties to a census contract conforms more or less to the common price of other similar *census*

---

[46] *Ibid.*, 29.

[47] For a continuation of this line of reasoning in the early fourteenth century, albeit with much added detail and mathematical rigor concerning the doubt and probability built into such contracts, see the comments of Alexander Lombard, *Tractatus de usuris*, 152–7.

[48] Innocent IV, *Super Libros Quinque Decretalium* (Frankfurt, 1570, reprint Minerva, 1968), V.19.5, *In civitate*.

[49] *Ibid.*, 517rb: "Ex forma huiusmodi contractus, non potest censeri usurarius ex forma, quia venditio est, et non mutuum, et in mutuo tantum intervenit usura." Cf. Noonan, *Usury*, 155.

contracts (*communi aestimatione non excedat*). The terms of payment agreed to in such contracts are to be determined by the estimation of the parties themselves that they have arrived at a just equivalence (at best approximate) between the promised annual return and the original "buying" price offered.[50] The shared estimation of equal benefit at the time of the sale at the common price has now been deemed sufficient, in itself, to satisfy the requirement for *aequalitas* in such contracts.[51]

Pope Innocent's position here at the middle of the thirteenth century, while applied only to contracts of sale, nevertheless confirmed the general principle (as stated in *Naviganti*) that probable doubt relaxes and reshapes the requirement of equality in all contractual forms. It reveals with great clarity the difficulties that arguments constructed to maintain the ideal of perfect numerical equality in the *mutuum* would face from this time forward. If probable doubt excuses usury, the question arises: in what loan contract – indeed, in what economic exchange of any kind – is doubt not present? When even the broad mathematical limits of legal sale price can be ignored because of the uncertainty and approximation built into census contracts, the definition of exchange equality becomes ever more destabilized, and the quest for some test of equality between exchangers ever more problematic. But the test remained and the search remained.

For Pope Innocent, the test became whether the terms agreed to (i.e., the sum of the annual payment in proportion to the sum originally given) fell within the price bounds of "common estimation," and if they exceeded those bounds, the contract was to be judged unequal and illicit.[52] But how was a judge or priest or confessor to make this determination? From the mid thirteenth century at the latest, those who were called upon to judge the liceity of such contracts were required to make themselves intimately familiar with the vagaries of the marketplace if they were to be knowledgeable about "common prices" and their variation

---

[50] I consider the growing recognition of the role of "common estimation" in the determination of just price and value, so crucial to the development of medieval price theory, in Chapter 2 below.

[51] Innocent IV, *Libros Quinque*, V.19.5 (517rb): "Ex hac decretali satis innuitur, quod si aliquis pro certa pecuniae quantitate emeret aliquem redditum grani, vel vini, vel alium consimile perpetuo sibi et suis haeredibus dandum a venditore et suis haeridibus, vel ad certum tempus, vel ad tempus vitae alicuius, quod licitus est huiusmodi contractus, dummodo *redditus* annuus communi aestimatione non excedat redditum quem haberet, vel habere posset, si terram de tanta pecunia emisset. Et si excedat communiter, non est licitus contractus." See Veraja, *Contratto di censo*, 37–9. For the opinion of the eminent Italian jurist, Baldus de Ubaldus, writing at the end of the fourteenth century, on this form of equalization, see Franklin, "Ancient Legal Sources of Seventeenth-Century Probability," 128–32.

[52] Innocent IV, *Libros Quinque*, V.19.5 (517rb): "Et si excedat communiter, non est licitus contractus." On this subject, see McLaughlin, "Teaching of the Canonists," 118–19.

over time. They were, in effect, required to recognize the complex and ever-shifting workings of commercial agreement and exchange, required to consider the changing relations between parties to a contract and their varying chances of gaining or losing, and required to comprehend the intricate movement of prices and its causes. The capacity to comprehend these subjects, in turn, required observers, whether lawyer or theologian, to "think" with probabilities, proportionalities, estimations, and sliding scales. As they did so, not only did their determinations concerning which contractual forms conformed to the requirement of equality change, but so too did their very sense of what *aequalitas* might look like.

Models of equality and equalization in Aristotle's analysis of economic exchange, *Nicomachean Ethics*, Book V

Interpretations and positions on how to fit doubt and risk to the requirements of equalization in the loan contract continued to evolve over the second half of the thirteenth century. Two contributors to this debate, the theologians Thomas Aquinas and Peter of John Olivi, offer revealing views into its shape and direction, and I will focus on their opinions in the pages that follow. Before considering them, however, I turn to a crucial intellectual development of the mid thirteenth century that intervened between the debates thus far considered and the theological speculations on equality and usury found in the writings of Thomas and Olivi: the appearance of Robert Grosseteste's first complete Latin translation of Aristotle's *Nicomachean Ethics* from the Greek (1246–7), which included the first Latin translation of Aristotle's profoundly insightful analysis of money and exchange in Book V.[53]

The first point to make concerning this text is that Aristotle, fully as much as Gratian and the scholastics who followed him, situated his discussion of economic exchange squarely within the context of justice, equality, and forms of equalization. Indeed, in *Ethics* Book V Aristotle analyzed forms of equality and equalization with a thoroughness and acuity far surpassing any discussion of the subject previously available within scholastic culture. Due in large part to its penetrating focus on these topics, the impact of Aristotle's discussion in *Ethics* V was profound and long-lasting, not only on scholastic economic thought but on all disciplines centered on the concern to attain and maintain *aequalitas*,

---

[53] For more on the history of this text and its Latin translation, with a focus on its pivotal place in scholastic thinking on justice and equality, see my *Economy and Nature in the Fourteenth Century*, esp. 37–78.

which is to say on the great majority of scholastic disciplines.[54] In the area of economic thought, the primary contribution of Aristotle's discussion was to add definitional precision and theoretical structure to a scholastic analysis of exchange *aequalitas* that, with its grounding in the close observation of economic life and its inheritance from Roman and canon law, had already achieved a high degree of sophistication *before* its reception. From its reception forward, the text of *Ethics* V provided an additional analytical lens through which to view and interpret the ever-evolving dynamic of urban exchange as a process of equalization.

In Book V, chs. 3–5, Aristotle considers the process of economic exchange and the function of money within that process as intellectual problems with their own proper modes of description and analysis. Within the *Nicomachean Ethics* as a whole, Book V containing the analysis of money and exchange was given particularly close scrutiny by scholastic readers, since it was at the same time the site of Aristotle's most detailed discussion of justice, a subject of paramount concern to medieval thinkers. Aristotle's decision to place his discussion of money and economic exchange in the context of his detailed analysis of *justitia* had important consequences, not least for the history of economic thought. The conjuncture gave great support to the position that economic activities, such as producing, exchanging, buying, selling, and the use of money itself, could be sites of order and justice, governable by the logic and mathematics of equality and equalization.[55] Aristotle's unambiguous provision of equalization and order as the context of economic exchange served as a textual bridge between the everyday experience of economic life and intellectual models that could be constructed to comprehend and represent it. The text of the *Ethics* thus contributed to the transformation of the medieval conception of money and the marketplace from sites of corruption, dislocation, and imbalance to potential sites of equalization and justice, deserving of a place at the center of social organization.

Justice as mathematical equalization in *Ethics* V

The first thing to note about Aristotle's definition of justice is how thoroughly mathematical it is and how central the concept of proportionality

---

[54] Due to its importance and lasting influence, I have occasion to refer to Aristotle's analysis of equality and forms of equalization at many points in the chapters that follow.

[55] Fabian Wittreck, *Geld als Instrument der Gerechtigkeit: Die Geldrechtslehre des Hl. Thomas von Aquin in ihrem interkulturellen Kontext* (Paderborn: Ferdinand Schöningh, 2002).

is to it. He writes: "The just, then, is the proportionate; the unjust is that which violates proportion."[56] For Aristotle, all forms of justice are directed toward the attainment of an appropriate mean or *medium*. Working from this base, he separates justice into two particular forms, (1) distributive justice (*iustitia distributiva*), and (2) rectificatory or directive justice (*iustitia directiva*), each form characterized by the mathematical process of equalization proper to it. Distributive justice, the first species he considers, is characterized by proportional equalization. To illustrate this form, Aristotle provides an example in which a central authority (e.g., the *civitas*) distributes benefits or rewards to its citizens in proportion as they have proved themselves worthy of reward through service or contribution. Since the quality and amount that men contribute and are capable of contributing is inherently unequal, distributive reward requires the establishment of (in Aristotle's terms) a "geometrical" rather than an "arithmetical" equivalence: that is, a proportional equivalence in which greater service justly receives a proportionally greater reward.[57] In this context Aristotle states a rule: in cases where the contribution has been unequal, to award all with an identical (i.e., "arithmetically" equal) reward would be manifestly *unequal* and unjust.[58] Aristotle extends the form of distributive justice to cover certain economic practices current in his society. He specifically includes partnerships under *iustitia distributiva*, noting that funds drawn from the partnership "will be according to the same proportion as the funds [the partners] put into the business bear to one another."[59] Note the echoes here between Aristotle's *iustitia distributiva* and the proportional equivalences that canonists from the late twelfth century (which is to say, long before the text of the *Ethics* was in circulation) brought into play in their analysis of credit contracts.

---

[56] The Latin I cite in the notes is taken from the revised version of Robert Grosseteste's mid-thirteenth-century (1246–7) translation, dated to *c.* 1260: *Ethica Nicomachea, translatio Roberti Grosseteste Lincolniensis, recensio recognita*, ed. R. A. Gauthier, in *Aristoteles Latinus*, vol. XXVI, 1–3, fasc. 4 (Leiden: Brill, 1973) (henceforth, *Arist. Lat.* XXVI). This revised version remained the most widely used Latin text of the *Ethics* through the fifteenth century. For the English translation I rely primarily on W. D. Ross, in *The Basic Works of Aristotle*, ed. Richard McKeon (New York: Random House, 1941), although I emend his translation at some points to bring it into line with the medieval Latin text. *Ethica* [1131b16], in *Arist. Lat.* XXVI, 459: "Iustum quidem igitur hoc proporcionale. Iniustum autem quod preter proporcionale."

[57] *Ethica* [1131b12–14], *Arist. Lat.* XXVI, 459: "Vocant autem talem proporcionalitatem geometricam mathematici."

[58] This rule holds profound implications for the determination of equality in usury theory. It will be discussed below in regard to the position on usury adopted by Thomas Aquinas.

[59] *Ethica* [1130b29–30], *Arist. Lat.* XXVI, 459: "et enim a pecuniis communibus si fiat distribucio, erit secundum proporcionem eandem quam habent ad invicem illatam."

Where distributive justice establishes a proportional equivalence between assumed unequals, Aristotle's second-named form of justice, *iustitia directiva*, applies "arithmetical" equalization to cases in which the participants are assumed to be and are treated as equals.[60] In cases governed by *iustitia directiva* there is presumed to be an equalizing mid-point between the claims of two contesting parties. The judge, who considers the relative gain and loss of two parties after the fact of an unequal exchange, reaches this mid-point through the arithmetical processes of addition and subtraction – adding to the one who has excessively lost and taking from the one who has excessively gained.[61] In the text of the *Ethics*, "directive" justice is also called "rectificatory" or "corrective" because it applies to those cases in which equality is restored through the interventions of a judge or orderer, after the exchange itself has taken place. The image Aristotle employs here is of the judge bisecting the line of gain and loss to arrive at a balancing point.[62]

Although Aristotle here writes of the comparison and bisection of lines, the image of the mechanical scale – the iconographic representation of justice – lies in the background. Indeed, his discussion of *iustitia directiva* provided a name, defining characteristics, and mathematical precision to a model of arithmetical equalization that had previously remained unnamed, even though it had occupied a central place in usury theory from the time of Gratian's *Decretum*. At the very same time, however, *Ethics* V provided the name, defining characteristics, and mathematical logic governing an *alternative* model of equalization, *iustitia distributiva*, whose proportional requital is utterly inconsonant with the kind of arithmetical equality traditionally required in usury theory. And yet here, in Aristotle's scheme, it is fully and equally identified as a species of justice and equality.

After describing the mathematical forms of distributive and directive justice, Aristotle introduces the concept of reciprocity (*contrapassum*), and it is this third, hybrid form of equalization that he identifies with the types of economic exchange common to life in the *civitas*: buying, selling, the exchange of labor and services, and the production of goods for exchange between individual exchangers.[63] Since Aristotle's discussion of economic *contrapassum* is particularly germane to the determination of value in exchange, I will withhold my treatment of it until the following chapter dedicated to the scholastic discourse on price and value. Aristotle then follows his exploration of *contrapassum* in exchange with a rich,

---

[60] *Ibid.*: "Reliqua autem una directivum."   [61] *Ethica* [1132b24–9].   [62] *Ibid.*
[63] On Aristotle's exclusion of commercial exchange from his discussion, see Kaye, *Economy and Nature in the Fourteenth Century*, 52–5.

insightful, and remarkably compressed analysis of the form and function of money in exchange. This topic, too, pertains directly to the following chapter on price and value, and I consider it there, but since questions relating to the equalization of monetary sums in the *mutuum* are dependent on assumptions concerning money itself, it is also highly relevant to the subject of usury.

Money as an instrument of equalization in *Ethics* V

In a passage that is often expanded upon by medieval commentators, Aristotle equates the very survival of human industry, and thus the survival of the *civitas* itself, with the establishment of *proportional equivalences* in economic exchange.[64] Aristotle's fixation (not at all too strong a word) on the finding of equality in economic exchange necessarily brought him to questions of measurement and commensurability. How, he asked, can equivalences be established between diverse people exchanging diverse goods of diverse quality involving diverse labors and skills of production? This question was paramount, since he believed that without a means to insure equalization between exchangers, exchange would not take place, and without exchange, the *civitas* would not hold together.[65]

For it is not two doctors that associate for exchange, but a doctor and a farmer, and in general people who are different and unequal; *but these must be equated.* This is why all things must somehow be comparable for there to be exchange (my emphasis).[66]

In Aristotle's scheme, it is money that provides the solution to the thorny problem of comparison and commensuration in exchange.

It is for this end that money has been introduced, and it becomes in a sense an intermediate (*aliqualiter medium*); for it measures all things, and therefore the

---

[64] *Ethica* [1133a15–17], *Arist. Lat.* XXVI, 462–3: "Oportet igitur hec utique equari. Est autem hoc et in aliis artibus. Destruentur enim si non fecerit faciens et quantum et quale et faciens hoc et tantum et tale." This statement is considered to be an interpolation by certain modern editors. Nevertheless, it appears in both the first Grosseteste translation of the *Ethics* and in its authoritative revision, and it was often glossed by medieval commentators. On this subject, see Odd Langholm, *Economics in the Medieval Schools: Wealth, Exchange, Value, Money, and Usury According to the Paris Theological Tradition* (Leiden: Brill, 1992), 189.

[65] *Ethica* [1132b31–4], *Arist. Lat.* XXVI, 462: "per contrafacere enim proporcionale commanet civitas."

[66] *Ibid.*, 463: "Non enim ex duobus medicis fit communicacio, set ex medico et agricola, et omnino alteris, et non equalibus; *set hos oportet equari* [my emphasis]. Propter quod omnia comparata oportet aliqualiter esse, quorum est commutacio."

excess and the defect (*et superhabundanciam et defectum*) – how many shoes are equal (*equale*) to a house or to a given amount of food.[67]

But in what sense are multiple pairs of shoes said to be "equal" to a house? What is the meaning of "equal" here, given the inescapable value inequalities (*superhabundanciam et defectum*) attached to the skill of every producer and to the "labor and expenses" attached to all goods in exchange? Aristotle's answer is that the equality aimed for is never arithmetical, never fixed at 1:1, but always fluid and geometrically proportional.[68]

If, then, first there is proportionate equality of goods (*proporcionalitatem equale*), and then reciprocal action (*contrapassum*) takes place, the result we mention [just exchange] will be effected. If not, the exchange is not equal, and does not hold (*non equale, neque commanet*); for there is nothing to prevent the work of the one being better than that of the other; they must therefore be equated.[69]

Nowhere, as we have seen, were medieval thinkers more in line with Aristotle than in their agreement that just exchange was a process of equalization. Although before the reception of the *Ethics*, canon law decisions on credit contracts never specified what forms of equality they were employing with the clarity and mathematical precision that Aristotle brought to the subject, nevertheless, like Aristotle, they were moving toward the recognition that only a modified form of proportional equalization, such as that embedded in mutual agreement, could accommodate the open-ended nature of risk and doubt and the inequality of gain and loss built into the loan contract. With the intellectual ground well prepared for it, the text of the *Ethics* had a deep and lasting influence on the scholastic discourse of *aequalitas* in exchange, but its influence extended far beyond the economic sphere as well. Every medieval discourse that was constructed around the ideal of equality, or the finding of the mean, or the establishment of justice, or the maintenance of order, made use of it, and there were very few scholastic discourses that did not. After the

---

[67] *Ibid.* (continuing) "propter quod omnia comparata oportet aliqualiter esse, quorum est commutacio; ad quod nummisma venit, et fit aliqualiter medium. Omnia enim mensurat, quare et superhabundanciam et defectum. Quanta quedam utique calciamenta, equale domui vel cibo." Note the use of the term *superhabundanciam* here to express the idea of excess – a term well known to scholastics from its place in the *Decretum* as the definition (initially by St. Jerome) of usurious inequality.

[68] *Ibid.*, 462: "Set in concomitacionibus quidem commutativis continet tale iustum contra-passum secundum proportionalitatem et non secundum equalitatem; per contrafacere enim proporcionale commanet civitas."

[69] *Ibid.*: "Si igitur primum sit secundum proportionalitatem equale, deinde contrapasssum fiat, erit quod dicitur. Si autem non, non equale, neque commanet. Nichil enim prohibet melius esse alterius opus, quam alterius. Oportet igitur hec utique equari."

Latin translation of the *Ethics* in the mid thirteenth century, and the subsequent dissemination of its lessons in the schools, scholars had the great advantage of the clarity and mathematical framing Aristotle brought to the modeling of forms of equalization. But perhaps it is already apparent: along with the benefits of clarity, Aristotle's lessons here would bring serious problems and hurdles to a theorization of usury still linked to the authority of Gratian's canons in the *Decretum*. We can, I think, see this dual heritage clearly in the writings on usury of Thomas Aquinas.

Models of equality and equalization in Thomas Aquinas' writings on usury

The importance of St. Thomas Aquinas (1225–74) to the development of usury theory has at times been overstated. He derived many of his technical arguments directly from Roman and canon law, with further borrowings from earlier theological writings on the subject and, after 1250, from the writings of Aristotle. Although he came back to the question of usury a number of times, and although he clearly thought the question important, he devoted only a tiny fraction of his writings to it or, in general, to subjects we would now consider to have an "economic" component. While his discussion of usury was largely derivative, I want to argue that the arguments he put forth represent an extremely careful and narrow choice taken from the wide array of arguments available to him. Indeed, the closer one looks at his writings, both early and late, the more careful and more narrow his choices appear. His caution, I believe, resulted in large part from his remarkable sensitivity to the changing definitions of the major terms in the equation of usury: money, nature, and equality itself. The profound shift in meaning of these three constituent terms over the course of the thirteenth century, when fully comprehended, rendered many of the oldest and most commonly held positions on usury, some dating back to the *Decretum*, untenable. It is not, then, Thomas' status as an innovative "economic" thinker that has led me to focus here on his writings, but rather his sensitivity to changing definitions and their implications.

In a number of respects, the positions held by medieval theologians on usury differed from those of the lawyers. Although often informed and influenced by canon law on the subject, theologians were generally more conservative with respect to the justification of *interesse*.[70] Thomas accepted the principle of *damnum emergens*, the lender's right to

---

[70] Ibanès, *La doctrine*, 41–2.

compensation for actual damages caused by the contractual failure of the borrower.[71] But he was considerably more sensitive than Hostiensis to the philosophical implications of *lucrum cessans*.[72] He denied the lender's right to require compensation for lost future profits that were merely possible, on the basis that doing so involved selling what had only *probable* rather than real existence. He wrote: "one should not sell something which one has not yet got and which one may be prevented in many ways from getting."[73] Thomas' distinction between what is "merely" probable and what is real was crucial to his position on equality in the loan contract.

Before the full text of the *Ethics* became available in Latin, Thomas had been fully engaged in the process of integrating the thought of Aristotle with the intellectual tradition of Christian theology and law. He was introduced to the *Ethics* through the lectures of his mentor, Albertus Magnus, in Cologne (*c.* 1250), shortly after its first complete Latin translation appeared. Albert used these lectures as a basis for writing the first scholastic commentary on this work, which he followed with a second commentary a decade later (*c.* 1270), and only then did Thomas follow suit with his own (*c.* 1271).[74] Thomas' commentary to Aristotle's analysis of money and exchange in Book V of the *Ethics* reveals not only that he fully grasped the elements in Aristotle's argument but that he was capable of clarifying the text and reinforcing its insights. In this he was aided by his thorough knowledge of Roman and canon law writings on economic questions and by his own close observation of economic life.

---

[71] The Latin edition of Thomas Aquinas, *Summa theologica* (hereafter, *ST*) is the Leonine edition (Rome: Commissio Leonina, 1888–1906), which can be accessed at www.corpus thomisticum.org. Since the Latin edition is readily available, I include the Latin text in the notes only where I quote directly from it or where the wording is particularly revealing. English translations are for the most part from *Summa theologica* (New York: Blackfriars, 1964–81), with modifications noted. *ST*, II, II, 78, 2, ad 1: "ille qui mutuum dat potest absque peccato in pactum deducere cum eo qui mutuum accipit recompensationem damni, per quod subtrahitur sibi aliquid quod debet habere; hoc enim non est vendere usum pecuniae, sed damnum vitare."

[72] Ibanès, *La doctrine*, 26–7; Noonan, *Usury*, 117.

[73] *ST*, II, II, 78, 2, ad 1: "Recompensationem vero damni quod consideratur in hoc quod de pecunia non lucratur non potest in pactum deducere, quia non debet vendere id quod nondum habet, et potest impediri multipliciter ab habendo."

[74] I am following the edition, *Sancti Thomae de Aquino Sententia libri ethicorum*, vol. XLVII in *Opera omnia* (Rome: Commissio Leonina, 1969) (henceforth, *Ethics*). There has been controversy over the dating of this work. I follow R.-A. Gauthier, "La date du commentaire de saint Thomas sur l'Ethique à Nicomaque," *Recherches de théologie ancienne et médiévale* 18 (1951), 66–105. For a more recent confirmation, see Jean-Pierre Torrell, *Saint Thomas Aquinas: The Person and his Work*, vol. I, trans. Robert Royal (Washington, DC: Catholic University of America Press, 2005), 227–8.

Problems introduced by Aristotle's analysis of exchange equalization

Thomas' commentary to Aristotle's discussion of money in the *Ethics* provides evidence of his comprehension of each of its major points: that money functions (1) as a common measure, graded and numbered to facilitate its measuring function;[75] (2) as a divisible measuring line, capable of being added to and subtracted from, so that ever-fluctuating gain and loss in economic exchanges can be equalized;[76] (3) as a medium of *relation*, serving as the mid-term in the exchange of goods, permitting the wide array of goods and services to find comparison and commensuration;[77] (4) as an instrument of proportionalization, facilitating the dynamic equalization (*contrapassum*) of exchange;[78] (5) as a continuous connecting *medium*, literally binding the *civitas* as it brings together producers and consumers of widely varying goods and services.[79] Moreover, Thomas noted and supported Aristotle's observation that while the value of money should ideally remain stable (the better to serve as the universal medium of measurement and commensuration), in fact it often did not, fluctuating (as the values of goods themselves were understood to fluctuate) in response to changing conditions.[80] Although Thomas seems to accept each of these characteristics without hesitation in his *Commentary* on Aristotle's *Ethics*, the logical implications of any one of them would, I maintain, render it difficult if not impossible for him to also accept the assumptions about money that

---

[75] Aquinas, *Ethics* V.9, 294, comment to [1133a19–30]: "Et ad hoc inventum est nummisma, id est denarius, per quem mensurantur pretia talium rerum, et sic denarius fit quodam modo medium, in quantum scilicet omnia mensurat et superabundantiam et defectum."

[76] *Ibid.*, 295, comment to [1133b19–23]: "res tam differentes impossibile est commensurari secundum veritatem ... unde oportet esse unum aliquid quo omnia huiusmodi mensurentur ... unde etiam vocatur nummisma."

[77] *Ibid.*, 294, comment to [1133a19–30]: "oportet quod omnia illa quorum potest esse comutatio sint aliqualiter ad invicem comparabilia ... Et ad hoc inventum est nummisma."

[78] *Ibid.*, 295, comment to [1133a31–b4]: "quando fit commutatio rerum oportet ducere res comutandas in diametralem figuram proportionalitatis."

[79] Aquinas, *Ethics* V.8 (1969), 291, comment to [1132b33]: "quod iustum commutativum contineat contrapassum secundum proportionalitatem, quia per hoc commanent cives sibi invicem in civitate quod sibi invicem proportionaliter contrafaciunt." In Aristotle's analysis, seconded by Aquinas, money is the instrument that facilitates the proportional equalization which binds the *civitas*.

[80] Aquinas, *Ethics*, V.9, 295, comment to [1133b10–14]: "non semper est eiusdem valoris; sed tamen taliter debet esse institutus ut magis permaneat in eodem valore quam aliae res." On the limited fluctuation of the value of money compared to other goods, see Wittreck, *Geld als Instrument der Gerechtigkeit*, 237–44.

underlay Gratian's insistence on arithmetical equality in contracts of loan. Yet Thomas set himself the task of constructing an absolute argument against usury in a way that would be consistent with the ancient canons.[81] The strength and lasting influence of his argument mask the serious problems he was forced to work around and overcome. Behind the seeming naturalness of the product lies the reality of very strenuous and purposeful construction.

The engineering of Thomas' argument

The two most complete of Thomas' later treatments of the question of usury appear in the *De malo* (*c.* 1268–70), question 13, article 4 and in *Summa theologica* II, II, question 78 (*c.* 1270–2).[82] Some general statements can be made about both. Although he suggests that men should be motivated to lend by friendship and charity without hoping for reward, his goal is not to show that demanding usury is a sin against charity. Rather, it is to demonstrate that usury is a sin against *justice*, and in particular that aspect of justice that is quantifiable and knowable – *aequalitas* – an *aequalitas*, moreover, that is as precisely numerable and knowable as the equality found in Gratian's canons. Thomas makes this crystal clear in the opening words of the first *responsio* in *Summa theologica* II, II, 78: "It is said," he writes, "that to accept usury for the money that has been lent is in itself unjust, because it is to sell that which does not exist, which clearly constitutes inequality (*inaequalitas*) and is contrary to justice."[83]

To support this claim, Thomas constructs an argument that rests in part on Roman law and in part on definitions developed within the canon law tradition after Gratian.[84] He posits that in the loan (*mutuum*), the lender transfers ownership of money to the borrower (which distinguishes the *mutuum* from the rent contract, or *locatio*, in which ownership is

---

[81] The dimensions of this project are explored in Giacomo Todeschini, "Ecclesia et mercato nei linguaggi dottrinali di Tommaso d'Aquino," *Quaderni storici* 105 (2000), 585–621.

[82] There is debate over the exact chronology of these questions. I generally follow J. A. Weisheipl, *Friar Thomas d'Aquino: His Life, Thought, and Works* (Washington, DC: Catholic University of America Press, 1983). Weisheipl (210–12) discusses the contested datings of *De malo* but notes the general consensus that the treatment of usury in the *De malo* was completed before Thomas began work on *ST*, II, II (1270–2). Cf. Todeschini, "Ecclesia," 586; Noonan, *Usury*, 51, n. 48. The editon of the *De malo* I use is *Quaestiones disputatae De malo*, vol. XXIII in *Opera omnia* (Rome: Commissio Leonina, 1982).

[83] Thomas, *ST*, II, II, 78, 1, resp.: "Dicendum quod accipere usuram pro precunia mutuata est secundum se injustum, quia venditur id quod non est; per quod manifeste ineaequalitas constituitur, quae justitiae contrariatur."

[84] McLaughlin, "Teaching of the Canonists," 99 ff.

retained by the owner). He argues that in abandoning his ownership of the money, the lender loses his right to then charge the borrower for its use.[85] Thomas defines usury as, in essence, the lender's selling the use of the money he lends that is no longer his to sell, since it has already been transferred to the borrower. The money the lender provides is, in effect, *consumed* in the act of lending, or so Thomas argues. In support of this argument he could draw on the canons in Gratian that linked money with other measurable and "fungible" commodities such as wine, wheat, and oil, which are literally consumed in their use.[86]

It is clear that money falls under the category of a fungible good in one of its senses: it can be freely replaced by another of like kind and identical quantity in the satisfaction of an obligation. But that it fulfills its second accepted sense, that it is consumed in its use, is considerably more questionable and difficult to establish – and certainly to establish with the kind of universal validity that Thomas is searching for. To bolster this problematic point, Thomas employs the authority of Aristotle: "According to the Philosopher [Aristotle] money was invented primarily to facilitate exchange, and in performing this function it is consumed in its use."[87] Although Thomas leans on the authority of Aristotle here, nowhere in the *Ethics* does Aristotle link money's facilitation of exchange with its consumption. Nevertheless, from this statement on, Thomas considers that he has established this essential element in his case against usury.[88] With this point assumed, Thomas can argue that when a person lends money, he transfers at the same time its substance, its use, and its ownership (*dominium*) to the borrower. If the usurer then charges the borrower *ultra sortem* for the use of the money loaned, he is either selling what does not exist, or what is not his to sell, or he is selling the same thing twice (*unde vendit id quod non est vel vendit idem bis*). In either case, he creates an unwarranted and *unnatural* excess (*superhabundantia* in

---

[85] As I noted above, in Roman law fungible goods have two qualities that set them apart from all other goods whose use can legitimately be charged for: (1) they can be freely exchanged (or replaced) by another of like kind and identical quantity in the satisfaction of an obligation, and (2) such substitution is necessary because the fungible (wheat, wine, etc.) is consumed in its use, so the original cannot be returned.

[86] Gratian, *Decretum*, II, 14, 3, c. 1 and c. 4. On Thomas' argument for money as a consumed good, see Ian Wei, *Intellectual Culture in Medieval Paris: Theologians and the University, c. 1100–1330* (Cambridge University Press, 2012), 315–18.

[87] *ST*, II, II, 78, 1, resp. "Pecunia autem, secundum Philosophum, principaliter est inventa ad commutationes faciendas, et ita proprius et principalis pecuniae usus est ipsius consumptio, sive distractio secundum quod in commutationes expenditur."

[88] Thomas follows the same pattern in the *De malo* (q. 13, art. 4, resp.), joining the argument equating consumption and use to a generalized citation from Aristotle: "ita etiam et proprius usus pecunie [est] ut expendatur pro commutatione aliarum rerum: sunt enim inventa nummismata commutationis gratia, ut Philosophus dicit in II *Politice*."

Gratian's terms) and in doing so he violates the equality built into both natural justice and nature itself.[89]

My purpose here is not to focus on the problems that exist in Thomas' argument against usury.[90] What I find more telling is what he does *not* say, the Aristotelian insights he intentionally omits and ignores, and even the traditional Christian elements in the argument against usury that he jettisons in his attempt to construct a natural law case against it. Here, I want to argue, that the negative aspects of Thomas' argument – the traditional points he abandons in his case against usury – can tell us as much about the pressures on the redefinition of economic *aequalitas* in the thirteenth century as can the already noted positive contributions of canonists such as Hostiensis and Pope Innocent IV. For someone who was not only fully familiar with Aristotle's treatment of justice, equality, and exchange in *Ethics* V, but who actually refined and expanded on Aristotle's analysis in his commentary, it is striking that Thomas abandoned the most insightful aspects of this discussion in his final formulations on usury. Aristotle had established one point beyond doubt: that it was impossible to talk about justice or equality in exchange without talking about proportionality.[91] Yet there is not a single word about proportionality in all of Thomas' writings on usury.

Indeed, how could there be? Attaching even the slightest notion of proportionality to the *mutuum* would destroy the ancient requirement for a perfect and simple numerical equality that lay at its core. If the lender is likely to give more or suffer more from the loan than the borrower, or if the borrower is likely to benefit more from the loan than the lender (both of which are more than likely), then the application of proportional equalization to the *mutuum* would *require* a numerically *unequal* return, and

[89] The argument in *ST*, II, II, 78, 1, resp. is identical to that in *De malo*, q. 13, art. 4, resp.: "Set in illis rebus quarum usus est earum consumptio non est aliud usus rei quam ipsa res, unde cuicumque conceditur usus talium rerum conceditur etiam et ipsarum rerum dominium et e converso... usus autem pecunie ut dictum est, non est aliud quam eius substantia, unde vendit id quod non est vel vendit idem bis, ipsam scilicet pecuniam cuius est consumptio eius, et hoc est manifeste contra rationem iustitie naturalis."

[90] Many of the problems in his presentation were realized in the following generations: Johannes Andreae, the great canonist, and the theologian Henry of Ghent were among those who recognized that money cannot be said, by definition, to be consumed in its use. This, they saw, held especially true in the loan contract, where the lender actually retains the money he lends by contract, and sells to the borrower not the money *per se* but only the *right* to use the money for a particular length of time. On this, see Noonan, *Usury*, 60–5; Odd Langholm, *The Aristotelian Analysis of Usury* (Bergen: Universitetsforlaget, 1984), 81 ff. Other critics, such as Duns Scotus and Peter Olivi, questioned the necessary identification of money's use, substance, and ownership from a Franciscan perspective, as discussed further below.

[91] On Thomas' recognition of this point, see *Ethics* V.8, 291: "quod iustum commutativum contineat contrapassum secundum proportionalitatem, quia per hoc commanent cives sibi invicem in civitate quod sibi invicem proportionaliter contrafaciunt."

would *require* the introduction of a proportioned *interesse* into the structure of the loan contract in recognition of the inequalities involved.[92] A second major omission: in all of Thomas' writings on usury, there is no hint of the central insight from the *Ethics* that economic value is *relative* value, determined by a variable need or *indigentia* that is relative to time, place, and circumstance.[93] But of course notions of relative value and of a relative need measurable by money would destroy the requirement for numerical *aequalitas* in the loan contract, where the needs of the borrower and lender are utterly different, as are their gains and losses from the exchange.

It was not, however, only the lessons about exchange equalization from Aristotle's *Ethics* that Thomas ignored. He also passed over the many developments within thirteenth-century canon law that destabilized, and indeed subverted, the simple definition of arithmetical equality so clearly and unproblematically asserted in the *Decretum*. And there is yet an even more revealing omission. In his most mature positions in the *De malo* and the *Summa theologica* (*ST*), he has jettisoned most of the traditional Christian *moral* and *ethical* argument against usury, based in the ethics of the *personal* exchange between lender and borrower, which had been so central to the reasoning in the *Decretum* and in later canon law. Why would he do this?

There is ample evidence that Thomas was well aware of the actual preexisting inequalities between borrower and lender built into the *mutuum*. One of the striking things about his later treatments of usury is his clear and unabashed recognition that borrowers gain from the loans they receive, even from loans contaminated by usury, even from loans that contractually require a repayment beyond the sum lent. The clearest statements of this recognition in the *ST* and the *De malo* come when he explains why moderate usury is acceptable within Roman law.

Summa theologica: Human law allows usury not because it judges it to be commensurate with justice but because to deny it would be to impede the utility (*utilitates*) of many.[94]

---

[92] Traces of this reasoning can be seen in the Roman law, which permitted the unequal positions of lender and borrower to find reflection in a permissible proportional interest on loans.

[93] For Thomas' comprehension and acceptance of this point, see *Ethics* V.9, 294b–95a: "Hoc autem unum quod omnia mensurat, secundum rei veritatem est indigentia, quae continet omnia commutabilia, in quantum scilicet omnia referuntur ad humanam indigentiam; non enim appretiantur res secundum dignitatem naturae ipsorum; alioquin unus mus, quod est animal sensibile, maioris pretii esset quam una margarita, quae est res inanimata; sed rebus pretia imponuntur secundum quod homines indigent eis ad suum usum." Discussed in greater detail in Chapter 2 below.

[94] *ST*, II, II, 78, 1, ad 3: "Et ideo usuras lex humana concessit, non quasi existimans eas esse secundum iustitiam, sed ne impedirentur utilitates multorum." The official Dominican translation of this passage from Latin to English (New York: Blackfriars, 1964) appears

De malo: The positive law permits usury because of the many benefits (*multas commoditates*) that result from the lending of money, even from usurious lending.[95]

Given his recognition of the "*utilitates*" and "*commoditates*" offered by usurious contracts, and his awareness of the lessons of proportionality and relativity conveyed in Aristotle's *Ethics*, and his knowledge of canon law decisions expanding exchange *aequalitas* through the recognition of probability, risk, and doubt, it would be hard, if not impossible, for him to deny that the probability of benefits to the borrower and losses to the lender would in many cases require an arithmetically *unequal* return, if this relationship itself were made the basis of the equation.

But if he can no longer locate the inequality of usury in the personal relationship between lender and borrower, where then can he locate it? When we look closely at the kind of inequality that forms the basis of his case, we can see that it is not, in essence, personal, social, moral, or ethical: it is formal and definitional. At its core is the rigid definition of money that insists on its being consumed in its use and that charging separately for its use involves either selling something that does not have a separable existence or selling the same thing twice.[96] I suggest that Thomas chose this highly selective and narrow path because social and economic pressures on the conceptualization of *aequalitas* made him aware of new definitional traps on every side. His options were extremely limited if his intent was to continue to support the traditional ideal of perfect numerical equality between sum lent and sum returned in the intellectual culture of the later thirteenth century. He had first to elim-inate the actual elements and processes of equalization at work between real individuals in real exchanges, which he accomplished by shifting the basis of his argument to the realm of highly restricted formal defi-nition. Then a more difficult task faced him: to choose and construct an abstraction that could serve him as an absolute and impersonal arbiter of *aequalitas* in the *mutuum*, one that would hold true despite the ever-shifting contexts of exchange. It must be an abstraction capable of standing detached from actual economic transactions – detached from inescapable inequalities and uncertainties, relativized and ever-shifting

intent to overlook Thomas' acceptance of usury's evident benefits: "Human law, there-fore, allows the taking of interest, not because it deems this to be just but because to do otherwise would impose undue restrictions on many people."

[95] *De malo*, q. 13, art. 4, ad 6: "Et hoc modo ius positivum permisit usuras propter multas commoditates quae interdum aliqui consequntur ex pecunia mutuata, licet sub usuris."

[96] The sense of the personal remains present in Thomas' insistence that the borrower may voluntarily choose to recompense the lender in recognition of the aid and charity repre-sented by his loan, but this voluntary recompense is defined as outside the law and outside the equalization required by nature.

values, monetary instabilities, and the like. He chose overarching Nature as that abstract arbiter.[97]

In his final position on the question of usury, Thomas defines the slightest numerical difference between sum lent and sum required in return as a violation of "natural equality," and hence, *in itself* (i.e., divorced from any and all particular contexts) as a sin against "natural justice" (*secundum se peccatum: est enim contra iustitiam naturalem*).[98] Nature has become the judge with the authority to define *aequalitas* and *justitia* in a way that brooks no alteration or expansion.[99] And nature is also now, first and foremost, the injured party. Since Thomas recognized that borrowers can in many cases benefit from even usurious loans, the inequality at the root of usury violates first and foremost the order of nature: in effect, the balance of nature as he defined it. For this reason, I think it is fair to say that in his later writings Thomas centers the dislocation of usury more in the realm of *physics* than in the ethics of commutative justice.

There is no denying the success and influence of Thomas' definitional "solution" here, placing impersonal nature as the arbiter of usury. It remained viable for centuries, particularly among his fellow Dominicans. My point is that there is also no denying what Thomas was forced to give up in formulating this position: the rich insights into the nature of money and exchange he had learned from Aristotle; the recognitions he had inherited from canon law that exchange was embedded in multiform contexts in which the play of probabilities, doubts, and risks necessitated approximate and proportionalized solutions and vitiated expectations for numerical exactitude in the return; and, most pointedly, the moral, ethical, and social arguments against usury that had informed its condemnation from the time of Gratian.

But Thomas' was only one solution, only one moment in the history of *aequalitas* and balance. Very soon, as it happened, in the vibrant intellectual culture of late thirteenth-century scholasticism, it was followed by other solutions, rooted in other visions of equality and equalization, other "senses" of the potentialities of balance in nature, that proved to be very different from Thomas'. In the field of medieval economic thought, we can see a strikingly new model of equalization emerging in the last quarter

---

[97] Thomas' "nature," as it finds expression here and elsewhere in his thought, is an abstraction whose imaginative construction is deeply indebted to Aristotle's writings on the subject.

[98] *De malo*, q. 13, art. 4, resp.: "[usura] nec ideo est peccatum quia est prohibitum, set potius est prohibitum quia est secundum se peccatum: est enim contra iustitiam naturalem."

[99] *ST*, II, II, 78, 1, resp.: "usus autem pecunie ut dictum est, non est aliud quam eius substantia, unde vendit id quod non est vel vendit idem bis, ipsam scilicet pecuniam cuius est consumptio eius, et hoc est manifeste contra rationem iustitie naturalis."

of the thirteenth century, most directly and forcefully in the writings of the Franciscan theologian Peter of John Olivi (c. 1248–98).

Equality, equalization, and equilibrium in the writings on usury of Peter of John Olivi

The core of Peter Olivi's economic writings are found in a single work: *The Treatise on Buying and Selling, on Usury, and on Restitutions (Tractatus de emptionibus et venditionibus, de usuris, de restitutionibus).*[100] In his responses to questions attached to risk and doubt, and in his acceptance of approximation, common estimation, probabilistic reasoning, proportionalization, and, above all, the dynamic factor of multiplication, he stretched the boundaries of *aequalitas* and the model of equalization past anything we have seen so far. Indeed, I want to argue that the word "equilibrium," with its modern connotations of systematic self-regulation and self-ordering, can for the first time in the history of scholastic economic thought be applied to Olivi's understanding of exchange *aequalitas* – including the *aequalitas* required in contracts of loan.

It is true that in constructing his arguments concerning usury and economic exchange in the *Tractatus*, Olivi makes use of a number of decisions that had evolved within both Roman and canon law over the course of the thirteenth century; reflections of opinions offered by Hostiensis, Innocent IV and other legists are clearly visible in his writings. But it is essential to recognize that Olivi wrote as a theologian, not as a

---

[100] This is the name chosen by Giacomo Todeschini, *Un trattato di economia politica francescano: il "De emptionibus et venditionibus, de usuris, de restitutionibus" di Pietro di Giovanni Olivi* (Rome: Istituto storico italiano per il medio evo, studi storici, 1980) (hereafter *Tractatus*). Todeschini's was the first complete edition of this work (and the first edition of the section *De usuris*), and it, along with Todeschini's introduction, remains the best source for Olivi's thinking on economic questions. Todeschini preceded his edition with a series of articles that have provided the basis for the analysis of Olivi and Franciscan economics up to the present time. See his "'Oeconomica francescana' I: proposte di una nuova lettura delle fonti dell'etica economica medievale," *Rivista di storia e letteratura religiosa* 12 (1976), 15–77; Giacomo Todeschini, "'Oeconomica francescana' II: Pietro di Giovanni Olivi come fonte per la storia dell'etica-economica medievale," *Rivista di storia e letteratura religiosa* 13 (1977), 461–94. In addition to the *Tractatus*, Olivi wrote two quodlibetal questions on the subject of usury, which confirm and on some points expand his economic positions in the Tractatus. For the standard edition of these questions, with introduction, see Amleto Spicciani, "Gli scritti sul capitale e sull'interesse di Fra Pietro di Giovanni Olivi: Fonti per la storia del pensiero economico medioevale," *Studi francescani* 73 (1976), 289–325. A new Latin edition and French translation of Olivi's complete treatise appeared too late for me to utilize it in my discussion of Olivi's economic thought: Pierre de Jean Olivi, *Traité des contrats*, ed. and trans. Sylvain Piron (Paris: Les Belles Lettres, 2012).

lawyer. As a theologian, Olivi is most concerned with the question of whether the economic activities of men and the economic contracts they devise can (or cannot) be integrated into a governing reason or *ratio* consistent with God's plan for mankind. Where the lawyers proceeded case by case, guided by authoritative precedents, Olivi's thinking reflects both his imagination of an overarching *ratio* and his confidence that much of the economic behavior he observes can be viewed as belonging within and to that rational whole. Only on this basis, only on the basis of its conformity to an overarching rationality as he came to imagine it, could he justify such activity.[101]

As strange as it might appear to the modern reader, at the same time that he was expanding the bounds of *aequalitas* beyond anything previously imagined, Olivi continued to condemn usury and the inequality he located at its core in the strongest possible terms. In the introduction to his treatment of usury in the *Tractatus*, he offers nine separate arguments against it, drawn from traditional biblical, legal, theological, and philosophical sources. He asserts that it violates the justice required by both divine law and "natural equity"; that it poses the greatest threat to the social bonds of community; that it corrupts the usurer as it corrupts the ties of friendship; that it is a sin against grace and charity; that it leads (as "experience teaches") to the "total devouring" of the wealth of others; and yet other reasons besides.[102] In short, he claims: "It is not possible to demand anything more in return (*ultra sortem*) without violating both equity and equality."[103] His identification of usury as a violation of the requirement for equivalence in exchange could not be clearer.

---

[101] Amleto Spicciani, "Pietro di Giovanni Olivi: indigatore della razionalità economica medioevale," in *Usure, compere e vendite: la scienza economica del XIII secolo, Pietro di Giovanni Olivi*, ed. Amleto Spicciani, P. Vian, and G. Andenna (Milan: Europía, 1998), 21–72. This volume also contains Spicciani's Italian translation of Olivi's *Tractatus*.

[102] The diatribe *contra usuram* goes on for pages (*Tractatus*, 70–7), making use of traditional arguments, including the canons cited by Gratian in the *Decretum*, decisions from the *Decretales Gregorii IX*, a partial use of Thomas' argument from the *ST*, and Aristotle's position condemning usury from Book I of the *Politics*.

[103] Olivi, *Tractatus*, 70–1: "Equitas enim est quod pro equali non exigatur plus quam equivalens, seu equale. Non potest amplius exigi absque aperta lesura equitatis et equalitatis." For the position that the innovation of Olivi's economic thought has been overestimated (by Todeschini and others), that Olivi's treatment of usury was both more fragmentary and "traditional" than not, and that it leant heavily on the canon law tradition, see Julius Kirshner and Kimberly Lo Prete, "Peter John Olivi's Treatises on Contracts of Sale, Usury and Restitution: Minorite Economics or Minor Works?" *Quaderni fiorentini* 13 (1984), 233–86. I think it fair to say that while it is helpful to underscore Olivi's debt to canon law (particularly to the writings of Hostiensis), scholarship over the past quarter-century generally supports Todeschini's position with respect to Olivi's originality and importance. The debate has been a productive one.

Moreover, Olivi extended the charge of usury beyond the simple loan contract to cover all agreements that include within them some form of unjust (i.e., unequal) lending, as he defined it. Olivi's restatement of the most traditional objections and rigorist claims in the midst of his expansive reimagining of the potentialities of equalization, reveals with exceptional clarity the tensions and pressures attached to the question of equality in this period and the high stakes involved in its shifting determination.

Equilibrium and the ideal of the Common Good in Olivi's thought

One matrix for the reimagining of *aequalitas* by Olivi and others over the course of the thirteenth century is a concept that grew to occupy a place of immense importance within medieval thought in this period: the concept of the Common Good (*bonum commune*). As he writes in the *Tractatus*:

According to the order of law, justice, and Christian charity (*caritatis*), the common good (*commune bonum*) is preferred and ought to be preferred to any private good.[104]

Notable here is the divine sanction Olivi allows to the Common Good. In his view, it conforms not only to the order of civic law and justice but equally to the "order" of Christian *caritas*, the highest religious value and virtue.[105] It reminds us that this treatise was written by a man who identified himself, above all, as a Christian and a Christian thinker. His concern as a deeply committed Franciscan friar and as a confessor and teacher of future confessors, must be for the souls of buyers and sellers, not merely for the comprehension and justification of their economic actions. His redefinition of justice and equality must have an ethical and religious basis, not merely a practical or purely intellectual one. That it does, that he is able to identify common economic practices with the Common Good, and to identify the order of the Common Good with

---

[104] Olivi, *Tractatus*, 51: "Item secundum ordinem iuris et iustitie et caritatis commune bonum prefertur et preferri debet bono privato."

[105] For an early appreciation of the importance of the Common Good to Olivi's analysis of economic activity, see Todeschini, "Un trattato di economia politica francescana," esp. 12–20. Todeschini speaks here (31) of "A subtle play of relation" in Olivi's thought," between *valor, pretium, bonum commune, caritas* and *lucrum*." See also, Giacomo Todeschini, *Franciscan Wealth: From Voluntary Poverty to Market Society*, trans. Donatella Melucci (Saint Bonaventure, NY: Franciscan Institute, 2009), 112–16. Kirshner and Lo Prete, who find a number of points on which to disagree with Todeschini's reading, nevertheless agree on this point ("Minorite Economics?" 269–70): "A just profit can thus be retained from the exchange of goods as a result of the service a merchant performs for society."

the order of both *justitia* and *caritas*, is testament to the scope, power, and influence this ideal had come to possess by the last quarter of the thirteenth century.

The ever-increasing importance allowed to the *bonum commune* over the course of the thirteenth century was closely tied to the rapid advance of urbanization, communication, commercialization, administration, and political organization that occurred over this same period. The strength of this ideal draws, in part, from the idea, emphasized by Aristotle in the *Politics*, that life within a political community is essential not only for human survival but for the perfection of human virtue. With remarkable unanimity, medieval Christian thinkers gave their assent to this assertion. So central does this concept become after the mid thirteenth century, that writers (including leading theologians like Albertus Magnus and Thomas Aquinas) offer their assent, seemingly without hesitation, to Aristotle's dictum in the *Politics* that the common good of the political community is "manifestly greater and more divine" (*melius vero et divinius*) than the private good of any single individual.[106] We have seen that for canon lawyers, *aequitas*, could be identified with God himself (*aequitas est nihil aliud quam Deus*).[107] So, too, theologians from the mid thirteenth century forward found it possible to identify the good of the whole community, the Common Good, with the order and governance of the universe itself, and thus, *per similitudinem*, with God.[108] It is an extraordinary claim, and it had extraordinary repercussions, not least within the intellectual sphere.

As its name implies, the Common Good represents an aggregate whole – the sum of its moving, acting, and interacting parts, which in this case are the citizens of the *civitas*. In its essence, it privileges the aggregate over the individual, the whole over the part. In the words of St. Thomas (writing approximately two decades before Olivi composed

---

[106] Aristotle, *Politics*, I.2 [1094b8–10]. Thomas Aquinas, *ST*, II, II, 31, 3: "The common good of the many is more divine than the personal good of an individual." I discuss attitudes toward the Common Good in greater detail in Chapters 5, 6, and 7 below, with respect to equality and equilibrium in medieval political thought. Chapter 5 deals specifically with the place of this ideal in the thought of Albertus Magnus and Thomas Aquinas.

[107] Gouron, "Some Aspects,"164; Grossi, *L'ordine giuridico*, 211.

[108] Saint Thomas Aquinas, *Summa contra gentiles*, ed. C. Pera (Turin: Marieti, 1961), based on the earlier Leonine edition (henceforth, *SCG*), Book III, trans. Vernon J. Bourke (New York: Hanover House, 1955–7), III, 17, 6: "Furthermore, a particular good is ordered to the common good as to an end; indeed, the being of a part depends on the being of the whole. So, also, the good of a nation is more divine than the good of one man. Now, the highest good which is God is the common good, since the good of all things taken together depends on Him." For the explicit linking of the Common Good of the political community to the divine, see Remigio Girolami, *De bono communi*, in "Remigio Girolami's *De bono communi*," ed. Minio-Paluello, *Italian Studies* 11 (1956), 56–71.

the *Tractatus*): "a particular good is ordered to the common good as to an end; indeed, the being of a part depends on the being of the whole (*esse enim partis est propter esse totius*)."[109] To "think with" the Common Good, which became ever more common in the fields of political and economic thought after the mid thirteenth century, meant to think in terms of aggregates and multiples. It meant learning to imagine and comprehend the workings of composite communities, whether the *civitas* or the multitude of exchangers in the marketplace, composed of myriad individual parts ordered within a larger functioning system. It raised new questions: how do composite communities act, how do they find direction, how do they arrive at decisions and judgments, how are they ordered and regulated, how might they order and regulate themselves? From the mid thirteenth century on, each of these questions directed toward the communal whole continued to center on the notion of *aequalitas* and its requirements, just as they had in earlier times when they were directed toward the actions and judgments of individuals. But since the new object of investigation was a systematic unity rather than an individual, new questions were added: how does the unity hold together, how do its parts *fit* together and *function* together, how do the parts *relate* to the whole, how does the system order and equalize *itself* in the absence of direction from outside or above; in short, how does it *work*?

By the last quarter of the thirteenth century, the act of reasoning or calculating in terms of the maintenance of *aequalitas* within this functioning unity came to entail imagining a fundamentally new principle of order, based on a new *sense* of the potentialities of balance, which closely approaches the modern connotation of the term "systematic equilibrium." The meaning of the word "equilibrium" did not change in this period. It continued to be applied to two perfectly equal weights balanced at a single achievable point, on the model of the mechanical scale, as it had for millennia past. What changed was the unworded sense of what balance was and could be when expanded past the individual to the systematic whole. It is this unworded sense of balance to which the modern connotations of the word equilibrium apply: a sense of multiple moving and intersecting parts, capable of continually reordering and reequalizing

---

[109] *SCG*, III, 17; *ST*, I, II, 90, 3, ad 3: "And therefore, as the good of one man is not the last end, but is ordained to the common good; so too the good of one household is ordained to the good of the *civitas*, which is a perfect community." There are very many quotations from the works of Thomas that could be used to illustrate the power of the ideal of the Common Good and its multifarious applications. I have chosen to use his words to indicate its contours because of his extraordinary sensitivity to the logical implications of the terms he employs and his capacity to give intellectual shape to concepts of this magnitude.

themselves through their intersections and interactions, and doing so around approximate ranges or "latitudes" rather than around perfectly knowable points. Rather than the 1:1 arithmetical equalization required by Gratian's canons, or even the neat bisection of the line of gain and loss that Aristotle associated with *justitia directiva*, the new sense of balance/ equilibrium, to which the old word *aequalitas* continued to be applied, was grounded in proportions that were understood to shift constantly in relation to shifting contexts and conditions. As Olivi's writings will show, the goal of equalization could now incorporate notions of probability, but it could only do so by abandoning requirements for fixity and certainty. And yet Olivi found it possible to equate this new and newly dynamic form of *aequalitas* with the maintenance of the Common Good.

In short, the evolving ideal of the Common Good was pressured and shaped by the same factors that shaped the expansion of *aequalitas* over the course of the thirteenth century. But where the elements and assumptions constituting *aequalitas* remained for the most part unarticulated and beneath the level of debate, conceptions of the Common Good were continually rearticulated and expanded upon. As the concept continued to evolve and to strengthen, the immense and far-reaching discourse on the "good" in both the Christian and the Aristotelian traditions came ever more to be viewed through its lens. In many cases, acts, habits, laws, virtues, and subordinate ideals were reconceived and reordered to the evolving requirements of this great and growing ideal. As Thomas writes: "A law properly speaking, regards first and foremost the order to the common good."[110] And again, "There is no virtue whose act is not ordainable to the common good, either mediately or immediately."[111] In short, when the ideal of the Common Good, with its particular logic, values, and forms of analysis, was superimposed on questions that had long been asked within scholastic culture, the effects were often profound and transformative. So it was with the question of usury.

Olivi and the Franciscan Order

Deep links between the Franciscan Order, the commercial classes of the towns, and the ideal of the Common Good were established generations before Olivi wrote his *Tractatus* on contracts. Franciscans lived among townspeople, preached to them, received alms from them, frequently drew their members from among them, and often were called upon to confess them. All of these factors linked the Franciscans to the life of

---

[110] *ST*, I, II, 90, art. 3.   [111] *Ibid.*, I, II, 96, 3, ad 3.

the city and encouraged brothers to observe the details of town and commercial life with care. The many years Olivi spent in urban environments were typical in this respect. Born in southern France in the diocese of Béziers (1248), he entered the Franciscan Order at the relatively young age of twelve, where he received his early education.[112] At eighteen (1266) he was sent to the great urban center of Paris to study theology. He remained a student at Paris for at least six (and perhaps as many as eight[113]) of his formative years, after which he returned to southern France. He spent the later 1270s and early 1280s teaching in Franciscan convents within the expanding and economically precocious towns of Narbonne and Montpellier.[114] Both were centers of commerce in this period; both were at or approaching their commercial and demographic zenith in these last decades of the thirteenth century.[115] In 1283, while teaching in the Franciscan convent in Montpellier, certain of Olivi's theological positions were condemned by a commission of scholars from Paris, and his status within the Order was seriously compromised. After several years of contesting the charges, however, he succeeded in defending himself and his writings, and by 1287 he was back in good graces. At this point he was appointed to teach at the important Franciscan school at Santa Croce in the great commercial capital of Florence, where he remained for two years. After 1289, he was back again at the Franciscan *studium* in Montpellier, which had close contact with the University of Montpellier and its renowned medical school. In these years he very likely came into contact with the

---

[112] For the biography of Olivi, see David Burr, "The Persecution of Peter Olivi," *Transactions of the American Philosophical Society*, n.s. 66, no. 5 (1976), 1–98; David Burr, *Olivi and Franciscan Poverty: The Origins of the Usus Pauper Controversy* (Philadelphia: University of Pennsylvania Press, 1989). Additional details are provided in Sylvain Piron, "Marchands et confesseurs: Le Traité des contrats d'Olivi dans son contexte (Narbonne, fin XIIIe–début XIVe siècle)," in *L'argent au Moyen Âge* (Paris: Publications de la Sorbonne, 1998), 289–308.

[113] This is the conjecture of Sylvain Piron, "The Formation of Olivi's Intellectual Project," *Oliviana* 1 (2003) (online journal).

[114] Burr, "Persecution," 6 and n. 10.

[115] See Kathryn Reyerson, *Business, Banking and Finance in Medieval Montpellier* (Toronto: Pontifical Institute of Mediaeval Studies, 1985), 115; Jacqueline Caille, "Urban Expansion in the Region of Languedoc from the Eleventh to the Fourteenth Century: The Example of Narbonne and Montpellier," in *Urban and Rural Communities in Medieval France: Provence and Languedoc, 1000–1500*, ed. Kathryn Reyerson and J. Drendell (Leiden: Brill, 1998), 51–72. I discuss the commercial setting of Montpellier further in Chapter 4, with reference to the contemporary residence there of Arnau de Vilanova, who made great contributions to the intellectual shaping of the new model of equilibrium from the direction of medical theory.

eminent scholastic physician and medical author, Arnau de Vilanova.[116] Olivi wrote his *Tractatus* in the middle 1290s while teaching either at Montpellier or Narbonne.[117] One thing is clear: whether at Paris, Florence, Narbonne, or Montpellier, Olivi spent his entire life in cities that were undergoing rapid expansion, both demographically and commercially.

In every page of his *Tractatus*, Olivi demonstrates his acute awareness of the commercial and contractual life that surrounded him. His sensitivity to contractual forms may well be linked to the vibrant notarial cultures that pervaded the cities he inhabited – Florence, Narbonne, and Montpellier, in particular. These civic spaces were characterized by the habit of organizing the minute details of economic life into contract form.[118] But the depth of Olivi's contractual awareness raises a series of questions that cannot, I think, be explained by his urban setting alone. How did it happen that this rigorist Franciscan theologian, committed to the ideal of evangelical perfection, sworn to a strict vow of poverty, convinced that the preoccupation with temporal affairs and the distractions of the senses was the primary path toward sin and error, possessed at the same time such a capacious understanding of mercantile contracts and practices, and such a capacious willingness to judge existent practices favorably as legitimate forms of equalization?[119] One answer surely lies in his unhesitating recognition that commerce and the commercial classes that pursued it, served the Common Good.

[116] I discuss the intellectual links between Olivi and Arnau (and between economic thought and medical thought) further in Chapter 4 below.

[117] Piron, "Marchands et confesseurs," 291–2, has suggested the dates 1293–5.

[118] On notaries in Montpellier in this period, see Kathryn Reyerson, *The Art of the Deal: Intermediaries of Trade in Medieval Montpellier* (Leiden: Brill, 2002), 79–83. For the focus on contractual specificity, see *Medieval Notaries and their Acts: The 1327–1328 Register of Jean Holanie*, ed. and trans. Kathryn Reyerson and Debra A. Salata (Kalamazoo, MI: Medieval Institute Publications, 2004).

[119] For Olivi's leadership in the Franciscans' debate over the question of poverty, see Burr, *Olivi and Franciscan Poverty*, esp. 57–80. Despite his rigorist position, Olivi recognized that the degree of poverty embraced by each of the brothers must be determined relative to the needs and capacity of each, which he understood to vary. It is noteworthy that to express this sense of relativism and latitudinarianism in spiritual matters he used the identical word to signal the idea of proper and relative fit, *idoneitas*, that he used with respect to similar concerns in economic matters. On this point, and on the linkage between spiritual and economic vocabularies in Olivi's writings, see Todeschini "Oeconomica francescana II," 491 ff; Giacomo Todeschini, "Olivi e il *mercator* cristiano," in *Pierre de Jean Olivi (1248–1298): pensée scolastique, dissidence spirituelle et société*, ed. Alain Boureau and Sylvain Piron (Paris, 1999), 217–37; Todeschini, *Franciscan Wealth*, 96–103.

Problems attached to *aequalitas* in the loan contract

In the long history of scholastic economic thought, the analysis of usury was considerably more cautious, strict, and ideal-driven than the analysis of price and value in buying and selling. We can see this division reflected in Olivi's *Tractatus*. Where the section *De emptionibus et venditionibus* begins with the enunciation of principles of huge scope and implication (discussed in Chapter 2 below), the section *De usuris* begins much more cautiously and derivatively with a series of arguments against usury drawn from the past.[120] Clearly, Olivi intends to establish from the beginning that whatever he might say concerning equalization in the loan contract, his starting point is the principle that usury – the demanding of anything in return beyond the sum lent – is in itself (*in se*) a sin against both divine and natural *aequalitas*.[121] As he writes: "It is not possible to demand more in return (than the sum lent) without breaching both equity and equality."[122] After dedicating page after page to these traditional arguments, Olivi suddenly halts and suggests that with all the certainty attached to its sinfulness and illegality, there are still a number of doubts (*dubia*) pertaining to the question of usury. Over the concluding pages of the section on usury in the *Tractatus*, he considers seven of these doubts.[123] All of the seven *dubia* focus on the strict requirement for equality in the loan contract; all make use of concrete examples from commercial life to illustrate the problems and questions associated with this strict requirement; and in response, all expand *aequalitas* in the direction of equilibrium. I consider here the two I judge to be particularly revealing of Olivi's attitudes.

In *dubium* 5, Olivi asks whether and to what extent contracts involving doubt concerning an unknown and unknowable future might affect the rules governing equality. We have seen this question raised earlier in canon law, and we have seen the difficulties presented by the introduction of future risk and doubt to the determination of a licit *aequalitas* in contracts of loan. Olivi is not so much breaking new ground here as providing both a general framework and an approximate mathematical scheme that can be applied to the problem. He asks whether a right to possession in the future can be bought for a price less than the thing itself

---

[120] Olivi, *Tractatus*, 69–77.

[121] *Ibid.*, 68: "Dicendum quod mutuo seu propter mutuum recipere aliquid plus vel prevalens, est contra ius divinum et naturale."

[122] *Ibid.*, 71–2: "Non potest amplius exigi absque aperta lesura equitatis et equalitatis."

[123] *Ibid.*, 77–88.

would command at present.[124] He not only declares that it can, but he imposes a rough mathematical scale on the differences permitted. "To the extent," he writes, "that a future right to possession extends further into the future, it can, all things being equal (*ceteris paribus*), be bought for a [proportionally] lower price."[125] He adds to this the general rule:

> The right to receive a thing that is actually present, and the actual possession itself, is worth more, all things being equal (*ceteris paribus*), than either the right to receive something in the future or the right alone without actual possession.[126]

He then broadens the principle yet further: "The certitude of actual possession is worth more than the certitude of possession in the future."[127] Based on these general principles, which are in turn grounded in his recognition that varying degrees of probability can be contractually expressed by proportionately varying prices, he concludes that when it is a right (*ius*) to receive something in the future that is being bought and sold, it is permissible to buy it for less than its present value would command.[128]

He concludes, in sum, that when doubt and risk intervene in contracts involving some form of credit, it is permissable to violate the requirement of strict arithmetical equality and to substitute instead a sliding scale of equalization, proportioned to the length of intervening time the credit sum would be at risk, compounded by the degree of uncertainty and probability involved in the contract. *Aequalitas* here is the estimative product of intersecting sliding scales. In order to arrive at this solution, Olivi had to overcome traditional scholastic objections

---

[124] *Ibid.*, 83: "Quintum ex predictis patens est quod ius futuri etc." The distinction he makes here between the possession of a thing and the possession of a right (*ius*) to the thing was developed in the canon law tradition justifying the census contract before Olivi wrote the *Tractatus*. It proved to be an important conceptual tool in dealing with questions involving future doubt and risk, and it was expanded by writers on economic questions both before and after Olivi.

[125] *Ibid.*: "quanto ius futurorum procedit in longinquiora futura, tanto ceteris paribus potest minori pretio emi."

[126] *Ibid.*: "Constat autem quod ius et naturalis possessio rei presentis plus valet ceteris paribus, quam solum ius rei future, aut quam solum ius absque actuali possessione non statim tradita vel tradenda."

[127] *Ibid.*: "Certitudo autem rei presentis et presentialis possessionis eius maior et prestancior est quam certitudo rei future possessionis aut quam certitudo future possessionis rei presentis." Cf. Piron, "Le traitement de l'incertitude," 83–5.

[128] Olivi, *Dubium* 3, *Tractatus*, 81–3. See also his determination (*Tractatus*, 84) that since it is more certain that money lent to the city will be repaid with interest than that profit will accrue from actual trade, the indemnification owed by the city should be proportionally discounted with respect to the sum lent: "Idcirco tamen debet sibi de probabili lucro subtrahi, quantum prefata certitudo preponderat incertitudini et periculo, quod circa capitale et lucrum potest in mercationibus."

(strongly voiced within the traditional discourse on usury) to the selling of time. In traditional theory, time was common to all things in creation and possessed by no one except God. To sell time (as one does when one charges a borrower for the time he possesses the money lent, or the time he takes to pay back the loan, or the time difference between payment and receipt) is to sell what one does not possess and is not one's own to sell, creating the injustice and inequality that constitutes the sin of usury. Olivi countered this objection (in a previous *dubium*), by arguing for a crucial (and bold) distinction between common time, which can never be sold, and "specific time" which is attached to specific contracts and specific elements of economic exchange involving future return.[129]

Envisioning the equalization of the probable and the open-ended: commercial *capitale*

Olivi's *dubium* 6 is his most powerful and includes his most potentially destabilizing arguments. From the time that it was first edited by Todeschini, it has rightfully occupied a central place in the history of usury theory. It contains two major parts. The first asks the question whether loans that are forced upon the lender (e.g., loans that the *civitas* demands from its citizens on behalf of the Common Good) can legitimately require and receive "interesse" added to the value of the loan itself.[130] Olivi answers in the affirmative: no matter why the lender was forced to loan by the city, he has the right to require an indemnity, but only on the condition that he has suffered actual financial loss from the loss of the *use* of his money, that is, only if he would otherwise have put the money he lent to productive and profitable use. In that case, the lender may justly demand *the equivalent of the profit he would likely have gained*, had he

---

[129] On the break with tradition that this reasoning represents, see Kirshner and Lo Prete, "Minorite Economics?" 262–6.

[130] This and related questions pertaining to forced loans and the administration of municipal debt continued to be asked and answered with great sophistication throughout the fourteenth century. The plethora of answers has given rise to a number of important studies. On the history of this discussion, see Julius Kirshner, "Storm over the *Monte Comune*: Genesis of the Moral Controversy over the Public Debt of Florence," *Archivum Fratrum Praedicatorum* 53 (1983), 219–76; Julius Kirshner, "*Ubi est ille?* Franco Sacchetti on the Monte Comune of Florence," *Speculum* 59 (1984), 556–84; Lawrin Armstrong, "The Politics of Usury in Trecento Florence: The *Questio de monte* of Francesco da Empoli," *Mediaeval Studies* 61 (1999), 1–44; Lawrin Armstrong, *Usury and Public Debt in Early Renaissance Florence: Lorenzo Ridolfi on the* Monte Comune (Toronto: Pontifical Institute of Medieval Studies, 2003), esp. 28–84; Munro, "The Medieval Origins of the Financial Revolution," 511–18.

retained the use of his money.[131] How can Olivi say this? If money is presumed to be sterile, not lucrative in itself (*ex se sola non est lucrosa*), incapable of generating more of itself by itself, which had long been a primary precept of medieval economic thought, then how can Olivi argue that the sum lent, whether from the threat of violence or from any other cause, *requires* an indemnification *ultra sortem* simply to maintain equality in the contract, and, moreover, an indemnification "equivalent" to the *probable profit* the money would likely have earned?

He can make this claim because he has come to a realization that is startling in its implications: all money is not equal.[132] It exists in two forms, and each requires its own form of equalization. On the one hand, there is money as it had been traditionally identified, as it had appeared in Gratian's canons, as it had received clear definition in Aristotle's discussion in *Ethics* V, and as Thomas reaffirmed in his questions on usury. Here money (*pecunia numerata*) is the numbered measure and commensurating medium of all goods in exchange. In this form (which Olivi frequently designates as "simple money") it is and must remain fixed in order to perform its proper functions of commensuration and equalization.[133] As *pecunia numerata*, money falls under all the traditional restrictions of usury theory: to demand, accept, or desire anything *ultra sortem* for its loan is to create an insupportable inequality and to commit the sin of usury.

The second form that money takes, according to Olivi, is money as commercial investment, employed by merchants for the express purpose of gaining profit through trade. He himself gives this second form the name "capital" (*capitale*), and he outlines the essential ways in which it differs from "simple" money. Where *pecunia numerata* is fixed and (ideally) stable, *capitale* is, in essence, fruitful, expansive, and multiplicative. He writes:

The reason why [money of a certain kind] can be bought or exchanged for a price [more than itself] is because ... money which in the firm intent of its owner is directed toward the production of probable profit (*ad aliquod probabile lucrum*) possesses not only the qualities of money in its simple sense but beyond this a kind of seminal cause of profit within itself (*quamdam seminalem rationem lucrosi*), which we commonly call "capital." And therefore it possesses not only its simple

---

[131] Olivi, *Tractatus*, 84: "Et ideo eo ipso quod potest iuste exigere interesse damni, potest iuste exigere equivalens damnificationis talis lucri."

[132] Kirshner, who questions the originality of Olivi on many points, recognizes, nevertheless, the "significant departure from tradition" represented by Olivi's definition of *capitale* and its consequences in his thought. On this see Kirshner and Lo Prete, "Minorite Economics?" 262–74, at 266.

[133] E.g., Olivi, *Tractatus*, 85: "habet rationem simplicis pecunie."

numerical value as money/measure but it possesses in addition a superadded value (*valor superadiunctus*).[134]

Olivi is clear to emphasize, here and elsewhere, that money per se cannot be the cause of its potential for expansion and multiplication. Rather, capital is money that has "taken on" (*assumit*) its quality of fruitfulness and its multiplicative power.[135] The accumulative source of power in capital is the "industry" of the merchant (*ad lucra per mercationum industriam cumulanda*).[136] Money as capital literally "retains" (*retentor*) the profitable industry of the merchant. It is the merchant who, through his activity (an activity that Olivi everywhere defines as beneficial to the Common Good), fructifies money and transforms it into capital.

Olivi's conception of the merchant's *industria* – that which transforms simple money into productive capital – is remarkably capacious. It comprehends a host of qualities that grow out of the merchant's hard-earned professional knowledge. It includes his skill in judging the value of commodities, his grasp of different monies and markets that permits him to know where goods can be bought for less and sold for more, his care in managing his affairs, and his courage in facing the risks associated with commerce. I will consider these qualities and their role in the legitimization of mercantile profits in the chapter that follows. Here I want only to look at the assumptions that underlie a reevaluation of this magnitude. At the forefront of these stands the weight Olivi allows to probability and his attempt to integrate probability into a mathematics of equalization.

As we have seen, the merchant who loses the use of his money, by virtue of being forced to lend it, is, according to Olivi, permitted to charge an indemnity "equivalent" to the "probable profit" he would have made had he retained the use of his money. In *dubium* 6, Olivi provides additional guidelines for integrating exchange probabilities into a mathematics of proportional equalization. For example, a merchant who, out of "special" grace and charity sells his wheat soon after harvest when the community values it less (*communiter minus valet*), rather than holding off its sale, as he had intended to do, for a time when the price would most "probably"

---

[134] *Ibid.*: "Causa autem quare sub tali pretio potest illud vendere vel commutare est . . . quia illud quod in firmo proposito domini sui est ordinatum ad aliquod probabile lucrum non solum habet rationem simplicis pecunie seu rei, sed ultra hoc quamdam seminalem rationem lucrosi quam communiter capitale vocamus, et ideo non solum habet reddi simpliciter valor ipsius sed etiam valor superadiunctus." On this, see Franklin, *Science of Conjecture*, who notes (265): "What is especially original in Olivi is his use of the concept of the probable."

[135] Olivi, *Quodlibet I*, q. 17, in Spicciani, "Gli scritti," 319–20.

[136] *Ibid.*, q. 16, in Spicciani, "Gli scritti," 317.

be greater (*probabiliter magis caro*), is allowed to request the price that the future sale would "probably" (*probabiliter*) have brought.[137] Olivi then concludes *dubium* 6 with a general statement of his expanded vision of *aequalitas* (and hence of liceity) in the loan contract. The case he presents is of someone who is firmly determined to invest his money in profitable trade but who instead lends it to another in need, solely out of piety and concern for the other's condition. May this person require a return on his loan *ultra sortem* without committing usury? Olivi's answer is yes: the lender may require of the borrower an additional sum in return, equivalent to the lost probable profit that the lender would likely have earned on his money, had he invested it in commerce rather than loaned it.[138] And he may stipulate this as an integral part of the contract itself at the time of its formulation.

Almost all the cases Olivi offers in *dubia* 5 and 6 reflect questions that had been debated within the canon law on usury for a generation and more before he wrote the *Tractatus*, including the question: should the lender who could have invested his money in commerce at a probable profit be indemnified for the loss of this profit? As we have already seen, the influential legal scholar Hostiensis, writing toward the middle of the thirteenth century, generally accepted the right to such an indemnification under a form of *interesse* entitled *lucrum cessans*. But despite Cardinal Hostiensis' authority and his excellent standing within the Church, the matter was far from decided. St. Thomas, for one, refused to allow probability the ontological status conferred on it by Hostiensis and Olivi. He denied the legitimacy of *lucrum cessans* by making a strict distinction between what was "merely probable" (the profit expected from investment) and what was real (the actual sum lent).[139] After Hostiensis, the question continued to be debated for centuries, with scholastic

---

[137] Olivi, *Tractatus*, 84.

[138] *Ibid.*, 85: "Item ex hoc patet quod quando aliquis pecuniam de qua firmiter mercari proponitur, prestat alicui ex sola pietate et necessitate illius, sub tali pacto quod quantum consimilis summa apud talem equivalentem mercatorem lucrabitur vel perdet, tantum ipse lucretur vel perdat, non committit usuram, sed potius facit aliquam gratiam salva tamen sua indemnitate." Olivi takes up a similar case again in *Quodlibet I*, q. 17 (Spicciani, "Gli scritti," 320), and here he openly declares that when merchants make such loans, even when they require indemnity *ultra sortem* for their lost profit, they are still being "immensely helpful to friends," and are performing "works of piety and equity" (*opus pietatis simul et aequitatis*). Note that the right to indemnification for lost probable profit extends only to those who had a previous "firm intent" to invest their money in commerce, and, as Olivi also specifies, to those who possessed the knowledge to do so and the habit of doing so. In short, it extends only to those merchant servants of the Common Good who are habitually engaged in commerce but are not habitual lenders. For these merchants, traditional strictures against demanding any "excess" *ultra sortem* has, as Todeschini points out in many places, effectively disappeared.

[139] *ST*, II, II, 78, 2, ad 1: "he [the lender] must not sell that which he has not yet, and may be prevented in many ways from having." There are writers on economic questions, after

economic thinkers lining up on both sides of the question, but with the majority arguing against the acceptance of *lucrum cessans*.[140]

Olivi's full embrace of probability in *dubia* 5 and 6 clearly differs profoundly from Thomas' position. It is important, however, to recognize in what ways it also differs from the canon law position accepting *lucrum cessans* enunciated by Hostiensis.[141] Hostiensis insisted that *lucrum cessans* be considered an "external title" to the loan, dependent on the merchant lender's request to be indemnified on demonstration of his lost profit.[142] Olivi, in contrast, has normalized the probability of profit and fully integrated it into the loan contract itself. For Olivi probability is not an external or separable circumstance. Rather, in his vision, the probability of profit exists, in some real sense, as a "seminal" power *within* the capital itself, and consequently all loans involving capital must integrate this seminal and superadded value into the requirement for equality and equalization in the exchange. Such an integration could only have been imagined following a radical re-visioning of *aequalitas* itself.

Envisioning a model of equilibrium in exchange

The clearest illustration of Olivi's reevaluation of probability in the *mutuum* and his attempt to apply proportional mathematics to its estimation is found in a separate "case" he added to the *Tractatus* several years after its initial composition.[143] The case itself is highly detailed in its consideration of commercial risk and doubt, with the convoluted logic of the decretal *Naviganti* visible in its background. But it brings Olivi to enunciate a series of principles concerning probability and

Thomas, who continue to support this position, and others who cite it authoritatively yet alter it in interesting ways. See, for example, Gregory of Rimini's position in *Tractatus subtilissimi doctoris Gregorii de Arimino: De Imprestantiis Venetorum. Et de Usura* (Reggio Emilia: Ludovici de Mazalis, 1508), article 4, n.p. Here Gregory confirms Thomas' argument and cites him directly on this point. As he goes on, however, he recognizes that some proportion between real loss and merely possible loss exists and can be determined, with the implication being that a discounted value can be assigned to merely possible loss: "quia minus est habere aliquid in virtute quam habere actu: tamen tenetur facere aliquam recompensationem secundum conditionem personarum et negociorum." See also Ovidio Capitani, "Il 'De peccato usure' di Remigio de Girolami," *Studi Medievali* 6, 3rd series (1965), 537–662, at 566–7.

[140] On the history of this discussion, see Armstrong, *Usury and Public Debt*, 61–5; Amleto Spicciani, *Capitale e interesse tra mercatura e povertà nei teologi e canonisti dei secoli VIII–XV* (Rome: Jouvence, 1990), 40–8; Munro, "Medieval Origins of the Financial Revolution," 511–12; Wei, *Intellectual Culture*, 319–21.

[141] Kirshner and Lo Prete, "Minorite Economics?" 269–74.   [142] Noonan, *Usury*, 118.

[143] The case was first edited by Spicciani under the title "*De contractibus usurariis: casus*," in *Gli scritti*, 321–5. Todeschini added this text as an appendix to his edition of the *Tractatus*, 109–12. For an estimate of the date and circumstances of its composition, see Piron, "Le traitement de l'incertitude," 21.

equalization that are unrivaled in the medieval period for their clarity and perceptiveness. These principles enunciate virtually all the major elements constituting what I am calling the "new model of equilibrium," a model whose evolution we have been tracing in this chapter and will continue to trace in each of the chapters that follow. They are: the assigning of an "appreciable value" to probability; the recognition of value relativity; the acceptance of determinations based on estimations and approximations; the application of graded and divisible "latitudes," open to continual expansion and contraction, to the measurement of qualities and values; the implementation of a mathematics of proportionality; the integration of multiplication into the mathematics of equalization; the vision of a self-equalizing system in which order is attained through the dynamic intersection and interchange of parts within the whole; the expansion of the scale of ordering from the individual to the aggregate; all of which are directed toward the attainment and maintenance of balance/*aequalitas*.

In the appended *casus*, Olivi presents the clearest statement of his position that the probability of commercial profit possesses a real and "appreciable" value (*appreciabilis valor probabilitatis*) that can be estimated and measured by money price and can therefore be licitly bought and sold for that price.[144] Merchants, he recognized, presuppose that superadded value "truly" (*vere*) exists within the *capitale* itself as a "cause" or "reason" or "seed" of fructifying profit, and they buy and sell it as if this were the case, without committing usury.[145] He also provides an answer to a fundamental question that he had previously left open: how is the price attached to probable profit to be determined? And by whom? The importance of this answer is clear: without it, the "equivalence" between buyer and seller that he repeatedly insists upon lacks the order and precision it requires. In a characteristic move, he de-centralizes judgment. Rather than assigning the responsibility for determining capital's superadded value to any overarching authority standing outside or above the field of exchange, he assigns it to the conjoined judgments of the individual merchant exchangers themselves. He does so because he recognizes that the value of capital can never be determined precisely or absolutely; nor

---

[144] Olivi, *Tractatus*, 110: "Secundum est, appreciabilis valor probabilitatis seu probabilis spei lucri, ex capitali illo per mercationes trahendi. Ex quo enim haec probabilitas habet aliquem valorem, aliquo temporali precio appretiabilem potest licite illo vendi pretio."

[145] *Ibid.*: "Ergo praedictum interesse probabilis lucri, quodam modo causaliter, et quasi seminaliter continebatur in praedicto capitali: alias enim non posset licite exigi ... prout causaliter continentur in capitali, in quantum est capitale, idest in quantum vere et non ficte est in mercationes fiendas deputatum et destinatum; ergo hic non est peccatum usurae."

can it be fixed for all times and situations. Its value can only be determined by and in the act itself of buying or selling capital, not by law or theory. It can only be a relative determination, calculated in relation to the actual and always changing circumstances of exchange. Since only the merchant borrowers themselves know how much the borrowed capital is worth to them in any given situation, only they know how much they are willing to pay for it *ultra sortem*.

In sum, Olivi recognized that merchants *lived in the world of the probable*. Through their continual experiences and experiments with commercial risk and doubt, they had learned how to *estimate* its ever-shifting value at any point in time. They had learned how to *rationally discount the probable*, paying proportionally less as the uncertainty and doubt attached to risk increased. He writes:

> the probability of profit is sold at a lower price than the buyer [i.e., the merchant borrower] expects to make in the future from the capital he has bought ... it is understood that the buyer [borrower] of capital always expects to profit more from it in the future than he will pay for it.[146]

The merchant borrower, being knowledgeable in the art of trade (*in arte mercandi et lucrandi industrius*) (as Olivi assumes), can be expected to "buy" capital for a price that is *rational*, even if it is, necessarily, an estimated price based on probabilistic reasoning. Recognizing that merchants have succeeded in integrating probability and rationality in practice, Olivi does so in theory.

Notice that throughout this *casus*, Olivi has transferred the terms of acquiring capital from a loan to a sale. In doing so, he employs the same strategy that Pope Innocent IV had earlier applied to the census contract. In both cases, the transfer permits the test of equality to be shifted from a precise balancing point to a continuous range, and from an arithmetical to a proportional equivalence.[147] The guarantee of equality and rationality in this type of open-ended exchange, in which hugely varying degrees of risk and probability are involved, is provided solely by the voluntary agreement of both parties to the contract.[148] Mutual agreement implies mutual

---

[146] *Ibid.*, 123: "probabilitas illa minori pretio venditur quam lucrum ex mercationibus capitalis creditur suo tempore futurum et valiturum, constat quod in eius venditione semper creditur probabiliter quod emptor eius sit finaliter lucraturus seu plus quam in emendo dedit habiturus."

[147] I discuss the implications of this transference in the chapter that follows.

[148] Olivi, *Tractatus*, 112: "Dicendum quod immo causaliter, seu aequivalenter aut prae-valenter, ex ipso educitur, pro quanto scilicet futurum lucrum suarum mercationum iam quasi esse in ipso praesupponitur, et tamquam iam praesuppositum venditur et emitur; et certe, ipse emptor, cum sit in arte mercandi et lucrandi industrius et voluntarius, non emeret illud lucrum nisi bene sciret illius emptionem probabiliter esse sibi lucrosam."

recognition of gain, which, *in itself*, provides the necessary basis of *aequalitas* in exchange. Clearly, no matter how knowledgeable the merchant, his calculations of future profit would prove wrong from time to time. But failure in these individual cases does not render the agreements under which they were contracted usurious in Olivi's eyes. In his search for equality, he is looking past individual exchanges to the "common" course of exchange in his society. His vision has expanded to comprehend the aggregation of myriad personal decisions that constitute the working *system* of exchange.

The emergence of the "new" model of equilibrium at the end of the thirteenth century

Olivi's concept of *capitale* grew out of his recognition that bringing the world of commerce within the bounds of philosophical and theological rationality required the intellectual imagination of new forms of equalization. Such forms existed in the urban marketplaces of southern France and Italy *before* they found expression in Olivi's thought. He makes this clear when he notes that the concept of productive capital was in common use (*communiter capitale vocamus*) before his decision to provide it with a philosophical rationale and to bring it within the bounds of licit equalization. I do not, however, mean to suggest that the new model of equilibrium was present in the understanding of even those merchants whose economic practice conformed to it. While the model of equilibrium envisioned by Olivi was, to my mind, indubitably the product of a particular socioeconomic environment at a particular time, one that was in place in the most urbanized centers of Europe by the last quarter of the thirteenth century, it was at the same time an *intellectual product*. It was a mixture of experience, observation, and the highest intellection. It grew out of a desire to make sense of how things actually appeared to work in the urban marketplace, yes, but training in philosophy and theology provided the very ground for "making" sense. For Olivi, to make sense was to rationalize, to integrate observations of everyday life and transcendent values into a rational and logical plan capable of meeting the stringent test of theological (not merely legal) approval.[149] In Olivi's case, this meant redefining the boundaries of equality so that the commercial activity of merchants, which he firmly believed contributed greatly to the Common Good, could be

---

[149] Spicciani, "Pietro di Giovanni Olivi: indigatore della razionalità economica medioevale," 21–72.

incorporated within that "order of law, justice, and Christian charity" it was the theologian's responsibility to define.[150]

The great expansion of commerce in the thirteenth century, the equally great successes of the calculating merchant, and the recognition that mercantile activity, taken as a whole, served the community as a whole, led Olivi to recognize – to *seek* to recognize – the rationality of commercial exchange. There were great hurdles to overcome, given that the system of exchange was built around elements that had previously appeared inherently destabilizing and inimical to rationalization, if not sinful: the probable, the uncertain, the dynamic of multiplication, the acceptance of superadded values, the building of agreements on the sands of approximation and estimation, and not least of all, the personal search for advantage and profit, the personal desire for *unequal* gain.[151] The task facing Olivi was to formulate new explanations, consistent with the scholastic requirements of *ratio*, *aequitas*, and *aequalitas*, that were capable of comprehending the logic of commercial activity. The end result was his vision of exchange as a supra-personal system in dynamic equilibrium.

Olivi's *Tractatus* does not reveal what was current or dominant in scholastic economic thought at the end of the thirteenth century; his insights into the potentialities of balance were fuller and deeper than those of any of his contemporaries, and the likes of his genius are rarely found.[152] Many of Olivi's contemporaries, even those with impressive accomplishments in philosophy and theology, were unable either to grasp the full contours of his model of exchange equilibrium or to accept them – not surprising, perhaps, given the many traditional boundaries transgressed in their realization. But if Olivi's vision does not reveal the common view of things, it reveals something of equal importance: what it was *possible to think and imagine* concerning the boundaries of equality and the workings of systematic equilibrium here at the cusp of the fourteenth century. I conclude this chapter with Olivi's writings not because they provide some kind of conclusion to the scholastic discourse on usury but because in them the "new" model of equilibrium appears, at this early

---

[150] Cf. Olivi's opening argument of the *Tractatus* (cited above) where mercantile activity is identified with the Common Good and the Common Good is identified, in turn, "secundum ordinem iuris et iustitie et caritatis." On this linkage see Todeschini, "Olivi e il *mercator* cristiano," esp. 229–37.

[151] The Olivian notion of "capitale" in itself is remarkably (and dangerously) open-ended and resistant to traditional bounds. Todeschini notes this ("Olivi e il *mercator* cristiano," 226–7) and cites a phrase that Olivi attached to money in another of his writings: "multiplicabilis, aggregabilis in infinitum … ad omnem contractum valde ductilem."

[152] Olivi's contemporary, the theologian Godfrey of Fontaines, is one of those who does indeed share many of his insights. I discuss Godfrey's opinions in the chapter that follows.

date, with remarkable fullness and clarity of detail. When scholastic writers projected the ideal of *aequalitas* beyond the loan contract to encompass the proper determination of prices and values in the economic landscapes of the thirteenth and fourteenth century, yet more crucial elements of the model emerge, with equal and at times even greater clarity. I provide evidence for this statement in the following chapter.

2 Equality and equalization in the economic sphere, part 2: The scholastic discourse on price and value to 1300

Money, then, acting as a measure, makes goods commensurate and equates (*equat*) them; for neither would there have been association if there were not exchange, nor exchange if there were not equality (*equalitas*), nor equality if there were not commensurability.

(Aristotle, *Nicomachean Ethics*, Book V, *Translatio Recognita, c.* 1260)

The just price of things is sometimes not precisely determined (*non est punctualiter determinatum*) but rather consists in an estimate (*quadam aestimatione consistit*). Therefore a small (*modica*) addition or subtraction does not seem to destroy the equality of justice (*aequalitatem justitiae*).

(Thomas Aquinas, *Summa theologica*, II, II, 77, 1, *ad* 2, *c.* 1272)

The valuation of things in exchange can rarely or never be achieved except through the use of conjecture or probable opinion (*nisi per coniecturalem seu probabilem opinionem*), and it is never a precise point nor precisely measurable, but rather it falls within some fitting latitude (*sub aliqua latitudine competenti*), within which the understanding and judgment of men differ.

(Peter of John Olivi, *Tractatus de emptionibus et venditionibus, de usuris, de restitutionibus, c.* 1295)

Throughout the medieval period the ideal of equality as the proper end of all exchange remained as central to the scholastic discourse on price and value as it was to the discourse on usury.[1] But, as we saw in the case of usury in the previous chapter, so too with price: assumptions concerning what actually constituted equality in its determination changed profoundly over the twelfth and thirteenth centuries along with the definition of *aequalitas* itself. These changes occurred within a highly refined intellectual culture, but their roots were social and material as well as intellectual. They followed upon a long period of vigorous economic and demographic expansion in Europe, extending from the eleventh to

---

[1] I visited this subject earlier in my *Economy and Nature in the Fourteenth Century* under the heading "Equality, the Mean, and Equalization in Exchange." In what follows, I make selective use of my earlier findings, reframing and adding to them to suit the changed focus of my discussion here.

the end of the thirteenth century. Exponential growth in many related areas occurred over this period: raw population, urban population, urban power and wealth, agricultural and craft production, number and size of market sites, commercial goods in circulation, and the minting and circulation of coins, to name but a few. Each of these processes was accompanied and accelerated by the development of increasingly sophisticated commercial techniques, contracts, and enterprises on the part of a merchant estate that grew ever larger, more successful, more self-confident, and more self-conscious over the course of these two centuries.

The story of this economic "revolution" has been told many times.[2] The expansion of coinage alone conveys some idea of its scope. Evidence from well-documented English sources reveals that in the century between 1180 and 1280 the number of silver pennies in circulation multiplied more than tenfold. The scale of this expansion becomes even more notable when it is placed in historical context, as here by the historian and numismatist Peter Spufford: "It is astonishing to realise that the weight of silver generally minted each year in thirteenth-century England was not regularly exceeded until after the Napoleonic Wars."[3] The speed with which the economy multiplied in England over this period was matched and at times surpassed by other European economies: the urban centers of Flanders, the Paris basin, southern France and western Spain, and most dramatically, the communes of northern Italy. Multiplication in numbers translated into multiplication of effect: the joined processes of urbanization, commercialization, monetization, and market development had an impact on almost every aspect of medieval life. By the mid thirteenth century, the everyday use of coins in exchange had extended from the urban centers to the far reaches of the countryside, from the counting houses of bankers to the treasuries of popes, kings, communes, and monasteries, and from the calculations of merchants to everyday economic decisions made by aristocrat, artisan, monk, student, and peasant.

But what did these calculations look like? In the historical view that generally held until the mid twentieth century, and that is still often reflected in the popular understanding, corporatist and religious ideals

---

[2] See, for example, Robert Lopez, *The Commercial Revolution of the Middle Ages* (Englewood Cliffs, NJ: Prentice Hall, 1971), for an early claim that the term "revolution" was fully applicable to the expansion of the medieval economy in this period.

[3] Peter Spufford, *Money and its Use in Medieval Europe* (Cambridge University Press, 1988), 204–5. Spufford notes that in the recoinage of 1279–81, 120 million new pennies were struck in the London and Canterbury mints alone. Cf. Nicholas Mayhew, "Modelling Medieval Monetisation," in *A Commercialising Economy: England 1086 to c. 1300*, ed. Richard Britnell and Bruce Campbell (Manchester University Press, 1995), 55–77. Mayhew notes (65–8) that estimates of coinage growth do not take into account the volume of credit operations, which also increased greatly over this period.

were assumed to have held sway in the medieval economic sphere, to the extent that economic actors were only dimly aware of how the values and prices of the goods they bought and sold were determined.[4] Working from such a picture, historians of an earlier period imagined that the just price (*iustum pretium*), so often mentioned by scholastic writers, was an ideal price attached to goods and services in exchange. It was imagined to be a more or less objective measure of true value, determined primarily by the labor and expenses involved in a good's production and by the measure of its usefulness to the community. Such a price would allow producers a modest surplus befitting their social position. The just price thus conceived would necessarily be more or less fixed, independent of the fluctuations and vagaries of time and place and of scarcity and need. It belongs to a time when economic actors were innocent of calculation, ignorant of the economic pressures on price, and averse to the rough give-and-take of bargaining in the marketplace. Viewed in this way, the theory of the just price was a sister to usury theory: another manifestation of the medieval desire to control economic activity in the name of religious ideals and ethical and social norms. The problem with this picture and this understanding of the medieval just price, is that the surviving textual evidence does not support it and points in a very different direction.

Since John Baldwin's path-breaking study (1959), historians have come to doubt that the just price ever existed, whether in fact or in theory, as a normative and fixed determination detached from market pressures.[5] In the strong early words of the eminent economic historian Raymond De Roover:

According to the majority of the [scholastic] doctors, the just price ... was simply the current market price, with this important reservation: in cases of collusion or emergency, the public authorities retained the right to interfere and to impose a fair price.[6]

While no historian today would defend the older vision of a "just price," in recent years articles have appeared in which economic historians have criticized the use of the term "market price" to characterize either the formation or the understanding of price in the medieval period, going so

---

[4] For the citation and criticism of numerous examples of this older interpretation, see Raymond De Roover, "The Concept of the Just Price: Theory and Practice," *Journal of Economic History* 18 (1958), 418–34.

[5] John Baldwin, "The Medieval Theories of the Just Price: Romanists, Canonists, and Theologians in the Twelfth and Thirteenth Centuries," *Transactions of the American Philosophical Society*, n.s. 49, no. 4 (1959), 1–92.

[6] De Roover, "The Concept of the Just Price," 420.

far as to level the charge of "anachronism" and "presentism" against those who have dared to use it.[7] In my view, those who have leveled these charges should be wary that they are not guilty of these same sins of assuming that there is one point (and place) in history when a "true" market price can be said to exist and that all others are unworthy of the name. The view I express in this chapter is that at a certain point in the history of the scholastic analysis of price, the term becomes applicable and useful (when qualified), and so too does the notion (grasped at the time) of a market that functioned and ordered itself according to its own principles rather than in conformance to normative expectations or requirements.[8] I trust that my reasons for saying this will become clear as the chapter unfolds.

Does the scholastic understanding of market price have its own characteristic valences and shadings that differ from those attached to the "market price" of classical economics or the economics of today? Certainly. The medieval understanding of the marketplace and market prices never attained the heights of idealization it assumes in classical economic thought. Prejudice was alive and well in this period against those (particularly those of lower status) whose lives were dominated by the concern to amass wealth and to profit at every opportunity. Many philosophers and theologians writing on the subject continued to maintain that achieving a truly "just" price requires buyers and sellers to remain personally responsible for judging and aligning price with value in their exchanges. Moreover, minute regulations regarding the size, weight, and quality of manufactured goods and foodstuffs (ale, bread, etc.) were issued for every market, and through the fourteenth century and beyond, maximum price edicts remained a traditional governmental response to economic crises.[9] As a rule, however, market-wide price restrictions were temporary solutions. Only when authorities recognized that the normal factors influencing the establishment of a "common price" in the marketplace were being unfairly manipulated by monopolists, or hoarders, or

---

[7] See the recent argument against the use of the term with regard to scholastic economic thought in Odd Langholm, "Buridan on Economic Value," *History of Political Economy* 38 (2006), 269–89. Similarly, Piron, "Le traitement de l'incertitude commerciale dans la scolastique médiévale," 14.

[8] I provide support for this statement in "Monetary and Market Consciousness in Thirteenth and Fourteenth Century Europe," in *Ancient and Medieval Economic Ideas and Concepts of Social Justice*, ed. S. Todd Lowry and Barry Gordon (Leiden: Brill, 1998), 372–403.

[9] Attempts to control market prices in goods and wages came into play with renewed force after the extreme market dislocations resulting from the Black Death. I discuss this case and its effects further in Chapter 7 below.

profiteering resellers, did they routinely intervene.[10] In the all-important area of grain, wine, and other agricultural and animal products, prices were expected to fluctuate seasonally (or more often) in relation to the bounty or scarcity of goods, and they were permitted to do so.[11]

That prices were established within markets and by market conditions in some measure independent of the needs and estimations of individual buyers and sellers (and, for that matter, independent of what the authorities might wish or command) was clear to nearly everyone connected to the monetized marketplace. Here I am not speaking only of the commercial actors themselves, who were trained, most often from youth, in the ways of prices and markets, and whose comprehensive knowledge in this area permitted them to remain on the positive side of the ledger over a lifetime of trading. The documents they have left clearly illustrate their extraordinary sensitivity to the principles and workings of price formation.[12] But small-scale producers and consumers shared in this understanding as well. Included in this number were the many clerks and monks who oversaw the production and consumption accounts of their religious institutions; the many university students who were charged with complex administrative and economic responsibilities on behalf of their colleges during their student years and into their teaching years; and, I would add, virtually all the scholastic authors who felt sufficiently knowledgeable in the area to contribute to economic debates.[13]

[10] R. H. Britnell, *The Commercialisation of English Society, 1000–1500* (Cambridge University Press, 1993), 93–4.
[11] De Roover, "Concept of the Just Price," 421; Baldwin, *Just Price*, 32–4; Michael Postan, *The Medieval Economy and Society: An Economic History of Britain 1100–1500* (Berkeley: University of California Press, 1972), 21–2; Harry Miskimin, *Money, Prices, and Foreign Exchange in Fourteenth-Century France* (New Haven, CT: Yale University Press, 1963), 21.
[12] See, for example, the commercial handbook of the Florentine merchant and banker, Francesco di Balduccio Pegolotti, written over the course of his career to c. 1340, *La pratica della mercatura*, ed. Allen Evans (Cambridge, MA: Medieval Academy of America, 1936); and the earlier document (c. 1310), *Zibaldone da Canal*, in *Merchant Culture in Fourteenth Century Venice*, ed. and trans. John Dotson (Binghamton, NY: Medieval and Renaissance Texts and Studies, 1994). For a concise document that reveals this knowledge in the highest degree, see "Reports from the Fairs of Champagne," in *Medieval Trade in the Mediterranean World*, ed. Robert Lopez and Irving Raymond (New York: Columbia University Press, 1955), 388–94. See also below in this chapter for Peter Olivi's asssumptions concerning the merchant's highly schooled and sophisticated understanding of the determinants of price.
[13] I discuss the penetration into the monastery of insights relating to market exchange in "Monetary and Market Consciousness," esp. 374–8. A number of studies take this theme back to the twelfth century, e.g., Constance Bouchard, *Holy Entrepreneurs: Cistercians, Knights and Economic Exchange in Twelfth-Century Burgundy* (Ithaca, NY: Cornell University Press, 1991). For the involvement of students in the institutional life of the medieval university, and consequently in the urban marketplace, see my *Economy and Nature in the Fourteenth Century*, esp. 28–36.

Underestimating the degree to which medieval people in general, and writers on economic questions in particular, were conscious of a marketplace in which prices were established by "common estimation" and "common consent," determined with respect to common scarcity and need, was a mistake committed by historians of the past who imagined a Middle Ages innocent of such knowledge and incapable of such calculation. It is a mistake we should be concerned to correct. In what follows, I presume that my readers are capable of grasping the range of meanings attached to terms such as "common price" and "market price" once they have been qualified by the actual words of the scholastic writers themselves, as cited in both text and notes.

Early guidelines on price equalization from Roman and canon law

The origins of medieval legal thinking on market price and just price can be found in Roman law. In the *Digest* and *Codex* of Justinian's *Corpus iuris civilis*, the establishment of an equality between buyer and seller was accepted, almost without exception, as a dynamic back-and-forth process. Equalization was recognized as a *product* that emerged out of the conflicting desires of the buyer to pay as little as possible and the seller to charge as much as possible. As John Baldwin has written: "The fundamental Roman law principle of sale and price was that of freedom of bargaining."[14] The liberties allowed in this process of bargaining were quite extensive. Roman law permitted buyer and seller to outwit each other in order to obtain price advantage, up to the point of committing outright fraud. Not only was such rough bargaining permitted within Roman law, it was accepted as the "natural" state of affairs in buying and selling.[15] A ruling in the *Digest* declares: "In sales and purchases it is naturally allowed (*naturaliter concessum est*) to buy a thing of greater value for a smaller price and to sell a thing of lesser value for a greater price."[16] Despite the deception permitted in Roman law, there is no discussion there of a distinction between the selling price of a good (arrived at through bargaining) and its legal value. With one minor exception

---

[14] Baldwin, *Just Price*, 17.
[15] *Digest*, 4.4.16.4: "in pretio emptionis et venditionis naturaliter licere contrahentibus se circumvenire." See also *Codex*, 4.44.10; *Codex*, 4.44.5; Kenneth Cahn, "The Roman and Frankish Roots of the Just Price of Canon Law," *Studies in Medieval and Renaissance History* 6 (1969), 3–52, at 12.
[16] *Digest*, 19.2.22.3: "Quemadmodum in emendo et vendendo naturaliter concessum est quod pluris sit minoris emere, quod minoris sit pluris vendere et ita invicem se circumscribere, ita in locationibus quoque et conductionibus iuris est."

(discussed below) a legally sufficient equality between price and value was assumed to exist in all sale agreements entered into freely by both parties.[17] This assumption was expressed in the often-repeated Roman law tag: "A thing is worth what it can be sold for" (*Res tantum valet quantum vendi potest*).[18]

Roman law contained one small exception to this rule. It appeared in two judgments, both limited to a sale of real estate by a minor (who is here presumed to be in possession of less than adequate or normal knowledge) at less than half the amount of the estate's "just price" calculated at the time of the sale.[19] In such a sale the minor seller was seen to have suffered excessive damage, and the buyer was left the choice of either furnishing the difference between the selling price and the "just price" or cancelling the sale. Even within the Roman law judgments proposing this exception, there is a spirited defense of the fundamental principle of free bargaining. There is also, however, the contradictory implication that there may actually exist some "just price" for the land apart from its selling price, and that in certain limited situations, agreed prices are not just. Medieval lawyers greatly expanded this limited exception to the rule of free bargaining under the heading *laesio enormis* (excessive damage).[20] In Roman law the rule protected only the underage seller of a piece of property. In twelfth-century legal commentaries, the principle was gradually extended from the sale of real estate by a minor to all sales of all goods in which less than one half of the "true" value of the good had been covered by the sale. It was then expanded still further to include deceived buyers as well as sellers.[21] The new, expanded principle allowed that any payment exceeding one half above or one half below the "just price" provided either buyer or seller grounds to rescind the sale.

While the rule of *laesio enormis* required the "just price" to occupy the center of the continuum of legal price, it gave no guidance on how

---

[17] Adding weight to this rule was the more general principle, central to Roman law, that a willing party is not injured. See *Digest*, 39.3.9.1.

[18] *Digest*, 36.1.16; *Digest*, 35.2.63; *Digest*, 9.2.33. On this, see Odd Langholm, *Economics in the Medieval Schools: Wealth, Exchange, Value, Money, and Usury According to the Paris Theological Tradition 1200–1350* (Leiden: Brill, 1992), 93; Louis Baeck, *The Mediterranean Tradition in Economic Thought* (New York: Routledge, 1994), 143. Baeck interprets this position as indicating that "Within the constraints set by the social cohesion of the community, market prices are perceived to express the real value of commodities."

[19] *Codex*, 4.44.8: "nisi minus dimidia iusti pretii, quod fuerat tempore venditionis." See Baldwin, *Just Price*, 18–19, 22.

[20] The actual term *laesio enormis* did not get attached to this exception until the fourteenth century. On this see Baldwin, *Just Price*, 18, n. 68.

[21] *Ibid.*, 22. On the adoption of this rule within canon law, see *ibid.*, 43–4. An important early statement of the expanded rule in canon law appears in the decretal *Quum Causa* of Innocent III, *Decretales*, X.3.17.6; ed. Friedberg, vol. II, col. 520.

to determine it. Roman law at times recognized the necessity for a third party or "good man," acting as judge, to estimate the true value of goods, especially for the settling of estates, but Roman jurists never precisely specified the criteria that should be applied for such estimates. In the absence of such specification, the prevalent historical view holds that, in effect, the just price of Roman law was identical with the *common price* in the marketplace: in John Baldwin's words, "a normal and customary price ... determined in commerce of free exchange which is regular and orderly."[22] This view is in line with the general tenor of Roman law on the subject of price. Roman jurists fully grasped the concept of a "common price," established independently of individual will and condition. On several occasions they explicitly identified this common price with a legally sufficient price. Two nearly identical texts from the *Digest* clearly formulate this understanding: "The prices of things are determined not by their value and utility to individuals, but by their value determined commonly" (*pretia rerum non ex affectu nec utilitate singulorum sed communiter funguntur*).[23]

Beginning in the twelfth century, medieval Romanists and canonists regularly cited and agreed with this opinion in their writings on just price. They recognized that price freely and commonly arrived at in the marketplace was the best single guide to the determination of economic values and hence the best guide to assuring equalization in exchange – an ideal that remained unquestioned. To take but one highly influential example, the jurist Accursius, professor of Roman law at Bologna and author of what became the standard gloss (*Glossa ordinaria*) on the *Corpus iuris civilis* (*c*. 1220–50), joined together the positions on price from the *Code* and the *Digest*. He supported the general rule from the *Code* that in a sale between individuals, price was an agreement arrived at through the process of free bargaining: *Res tantum valet quantum vendi potest*.[24] But he gave even greater weight to the opinion in the *Digest*, which held that "The prices of things are determined not by their value and utility to individuals, but by their value determined commonly."[25] His resulting synthetic position, often repeated by future legists, was that the value of a commodity is determined by its *common price*, the price at which it can *commonly* be sold: in his words: "*res tantum valet quantum*

[22] Baldwin, *Just Price*, 20.
[23] *Digest*, 35.2.63; also *Digest*, 9.2.33. On this, see Noonan, *Usury*, 81–99; Cahn, "Roots," 30–2.
[24] Accursius, Gloss on *Codex*, 4.44.8; Baldwin, *Just Price*, 21.
[25] Accursius, Gloss on *Digest*, 35.2.63; Langholm, *Economics in the Schools*, 260 ff.

vendi potest, scilicet communiter."[26] In short, for Accursius and the civil lawyers who followed him, the common estimation of value in the marketplace provided the best guide to aligning price with economic value and hence to the establishment of exchange equality.

The implications of this recognition are profound; to hold it is to recognize that common valuation serves not only as a dependable guide to just value, but that in most cases it is to be trusted *above* individual judgments on these matters. Indeed, the implications are that common valuation serves as a *corrective* for individual judgments and valuations – a corrective for the wide variations in individual circumstances and needs upon which individual decisions about price are made. It is precisely these implications that were worked out over the course of the thirteenth century in writings on price and value. At the end of the century, legists and even certain philosophers and theologians could argue that since individual needs, interests, and judgments are liable to vary so greatly with varying personal situations, the proper process of equalization in exchange actually *requires* the guidance of a "common" price and a "common" estimation of value.[27] This is where the logic of the Roman law on buying and selling pointed, but its full realization would come only at the end of the thirteenth century, a testament to the continued sensitivity of scholastic writers to the actual details of their social and economic environment as well as to their freedom (in this area of economic thought) to record what they themselves saw and experienced.

In the previous chapter on equality in usury theory, we saw that the ancient Roman law acceptance of a proportional indemnification *ultra sortem* in the loan contract (i.e., the legitimacy of charging a legally regulated interest on a loan) was, in the Christian tradition, unreservedly denied on the basis of both divine and natural law. Biblical injunctions and writings of the Church Fathers were marshaled to create a unified position of unquestioned authority in opposition to permitting lending at interest. Proportionality was denied. Justice in the loan contract required a perfect arithmetical equality between sum lent and sum required in return, with no respect paid to the varying positions of borrower and lender. In theory, the smallest deviation from this equality created an inequality and injustice that was condemned in the eyes of God and Nature and forbidden by the laws of the Church. This negation, first fully expressed in the canons of Gratian's *Decretum*,

---

[26] Accursius, Gloss on *Digest*, 35.2.63: "communi pretio aestimantur res; quod ergo dicitur res tantum valet quantum vendi potest, scilicet communiter." On this see Ibanès, *La doctrine*, 35–41.

[27] See below for the formulation of this position in the writings of Peter Olivi.

set the course for the scholastic discourse on usury for centuries to follow.

Markedly different, however, was the Christian response to the ancient Roman law acceptance of free (and at times rough) bargaining in exchange. The desire to profit or gain advantage in contracts of buying and selling never earned the same degree of condemnation or the same association with unmitigated inequality and injustice. Biblical injunctions and canons of the Fathers were rarely brought to bear to declare bargaining unlawful or sinful. There were, indeed, certain hesitations expressed by certain thinkers, and conditions were attached at points to the general legal rule permitting bargaining to the limit of fraud. Avarice was universally condemned and open-handedness was an often-expressed value in both aristocratic and clerical circles. But the practical "naturalism" of the Roman law decision in the area of buying and selling – the general acceptance of the "what is" of economic life rather than the imposition of the "what should be and must be," of divine law – continued to be part of the discussion on price and value throughout the medieval period. This, in itself, allowed the analysis of price and value to follow a freer and wider path in its development than was possible in the case of usury theory. At the same time, scholastic commentators remained united in agreement on one transcendent ideal over this whole period: the goal and required end of all transactions involving buying and selling is and must be *aequalitas*. The question became, once again, how to define it.

Equality as a range along a numbered continuum of value

The lawyer's rule of *laesio enormis*, which determined that the bounds of legal price extended one half above and one half below the "common" price, rests on the assumption that economic value can be represented as a numbered continuum, divisible as a line is divisible. With the extension of the principle of *laesio enormis* in jurisprudence to cover all sales by the end of the twelfth century, general rules and numerical illustrations were devised to aid lawyers in determining legitimate ranges for all prices. At the beginning of the thirteenth century, the renowned commentator and professor of Roman law at Bologna, Azo, provided these simple guidelines: if the "just" price (i.e., the common price of Roman law) is 10 and the lower legal limit of sale price is 5, the upper limit should be 15.[28] This position was approved by Accursius, and from the authority

[28] Baldwin, *Just Price*, 23.

of his gloss (*c.* 1230), it became the standard application of the rule in both civil and canon law.[29] What this development reveals is that legal writers of the thirteenth century, both Romanists and canonists, routinely considered the just price in all exchanges as an approximative range along a numbered continuum of value, framed by an upper and lower limit, rather than as a precise and knowable point. As far as jurists were concerned, the perfect arithmetical equality required in the loan contract was not only not required in the determination of price, it was increasingly understood to be unknowable and therefore effectively unattainable.

The requirement for equality in the theological tradition

What did the theologians, concerned more with the strict requirements of divine law than with the approximations of human law, make of the legal latitudinarianism on the question of just price? How did it fit their focus on questions of personal salvation and on the personal ethics involved in exchange? There were clear theological problems associated with a body of decisions that accepted the desire for personal advantage and some degree of deceit as the basis of economic exchange. There were problems with the wide, merely approximative ranges of legitimate equalization permitted by the rule of *laesio enormis*. And there were exceptional problems associated with a vision of exchange in which equality and justice were seen to result from a supra-personal process of common estimation and valuation rather than from individual decisions based in conscience and charity.[30] It is not surprising, then, that the earliest theological discussions of just price established a clear distinction between a price equality (just price) legally sufficient within the wide bounds of *laesio enormis*, and a price equality that conformed to the stricter moral requirements of divine law. The first theologians to discuss the contract of sale in the early thirteenth century were well aware that civil and canon law allowed deception within limits; they were aware that in legal theory "a thing is worth what it can be sold for"; they were aware that all sales in which the price fell within the broad bounds of *laesio enormis* were

---

[29] *Ibid.*, 45. The great canon lawyer, Cardinal Hostiensis, writing in the mid thirteenth century, aligned his position on the computation of *laesio enormis* with that of Azo and Accursius. Hostiensis, *Summa aurea* (Venice, 1574, reprint Turin: Bottega d'Erasmo, 1963), Book III, cols. 943–4.

[30] For a clear recognition of the metaphysical problems presented by the privileging of systematic equalization in exchange within the legal tradition, see Amleto Spicciani, *La mercatura e la formazione del prezzo nella riflessione teologica medioevale* (Rome: Accademia dei Lincei, 1977), 234.

considered final and legal. They insisted, however, that the *lex divina* made no such allowances.[31]

Theologians, therefore, continued to think it quite possible that an individual could knowingly buy for less than the just price or sell for more, even when buying or selling within the legal mathematical limits. In their opinion, such sales violated the essence of *aequalitas* required in all economic exchanges, and for that reason they should be subject to the same penalties as usurious loans.[32] It was, they held, the *personal* responsibility of both buyer and seller to aim for and to achieve a just price. Even though theologians of the first half of the thirteenth century never decided nor even discussed how this precise point of exchange equality was to be determined in practical terms, they insisted that the smallest deviation from it required restitution.[33] For these reasons, through the middle of the thirteenth century, the scholastic discourse on price and value was characterized by a disjunction between legal and theological positions on the determination of just price. Then, with the publication of a single work, the shape and sophistication of the discourse changed dramatically. In 1246–7, Aristotle's remarkable discussion of money and exchange appeared in Latin for the first time in Robert Grosseteste's full translation (from the Greek) of the *Nicomachean Ethics*.[34] Soon after its translation, the *Ethics* came to occupy a central place in the curriculum of the medieval university, and within two decades, influential commentaries by Albertus Magnus and Thomas Aquinas had been produced to deepen its study.[35]

---

[31] For an overview of the early theological position on price, see John Baldwin, *Masters, Princes, and Merchants: The Social Views of Peter the Chanter and his Circle*, 2 vols. (Princeton University Press, 1970), vol. I, 261–75; Baldwin, *Just Price*, 68–71. Langholm considers this question in relation to individual theologians at many points in his *Economics in the Schools*.

[32] Baldwin, *Just Price*, 69; Baldwin, *Masters*, 265.

[33] Baldwin, *Just Price*, 69, n. 127, quoting from the *Poenitentiale* of Thomas of Chobham: "In venditione autem secundum humanas si aliquis deceperit aliquem ultra medietatem iusti precii tenetur restituere illud quod ultra medietatem recipit. sed si minori quantitate decipit emptorem non tenetur restiturere. sed secundum legem dei si decipit emptorem in uno denario ultra iustum precium tenetur restituere."

[34] On Grosseteste's Latin translation of the *Ethics*, see D. A. Callus, "The Date of Grosseteste's Translations and Commentaries on the Pseudo-Dionysius and the *Nicomachean Ethics*," *Recherches de théologie ancienne et médiévale* 14 (1947), 200–9. For more on the history of the medieval Latin translations of the *Ethics*, see René Antoine Gauthier and Jean Yves Jolif, *L'Éthique à Nicomaque: Introduction, traduction et commentaire*, 2 vols. (Louvain: Publications universitaires; Paris: Béatrice-Nauwelaerts, 1970), vol. I, 115–30.

[35] For the important place of the *Ethics* within the university curriculum, see Zénon Kaluza, "Les cours communs sur *L'Éthique à Nicomaque* à l'université de Paris," in *"Ad Ingenii Acuitionem": Studies in Honour of Alfonso Maierù*, ed. Stefano Caroti, Ruedi Imbach, Zénon Kaluza, et al. (Louvain-La-Neuve: Collège Cardinal Mercier, 2006), 147–81. For a general discussion of the economic opinions expressed by Albert and Thomas in their commentaries (with bibliography), see Kaye, *Economy and Nature in the Fourteenth Century*, 56–78.

Price and value in Aristotle's discussion of exchange:
Nicomachean Ethics, Book V

In the preceding chapter, I considered aspects of Aristotle's economic analysis in *Ethics* V that touched on the question of usury; here I focus on those elements that are germane to the subject of price and value.[36] I note first that Aristotle placed his discussion of money and economic exchange in *Ethics* V at the center of his most detailed analysis of justice and the forms of equalization that comprise it. His decision to do so had significant ramifications. On the one hand it played a crucial role in countering ingrained notions of buying and selling as sites of inevitable deception, greed, and corruption; on the other it indicated that economic exchange could be understood as a rational system characterized not only by an order that could be represented in mathematical terms but by justice itself. This, in turn, had the almost immediate effect of encouraging further philosophical investigations into the logic of exchange. Moreover, Aristotle's insistence in *Ethics* V, that all exchange must be ordered to the end of equality, fully corroborated the Christian tradition on the subject.[37] Indeed, for Aristotle, economic exchange was by definition a process of equalization. The text of the *Ethics* thus served as a sturdy textual bridge between the everyday experience of exchange in the marketplace and the scholastic construction of intellectual models capable of comprehending and representing its ordering and equalizing principles.

As I noted in the previous chapter, Aristotle divided justice into two particular forms in *Ethics* V. Each form was defined both by the species of equality proper to it and by the mathematical process involved in attaining that equality. Briefly, the first form, *iustitia directiva* (sometimes designated *iustitia correctiva*), is directed toward attaining an arithmetical equality through the process of addition and subtraction. In the case of an unequal exchange having occurred, *iustitia directiva* is accomplished by subtracting a sum from the party that had gained overmuch and adding it to the party that had lost. The model for this form is the mechanical scale (the traditional iconographic representation of *iustitia*), in which a

---

[36] The Latin text of the *Ethics* I cite in the notes is taken from the revised version (*c.* 1260) of Grosseteste's translation: *Ethica Nicomachea, translatio Roberti Grosseteste Lincolniensis, recensio recognita*, ed. R. A. Gauthier, in *Aristoteles Latinus*, vol. XXVI, 1–3, fasc. 4 (Leiden: Brill, 1973). Hereafter, this edition will be cited as *Arist. Lat.* XXVI. I use the English translation of the Greek *Ethics* by W. D. Ross, in *The Basic Works of Aristotle*, ed. Richard McKeon (New York: Random House, 1941), where it accurately conveys the sense of the Latin translation.

[37] The search for equality and the mean provides the central theme of the *Ethics*; economic exchange is only one of many aspects of human life that Aristotle treats as belonging to that search.

subjective orderer adds and subtracts weights to either side of the scale until a definable point of equality and balance is achieved. Aristotle does not, however, intend this form to be applicable to the active process of economic exchange itself. Rather, it is the form followed by a judge, whose task, after the fact of an unequal exchange, is to restore equality by bisecting the line of gain and loss existing between the two parties.

The second form, *iustitia distributiva*, is different in almost all respects from the first. Its end is *proportional* equalization rather than the establishment of a perfect arithmetical equality, and it is directed to this end through the mathematical processes of division and multiplication (in Aristotle's terms) rather than addition and subtraction. To underscore the identification of justice with equality, and at the same time to demonstrate that economic exchange, as a process of equalization, possesses a mathematically definable order, Aristotle represents the process of proportionalization governed by *iustitia distributiva* as an equation in four lettered terms.[38]

The conjunction then, of the term A with G and of B with D is what is just in distribution, and this represents the just medium ... For the medium is proportional and the just is proportional. Mathematicians call this kind of proportion geometrical. In geometrical proportion, the whole is compared to the whole as the part to a part.[39]

After describing the mathematical forms of distributive and directive justice, Aristotle introduces the concept of "reciprocity" (*contrapassum*), and it is in this context that he begins his discussion proper of economic exchange. Once again, he is careful to make explicit one of his central lessons and one of his deepest insights: that the equality (*medium*) that constitutes justice in economic exchange (buying and selling) is a proportional rather than an arithmetical equality.

Now "reciprocity" (*contrapassum*) fits neither distributive nor rectificatory justice ... But in associations for exchange just reciprocity (*iustum contrapassum*) prevails, determined on the basis of proportionality rather than on the basis of precisely equal return.[40]

---

[38] *Ethica* [1131b4–6], *Arist. Lat.* XXVI, 459: "Est autem et iustum in quatuor minimis, et proporcio eadem; divisa enim sunt similiter et quibus et que; erit ergo ut A terminus ad B, ita G ad D, et permutatim ergo ut A ad G, B ad D; quare et totum ad totum."

[39] *Ethica* [1131b9–14], *ibid.*, 459: "Ergo A termini cum G et B cum D coniunccio in distribucione iustum est, et medium iustum ... Proporcionale enim medium, iustum autem proporcionale. Vocant autem talem proporcionalitatem geometricam mathematici. In geometria enim accidit et totum comparari ad totum quod quidem pars alterum ad alterum."

[40] *Ethica* [1132b24; 31–4], *ibid.*, 462: "Contrapassum autem non congruit, neque in distributivum iustum, neque in directivum ... Set in concomitacionibus quidem commutativis continet tale iustum contrapassum secundum proporcionalitatem et non secundum equalitatem."

Aristotle's geometry of exchange equalization

Aristotle then does something extraordinary: he fits the complex interchange between any two producers and their two varied products into a
geometric diagram – what the Latin translator refers to as a "figure of
proportionality" (*figura proporcionalitatis*).[41] In a large number of Latin
manuscripts of the *Ethics* and its scholastic commentaries, the geometric
"figura" of proportional equalization that Aristotle describes is graphi-
cally rendered as an accompanying figure drawn in the margin: a
rectangle with crossed diagonals, with each corner of the square lettered
and labeled – builder (A), shoemaker (B), house (G), shoe (D). The
crossed diagonals, which represent the direction of the exchange and
emphasize its dynamic qualities, are often labeled as well.

The frequency with which this labeled *figura proportionalitatis* appears
(often as the only drawn figure in the entire manuscript) is a good indication
of the seriousness and concreteness medieval scholars accorded Aristotle's
geometry of exchange.[42] The rectangular figure with its crossed diagonals
formed, for thinkers of the thirteenth and fourteenth centuries, an ideal
analogue to the developing conception of the marketplace as a working
system of proportional equalization, with its own working logic, its own
mathematical and geometric form, and its own governing *ratio*.[43] Once
established, Aristotle refers to his "figure of proportionality" six more
times in the short remainder of his economic discussion in Book V. In
short, the equalizing geometry underlying Aristotle's scheme could hardly
be ignored. And yet it carried with it a number of implications that might
well have been disquieting to thirteenth-century readers, particularly theologians. For one, the sheer impersonality of a system in which exchangers
could be represented by lettered terms and treated as elements in what is

---

[41] *Ethica* [1133a34], *ibid.*, 463: "In figuram autem proporcionalitatis." *Ethica* [1133a6–11],
ibid., 462: "Facit enim retribucionem eam que secundum proporcionalitatem secundum
dyametrum coniugacio. Puta edificator in quo A, coriarius in quo B, domus in quo G,
calciamentum in quo D. Oportet autem accipere edificatorem a coriario illius opus, et
ipsum illi retribuere quod ipsius."

[42] *Arist. Lat.* XXVI, 236, 238, and notes.

[43] The crossed diagonals of Aristotle's *figura* can be seen as a geometrical representation of
what Roman law recognized as the dynamic act of free bargaining. Aristotle never
mentions the act of bargaining, and he provides no clues as to how any two producers
reach their particular point of equalization, but certain of his modern commentators
assume that he understood free bargaining to be the general rule in exchange. See, for
example, S. Todd Lowry, "Aristotle's Mathematical Analysis of Exchange," *History of
Political Economy* 1 (1969), 44–66, at 51; also, *Ethica* [1136b7–15]. For an argument
against this conclusion, see M. I. Finley, "Aristotle and Economic Analysis," in
Jonathan Barnes *et al.* (eds.), *Articles on Aristotle*, vol. II: *Ethics and Politics* (London:
Duckworth, 1977), 140–58, at 147.

essentially a mathematical equation; for another, that exchange *aequalitas* could be envisioned as a quasi-mathematical *product* of the systematic geometry of exchange; and, for a third, the implication that the geometry of exchange represents a *self-ordering process of proportionalization and equalization*, capable of functioning in the absence of an overarching or intervening orderer imposing judgment from above or from outside the process itself.[44] But if these powerful elements were disquieting or difficult to integrate into traditional models of equalization, in the end they were neither abandoned nor even diluted. They were employed, instead, as part of the scholastic effort to make sense of the ever-increasing speed, volume, and variety of exchange that, along with its ever-widening social and political effects, characterized the last decades of the thirteenth century. Used in this way, Aristotle's geometry of exchange arguably achieved deeper significance and exercised greater influence than Aristotle had intended for it. Moreover, as insights into the self-ordering and self-equalizing potential of exchange were grounded in contemporary observation and experience, they lost their incongruity and became, in a sense, naturalized. Indeed, I want to argue that, by the last decades of the thirteenth century, the same insights that had once been incongruent with existing models of equalization were precisely those that became foundational elements of the new model of equilibrium – a model which was emerging just at this time.

Money as an instrument of equalization in *Ethics*, Book V

With the image of the rectangular *figura* of exchange firmly established, Aristotle then turns to show how the instrument of money functions within and makes possible the geometry of exchange. As the universal *medium* of economic measurement and commensuration, money forms the middle term in all exchange equations. He notes that it is impossible for things that differ greatly, such as a bed and a house, to be made commensurate in themselves.[45] Money, however, makes such commensuration possible, because it serves as a common measure of all goods in exchange.[46] He then constructs a second rectangular *figura*, through which he illustrates how money, acting as a numbered continuum capable of

---

[44] I offer evidence below in this chapter that these determinations were indeed disquieting to the early readers of the *Ethics*.

[45] *Ethica* [1133b18–20], *Arist. Lat.* XXVI, 464: "Secundum quidem igitur inpossibile tantum differencia, commensurata fieri, convenit sufficienter."

[46] *Ethica* [1133b20–3], *ibid.*, 464: "Unum utique aliquid oportet esse; hoc autem ex supposicione; propter quod et nummisma vocatur, hoc enim omnia facit commensurata. Mensurantur enim omnia nummismate." This passage contains many important variants in the medieval Latin translation. See the editor's notes on this point, *ibid.*, 464.

fluid expansion and contraction, makes possible the commensuration of unequal goods, which, he maintained, was the precondition of exchange.[47] Again in this figural representation, exchangers and their products are so interchangeable that they can be represented by mathematical terms and geometrical figures; again it appears that the necessary end of proportional *aequalitas* is represented not by a conscious agreement between individual exchangers but by the crossed diagonals of the rectangle of exchange. Money is the essential *medium*, the continuous measuring and connecting *line* that makes the geometry of exchange possible.[48] As we move forward from the mid thirteenth century, and as we begin to see a more complex vision of systematic equilibrium emerging in scholastic economic thought, we must keep in mind Aristotle's extraordinary creation here.

The place of relativity in Aristotle's model of equalization

Money is the instrument that makes equalization – the *sine qua non* of all economic exchange – possible. But what precisely does money measure? Aristotle's answer here proved very important to his medieval commentators. In the course of his discussion there are hints that money measures certain qualities existing in some sense within the commodities themselves, whether the quality of workmanship in the product;[49] or the level of skill involved in its production;[50] or the different expenditures of labor required in production.[51] Nevertheless, judging by the weight Aristotle allowed to such "internal" factors in his discussion, they held second place in his understanding of economic value.[52] Indeed, Aristotle states and repeats that money does not so much measure the skill and labor put into

---

[47] *Ethica* [1133b 23–6], *ibid.*, 464: "Mensurantur enim omnia nummismate. Domus in quo A, mnarum quinque, lectus in quo B, minus dignus; lectus autem quinta pars domus utique erit. Manifestum igitur quanti lecti equale domui, quoniam quinque."

[48] On the many ways that scholastic authors identified money with the geometric line, see my *Economy and Nature in the Fourteenth Century*, esp. 158–9.

[49] *Ethica* [1133a13–15].

[50] *Ibid.* [1133a17–19], as in Aristotle's example, an exchange between a farmer and a doctor.

[51] *Ibid.* [1133b23–5].

[52] Modern commentators have weighed the "objective" value components of labor and expenses against the "subjective" component of human need in Aristotle's analysis in *Ethics* V. On this question, see Joseph Soudek, "Aristotle's Theory of Exchange: An Inquiry into the Origin of Economic Analysis," *Proceedings of the American Philosophical Society* 96 (1952), 45–75, at 60, 65–8; Odd Langholm, *Price and Value in the Aristotelian Tradition* (Bergen: Universitetsforlaget, 1979), 50. For a balanced presentation of the textual evidence on both sides of this question, see Barry Gordon, "Aristotle and the Development of Value Theory," *Quarterly Journal of Economics* 78 (1964), 115–28.

the production of commodities, or their internal qualities, as it does the external and ever-shifting demand or need (*indigentia*) attached to objects in exchange. Since, his argument goes, all things in exchange share the common quality of being needed by someone, money as a measure of need (*indigentia*) creates the possibility of universal commensuration and hence the ground of exchange equalization.[53] At its core, the quality of human need (*indigentia*) is variable and relativized, continually growing and diminishing in relation to changing persons, times, places, and conditions. It is this variable and relativized quality of *indigentia* that functions as the primary determinant of value in Aristotle's discussion of economic exchange.[54] At the center of Aristotle's geometry of exchange, then, with all its promise of analytical precision, lies the recognition that economic value is relative value, always varying in relation to varying contexts and, therefore, always at best approximative.

Although relativity is central to Aristotle's economic analysis, there is evidence of discomfort with and resistance to it as a key to the determination of value by his first medieval readers. Value fluidity was difficult to conceptualize within a Christian worldview that envisioned an ontologically graded universe within which every object and subject had its fixed place in the order of being from God down to the least of his creations.[55] The textual weight of Aristotle was great, but it required the confluence of textual authority and lived experience to open the door to relativized determinations in medieval thought – a door that would be flung wide open in the fourteenth century.[56] The scholar's daily life, whether in the city of Paris, Bologna, Padua, Montpellier, or Oxford, would have shown him beyond doubt that the same object or commodity, although unchanging in itself, was valued differently from day to day or week to week; that the price of his bread or meat or wine was constantly redetermined relative

---

[53] *Ethica* [1133a26–30], *Arist. Lat.* XXVI, 463: "Oportet ergo uno aliquo omnia mensurari, quemadmodum dictum est prius. Hoc autem est secundum veritatem quidem continet. Si enim nichil indigerent, vel non similiter, vel non erit communicacio, vel non eadem indigencia que puta propter commutacionem necessitatis nummisma factum est secundum compositionem." For the confusion engendered by variant Latin translations of this passage, see Odd Langholm, "Scholastic Economics," in *Pre-Classical Economic Thought*, ed. S. Todd Lowry (Boston: Kluwer, 1987), 122–3.

[54] For a fuller discussion of the place of relativized *indigentia* in Aristotle's analysis of economic value, see Kaye, *Economy and Nature in the Fourteenth Century*, 47–51. For the further development of this understanding in later scholastic commentaries, see *ibid.*, 147–52.

[55] In Chapter 5 below I discuss the strength of this view in the thought of Albertus Magnus and Thomas Aquinas. For a discussion of Thomas' resistance to the implications of value relativity in the loan contract, see Chapter 1 above, and for his position on relativity in the determination of price and value, see below in this chapter.

[56] Fourteenth-century relativism is discussed further in Chapters 4, 6, 7, and 8.

to such external factors as time and place.[57] And the scholar's recognition of relativized values in the marketplace would be further expanded were he to be involved, as was so often the case, in the administration of his school, religious order, Church, or secular government, requiring his direct and frequent participation in the marketplace on behalf of his institution.[58]

After the mid thirteenth century, with the wide circulation of the *Ethics* and its commentaries in the schools, scholars had, in addition to their economic experiences, the text of *Ethics* V to frame and clarify the implications of relativity and to authorize its application to intellectual problems. Indeed, by the 1270s, the fact that the same measure of wheat (or any other food crop) was worth considerably more in the summer, when it was scarce (and therefore more needed and more "useful") than in the fall, when it was plentiful, was being seen as a "natural" component of its commodity value, as natural as those qualities that made the commodity useful (and valuable) in the first place.[59] Following the dissemination of *Ethics* V, scholastics were not only sensitized to thinking of economic value in relativized terms, but they were seeing how relativity and its essential indeterminacy might be integrated into other discourses organized around the requirement of proportional equalization, which is to say almost every scholastic discourse.

With respect to the definition of *aequalitas* itself, following the translation and wide circulation of the *Ethics* within the university, proportional equality, with its ever-shifting determinations and inescapable approximations, could now be held to be every bit as "equal" as the 1:1 arithmetical equality achieved through the mechanical scale, and every bit as deserving of a place under the heading of "justice." Aristotle provided the authority: "For the medium is proportional and the just is proportional."[60] These lessons

---

[57] See, for example, the comments made by Jean Buridan in his mid-fourteenth-century *Quaestiones in decem libros ethicorum Aristotelis ad Nicomachum* (Oxford: H. Cripps, 1637), Book II, q. 16: "nec semper aequali pecunia bladum aequale emitur, nec ubique similiter: sed magis et minus, secundum nostram exigentiam vel abundantiam. Sed hoc usque ad quintum librum dimittatur . . . Et non aequaliter venditur pannus in foro Brugis, et in foro Parisius."

[58] For evidence of the participation of scholars in such administrative tasks, see Kaye, *Economy and Nature in the Fourteenth Century*, 28–36.

[59] Giles of Lessines, *De usuris in communi, et De usurarum in contractibus*, ed. S. E. Fretté as part of Thomas Aquinas, *Opera omnia*, vol. XXVIII (Paris: Vivès, 1889), 593: "Et hoc modo si causa temporis plus vendatur vel minus, non erit hujusmodi contractus usurarius: pluris enim aestimatur et juste mensura tritici in aestate quam in autumno ceteris paribus, hoc est quantum est de natura temporis; et ideo si quis accipiat plus de blado vendito pro tempore aestatis, quam dederit in autumno, quando bladum emit, non judicatur usurarius."

[60] *Ethica* [1131b9–12], *Arist. Lat.* XXVI, 459: "Ergo A termini cum G et B cum D coniunccio in distribucione iustum est, et medium iustum . . . Proporcionale enim medium, iustum autem proporcionale."

would have profound effects on medieval thinking in the decades to come, both within the economic sphere and beyond it.

Economic equalization in the writings of Thomas Aquinas

Soon after the first Latin translation of the *Ethics* appeared, Albertus Magnus presented a series of lectures on it in Cologne. Shortly after, he authored the first scholastic commentary on the complete text (*c.* 1250).[61] In the audience for his lectures was his student, Thomas Aquinas, who more than a decade later wrote his own commentary.[62] It is noteworthy that both Albert and Thomas followed Aristotle's striking exposition of the geometry of exchange, including his use of the geometrical *"figura proportionalitatis"* to illustrate its workings, without difficulty, and seemingly without hesitation.[63] Albertus did, however, at one point digress from the Aristotelian text and observe that economic exchange at times followed patterns unrecognized by Aristotle – patterns that did not conform to his geometric model because they were not the product of purely voluntary exchanges between producers. Demonstrating the acuity of his perceptions of economic life and the workings of the marketplace (*in foro*), he notes that during periods of great shortages, the prince may interfere in the market and set maximum prices so that the city as a whole does not suffer. He also recognizes that the normal equivalence established between buyer and seller in exchange can be upset by preexistent agreements or pacts that fix the selling price and do not permit it to vary as it normally would.[64] In recognizing these exceptions, Albert demonstrates his association of the geometrical process of exchange equalization with the free, direct, and dynamic interchange of goods and people in the marketplace.

---

[61] Albertus' first commentary on the *Ethics* has been edited as volume XIV of the recent Cologne edition of his *Opera omnia: Alberti Magni super Ethica commentum et quaestiones*, ed. Wilhelm Kübel (Monasterii Westfalorum: Aschendorff, 1972) (henceforth *Ethica*, ed. Kübel). His second commentary on the *Ethics* is found in volume VII of his *Opera omnia: Ethicorum libri decem*, ed. A. Borgnet (Paris, 1891) (henceforth *Ethica*, ed. Borgnet). See Jean Dunbabin, "The Two Commentaries of Albertus Magnus on the Nicomachean Ethics," *Recherche de théologie ancienne et médiévale* 30 (1963), 232–50. I discuss the economic insights contained in Albert's commentaries in *Economy and Nature in the Fourteenth Century*, 56–78.

[62] *Sancti Thomae de Aquino Sententia libri ethicorum*, vol. XLVII of *Opera omnia* (Rome: Commissio Leonina, 1969) (henceforth *Ethics*).

[63] Albert, *Ethica*, ed. Kübel, 343a–b: "sicut vides in figura exterius"; Thomas, *Ethics*, 292a: "deinde fiat contrapassum ... scilicet retributio secundum proportionalitatem facta per diametralem coniunctionem."

[64] Albert, *Ethica*, ed. Borgnet, 355b.

Not surprisingly, the focus on equality in exchange remained a constant in the work of both theologians, both in their commentaries on the *Ethics* and in their other writings on economic subjects. This can be clearly seen in the opening words of St. Thomas' opinion on economic exchange in his *Summa theologica:*

Considered in itself, the transaction of buying and selling is seen to have been introduced for the common utility (*pro communi utilitate*) of both [buyer and seller] ... Therefore the contract should be instituted according to an equality of things (*secundum aequalitatem rei*) between them. The value of things which come into human use are measured by their given price, and for this reason money was invented as [Aristotle] said.[65]

So far so good. Aristotle never discussed the details of how the equalizing price was to be decided aside from its determination within the systematic geometry of exchange. By the time Thomas was writing the *Summa theologica*, both Roman and canon lawyers accepted (as we have seen) that the price agreed to between individual exchangers can be achieved through the process of free bargaining. Whatever price the participants arrived at, assuming that it fell within the broad bounds of *laesio enormis*, would be a legal price reflecting an effective equalization between the needs of buyer and seller. But neither of these solutions was sufficient in Thomas' eyes nor in the eyes of a number of other theologians of his generation. Based on the premises he introduced above, he continues:

And therefore if either the price exceeds the quantity of the value of a thing or, conversely, if the value of the thing exceeds the price, the equality that justice demands is destroyed (*tolletur justitiae aequalitas*). And therefore, to buy a thing for less or to sell a thing for more than it is worth is in itself unjust and illicit.[66]

Equality is at the center of Thomas' view of economic exchange in three ways: (1) there is an assumed equality of need between buyer and seller before the sale; (2) there is an assumed equality of benefit between buyer

---

[65] The Latin edition of the *ST* is the Leonine edition (Rome: Commissio Leonina, 1888–1906), which can be accessed at www.corpusthomisticum.org. Since the Latin edition is readily available, I include the Latin text in the notes only where I quote directly from it or where the wording is particularly revealing. English translations are for the most part from *Summa theologica* (New York: Blackfriars, 1964–81), with modifications noted. *ST*, II, II, 77, 1, resp.: "Uno modo secundum se, et secundum hoc emptio et venditio videtur esse introducta pro communi utilitate utriusque ... et ideo debet secundum aequalitatem rei inter eos contractus institui. Quantitas autem rerum, quae in usum hominis veniunt, mensuratur secundum pretium datum; ad quod est inventum numisma, ut dicitur."

[66] *ST*, II, II, 77, 1, resp.: "Et ideo si vel pretium excedat quantitatem valoris rei vel e converso res excedat pretium, tolletur justitiae aequalitas. Et ideo carius vendere aut vilius emere rem quam valeat est secundum se injustum et illicitum."

and seller as the result of the sale; (3) there must therefore be an equality between the price paid and the value of the thing bought. But while his emphasis on equality in exchange is clear and unmistakable, his model of economic equalization is not. He never makes explicit in any of his writings how either the "equality of things" or the "just price" of a commodity in exchange can or should actually be determined.[67] He is uncharacteristically vague on this point, especially in contrast to his teacher, Albertus Magnus, who specifically identified the "just price" of a good or service with its common market price, writing:

The "just price" is the value which, according to the estimation of the marketplace (*secundum aestimationem fori*), can be assigned to a particular good for sale at a particular time.[68]

Equality, just price, and market price

Thomas' lack of clarity on the just price resulted neither from his lack of interest in economic questions, nor from his lack of knowledge about how prices are determined in the marketplace. In his discussion of the question in the *Summa theologica*, he demonstrates his acuity and sophistication as an economic observer. Through the examples he offers, he makes clear his awareness that market value is determined relative to common scarcity, common need (*indigentia*), and common estimation (*aestimatio communis*), and that it properly varies in each particular market in relation to varying time, place, and circumstance.[69] In his commentary to Book V of Aristotle's *Ethics*, he again demonstrates how fully he comprehends Aristotle's injection of relativity into the heart of the process of geometrical equalization in exchange. He writes:

The one thing that measures all things, according to the truth of things, is need (*indigentia*), which is attached to all things in exchange, to the degree that all things in exchange have reference to human need (*ad humanam indigentiam*). Things in exchange are not valued according to the dignity of their inherent natures (*secundum dignitatem naturae ipsorum*). If they were, a mouse, which possesses sensitive life, would be priced higher than a pearl, which is inanimate. Rather, the price of things is determined according to how much men need them for their use (*secundum quod homines indigent eis ad suum usum*).[70]

---

[67] He comes perhaps closest in *ST*, II, II, 77, 3, ad 4, discussed below.

[68] Albertus Magnus, *Commentarius in IV sententiarum*, dist. XVI, art. 46, in *Opera omnia*, vol. XXIX, ed. A. Borgnet (Paris: Vivès, 1894), 638: "Justum autem pretium est, quod secundum aestimationem fori illius temporis potest valere res vendita."

[69] See especially *ST*, II, II, 77, 3, ad 4.

[70] Thomas, *Ethics*, 294b95a: "Hoc autem unum quod omnia mensurat, secundum rei veritatem est indigentia, quae continet omnia commutabilia, in quantum scilicet

Moreover, throughout his discussion of economic questions, he demonstrates his knowledge of decisions from both canon and civil law that legitimate the practice of free bargaining, that recognize the commanding role of common estimation (*estimatio communis*) in the establishment of market price, and that equate legal and legitimate price with its common estimation in the marketplace.[71] Why then did he refrain from explicitly identifying just price with the common market price (*secundum aestimatione fori*) as his teacher Albert had? It is a question that remains alive among historians.[72]

I suggest that Thomas' failure to identify just price with the common price resulted not from a lack of economic understanding nor from a conflict of economic models but from his recognition that such a linkage brought with it serious theological, ethical, and metaphysical difficulties. One of the most important metaphysical principles for Thomas is that order always implies the existence of an active, intelligent orderer. The equation of order with intelligence is so central to his thought that it provides the basis for his arguments on behalf of God's necessary existence with which the *Summa theologica* begins.[73] This principle is threatened with the acceptance of an economic system in which a "just" equality is created as an accidental product of competing desires within an impersonal process, and where value (price) is detached from individual judgment. Similarly, judged from within his philosophical and theological value system, which greatly privileged hierarchy and permanence, the acceptance of a shifting, relational estimation as a "just" solution to the problem of economic value would present great difficulties. The legists did not focus on the theological implications of the geometrical model of equalization, but Thomas was required to.

The ethical implications were equally disturbing to Thomas. If just price equals common or market price and is divorced from individual judgment and direction, the individual's responsibility in economic activity is effectively eliminated. For Thomas to accept that ideal ends (whether defined as *aequalitas* or *iustitia*) could follow from the base

omnia referuntur ad humanam indigentiam; non enim appretiantur res secundum dignitatem naturae ipsorum; alioquin unus mus, quod est animal sensibile, maioris pretii esset quam una margarita, quae est res inanimata; sed rebus pretia imponuntur secundum quod homines indigent eis ad suum usum." He repeats this insight at *ST*, II, II, 77, 3, ad 3.

[71] E.g., *ST*, II, II, 77, 1, ad 1: "Sic igitur habet quasi licitum, poenam non inducens, si absque fraude venditor rem suam supervendat aut emptor vilius emat; nisi sit nimius excesus, quia tunc etiam lex humana cogit ad restituendum, puta si aliquis sit deceptus ultra dimidiam justi pretii quantitatem."

[72] See my *Economy and Nature in the Fourteenth Century*, 97–8, for competing interpretations.

[73] *ST*, I, I, 2, art. 3.

motive of deception and the base desire to buy cheaply and sell dear, would be for him to sever the link between the ethical order and the natural order, a link that he sought to strengthen at every point. The economic position Thomas adopted in the *Summa theologica* was crafted to take these serious philosophical difficulties into account – each of which centered on problems associated with the proper definition and determination of *aequalitas* in exchange.[74]

While the civil law permits mutual deception within the broad range of *laesio enormis*, Thomas makes clear that the divine law does not.[75] A market price based on *communis aestimatio* cannot in itself guarantee an exchange equality sufficient to merit the word "just." He supports this position with a more general one: what is common in the world is not necessarily identical with what is "natural" or what is just. Rather, he argues, the common way can at times lead in the unnatural direction of vice and sin, and he illustrates this general point with the specific example of the "common" desire to buy cheap and sell dear.[76] Individuals, he asserts, must work to overcome such common desires. For Thomas, a truly just equality between buyer and seller, which is to say a truly just price, requires each exchanger to consciously order each transaction to the end of *aequalitas justitiae*.[77] But how was this equivalence to be determined, and with how much precision could it be determined? To answer this Thomas introduced into his theological and philosophical discussion a refinement of the legal rule of *laesio enormis*:

> The just price of things is sometimes not precisely determined (*quandoque non est punctualiter determinatum*), but rather consists in an estimate (*quadam aestimatione consistit*). Therefore a small (*modica*) addition or subtraction does not seem to destroy the equality of justice.[78]

The modest phrasing of this conclusion disguises its import. Here, even within the constraints of reconciling economic observations with divine law, Thomas visualizes a true and just equality, one pleasing to God and

---

[74] See Chapter 1 for my reading of Thomas' "engineered" position on usury. Once again I see him adopting a highly crafted position that permits him to defend traditional positions and core beliefs while opening the door to some of the destabilizing implications of Aristotle's insights in *Ethics* V.

[75] *ST*, II, II, 77, 1, ad 1.

[76] *Ibid.*, ad 2: "Unde patet quod illud commune desiderium non est naturae sed vitii, et ideo commune est multis, qui per latam viam vitiorum incedunt."

[77] *Ibid.*: "Unde secundum divinam legem illicitum reputatur, si in emptione et venditione non sit aequalitas justitiae observata. Et tenetur ille qui plus habet recompensare ei qui damnificatus est, si sit notabile damnum."

[78] *Ibid.*, ad 1: "Quod ideo dico, quia justum pretium rerum quandoque non est punctualiter determinatum, sed majus in quadam aestimatione consistit; ita quod modica additio vel minutio non videtur tollere aequalitatem justitiae" (my emphasis).

consistent with the requirements of justice and virtue, not as a precise *point* but as a *range* along a continuum of value, however small he might wish that range to be. Moreover, estimation replaces knowing as the intellectual process through which this range is recognized. Within Roman and canon law, approximation and estimation were well understood to be adequate in the determination of price. Here, they receive Thomas' imprimatur in the much more demanding realm of philosophy and theology.

Thomas' acceptance of estimation and approximation within a range of value as consistent with the requirements of the *lex divina* had important philosophical implications. In an intellectual tradition preoccupied with the ideal of *aequalitas*, changes in its definition, or in the understanding of how it might be achieved, had multiple consequences, expanding far beyond the economic sphere. When Thomas, for example, projected this equalizing range (or "latitude" as it later came frequently to be called) onto the plan of nature, he (and others after him) began to step away from an earlier philosophical vision of natural activity centered on discrete and knowable points of perfection, toward a much more dynamic and fluid vision of the world. In the century following Thomas, the insights that came to cluster around the equalizing "latitude" or line range, would come to occupy a central place in proto-scientific speculation. The instrument of the measuring latitude itself would take its place as a foundational element in a new and highly productive (in intellectual terms) conception of nature within university speculation.[79] Indeed, as I will try to show in this and succeeding chapters, the capacity to see and think with fluid latitudes rather than with discrete points, and to imagine systems functioning and equalizing around approximating ranges, becomes one of the defining characteristics of the "new model of equilibrium" as it manifests itself in multiple disciplines from the last decades of the thirteenth century.

Another debate over the definition of *aequalitas* in the census contract

I began my discussion of the census contract in the previous chapter, taking it from its earliest appearance in canon law to the writings on the subject by the brilliant professor of law, Sinibaldo Fieschi, scion of a noble Genoese family that was heavily engaged in commerce, who was elevated to the papal throne as Pope Innocent IV (1243–54). As we saw, the census

---

[79] See Chapters 4 and 8 for discussions on this point.

contract was a peculiar hybrid between a contract of loan (*mutuum*) and of sale (*emptio-venditio*). In its basic form, the *census* was an agreement between two parties, in which one party (A) offers the rights to a piece of fruitful property valued at a particular sum of money to another (B), and in return B agrees to pay A a lesser sum yearly over the duration of the contract, derived from the fruits of the property. In a typical example, the property that A transfers to B might be valued at 100 solidi, and in return B contracts to pay A 10 solidi per year, either for as long as A (or his named heirs) lives (*redditus ad vitam*), or in perpetuity (*redditus perpetuus*).[80] Clearly, and as noted previously, the probability of a numerical equality resulting from this contract is small to none. In the case of *redditus ad vitam*, the party receiving the annual payment would have to die precisely ten years after making the contract in order for the return to exactly equal the original value of the land. In the case of *redditus perpetuus*, not only is achieving an arithmetical equality between sum proffered and sum returned out of the question, there is no recognizable basis for numerical equality at all. Is this not a usurious contract in its clearest definition (from Gratian): "where more is expected in return than was given"?[81]

Although the census contract was originally attached to the transfer of fruitful property, beginning in the twelfth century it began to take another characteristic form, which involved citizens transferring sums of money to their municipal authorities (at times as forced loans) in return for the guarantee of a fixed annual return.[82] Clearly the same impossibility that a knowable and arithmetically equal return could result from the census on land also attached to the municipal loan. And yet these loans became more and more frequent over the thirteenth and fourteenth centuries, and they came to involve ever subtler financial calculations and maneuverings pertaining to profit and loss on the part of both citizens and city governments.[83] Not surprisingly, as the use and monetary value of these contracts increased, so too did the heated debates over their legality and morality.[84] Reasoned positions were put forward on both sides of this

---

[80] Fabiano Veraja, *Le origini della controversia teologica sul contratto di censo nel XIII secolo* (Rome: Edizioni di storia e letteratura, 1960). For an excellent recent treatment of this form of contract and the theological questions it brought to the fore, see Wei, *Intellectual Culture in Medieval Paris*, 323–45.

[81] Gratian, *Decretum* II, c. 14, q. 3, c. 1: "si plus quam dedisti expectes accipere, fenerator es."

[82] John Munro, "The Medieval Origins of the Financial Revolution: Usury, Rentes, and Negotiability," *International History Review* 25 (2003), 505–62.

[83] *Ibid.*, 514–18.

[84] See, for example, Julius Kirshner, "Storm over the *Monte Comune*: Genesis of the Moral Controversy over the Public Debt of Florence," *Archivum Fratrum Praedicatorum* 53 (1983), 219–76; Armstrong, "The Politics of Usury in Trecento Florence"; Armstrong, *Usury and Public Debt in Early Renaissance Florence.*

question. The elaborations of these positions reveal with particular clarity the shape and logic of available models of equalization in this period.

As previously noted, Pope Innocent made the decision to consider the contractual form of the *census* as a sale and not as a loan. On the basis of this redefinition, he could declare that the perfect numerical equality demanded in contracts of loan did not apply. Conforming to the position already established in both Roman and canon law, Innocent judged that since the contract was now defined as one of sale (*emptio-venditio*), all that is required is that the price agreed to by the parties to a *census* contract (i.e., the amount and duration of the annual payment) conforms, within the broad limits of *laesio enormis*, to the common price of other current *census* contracts at the moment of the agreement. The acuity and economic sophistication of Innocent's decision is clear, but it was by no means the end of the matter. In the 1270s and 80s the debate over the liceity of this essentially indeterminate and open-ended contract flared once more, this time between two renowned theologians at the University of Paris, Henry of Ghent and Godfrey of Fontaines.[85] In the details of this technical economic debate, we can learn a great deal about developments in the modeling of *aequalitas* in this last quarter of the thirteenth century.[86]

It was very common in this period for religious institutions of all kinds and sizes to engage in census contracts and to support themselves through them. Nevertheless, Henry of Ghent, speaking for a rigorist and consciously conservative position in economic matters, declared such a contract to be inescapably usurious. He argued that it

directly violates the equity of natural commutative justice, which requires a perfect equality (*aequalitas omnimoda*) between the sum given and the sum received, as is clearly stated.[87]

---

[85] I analyze this debate in *Economy and Nature in the Fourteenth Century*, 101–15. For a recent treatment of it that exhibits numerous parallels with my earlier discussion, see Elsa Marmurszstejn, *L'autorité des maîtres: scolastique, normes et société au XIIIe siècle* (Paris: Les Belles Lettres, 2007), 196–215.

[86] The debate was carried on through a series of published quodlibetal questions. Henry delivered his first opinion on the subject in his first quodlibet, dated to 1276. Successive quodlibets touching on this subject were published from 1276 to 1292. Godfrey's responses came in quodlibetal questions published over the period 1285–96/7. This was far from the only question that Henry and Godfrey disagreed on. Henry was a force behind the promulgation of the Condemnations of 1277 at the University of Paris, while Godfrey was opposed. On their intellectual relations, see Georges de Lagarde, "La philosophie sociale d'Henri de Gand et de Godefroid de Fontaines," in, *L'organisation corporative du Moyen Âge à la fin de l'Ancien Régime* (Louvain: Bibliothèque de l'Université, 1937), 57–134, esp. 57–60.

[87] Henry of Ghent, *Henrici de Gandavo, Quodlibet I*, ed. Raymond Macken, in *Opera omnia*, vol. V (Leuven University Press, 1979), q. 39, 214: "Quod si fiat, accipit aliquid pro quo

Since Henry held that equality in exchange was a requirement established by natural law, not merely by human law, Pope Innocent IV's
redefinition of the census as a contract of sale did not, to his mind, render
its essential inequality any more permissible. Indeed, even when directing his comments explicitly to contracts of buying and selling, Henry
not only held to the ancient ideal of 1:1 arithmetical equality in the
exchange, but he thought it justifiable to reassert the ancient equalizing
model of the mechanical scale, balancing around a single, knowable,
balancing point.[88]

And if equality is to be saved (*debet servari aequalitas*), all things given and accepted
must be equal in value. And to do this, both buyer and seller ought to be judges,
acting as two arms of a scale, as animate justice, so that he who senses he has
received the heavier weight of price might give some of it back to the other, so that
equality is established (*fiat equale*), and so that the exchangers stand in relation to
each other like arms of a scale, equally elevated and lowered.[89]

Henry's use of the mechanical scale to represent equality in buying and
selling indicates the degree to which he recognized economic exchange as
a process directed toward the establishment of a knowable, definable, and
perfect balance between exchangers. *Aequalitas* here is represented in its
most traditional and rigorist form, consciously linked to its representation
in Gratian's *Decretum*.[90] Note, however, that at the same time Henry
makes use of a mechanical metaphor for exchange equalization, he insists
on the place of subjective judgment and ordering (*iustitia animata*) in
establishing a true equality and thus a truly just price. Both exchangers
must consciously *aim* at equality as the end, and they must use their
personal judgment to arrive at it. Henry's hybrid position here closely
resembles Thomas' in the *Summa theologica* considered above. Both
thinkers were conscious of a supra-personal mechanism for price

---

nihil dedit, et ita cum suo alienum tollit, quod est directe contra aequitatem naturalis
iustitiae commutativae, in qua debet esse aequalitas omnimoda in pretio dati et recepti, ut
dictum est." See also *ibid.*, q. 39, 215.

[88] Henry of Ghent, 1.40, 221: "In isto ergo contractu emptionis et venditionis sic debet servari
aequalitas inter mutuo dantem et recipientem, quod neuter plus recipiat quam det."

[89] *Ibid.*: "Et si debet servari aequalitas, aequale debet esse omnino in valore datum et
receptum hinc et inde. Et in hoc ambo debent esse iudices tamquam duo brachia librae
et animatae iustitiae, ut qui in pondere pretii sentiat se plus recepisse de eo quod est
alterius, rescindat et reddat ei de suo, quousque fiat aequale, et sic stent quasi brachiis
librae elevatis et depressis aequaliter."

[90] Langholm (*Economics in the Medieval Schools*, 256) has called Henry's statement, "most
likely the first clear statement of the principle of equilibrium in the history of economics."
I hope it is clear from the many examples we have already seen, dating back to the twelfth
century, that this opinion cannot stand. For the same reason I trust that it is also clear that
Henry's use here of the model of the mechanical scale is retrograde – intentionally
retrograde – rather than forward-looking in any sense of the term.

determination in the marketplace (i.e., common estimation), but both sought to reconcile this mechanism with the ethical requirement of individual responsibility and with the metaphysical requirement that order everywhere implied and required an intelligent orderer. What is absent from Henry's picture is the dynamic geometry and crossed diagonals from *Ethics* V, or the legists' longstanding position on price as a product of the essentially crossed purposes of buyer and seller, each desiring and acting in the direction of self-interest.

The theologian Godfrey of Fontaines was one of a number of thinkers who took exception to Henry's argument.[91] His acute understanding of the contract as a whole reveals both the evolution of newer theological attitudes toward economic analysis and, most important for our purposes, an expanded vision of the potentialities of equality and equilibrium underlying this analysis. Godfrey in no way sought to distance himself from the traditional requirement for *aequalitas* in exchange.[92] While admitting to the difficulty of determining whether the census contract was properly a loan or a sale, he came down on the side of Innocent IV and the canon law tradition and concluded that it was in fact a licit contract of sale.[93]

Once Godfrey defined the census as a contract of sale rather than as a *mutuum*, certain conclusions followed. It was no longer necessary to arrive at Henry of Ghent's perfect point of balance and arithmetical equality. Far from it. Godfrey argues that the equivalence required has nothing to do with an actual numerical equality between the sum offered and the sum eventually received in return, but that it simply must represent a "fitting" and "sufficient proportionalization" of estimated benefits on the part of both parties.[94] If both parties make a reasoned estimate that they will benefit from the contract, the requirement for equality is

---

[91] The following argument appears in *Godefroid de Fontaines, Quodlibet V*, in *Les philosophes belges*, vol. III, ed. M. De Wulf and J. Hoffmans (Louvain: Institut Supérieur de Philosophie, 1914), quest. 14, 63–9, "Utrum licitum sit emere redditus ad vitam et recipere de redditibus emptis ultra sortem." On Godfrey's biography and the dating of his quodlibetal questions, see John Wippel, *The Metaphysical Thought of Godfrey of Fontaines: A Study in Late Thirteenth-century Philosophy* (Washington, DC: Catholic University of America Press, 1981).

[92] *Godefroid de Fontaines, Quodlibet III*, in *Les philosophes belges*, vol. II, ed. M. De Wulf (Louvain: Institut Supérieur de Philosophie, 1904), quest. 11 (longae), 219: "debeat aequalitas secundum iustitiam conservari."

[93] Godfrey of Fontaines, V.14, 66: "Ex praedictis ergo videtur quod talis contractus sit contractus emptionis." Also, Godfrey of Fontaines, V.14, 64: "Si autem sit contractus emptionis et venditionis, et fiat rationalis adaequatio inter rem emptam et pretium datum, est licitus contractus."

[94] *Ibid.*, V.14, 67: "est dicendum quod videtur posse fieri conveniens aestimatio, non quidem omnimode aequalitatis rei ad rem secundum se, sed sufficientis proportionis secundum quod in usum hominum natae sunt venire" (my emphasis). Note the link

fulfilled.[95] What, then, guarantees that such estimated proportionalization will conform to the inarguable requirement of just equality? Only
that the sums agreed to conform to what is commonly found in other
documents of similar kind, or, as Godfrey frequently writes: only that
other buyers and sellers can be found who would be willing to make a
similar agreement on similar terms.[96] If this condition is met, then in
Godfrey's judgment the required *aequalitas* in exchange is fully present,
both in contracts of "return for life" (*redditus ad vitam*) and "perpetual
return" (*redditus perpetuus*), even though no one can possibly know who
will benefit more from the contract in the end.

Paradoxically, the only real certainty in such contracts is that the
result will *not* produce an arithmetical equality. Where for Henry of
Ghent this is taken as a proof of usurious inequality, Godfrey, through
a striking realignment, turns this negative into a positive. True, he
admits, in contracts of buying and selling, especially those that are
extended over time, neither party can know, at the time of sale, which
will benefit more over the long run. Doubt and uncertainty are inescapable. But this very condition of guaranteed uncertainty produces *in itself*
an *aequalitas* sufficient to render the exchange licit, assuming that there
is an *equal measure of doubt* between buyer and seller (*aequaliter est
dubium ex parte vendentis et ementis*).[97] When this final point is added
to the whole of Godfrey's argument, when the requirement for equality
in the census contract (or any contract of sale) can be satisfied by
the equality of doubt it contains, and when a sufficient equality in the

between proportionality and Godfrey's dynamic concept of equalization. Henry of Ghent,
as we have seen, made a concerted effort to eliminate the problematic concept of
proportionality from his discussion of equality in economic exchange.

[95] *Ibid.*, V.14, 65: "declarandum est quomodo est ibi vere contractus emptionis et quomodo
potest ibi fieri vere conveniens adaequatio."

[96] *Ibid.*, V.14, 67: "ideo sufficit quod sit talis adaequatio secundum quam possit inveniri ut
in pluribus emens, cum invenitur vendere volens, et hoc sive haereditarie sive ad vitam."
And again, *ibid.*, V.14, 67: "Etiam ita in venditione reddituum ad vitam non debet fieri
secundum proportionem ad vitam ementis, quia hoc esset fieri adaequationem rei ad rem
ut secundum se ad invicem comparantur, sed secundum illum modum secundum quem
ementes inveniuntur."

[97] *Ibid.*, V.14, 63: "Contrarium arguitur per contrarium, quia ille contractus videtur licitus
in quo constituitur aequalitas inter ementem et vendentem. Sed ita contingit in proposito:
nam *aequaliter est dubium ex parte vendentis et ementis* de plus vel minus recipiendo; ergo
et cetera" (my emphasis). Godfrey's contemporary, the Franciscan Matthew of
Acquasparta, offers a similar judgment, also in response to the question of the liceity of
contracts *redditus ad vitam*. His opinion, taken from Quodlibet I.9, is cited in Veraja, *Le
origini della controversia teologica*, 201–2: "Quidam enim simpliciter dicunt contractum
esse iustum et licitum: quoniam, quamvis ibi sit inequalitas aliqua, tamen illa incerta est.
Unde propter eventus incertitudinem ista inequalitas habet quamdam equalitatem ... et
ideo incertitudo eventus mortis facit in isto contractu quamdam equalitatem." Matthew
will insist, however, that the two parties should at least aim to equalize the contract.

contract is guaranteed merely by the willingness of others to assume a similar doubt at a similar price, we have achieved a new, protean, and potent understanding of the ancient ideal of *aequalitas*. It is this vastly expanded understanding that informs the new model of equilibrium.

Aequalitas into equilibrium in the economic thought of Peter of John Olivi

Godfrey of Fontaines was a close contemporary of the Franciscan theologian Peter of John Olivi. They were both students at the University of Paris in the early 1270s (at the same time that Thomas Aquinas was in residence there as master of theology),[98] but their life paths differed in significant ways, both before and after their student years. From the age of twelve, Olivi was attached to the Franciscan Order, while Godfrey remained a secular teaching master at Paris who came to oppose the growing institutional powers of the Mendicant Orders at the university. Olivi never received a higher degree at Paris and left sometime before the mid 1270s, while Godfrey went on to complete his course of study, becoming a Regent Master in theology at Paris in 1285, and remaining in this position for the most part throughout the 1290s. Given that both men were exceptionally acute observers of economic life, it is not surprising that both retained close contact to urban centers throughout their lives: Godfrey to Paris, Liège, Tournai, and to a lesser degree Cologne; Olivi to Paris, Florence, Montpellier, and Narbonne. Their major economic writings appeared roughly within the same half-decade, 1288–93.[99] In short, although living very different lives, both men belonged to the same intellectual generation, and both share in its strongest and most adventurous characteristics. Godfrey's intellectual accomplishments in the sphere of economic thought, and his approach to the "new" model of equilibrium within it, can thus provide a partial context for approaching the startling economic insights – and startling previsioning of systematic equilibrium – that appear in the writings of Peter Olivi. In the previous chapter we witnessed a number of these with respect to the requirements for equality in the loan contract. We now turn to consider Olivi's position on equality and equalization in contracts of sale.

---

[98] This was the period (1269–72) in which Thomas was at work completing his *Summa theologica* and most probably his commentary on Aristotle's *Ethics* as well.

[99] For the date of Godfrey's fifth quodlibet, see Wippel, *Godfrey*, xxiii, xxvii.

The Common Good, the Christian merchant, and *aequalitas* in exchange

As I suggested in the previous chapter, the concept of the Common Good (*bonum commune*), which by the late thirteenth century occupied a place of great importance within medieval thought, constituted a crucial matrix for Olivi's reimagining of *aequalitas* in economic exchange.[100] Before discussing the impact the concept of the Common Good had on Olivi's positions on the determination of price and value, it is well to consider some of the broader economic effects that followed from the triumph of this ideal.

The status of the merchant in Christian society, and the activity of commerce itself, were great beneficiaries of the new lens provided by the Common Good. The (slow) realization within scholastic culture, over the course of the twelfth and thirteenth centuries, that the merchant had a right to profit by doing what he habitually does – buying a good for one price and reselling it later for more than it had originally cost – occurred only as thinkers came to appreciate the merchant's role in serving and benefiting the Common Good and common profit of all, not simply his own personal good and profit.[101] Before this recognition and appreciation, many jurists, theologians, and moralists expressed the opinion that the commercial act represented a form of inequality in itself. Reselling a good for more than it had originally cost, without the good having been improved in some way through honest labor, was associated by some with the production of *superhabundantia* – the same unwarranted excess that Gratian's canons condemned in the case of the *mutuum*. Others associated commercial profits with outright theft. Gradually, however, the recognition grew that the merchant's transportation of commodities from where they were plentiful to where they were needed was itself a form of improving labor. Gradually, too, the merchant's skill and knowledge came to be recognized as adding real economic value to the prices of the goods he transported. Reasons that scholastics offered in defense of these attitudinal changes most often cited the

---

[100] Todeschini has made this point from his earliest writings, e.g., Un trattato di economia politica francescano: il "De emptionibus et venditionibus, de usuris, de restitutionibus" di Pietro di Giovanni Olivi (Rome, 1980), 15 ff. (henceforth Olivi, *Tractatus*).

[101] Spicciani, *La mercatura*, 173–9, 221–30; Giacomo Todeschini, "Participer au bien commun: la notion franciscaine d'appartenance à la civitas," in *De Bono Communi: Discours et pratique du Bien Commun dans les villes d'Europe occidentale (XIIIe–XVIe siècles)*, ed. Elodie Lecuppre-Desjardins and Anne-Laure Van Bruaene (Turnhout: Brepols, 2010), 225–35.

recognition that where merchants and commercial pursuits flourished, so too did the Common Good.[102]

The reevaluation within scholastic thought of both commerce and the money that fueled it, from principles of inequality and imbalance to principles of equalization and balance, was an extraordinary accomplishment. It was achieved in large part by shifting focus from the individual (who still remained open to greed and corruption) to the idealized community he was increasingly recognized to serve and benefit. It was achieved by looking past the multiplying riches of individual merchants and past the merchant's personal profit (which continued to be looked upon with suspicion) to the multiplying wealth and supra-personal "common profit" that merchants brought to the *civitas*. Olivi's speculation in the area of price and value was deeply influenced by this broad cultural shift from a focus on the personal and the individual part to a focus on the commonality and the systematic whole. In his *Treatise on Buying and Selling, on Usury, and on Restitutions* (*Tractatus de emptionibus et venditionibus, de usuris, de restitutionibus*), he clearly (and often) articulates this position:

According to the order (*secundum ordinem*) of law, justice, and charity, the Common Good (*commune bonum*) is to be and ought to be preferred to private good.[103]

From the opening words of his *Tractatus*, we can see him working out the implications of this preference. He begins by asking a question that had been posed many times before over the previous century – a question, I would add, that only makes sense if the requirement for equality remained in his mind the *sine qua non* of economic liceity. "Concerning contracts of buying and selling, we ask first whether things may be sold, licitly and without sin, for more than their value or can be bought for less."[104] His first response, which follows immediately, is revealing:

Yes, it appears that they may. Because otherwise the whole community (*tota communitas*) of buyers and sellers would be sinning against justice; since virtually all desire to sell dear and buy cheap.[105]

---

[102] I discuss this change of attitude and the reasons that were offered for it in *Economy and Nature in the Fourteenth Century*, 139–41. See also John McGovern, "The Rise of New Economic Atttitudes: Economic Humanism, Economic Nationalism During the Later Middle Ages and the Renaissance, A.D., 1200–1550," *Traditio* 26 (1970), 217–53, esp. 223–6.

[103] Olivi, *Tractatus*, 51: "Item secundum ordinem iuris et iustitie et caritatis commune bonum prefertur et preferri debet bono privato."

[104] *Ibid.*, 51: "Circa venditionum et emptionum contractus queramus primo an res possint licite et absque peccato vendi plus quam valeant vel minus emi."

[105] *Ibid.*: "Et videtur quod sic. Quia aliter fere tota communitas vendentium et ementium contra iustitam peccarent, quia forte omnes volunt care vendere et vile emere." See also, *ibid.*, 61: "Ita quod emptor vult sibi plus rem emptam quam pretium eius, et venditor econtrario."

In further support of this position, he offers an analysis of the exchange process which takes into consideration the *thinking* common to those who engage in it:

It is licit for me to set any price I choose on my goods (*precium ponere quod volo*), and no law forces me to give or exchange my goods for a price other than one that pleases me (*pretio mihi placito*) and that is set by me (*a me pretaxato*); and similarly, no one is compelled or required to buy a thing for a price greater than one that pleases him. If therefore, the contract of buying and selling is voluntary [as it is], so the price of things agreed to is also voluntary.[106]

Olivi presents us here with a fascinating image of the marketplace as a site where opposing wills and desires clash, intersect, link together, and yet, somehow, find order and equalization. The roots of this image can, no doubt, be traced back to the Roman law of bargaining. Indeed, to demonstrate that this position meets the requirement of *human* justice, he immediately supports it with the well-known "rule" of price from Roman law: "A thing is worth what it can be sold for" (*Res tantum valet quantum vendi potest*).[107] I venture to say, however, that Olivi's statement here incorporates a sense of systematic activity and systematic equalization that owes as much or more to the intellectual culture of the late thirteenth century than it does to Roman law. As I noted in the previous chapter, while Olivi is clearly knowledgeable about the law, he is writing as a theologian and not a lawyer. He is searching to find an overarching rationality in the systematic process of exchange which can comprehend both human actions and divine injunctions.

In good scholastic fashion, he offers a position that contradicts his opening arguments: buying a thing for less than it is worth or selling it for more does indeed violate commutative justice, because such justice requires the establishment of a "real equivalence" (*in reali adequatione redditi*) between goods and their prices. But this position is then immediately questioned in turn: how can there be a real equivalence between the price of a thing and its inherent nature (*realem bonitatem nature*) when such natures are not at all what price actually measures?[108] Here is the crux. Olivi is unwilling to abandon the requirement that all individuals aim for justice in each of their exchanges, but he has given up entirely on the idea that a perfect equivalence or balance between price

---

[106] *Ibid.*, 51: "Item licitum est mihi rei mee precium ponere quod volo, nec aliquod ius me compellit dare aut commutare res meas absque pretio mihi placito et a me pretaxato; sicut econtrario nullus compellitur vel cogitur rem alterius emere ultra pretium sibi placitum. Si igitur contractus vendendi et emendi est mere voluntarius, igitur taxatio pretii rerum venalium erit mere voluntaria, ac per consequens."
[107] *Ibid.*: "Iuxta illud vulgare verbum: Tantum valet res, quantum vendi potest."
[108] *Ibid.*, 54.

and value exists and is achievable, even between exchangers who are seeking justice.

For Olivi, the supremacy of the Common Good (composed of the intersecting wills and desires of its human parts) introduces its own economic imperatives and its own proper forms of economic understanding. He expresses this understanding most clearly:

> Since, therefore, the final end and reason for all civil and human contracts is the Common Good of all, it is in relation to the Common Good that equity in the determination of price is established, and it is with respect to the furthering of the Common Good that equity is measured.[109]

In his subsequent elucidation of this understanding, Olivi makes use of a number of positions that had been voiced before him in canon law decisions on price and value. But again, in an unprecedented way, he extends and joins these varied judgments into a rational and logical totality, into a *systematic* totality. He writes:

> The common welfare (*communi saluti*) of men after the Fall requires that the prices of things in exchange not be considered as a precise and unchanging point (*non sit punctualis*), nor as reflecting some "absolute" and inherent value in the thing itself (*nec secundum valorem absolutum rerum*). Rather, price is determined with respect to the common consensus (*ex communi consensu*) concerning value, freely (*libere*) arrived at on the part of both buyers and sellers. This way involves a lesser danger of fraud.[110]

His analysis here hinges on the weight he allows to working aggregates: the common good (*commune bonum*), the common welfare (*commune saluti*), and common agreement (*communi consensu*). The concepts support and reinforce each other. The requirement for exchange *aequalitas* on which the health of the community rests is satisfied through the aggregation of myriad free choices and judgments exercised by individual exchangers, even though singular exchanges within the aggregate may deviate somewhat from equality. It is from this premise that he can insist that the common estimation and determination of price is not a mere abstraction. Rather it is the active *aggregate product* of the civil community acting in common and in concert; in his words, "a common estimation, commonly

---

[109] *Ibid.*, 55: "Quia igitur in contractibus civilibus et humanis, ratio finalis est commune bonum omnium, idcirco equitas taxationis pretiorum fuit et est mensuranda per respectum ad commune bonum, prout, scilicet, expedit communi bono."

[110] *Ibid.*, 51: "sed communi saluti hominum post lapsum expedit quod taxatio pretii rerum venalium non sit punctualis nec secundum valorem absolutum rerum, sed potius ex communi consensu utriusque partis vendentium, scilicet, et ementium libere pretaxetur. Hoc enim minora pericula fraudum includit."

made by the community of citizens."[111] In his vision, the community represents the whole within which all the myriad individual intersecting and competing exchanges – economic and otherwise – find equalization. The conception that a systematic whole (in this case, the community of exchangers) is capable of transmuting individual inequalities into an aggregate *aequalitas*, is, as I have noted previously, a foundational element of the new model of equilibrium. In many ways, then, the Common Good functions in Olivi's thought as the named conceptual correlative of the new model of equilibrium.

Common estimation, common consent, common need, common price

More, I think, than any thinker before him, Olivi is able to comprehend and accept the (real) complexities and uncertainties that accompanied economic exchanges in his society. He does not shrink from them. He does not seek to reduce or blunt them. Nor does he ever abandon the ideal of and requirement for *aequalitas*. He continues to insist that according to the requirements of both human and natural justice, the purpose of exchange is to serve equality (*equalitatem servare intendit*). He is able to take these complexities, ambiguities, and seeming contradictions on their own terms because he has imagined a working system capable of unifying and equalizing in the whole what could never be perfectly equalized in the part. He provides three keys to the functioning of this system: common (informed) estimation (*secundum communem estimationem*); common (informed) consent (*ex communi consensu*); and the resultant common determination of price in the marketplace (*communis taxatio*). As the names he attaches to these solutions indicate, all of them are clustered and shaped within the capacious organizing ideal of the Common Good.

One way to demonstrate the weight Olivi allows to "common estimation" in the determination of value is to examine his attitude toward value decisions made on the basis of individual needs and private estimations alone. After having stated and restated the rule that equality in exchange is satisfied by the informed agreement of exchangers, he considers whether and under what conditions there are limits to this rule. He poses this question: since economic value is determined in relation to human use and need (a principle he accepts without reservation), can the seller of

---

[111] *Ibid.*, 56: "Sciendum igitur quod quia precium rerum et obsequiorum est taxandum sub respectu ad ordinem boni communis, idcirco in huiusmodi est primo et principaliter attendenda *communis taxatio et extimatio a communitatibus civilibus facta communiter*" (my emphasis).

healing potions and medicinal herbs charge a sick buyer on the verge of death as much as he is willing to pay? Or, put another way, can these medicines be licitly sold for a price equivalent to the value the sick man places on his life?[112] Clearly if the rule of free bargaining holds in all cases, and if the rule similarly holds that "the equity of commutative justice requires that however much utility is conveyed to me, I am held to give back so much in return," then the answer must be yes.[113] But Olivi will answer no. The reason these rules do not hold in this case is that the agreed price here is a "private and particular" price rather than a "common" price. Moreover, in cases of extreme personal need, such as the price a sick man will pay for life itself, or the price a man dying of thirst will pay for water, the upper limits approach infinity. This being the case, in his judgment there can be no rational form to the exchange, no regular range of licit valuation that can be applied, and therefore, as Olivi understands the term, no real price at all (*quasi impretiabile*).[114] These extreme cases point out the general rule: legitimate price can only be based on common estimation, not on estimation determined by personal and particular need and circumstance. It must be an aggregate estimation, an aggregate *product*, an aggregate *aequalitas* that takes into consideration the intersecting results of various exchanges under various conditions of need and use by various buyers and sellers within a given market. In short, there must be a market price for there to be a price at all.[115]

At no time does Olivi suggest that the equalization occurring within the system of exchange is to be accepted without reference to morality and rationality. This in itself clearly distinguishes his conception of market price. What he does argue, however, is perhaps even more remarkable: that for the most part the system of market exchange will function within acceptable and rational limits, and will arrive at a just *aequalitas*, even though at its foundation lies the conflicting desire for unequal gain: the desire to buy for less and sell for more. Even more remarkable in a theological context is the clear lesson that common equivalences

---

[112] *Ibid.*, 55: "An dans iuste possit a me exigere pretium sanationis equivalens sive impretiabile."

[113] *Ibid.*: "Videtur quod sic quia ut supra dictum est, "valor et pretium rerum venalium potius pensatur in respectu ad nostrum usum et utilitatem ... Item equitas iustitie commutative est ut quantum utilitatis mihi confert, tantum idem tibi conferam."

[114] *Ibid.*, 55: "pretium esset quasi impretiabile. Nam ciphus aque sitienti et nisi aquam habeat morituro, valet in casu isto infinitam substantiam auri et longe amplius."

[115] "Market price" here has the meaning of a common price established in the marketplace, based on a community-wide estimation of value, judged relative to time, place, and conditions of scarcity or abundance – all of which are stated components of Olivi's analysis of price.

systematically arrived at through the principles of free bargaining and informed consent are to be trusted *more* than equivalences arrived at through conscious private judgments based on personal circumstances. Olivi's argument here, woven into the logic of the Common Good, most likely makes excellent economic sense to a modern reader. But consider its transformative implications: in the arena of economic value, individual and personal judgment – the traditional philosophical and theological site of rationality – is denied validity, while "fitting" rationality can be found only in the recognition of and adherence to an ever-shifting, depersonalized, aggregate estimation.

It is true that Olivi allows a prominent place to the estimations and judgments on value made by professional merchants in the formation of the "common estimation."[116] This again creates some distance between his concept of common price and classical definitions of market price. But merchants, like all exchangers, must base their estimations on the circumstances in play within particular markets at particular times. While they contribute to the aggregate *aestimatio communis* that defines the common or market price in Olivi's vision, they are also certainly guided by it. Olivi counsels the same for everyone in every transaction, including merchants: "Individuals in all their personal contracts or demands must follow the form and rule of common estimation and price determination (*debent sequi formam et regulam communium extimationum et taxationum*)." Only in this way can individual exchangers, including merchants, avoid shameful or irregular outcomes in their economic exchanges.[117]

Integrating value relativity into exchange equality: the determinants of economic value according to Olivi

Olivi fully accepts the metaphysical position that everything in existence possesses a proper nature, and that these natures do indeed possess an inherent and determined degree of value or goodness (*bonitas*), which determines their place in the plan of creation. But while it is perfectly true and valid to grade inherent natures on an ontological scale, such gradation has, he asserts, *nothing* to do with how economic value is determined in exchange. In exchange, the values of things are entirely

---

[116] Todeschini, "'Oeconomica francescana' I," 15–18. One locus of this observation is Olivi, *Tractatus*, 63: "sic industria mercatoris in rerum valore et pretio prudentius examinando, et ad subtiliores minutias iustum pretium producendo ... quod per hoc adiscent subtilius pensare rerum pretia et valores." Cf. Piron, "Le traitement de l'incertitude," 17, 33.

[117] Olivi, *Tractatus*, 57: "Singuli autem in suis singularibus contractibus vel exactionibus sumptuum, debent sequi formam et regulam communium extimationum et taxationum, ne pars turpiter et irregulariter et inobedienter disconveniat suo toti."

determined relative to their usefulness to humans.[118] He finds this position to be so true that he can frame it as an equation: "insomuch as things are of more use to men (*sunt usibus nostris utiliora*), by so much are they valued higher."[119] Under this equation, the "higher" order of valuation, determined according to inherent individual natures simply does not apply in the economic sphere, and, indeed, is often found turned on its head there. In the whole of the discussion where Olivi asserts the distinction between "natural value" and relativized "economic value," he is saying little that had not been said many times before within scholastic writings.[120] What distinguishes his treatment here as elsewhere, is the degree to which he allows the logic of this position to fully determine his economic analysis. He states without hesitation that justice in exchange is rightly judged "*only* in terms of equivalences determined with respect to human use and utility.*"[121] And he never hedges on this principle.

But granted that economic value is determined relative to human utility and need, what are the general factors that affect the scale or measure of this value? Or, phrased another way, what are the general factors that *condition* human utility and need? Olivi's detailed response to this question in the *Tractatus* represents the most sophisticated analysis of the determinants of economic value in all of scholastic literature before the sixteenth century. As such, it has received much scholarly attention. Until the 1950s, however, this analysis was credited not to Olivi, its true author, but to the Franciscan preacher, San Bernardino of Siena (1380–1444), who in the mid fifteenth century copied Olivi's economic arguments in full and without ascription into his written sermons.[122] Nothing speaks

---

[118] *Ibid.*, 52: "Secundo modo sumitur in quantum ad usum nostrum."

[119] *Ibid.*: "hoc modo quanto aliqua sunt usibus nostris utiliora, tanto plus valent." Note the similarities here to the argument made by Godfrey of Fontaines at roughly the same time (*Quodlibet* V.14, 67): "posse fieri conveniens aestimatio, non quidem omnimode aequalitatis rei ad rem secundum se, sed sufficientis proportionis secundum quod in usum hominum natae sunt venire."

[120] As seen earlier in the recognition by Aristotle, Albertus Magnus, and Thomas Aquinas that the primary determinant of economic value was the purely relative quality of "common need" (*indigentia communis*) common to all goods in exchange.

[121] Olivi, *Tractatus*, 55: "iustitia commutativa non consistit in reali equivalentia rerum secundum absolutum valorem naturarum suarum pensata, sed *solum* in equivalentia ad nostrum usum et utilitatem ut superius dicto relata" (my emphasis).

[122] Due to Olivi's identification as a leading theoretician of the rigorist wing of the Franciscan Order, many of his works were condemned and publicly burnt soon after his death (1298) for political and doctrinal reasons having nothing to do with his economic writings. His identification with heterodox theological positions increased over the first decades of the fourteenth century as the struggle between the Papacy and the rigorists became ever fiercer; in 1318 his grave was desecrated, his bones disinterred and scattered. After the censure of his corpus, certain of his texts continued to circulate,

more eloquently to the precocity of late thirteenth-century economic thought than that Bernardino's mid-fifteenth-century comments, copied from Olivi's *Tractatus* nearly a century and a half after their original composition, were long judged by modern economic historians to be the highpoint of pre-modern economic thinking.[123]

Olivi arrived at and outlined three primary determinants of economic value in the *Tractatus*. As San Bernardino copied Olivi's thoughts on this subject, he labeled each of these three determinants with a single word. Olivi's first factor entails the real virtues, qualities, and properties of things that make them better or more useful to men.[124] Bernardino captured Olivi's intent here by labeling this first factor, "*virtuositas*." Olivi's second factor (which Bernardino labeled "*raritas*," and we would label "supply") is the "scarcity" of a thing, which leads to difficulties in its procurement, bringing about an increase in the need (*indigentia*) for it and hence an increase in its value and price.[125] Olivi goes into particular detail with regard to the factor of *raritas*, finding the linking of scarcity and price so inarguable and of such common knowledge, that he offers a "common saying" (*commune verbum*) to express the rule, "where things are rarer they are dearer," and conversely, where something is more commonly abundant – even gold itself – its price is diminished.[126] Olivi's third factor, designated by Bernardino "*complacabilitas*," regards the variable "pleasingness" attached to the

---

but they did so clandestinely. This explains Bernardino's access to the *Tractatus*, and it may also explain his failure to credit Olivi with these insights. On the fate of Olivi's writings, see David Burr, "The Persecution of Peter Olivi," *Transactions of the American Philosophical Society*, n.s. 66, no. 5 (1976), 1–98; Spicciani, *La mercatura*, 181–9; Sylvain Piron, "Censures et condamnation de Pierre de Jean Olivi: enquête dans les marges du Vatican," *Mélanges de l'École française de Rome – Moyen Âge*, 118 (2006), 313–73.

[123] Raymond De Roover, *San Bernardino of Siena and Sant'Antonino of Florence: The Two Great Economic Thinkers of the Middle Ages* (Boston: Kress Library of Business and Economics, 1967). Olivi's authorship was first recognized and proposed in D. Pacetti, "Un trattato sulle usure e le restituzioni di Pietro de Giovanni Olivi falsamente attibuito a fr. Gerardo da Siena," *Archivum Franciscanum historicum* 46 (1953), 448–57. For more on this subject, see Todeschini, "'Oeconomica francescana' II," 488–94; Spicciani, *La mercatura*, 181–219; Raymond De Roover, *La pensée économique des scolastiques: doctrines et methodes* (Montreal: Institut d'études médiévales, 1971), 48–50; Kaye, *Economy and Nature in the Fourteenth Century*, 123–7, 141–8.

[124] Olivi, *Tractatus*, 52–3: "secundum quod res ex suis realibus virtutibus et proprietatibus est nostris utilitatibus virtuosior et efficacior."

[125] *Ibid.*, 53: "secundum quod res ex sue inventionis raritate et difficultate sunt nobis magis necessarie, pro quanto ex earum penuria maiorem ipsarum indigentiam et minorem facultatem habendi et utendi habemus."

[126] *Ibid.*, 56: "observat in hiis communem cursum copie et inopie, seu paucititatis et habundantie. Unde et commune verbum est: quod omne rarum est carum et preciosorum preciosum. Et ideo ubi aurum vel triticum communiter multum habundat non tanti pretii extimatur."

quality and use of things, which, Olivi reasoned, translates into variable estimations of value, particularly for luxuries.[127]

Following his analysis of the three main determinants of price, Olivi notes that they all point to an inescapable conclusion: the judgment of value is immensely complex, difficult, and imprecise, based as it must be on highly variable factors, which are, in turn, judged differently by different persons and even by the same person at different times and in different situations. The inescapable complexity and variability in itself has implications for the way we judge value. He writes:

the valuation of things in exchange can rarely or never be achieved except through the use of conjecture or probable opinion (*nisi per coniecturalem seu probabilem opinionem*), and it is never a precise point nor precisely measurable, but rather it falls within some fitting latitude (*sub aliqua latitudine competenti*), within which the understanding and judgment of men differ.[128]

Here is Olivi's answer to Henry of Ghent, Thomas Aquinas, and others who continued to insist on the existence of a measurable and knowable point of exchange equalization that lay within the power of humans to approach, if they only so desired. Not yet content with the clarity and force of this statement, Olivi strengthens it by restating it in various forms throughout the portion of the *Tractatus* devoted to contracts of sale, including twice in the sentences that immediately follow. "And therefore," he writes, "various degrees (*varios gradus*) and little certainty and much ambiguity (*multumque ambiguitatis*) are attached to opinions concerning value."[129] And again, since the values of things are determined in relation to human utility and need, which themselves vary, they are therefore "measured by the probable judgment (*ad probabilem iudicium*) of human estimation, within the [broad] limits of a fitting latitude (*infra limites latitudinis*

---

[127] *Ibid.*, 53: "secundum magis et minus beneplacitum nostre voluntatis in huiusmodi rebus habendis."

[128] *Ibid.*: "Item tertio sciendum quod huiusmodi pensatio valoris rerum usualium vix aut numquam potest fieri a nobis nisi per coniecturalem seu probabilem opinionem, et hoc non punctualiter, seu sub ratione seu mensura indivisibili in plus et minus, *sed sub aliqua latitudine competenti*, circa quam etiam diversa capita hominum et iuditia differerunt in extimando" (my emphasis). I note that Olivi's joining of "conjecture" and probabilist opinion to the notion of a graded "latitude" or range of permissible values here in an economic context is paralleled by similar joinings both in scholastic medical thought and in fourteenth-century natural philosophy. I discuss these parallels and their implication for the history of ideas in Chapters 3 and 4 on medicine and Chapter 8 on natural philosophy.

[129] Olivi, *Tractatus* 53: "Et ideo varios gradus et paucam certitudinem, multumque ambiguitatis iuxta modum opinabilium in se includit, quamvis quedam plus et quedam minus."

competentis)."[130] In essence, uncertainty regarding the estimation of economic value is the inescapable ground of exchange, as are probabilistic judgments and solutions.[131]

Olivi's repeated stress on uncertainty and probabilism in the establishment of value underscores how clearly he grasps the complexities involved in the "simple" valuation of goods in exchange. Notably, he neglects to explicitly associate his "fitting latitude" of price with the numerical limits of one half above or one half below the common price as imposed by the legal doctrine of *laesio enormis*. He is well aware of this doctrine, of course, and he introduces it as the legal rule, providing actual numbers to indicate its range, but he does not find it entirely suitable. He rejects it not because it is too broad, but because it is not elastic enough to match the actual variations in common estimation and price. In support of this position, he offers the example of a price agreed to by a buyer and seller that falls outside the mathematical range of *laesio enormis*. On this ground alone, he writes, such a price does not merit the charge of fraud. Rather, he asserts, there is a higher and better way of determining the upper and lower limits of just value, and that is the *informed consent* by the parties to an exchange. Even when both parties recognize that a price lies outside the range of *laesio enormis*, if they then knowingly and freely agree to this price, the agreement remains acceptable and free from the charge of fraud.[132] Far from being naïve about what each party is aiming for, Olivi is quite clear that buyers want to receive more than the agreed price and sellers want to pay less.[133] He is also fully cognizant of the doubt and probability that attend every exchange. But if both parties participate in the agreement freely, then the agreed price is *ipso facto* rational, fitting, and licit.[134] Here we have a vision of exchange equalization that is truly deserving of the adjective "dynamic."

---

[130] *Ibid.*, 53: "His igitur prenotatis, dicendum quod res non possunt licite vendi plus quam valeant nec minus emi, pensato earum valore etiam in respectu ad usum necessarium et ad probabilem iudicium humane extimacionis, mensurantis valorem rei infra limites latitudinis competentis."

[131] *Ibid.*, 61: "Quarta ratio sumitur ex incertitudine humane extimationis."

[132] *Ibid.*, 54.

[133] *Ibid.*, 61: "Ita quod emptor vult sibi plus rem emptam quam pretium eius, et venditor econtrario."

[134] Olivi adds another important caveat that receives its single mention on this same page: if parties to an exchange knowingly buy or sell without paying any attention to law or justice, the resulting agreed price is illicit whether or not it falls within the legal bounds of *laesio enormis*.

Private actions weighed against the Common Good

We have already seen Olivi's adamant position that personal need or scarcity, as in the case of the sick man who needs medicine to survive, cannot in itself be a licit cause of price increase. But are there limits to common need, communal estimation, and common consent as the basis of price? He approaches this problem through the following question: is it licit for those in possession of a necessary good (e.g., wheat) to raise its selling price sharply in times of great common scarcity? He notes at first that some consider this kind of activity an open violation of both the Common Good and the demands of piety. He, however, takes the opposite position. It is rather, he argues, when prices do *not* rise as common need rises that the Common Good is actually injured; and, conversely, the Common Good is actually served when prices rise in proportion to scarcity, as long as they do so within some "rational" limit.[135]

Olivi provides a number of reasons to support this position, but perhaps the most telling in terms of his sense of equalization is that if prices do not rise in times of scarcity, then the possessors of goods (in the case of wheat, the farmers) will hoard their produce to the harm of those in need, and thus to the detriment of the Common Good; while if prices do rise, possessors will be induced to sell, thus relieving common need and scarcity.[136] Olivi is clearly aware of the problematic practice of price gouging, and he is careful to insist that there are limits to how far above the "common determination" (*a taxatione communi*) prices can rise and still remain licit and "rational."[137] But the general principle that price not only can but *should* rise to reflect scarcity remains in place. Here I think we have a clear view into Olivi's conception of exchange as a system in dynamic equilibrium. At the same time, in his valorization of a form of behavior (charging a markedly higher price for necessities in times of scarcity) that had traditionally been the object of both moral and religious censure, we can again see its potentially transformative implications.

Merchants as animate instruments of equalization: fitting commercial profit within exchange equilibrium

When reading Olivi's comments in the *Tractatus*, with their capacious understanding and acceptance of commercial life, it is at times possible to

---

[135] *Ibid.*, 58: "Secundo quia si tunc pretium non habet augeri, hoc ipsum esset in preiuditium boni communis."

[136] *Ibid.*, 58: "Quia habentes non sic prompte communiter non habentibus et egentibus res huiusmodi vendere vellent; et ideo minus bene communi egestati provideretur."

[137] *Ibid.*

forget that they spring from a profoundly religious thinker, fully committed in thought and deed to a life in emulation of Christ, fully committed to the personal renunciation of physical possessions, pleasures, and desires in emulation of the founder of his Order, St. Francis.[138] The great majority of his writings were devoted to questions of a theological and spiritual nature, with a smaller portion devoted to the philosophical questions of his day. The *Tractatus* represents but a tiny fraction of his writings as a whole. This alone should indicate that for Olivi, as for virtually every scholastic who wrote on the subject, the vision of the Common Good was attached to the highest truths of theology and philosophy and to the highest demands of reason. The ideal was grounded in the life and practice of the urban communes to which Olivi was nearly continuously attached (as were many of its other champions), but it was never simply a practical concept, either in derivation or in application. Nor could Olivi justify the expanded range of licit equalization in exchange required by "the order of the Common Good" on purely practical grounds; nor could he justify them on the grounds that this form of equalization was judged to be sufficient within the law. Although many of his economic decisions generalize positions accepted within canon law, Olivi was writing as a theologian, not as a lawyer. He wrote the *Tractatus* as a guide to his fellow Franciscan confessors; its ultimate concern was for the souls of those who were daily engaged in the contests of exchange agreement, particularly merchants. He must show not only that merchants multiplied the wealth of the community, but also that their commercial actions were consistent with the order of law, justice, and Christian charity that (as he announced from the opening of the *Tractatus*) defined the order of the Common Good.[139]

For centuries Christian lawyers, moralists, and theologians had asked the question: is it licit for merchants to resell a good, unchanged in its inherent qualities or nature, for more than they had originally paid for it? Olivi believed that they were justified in doing so. His discussion supporting this position represents a true landmark in the analysis of commercial activity, unmatched in its acuity for centuries.[140] He begins with the observation, which he never questions, that the labor of the merchant does indeed serve the interests and the common profit of the community. He must then show in what ways this labor can be seen to be productive, honest, and deserving of reward – as productive and honest in its own way

---

[138] Spicciani, *La mercatura*, 152–4.
[139] Olivi, *Tractatus*, 51: "Item secundum ordinem iuris et iustitie et caritatis commune bonum prefertur et preferri debet bono privato."
[140] *Ibid.*, 62–6.

as is the labor of the artisan. He notes the expenses the merchant incurs in his initial investments, the considerable risks he assumes both with regard to his wares and to his bodily welfare, and the labor he expends in physically transporting goods from where they are plentiful to where they are scarce.[141] To this list of elements deserving of recompense, Olivi adds specific qualities possessed by the merchant that permit him to succeed in his profession: his highly developed skills in estimating prices and values, his capacity to anticipate future conditions and make calculations on their basis, and even the long training that his profession requires.

Olivi accepts as a given that the precondition of all commerce is the reality that one region or city or community lacks and needs what another has in abundance.[142] Not all individuals, however can be expected to make the dangerous and difficult journeys to other lands that the securing of necessities requires, nor do all have the skill and knowledge to do so. For this reason, the community dispatches a certain few to perform this difficult task, recognizing, at the same time, that they should be allowed to profit from performing it (*lucri emolumentum debetur*).[143] On the basis of all these factors, he concludes that just as the artisan can add the value of his labor, skill, and expenses to the value of the goods he produces, so the value of the merchant's labor, skill, knowledge, and expenses can be translated into a numerable price and legitimately added to goods without upsetting the requirement for *aequalitas* in exchange.[144]

In this part of his argument, Olivi presents the merchant almost as if he functioned as an instrument of equalization in himself, habitually buying in lands where the merchandise is abundant and valued less (*habundans et vile*), and carrying it to where it is scarce and valued more (*carum et necessarium*). In doing so he serves the benefit of both

---

[141] *Ibid.*, 63: "Prima autem ratio est ex manifestis commodis et necessitatibus provenientibus communitati ex actu et offitio mercandi. Et similiter cum hoc ex honerosis laboribus ac periculis et expensis et industriis ac pervigilibus providentiis que exigunt offitium illud."

[142] *Ibid.*: "Constat enim quod multa desunt uni urbi vel patrie que habundant in altera."

[143] *Ibid.*: "Pauci enim habent ad hoc industriam et peritiam competentem, propter quod communitati expedit ut huic offitio aliqui ad hoc inductrii mancipentur, quibus ubique aliquid lucri emolumentum debetur." On this, see Giovanni Ceccarelli, "Le jeu comme contrat et le *risicum* chez Olivi," in *Pierre de Jean Olivi (1248–1298): pensée scolastique, diffidence spirituelle et société*, ed. Alain Boureau and Sylvain Piron (Paris: J. Vrin, 1999), 239–50 at 242: "[For Olivi] le marchand joue pour la communauté le rôle de médiateur rémunéré entre *bonum commune* et *periculum*."

[144] Olivi, *Tractatus*, 63: "sicut ars et industria artificis sibi licite lucrosa, sic industria mercatoris in rerum valore et pretio prudentius examinando, et ad subtiliores minutias iustum pretium producendo, potest licite sibi valere ad lucrum et maxime cum in hoc, salva latitudine iusti pretii, aliis communiter prosit, etiam in solo hoc quod per hoc adiscent subtilius pensare rerum pretia et valores."

communities. Olivi frames this point with particular clarity, but he is breaking no conceptual ground here: one can find statements recognizing the equalizing function of merchant activity, as well as its essential service to the community, dating back to the early thirteenth century.[145] And while his overall observations on the value of mercantile labor are exceptionally full and acute, as long as he continues to credit legitimate increases in selling price to the merchant's labor, skill, and expenses, he is working within a vision of commercial equality and equalization that had precedent in scholastic thought.

Olivi is remarkable, however, for his capacity to comprehend the global logic of situations, and equally remarkable for his courage in following this logic through to its ends, potentially destabilizing though it may be. His observations of urban communal life required that he add one more element to the equation, one that contained a multiplying factor and a dynamic open-endedness that transcended traditional scholastic models of equalization: the element of mercantile *profit*. What he seeks to establish is not merely the fact of profit – that is obvious to all – but the *rationality* of profit within the system of exchange that he observes and has taken upon himself to theorize.[146] Only in this way can the existence of commercial profit be truly aligned with the rational "order" of the Common Good. He thus concludes the section of the *Tractatus* dedicated to buying and selling with seven arguments intended to demonstrate "the rationality of profit."

After having established the point that the merchant's labor is essential to maintaining the health of the community, he notes, in general, that only a few men possess the knowledge and skill required to carry out these necessary tasks.[147] Merchants are often exposed to great danger, both with respect to their persons and to recovering the "capital" they have invested.[148] Who will leave the comforts of home to take on the great risks and hardships of commercial voyages to foreign lands? Only those, he argues, who can expect a reward that is in some way equivalent to them. In support of this point, he cites 1 Corinthians 9:7: "No one serves as a soldier at his own expense."[149] But what kind of equivalence can be found

---

[145] E.g., Thomas of Chobham, *Summa confessorum*, 6, 4, 10 (*c.* 1216), ed. F. Broomfield (Louvain: Nauwelaerts, 1968), 301–2.

[146] Olivi, *Tractatus*, 63: "ex eo quod salvo eorum rationabili lucro."

[147] *Ibid.*, 63: "Pauci enim habent ad hoc industriam et peritiam competentem . . . Si etiam non essent industrii in rerum valoribus et pretiis et commoditatibus subtiliter extimandis, non essent ad hoc idonei."

[148] *Ibid.*: "multis periculis exponunt . . . nec sunt certi an de mercibus emptis suum rehabeant capitale."

[149] *Ibid.*: "Quia secundum Apostolum, I Corintios, 9:7: 'Nemo militat suis stipendiis umquam.'"

for so large a collection of risks and uncertainties, given that both reason and justice require that an equivalence be found? His answer is mercantile profit. "Without the promise of profit (*absque lucro*), no one would be willing to undertake the risks and dangers involved."[150] To this quasi-psychological argument for the necessity of high profits he adds a second based in economic logic: "if merchants were not highly remunerated for their work, they would not be able to buy and transport great amounts of merchandise and precious goods from afar."[151] With this statement alone, we can see that Olivi's argument for commercial profit differs from previous scholastic arguments based in the acceptance of honest wages for honest labor.

In Olivi's understanding, where remuneration in other fields rests in the realm of addition, commercial profit exists in another and higher realm of equalization, the super-added realm of *multiplication*. How else is the merchant to accumulate the wealth necessary to "buy and carry back great amounts of merchandise and precious goods"? With this in mind, we can see how, in Olivi's overall understanding, his concept of profit (*lucrum*) in contracts of commercial buying and selling mirrors his concept of capital (*capitale*) in contracts of commercial borrowing and lending, which he had outlined in the section of the *Tractatus* devoted to usury.[152] Both concepts assume and justify the production of "super-added" value (*valor superadiunctus*); both are situated in the realm of multiplication rather than addition; both are essentially open-ended, lacking definable bounds; and both are grounded in a powerful new sense of what a just balance and equality might look like. For these reasons, before Olivi, neither merchant capital (*capitale*) nor merchant profit (*lucrum*) had been fully invested with rationality because neither had been fully integrated (in thought) into the process of licit equalization in exchange. Yet Olivi, rather than fearing the runaway potential of multiplication attached to both, has found a way to accept them.

At the conclusion of his argument defending the rationality of commercial profit in the *Tractatus*, he is confident he has demonstrated that "a commensurable profit both can be and should be awarded under such circumstances," and that such profit, when added to the price of commercially resold goods, can still remain within a fitting and

---

[150] *Ibid.*: "Quia secundum Apostolum, I Corintios, 9: 'Nemo militat suis stipendiis umquam,' et vix umquam invenietur qui absque lucro vellet huic operi inservire."

[151] *Ibid.*: "Si etiam non essent pecuniosi non possent grandes et caras merces prout terris expedit providere."

[152] For the place of *capitale* in his vision of exchange equalization, see Chapter 1 above.

rational measure.[153] Olivi has found a way to integrate the destabilizing multiplier of commercial profit into his rational model of exchange equilibrium, just as profit can and must, in his view, be integrated into the order of the Common Good. Once more, the ideal of the Common Good and the new model of equilibrium work in tandem, and once more, in doing so, they gain the power to overturn older assumptions concerning the limits of *aequalitas* and the potentialities of balance. And once more, too, they open up new ways of seeing and comprehending the workings of the world.

From a world of points to a world of lines

How new was Olivi's vision of exchange equalization, and in what major ways did his vision differ from those that preceded his? When we compare Olivi's position on the subject of price and value to that of Thomas Aquinas considered earlier, the distance that separates their assumptions (and their modeling) of what constitutes legitimate equalization is clear. Little more than two decades separated their writings on the subject. Thomas' position was itself somewhat expanded compared to those within the theological tradition before him. On the one hand, Thomas insisted, as had earlier theologians, that any exchange in which a thing was sold for more or bought for less than it was worth "destroyed the equality of justice" (*tolletur justitiae aequalitas*) and was in itself unjust and illicit.[154] On the other hand, as a close observer of the economic life of his time, he could not escape the recognition that "The just price of things is *sometimes* (*quandoque*) not *precisely* (*punctualiter*) determined, but rather consists more in an estimate (*quadam aestimatione consistit*)." We can see him taking small steps away from asserting that economic values can be perfectly "known," toward accepting, at least in some cases, that they can only be approximately "estimated." In similar fashion, he has stepped away from assuming the existence of knowable points of value in the direction of accepting that there may, at times, be variable ranges within which the estimation of values will fluctuate. But in both cases he appears to be moving, if not reluctantly, then very cautiously. Even as he recognizes that a space exists between a knowable point and an estimated range of value, he is careful to limit its extent. And so he concludes:

---

[153] Olivi, *Tractatus*, 63: "Ex his autem aperte concluditur quod lucrum predictis circumstantiis competens inde possint et debent reportare. Ex quo ulterius sequitur quod usque ad aliquam mensuram congruam possunt suarum mercium pretium augere."

[154] *ST*, II, II, 77, 1, resp.: "Et ideo si vel pretium excedat quantitatem valoris rei vel e converso res excedat pretium, tolletur justitiae aequalitas. Et ideo carius vendere aut vilius emere rem quam valeat est secundum se injustum et illicitum."

"Therefore a *small* (*modica*) addition or subtraction does not seem to destroy the equality of justice."[155]

Olivi, by contrast, has eliminated the contradiction between an ideal equality and the real equalizations that take place in the marketplace by boldly identifying the normal "what is" of exchange *aequalitas* with the "what should be" of *aequalitas iustitiae*. The overarching ideal of the Common Good provided him with a bridge to this position. Where Thomas wrote that the just price is "sometimes" not a precise and knowable point, Olivi asserts that it never is; where Thomas admitted that knowledge must at times give way to estimation, Olivi states that conjecture and probable opinion in the determination of economic value is the rule, not the exception; where Thomas permitted, at times, a "small" addition or subtraction, Olivi assumes that opinions and judgments will at all times vary along a latitude. Where Thomas restricts the distance between some imagined point of justice and its permissible range, Olivi extends the range without even stipulating its bounds, permitting it to transcend even the broad limits of *laesio enormis* if reached through a process of informed common consent. For Olivi it is no longer a choice between points and lines; lines are all there are – myriad divisible latitudes of value, ever expanding, contracting, intersecting, and interacting, and in their totality constituting the balance of the whole.[156]

In the two decades separating Olivi's writings from those of Thomas, addition and subtraction has given way to multiplication, arithmetic has given way to a fluid geometry, and a world imagined to be composed of discrete points and perfections has opened out into a world of lines. This is the world of the monetized marketplace, sufficiently well established by the end of the thirteenth century to impress itself on the minds and on the senses of acute observers. In the *Tractatus*, Olivi never directly addresses the question of money's functions in exchange as the universal medium and measure of ever-changing values.[157] Nor does he address its instrumental "shape" as a numbered continuum, capable of fluid expansion and contraction. Perhaps he assumed that these points had been so clearly established by Aristotle in *Ethics* V, and had been so clearly articulated by its early commentators (including Thomas) that they did not require repeating. Nevertheless, the "shape" and function of money as

---

[155] *ST*, II, II, 77, 1, ad 1: "Quod ideo dico, quia justum pretium rerum quandoque non est punctualiter determinatum, sed majus in quadam aestimatione consistit; ita quod modica additio vel minutio non videtur tollere aequalitatem justitiae."

[156] E.g., Olivi, *Tractatus*, 64: "Tertia ratio est a pari seu equivalenti et simul cum hoc ex altitudine iusti pretii divisibili in maius et minus."

[157] Although he does specifically contrast the "simple" definition of money as medium and measure to his concept of fruitful *capitale*.

a numbered measuring continuum is implied in all of his foundational economic insights: the "fitting latitude" of price whose limits shift with shifting conditions of scarcity and need; the fluctuation of value within the upper and lower limits of this latitude; the description of just price as possessing an "altitude divisible into more and less" (*ex altitudine iusti pretii divisibili in maius et minus*) as the common estimation of value increases and decreases.[158] In Chapter 4, I come back to this image of a "world of lines" and its connections to the new model of equilibrium, when I discuss its place in scholastic medical theory at the end of the thirteenth century. In Chapter 8, I come back to it yet again with respect to the new image of nature and natural activity that emerged within scholastic natural philosophy over the first half of the fourteenth century. Here I want only to suggest that in the writings of the most innovative medical writers and natural philosophers of the late thirteenth and fourteenth century, we will again see the dynamic integration of estimation, conjecture, relative determinations, multiplication, probabilistic thinking, and measurement by latitudes that characterized both the new "world of lines" and the new model of exchange equilibrium as envisioned and rationalized by Olivi.

The model of equilibrium in the late thirteenth century

Scholastic thought is commonly associated with caution, if not sclerosis. What is very apparent in the writings of the leading economic thinkers of the last quarter of the thirteenth century, however, is not pervasive caution, but striking intellectual adventurousness and creativity. What we have seen in the case of Godfrey of Fontaines and Peter of John Olivi is that by shifting the essential requirement for exchange equality from the personal to the communal and from the individual part to the working totality, they moved from a traditional model of conscious 1:1 equalization to a dynamic model of systematic equilibrium. They began to imagine the workings of a systematic whole (the community of exchangers) capable of ordering and equalizing itself – capable of *balancing* itself – in the dynamic intersection and interaction of its moving parts. With this new modeling of balance and its potentialities, we can, I think, truly speak of a break with the past. A clear indication of this break is that within the newly perceived possibilities of systematic equilibrium, elements that had traditionally been feared and rejected as dangerously open-ended and destabilizing – doubt, probability, approximation, value relativity,

---

[158] Olivi, *Tractatus*, 64: "Tertia ratio est a pari seu equivalenti et simul cum hoc ex altitudine iusti pretii divisibili in maius et minus."

multiplication, the desire for profit, and the like – could now be integrated as rational elements within the logic of a working system whose productive power and benefits to the Common Good were difficult to deny.

Not all thinkers of the time embraced this new model of equalization. Henry of Ghent's full-bore opposition to what he considered dangerous intellectual innovations in economic thought (and other spheres of thought as well) clearly demonstrates the lack of unanimity concerning its innovations. Indeed, the decades of the 1270s and 80s saw many instances of conservative reaction – a number of them concerted and successful – in the area of university thought. As in all periods, a few thinkers lead the way, while most remain incapable of reaching the requisite level of intellectual adventurousness or insight. These either resign themselves to follow (more or less competently) or they determine to oppose. As with most studies in intellectual history, this one too is focused on the few.

The progress in economic thinking resulting from the integration and application of the new model of equilibrium by no means ends with the writings of Peter Olivi. From Olivi's time through the mid fourteenth century there are writers who continue in this tradition and continue to shape the definition of *aequalitas* in exchange. Notable in this respect are those from Olivi's own Franciscan Order who carried on the project of judging the liceity (equality) of economic contracts in current use, involving both individuals and corporate entities: Duns Scotus, Alexander Lombard, Francesco da Empoli, Gerald Odonis, and Francesc Eiximenis, were among the most important of these.[159] Not surprisingly, insights taken from the *Tractatus* instruct these later Franciscan writings, although for reasons already mentioned, always without ascription. From outside the mendicant orders, the speculations on economic questions by the fourteenth-century Paris Masters Jean Buridan and Nicole Oresme contained brilliant further insights into the determinants of relativized economic value and the logic of exchange, while furthering at the same time the conceptions of the marketplace as an

---

[159] See, for example, Alan B. Wolter, *John Duns Scotus' Political and Economic Philosophy* (St. Bonaventure, NY: Franciscan Institute Publications, 2001); Alexander Lombard, *Un traité de morale économique au xive siècle: Le Tractatus de usuris de Maître Alexandre d'Alexandrie*, ed. A.-M. Hamelin (Louvain: Nauwelaerts, 1962); Armstrong, "The Politics of Usury in Trecento Florence"; Giovanni Ceccarelli and Sylvain Piron, "Gerald Odonis' Economics Treatise," *Vivarium* 47 (2009), 164–204; Paolo Evangelisti, "Contract and Theft: Two Legal Principles Fundamental to the *civilitas* and *res publica* in the Political Writings of Francesc Eiximenis, Franciscan Friar," *Franciscan Studies* 67 (2009), 405–26.

arena of systematic equilibrium and the merchant as an animate instrument of equalization.[160]

While Olivi's *Tractatus* can represent only a segment of scholastic economic thinking in this creative period, I have concluded with it because I believe it offers a particularly clear view into the new model of equilibrium at work. I note that almost every one of the more than a score of elements I link to the new model in the Introduction to this work can be seen intersecting and interacting within the overall logic of Olivi's presentation. But I have focused these first two chapters on Olivi's writings from the 1290s for another reason as well. Through them, I hoped to convey a central point concerning the history of balance: that the *sense* and *experience* of the dynamic of urban life and urban exchange in this early period served as a primary site for the *formation* of the new model of equilibrium, as well as a primary site of its reflection. In short, for Olivi, as for others, the recognition of systematic self-ordering, self-equalizing, and self-balancing that defines the new model was activated and shaped in no small part by the experience and observation of urban economic life. (I take up this theme again in Chapter 5.) In the chapters that follow, I hope to show that the new understanding (or faith) in the potentialities of systematic balance exhibited by Olivi extended far past the sphere of scholastic economic speculation to speculation in a host of other fields and disciplines, making possible fruitful new ways of conceiving the working order of the human body, the political body, and the cosmos itself. The following two chapters provide evidence for this claim in the sphere of scholastic medicine.

---

[160] These two thinkers play a prominent role in the chapters to come: Oresme's political philosophy is the subject of Chapter 7, and the role of the new equilibrium in the natural philosophy of Buridan and Oresme is examined in Chapter 8. For a discussion of their contributions to economic thought, see my *Economy and Nature in the Fourteenth Century*, esp. 127–62.

3   Balance in medieval medical theory, part 1: The legacy of Galen

> The sign of the healthiest bodies is that they are equally [proportionally] balanced in their members (*aequalitas membrorum*) with respect to the four elemental qualities: heat, cold, dryness, and wetness; and that there is an equality in the organic members (*aequalitas membrorum*) in terms of their quantity, construction, number, and the form of their component parts, both with respect to their instrumental functions and in their relationship to the whole.   Galen, *Tegni* or *Ars medica* (*c.* 193 CE)

> One fundamental mode of healing is to introduce the opposite (*contrarium*) of that which is to be corrected; all causes promoting health are of this mode. For hot dispositions, a cold cause is the opposite; for cold dispositions, a proportionally hot one; and so on proportionally (*proportionaliter*). For if everything that is ill-proportioned (*immoderatum*) is contrary to nature, and everything that is moderate is in accord with nature, then nature requires that everything immoderate be restored to moderation (*ad moderatum reduci*) by something which is equally ill-proportioned in the contrary direction.
> Galen, *Tegni* or *Ars medica*

In the previous two chapters I argued that the sense and conception of balance and its potentialities expanded continually over the twelfth and thirteenth centuries in response to momentous changes in the social and economic landscape of urban Europe. Since "internalist" readings of intellectual innovation (focused on the reading, absorption, and passing on of texts) have generally prevailed in the history of medieval thought, I have sought, both in the previous chapters and in my past writings, to balance and expand the explanatory frame by imagining how the lived *experience* of socioeconomic environments may also have shaped the form and direction of scholastic thought, including some of its most abstract and most seemingly "detached" speculations. At the same time, however, I have been intent to stress that intellectual innovation of the kind that characterizes the most adventurous scholastic speculation was produced through a complex interchange between the intellectual environment of the medieval universities and the social environment of the cities that surrounded them; between insights embedded in and inherited from texts, and the socioeconomic contexts in which texts were read and taught. I hope, in what follows, to do some justice to the complexities of this interchange, specifically as it affected both the emergence of the "new" model of equilibrium and its impact on scholastic thought.

Aristotle's writings, above all other writings, whether pagan, Islamic, or Christian, are generally assumed to have played the largest role in the formation of scholastic thought. I always assumed the same. That has changed somewhat, as my focus has turned to the history of balance and an analysis of its leading place in the process of intellectual imagination and innovation. I would now posit that in the critical area of the conceptualization and theorization of balance and equalization there was no pre-modern thinker that rivaled Galen of Pergamum (c. 129–c. 216? CE), and no textual tradition more important to the formation of the new model of equilibrium than the medical Galenism that passed from Rome, to Greek Alexandria, to the Islamic world, and on to Latin Christian culture in the mid twelfth century and after. In the following two chapters, I hope to convey the admiration I have gained both for Galen's modeling of balance (Chapter 3), and for the role of scholastic medicine in further shaping and communicating that model in the sphere of medical thought and beyond (Chapter 4).

Overview of Galen's corpus and its reception

The reception of Galen's medical writing by Latin Christian culture occurred in numerous overlapping stages. The way was prepared, from the late eleventh century, by the circulation of Latin translations of Arabic medical works which had drawn heavily on Galen and which were often explicitly crafted as introductions to Galenic medicine. Then, the first Latin translations of authentic Galenic texts began circulating in the mid twelfth century. This initiated a centuries-long translation project, with an important group of Galen's texts only finding their place in the Latin medical curriculum at the end of the thirteenth century, and with newly translated texts appearing well into the first century of printing. From the first, the challenging Galenic texts often circulated along with learned commentaries by Arabic and Latin authors. These commentaries themselves became part of an evolving history as newer ones folded older ones into their exposition of the Galenic system. Particularly important in this respect was the translation and reception of Avicenna's immense and magisterial *Canon* of medicine, which was, in essence, a systematic presentation of the totality of the Galenic system as filtered through the lens of Aristotelian logic and natural philosophy. Indeed, the reception and progressive comprehension of Galenic thought – the ways in which

Galen's profound insights could be read and understood – were inextricably tied to the flowering of Aristotelian learning within the medieval schools over the course of the thirteenth and fourteenth centuries.

The sometimes considerable gaps in time between the translation of certain Galenic texts and their general circulation, as well as the gaps between the circulation of Galenic concepts and their full comprehension (as witnessed by the commentaries), tell us a good deal about the difficulties that had to be overcome in order for certain technical elements within Galen's teaching to be grasped and applied. This is particularly true of his highly developed conceptualization of balance. At the core of medieval medicine as an intellectual discipline, and therefore, at the core of my analysis of the developing understanding of balance within scholastic thought, lie Galen's texts, his observations and insights, his theoretical framework, and his genius.

Galen's life and writings

Galen was born and educated in the Greek-speaking city of Pergamum in Asia Minor, and was schooled from youth in both philosophy and medicine.[1] In his early twenties he left Pergamum for further study in the great city of Alexandria, remaining there for five years.[2] He then returned to Pergamum to immerse himself in the practice of medicine, and while there he was appointed physician to the school of the gladiators.[3] In 162 CE, at the age of thirty-three, he traveled to Rome, where he lived for long periods over the more than forty years remaining to his life. In Rome he built for himself a great reputation as a practicing *medicus*, which by the last decades of the second century earned him the exalted position of physician to the Emperor Marcus Aurelius, to his son and successor, Commodus, and most probably to the Emperor

---

[1] There is, apparently, no reason to assign Galen the first name, Claudius, although it was common do so in medieval manuscripts and early printed editions of his writings and is still found in the present day. Many of the major dates in Galen's life are still debated, including his years of birth and death and the chronology of his travels. On this, see Vivian Nutton, "The Chronology of Galen's Early Career," *Classical Quarterly* 23 (1973), 158–71. Nutton has suggested that Galen may have lived until 216 or 217 CE, almost two decades longer than the traditional estimate. For his reasoning, see "Galen in the Eyes of his Contemporaries," *Bulletin of the History of Medicine* 58 (1984), 315–24, esp. 323.

[2] On this particular aspect of Galen's biography, see Vivian Nutton, "Galen and Egypt," in "Galen und das hellenistische Erbe," ed. J. Kollesch and D. Nickel, special issue of *Sudhoffs Archiv* 32 (1993), 11–31.

[3] Galen boasts of his medical successes in keeping gravely wounded gladiators alive in *De optimo medico cognoscendo*, English translation (from the Arabic), *Galen: On Examinations by Which the Best Physicians Are Recognized*, ed. and trans. Albert Iskandar (Berlin: Akademie Verlag, 1988), 105.

Severus as well.[4] Galen himself (with typical modesty) tells us that Marcus Aurelius referred to him as "first among physicians, unique among philosophers."[5] This brief biographical sketch brings to light three central points: throughout his life Galen combined the study of medicine with the study of philosophy (Platonist, Stoic, and Aristotelian); throughout his life he combined a concern for both the theory and the practice of medicine; and he passed virtually his entire life in highly advanced urban environments (Pergamum, Alexandria, Rome) linked together within a colossal empire at the furthest point of its expansion.

Galen was an extraordinarily prolific author. The standard modern edition of his collected works in Greek (which number more than 120) fills twenty volumes, and this does not include those of his writings that survived without a Greek text (in Arabic, Syriac, Hebrew, or Latin), or the scores that have been lost.[6] Very few of his many philosophical writings have survived, but the evidence that remains shows him to be as committed a synthesizer in the realm of philosophy as he was in the realm of medicine. There were some elements of his intellectual heritage that he flatly rejected, but overall he succeeded in bringing together a huge amount of potentially antagonistic material. He brought into alliance much of the Greek philosophical tradition: Stoic, Platonist, and Aristotelian, accepting Plato as his master, while at the same time relying heavily on Aristotle for his logic and his principles of natural philosophy.[7] He synthesized the work of the Hippocratic medical authors of ancient Greece (with whom he strongly

[4] The fullest biography of Galen in English is George Sarton, *Galen of Pergamon* (Lawrence: University of Kansas Press, 1954), but as research into Galen's biography continues, many details of Sarton's exposition have been questioned. For an excellent shorter view, see Michael Frede, "Introduction" to *Three Treatises on the Nature of Science*, ed. and trans. Richard Walzer and Michael Frede (Indianapolis: Hackett, 1985); Luis García Ballester, *Galeno en la sociedad y en la ciencia de su tiempo* (Madrid: Ediciones Guadarrama, 1972), 26–53; R. J. Hankinson, "The Man and his Work," in *The Cambridge Companion to Galen*, ed. R. J. Hankinson (Cambridge University Press, 2008), 1–33.
[5] Cited in Jonathan Barnes, "Galen on Logic and Therapy," in *Galen's Method of Healing*, ed. F. Kudlien and R. J. Durling (Leiden: Brill, 1991), 50–102, at 50. Galen was recognized by the most eminent philosophers both of his day and afterwards as an important (if sometimes mistaken) philosophical thinker as well as the preeminent medical theorist. On Galen the philosopher, see Ben Morison, "Logic," in *Cambridge Companion to Galen*, 66–115.
[6] C. Galenus, *Opera omnia*, ed. K. G. Kühn, 22 vols. (Leipzig: Teubner, 1821–33). Kühn's edition (volume, page, and line number) still serves as the standard for citations to Galen's works, and I will refer to it in my citations below. Newer estimates of Galen's output, which are based on newly available Galenic texts primarily in Arabic and Syriac, put the number of his treatises at over 300. In the great Roman fire of 191 CE, Galen (and posterity) lost a good portion of his library, including almost all of his many works on philosophy (García Ballester, *Galeno*, 46). For a tentative listing of these lost works, see Morison, "Logic," at 66–8.
[7] Jonathan Barnes, "Galen and the Utility of Logic," in "Galen und das hellenistische Erbe," ed. J. Kollesch and D. Nickel, special issue of *Sudhoffs Archiv* 32 (1993), 33–52; Frede, "Introduction" to *Three Treatises*. For Galen's debt to stoicism, see Helen Karabatzaki,

identified) with writings of Herophilus (*c.* 325–*c.* 280–255 BCE) and his followers in the Alexandrian school of medicine, adding to these certain of the theorists and medical practitioners of his own Hellenistic period. He insisted that the *medicus* (the practicing physician) must join the universality of philosophy to the particularity of art and technique; must draw on both the reasoning intellect and the observing senses to understand the causes of sickness and health. In doing so, he synthesized the disciplines of philosophy and medicine as no one had before him and, with the possible exception of Avicenna, as no one has since.[8]

Judged in terms of its intent to unite a tangled mass of precious yet disparate elements of Greek and Hellenistic culture, Galen's system (such as it was) was extraordinarily successful.[9] This success is marked both by the explanatory power it achieved and by its adoption as the authoritative basis of medicine for almost fifteen hundred years after its construction. At the same time, the joining of disparate elements within Galen's oeuvre was accomplished at the cost of the loss of a measure of internal coherence. Judged against Aristotle (as it might well have been by Latin scholars of the thirteenth century and after), Galen's "system" looks somewhat provisional and at times self-contradictory. Numerous commentators, from his contemporaries to ours, have noted places where Galen's positions (both clinical and theoretical) differ in detail from work to work and sometimes even within the same work.[10] But while some anomalies may

"Stoicism and Galen's Medical Thought," in *Philosophy and Medicine*, ed. K. J. Boudoris (Athens: Ionia Publications, 1998), 95–113. Karabatzaki (107, nn. 4, 5, and 6) provides a considerable list of lost works Galen dedicated specifically to the subject of Platonic, Aristotelian, and Stoic philosophy, and Barnes (above) calls Galen a "votary of logic," crediting him with approximately fifty works on the topic. Also P. N. Singer, "Aspects of Galen's Platonism," in *Galeno: obra, pensamiento e influencia*, ed. J. A. López Férez (Madrid: Universidad Nacional de Educación a Distancia, 1991), 41–55.

[8] This joining is a continual theme in his writings. See his treatise, "The Best Doctor is Also a Philosopher," in *Galen: Selected Works*, ed. and trans. P. N. Singer (Oxford University Press, 1997), 30–4. His synthetic program is clearly apparent in his *De placitis Hippocratis et Platonis*, English translation, *On the Doctrines of Hippocrates and Plato*, ed. and trans. Phillip de Lacy, 3 vols. (Berlin: Akademie Verlag, 1978–84). For Galen's recognition of certain differences between the two authors, G. E. R. Lloyd, "Galen on Hellenistics and Hippocrateans: Contemporary Battles and Past Authorities," in "Galen und das hellenistische Erbe," ed. J. Kollesch and D. Nickel, special issue of *Sudhoffs Archiv* 32 (1993), 125–43, esp. 135–8. On Galen's constant joining of philosophy and medicine, Barnes, "Galen on Logic and Therapy," 50.

[9] Marzia Mortarino in the introduction to her Italian translation, *Galeno: sulle facoltà naturali* (Milan: Mondadori, 1996), v–lv, esp. xli, uses the phrase "cultural project" to capture Galen's synthesis of varied conceptual instruments, specialized techniques, and philosophical and medical traditions.

[10] For the general recognition of major inconsistencies, see, for example, Owsei Temkin, *Galenism: Rise and Decline of a Medical Philosophy* (Ithaca, NY: Cornell University Press, 1973), 6: "His works are studded with propositions that are hard to reconcile, even where they do not contradict one another." For inconsistencies on particular points, see, for

indeed have resulted simply as by-products of an overly ambitious synthetic project, I think it is important to suggest that a perfectly consistent "system" is almost surely *not* what Galen sought. There are strong indications that as a committed anti-dogmatist he recognized the dangers of theoretical consistency. He recognized that consistency could mask the complexity and variability of the real and thus could easily work against the close observation of particulars, which he placed at the core of successful medicine.[11] He clearly believed, and acted frequently on the belief, that it better served truth to alter his positions in the light of new findings than to maintain previous positions in the name of consistency.[12] In any case, and despite the inconsistencies real and perceived, it is clear that Galen saw his work as a connected whole and often wrote about it in these terms.[13]

As a written corpus, sealed with the death of its author, the Galenic system is in some sense closed and static. When one reads Galen, however, one senses not rigidity but rather a delicacy and lightness of touch, and not fixity but rather, quite remarkably, a sense of openness, rhythm, and motion that his rhetorical strategies imparted to his texts and his method. Unable to be present to future students in the teaching of this complex art, unable to demonstrate to them by doing, through motions, gestures, and actions, he found a way to insert himself as an active and deliberating subject into his texts.[14] Within each text and from text to text there is motion in the continual division, rearrangement, and subtle

example, Luis García Ballester, "On the Origin of the 'Six Non-Natural Things' in Galen," in "Galen und das hellenistische Erbe," ed. J. Kollesch and D. Nickel, special issue of *Sudhoffs Archiv* 32 (1993),105–15.

[11] Although Galen was severely critical of dogmatism in the general sense of the term, R. J. Hankinson places him partly in the camp of the Dogmatist physicians, insofar as he accepted that a causal understanding of the body was possible and necessary for proper treatment. On this, see Hankinson, "Causation in Galen," in *Galien et la philosophie*, ed. Jonathan Barnes, Jacques Jouanna, and Vincent Barras (Geneva: Fondation Hardt, 2003), 31–72; R. J. Hankinson, "Epistemology," in *Cambridge Companion to Galen*, 157–83, esp. 165–9.

[12] Temkin (*Galenism*, 7 n. 24) notes that even after changing positions, Galen would continue to advise the reading of earlier works which contained the superseded opinions, without warning his readers concerning the now outdated material.

[13] See, for example, the short concluding section of the *Tegni* (considered below) in which he outlines his major areas of theoretical and practical concern and suggests a grouping of his writings specific to each area.

[14] Galen's frequent public displays of his craft (particularly anatomical demonstrations) and his skilled exploitation of stagecraft to impress his audiences speaks to the close connection between rhetoric and gesture in his professional life. On Galen and public performance, see Heinrich von Staden, "Galen and the 'Second Sophistic,'" in *Aristotle and After*, ed. Richard Sorabji (University of London Institute of Classical Studies, 1997), 33–54. Also, Vivian Nutton, "Galen and Medical Autobiography," *Proceedings of the Cambridge Philological Society* 198 (1972), 50–62, at 52: "Galen is both teacher and model, both author and exemplar." Also, Hankinson, "The Man and his Work," 12–14.

reshaping of the constituent parts of his argument.[15] Certain individual works – even relatively short ones (e.g., the *Tegni* and the *De complexionibus* discussed below) – seem constructed to communicate (indeed to inculcate) a sensitivity to rhythm, flux, and the play of moving elements as they alternate and juxtapose principles, observations, objections, and distinctions. In the process, fixity and certainty are (seemingly) intentionally undermined, even as the system is expounded.

I would suggest that Galen's capacity to formulate a rhetorical method that remains so labile and light on its feet is linked to his social experience as a wandering intellectual, traveling from one urbanized cultural capital to another within the late Empire, and living for years as a provincial at the very center of urbanity in Rome itself.[16] Simply to maintain one's position in this context, one would likely have had to remain open and fluidly adaptable to widely varying cultural signs, norms, and demands, and Galen, as we know, fared far better than mere maintenance. But I do not want to suggest that his rhetorical strategies and his larger method were mere accidents of biography. Galen's consistent application of these strategies over a long and productive lifetime suggests that they were structured for a purpose: to bring intellectualized theory into congruence with the sensory experience of widely varying and ever-shifting particulars.

The balance Galen maintained over a lifetime between theory and practice, between the universal and the particular, between medicine as science and medicine as art, was an exceedingly delicate one. Only, he maintained, through the use of philosophically guided reason could the physician organize and judge the myriad signs and symptoms he perceived. But only if theory remained open and supple could it organize the particulars of sensory life without distorting them through the imposition of its own structures. In Galen's system, the physician himself must in some sense embody this delicate and ever-shifting *balance* – this attitude of lightness, openness, and adaptability with respect to human differences and to the ever-changing states of the human body. To a remarkable degree, Galen succeeded in building this structured adaptability and

---

[15] R. J. Penella and T. S. Hall, "Galen's 'On the Best Constitution of Our Body': Introduction, Translation, and Notes," *Bulletin of the History of Medicine* 47 (1973), 282–96, at 282: "Galen developed a reservoir of broad interpretive ideas which he drew upon repeatedly, arranging them in ever new patterns as treatise after treatise took form in his mind."

[16] While the prestige Galen achieved at the Roman court was remarkable, his movement from city to city within the Empire was fairly typical for ambitious intellectuals in his period. For the argument that this pervasive wandering colored the intellectual climate of Galen's age, see G. W. Bowersock, *Greek Sophists in the Roman Empire* (Oxford: Clarendon Press, 1969).

this overarching sensitivity to balance into his system of medical knowledge and practice.

The question of "balance" in Galen's system

Often the first image that comes to mind when we speak of balance is that of the mechanical scale. Here, weights are added to the two arms of a scale until they are equally balanced over a balancing point. Here, too, balance is associated with a precise quantitative equality – two quantitatively equal and numerable weights on each side of the balancing point. This is *not* the balance at play in Galenic medicine. Rather, the first thing to recognize about Galen's conception of balance is that complex notions of proportionality, and thus of quantitative *in*equalities – the proportional blending of quantitative *un*equals – always lie at its core. The essential role of quantitative inequality in Galenic balance in large part explains what might otherwise remain puzzling: in all the millions of words that constitute Galen's medical writings, the specific words for "balance" appear only very rarely.[17] In ancient Greek, the word *isorrhopia* (and its roots) retains a technical and highly specific meaning related to the apparatus (and image) of the mechanical scale balancing two equal weights. Neither the Greek term *isorrhopia* nor its medieval Latin equivalents, "aequilibrium" "aequilibrare" etc., are adequate to convey the *proportional* equalization of *unequal* weights, measures, and effects so central to Galen's meaning. Nor can these technical Greek or Latin terms be applied to the complex process of equalization as it occurs within an ever-moving and multivalent system such as Galen understood the animal body to be.[18]

It is only in recent centuries that the English words "balance" and "equilibrium" have expanded to encompass these broader, metaphorical meanings, including the idea of the continual reproportionalization of

---

[17] I am indebted to Heinrich von Staden for underscoring Galen's failure to use the technical term "balance" or "equally balanced" (*isorrhopia*). Von Staden also speaks to a scholarly hesitation to associate Galen with the concept of "balance" (especially such common notions as the "balance of the humors"), specifically because the "ordinary" sense of the word still signifies and carries with it the simplified image of a scale balancing two equal weights or quantities. For Galen's great concern for concision in his vocabulary and his metaphors, see Von Staden, "Science as Text, Science as History: Galen on Metaphor," in *Ancient Medicine in its Socio-Cultural Context*, ed. P. J. van der Eijk, H. F. J. Horstmanshoff, and P. H. Schrijvers, vol. II (Amsterdam: Rodopi, 1995), 499–518. Also, Ben Morison, "Language," in *Cambridge Companion to Galen*, 116–56.

[18] García Ballester, *Galeno*, 47–8; Paola Manuli, "Galen and Stoicism," in "Galen und das hellenistische Erbe," ed. J. Kollesch and D. Nickel, special issue of *Sudhoffs Archiv* 32 (1993), 53–61, esp. 56.

moving elements within a functioning system.[19] Lacking any single word
with the breadth of meanings attached to the modern words "balance" or
"equilibrium," Galen (and his medieval Latin translators) used a multiplicity of related terms. Once again, forms of "equality" (*aequalitas*) and its
cognates (*aequalis, aequus, aequare, aequabilis, adaequatio, aequivalentia,
coaequale*, and others) are the words most often found in place of our
"balance" in Latin translations of Galen. But in addition to these, Galen
frequently employed a number of technical terms, which (as he was careful to instruct) carried within themselves both the *idea* of proportional
balance, and the active *sense* of a dynamic process of systematic balancing.
Among these terms (as they were translated in Latin texts), are *complexio,
temperamentum, proportio, medium, mediocritas, symmetria, mixtio, justitia*,
and, taken directly from the Greek, the term "*eucraton*," which denoted a
well-proportioned and well-balanced mixture.[20]

Galen's very hesitation to use the word *isorrhopia* indicates that his
"sense" of balance – the form he imagines when he describes the shifting
proportional relationship of elements within a moving system – is far
more complex than that represented by the image of a scale balancing
two equal weights at a fixed balancing point.[21] It indicates as well that
in studying the history of balance, it is often necessary to discern,
describe, and provide words for "forms," "shapes," and "senses" of
balance that were never explicitly verbalized in the texts themselves.
The riches of Galen's new concepts and perceptions in this area outran
the vocabulary available to him. Indeed, only in the seventeenth century
did the English words "balance" and "equilibrium" come to possess
much of the metaphorical breadth that they possess today; only
then did the meanings attached to these words begin to do justice
to the subtlety and complexity of Galen's vision of systematic

---

[19] See the *Oxford English Dictionary* for "balance" n. and v.

[20] It is noteworthy that in her recent French translation of Galen's *Ars medica*, the Galen
scholar Véronique Boudon frequently translates each of these Latin near-equivalents with
the French "équilibré" or "juste équilibre." Her equation of "balance" with Galen's
"good blend" is apparent in her statement: "La médecine de Galien repose tout entière
sur le juste équilibre ou le parfait mélange (*krasis*) des quatre qualités." See
Boudon, *Galien*, vol. II: *Exhortation à l'étude de la médecine: Art médical* (Paris: Les
Belles Lettres, 2000), at 401.

[21] Galen does, however, make frequent use of the term "*symmetria*," and Boudon
(*Art médical*, 283, n. 3) notes that he "habitually employs it to translate the idea of just
balance (*juste équilibre*) relative to the size, number, complexion, and situation of the
organs" (my translation). For a study that traces the history of the term and the concept
of symmetry in the mathematical realm from ancient Greece to the end of the eighteenth
century, see Giora Hon and Bernard Goldstein, *From* Summetria *to* Symmetry: *The
Making of a Revolutionary Scientific Concept* (New York: Springer, 2010).

balance.[22] For this reason, I feel justified in attaching the term "balance" to Galen's speculations, even if he and his pre-modern commentators did not and could not.

Introduction to Galen's *Tegni* and *De complexionibus*

The elements that underlay Galen's sense of balance are best uncovered through a close analysis of his particular works. I will concentrate on two central texts and on one concept that formed the primary subject of several of Galen's writings and was foundational to the medieval conception of *aequalitas* as applied to the living body. The first text I consider is that of the *Art of Medicine (Techne iatrike)*, Latinized variously as *Ars medica, Ars parva,* or *Tegni.*[23] In the latter part of this chapter, I turn to Galen's *On Complexions (Peri kraseon)*, Latinized as *De temperamentis* or *De complexionibus*. The concept that is pivotal to both works and to the scholastic understanding of *aequalitas* is that of *krasis (crasis)*, or "blended mixture," Latinized as *mixtio* or, more technically, as *complexio*.

There are a number of factors that support the use of the *Tegni* as a representative text. It was one of Galen's later works (193 CE), and he wrote it with the stated intention that it serve as the introduction to the principles that underlay his "art."[24] Although Galen could be extremely prolix, he crafted the *Tegni* as a concise work, the better to serve as a general introduction and to facilitate memorization.[25] No doubt in part because it provided a short and graspable overview of the Galenic corpus, the *Tegni* was widely circulated and commented upon, first within the Hellenized Mediterranean (particularly at Alexandria, through the seventh century CE), and then, beginning in the ninth century, within the Islamic world. For similar reasons the *Tegni* was one of the first of

---

[22] For the metaphorical expansion of these words in English, see Joel Kaye, "The (Re)Balance of Nature, 1250–1350," in *Engaging with Nature: Essays on the Natural World in Medieval and Early Modern Europe*," ed. Barbara Hanawalt and Lisa Kiser (University of Notre Dame Press, 2008), 85–113, at 86–7.

[23] Other common names for the *Tegni* are: *Microtechne, Microtegni, Ars medicina, Ars medicinalis.* Hereafter I refer to it primarily by the title *Tegni*.

[24] Hankinson ("The Man and his Work," 22) has called the *Tegni*, "the fundamental medical text of the Late Middle Ages and Renaissance." The most thorough treatment of the *Tegni* and its medieval reception in English is Per-Gunnar Ottosson, *Scholastic Medicine and Philosophy: A Study of Commentaries on Galen's Tegni (c. 1300–1450)* (Naples: Bibliopolis, 1984).

[25] In the first Latin edition of Galen's *Opera omnia* (Venice: Philippus Pincius, 1490), it occupies fols. 10ra–15vb, double columned and abbreviated. In its most recent English translation in *Galen: Selected Works*, trans. P. N. Singer (Oxford University Press, 1997), it occupies approximately fifty pages, 345–96.

Galen's works to be translated into Latin and the first to gain wide circulation within Latin Christian culture.[26] It was intended by Galen to be the textual key to the Galenic corpus, and it remained so throughout the medieval period. It is a key, as well, to Galen's remarkably rich and refined conception of balance.

As early as the mid twelfth century, a grouping of medical texts began to circulate in Latin Europe, having been compiled and translated into Latin most probably at the medical school at Salerno.[27] At first this collection, soon to be commonly known as *Ars medicine* or *Articella*, contained no authentic Galenic work, although it did include a very short and schematic introduction to Galenic theory, the *Isagoge Johanittii*, along with two works by Hippocrates and two later (post-Galenic) Greek works on the pulse and on the examination of urine.[28] In total, the earliest *Articella* grouping occupied less than fifty folios.[29] Toward the later twelfth century, within a short period after the *Articella*'s original compilation, a new work was added to the collection and circulated as an integral part of it for centuries to follow – Galen's *Ars medica* or *Tegni*. It would be difficult to exaggerate the importance of the *Articella* (and thus of the *Tegni*) to medical education in the medieval period. As the collection gradually expanded to include several longer works and commentaries (including an important commentary on the *Tegni* itself), it remained for centuries the most widely read and widely commented-upon text in medicine.[30]

At the University of Paris and at many other universities with higher faculties in medicine, the *Tegni* maintained its commanding position at

---

[26] The early translation history of the *Tegni* remains uncertain. There was almost certainly a Latin translation from the Greek circulating from the sixth century, but it has not survived. For the indications of its existence, see N. Palmieri-Darlon, "Sur les traces d'une ancienne traduction latine de l'*Ars medica*," *Latomus* 56 (1997), 504–11.

[27] Paul Oskar Kristeller, "Bartholomeus, Musandinus and Maurus of Salerno and Other Early Commentators of the 'Articella,' with a Tentative List of Texts and Manuscripts," *Italia medioevale e umanistica* 19 (1976), 57–87; Kristeller, "The School of Salerno," *Bulletin of the History of Medicine* 17 (1945), 138–94. For possible objections to a Salernitan origin, see Cornelius O'Boyle, *The Art of Medicine: Medical Teaching at the University of Paris, 1250–1400* (Leiden: Brill, 1998), 98–9.

[28] The earliest grouping contained Hippocrates' *Aphorismi* and *Prognostica*, Hunain ibn Ishaq's (Lat. Johannitius) *Isagoge in artem parvam Galeni*, Philaretus' *De pulsibus*, and Theophilus' *De urinis*.

[29] O'Boyle, *Art of Medicine*, 80 ff.

[30] Danielle Jacquart estimates, for example, that one half of all medical commentaries written between the twelfth and the sixteenth century in France were on the *Articella* (most of these in the thirteenth and fourteenth century at Paris and particularly at Montpellier), with the remaining half split between individual works of Galen, Avicenna, Rhazes, Averroes, etc. See Danielle Jacquart, *Le milieu médical en France du XIIe au XVe siècle* (Geneva: Droz, 1981), 209–10.

the center of the medical curriculum into the age of printing.[31] There can be no doubt, then, concerning its central importance to the development of medical learning and its central place within university education. Since Galen intended it to serve as the introduction to his art, the *Tegni* contains so much information and raises so many questions that even a cursory reading of the whole is out of the question here. In what follows, I limit my discussion only to those components that touch directly on the question of balance, and even these, because of their number and complexity, can only be considered in part. The text itself is available in many editions and has been translated into many modern languages so that readers who desire a sense of the whole are encouraged to examine it in its entirety.[32]

The earliest Latin translation of the *Tegni*, which came to be known as the *translatio antiqua*, was taken from a Greek source near the middle of the twelfth century. In the late twelfth century (1187), it was joined by a second version, this time translated from the Arabic and known as the *translatio arabica* (also, *translatio ex arabico*). Both versions continued in wide circulation through the fifteenth century. Indeed, as a testament to the importance of the *Ars*, both versions often appeared together in their entirety within the same manuscript, presumably so that the one could be read "against" and in concert with the other.[33] The *translatio antiqua* and *translatio arabica* remained the standard versions of the *Tegni* for centuries until emended by humanist translations.[34] The person responsible for the *translatio antiqua* remains unknown to us, as do the specific conditions

[31] Only in the 1270s is the required study of the *Articella* recorded within the statutes of the Medical Faculty at Paris, although it was almost certainly in use earlier. It was also, most probably, required reading at this time at the other two leading centers of medical education, Montpellier and Bologna, although there is no statutory evidence to support this. On this, see O'Boyle, *Art of Medicine*, 100 ff.

[32] See "The Art of Medicine," in *Galen: Selected Works*, ed. and trans. Singer, 345–96. In those cases where Singer's translation accords well with the Latin texts available to medieval readers, I utilize and cite it. Singer's translation, however, was taken from the Greek text of Kühn's edition, necessitating, at times, that it be either modified or replaced with my own translation to bring it into line with the Latin versions. If Singer is not cited, the translation is my own; if modified, I will note it. There is also the excellent recent French edition and translation by Véronique Boudon, *Art médical*, 274–392. For a listing of other modern language translations, see Gerhard Fichtner, *Corpus Galenicum: Verzeichnis der galenischen und pseudogalenischen Schriften* (Tübingen: Institut für Geschichte der Medizin, 1989), 11–12, and Boudon, *Art médical*, 266.

[33] The majority of the 150 Latin manuscripts of the *Articella* examined by Véronique Boudon contain both versions. On this see, Boudon, "La *Translatio antiqua* de *L'Art médical* de Galien," in *Storia e ecdotica dei testi medici greci*, ed. Antonio Garzya and Jacques Jouanna (Naples: D'Auria, 1996), 43–55, esp. 44.

[34] Even in the later printed editions, which utilized newer translations by Niccolò Leoniceno, Lorenzo Lorenziano, and others, the texts of either or both the *translatio antiqua* and *translatio arabica* often continued to appear alongside them, with each version identified as such.

of its construction from a Greek original.[35] The *translatio arabica* can be safely credited to Gerard of Cremona (*c.* 1114–87), who worked from an Arabic translation made originally in the ninth century by Hunain ibn Ishaq (Latinized, Johannitius).[36] Gerard translated the text of the *Tegni* together with an early eleventh-century commentary upon it (approximately three times as long as the *Tegni*) composed by the Cairo physician, Ibn Ridwan, and the two texts continued to circulate together into the seventeenth century.[37]

There are a number of differences between the two translations of the *Tegni* which undoubtedly help to explain the frequent inclusion of both in manuscript and printed versions of the *Articella*. The *translatio antiqua* was intended as a faithful, rather literal Latin translation from the Greek text of the *Ars* as it had come down to the twelfth century. As such it did not attempt to clarify or explicate the obscurities in the original. On the other hand, Hunain ibn Ishaq's ninth-century Arabic translation (the basis of Gerard of Cremona's twelfth-century Latin translation) emended and elaborated on the text's obscurities at a number of points, drawing on a long commentary tradition.[38] In what follows, I use the two versions in the way I imagine they were often used by medieval readers, consulting both and using the one to clarify and reinforce the other.[39]

---

[35] On this, see Richard Durling, "Corrigenda and Addenda to Diels' Galenica," *Traditio* 23 (1967), 461–76; Durling, "Lectiones Galenicae *Techne iatrike*," *Classical Philology* 63 (1968), 56–7; Boudon, *Art médical*, 246–8; Ottosson, *Tegni*, 24–5. For an earlier ascription of the translation to Constantine, see Lynn Thorndike and Pearl Kibre, *A Catologue of Incipits of Mediaeval Scientific Writings in Latin* (Cambridge, MA: Medieval Academy of America, 1963), col. 1585, and Boudon's criticism, *Art médical*, 245, n. 45.

[36] Hunain (Johannitius) was also the author of the *Isagoge Johannitii*, the brief introduction to Galenic thought that formed one of the original five texts of the *Articella*.

[37] Boudon, *Art médical*, 168–9, 246.

[38] *Ibid.*, 246–9. See also J. S. Wilkie and G. E. R. Lloyd, "The Arabic Version of Galen's *Ars Parva*," *Journal of Hellenic Studies* 101 (1981), 145–8.

[39] I have cross-checked a number of versions of the *translatio antiqua*, noting numerous minor changes in wording: *Opera omnia Galeni* (Venice: Philippus Pincius, 1490), 10ra–15vb (available to all on the website of the Bibliothèque Interuniversitaire de Médecine [BIUM]); *Articella nuperrime impressa cum quamplurimis tractatibus pristine impressioni superadditis* (London: Jacob Myt, 1519), 117v–135v (available online at openlibrary.org); and Harley Ms. 3140, 7v–21r, dated to *c.* 1300, and available online in digitized form from the British Library. Citations will be primarily from the Venice, 1490 edition. Citations to the *translatio arabica* (and to Ibn Ridwan's commentary) will be from *Hali Filii Rodbon in Parvam Galeni Artem Commentatio*, in *Plus quam commentum in Parvam Galieni Artem, Turisani Florentini Medici Praestantissimi* (Venice, 1557), fols. 175r–217r (also online at the BIUM website).

Reading the Latin *Tegni*: balance and the *neutrum* (neither) state

Galen begins the *Tegni* with a short technical discussion of methods and problems associated with conveying systematic knowledge. His aim, he declares, is to facilitate "the comprehension of the whole art [of Galenic medicine] and the memorization of its constituent parts."[40] Following his concise introductory section on method, Galen begins the *Tegni* proper by providing a broad definition of the medical art that was to be repeated many, many times over the following centuries: "Medicine," he writes, "is the knowledge (*scientia*) of what is healthy, what is sick, and what is neither."[41] Right from the opening words, then, Latin readers would see that Galen has claimed medicine as a "science," and that he has framed the whole of medicine as a kind of balance. At one end of the continuum lies health, at the other, sickness, and in the middle lies a vague area of indeterminate extent, the *neutrum* or "neither" state, which the doctor cannot categorize as either healthy or sick because the signs there are mixed (*dispositione quae non est sanitas neque aegritudo*).[42] Confronted with this tripartite scheme, we readers are immediately led to sense the body's ever-present potential to flow between the two extremes of health and sickness and, at the same time, to recognize that medicine is primarily concerned with discerning and regulating that flow. And right from the opening, we have entered disputed territory. Why add a third state labeled "neither" when it can clearly have no fixed definition and no definable

---

[40] All citations from the Latin text of the *Tegni* that follow will be cross-referenced to the page of K. G. Kühn's standard Greek edition of the *Opera omnia*, where it appears in volume I. In this case, the citation is: K, I: 306; *Antiqua*, 10ra: "et ratione tantum habundans est ad comprehensionem totius artis et memoriam eorum que secundum partem."

[41] K, I: 307; *Antiqua* (1490), 10ra: "Medicina est scientia sanorum et egrorum et neutrorum." *Arabica* (1557), 176r: "Dico ergo quod medicina est scientia rerum pertinentium continuatarum cum sanitate, et cum egritudine et cum dispositione in qua non evadit homini sanitas neque egritudo." I give the two readings here to illustrate the difference in style and presentation between the two translations. Note the explicit reference to health and sickness as continuous in the *translatio arabica*. On Galen's use of the term "science" here, see Véronique Boudon, "Art, science, et conjecture," in *Galien et la philosophie*, ed. Jonathan Barnes, Jacques Jouanna, and Vincent Barras (Geneva: Fondation Hardt, 2003), 269–305, esp. 277–8. On Galen as a "continuum theorist," see R. H. Hankinson, "Philosophy of Nature," in *Cambridge Companion to Galen*, 210–41, at 212.

[42] K, I: 308; *Arabica*, 177r; *Antiqua*, 10rb. While the Galenic texts support the translation of "neutrum" as "neither," the term also carries the implication of "between" or "neutral." For an important article on the *neutrum* that follows both of these readings, see Maaike van der Lugt, "Neither Ill nor Healthy: The Intermediate State between Health and Disease in Medieval Medicine," *Quaderni storici* 136 (2011), 13–46. Questions concerning the "neither" state in Galen's *Tegni* are treated extensively in Timo Joutsivuo, *Scholastic Tradition and Humanist Innovation: The Concept of Neutrum in Renaissance Medicine* (Helsinki: Academia Scientiarum Fennica, 1999).

limits? What is to be gained? A passionate debate on these questions began soon after the reception of the *Tegni* and continues into the present day.[43]

There was precedent for such a tripartite scheme in the work of the Alexandrian physician, Herophilus, a medical authority Galen clearly respected and cited numerous times.[44] But there had been no precedent for such a taxonomy in Galen's previous writings, and a number of statements in Galen's previous works can be taken to argue directly against positing a "neither" disposition between health and sickness.[45] Furthermore, Aristotle, whose writings Galen knew thoroughly and for the most part followed (when his own observations did not directly contradict them), had argued that one could properly speak only of the contraries health and sickness, specifically denying the existence of an "intermediate" or neutral state between these or, for that matter, between any two contraries.[46] Galen, however, not only added the third "neither" state to the opening definition of medicine, he then followed this tripartite division all the way through the *Tegni*, allowing the *neutrum* equal importance with sickness and health in the organization of the text. The controversial nature of Galen's decision to add the *neutrum* in opposition to Aristotle is evidenced by severe criticisms of the move made by some

[43] As Joutsivuo notes (*Neutrum*, 57–64) the very conception of health and disease as a continuum, and the very notion of a continuous motion or flow between these contraries through the *neutrum*, violates the logic of Aristotle's definition of them as qualitative "dispositions." See also Van der Lugt, "Neither Ill nor Healthy," 17. This was recognized by a number of medieval thinkers and commentators: Ibn Ridwan, Pietro d'Abano, and Turisanus, among others. The problem is clearly elucidated in Pietro d'Abano, *Conciliator controversiarum, quae inter philosophos et medicos versantur* (Venice: ad Iuntas, 1565; reprint, Padua: Editrice Antenore, 1985), diff. 72, fols. 109r–111r. I discuss this further in Chapter 4.

[44] For the life, works, and continuing medical influence of Herophilus, including his influence on Galen, see Heinrich von Staden, *Herophilus: The Art of Medicine in Early Alexandria* (Cambridge University Press, 1989). For Herophilus' tripartite division of medical science and its possible influence on Galen's plan in the *Tegni*, see *ibid.*, 89–114. In other works Galen ascribes the tripartite division to Herophilus, but nowhere does he do so in the text of the *Tegni* in reference to his own decision to add the neuter state. See also Boudon's comments on this question, *Art médical*, 396–8.

[45] Joutsivuo, *Neutrum*, 50. The break with Galen's past writings represented by the appearance of the *neutrum* and the tripartite definition of medicine, along with other stylistic and theoretical inconsistencies, has prompted one scholar to question Galen's authorship of the *Tegni*. See Jutta Kollesch, "Anschauungen von den *archai* in der *Ars medica* und die Seelenlehre Galens," in *Le opere psicologiche di Galeno*, ed. Paola Menuli and Mario Vegetti (Naples: Bibliopolis, 1988), 215–30. Véronique Boudon has responded to Kollesch with a full, and, I think, convincing defense of Galen's authorship: "*L'Ars medica* de Galien est-il un traité authentique?" *Revue des Études Grecques* 109 (1996), 111–56.

[46] Joutsivuo, *Neutrum*, 51; Van der Lugt, "Neither Ill nor Healthy," 17; Aristotle, *Categories*, 10 [12a4–9, 12b30–2].

of his most avid supporters in the centuries that followed.[47] Given its lack of congruence with his previous writings and its opposition to Aristotelian definition, it is fair to ask what Galen might have hoped to accomplish through the addition of a third "neither" disposition in this work dedicated to "the comprehension of the whole art."

Galen writes in general of the *neutrum* that it can be understood in three ways: (1) it can have no part in the contraries (of health and sickness); (2) it can participate sometimes in one contrary and sometimes in the other; or (3) it can participate in both contraries, sometimes equally in both and sometimes more in one than in the other.[48] When he then turns to give a brief definition of the neither body (*neutrum corpus*), he speaks of it as a medium (*medium*) between the most healthy and most sickly body.[49] He goes further to assert that the "neither" disposition exists not only in relation to the whole body but that every one of the body's myriad parts possesses its own *neutrum* disposition intermediate between its own health and sickness. Then, when later in the text he considers how the *neutrum* appears to the physician and can be read as a bodily sign, he replicates his earlier comments: either it provides no clear indication of health or disease, or it indicates a state alternating between health and morbidity.[50]

In short, through its consistent focus on the *neutrum* and its continual return to the subject in the manner of theme and variation, the text of the *Tegni* instructs its readers to pay the closest attention – to literally "see" – a disposition defined by its indeterminacy and marked by motion and change. Galen intended readers of the *Tegni* to memorize the specifics of body, sign, and cause that he presents, but here at the very beginning of the treatise, they are also being taught to "sense" the patterned motion that the doctor must learn to recognize. As the reader moves through the text, Galen manages to convey through writing not only what the physician must see but also how he must learn to look. He patterns his prose not only toward the learning of the body's structure but toward the *sensing* of its living rhythm. As the renowned historian of medicine, Luis García Ballester, has written:

---

[47] Avicenna, Averroes, and Pietro d'Abano among others. See Joutsivuo, *Neutrum*, 49–54; Van der Lugt, "Neither Ill nor Healthy,"17 ff. Von Staden, however, shows (*Herophilus*, 94–5) that the concept of *neutrum* had its philosophical defenders among the Stoics at the time of Herophilus and after, and notes (97) that Aristotle too at times made use of the concept of "neither," though not in the context of health and sickness.

[48] K, I: 308; *Antiqua*, fol. 10rb: "tripliciter unumquodque dicitur: hoc quidem eo quod neutro contrariorum participet: hoc vero eo quod utrisque: hoc autem eo quod aliquando quidem hoc aliquando vero illo: horum vero ipsorum secundum duos modos dicitur: aliquando quidem participando utroque contrariorum equaliter; aliquando autem amplius altero."

[49] K, I: 311; *Arabica*, 178r; *Antiqua*, 10rb.   [50] K, I: 313; *Arabica*, 178v; *Antiqua*, 10va.

For Galen the basic criterion of his medical practice was "the sensing of the body" [*aesthesis tou somatos*], a Hippocratic idea, expressed also as "the sensation the doctor has of his patient's body," and "the application of the doctor's senses to the precise knowledge of the patient's reality."[51]

If, then, Galen's goal in this introductory work is to impart a sense of the body's rhythm as well as a sense of its formal structure, it becomes clear that adding the *neutrum* to the conceptual scheme served his purpose well, even if it stretched certain philosophical definitions. Once he establishes health and sickness as a qualitative continuum with the *neutrum* as medium or mid-range, he opens up the possibility of thinking (and seeing) in terms of a continual flux and reflux along the continuum. In this way he adds considerable physical and spatial realism to his model. With the *neutrum* blown up, as it were, to equal status with the contraries health and sickness, diminutive motions around the center are magnified. They can no longer be ignored as too small to matter or to observe but can now be treated as real motions and real signs with real consequences, which with practice can (and must) be read by the physician. Motion through the *neutrum* would then represent the "tipping point" between health and sickness: an area the physician would do well to learn to recognize. In short, I posit that by adding the *neutrum* as a middle space, Galen brings to the fore the sense of health as an ever-shifting balance. This sense was central to his teaching of the "whole art," and yet it was one that could best be conveyed only indirectly, by setting up a system of signs that was itself animated and that itself moved with the rhythm of the living body.

The equation of health with balance: elements, qualities, and the *complexio*

The direct equation of health with balance and of illness with imbalance existed in Greek thought long before Galen's time (as it existed in many other ancient cultures beside the Greco-Roman), and it is clear that he borrowed much of the general theory behind this equation from earlier authors. As the historian of medicine, Heinrich von Staden, has written of medical theory before Galen: "A restoration of the balance between excess and deficiency will result in health: this view occurs frequently in Greek medicine and is also expressed as *isonomia* or *isomoiria*, an equal balance between the various elements, humours, properties of the body, or as a climatic equilibrium, or again as the right harmony or blend of opposites

---

[51] Luis García Ballester, "Galen as Medical Practioner: Problems in Diagnosis," in *Galen: Problems and Prospects*, ed. Vivian Nutton (London: Wellcome Institute, 1981), 13–46, at 25.

enclosed in the body."[52] In order to understand the terms Galen used and the general concepts he employed to signify health/balance, as they were translated into Latin (*aequalitas, coequale, medium, symmetria, temperamentum, mediocritas, moderatum,* etc.) it is helpful to consult the writings of his predecessors, particularly Hippocrates.

The Hippocratic corpus consists of sixty or so medical treatises written by a series of authors between the fifth and fourth centuries BCE and compiled under the name of its single eponymous author. Although there were a number of different philosophical theories circulating in these centuries concerning the physical structure of the universe, Hippocrates (standing for all the anonymous authors in the series) from the beginning adopted the theory of the four elements, and this theory then played a central role in the Hippocratic teachings on the composition and function of the human body. The theory held that everything existing on this earth and under the sphere of the moon was composed of a mixture of four primary elements: earth, water, air, and fire. Each of the elements in turn possessed a mixture of two out of the four natural qualities: hot, cold, wet, and dry. Thus, earth was essentially cold and dry; water was cold and wet; air was hot and wet; fire was hot and dry. The qualities possessed by each of the four elements determined not only their "form" but their activity, both in relation to the objects into which they were mixed in various propor-tions, and in relation to each other. Creation and change in the world were thought to be the product of the dynamic interaction between the four elements activated by the four primary qualities or "powers."[53]

In this scheme, heat and cold were conceived as "contraries," as were wet and dry. Not only did the presence of one contrary come at the expense of the other, but they were also theorized to be in constant opposition and tension, each working to overcome the other. Change in both the philosophical and the physiological sense was imagined as a product of the tension built into the mixtures of the elements and their

---

[52] Von Staden, *Herophilus*, 98. For a statement by Aristotle equating health with balance, see *De partibus animalum* [648b4]: "Thus, bodily health would be displayed when the body as a whole (and each of its parts) achieved and maintained a suitable balance (*symmmetria*) among its qualities."

[53] Jacques Jouanna reminds us that the Greek term "dunamis" carries the meaning of "force" or "power," which is only poorly conveyed through its Latin translation as "qualitas" and its English translation as "quality." Thus in the Hippocratic texts and after, the primary qualities contain within them not only the sense of action and activity, but of mutual opposition and struggle, even of war. See Jouanna's comments to Charlotte Schubert's article, "Menschenbild und Normwandel in der klassischen Zeit," in *Médecine et morale dans l'antiquité*, ed. Hellmut Flashar *et al.* (Geneva: Fondation Hardt, 1997), 121–55, esp. 154.

contrary qualities. The system of the four elements and four primary qualities might seem rather simplistic to the modern reader, but from the pre-Socratics through Plato, Aristotle, and the Hippocratic authors, through Galen, through the Islamic and Christian Middle Ages, past the Renaissance and into the seventeenth century, this system proved so plastic and was elaborated with such extraordinary subtlety (by Galen and others), that it was accepted, virtually without question, as the basis of all physical structure and activity in the terrestrial realm, including, importantly, that of the animal body.[54]

In theory, none of the four elements existed in its pure state but was always proportioned to each of the others as part of a mixture. An element might predominate proportionally, but it was always in mixture with the other three. Thus the earth beneath our feet was not pure elemental earth but a mixture predominated by the element earth; similarly for the air, water, and fire we experience. This held true both for the totality of the object world and for the animal body.[55] Blood for example, although obviously wet, was also blended with portions of earth, air, and fire, in due proportion; wetness and heat predominated in blood (as the doctor's sense experience indicated), but lesser proportions of their contraries, dryness and cold were also present. Like every other substance within the body, like the body in its totality, blood had its own proper *mixture* ("proper" defined in regard to its function), and its own proper proportional balance of the elemental qualities. As long as, and insofar as this proportional balance was maintained, the blood (or liver, or brain, or bones, or ligaments, etc.) were healthy.

A number of words and concepts keep coming up in Galen's elaboration of elemental theory: elements, qualities, mixtures, proportions, proportional equalities. Galen, following the Hippocratic school, united these into a single concept and term, *krasis*, which, beginning in the twelfth century, the Latins translated as *complexio*, and which in modern English can be rendered by the terms "balanced mixture," "proportionally balanced blend," or "temperament." The *complexio*, then, is a balanced blend (for Galen always a proportional blend) of the primary qualities (hot, cold, wet, and dry) that results from the mixture of the primary elements within the living body as a whole and in each of its

---

[54] Galen's fullest exposition of the theory of the elements and qualities is found in his *De elementis secundum Hippocratem*, English translation, *On the Elements According to Hippocrates*, ed. and trans. Phillip de Lacy (Berlin: Akademie Verlag, 1996).

[55] *Ibid.*, 97–101.

working parts.[56] The description by Luis García Ballester of Galen's notion of *complexio* does full justice to the central place of balance within it:

The quantitative and qualitative balance of the body as a whole, and of each of its parts, was to receive the name of *complexio*, or the more precisely expressed form of *equalis complexio*, balanced complexion, so as to distinguish it from the *inequalis* form.[57]

Yet another critical idea attached to the *complexio* is that in addition to its generality (each species of plant and animal – man, dog, bee, etc. – has its own proper complexion), it is also highly individual (i.e., this particular man, this dog, this bee), and its individuality is further extended to comprehend the changing conditions particular to every living body (i.e., this adolescent male living in this climate, at this time of the year, etc.). Nancy Siraisi expresses this element of individuality particularly well:

Among human beings, furthermore, each person was endowed with his or her own innate complexion: this was an essential identifying characteristic acquired at the moment of conception and in some way persisting throughout life. In this sense, complexion was a fundamental organizing principle of each individual human organism considered as a whole.[58]

Relativity and the "well-blended complexion" (*eucraton*)

In myriad ways, Galen used the concept of *krasis* (*complexio*) to refine, expand and thoroughly relativize the understanding of equality, proportionality, and balance in the *Tegni*.[59] At the beginning of the *Tegni*, Galen devotes a concise section (a short paragraph in Latin editions) to defining both the healthy body (*sanum corpus*) and the sick body (*egrum corpus*) *essentially* in terms of balance (*aequalitas*), whether its possession or its

---

[56] The best introduction to the role of the elements, qualities, and complexions in Galenic medical theory is Nancy Siraisi, *Medieval and Early Renaissance Medicine: An Introduction to Knowledge and Practice* (University of Chicago Press, 1990). For the central place of proportionality in Galen's conception of the complexion, *ibid.*, 101.

[57] Luis García Ballester: "*Artifex factivus sanitatis*: Health and Medical Care in Medieval Latin Galenism," in *Knowledge and the Scholarly Medical Traditions*, ed. Donald Bates (Cambridge University Press, 1995), 127–50, 137.

[58] Siraisi, *Medieval and Early Renaissance Medicine*, 102.

[59] Relativity (and relativist thinking) is a prime component of the "new" model of equilibrium that takes shape at the end of the thirteenth century. Compare the relativity employed by Galen here in the *Tegni* to the relativity applied to scholastic economic thought in Chapters 1 and 2 above; to the relativity applied to political thought by Jean de Jandun and Marsilius of Padua in Chapters 5 and 6 below; and to the relativity employed in scholastic natural philosophy by Jean Buridan and Nicole Oresme in Chapter 8 below.

lack.[60] A body, he writes, is generally healthy, when (a) from birth it enjoys a well-blended complexion (*eucraton*) in each of its primary parts (e.g., its blood, bone, muscle, cartilage, etc.) and its organs (e.g., its heart, liver, brain, etc.) and when (b) the organs composed of the primary parts exist in a relation of balance/equality (*coequale*) to each other and to the body as a whole.[61] Continuing on this theme, he notes that "The absolutely healthy body is that which is called "*eucraton*," "which he further defines as that body which from its very conception has maintained balance (*temperamentum*) within and between its primary members (*secundum temperamentum complexionis membrorum suorum*)."[62]

Galen has presented us here with three physiological levels of the body, from its base constituent elements and their qualities, through its material components, to its most complex working parts, all of which must be in balance, and remain in balance, both within themselves and each to each, for the body to be determined healthy. And what is already a complicated and many-layered conception of bodily balance is soon to become even more so. Immediately after Galen identifies health with both the well-balanced complexion (*eucraton*) and the maintenance of a working balance (*coequale*) between the body's parts, he finds it necessary to qualify what the reader should understand by the very terms "balanced complexion" and "equality" when applied to real (as opposed to ideal) human bodies.[63] Real bodies, he maintains, are never purely and always healthy (*simpliciter/absolute*); they are, at best, "healthy now" (*ut nunc*). The body that is "healthy now" does indeed possess balance (*temperantia*) and co-equality among its parts, but he adds this crucial qualification: "neither balance nor equality are to be conceived in terms of some abstract optimum, but rather in terms of what is proper (or optimum) relative to

---

[60] Although Galen makes use of the four humors and their proportional balance in his explanation of the body's functioning, the *complexio* and the proportions of the four qualities that define it are considerably more central to his physiological theory than are the humors. Ottosson writes (*Tegni*, 134): "The four humours are certainly also connected with the combined distemperaments in the Galenic theory, but it is the qualities, and not the humours as such, which are the vital factors." I discuss the relationship between the qualities and the humors in Galen's system further below.

[61] K, 1: 309–10; *Antiqua*, 10rb: "Sanum est simpliciter corpus *eucraton* quidem existens ex generatione: ex primis etiam simplicibus particulis; coequale vero his que ex his componuntur organicis."

[62] *Arabica*, 177r: "Dico ergo quod corpus sanum absolute est illud quod nominatur *eucraton*. Et illud quod nominatur absolute *eucraton* est illud cuius fabricatio ex principio creationis in ventre matris suae est secundum temperamentum complexionis membrorum suorum simplicium primorum ... primorum, et aequalitatem compositionis instrumentorum compositorum ex illis."

[63] On the emphasis Galen places on how things actually work, see Hankinson, "Epistemology," 180.

each particular body."[64] In Galen's system, which is directed toward the treatment of real individual bodies, neither balance, nor equality, nor health itself can be treated by the physician as absolute, uniform, or universally applicable goals or states. Optimum balance does indeed equal optimum health, *but only relative to the optimum that can be achieved within each particular body or each particular part*; and as each body is different from every other, so the optimum balance for each body, determined relatively, is also always different. He writes:

> Now, since there are not just one, but many kinds of healthy bodies – as distinguished above – each will have its own cause of preservation, since, conversely, every cause is a cause in relation (*ad aliquid*) to a particular object.[65]

We are not used to thinking of balance, much less of equality, in these relativized and shifting terms. This would have been even truer for Galen's contemporaries in the Hellenistic world, and truer still for his Latin Christian readers in the twelfth and thirteenth centuries. No mechanical scale could possibly function on these principles. And yet Galen will argue at various points in this single text that age, sex, geography, occupation, climate, season, personal habits, mental, moral, and emotional states, and a host of other shifting factors, might all affect which "balance" and which "*aequalitas*" is optimal at any given time, within any given environment, for any given individual. In Galen's view, the doctor is called on first and foremost to cure individuals, or as he often reminds his readers: "The cure comes first."[66] The physician is successful in his art insofar as he can effect individual cures, not insofar as his definitions have philosophical (i.e., universal) validity.

In the pursuit of every cure, the doctor must rely heavily on his senses of touch, sight, taste, and smell. Galen was quite aware of the pervasive distrust of the senses in the intellectual culture of his day, particularly in the realm of philosophy.[67] He never, however, failed to stress the crucial role of sense-based judgment in the doctor's way of knowing.[68]

---

[64] K, I: 310; *Antiqua*, 10rb: "[Sanum ut nunc est] secundum quod sanum est *eucraton* et coequale; non secundum optimam eucrasiam et coaequalitatem, sed propriam ipsius sani corporis." *Arabica*, 177r: "verumtamen ipsius temperantia et ipsius equalitas non sunt secundum meliorem dispositionem equalitatis, sed est ei temperantia proprium."

[65] K, I: 366; *Arabica*, 198v: "quoniam omnis causa non est causa nisi per semitam comparationis ad aliquid." *Antiqua*, 13va: "Cum igitur sit non unum sanum corpus: sed plura quemadmodum determinatum est prius: secundum unum quodque eorum erit conservativa: quoniam et omnis causa ad aliquid est."

[66] *De locis affectis*, 2.10, cited in García Ballester, "Galen as a Medical Practitioner," 13–46, at 13.

[67] This was even truer for the scholastic culture that received his writings.

[68] On the emphasis Galen places on sense knowledge and his positive judgments concerning its reliability, see Hankinson, "Epistemology," 165–9.

Throughout his writings, he argues that while the physician must rely on philosophy for the knowledge of universal first principles, which transcend particular cases and the senses themselves, he must at the same time continually bring the abstractions of theory into line with the stark transience and particularity of the human body, which can only be known through the senses. His recognition that the proportionally balanced "blend" of qualities that produces health (the physician's standard and goal) must always be considered relative to the ever-changing individual body, necessitated that an extraordinary delicacy and complexity be built into his modeling of balance.

Reading the body as a system in dynamic equalization: the necessary role of approximation and estimation

After his preliminary discussion of the composition of healthy, sick, and "neither" bodies, Galen turns to consider the signs each of these offer the practicing physician. The ability to "read" and correctly interpret the signs of the body lies at the foundation of the physician's art, yet Galen is brutally and consistently honest about the difficulties of this task. External signs can provide, at best, only an approximation of what is actually taking place in the body's invisible interior. And the signs themselves are often ambiguous and difficult to interpret. Rather than attempt to construct an abstract model to fix, regularize, and render them more "knowable" in the philosophical sense, Galen takes them on their own terms by marshaling a cluster of conceptual elements. Chief among these are relativity, gradation, approximation, and estimation. All are predicated on the abandonment of the absolute. Unstable in themselves, they are well matched to the instability of the body and its signs.[69]

Even though the signs the body presents to the physician are often ambiguous and in the "neither" state, the doctor must learn to read them. In order to do so, he must learn how to recognize shapes in a perpetually foggy landscape; he must learn to sense the speed and anticipate the directions of the body's motions toward or away from health; and this requires an ever greater refinement of the doctor's sense of balance. Just several paragraphs after his first discussion of the healthy (balanced) body, he recapitulates with slight expansion:

---

[69] For the importance of approximation and estimation as ways of knowing within the new model of equilibrium, see the list of the model's components in the Introduction, and note their appearance in every discourse under consideration.

The sign of the healthiest bodies is that they are equally [proportionally] balanced in their members (*aequalitas membrorum*) with respect to the four elemental qualities: heat, cold, dryness, and wetness; and that there is an equality in the organic members (*aequalitas membrorum*) in terms of their quantity, construction, number, and the form of their component parts, both with respect to their instrumental functions and in their relationship to the whole.[70]

But what are the signs of this essential equality? How does the physician recognize the balanced state (*aequalitas/medium/mediocritas*) proper to each individual part, organ, and member within each individual body? This is a question that concerned Galen greatly. Here in the *Tegni* his first answer is admirably concise and admirably honest in its notable imprecision.

With respect to the sense of touch, a middle ground (*mediocritas/aequalitas*[71]) between hardness and softness; with respect to the sense of sight, good color; with respect to smoothness and roughness, a middle ground (*mediocritas/aequalitas*); and with respect to function, perfect performance, which we call "virtue."[72]

If these are the beacons Galen can offer the physician in the sea of ambiguity and change, they are dim indeed. There is no escaping that both the signs of health and the instruments the physician possesses to "read" them are those proper to a world of approximation. The doctor must be trained to draw conclusions from them as best he can. He must use the sensitive fingers and palm of his hand, his visual sense of color gradation, his "sense" of correct function, even his aesthetic sense, to recognize the various qualitative mid-points and "equalities" that indicate health.

Approximation and estimation by means of the measuring latitude (*latitudo*)

Sick bodies fall away from the balance of health (*laesio in complexione membrorum*) in various degrees, resulting in varying impairments of function, and all these, too, must be estimated by the physician through their signs.[73] His primary task is to restore balance to the body that has lost

---

[70] K, I: 314–15; *Arabica*, 179r: "A substantia quidem ipsa tunc, quando corpus est secundum meliorem formam. Nam ex signis eius est aequalitas membrorum eius partium similium, in calore, et frigore, humiditate, et siccitate; et aequalitas membrorum eius instrumentalium in quantitatibus partium, ex quibus sunt composita, et numero eorum, et forma cuiuslibet partium, et in loco, et forma instrumentalis totius, et loco eius."

[71] Where the *translatio antiqua* has "mediocritas," the *translatio arabica* (179r) has "aequalitas."

[72] K, I: 315; *Antiqua*, 10va: "quantum quidem ad tactum in diuritia et molitia mediocritas: quantum vero ad visum bonus color: et secundum lenitatem et asperitatem mediocritas, secundum vero effecta perfectio quam et virtutem eorum nominamus."

[73] K, I: 315; *Arabica*, 179r: "in similes partes habentium lapsa sunt a temperantia."

it. In expanding upon this idea in the *Tegni*, Galen brings in a concept central to many of his writings – that of the latitude of health (*latitudo sanitatis*) – which beautifully expresses the world of relativity, proportionality, gradation, and approximation he must teach the physician to inhabit.[74] The *latitudo sanitatis* underscores the continual necessity on the part of the physician to approximate the distances which separate the particular member or body from the healthy balance proper to them, and it renders the notion of distance concrete and semi-sensible as a linear continuum open to quantified gradation. Since the latitude can be so readily visualized, its use as a concept permits Galen to deepen and compound the sensitivity to motion, measurement, and gradation so central to his diagnostic project. No sooner does he introduce the notion of a "latitude" of health than we find that this latitude is itself divided into three, with each of the three states – health, sickness, and "neither" – possessing its own proper latitude.

The latitude of health as a whole is divided into three parts, each of which has its own latitude; the first is [a latitude] of healthy bodies, the second is of "neither" bodies, the third of sick bodies.[75]

Perfect health, in Galenic theory, exists as a theoretical abstraction. Yes, the doctor must be able to consider (or "think with") the notion of perfect health, but he does so primarily so that he can form relative judgments as to how particular approximative states relate to theoretical ideals.[76] In distinction to attitudes common to much of pre-modern thought, the "failure" of the ideal in Galen's writings is not merely attributable to the failure of the senses to grasp it. His point is that in the world of living bodies, there is no ideal, there are no perfections to grasp. The individual body is always becoming, always in motion either toward or away from balance/health on numerous levels, and it is the individual body which must be cured. Galen recognizes that when the body is moving from health in the direction of sickness, there is a range within which it might

---

[74] Applying and thinking in terms of approximative latitudes rather than precise points is another of the prime components of the new model of equilibrium. Compare Galen's conceptualization and use of the measuring latitude here in the *Tegni* to its use by Peter Olivi in his analysis of price and value in the marketplace in Chapters 1 and 2 above, and its pervasive use in scholastic speculations on nature in Chapter 8 below.

[75] K, I: 316–17; *Antiqua*,10va–b: "Et dividitur totius sanitatis latitudo in tres partes latitudinem habentes: et ipsam multam quarum quidem prima erit sanorum corporum, secunda vero neutrorum, tertia egrorum." *Arabica*, 179v: "Sic ergo latitudo totius sanitatis dividitur in tres partes."

[76] Boudon, *L'Art médical*, 401. The complex diagram of the *latitudo sanitatis* offered in Joutsivuo, *Neutrum*, 156, provides a good indication of how seriously medieval readers took this concept.

still "appear" healthy, because the signs still remain within the latitude of health; similarly there is a range within which the signs of the sick body moving toward health might still appear to fall within the latitude of sickness. Like the mid or "neither" state Galen posited at the opening of the *Tegni*, the concept of the latitude serves yet again to sensitize the physician to the perception of motion between health and sickness and to refine yet further his sense of the body's perpetual flux along this "latitude."[77] Indeed, Galen specifically refers to the separation between sickness and health as a quantifiable "distance," thus explicitly identifying the motion between sickness and health with motion across space.[78]

Galen's "latitude" represents not only the space (real, conceptual, and didactic) that exists within each of the three categories (health, sickness, and neither), but it also reifies the irreducible fact that the approximative range is all the physician really has to work with. The multiform ever-transient body can approach or depart from, but never arrive at, a singular balancing *point* designated as perfect health. For Galen, health itself, when considered in the individual case, must be understood as a continuum or *latitude*, rather than as a point or a singular perfection to be achieved.[79] Within the Galenic model, the consistent direction is from perfections to approximations, from absolute to relativized determinations, and from balancing points to gradable latitudes of equalization.[80] Each of these directions came to characterize the "new model of equilibrium" as it emerged in the last quarter of the thirteenth century.

The introductory section of the *Tegni* ends with Galen's elucidation of the concept of the latitude, at which point his exposition becomes considerably more complex in outline and more technical

---

[77] On this linkage, see Van der Lugt, "Neither Ill nor Healthy," 17–18: "the notions of complexion, of health as a scale, and the neutrum serve the same purpose. They reflect Galen's individualistic and relativistic conception of health."

[78] K, I: 317–18; *Antiqua*, 10vb: "Hec signa ergo eorumque sanantur corporum: sed egrorum sanorum et neutrorum existentium *quantitate distantie* differunt nobis ponentibus duos extremos terminos contrarios alter utrum optimam secundum compositionem et nunc factam egritudinem; considerantibus vero cui horum sint viciniora que probantur corpora" (my emphasis). *Arabica*, 180r: "Corporum autem quorum operationes debilitantur, tunc, si illa debilitas *elongatur longitudine multa valde a dispsitione sanorum*, discretio facilis est; et si *elongatur pauca longitudine*, tunc in esse eorum est ambiguitas" (my emphasis).

[79] As Galen writes in his treatise *On the Best Constitution of our Body* (ed. Penella and Hall, 293), "health is not something narrow or absolutely simple or indivisible, but rather is capable of wide variation."

[80] Compare to Olivi's model of equalization applied to market exchange in Chapters 1 and 2 above. Galen will still sometimes use phrases like "precisely balanced" or "perfectly balanced," but the very indeterminacy of the signs that indicate these states, e.g., "hair reasonably fair and generally curled," make clear that the balance indicated can never be more than approximate.

in detail.[81] Signs and times and states and causes are divided and subdivided and divided again (and again) as Galen descends from the general into a discussion of the particular parts of particular bodies, offering literally hundreds of his observations of bodily signs along with their proper interpretation. As Galen teaches the physician how to diagnose the signs of health in the brain, heart, liver, and testicles; in the nerves, arteries, and ducts; in the bones, ligaments, fat, flesh, blood, etc., he also continually reminds him of the approximative conceptual world within which he must learn to function. From this point on, rather than follow the course of Galen's exposition in the order he presented it, I turn to consider how he applies the cluster of terms and concepts he has already introduced pertaining to health/balance, such as (in their Latin translations) *complexio*, *crasis*, *eucraton*, *temperantia*, *aequalitas*, *coequalitas*, *medium*, *proportionalitas*, *latitudo*, and how by doing so he deepens and refines his modeling of balance itself.

The place of relativity and relational thinking in Galen's model of bodily equalization

Galen conceives of the body as a working whole, which is to say, as an ever-shifting relational system. It is not only that the body's parts function in relation to one another and to the whole, but, more importantly, that parts continually *move* and *change* in relation to each other within the whole. Motion itself is "in relation" in Galen's system. And Galen's relativity extends yet further (or deeper), past the interior structure and motion of the body, to encompass the body's ever-changing relationship to the world surrounding and impinging upon it. For Galen, changes occurring within the body (the primary focus of the physician's attention) can be understood only when viewed in relation to the body's physical, social, and moral environment.[82] For this reason, both therapeutic cure and the maintenance of health often require that the doctor prescribe a healthful "regimen" to regulate the relationship between the individual

---

[81] The highly condensed introductory section occupies less than one full folio from the 1490 edition.

[82] In recognizing the importance of "environmental" factors on health and of the doctor's responsibility to monitor and adjust these in the pursuit of healing, Galen was drawing directly on Hippocratic writings, especially the *Epidemics*, and *De aere aquis locis* (*Airs, Waters, and Places*), on both of which he wrote commentaries. "Moral" here, in the Galenic sense, corresponds roughly to "emotional" in the modern sense. On the bodily effects of the passions, Galen writes in the *Tegni* (K, I: 371; trans. Singer, 376): "Obviously one must refrain from excess of all affections of the soul: anger, grief, pride, fear, envy, and worry; for these will change the natural composition of the body."

body and its environment. In the long medical tradition that followed Galen's writings, the list of "environmental" factors impinging on health came to be standardized and known under the heading "the non-naturals" (*res non naturales*). Galen provides a list of these factors in the *Tegni*:

And if we make a classification of all the necessary factors which alter the body, to each of these will correspond a specific type of healthy cause. One category is contact with the ambient air; another is motion and rest of the body as a whole or of its individual parts. The third is sleep and waking; the fourth, substances taken; the fifth, substances voided or retained; the sixth, what happens to the soul. *The body cannot but be altered and changed in relation to all these causes* (my emphasis).[83]

Rather than a mere addendum to his focus on the body's interior, considerations of "external" factors were indispensable to Galen's therapeutic system.[84] By means of the non-naturals, Galen posited an interactive relationship between interior and exterior, between the body's contents and its ever-changing contexts.[85] Changes in the external environment were directly tied to the body's interior *complexiones* – the proportional balance of the four qualities that regulates the health of each part of the body as well as the body as a whole. By emphasizing the causal, ever-shifting relationships between external factors and internal states, Galen expanded his pivotal notion of balance beyond the individual body to encompass the living system of the body in the world. In García Ballester's words, "health [was] here being regarded as a balance between the individual's body and the environment – in the widest sense of the word – in which he or she moved on a daily basis."[86]

Having established the conception of this grand, ever-shifting balance, Galen then places it within a fully relational context by showing how each regimen the doctor might prescribe must be carefully proportioned to a particular body's particular needs at a particular time. What is healthful

---

[83] K, I: 367–8; (trans. Singer, 374, with last line modified), *Arabica*, 199r: "quia necesse est corpori, ut alteretur at mutetur ab omnibus istis causis."

[84] García Ballester, "'Six Non-Natural Things' in Galen," 105: "a substantial part of the causal and therapeutic system of Galenic pathology was based on them, while, at the same time, all the preventive doctrine for the preservation of health was built on them." García Ballester has found Galen's fullest and clearest exposition of the "non-natural things" in his *Epidemics* VI, a commentary on a Hippocratic work.

[85] García Ballester, "*Artifex*," 134.

[86] *Ibid.* The full list of external factors impinging on health considered by Galen extends to include the effects of reading, writing, performing calculations, walking before and after meals, clothes worn, adornment, condition of the house and interiors in which life is spent, frequency of sexual intercourse, and, of course, "affections of the soul" like anger, envy, worry, and terror. On this, see García Ballester, "'Six Non-Natural Things' in Galen," 109–10, and "Soul and Body: Disease of the Soul and Disease of the Body in Galen's Medical Thought," in *Le opere psicologiche di Galeno*, ed. Paola Manuli and Mario Vegetti (Naples: Bibliopolis, 1988), 117–52.

in one context may well be poisonous in another; what cures one individual may sicken another. He provides the following example: when the body is in need of motion, exercise is healthy and rest morbid; at other times rest is healthy and exercise morbid. He then extends this principle to eating, drinking, and virtually all other applications of regimen to the body.[87] And there is yet another level of balance and relativization to follow. In the best forms of exercise, the parts of the body "will be moved in proportion" (*proportionaliter moventur*), so that no part is worked either too hard or not hard enough. Food and drink, too, should be of the "best-balanced kinds, these being the most appropriate to the best-balanced natures (*maxime convenientia eucratis naturis*).[88]

What we have, then, are three nested systems: the immensely complex working system of the body, the system encompassing the body in its ever-changing environment, and the dynamic relationship between the body and the healing *medicus*, each working to maintain itself in balance, and each shot through with relativized elements and determinations. There is not a comfortably fixed or absolute component attached to any of them. As the old story goes, "It's relativity all the way down." Even the question of the physician's certainty has been relativized. He can never be fully certain of his diagnoses or his prescriptions, but if he is well trained and practiced in Galenic principles, his analysis will certainly be more certain than those put forward by the empirics, who have no belief or education in physical theory, just as it will be more certain than those put forward by doctors who imagine they can be guided entirely by theory and what they can read in books.[89] In reading the *Tegni*, one senses that Galen intended his readers to perceive the whole of his teaching, and thus the whole of the body's systematic activity, to be floating on a sea of relativity.

The place of proportion and proportional thinking in Galen's model of systematic equalization

"Proportion" is a word that appears continually throughout Galen's exposition in the *Tegni*. His multifaceted manipulation of proportionality is, in turn, closely tied to his relativized view of the body's structures and functions. A proportion is in essence a relation, and in Galen's thought it is a relation in constant flux, as it must be if it is to match the living

---

[87] K, I: 369; *Arabica*, 200r.   [88] K, I: 372; (trans. Singer, 376), *Antiqua*, 13vb.

[89] For a concise analysis of Galen's position on the question of certainty, along with the continuation of this thinking in scholastic medicine, see Michael McVaugh's "Introduction," to Galen, *Tractatus De intentione medicorum*, in *Arnaldi de Villanova Opera medica omnia*, vol. V.1, ed. Michael McVaugh (Barcelona: Seminarium Historiae Medicae Granatensis, 2000), esp. 139–44, 181–7.

rhythms of the human body. Proportionality, relativity, and flux are thoroughly intertwined in his system. If we look solely at the previous section on the non-naturals, we can see (1) that the body is itself fluidly proportioned to its changing environment; (2) that the physician's choice of which environmental course to prescribe must be carefully proportioned to the body's particular constitution and its needs at a particular time; and (3) that the specific regimen or prescription (of food, exercise, etc.) must be proportionally balanced (tempered) within itself so that when attached to the body it will have the effect of counteracting the body's shifting imbalances. This is only the beginning. For Galen, proportionality and relativity go to the very core of the body's internal and external activity. Therefore sensitivity to ever-shifting proportions is one of the primary skills the physician must master. It is also, consequently, one of the primary lessons of the *Tegni*.

The degree of Galen's commitment to this concept, and the degree to which he uses the rhetorical process of division to drive it ever deeper into the reader's consciousness, can best be seen through a small sampling of his statements in one short section concerning the heart.[90] He begins with a general statement of relativity/proportionality: when we speak of greater heat, cold, dryness, or moisture of a bodily part such as the heart, these terms are relative to that part itself, not to any other (*non ad aliam aliquam comparantes*).[91] He then notes that while the proportional predominance of heat is proper to the healthy heart, still the proportion must remain within a certain proper range or there will be morbid repercussions.[92] Moreover, the qualities of the heart (or any of the other major organs – the brain, the liver, and [in the *Tegni*] the testicles) will, according to Galen, be proportioned to other related structures in the body, either from birth or as a result of continued influence and activity over time. For this reason, the doctor looking for diagnostic signs of internal and hence invisible and insensible conditions (in this case, the heart's internal heat) can find them in the externally visible proportions of related bodily structures.

Thickness of the chest, too, is a sign of heat, unless, again, the brain provides a powerful counterbalance ... For this reason, too, a small head combined with a

---

[90] On Galen's use of division as a rhetorical strategy, see Teun Tieleman, "Methodology," in *Cambridge Companion to Galen*, 49–65, esp. 62.

[91] K, I: 331–2; *Antiqua*, 11va; *Arabica*, 184r.

[92] K, I: 332; *Antiqua*, 11va; *Arabica*, 184r. He mentions specifically that an overheated heart (signalled by the presence of an excessively hairy chest) leads to bad temper and rashness. The quantity, quality, and color of hair are extremely important markers in Galen's diagnostic.

broad chest is the clearest indication of heat in the heart; while a big head combined with a small chest is a very specific indication of a cold heart.[93]

And finally (and this is central to his conceptualization of balance), relativity and proportion extend past the structure of the body to the determination of its function, motion, and even its character.

Breathing will be proportionate (*est proportionalis*) to the pulses, provided that the smallness of the chest is in proportion to the coldness of the heart; if the chest is larger than accords with the quantity of coldness (*secundum quantitatem frigiditate cordis*), the breathing will be not only smaller, but also slower and less frequent. Such people are timid by nature, lacking in courage and hesitant; their chests are smooth, without hair.[94]

Again: "It's proportion all the way down." But if approximate judgments and shifting proportions are all the physician really has to work with, then he must learn to "know" things in a way very different from the philosopher.

The doctor's way of "knowing": approximation, estimation, and conjecture

We have seen that Galen continually tries to encourage a way of seeing and knowing specific to the physician's task, using the most imaginative rhetorical methods to do so. At one point in the *Tegni*, while still in the section devoted to signs, he gives the physician's particular mode of knowing a name: "artful conjecture." Conjecture born of training and experience must suffice for the physician, given the difficulty of seeing and reading those things that the doctor nevertheless must: signs of the body's hidden *interior motion* toward or away from health, signs of the body's *interior* defects, and, most critically, signs that an interior defect is moving in the direction of morbidity. He writes:

None of the other internal parts has ever provided me with any manifest diagnostic knowledge (*manifestam cognitionem*). One must, however, attempt the diagnosis (*cognoscere*) of their virtues and defects, if not by means of an absolutely firm kind of knowledge (*disciplinam certam*), then at least by "artful" conjecture (*secundum coniecturam quandam artificialem*).[95]

---

[93] K, I: 333; (trans. Singer, 358), *Antiqua*, 11va; *Arabica*, 185r–186v.

[94] *Ibid.*: "Spiritus vero siquidem tanto minor torax sit quanto cor frigidius pulsui est proportionalis ; si vero maior fuerit secundum quantitatem frigiditate cordis non minorem tamen sed tardiorem declarat natura tales et timidi et curiosi et nudum eis pectus pilis."

[95] K, I: 353; (trans. Singer, 367, modified), *Antiqua*, 12vb: "non tamen aliorum que intrinsecus sunt manifestam cognitionem dedit mihi aliquin. Tentare tamen oportet cognoscere ut possibile est virtutem et vitium eorum; et si non secundum disciplinam certam sed secundum coniecturam quandam artificialem." *Arabica* (192r–v) substitutes the phrase "per aestimationem propinquam" for "secundum coniecturam."

Clearly, the Galenic doctor's judgments cannot be said to be arbitrary. Galen believed that his diagnoses were far superior and far more certain than those made by *medici* following other modes of observation and practice – not to mention those made by unschooled vernacular practitioners. He offers this opinion again and again throughout his writings. For Galen, the physician's education in logic and the proper theoretical principles, his thorough knowledge of anatomy, and his guided experience, provides a sufficient scientific framework for him to make reasonable "conjectures" about the particular state and prognosis of a particular body.[96] But despite his insistence that the doctor who is properly educated and trained can benefit his patients, he refuses to make the situation of uncertainty look rosier than it is. The Galenic doctor's judgments can never be more than probabilistic and approximative (*per aestimationem propinquam*).[97] By admitting the inescapable limitations of medical knowledge while at the same time claiming authority for himself and his theoretical approach, Galen both creates and names a legitimate form of knowing that differs essentially from the way of knowing offered within the Aristotelian tradition or, for that matter, within any of the philosophical traditions of his own day. At the same time, Galenic "conjecture" and *aestimatio* can, I suggest, be seen to represent yet another case of Galen's "in-betweenness," yet another case where his straddling of categories mimics the "neither" state so central to the structure of the *Tegni* and to its project of situating the *medicus* within the art. Galen makes extensive use of relativized determinations throughout his writings because they fit so well with a number of his core observations: the ever-changing proportional balance of elements and qualities within the complexion of every part of the body and the body as a whole; the ever-varying relationship of the body's "instrumental" members to each other and to the whole; and the body's ever-shifting relationship to its changing environment. But I want to suggest that relativity also served another essential function within Galen's system: he manipulated it as a tool of destabilization. He employed it as an effective antidote to the absolutism and dogmatism that most systems of knowledge have built into them but to which

---

[96] Boudon discusses Galen's use of this concept in "Art, science, et conjecture," 288–96.

[97] See above where the *translatio arabica* (192v) declares that knowledge of the body's interior signs can only be "per aestimationem propinquam." See also, García Ballester, "Galen as a Medical Practitioner," 35; and Boudon, "Art, science, et conjecture," 289–90: "La conjecture ici définie comme un moyen terme entre connaissance exacte et ignorance complète."

he was philosophically opposed.[98] In effect, relativity keeps the physician ever on his toes.

Relativity, proportionality, and the doctor's *sense* of balance

The idea of proportional relation carries with it both mathematical and aesthetic connotations, and Galen exploits each. The mathematical dimension promises a kind of precision, but the aesthetic is based in a more diffuse "sense" of how things properly fit together or work together. Training the student to recognize and allow diagnostic weight to this generalized "sense" forms a critical element of Galen's message and is central as well to his "sense" of balance. The clearest instance of the aestheticization of proportion in the *Tegni* occurs when Galen, after discussing the proportional blend of qualities proper to each of the body's major parts, turns to a discussion of the body as a whole. He first presents the most general signs of the body's overall balance, which he explicitly identifies with health. These are: a skin color (complexion in the modern sense) balanced (*mediocriter*) between red and white; blondish hair, moderately curly, "and a good balance of flesh in terms of quantity and quality (*mediocritas vero carnositatis in quantitate et qualitate*)."[99] After these most minimal of indicators, he writes: "A body thus defined, occupies a position exactly (!) midway (*medium perfecte est*) between all excesses."[100] But without further detail and precision, how are we readers and student physicians to fully recognize these various medium points and ranges?

The only conceptual guide and instrument Galen offers is a general sense of proportion, possessing both aesthetic and mathematical overtones, which he expects the doctor to share and refine through long study and experience. After yet another brief reminder that the balanced *medium*, which is ever the goal of medicine, must always be considered relatively and proportionally (*per comparationem*), he chooses a revealing illustration of the "rule" for its determination.[101] He writes: "There is no medium of the bodily qualities except those which, according to the

---

[98] For an analysis of Galen's anti-dogmatist philosophical stance, which sees him (once again) as occupying a tenuous mid-position, straddling the claims of the medical rationalists and empiricists of his day, see Michael Frede, "On Galen's Epistemology," in Nutton, *Galen: Problems and Prospects*, 65–86, esp. 68–74.

[99] K, I: 342; *Antiqua*, 12ra; *Arabica*, 189r: "et quod caro est temperata in qualitate sua et quantitate sua."

[100] K, I: 342, *Antiqua*, 12ra; *Arabica*, 189r: "quoniam hoc corpus est medium inter omnes species superfluitatum."

[101] K, I: 342; *Arabica*, 189r: "quia omnis superfluitas non dicitur nec intelligitur nisi comparatione ad ipsam [medium]."

Canon of Polyclitus, are deemed the truest and most universal."[102] Polyclitus was an ancient Greek sculptor famous for the perfection of his creations, not a physician. His treatise, the *Canon* (now lost), presented a sculptor's view of the body's ideal proportions. And it is this aestheticized proportional ideal that Galen offers as the model for the doctor, without going into any details concerning the proportions employed or the mathematics underlying them.[103]

Given the central importance of determining and restoring *aequalitas/ mediocritas* to the entire art of medicine, Galen's reticence here, his plugging of Polyclitus into the breach of uncertainty, is stunning. But after putting Polyclitus' rule forward, all Galen says in clarification is that it represented "the truest and most universal medium, neither soft nor hard, neither hot nor cold, and to sight neither hairy nor hairless, neither thick nor thin, nor any other qualitative imbalance (*intemperantia*)."[104] Despite the promise of "precision" that introduces this discussion, we are left in the realm of approximative sense and feel, no matter how highly trained and intellectualized.[105] Galen writes often that his purpose in the *Tegni* is to present a general introduction to the art rather than to offer exhaustive details, since these are provided in other books he has written, to which the reader is often referred.[106] But his restraint here is still something to marvel at: his denial to his readers of any comfortable resting place in certainty in the midst of this swirling mass of signs and observations.[107]

[102] K, I: 342; *Antiqua*, 12ra: "Nihil igitur horum est mediocre: sed quale Policleti regula ad summum venit mediocritatis universe." *Arabica*, 189r: "Et non est aliquod horum corporum aequale, sed aequale est, quod est secundum exemplum, quod preparavit Polycletis, et nominavit ipsum Canonem, qui consecutus est ultimum aequalitatis totius."

[103] Galen utilizes the example of Polyclitus again in reference to ideal proportion in the *De complexionibus*, discussed below.

[104] K, I: 342; *Antiqua*, 12ra: "ad summum venit mediocritatis universe: ut tangentibus quidem neque molle appareat neque durum neque calidum neque frigidum: videntibus vero neque pillosum neque nudum neque crassum neque gracile: aut aliquam aliam habens intemperantiam."

[105] Cf. Galen's attitude toward the "perfection" of Polyclitus' bodily proportions in his *On the Best Constitution of our Body*, 294.

[106] E.g., K, I: 394: "Our present task is not to go through every individual point, but merely to call to mind the principal points, which are elaborated in detail in other works." Also, K, I: 387.

[107] While Galen denies perfect certainty, he does believe that the good physician can attain relative certainty in his diagnoses. Hankinson expresses his in-between position in the following terms ("Epistemology,"169): "evident facts of perception, suitably rationally organized and aided by evident a priori truths, will allow us to determine the proper structure of things, in virtue of which they exhibit the symptomatic behaviour that they do."

Restoring balance (health) to the body

The task Galen sets the doctor is not only to recognize the multiple forms and degrees of bodily ill-mixture but to restore the balance of health to the body that has lost it through the active preparation and administration of medicines and curative therapies. In this role, the physician serves, quite literally, as both an animate instrument of balance, and as an animate instrument balanced between the healing power of nature and the sick body.[108] With the prescription and application of medicines, we come finally to one area in which Galen keeps open the possibility of a degree of exactitude in his science.[109] Here proportion (which again is everywhere) flirts with mathematics; here the overwhelmingly qualitative nature of Galen's teaching takes on a quasi-quantitative dimension. Accepting Galen's fundamental principle that "every excellence and deficit in the body is determined by the blend of its primary qualities (*crasis*),"[110] the doctor's primary responsibility follows: when the body or any of its parts is not of good mixture (*sit distemperatum*), these parts must be balanced in accordance with that defect.[111] In Galen's clearest theoretical statement within the *Tegni* of the physician's role in balancing cure to defect, he writes:

One fundamental mode of healing is to introduce the opposite (*contrarium*) of that which is to be corrected; all causes promoting health are of this mode ... For hot dispositions, a cold cause is the opposite, for cold dispositions, a proportionally hot one: and so on proportionally (*proportionaliter*). For if everything that is ill-proportioned (*immoderatum*) is contrary to nature, and everything that is moderate is in accord with nature, then nature requires that everything

---

[108] At a number of places in the *Tegni*, Galen claims that the doctor's role is primarily to do what is necessary in order to permit nature to perform its healing work. In this view, Nature, as the principle of order par excellence, having formed the body, exerts continual influence in the direction of health and proper function (balance), if it is permitted free action. For example (K, I: 378): "In all cases it is Nature that is the true creator, and the doctor is merely her servant."

[109] Von Staden reminds us, however, just how fraught with inexactitude, approximation, and error was this critical function of the doctor in Galen's eyes. See his "Inefficacy, Error and Failure: Galen on *dokima pharmaka aprakta*, in *Galen on Pharmacology: Philosophy, History, and Medicine*, ed. Armelle Debru (Leiden: Brill, 1997), 59–83. In this same volume, see Philip van der Eijk, "Galen's Use of the Concept of 'Qualified Experience' in his Dietetic and Pharmacological Works," 35–57.

[110] K, I: 352; *Antiqua*, 12va: "Dicta est autem in tertio de causis [the third book of his treatise, *De causis*] que unicuique potentie virtutis et vitii dominatrix crasis est."

[111] K, I: 370; (trans. Singer, 375–6), *Arabica*, 240v: "Et medicationis qua sit sanatio intentio prima communis est contrarietas rei, ad cuius solutionem et expulsionem intenditur: et omnes causae facientes sanitatem sunt huiusmodi generis." *Antiqua*, 13vb: "Quando vero sit distemperatum continens in tantam et contemperantias minui oportet in quantum eucrasia eius corrupta fuerit."

immoderate be restored to moderation (*ad moderatum reduci*) by something which is equally ill-proportioned in the contrary direction.[112]

Since the application of qualitative contraries to correct imbalances is so central to his therapeutic method, scores of examples of this process are offered in the *Tegni*. They are most generally expressed in qualitative terms, although he sometimes speaks in terms of "equal distances" along the continuum that joins two contraries (e.g., the hot and the cold), or equal distances along the continuum between health and sickness.[113]

At one point in the *Tegni*, however, Galen takes a further step toward the quantification of qualitative imbalance and cure by applying specific numbers to the proportional application of contrary to contrary. The introduction of numerical quantification at this single point in the text offers the promise of a therapeutic exactitude otherwise absent within this work. He writes:

In order to restore health, we must find a medicine that is proportional to the magnitude of the ill-balance (*proportionale magnitudini discrasie*) of the complexion, so that if, for example, a body deviates from its normal nature by a figure of ten to the hot and by a figure of seven to the dry, then the healthful cause in such cases must be ten to the cold and seven to the moist.[114]

---

[112] K, I: 381; (trans. Singer, 381, modified), *Antiqua*, 14vb: "Curatio vero unum quidem habet modum. Et maxime communem intentionem ei scilicet quod solvendum est contrarium, huius enim generis sunt omnes perficientes salutem causae ... Calidae igitur dispositioni frigida causa contraria est, frigidae vero calida et aliis proportionaliter. Si enim immoderatum omne praeter naturam, moderatum vero secundum naturam, vero secundum naturam necesse est omne immoderatum ab immoderato secundum contrarium ad moderatum reduci." *Arabica*, 204v: "Quod est, quia, cum sit omne, quod est egrediens ab natura inaequale : et omne quod est naturale aequale sit, oportet necessario, quod res egredientes ab aequalitate non redeant ad aequalitatem nisi ex re alia egrediente ab aequalitate ei contraria."

[113] E.g., K, I: 374; *Antiqua*, 14ra: "Equale vero distans ab altera crasi eucratarum et mediarum que optimis naturis convenire."

[114] K, I: 383; (trans. Singer, 382, modified), *Antiqua*, 14va: "Secundum vero compositas discrasias ex simplicibus compositio ostenditur salubria precepta et hic habentibus nobis proportionale magnitudini discrasie ad illam conveniens invenire medicamen. velut si ita acciderit. si. x. quidem numeris secundum calidius excedit aliquid ab eo quod est secundum naturam, septem vero secundum siccius esse oportet: et salubrem causam in talibus dispositionibus frigidiorum, x. quidem numeris, vii. vero humidiorem." Note the absence in the *translatio antiqua* (and in the Kühn text) of the technical term "degree" (*gradus*) in connection to the numbers provided here by Galen. Note, too, that both the *translatio arabica*, and the early commentary by Ibn Ridwan apply the term *gradus* in this context. *Arabica*, 206r: "Et exemplum illius est, ut ponas quod membrum aliquod mutatur ab complexione sua naturali, et declinat ad caliditatem *decem gradus*, et ad siccitatem septem. Oportet ergo ut sint in causa sanante hoc membrum ex frigore *decem gradus*, et in ea ex humiditate *septem gradus*" (My emphasis). I am grateful to David Reisman for having confirmed that the Arabic technical term for degree appears as well in Hunain's Arabic translation of the *Tegni* at this point. See the following chapter for Ibn Ridwan's extensive use of the technical term and concept of degree.

It is here, with the application of mathematics to proportion for the prescription of medicines, that, beginning in the later thirteenth century, medieval medical writers made some of their most important additions to Galen.[115] I hope, however, it is clear that they, along with other innovators in other disciplines in this period, had been bequeathed an extraordinary foundation on which to build. They had access to a model of equalization that succeeded in integrating into a logically coherent system a host of potentially destabilizing elements, from the perpetual clash of oppositional elements and forces, to the ceaseless motion back and forth along continuous latitudes, to a thoroughgoing relativity and proportionality applied both to the body's functions and its relation to its environments. It was a model grounded in approximative determinations discernible only through educated conjecture, whose efficacy as a form of knowledge was confirmed by Galen's authoritative example. Where Galen applied these elements to the analysis of the body and its workings, scholastic authors who came to share in the new model of equilibrium would see their applicability to many other complex equalizing systems, such as the workings of the marketplace, the city, and the cosmos itself.

As I conclude this section on the *Tegni*, I think it well to reiterate that Galen intended this text to fulfill a very particular task within his vast oeuvre. It was constructed as an introduction, as an encapsulation, as an attempt to capture the rhythm of the living human body through the use of words and rhetorical strategies. Every element underscores the doctor's exceptionally delicate task of reading the body's ever-shifting signs and states and of balancing them, when necessary, with appropriate cures through the principle of proportional equalization. Since it was intended as a compact introduction, the details it provides in any given area are (as Galen specifically announces) a fraction of those found in more sizeable works he dedicated specifically to these areas. For this reason, certain of its elements are somewhat exaggerated in the *Tegni* with respect to his

---

[115] See, in particular, the notable expansion and quantification of Galen's principle of cure by contraries in the writings of the late thirteenth-century *medicus*, Arnau de Vilanova, discussed in Chapter 4. The pharmaceutical examples Galen presents in the *Tegni* receive deeper and more detailed exposition in the treatises he specifically dedicated to pharmacology, particularly his *De simplicium medicamentorum facultatibus et temperamentis* and *De compositione medicamentorum secundum genera*. On this subject, see Owsei Temkin, "Galenicals and Galenism in the History of Medicine," in *The Impact of Antibiotics on Medicine and Society*, ed. Iago Galdston (New York: International Universities Press, 1958), 18–37; Alain Touwaide, "La thérapeutique médicamenteuse de Dioscoride à Galien: du pharmaco-centrisme au médico-centrisme," in *Galen on Pharmacology*, ed. Debru, 255–82. Touwaide argues for a conceptual "revolution" in the less than a century that separated Galen's writings from those of Dioscorides.

other writings, including the near-obsessive return to balance/*aequalitas* in all its forms. But it is precisely this focus which makes the *Tegni* so powerful as a teaching text. And since it was the most widely read and studied of the Galenic texts in the thirteenth and fourteenth centuries, it provides us with our clearest vision of the totality of the model of Galenic balance available to university students and scholars in the period that saw the emergence and evolution of the new model of equilibrium.

The Galenic model of equalization *in nuce*: the complexion

If there is one element within Galen's presentation of the body in balance that can be taken to represent and recapitulate the whole *in nuce*, it is the complexion (*krasis, complexio*). In itself, the *complexio* functions as the base unit for the proportional balancing of the four primary qualities, which, in turn, determines bodily health or sickness. In Galenic theory, in addition to the complexion that is proper to the body as a whole, there is a separate complexion proper to each one of the body's many functional parts, with each of these myriad complexions having its own proportional "blend" of the four elements and qualities proper to its particular function. This is to say that not only the body as a whole, but each of its functional parts, possesses its own proper balance determined in relation to its proper function. Galen refers to complexions often in the *Tegni*, but they are never fully delineated since he assumes that the reader will go (or will have gone) to his other more specialized works for details concerning them.[116] Fortunately for our purposes of assessing Galen's influence on scholastic thought of the thirteenth and fourteenth centuries, his primary work on the complexions, the *De complexionibus*, was also translated from the Greek in the mid twelfth century, making it among the earliest of Galen's works available in Latin.[117]

Although the Latin translation of the *De complexionibus* (sometimes titled *De temperamentis*) was roughly contemporary with the translation of the *Tegni*, there were considerable differences in their reception

---

[116] The concluding section of the *Tegni* is a short essay by Galen introducing the reader to his previous writings and suggesting an order in which they should be read. Of his more detailed medical works, the *De complexionibus*, along with the *De elementis secundum Hippocratem*, are the first he suggests reading (K, I: 407), which speaks to their foundational status.

[117] The text to which I will primarily refer is Richard Durling's edition of this twelfth-century Latin translation from the Greek, *Galenus Latinus: Burgundio of Pisa's Translation of Galen's Peri Kraseon "De complexionibus"* (Berlin: Walter de Gruyter, 1976). For the Latin translation of this work from the Arabic, see below.

histories and in their volume of circulation. Since the *Tegni* was attached to the *Articella* by the early thirteenth century, it circulated widely as the *Articella* assumed the status of medical textbook, occupying a central place within the medical curriculum from the late twelfth century through the fourteenth century and beyond. The *De complexionibus* on the other hand, although circulating in Latin manuscript, was one of thirty-five or so Galenic texts which, while translated relatively early, and while representing Galenic medicine in far more detail than the *Tegni*, nevertheless only began to find a place within the medical school curriculum at the end of the thirteenth century.[118] Indeed, the very slowness with which these important technical works were received into the medical curriculum suggests that there were difficulties attached to reading and fully comprehending Galen's writings, difficulties that had to be overcome, and were overcome, only over the course of the thirteenth century.[119]

There are, however, two notable similarities between the reception history of the *De complexionibus* and the *Tegni:* both circulated in two versions, one translated from the Greek and one translated later from the Arabic, and both owed their Arabic translation to Gerard of Cremona. In the section that follows, I cite Galen primarily from the Latin text of Burgundio of Pisa's translation from the Greek. Where Gerard's translation from the Arabic differs in tone or meaning, I cite it as well.[120]

---

[118] García Ballester refers to this group of treatises as "the new Galen," in "The New Galen: A Challenge to Latin Galenism in Thirteenth-Century Montpellier," in *Text and Tradition: Studies in Ancient Medicine and its Transmission,* ed. Klaus-Dietrich Fischer *et al.* (Leiden: Brill, 1998), 55–83; reprinted in *Galen and Galenism: Theory and Medical Practice from Antiquity to the European Renaissance,* ed. Luis García Ballester and John Arrizabalaga (Aldershot: Ashgate, 2002), 55–83. In 1309, Montpellier (through the influence of Arnau de Vilanova) became the first medical school to require the study of the *De complexionibus* and certain other works within this group, including the *De malicia complexionis diverse,* which is also centered on the subject of the *complexio.* The *Articella* continued to maintain its place in the medical curriculum alongside these new works, and at certain schools, particularly at the University of Paris, it maintained its dominance.

[119] García Ballester believes ("New Galen," 59) that the full comprehension of the more technical Galenic works depended on the mastery of the Aristotelian corpus – the great university project of the thirteenth century. The question of the relationship between Galen's reception and the reception of Aristotle is discussed further in the following chapter.

[120] In the case of the *De complexionibus,* it was Gerard's version that was printed as part of the 1490 edition of the *Opera omnia,* and it is this edition that I also refer to below (Venice: Philippus Pincius, 1490), vol. II, 7vb–21ra. This volume too is available for viewing online, courtesy of the BIUM. Gerard's translation was supplanted in the sixteenth century by that of the English medical humanist, Thomas Linacre. Peter Singer has translated Kühn's Greek text into English as "On Mixtures," in *Galen: Selected Works,* 202–89. As with the *Tegni,* where the Singer translation conveys the meaning of the Latin translations, I use it and cite it, modifying or replacing it (and so noting) where I think necessary.

In the following discussion, I restrict my treatment to those insights which significantly refine or expand the model of balance I have already presented in my analysis of the *Tegni*.

Complexional balance defined: Galen's *De complexionibus*

The *De complexionibus* begins with primary definitions: bodies are a mixture of the qualities hot, cold, wet, and dry; different species have and are determined by their different mixtures; to say that a complexion is hot (or any of the other qualities) is not to say that it absolutely hot, but rather that heat predominates relative (or proportional) to the other three qualities in the mixture.[121] Following Aristotle, Galen situates all qualitative alteration and change in the dynamism of opposing contraries.[122] This holds for the primary qualities, hot and cold and wet and dry, and for all other contraries as well, e.g., white and black, musical and non-musical. The degree of presence of one contrary quality implies the degree of absence of the other, with the tension of opposition between the two always present.[123] Galen takes the reciprocal relationship between contraries to imply that all qualitative change is continuous and that it takes place across a gradable continuum bounded by contraries. Thus far, both the general definitions and many of the specific examples Galen uses have been taken directly from Aristotle, consistent with his belief that the doctor must rely on philosophy for the elucidation of those necessary first principles which lie beneath the perceptual level of the senses.[124]

In setting out the primary definitions necessary for an understanding of the *complexio*, Galen restricts his discussion to the mixture of the four primary qualities (heat, cold, wet, and dry). There is no mention at all here of the "four humors." This absence requires some explanation, since the

---

[121] In citing, I reference first the page from the Kühn edition (vol. I) and then the page from either Durling's text (1976) or the Gerard translation (1490). K, I: 509–10; (1976), 3–4.

[122] K, I: 514; (1976), 7: "Etenim oportet et generationem et alteratione et transmutationem ex contrariis in contraria fieri." I discuss this essential insight further in Chapter 8 on the transformation of balance in natural philosophy.

[123] K, I: 516; (1976), 8: "non possibile secundum unum idemque corpus contrarias qualitates."

[124] Galen, however, goes beyond (and perhaps against) Aristotle in his specific recognition of a graded continuum of qualitative change, which threatens Aristotle's insistence on the categorical separation between qualities and quantities. This subject is considered further in the chapter that follows with respect to the quantifying scheme of Arnau de Vilanova. For a general statement of the philosophical problems associated (for Aristotelians) with quantifying qualities, see Edith Sylla, "Medieval Quantifications of Qualities: The 'Merton School,'" *Archive for History of Exact Sciences* 8 (1971), 7–39, esp. 9; Kaye, *Economy and Nature in the Fourteenth Century*, 175–7.

typical modern textbook version of Galen's medical theory often simply equates it with "the balance of the humors." It is not that the humors have no place in Galen's thought; further on in the text of the *De complexionibus*, when he has gotten past first principles into the detailed physiology of the body, the humors are discussed at a number of points, and the compensation or balancing of their imbalances is an important subject of discussion.[125] Moreover, blood as the primary humor holds an obviously central place in any discussion of the body. Still, the place allotted the humors in Galen's medico/physical theory is often exaggerated in secondary accounts, especially in relation to the place held by the primary qualities.[126] In the earliest treatment of all four humors (found in the Hippocratic text, *On the Nature of Man* [*c.* 400 BCE]), they were fluid substances embodying the four possible qualitative mixtures: blood (hot and wet), yellow bile (hot and dry), black bile (cold and dry), and phlegm (cold and wet). In line with Galen's strong identification with the Hippocratic tradition, he accepted the existence of humors, but he never drew a simple equation between health and the balance (or proper blending) of the humors themselves, and in his most direct and technical discussions of complexion, he refers solely to proportional mixtures, and their possible permutations, involving the four primary qualities.

The relativization of qualities and equalities in the complexion

Although the outline of the Aristotelian theory of the four qualities was generally accepted in Galen's day, he was not at all pleased with how most (in his view) *mis*interpreted and misapplied it. In Galen's view, the failure of his contemporaries was essentially their failure to grasp the relativity that he believed was built into the Aristotelian system: "Aristotle knows that the terms hot, cold, dry, and wet can be taken in a multiplicity of ways; yet these people do not understand them to have multiple senses, but always one and the same simple sense."[127] In addition to Aristotle, Galen believed that the ancient doctors

---

[125] E.g., K, I: 583, 603, 616, 630–4, 642–3, 679–80.

[126] The place of the humors in Galen's thought is discussed in Ottosson, *Tegni*, 130–2; Penella and Hall, "Galen's 'On the Best Constitution of Our Body,'" 282 ff. In the judgment of Penella and Hall (283), Galen's treatment of the humors was "complex and less than completely consistent," considering them at different times as "nutrient substances, constituents of whole blood, tissue components, behavioral determinants, and normal and pathological residues or secretions."

[127] K, I: 535; (1976), 22: "Multifariam enim ille [Aristotle] scivit calidum dici et frigidum et siccum et humidum: ipsi autem non intelligunt ea multifariam sed semper similiter."

(Hippocrates and others) also understood that the terms "hot" and "wet," when attached to the animal body, were used as comparative rather than absolute terms.[128] For Galen, relativistic thinking is the key to the theory of complexion:

[compared to one another] dogs are drier, men are wetter. And yet if you compare ants or bees to dogs, you will find that they are drier and dogs wetter. The same animal, then, is drier in relation to man and wetter in relation to the bee, or hot in relation to man and cold compared to the lion [thought to be the hottest of the animals]. And there is nothing strange if contrary qualities are ascribed to the same thing [in different contexts], nor is it unfitting if the same body is said to be both hot and cold, though not in relation to the same thing.[129]

After continuing in this vein, describing the dog which is both cold and hot, both wet and dry when considered comparatively, he concludes with a clear general statement: "All the cases above are spoken of in a comparative and relative sense" (*Hec quidem igitur omnia adinvicem ex comparatione dicuntur*).[130]

It is Galen's remarkably developed sense of relativity (even if neither he nor his Latin translators specifically use the term "relativity" in this general sense) that led him to break with what he characterized as contemporary medical opinion.[131] And in his thorough application of relativity, he goes far beyond Aristotle as well.[132] Given the impossibility of contraries existing in the same subject at the same time (in an absolute

---

[128] K, I: 537; (1976), 23: "Et nimirum ita animalia calida et humida a veteribus medicis dicuntur, non secundum propriam complexionem simpliciter, sed arboribus et mortuis comparata." I note that Galen at times ascribes to his ancient authorities positions that he himself has crafted.

[129] *Ibid.*: "Et quidem utique animalium ipsorum adinvicem secundum species comparatorum, siccius quidem canis, humidius autem homo. Si autem formice aut api comparabis canem, sicciorem quidem illum, humidiorem autem canem invenies. Quapropter idem animal siccius quidem ut ad hominem existit, humidius autem ut ad apem: ita autem et calidum quidem ut ad hominem, frigidum autem ut ad leonem: et mirandum nichil, si que ad alterum quid dicta contrarias simul predicationes suscipiunt. Non enim inconveniens, si idem corpus calidum esse dicitur et frigidum."

[130] See also K, I: 544; (1976), 28–9: "Quia autem multa sunt genera, quemadmodum et individua, possibile est idem corpus et calidum et frigidum et siccum et humidum esse secundum multos modos." For a general discussion of relativity in Galenic discussions of qualitative contraries, see Hankinson, "Philosophy of Nature," esp. 220–3.

[131] For the explicit use of the word "relation" in the Latin text, K, I: 546; (1976), 30: "Quando autem aut arborem temperatam aut animal quodcunque dicimus, non adhuc simpliciter adinvicem in tali dictione contraria comparamus, sed ad arboris naturam aut animalis *relationem* facimus."

[132] Pertinent in this context is R. J. Hankinson, "Galen and the Logic of Relations," in *Aristotle in Late Antiquity*, ed. Lawrence Schrenk (Washington, DC: Catholic University Press, 1994), 57–75. Hankinson demonstrates Galen's attempt to work within an Aristotelian syllogistic framework and yet to expand it to cover relations, in particular the relational basis of geometric proofs, i.e., "things equal to the same thing are equal to

sense), Aristotle had posited only four possible complexions: hot and wet; cold and wet; hot and dry; cold and dry. To these, Galen argues, must be added a fifth: the *eucraton* or "well-blended mixture." Since the *eucraton* represents a true (proportionalized) medium between all of the qualitative contraries, it cannot be defined in terms of any of them.[133] Within Galen's thoroughly relativized conception of complexion, the existence of the fifth temperament was a logical requirement, since (as he argues) qualities can only be designated in a relative sense: what is "hot" in some particular context may be cold in another, and so with all the other qualities.[134] If, then, one wishes to speak of the four temperaments (hot and wet, hot and dry, cold and wet, cold and dry) one can do so only by establishing a medium of comparison in relation to which the dominant qualities and temperaments can be defined. He writes:

> they [Galen's contemporaries] have ignored and eliminated it [the fifth or balanced complexion] even though they cannot truly speak about any of the other complexions without it. To understand the hot complexion as one in which there is a superabundance of heat, or of a cold as one in which there is a superabundance of cold, is quite impossible unless one first presupposes the well-balanced mixture (*eucraton*).[135]

Nor, he continues, can the doctor restore health unless he knows the parameters of the well-blended complexion specific to each individual patient, since this defines the healthy state to which the patient must be restored. The physician must know the patient's natural *eucraton* so that he can estimate how far and in what direction the diseased state is from it and thus estimate the qualitative proportions of the curative agents necessary to correct the imbalances causing disease.[136]

---

each other." Very typical here is Galen's attempt to bend Aristotle (and logic) in the direction of increased sensitivity to relations and relativity. See also Barnes, "Galen and the Utility of Logic," 37, and his statement in Barnes, "Galen on Logic and Therapy," 56: "His attention to the logic of relations is Galen's original gift to the science of reasoning."

[133] Later in the text (K, I: 559), Galen will add four more possible *complexiones*, each defining a medium of the original four, for a total of nine.

[134] K, I: 544; (trans. Singer, 218): "absolute quality in its pure form does not arise in the context of mixtures, existing only in the primary objects known as elements." In theory, insofar as they exist in nature, even sensible earth, air, fire, and water, while predominated by their co-named element (and its qualities) still contain some admixture of all the other elements and qualities.

[135] K, I: 519; (1976), 10: "obliti sunt et finaliter derelinquerunt, velut nequaquam existentem, quamvis neque loqui quid sine ista de aliis possunt. Quod in calida siquidem complexione superhabundat calidum seu in frigida frigidum neque intelligere possibile est nisi prius supponamus *eucraton*." Singer (206) translates *eucraton* here and elsewhere as "well-balanced mixture." Galen later restates this point in the general case (K, I: 540; [1976], 26): all qualitative terms are applied in relation to the medium.

[136] K, I: 519; (1976), 10.

The scope of Galen's relativization moves to yet another level when he seeks to define or "fix" in some sense the medium complexion, the *eucraton*, both in a general sense and specifically in terms of the human body. This, he recognizes, is required if the medium is to serve its necessary role in comparison. Not only will each plant and animal species have its own proper complexion (*eucraton*), but, speaking as a physician, he must insist that each and every individual possesses his (or its) own proper blend, unique to itself. In order to prepare the reader for his discussion on how to actually determine the medium proper to each species and individual, Galen engages in an extraordinary excursus, elaborating on the principles of relativity, which stretches over fifteen pages in the standard Kuhn edition.[137] The principles he enunciates here are presented in such a clear and methodical way that this section of the text can, I think, be characterized as a virtual primer on relativity.

That Galen thought such a primer necessary is revealing in itself. While it is clear that he is fully at home in relational thinking, he appears to have identified it as an intellectual skill somewhat foreign to his contemporaries and difficult to master.[138] (This would certainly have been true for the Latin thinkers of the twelfth and thirteenth centuries who first received his writings.) Indeed, earlier in the *De complexionibus* he had distinguished those who can and cannot reason philosophically essentially on the basis of their grasp of relativity and relativistic concepts.[139] The points he covers in this section on relativity (in addition to those we have already mentioned) are too numerous to discuss in full, but a few stand out for their subtlety and for their importance as keys to his sense of balance.

Although his main concern is with the mixing of the four primary qualities, Galen clearly intends his discussion of relativity to extend to all qualitative terms: large and small, fast and slow, etc. To aid his readers, he formulates several general rules of relativist terminology, and within these the concept of the *medium* takes central place. Where *eucraton* is a technical term that refers primarily to the balanced blend of the primary qualities within bodily complexions, *medium* has a more universal application as the neutral comparative for all qualitative contraries. In his view, we call something hot or cold or large or small or fast or slow *when it exceeds the medium*, just as we call a horse hot when it exceeds the complexional

---

[137] K, I: 535–50; (1976), 22–32.
[138] Sophists, he notes (K, I: 549), use relativity to confound. He, however, will use it properly, as a tool to decipher nature's signs and causes.
[139] K, I: 534–5; (1976), 21–2.

medium of heat established for horses.[140] Galen's continual use of the term "medium" underscores the point that in his view qualitative contraries frame real qualitative continua. The medium complexion (*aequalitas complexionis*), then, is that which is "equally distant from both extremes," judged, however, not absolutely but *always* relative to the potential degree of these qualitative extremes within any given species and within any given context.[141] In essence, then, Galen's medium is defined relative to what is itself relative.[142] Although "equally distant" implies some simple act of bisection, the relativist reality is far more complex. The relativized medium, when attached to the human body, possesses for Galen a distinctive value: it is not only the neutral comparative between two contraries, it is a state which is good in itself and essentially identified with proper nature and proper balance.[143]

Imagining a relativized system in dynamic equalization

Every statement Galen has presented so far has been crafted to prepare the reader to consider the difficult problem central to his theory: given the enormous variety of genera, species, and individuals, how is the relativized medium, the *eucraton*, determined for each? The answer to this question is crucial for the physician, since his whole science of diagnosis and cure depends upon it. After yet another quick run-through of the rules governing relative terms, and after separating out the rare case when the medium is considered in its absolute sense as a precise point mathematically equidistant from each contrary, Galen argues that the medium

---

[140] K, I: 540; (1976), 25–6: "secundum genus aut speciem nominari tunc unumquodque non calidum solum aut frigidum aut siccum aut humidum, sed et magnum et parvum et velox et tardum et talium unumquodque, *quando super id quod commensuratum et medium fuerit*, ut puta animal calidum aliquod dicimus, quando super medium fuerit complexione animal, ut puta equus calidus, quando super medium equum fuerit" (my emphasis).

[141] K, I: 547, 10rb: "Equalitas complexionis reperitur in omnibus corporibus equalibus animalis et plante non secundum equalitatem quantitas elementorum ex quibus commiscentur, sed secundum quod querit nature cuiusque animalis et cuiusque plante." Notice the form of his presentation, typical of this section on relativity, in which he continually distinguishes between the absolute and relative sense, and he then continually chooses the relative determination.

[142] K, I: 540; (1976), 26: "Media … equaliter enim distant ab extremitatibus in illo genere et specie."

[143] K, I: 543; (1976), 28: "Quoniam autem in omnibus entibus medium extremitatum est quod commensuratum et secundum illud genus aut speciem *eucraton*." Also, K, I: 547: 10rb, for the direct connection between the medium complexion, the true nature of the living subject, proper function, and relativity: "Cum enim dicimus de aliqua plantarum aut animalium, quecumque planta et animal fuerit quod est equalis complexionis, non comparamus in hoc sermone contraria adinvicem absolute sed secundum naturam plante aut secundum naturam animalis."

complexion (*eucraton*) for each individual is determined with reference
to its proper *function*. The optimal nature of every species and every
individual plant and animal is evidenced by, and judged by, its optimal
activity.[144] The fig tree with the optimal complexion (the best blend
of primary qualities) is the one that produces the best and most fruit:
similarly with the horse that runs fastest, the dog that is ferocious in the
hunt yet gentle in the home, etc.[145]

To clarify even further the relative nature of the medium being sought,
Galen introduces an example from beyond the realm of medicine and
physics – one that will assume an important place in the medieval
Galenic tradition – the example of justice (*iustitia*). For Galen, the
medium sought in justice, like the complexional *medium*, represents
not a simple midpoint between equal weights and equal measures
(*non pondere et mensura id quod equale*), but rather an "equality" *secundum
iustitiam*, which is to say, an *aequalitas* fittingly proportioned to the
nature of the particular case.[146] Although Galen does not specifically
refer to Aristotle here, I think it likely that his illustration of proportional
equality by reference to *justitia* owes a good deal to Aristotle's discussion
of justice and the mathematics of equality in Book V of the *Ethics*.[147]
Here Aristotle identifies two kinds of justice defined by two different
forms of equality: (1) an absolute, arithmetical sense of equality, in
which the judge seeks to establish a precise mid-point between the
contraries of gain and loss (*iustitia correctiva*), and (2) a relativized
and proportional equality, in which unequal rewards and penalties
are proportioned to the varying circumstances of the case (*iustitia
distributiva*).[148] It is clear that this second form of justice, built around
the search for *proportional* equalization, is the one that corresponds to

---

[144] K, I: 547; (1976), 30: "propriam naturam habere optime, propriis actibus iudicatur."

[145] *Ibid.*

[146] *Ibid.*: "Tale autem aliquid et iustitiam esse dicimus, non pondere et mensura id quod
equale, sed decente et secundum dignitatem scrutantem. 10rb: "Nos namque non
proportionamus eis equalitate pondere et mensura, sed quantitate secundum iustitiam
que est necessaria et debetur unicuisque." For Galen's use of the concept of justice in
other medical contexts, particularly (as in his *De usu partium*) in relation to the structures
of the body, see Owsei Temkin, "Metaphors of Human Biology," in *The Double Face of
Janus and Other Essays in the History of Medicine* (Baltimore, MD: Johns Hopkins
University Press, 1977), 271–83.

[147] Scholastic medical writers made this connection explicit, as will be noted in the chapter
that follows. I discuss the important theme of connections between *justitia* and notions of
dynamic balance in Chapters 1 and 2 on equalization in economic thought, in the
following chapter on scholastic medicine, and in Chapters 6 and 7 in the context of
scholastic political thought.

[148] Aristotle, *Ethics* V, 1131a30–b30 *et seq.*

Galen's thinking about the proportional medium proper to the complexion.

Thus, for plants and animals, their equal complexion (*equalis complexio*) is determined not in relation to the primary elements that compose them, but by determining the medium relative to their proper nature and function.[149] For the physician, the equality he must learn to recognize and work with is essentially proportional and relative. To arrive at it, he must learn to get past the literal sense of equality as the arithmetical mid-point between two extremes or as the mid-point of balance between two equal weights. Galen clearly recognizes this task is a difficult one; hence the careful training and repetition he offers in this long section on relativity; hence his use of the concept of "justice" to underscore the relativization that necessarily occurs when the simple notion of an absolute *aequalitas* (or an absolute balance) is applied to the multifarious complexities of life.

Educating the physician to sense and work with relativized equalization

Up to this point, Galen's discussion has remained in the realm of theory. We have learned that the "equal complexion" is a relativist determination with both an internal and an external dimension: internally it is determined with reference to the actual qualitative mixtures proper to each complexion; externally with reference to excellence of function and activity. If it is evident that a plant or animal is functioning poorly, we know there must be an imbalance (inequality) in the mixture, but in which direction and to what degree? Without such knowledge, the physician is helpless. Here the physician himself, through the use of his senses, functions as the most reliable diagnostic and balancing device. And yet, as Galen clearly recognizes, when the physician enters the realm of the senses, he enters by necessity the realm of approximate knowledge, however well trained and refined it might be.

The full weight that Galen allows to refined estimation and conjecture is revealed in the "instrument" he puts forth as the one most trustworthy for the measurement of complexions: the human skin and, more particularly, the skin of the human hand. He advises his readers that if they want to know what the absolute medium is between hot and cold (so that they have a universal point of sensible comparison) they should take boiling

---

[149] K, I: 547; (1976), 30: "Equalitas igitur complexionis in omnibus contemperatis animalibus et arboribus est, non que secundum commixtorum elementorum corpus, sed que nature animalis et arboris decens."

water, mix it with an "equal amount" of ice, and then carefully feel the resultant medium.[150] To sense the medium between dry and wet, his advice is to mix dry earth with water and to feel the result with the hand. Then after examining and feeling the resultant equal mixtures, the physician is advised to memorize how they felt and looked. The resulting memory can, he maintains, serve ("without much difficulty"!) "as a measuring rule against which qualitative deficits and superabundances can be judged."[151]

Consistent with his teleological view of nature, Galen believes that the skin of the human hand is exactly midway between all the qualitative extremes (*media certissime existens omnium ultimorum*) because it was intended by Nature precisely for the purpose of tactile judgment, and particularly for the kind of qualitative judgment involved in the doctor's determination of complexion.[152] This bit of certainty, however, is more than balanced by a weight of qualifications: only the few, he asserts, only those with the utmost dedication, experience, and learning, gain the ability to properly sense and judge the medium.[153] As an example of one who had attained the fullest capacity to recognize equal proportions, Galen once again brings in the sculptor Polyclitus and his *Canon*. As Polyclitus mastered the form of the human body and established its perfect proportions, so through long study and experience physicians can master the art of "finding the medium."[154] It is an instructive comparison. But in contrast to the precise proportional details he has apparently found in the *Canon* of Polyclitus, the details Galen offers the physician for determining when complexions are properly balanced are again decidedly fuzzier. "His perceptive faculties will be in the best possible state, as will the motions of his limbs; his color will be good, and also his breathing; he will strike the balance (*semper et medius*) between somnolence and

---

[150] K, I: 561; (1976), 40–1.

[151] K, I: 561; (1976), 41: "Itaque neque hic difficile nichil et visu simul et tactu dignoscentem supponere memorie et hac regula et iudicio uti ad deficientium aut superhabundantium humidorum et siccorum dignotionem."

[152] K, I: 563–4. For other statements reflective of a consistent and pure teleology, K, I: 575; K, I: 636. On this subject, see Paul Moraux, "Galien comme philosophe: la philosophie de la nature," in Nutton, *Galen: Problems and Prospects*, 87–116, esp. 97–105; Hankinson, "Causation in Galen," 46–52. Just as the skin of the hand possesses the medium complexion among all of the body's parts, so too, in Galen's scheme, the human complexion represents the perfect medium complexion among all the animal species. K, I: 541; (1490), 10ra: "Homo est medium in complexione sua in toto genere animalium."

[153] K, I: 566; (1976), 45.

[154] *Ibid.*: "Et nempe quedam statua laudatur Polycliti regula nominata, quia omnium particularum certissimam eam que adinvicem commensuritatem habebat tale adepta nomen." For a rich discussion of yet other uses Galen makes of the example of Polyclitus, particularly in his *De usu partium*, see Jackie Pigeaud, "Les problèmes de la création chez Galien," in "Galen und das hellenistische Erbe," ed. J. Kollesch and D. Nickel, special issue of *Sudhoffs Archiv* 32 (1993), 87–103.

insomnia, between baldness and hairiness, and between the black and white colors of hair."[155]

If anything, the example of Polyclitus' proportions promises the doctor more certainty than Galen actually allows him. The sculptor's task involves distilling a universal rule from a great multiplicity of forms, yes, but the forms involved are static. The sculptor can decide how to organize his particulars into species in his search for the ideal: men, women, young men, young women, seated, standing, etc. In contrast, the physician must take individuals as they are, and, even more problematically, his individuals are ever changing, always in the process of becoming, always shifting in relation to both internal and external factors. The inescapable fact of motion itself vitiates any possibility of establishing fixed points within a fixed canon and necessitates that estimation within approximative latitudes is the best the doctor can hope for.

Galen fully recognizes this, even as he asserts that the human senses are equal to the task of judging complexional balances and are capable of basing conjectures upon it sufficient to the finding of successful cures. Still, the complexities involved in this project are truly enormous. To the physician who seeks to determine whether the medium complexional heat of an individual increases with age, Galen advises that he check the heat of a two-year-old, remember it, and compare it to the heat of that same child at four or five. If there is a change, he can then, using proportional reasoning, project what the increase will be when the individual is fully grown.[156] If that were not difficult enough, he suggests comparing a group of children with a group of adults in their prime, to see if there is a general tendency toward an increasing medium as age increases. But in choosing these groups, he warns that one must see that they are comparable: thin children with thin adults, fat with fat, etc. Moreover, for an accurate comparison, one should group only those with similar regimens; the well-exercised together, the well-bathed together, the hungry together, etc. And one must be sure to judge them all at the same time of day and the same season of the year. Given modern instruments of measurement and modern methods of standardization and recording, the outline of Galen's plan here represents a model of thoughtful experimentation.[157] But in Galen's mind, this search to determine a meaningful "common" *medium* or balance is being performed by the same doctor, using the same instrument of the skin of his hand, recording and comparing all of his experiences over decades, entirely through the "instrument" of his sense

---

[155] K, I: 577; (1976), 52 (trans. Singer, 233).   [156] K, I: 591; (1976), 62.

[157] The possible influence of Galen's experimental model here on medieval and early modern science provides much room for further research.

memory.[158] For Galen, approximation based on sense knowledge does not imply defect: it provides the basis – the only basis – for the skilled conjecture on which all medical cure depends. Given the pervasive distrust of the senses and sense knowledge in the upper levels of medieval university culture, I think it is well to consider what possible impression, and what possible lessons, might examples of this kind have imparted? For that matter, what impression and possible lessons would each of the elements of Galenic balance have imparted to scholastic readers?

I leave the *De complexionibus* here, having discussed only small portions of this treatise. Once again, as in the case of the *Tegni*, Galen has educated the physician to assume the role of a finely tuned animate instrument, designed for the purpose of judging and restoring bodily balance. In performing this function, he is guided by the senses, reason, experience, memory, conjecture and the whole "art." Yet, withal, he is bound within the epistemological limits presented by these very same factors.[159] Galen's "art" was extraordinary in many ways, but one way, certainly, was its capacity to grasp (and to show) that the same elements that limit the possibilities of knowledge also expand them. Only by recognizing his delicate position as a balancing agent, only by embracing the tools of relativity, proportionality, measurement by approximative latitudes, and skilled conjecture, can the physician anticipate and attune himself to the rhythm of the living body.

Is Galen's body in equilibrium?

With everything I have written about Galen's model of equalization and balance, I have hesitated to apply to it the word "equilibrium" because it lacks a crucial element I associate with all true models of equilibrium, including the "new" model of equilibrium that emerged in the second half of the thirteenth century. In the Introduction to this work, I defined this element as:

the striking imagination that the working system is capable of ordering itself and equalizing (balancing) itself simply through the dynamic interaction of its working parts ... The imagination of systematic self-ordering and self-equalizing is thus linked to the potentially subversive recognition that the interior dynamic of the systematic whole ... is capable of replacing overarching mind or intelligence as the basis of its order and equalization.[160]

---

[158] K, I: 591–3; (1976), 62–3.
[159] Galen offers a spirited defense of his sense-based method against the claims of pure logic and reason, at K, I: 588–91.
[160] First two in the list of the model's elements in the Introduction.

Galen never quite arrived at this point. Indeed, Galen wrote that the more he recognized the immense complexity of the body's inner workings, the more he was driven to believe in the *necessary* existence of a unifying and overarching "nature" (*natura*), "soul" (*anima*), or divine creator/crafts-man (*opifex*) responsible for ordering the organism as a whole. Moreover, motivated by this same sense of wonder, he found that he could only explain the body's marvelous functioning and equalizing capacities by imagining that each and every one of its parts was pre-designed to perform its required tasks by a creating power and intelligence.[161]

These beliefs are present in the *Tegni* and the *De complexionibus* in his general comments about the ordering power of "nature," but they are less prominent in these works than they are in other of Galen's writings.[162] In his great work, *De usu partium* (*On the Usefulness of the Parts of the Body*), they are ever present. Here either Nature, the Soul, or the Creator (these terms often appear interchangeable) act as a formative intelligent power to both shape and control each part of the body and the body as a whole. As he writes in its opening chapter, "In every case the body is adapted to the character and faculties of the soul."[163] Galen then proceeds to apply this reasoning to every bodily part he considers over this lengthy text.[164]

If, according to the criteria I set out, Galen's model of bodily structure and activity cannot be considered a model of equilibrium, it was no less extraordinary for its depth, logical coherence, and complexity. On the contrary, his teleological assumptions exist alongside and balance his naturalistic explanations rather than replacing them. It is the marvelous complexity and inner logic of bodily equalization, conceptualized as a dynamic interactive system, that drives him to say, "I could never be persuaded that these [the tens of thousands of coordinated functioning parts of the body] have come about without the work of an extraordinarily

---

[161] These core beliefs, repeated many times throughout Galen's writings, have been well recognized by historians. See, for example, Nancy Siraisi, "Vesalius and the Reading of Galen's Teleology," *Renaissance Quarterly* 50 (1997), 1–37; Hankinson, "Philosophy of Nature," 225–9.

[162] E.g., as already cited, K, I: 178: "In all cases it is Nature that is the true creator, and the doctor is merely her servant."

[163] Galen, *On the Usefulness of the Parts of the Body [De usu partium corporis humani]*, ed. and trans. Margaret Tallmadge May (Ithaca, NY: Cornell University Press, 1968), 68. *Claudii Galeni pergameni De usu partium corporis humani, Nicolao Regio Calabro Interprete* (Paris: Simonis Colinaei, 1528), 1: "Omnibus vero aptum ac habile est corpus, animae moribus et facultatibus."

[164] These beliefs, and his reasons for holding them, appear with particular clarity in his short treatise, *De foetuum formation* (*On the Construction of the Embryo*), in *Galen: Selected Works*, ed. and trans. Singer, 177–201.

intelligent and powerful craftsman."[165] One might well expect that given the Christian setting of the medieval university, the scholastic authors who commented on Galen from the mid thirteenth century and after would pay particular attention to the place and function he allows this creating and ordering intelligence. But one of the most surprising and telling attributes of those scholastic commentators (and of all who shared in the new model of equilibrium) is that, if anything, they consistently downplayed the role (especially the necessary role) of an ordering intelligent power in their overwhelmingly naturalistic exposition of the systematic workings of the Galenic body.[166] To their modeling of the body, even more than to Galen's, the term "systematic equilibrium" fully and properly applies.

Assessing the Galenic model of equalization

One of the most frequent criticisms of Galen, both by contemporaries and by modern scholars, is that his works are diffuse, prolix, full of detours and asides, and generally lacking in systematic rigor. But is this entirely unintentional? Is it the product of too much writing with too little care for presentation, or, more damning still, too little intellectual rigor? I suggest, rather, that it is yet another indication of the profundity of his teaching strategy – the result of his persistent attempt to maintain a balance between the hyper-systematization of Peripatetic logic and the contempt for systematization expressed by the empiricist physicians of his day.[167] Recognizing the hybrid nature of medicine on numerous levels, due to its position somewhere between science and art, he is faced with the task of using his texts both to create systematic knowledge and, as difficult as it might seem, to *destabilize* the system at the very same time. The doctor who cannot reason, observe, or act systematically will fail, but so too will the doctor whose categories are so ingrained, whose diagnoses are so certain, that they prevent the full range of vision necessary to grasp the ever-shifting individual case.[168] This is, of course, still true of doctors today.

---

[165] *Ibid.*, 198. *De foetuum formatione*, in *Galeni omnia quae extant opera*, vol. II (Venice: ad Iuntas, 1565), 325v: "Ut, siquis fines uniuscuiusque fabricate numerare velit, numeros omnium summam perfectionem assecutorum in myriadas, non chiliadas (hoc est non in millia, sed in dena millia) redigatur: quos ergo nequaquam, ut dixi, nisi a sapientissimo ac potentisimo opifice, factos esse crediderim."

[166] This point, which will be further discussed in Chapter 4, has been forcefully made by Roger French, *Canonical Medicine: Gentile da Foligno and Scholasticism* (Leiden: Brill, 2001), 139–41.

[167] On Galen's position between the empiricists and the rationalists, see Hankinson, "Epistemology," 172.

[168] This characteristic "mediating" position is explored in Frede, "On Galen's Epistemology," esp. 72–8.

By writing hundreds of works, by coming at the same or similar problems from multiple perspectives at different times in his life, by constant cross-referencing, even at times by knowing self-contradiction, Galen succeeds in the extraordinary project – the extraordinary balancing act – of constructing a systematic science (or a science sufficiently systematic to remain authoritative for more than fifteen hundred years) that at the same time works on the level of the transient and the particular – the ever-changing individual body.[169] And he does so in the face of the received Aristotelianism of his day which held firmly that there can be no true science of the particular.

It would be misleading, however, to posit a simple contrast between Galen's focus on the individual case as a practicing *medicus* and the philosopher's concern for universal knowledge. Galen spent much ink and energy attacking the medical "empirics" of his day who denied the necessity of theory and the knowledge of universals in the name of practical experience and observation. He insisted that the good *medicus* must also be grounded in philosophy, and he considered himself (and was considered by others) to be both physician and philosopher, with Plato and Aristotle alongside Hippocrates as his great models. While recognizing that cure, the end of medicine, must be directed to individuals, he held that the physician's knowledge of cures depended on his capacity to group and generalize from particulars. Sounding like the good Aristotelian he believed he was, he wrote: "Which of us has learnt the art of healing from the pleuritic John Smith? No one. Not even of curing a pleuritic patient. No, the arts consist in concepts of genera and species."[170]

For Galen, medicine was a hybrid creation of science and art. And the doctor, then, was an intellectual hybrid, able to rest neither in the universal nor the particular, neither in reason nor the senses, neither in theory nor practice, but required to remain sufficiently flexible to move lightly back and forth between them.[171] In effect, Galen's doctor inhabits the

---

[169] For examples in the *Tegni* where Galen supports positions that contradict earlier ones, see Kollesch, "Anschauungen von den *archai* in der *Ars medica*." Some of these self-contradictions are so basic that, as I noted above, on their basis Kollesch has questioned Galen's authorship. But Kollesch identifies Galen's insertion in the *Tegni* of "neuter" state between the states of health and sickness as one of these major "contradictions," while, as I have argued, the insertion appears very well suited to his specific purpose in writing the *Tegni*. See also Van der Lugt, "Neither Ill nor Healthy," 17–18.

[170] *De differentia pulsuum*, 2.7, cited and translated in García Ballester, "Galen as a Medical Practitioner," 19. See also Frede, "On Galen's Epistemology," 79–80. And from the other side, Aristotle, especially in his biological works, enunciated the principle: "first the phenomena must be grasped ... then their causes discussed." *De partibus animalium* [639b3; 640a14–15]. This is noted and cited in Von Staden, *Herophilus*, 118.

[171] Frede, "On Galen's Epistemology," 71–4.

space *between* science and art – a straddling space which to my mind looks very much like the "neither" state between health and sickness he posited at the very beginning of the *Tegni*: "sometimes in neither, sometimes in both, sometimes in one and then the other, sometimes participating equally in both contraries, sometimes in one more than the other."[172] No wonder that one of his most astute readers, Luis García Ballester, uses the word "tension" to describe the relationship between scientific knowledge and clinical experience in Galen's system.[173] I would suggest that the continuation of this tension and this back and forth over a lifetime, helps to explain the unparalleled sensitivity that Galen brought to the question of balance, and the unparalleled richness of his understanding in this area.

The legacy of Galenic balance

Comparisons between Galen and Aristotle are instructive on this point. Aristotle's passion for order and classification, his causal linearity and tendency toward hieratic gradation, his desire to get quickly beyond the evidence of the senses to arrive at reasoned universal judgments, his promise of certainty, and many other aspects of his thought, fit fairly comfortably with the Christian intellectual culture of the late twelfth and thirteenth century that first received his writings. His analyses of particular systems (moral, physical, biological, political, economic) were often constructed around a moderate relativity, generally in advance (to my view) of the previous applications of relativist thinking in these areas, but they were also almost always in the end bounded and solidified by a priori absolutes and unquestioned first principles. Balance as the political, moral, and physical ideal was often at the heart of Aristotle's thought (as it was in almost all premodern thought), whether as the mean of virtue, the equality of justice, or the earth fixed at the precise center of a great bounded circle of stars. But it was a balance that required only moderate stretching on the part of the medieval culture that received and soon comprehended it. Aristotle projected, in the end, a reassuring sense of balance – one could argue, too reassuring to generate substantial changes in its modeling of the kind that appear at the end of the thirteenth century in the new model of equilibrium.

---

[172] *Tegni, translatio antiqua*, 10rb: "tripliciter dicitur: hoc quidem eo quod neutra extremarum dispositionum participet: hoc vero eo quod utraquem: hoc autem quod aliquando quidem hac aliquando vero illa."

[173] García Ballester, "Galen as a Medical Practitioner," 19, and again, 20.

Compare to Galen. Once we problematize balance and come to think of it as having a history, once we allow this history a central place in the history of ideas, his position and role in this history looms exceptionally large. His tempering of his thought to the movement of life, his embrace of approximation, estimation, and conjecture as legitimate ways of knowing, his courage to work without the net of certainty and the absolute, his suspicion of perfections and the ideal, his acceptance not only of the senses but of "sense" and "feel" in their largest meanings, his consistent naturalism, his habitual application of proportionality to problems in equalization, his overarching relativity touching and transforming every aspect of his system, his determination to study and "know" without killing and fixing the object of his study (which makes him as modern as today), all (in retrospect) were strikingly forward-looking. All were strikingly foreign in the context of medieval thought through the mid thirteenth century. All had the potential to profoundly reshape the modeling of balance within Latin Christian culture. The question then remains: when did Galenic texts begin to circulate in Latin Christian culture, who read them, and how were they read? This is the subject of the following chapter.

4   Balance in medieval medical theory, part 2: The scholastic reception and refinement of Galenic balance to *c*. 1315

The complexion is that quality which results from the mutual interaction and interpassion of the contrary primary qualities [heat, cold, wetness, dryness] ... Their opposite powers alternately conquer and become conquered (*ad invicem agunt et patiuntur suis virtutibus*) until a quality is reached which is uniform throughout the whole (*in toto*): this is the complexion.   Avicenna, *Canon medicinae* (c. 1025)

Galen was intent to say that when the doctor speaks of coequality (*coequalitas*), he does not do so in terms of its perfection ... but he understands it instead to refer to a latitude that terminates at notable loss of physical function (*latitudo terminator ad magnam lesionem operationem*). So that when Galen speaks of the words "equality" and "distemperament," he does not understand them in the way they might sound or signify [as perfections], but rather he allows them a certain magnitude.   Taddeo Alderotti, *Commentary* on Galen's *Tegni* (c. 1280)

And just as among citizens there occurs strife and recriminations when those who are equal in dignity participate unequally in honors, or those who are unequal participate equally, just so in the complexion; when its proportioning (*aequatio*) does not fit its proper function (*non convenit operi*), there arise weaknesses and illnesses, and the complexion is said to be "proportionally unequal" (*inequalis ab iniustitia*).
Pietro Torregiano de Torregiani (Turisanus), *Plusquam commentum*
on Galen's *Tegni* (c. 1315)

Given Galen's identification of health with bodily balance (*aequalitas*) and illness with imbalance, it is not surprising that concern with the problem of attaining and maintaining a properly proportioned balance within the operational system(s) of the body is ever present within his writings. In the previous chapter, I argued that in addressing this concern, Galen envisioned the form and working principles of systematic equilibrium in ways that were deeper, richer, and in almost every way more advanced than any that had come before him, whether in the sphere of medicine or philosophy. As I turn to consider the reception of the Galenic model of balance/*aequalitas* by medieval learned culture, I confront two questions from the start: (1) were the early Latin readers of the newly translated Galenic texts (and the newly translated Arabic commentaries that sometimes accompanied these texts) capable of comprehending the full range of Galen's sense and treatment of balance, or were there stages in the process of comprehension over the twelfth and thirteenth centuries? And (2), did medieval *medici* at some later point in the reception history begin to expand upon Galenic insights into the form and potentialities of balance, and if they did so, what form(s) and direction(s) characterized their new thinking? To answer these questions, I focus the discussion that follows on those thinkers and texts I consider illustrative of major shifts in the reception of Galenic balance between approximately 1250 and 1315.

The Latin translations of Galen's *Tegni* and the accompanying commentary by Ibn Ridwan

Toward the middle of the twelfth century, the first Latin translations of complete Galenic works began to appear in Europe. By 1187 the *Tegni* had been translated into two Latin versions: one, the *translatio antiqua* rendered from the Greek by an anonymous translator in the first half of the twelfth century, and the other, the *translatio arabica*, rendered from an Arabic version into Latin by the indefatigable Gerard of Cremona (1114–87) at the very end of his life. The Arabic translation of the *Tegni* that formed the basis of the *translatio arabica* is attributable to Hunain Ibn Ishaq (808–73), one of the most important representatives of the grand Arabic translation program centered in Baghdad in the ninth century. Toward the end of the twelfth century, the *Ars medicinae* or *Articella* – that canonical collection of short medical texts (originally five), which formed a pillar of medical instruction into the age of printing – was expanded to include the full text of Galen's *Tegni*. Then, around 1250, the collection was expanded further to include commentaries on some of its original core texts. Primary among these were commentaries by Galen on the *Aphorisms* and *Prognostics* of Hippocrates and a detailed commentary on the *Tegni* itself. The newly added commentaries greatly increased the length and technical complexity of the collection, an increase that well befitted the *Articella's* new position at the center of the developing faculties of university medicine.[1]

The commentary on the *Tegni* that was attached to the *Articella* at this time, and that remained attached for centuries to follow, was authored by the eminent Cairo physician Ibn Ridwan (998–*c.* 1068), who also used as his base text Hunain ibn Ishaq's Arabic translation. Gerard of Cremona

---

[1] O'Boyle, *The Art of Medicine.* O'Boyle has calculated (130) that the added commentaries constituted approximately nine-tenths of the later *Articella's* total length.

translated both texts into Latin at the same time. The two – translation and commentary – formed a unity from the start. In the form of the *Articella* that became standard for centuries, Ibn Ridwan's commentary on the *Tegni* often appears intercalated with the text of the *translatio arabica*, with small portions of the *Tegni* followed by the gloss (at times considerably longer) of Ibn Ridwan's commentary. This situation persisted from the twelfth century into the sixteenth century and the age of printing.[2] Since Latin students of medicine were introduced to the *Tegni* through the lens of Ibn Ridwan's commentary, my study of Galen's reception and the reception of Galenic balance begins with a look at this text and its relation to the text of the *translatio arabica*.[3] When the *Tegni* is read through the lens of Ibn Ridwan's commentary, the dynamism, delicacy, and many-layered structure of Galen's model of balance is brought out to an exceptional degree.[4]

From his opening sentence, Ibn Ridwan impresses on the student/ reader that notions of proportionality and continuity will hold a central place in the discussion that follows.[5] In similar fashion, over the length of the commentary, he emphasizes and clarifies other pivotal elements of Galenic balance. Among these are Galen's focus on equalization and the establishment of proportional equalities as central to the determination and restoration of health;[6] Galen's recognition that the doctor must abandon the ideal of perfect knowledge in favor of observing shifting value ranges knowable only through estimation and

---

[2] E.g., *Articella seu Opus artis medicinae*, ed. Gregorius Vulpe and Franciscus Argilagnes (Venice: B. Locatelli, 1493), where, at the center of the page, the text from the *translatio arabica* is presented, followed immediately by the same passage from the *translatio antiqua*, and in the margins surrounding both passages appears the longer gloss of Ibn Ridwan's commentary.

[3] The printed text I am using is *Hali Filii Rodbon in Parvam Galeni Artem Commentatio*, which is contained within the larger volume, Turisanus, *Plus quam commentum* (Venice: ad Iuntas, 1557), 175r–217v. All citations of Ibn Ridwan's commentary on the *Tegni* that follow are drawn from this edition. Ibn Ridwan's name, when Latinized, took a number of forms, but one common form was 'Hali filii Rodbon," and he was often referred to as either "Haly" or "Hali."

[4] Ibn Ridwan's sensitivity to Galen's overall plan speaks to the sophistication of the Alexandrian Greek tradition of medical commentary that informed his own, and to the grand achievements of Arabic medicine of the ninth, tenth, and eleventh centuries.

[5] Ibn Ridwan, *In Parvam Galeni Artem*, 176r: "Medicina est scientia rerum proportionatarum continuatarum cum sanitate hominis: et rerum proportionatarum continuatarum cum aegritudine hominis: et rerum proportionatarum continuatarum cum dispositione, in qua non evadit homini sanitas neque aegritudo." Compare to *translatio arabica*, 176r: "Dico ergo quod medicina est scientia rerum pertinentium continuatarum cum sanitate, cum aegritudine, et cum dispositione in qua not evadit homini sanitas neque egritudo."

[6] E.g., Ibn Ridwan, *In Parvam Galeni Artem*, 179r: "Et in corpore quidem toto, quoniam proportionalitas complexionum membrorum similium partium est proportionalitatis, ex qua sit complexio corporis aequalis."

approximation;[7] Galen's assertion that the range of proportional
equalization which constitutes health (whether defined as *aequalitas
ad iustitiam* or *temperantia*) is to be conceived of as a continuous and
gradable line range or "latitude";[8] Galen's sense that there is real
motion along the continuous latitude linking health and sickness,
which the doctor must learn to recognize;[9] Galen's emphasis on
relativity with regard both to the dispositions and functions of the
body and to the physician's way of knowing;[10] Galen's recognition
that the body exists in delicately balanced relation with its environment through the effects of the "non-naturals" – a relation that can be
manipulated and rebalanced by the doctor through proper regimen.[11]
Finally, as a practicing physician, Ibn Ridwan is particularly careful
to elucidate Galen's method of restoring the balance of health by
equalizing bodily imbalances through the prescription of contrary
medicines and cures.[12]

These highly sophisticated concepts, taken together, form the essential
elements in the Galenic model of equilibrium as it was applied to the
working system of the human body. Hunain ibn Ishaq's crystallization

[7] The phrase describing the doctor's way of knowing presented in the *translatio antiqua* as
"secundum coniecturalem artificialem," is rendered in both the *translatio arabica* and Ibn
Ridwan's commentary (192v) as "per aestimationem propinquam." Hence the repeated
phrase (192v): "aestimavit Gal. aestimatione propinqua veritati." Also, 211v: "Et melior
medicorum est, cuius aestimatio artificialis in hoc est propinquior veritati."

[8] E.g., Ibn Ridwan, *In Parvam Galeni Artem*, 177v: "Manifestum ergo est quod complexioni
uniuscuiusque membrorum partium similium est latitudo, et sanitas est in complexione,
ut proportionentur complexiones membrorum partium similium."

[9] Gerard of Cremona's translation of both the *Tegni* and Ibn Ridwan's commentary
encourages the sense that qualitative motion is continuous by speaking specifically of
qualitative "distances" and "degrees." E.g., Ibn Ridwan, *In Parvam Galeni Artem*, 204b:
"quod oportet ut sit causarum medicationis longitudo ab aequalitate, sicut longitudo
aegritudinis ab aequalitate aequaliter, et sit unaquaeque earum declivis ad contrarium.
Cuius exemplum est aegritudo frigida, et longitudo eius ab aequalitate gradus tres sint,
oportet ergo ut sit causa sanans eam calida, et longitudo eius ab aequalitate gradus tres."
Ibn Ridwan here (and elsewhere) also uses numbers along with the term *gradus* at loci
where they did not appear in the original text of the *Tegni*, to make concrete the examples
of equalization he provides, e.g., 206r.

[10] E.g., Ibn Ridwan, *In Parvam Galeni Artem*, 179r: "quod aequalitas complexionis in
unoquoque membrorum partium similium est complexio conveniens eis." At many
points in the text (e.g., 213r), Ibn Ridwan seconds Galen's insistence that each individual
possesses his own particular complexion of health, the proportional *aequalitas* of which is
determined relative to each individual nature and to multiple internal and external factors,
and that the doctor must work to restore each patient to his own proper equality/balance.

[11] E.g., *ibid.*, 200r: "Et docuit in hoc capitulo canonem suum, qui est si declinet aliqua
causarum sex ab aequalitate, sciatur, quanta est quantitas declinationis eius, et summa
quantitatis eius: deinde inquiratur rectificatio illius declinationis, et destruatur illud."

[12] E.g., *ibid.*, 206r: "Vult ut consideres quantae longitudinis sit membrum infirmum et
aestimes secundum quantitatem quae necessaria est, ut addatur in virtute eius medicinae,
donec perveniat ad membrum et remaneat in ea virtus aequalis virtuti aegritudinis."

of them in his Arabic translation of the *Tegni*; Ibn Ridwan's insistent magnification of them in his commentary; and Gerard of Cremona's consistent translation of them into Latin terms that convey the essential place of continuity, proportionality, relativity, and degree in the process of equalization, would likely have provided a significant aid to the comprehension of Galenic balance for the Latin readers of the *Tegni* over the centuries.

The reception of Galenic *aequalitas* through Avicenna's *Canon* of medicine

As manuscript texts of the *Tegni* and its commentary proliferated in the second half of the thirteenth century, a second textual influence on the reading of Galen moved to the center of the medical curriculum: the *Canon* (*Qanun*) of Avicenna (*c.* 980–1037).[13] The *Canon* was first translated into Latin from the Arabic in the 1180s by Gerard of Cremona, the same remarkable scholar responsible for the *translatio arabica* of the *Tegni* and the Latin translation of Ibn Ridwan's commentary.[14] The *Canon* is the product of an author who was instructed from youth in both medicine and philosophy (logic, ethics, metaphysics, mathematics, astronomy, and many areas of natural philosophy). Although Avicenna read widely in Greek, Persian, and Arabic sources, his two greatest intellectual influences were Galen (in the field of medicine) and Aristotle (in all fields of philosophy).[15] In essence, the *Canon* presents a synthesis of Galenic medicine with Aristotelian physics, all shaped by Avicenna's rare capacity

---

[13] For an overview of the contents and reception of the *Canon*, see Nancy Siraisi, *Avicenna in Renaissance Italy: The Canon and Medical Teaching in Italian Universities after 1500* (Princeton University Press, 1987); Danielle Jacquart, "Medical Scholasticism," in *Western Medical Thought*, ed. Mirko Grmek et al. (Cambridge, MA: Harvard University Press, 1998), 197–240, at 215–21; Joël Chandelier, "La réception du Canon d'Avicenne: médecine arabe et milieu universitaire en Italie avant la peste noire" (PhD thesis, École Pratique des Hautes Études, 2007).

[14] In what follows, I cite from the edition, *Canon. Avicennae Arabum medicorum principis. Ex Gerardi Cremonensis versione* (Venice: apud Iuntas, 1608). (Note that this edition is paginated, with each folio side numbered.) On Gerard as translator of the *Canon*, see Chandelier, "La réception du Canon," 19–22.

[15] Galen is cited as Avicenna's medical authority countless times in the *Canon*, but the explicit citations still do not do full justice to his importance. See, for example, Gotthard Strohmaier's judgment on this point, "Galen in Arabic: Prospects and Projects," in *Galen: Problems and Prospects*, ed. Vivian Nutton (London: Wellcome Institute, 1981), 187–96, esp. 192. At the same time, almost wherever Galen and Aristotle disagree on theoretical points (e.g., the status of the neuter state, the primacy of the brain or the heart), Avicenna comes down on the side of Aristotle. On this, see Siraisi, *Avicenna in Renaissance Italy*, 30–3.

to unify, condense, and organize an immense amount of knowledge into a form amenable to systematic presentation.

At more than a million words, the Latin *Canon* dwarfed any and all of the Galenic texts then in circulation. At the same time, it organized and concentrated into one work the basic teachings contained in a myriad of Galen's scattered writings.[16] The result is a work which has been variously termed a "comprehensive textbook" of Galenism and an "encyclopedia" of Greco-Arabic medicine.[17] In all, with its logical structure, its comprehensive nature, and its grounding in the authority of both Galen and Aristotle, it was perfectly suited to the intellectual culture of the medieval university.[18] For this reason, the story of the *Canon's* reception, including the delay of more than a half-century between its translation (*c.* 1187) and its move to the center of the medical curriculum (*c.* 1250), is directly tied to the remarkable growth of the medieval university over this same period, and to the impact of Aristotle's writings on that growth.[19]

Avicenna's presentation of Galen moves consistently from the universal to the particular, from first principles to their working out in medical practice.[20] It is not surprising then that he introduces the broad theoretical principles underlying the science of medicine at the very beginning of the *Canon*, Book I, Fen I, *doctrinae* 1–4. This opening section contains Avicenna's fundamental theoretical statements on the subject of Galenic balance in remarkably condensed form: *doctrina* 1 on the definition of

---

[16] In the judgment of the great fourteenth-century commentator on the *Canon*, Gentile da Foligno, the work was unprecedented in its comprehensiveness, in the immense study and learning it contained, and in the exquisite logic of its organization, which was so well suited to memorization ("valde convenienti ad tenendum in memoria"). Gentile da Foligno, *Primus Avicenne canonis cum argutissima Gentilis expositione* (Pavia: Jacob de Burgofranco, 1510), 2rb. On the life and thought of Gentile da Foligno, see French, *Canonical Medicine.*

[17] Siraisi, *Avicenna in Renaissance Italy*, 19–21; Michael McVaugh, "The Nature and Limits of Medical Certitude at Early Fourteenth-Century Montpellier," *Osiris* 6 (1990), 62–84, at 63. For the differences between the *Canon* and earlier Arabic attempts at medical encyclopedias (e.g., *Kitāb aṭ-Ṭibb al-Manṣūrī* [*Liber ad Almansorem*] and *Kitāb al-Malakī* [*PanTegni* or *Liber regalis*]), see Chandelier, "La réception du *Canon*," 8–10.

[18] On the history of the utilization of the *Canon* and other works of Islamic medicine in the context of the medieval university, see Danielle Jacquart and Françoise Micheau, *La médicine arabe et l'occident médiéval* (Paris: Éditions Maisonneuve et Larose, 1990), esp. ch. 5, 167–203.

[19] Siraisi, *Avicenna in Renaissance Italy*, 43–64; Danielle Jacquart, "La réception du Canon d'Avicenne: comparaison entre Montpellier et Paris au XIIIe et XIVe siècles," in *Histoire de l'école médicale de Montpellier*, Actes du 110e Congrès national des sociétés savantes (Paris: Éditions du CTHS, 1985), 69–77; French, *Canonical Medicine*, 11–19; Chandelier, "La réception du Canon," 60–159.

[20] Avicenna announces this aim in his prologue (1608) 1b: "Post ostendam regulam unversale in medicando. Deinde descendam ad medicandum particulariter." On the prologue itself, Chandelier, "La réception du Canon," 281–8.

medicine as an intellectual discipline; *doctrina* 2 on the action of the four primary elements (i.e., earth, air, water, fire) underlying all material substance and change; *doctrina* 3 on complexions; and *doctrina* 4 on humors.[21] The compression of this introductory section is stunning. In the 1507 Venice edition of the *Canon*, for example, fen I, *doctrinae* 1–4 occupy six (two-sided) folios, out of 543 for the entire work, and *doctrina* 3 on the pivotal concept and construct of the Galenic complexion, distills and organizes into a folio Galen's writings on the subject, drawn from the *De complexionibus*, the *Tegni*, and other discussions scattered over his numerous works.[22]

This compression, made possible by Avicenna's capacity to summarize and organize knowledge, was often cited as the *Canon*'s great advantage by its Latin readers.[23] Compression of this sort, however, has a dual effect: it focuses the reader's mind on the crystallized theoretical positions it presents, including crystallized elements of Galen's model of equalization, but at the same time, it obscures some of the richness and delicacy of that model, especially since, as we have seen, Galen's capacity to communicate his complex sense of balance was linked to the discursive form of his presentation.[24] Gone from Avicenna's introductory chapters are Galen's continual attempts at shading, his rhetorical techniques directed toward "dividing" propositions and then dividing them again to the end of reaching ever finer distinctions, and his overriding concern to sensitize the reader to the particularities of individual cases and individual histories. Completely absent is Galen's occasional flirtation with willful destabilization. Throughout its early chapters introducing Galenic theory, the *Canon* remains focused on establishing, in good Aristotelian fashion, universal rules based on generalized observations and first principles.

The complexion as a model of equilibrium *in nuce*

In the opening of *doctrina* 1, Avicenna demonstrates how Galenic medicine can and must be framed in terms of Aristotle's four causes: material, efficient, formal, and final. This was an argument that Galen never made,

---

[21] For a general description of the plan of the work, see Siraisi, *Avicenna in Renaissance Italy*, 21–30. For the place that Avicenna allots to medicine in his classification of the sciences, see Dimitri Gutas, "Medical Theory and Scientific Method in the Age of Avicenna," in *Before and After Avicenna*, ed. David Reisman (Leiden: Brill, 2003), 145–62.

[22] *Liber Canonis Avicenne revisus et ab omni errore mendaque purgatus . . .* (Venice, 1507).

[23] Gentile da Foligno, *Primus Avicenne Canonis*, 2ra–2rb.

[24] Siraisi, *Avicenna in Renaissance Italy*, 38: "Avicenna's drastic condensation of Galenic material is accompanied on occasion not only by oversimplification . . . but also by inconsistency, the latter sometimes merely echoing Galen's own."

and it demonstrates Avicenna's synthetic plan from the opening paragraphs. Avicenna locates the material causes of health and sickness in three areas: the bodily members, the four humors, and the four primary elements. The doctor, he then tells us, is concerned with these only insofar as they continually undergo alteration in relation to each other as parts of what he calls (in Gerard of Cremona's translation) functioning "unities."[25] For Avicenna, a "unity" (*unitas*) is, in effect, a physical system composed of moving parts in ever-shifting relation. He writes:

> And this unity (*unitas*) to which the multitude of parts converge, is either its complexion or its form; "complexion" (*complexio*) pertains to the alteration of parts within the unity (*secundum alterationem*), "form" pertains to its composition (*secundum compositionem*).[26]

The clear identification here of the Galenic complexion with the process of alteration is crucial. It establishes that for Avicenna the *complexio* is, by definition, a *dynamic* unity – always undergoing change in the relation of its parts, and yet always maintaining its identity as a functioning whole. When Avicenna then defines the "formal" cause of health as "the complexions, the faculties (*virtutes*) that follow from them and the compositions," the active and causal nature of the complexion is fully established in its primary place, both within the living body and within the theoretical structure of the medical science.[27] In stating this, Avicenna accurately represents Galen's position: that the complexion – the proportioned mixture of the four primary qualities (heat, coldness, wetness, and dryness) ever in the process of alteration and reproportionalization – represents the foundation of systematic equalization within the Galenic body.[28] But I want to argue that with Avicenna's complexion as functioning unity, we move to a model of systematic activity deserving of the term "equilibrium." It is not that Avicenna does not believe in Aristotelian final cause or in an overarching Aristotelian Nature capable of ordering all activity both within the body

---

[25] Avicenna, *Canon* (1608), 7b–8a: "In cuiusque autem rei compositione et alteratione quae sic componitur ad aliquam huiusmodi pervenitur unitatem."

[26] *Ibid.*, 8a: "Et haec unitas, ad quam huiusmodi revertitur multitudo, aut est complexio, aut forma. Complexio vero est secundum alterationem et forma secundum compositionem." Book I of the *Canon* has been translated into English (with the addition of an idiosyncratic commentary) by O. Cameron Gruner, *A Treatise on the Canon of Medicine of Avicenna Incorporating a Translation of the First Book* (London: Luzac, 1930). Michael McVaugh has somewhat modified Gruner's translation in his presentation of select portions of Book I, Fen I, for *A Source Book in Medieval Science*, ed. Edward Grant (Cambridge, MA: Harvard University Press, 1974), 715–20. Where I rely on the Gruner/McVaugh translation, I so note, and I note as well when I have made modifications.

[27] Avicenna, *Canon* (1608), 8a: "Formales vero causae sunt complexiones et virtutes, quae post eas eveniunt, et compositiones."

[28] See the discussions on this subject in the previous chapter.

as a whole and within each individual complexion, as Galen so clearly did. But in Avicenna's presentation, the complexion functions as a system that orders and equalizes *itself* on its own terms, through the workings of its own internal logic, in reaction to its own internal and external environments.

His introductory section on the complexion begins, as usual, with a broad, universalizing definition:

> The complexion is that quality which results from the mutual interaction and interpassion of the contrary primary qualities [heat, cold, wetness, dryness] residing within the primary elements [earth, air, water, fire]. These elements are so minutely intermingled as each to lie in very intimate relationship to one another.[29]

Avicenna here allows the complexion a spatial, temporal, and sensory reality, despite his recognition (after Galen) that the primary elements composing it lie beneath the level of sense perception and can only be known through their effects. The sensual reality of the complexion – the complexion as a *physical model* of equilibrium – is embodied yet further in the sentence that follows:

> Their [the four qualities'] opposite powers alternately conquer and become conquered until a quality is reached which is uniform throughout the whole: this is the complexion.[30]

The English phrase "alternately conquer and become conquered" (as translated here by Michael McVaugh), to describe the action of the qualities within the complexion, is admittedly somewhat stronger than Gerard of Cremona's Latin translation (*ad invicem agunt et patiuntur suis virtutibus*), but it captures Avicenna's recognition that the complexion is always "in act," always the unified product of a vigorous process of opposition, always a blending at a particular moment that represents the continuous reproportionalization of its component parts. The vision of qualitative interaction he conveys here captures the sense of the Greek term *dunameis*, which the Latins translated weakly as "qualitas/qualitates" (as in the four primary "qualities"), but which in Greek carries the sense of "capacity," or "force," or "power to effect," here applied to the dynamically balanced components composing all of material reality.

What emerges in Avicenna's lapidary introductory paragraphs, which were easily and frequently copied, is an image of the complexion

---

[29] McVaugh trans., *Source Book*, 717, *Canon* (1608), 11b: "Complexio est qualitas, quae ex actione ad invicem et passione contrariarum qualitatum in elementis inventarum. Quorum mentes ad tantam parvitatem redactae sunt, ut cuiusque earum plurimum contingat plurimum alterius provenit."

[30] *Ibid.*: "Quum enim ad invicem agunt, et patiuntur suis virtutibus accidit in earum summa qualitas in toto earum similis, quae est complexio."

embracing so many sensory correlatives, so palpable in its workings, so compressed, so "clear and distinct" in its imagery, as to multiply its potential impact as a *model* of dynamic equilibrium. In addition to conveying knowledge and meaning, Avicenna's image of the Galenic complexion also conveys a larger *sense* of the dynamic *potentialities* of balance. Distillation has increased its potency to act as a model (as I am defining the term): that is, to impress its readers on the level of intuition and experience as well as on the level of cognition.[31] No doubt, the palpable model of equilibrium that attached to the *complexio* and that encouraged this kind of "sensing" was there to a great extent in Galen's *Tegni* and *De complexionibus*, brilliantly shaped both conceptually and rhetorically. But here it has been focused and compressed into a working unity, polished like a gem, and like a gem endowed with formidable presence and power.

In the writings of both Galen and Avicenna, the *complexio* is active on multiple levels within the body simultaneously. Each individual bodily organ and each of the myriad bodily members possesses its own form of "equal" or "tempered" or "well-proportioned" complexion (*equa complexio*), a complexion proper to itself and its particular function alone, yet understood to be changing continually relative to changes in the body as a whole as it ages or responds to changes in its environment. Furthermore, the proper functioning of the body and each of its myriad parts requires that every one of these diverse (and ever-shifting) "proportioned equalities" – the predominantly hot-complexioned heart, the cold-complexioned brain, the moist-complexioned liver, the dry-complexioned bones, etc. – be unceasingly proportioned and re-proportioned to each other's changes, in order for the body to maintain itself in balance (health). When one recognizes that the dynamic equilibrium governing the functioning *complexio* is multiplied over and over again through layer after layer within the systematic whole, one begins to appreciate the extraordinary complexity and coherence that marks the Galenic model of balance.

---

[31] The process of intellectual distillation was accelerated yet further in the following decades with the production of comprehensive "summaries" of Galen's writings, written with student medical exams in mind, such as the *Revocativium memoriae* (c. 1285) by Jean de Saint-Amand. As became common with these kinds of works, Saint-Amand's guide contained a remarkably detailed alphabetized index to Galen's translated works, composed of some 4,400 statements arranged in 582 topics. On this see McVaugh, "The Nature and Limits of Medical Certitude," 64 and n. 8; Danielle Jacquart, "L'œuvre de Jean de Saint-Amand et les méthodes d'enseignement à la Faculté de médecine de Paris à la fin du XIIIe siècle," in *Manuels, programmes de cours et techniques d'enseignement dans les universités médiévales*, ed. Jacqueline Hamesse (Institut d'études médiévales de l'Université catholique de Louvain, 1994), 257–75.

Proportional "*iustitia*" as the model for bodily equilibrium and balance

Having established the complexion as a unity composed of proportioned (and continuously re-proportioned) parts, Avicenna proceeds to outline two of its conceivable permutations. There is the perfectly equal complexion in which the primary qualities are found in precisely equal quantities, and which thus represents a perfect "medium" between all the contraries.[32] And there is the complexion that declines sharply from the medium toward one or another of the contraries, i.e., toward the absolutely hot, cold, wet, or dry.[33] After elucidating these two possibilities, Avicenna abruptly asserts that neither of these – neither the perfectly equal nor the truly unequal – exist in their "pure" state within the living body.[34] Having created a space of uncertainty, Avicenna fills it with a series of statements that are the most conceptually difficult he has so far presented in these introductory chapters. He writes:

You should know that the term "equal," as commonly used by doctors in their writings, does not refer to a precise equality (*aequalitas*) by weight, but rather to an equality determined by division according to justice (*denominatur ab iustitia in divisione*).[35]

There is no novelty here in Avicenna's use of the term "*iustitia*" in a medical context, and no novelty in *iustitia* serving to distinguish between a simple equality by weight and a complex proportional equality. As I noted in the previous chapter, Galen (and his Latin translator) had used the term "*iustitia*" for similar purposes in the *De complexionibus*.[36] There the metaphor of justice served to reinforce Galen's general insistence on the relativity of bodily conditions and the relativity of the physician's resultant judgments. It is his way of underscoring that the equality that concerns the doctor is *always* the proportional equality relative to, or proper to, a particular individual, or part, or function, at a particular

---

[32] Avicenna, *Canon* (1608), 11b: "complexio aequalis ita, ut quantitates qualitatem contrariarum in complexionato sint aequales, non superantes, neque superatae, et sit complexio qualitas in medio earum vere."

[33] *Ibid.*: "Alter vero modus est ut non sit complexio qualitatum contrariarum media absolute, sed ad unam magis declinet extremitatum."

[34] *Ibid.*: "Quod autem in doctrina medicine consideratur aequale, aut extra aequalitatem, non est hoc neque illud."

[35] *Ibid.*: Debes autem scire, quod aequale, de quo medici in suis inquisitionibus tractant, non est denominatum ab aequalitate in qua *aequalitas* cum pondere aequaliter existit, sed denominatur ab iustitia in divisione." My translation here differs somewhat from that of McVaugh (*Source Book*, 717).

[36] Galen, *De complexionibus* (1976), 30: "Tale autem aliquid et iustitiam esse dicimus, non pondere et mensura id quod equale, sed decente et secundum dignitatem scrutantem."

time. "*Iustitia*," in this case, functions as an ideal for the doctor just as it does for the judge, both of whom must weigh the particular conditions of each individual case and arrive at the particular form of equalization that will produce a "just" and proportioned solution relative to each case.

I suggested in the previous chapter that Galen's use of "*iustitia*" to signal proportionalization and relativity may well have had its source in Aristotle's discussion of justice and exchange in Book V of the *Nicomachean Ethics*. But what I could only surmise in the case of Galen I can suggest with more certainty for Avicenna, whose program is, after all, to integrate, insofar as possible, Galenic medicine and Aristotelian philosophy. As every reader of the *Canon* who had also read the *Ethics* would know (and given the centrality of the *Ethics* to the university curriculum by the mid thirteenth century, this would surely include a good proportion of the *Canon*'s Latin readers), the "geometrical" and "proportional" form of justice and equality Avicenna here applies to the process of equalization within the bodily complexion is the same form of equality that Aristotle applied to essential aspects of both political and economic life within the *civitas*. In Aristotle's view, proportional equalization (*iustitia distributiva*) governs the just distribution of benefits and rewards between the *civitas* and its citizens. Even more central to the experience of urban life, Aristotle held that a form of proportional equalization governs the exchange of all goods and services within the economic sphere, or what medieval writers at times referred to as "the marketplace" (*in foro*).[37] I think it likely that Avicenna was aware that by using the term *iustitia*, he was, in effect, linking equalization in the medical sphere (the medical body) to equalization in the political and economic spheres (the body politic); likely, too, that the readers of the *Canon* would have been similarly awake to the implications of this linkage. In any case, later scholastic commentaries on the *Tegni*, such as that written by Pietro Torrigiano de Torrigiani (Turisanus) *c.* 1315–20, provide clear proof that the pivotal Galenic concept of "*aequalitas ad iustitiam*" was being linked quite consciously by scholastic *medici* to Aristotle's discussion of proportional equalization within the *civitas* in *Ethics* V.[38] Here I want only to suggest that when both Galen and Avicenna use the freighted term *iustitia* to define the form of equality applicable to the Galenic body, they cannot help but indicate intellectual links between the form of balance

---

[37] Aristotle, *Ethica Nicomachea*, V, 3–5 [1131a10–1133b18]. On the central place of proportional equalization in Aristotle's discussion of economic exchange, see Chapter 2.

[38] *Plus quam commentum in Parvam Galeni Artem, Turisani Florentini Medici Praestantissimi* (Venice: ad Iuntas, 1557), 8r, 14r–v. I provide evidence for this statement later in this chapter in a section dedicated to Turisanus and his *Plus quam commmentum*.

underlying the self-proportioning system of the body, the self-governing
and self-regulating *civitas*, and the self-equalizing dynamic of economic
exchange in the marketplace.

The first scholastic commentaries on Galen: Taddeo Alderotti

The first detailed scholastic commentaries on complete treatises of Galen,
including the *Tegni*, were written by the physician and professor of
medicine at the University of Bologna, Taddeo Alderotti (*c.* 1210–95).[39]
Taddeo brought to his reading of Galen a wide knowledge of Aristotle's
works on logic, physiology, and natural philosophy. To this he added a
comprehensive knowledge of virtually all the learned medical literature
then available in Latin. The primary works already considered in this
chapter, Ibn Ridwan's commentary on the *Tegni* and Avicenna's *Canon*,
were well known to him. Indeed, in addition to writing the first scholastic
commentary on Galen's *Tegni* (which made heavy use of Ibn Ridwan's
commentary), he wrote detailed commentaries on portions of the *Canon*
as well.[40] Although he chose to focus on only small sections of this
immense work, he was deeply influenced by it; Avicenna appears repeatedly as a trusted authority in all of his writings.[41]

   With Taddeo Alderotti, then, we can see for the first time how Galen
was read and understood after the reception of the *Canon* and at a time
when the study of Aristotle had moved to the center of the university
curriculum. Most of his writings date to the decades of the 1270s and 80s,
a period when "the new model of equilibrium" (as I have identified it)
was just beginning to emerge in many areas of scholastic speculation.[42]

[39] Taddeo, born in Florence, is also known as Taddeo da Firenze and Thaddeus
Florentinus. Villani includes a short biography of Taddeo in his *Liber de civitatis florentiae
famosis civibus*, and he also finds a place in Dante's *Divina Commedia*, at *Paradiso* 12: l.
82–4. The most comprehensive and important study of Taddeo and his circle is
Nancy Siraisi, *Taddeo Alderotti and his Pupils: Two Generations of Italian Medical Learning*
(Princeton University Press, 1981).

[40] The citations of Taddeo's commentary on the *Tegni* that follow are taken from *Micratechne
Galeni*, in *Thaddei Florentini Medicorum sua tempestate principis in C. Gal. Micratechne
Commentarii* (Naples, 1522).

[41] Taddeo wrote commentaries on, among other works, the *Tegni* and *De crisi* of Galen, the
Aphorisms, De regimine acutorum, and *Prognostica* of Hippocrates, and the *Isagoge* of
Johannitius. For a bibliography of Taddeo's writings, including his commentaries on
sections of the *Canon*, see Siraisi, *Taddeo Alderotti and his Pupils*, 39–40, 105, n. 26, 416–18.

[42] See Chapters 1 and 2 above for the emergence of the "new" model in scholastic economic
thought in this period, particularly in the economic writings of Peter of John Olivi. For an
introduction to the form and functioning principles of this model in the area of natural
philosophy, see Chapter 8 below, and Kaye, "The (Re)Balance of Nature."

As one who was trained in Galenic medicine, Taddeo was particularly sensitive to the forms and potentialities of bodily *aequalitas*. For these reasons, Taddeo's writings are well situated to shed light on an important moment in the history of balance.

Most of the surviving records of Taddeo's life derive from his active involvement in the economic and civic life of Bologna and Florence. Surviving documents record the generous monetary rewards he received from the commune of Bologna for his services as a physician, as well as numerous transactions in communal real estate and finance. A number of these records indicate that Taddeo's financial activity included money-lending: born poor, he died a wealthy man.[43] Taddeo's authorship of a vernacular translation of Aristotle's *Nicomachean Ethics* provides further evidence of his interest in the political, social, and economic life of his society. This translation is thought to be one of the earliest philosophical writings (as opposed to legal writings) to derive from the intellectual milieux of the University of Bologna.[44] In this one figure, then, we have the intersection of medicine, political and city life, economic speculation, and university culture, all at a highly expansive moment of the European economy. As it turns out, just such a combination of life influences frequently appears in the biographies of thinkers who contributed to the construction of the new model of equilibrium.[45]

In the 1260s, when Taddeo first came to be associated with the University of Bologna, its institutional structures for the study of both philosophy and medicine were quite weak, dwarfed as they were by the great school of law. Over his decades there, Taddeo worked to create a Faculty of Medicine that could take its place beside the Faculty of Law. Two steps were necessary for this process to succeed. The first was to construct professional organizations for physicians on the model of those previously invented by the lawyers at the university. The second was considerably more difficult: to raise the status of medicine as a discipline so that it could take its place in the university curriculum beside the study of philosophy and law. The stakes were high, and the potential rewards, both intellectual and material, were considerable, as Taddeo's example indicates.[46]

---

[43] For a brief biography of Taddeo, focusing on his "combination of professional success and business acumen," see Siraisi, *Taddeo Alderotti and his Pupils*, 27–31.

[44] On Taddeo's Ethics, see *ibid.*, 10, 77–82.

[45] See below for the biographies of Marsilius of Padua, Pietro d'Abano, Jean Buridan, Nicole Oresme, and others. For the routine involvement of scholastic masters in the economic and administrative life of their times, see Kaye, *Economy and Nature*, 28–36.

[46] For evidence of Taddeo's lucrative practice, see Siraisi, *Taddeo Alderotti and his Pupils*, 36–9.

In the hierarchy of knowledge generally accepted in this period, the more a discipline mixed in the world of practice and contingent particulars, and the closer it was to being classified as an "art," the lower its status and its place on the scale of intellectual value. In this scheme, medicine had a great weight to overcome. Galen's emphasis on the practical, the particular, and the contingent side of medicine, made it impossible for the learned physician to deny its links to the mechanical and practical arts. But Galen was a philosopher as well as a doctor. He insisted that the proper exercise of medicine required that contingent practice be grounded in the timeless truths about nature provided by philosophical (primarily Aristotelian) physical theory. He had often visited the question of medicine's crucial role in bridging the gulf between theoretical science and practical art, and his concern was echoed in scholastic culture, where detailed discussions of medicine's "in-between" position appeared again and again in treatises through the seventeenth century.[47] Not surprisingly, since Taddeo was directly concerned with raising the status of medicine as an intellectual discipline at Bologna, he considers this question at many points.[48]

In the end, Taddeo fully accepts that the most that doctors can ever achieve is approximate measurement and approximate knowledge through the evidence of the senses, trial and error, and the employment of "artful conjecture" (*per coniecturam artificialem*).[49] Taddeo's stances on this question make clear that the systematic equalization governing the Galenic body resists through its very complexity the attractions of the universalized and absolutist determinations associated with Aristotelian natural philosophy in his time.[50] Its comprehension demanded instead its own forms of seeing and knowing. Hence Taddeo's insistence that

---

[47] For the history of this discussion within scholastic medicine, see *ibid.*, 118–39; Cornelius O'Boyle, "Discussions on the Nature of Medicine at the University of Paris, ca. 1300," in *Learning Institutionalized. Teaching in the Medieval University*, ed. John Van Engen (University of Notre Dame Press, 2000), 197–228; McVaugh, "Nature and Limits of Medical Certitude," esp. 68–74. Avicenna's treatment of this question in the introduction to the *Canon* proved to be extremely influential for later Latin writers. On this see French, *Canonical Medicine*, 68–75.

[48] E.g., Taddeo, *Tegni*, 2ra: "Nam inquantum medicus dicitur vel docet incidere aut farmacare: vel farmacat; vel incidit facit vel docet operationem componendo farmatiam cum corpore nostro sicut carpentarius in faciendo domum dicitur activus. Sed inquantum res naturales et non naturales et contra naturam considerat dicitur speculator." The discussion of this question then continues for two folios.

[49] *Ibid.*, 203rb: "Dico quod talis distinctio in egritudinibus invenitur non tamen secundum certam naturam et veram mensuram sed per coniecturam artificialem."

[50] Mark Jordan, "The Disappearance of Galen in Thirteenth-Century Philosophy and Theology," in *Mensch und Natur im Mittelalter*. Miscellanea Mediaevalia XXI (Berlin and New York: Walter de Gruyter, 1992), 703–17.

medicine was a mixed "*scientia mechanica*" rather than a pure "*scientia speculativa.*"

> For medicine belongs under the heading of speculative natural science by reason of the theory it requires, but by reason of the practice it requires, it belongs under the heading of mechanical science (*comprehenditur sub mechanica scientia*), as we noted above, and this is the whole truth.[51]

Given that no one in Taddeo's time could have guessed that "modern" science would one day embrace and take as its own the epistemological "disabilities" that characterized Galenic medicine, Taddeo's actions here in exposing the problems of medical authority and reasserting the uncertainty of medical knowledge were clearly not intended to lend the medical profession a fake, if potentially lucrative, air of certainty. In Taddeo's honest recognition of these limitations, he is a worthy disciple of Galen.

Taddeo Alderotti's grasp of the Galenic *complexio*

Taddeo's consistent endeavor in his commentary on the *Tegni* is not so much to support Galen against possibly contrary positions assumed by other medical authorities (more than a dozen of whom are frequently cited, with Avicenna and Aristotle cited most frequently) as much as it is to read Galen in the light of other authoritative voices in order to clarify rather than confirm or criticize his points.[52] This approach can be clearly seen in his treatment of the *complexio* – the theoretical focal point of the Galenic body. Taddeo, like Avicenna, fully grasps the centrality of the *complexio* to the whole scheme of Galenic medicine. The doctor's main task is to help nature promote or maintain the proper balance (or proportional "*aequalitas*" in Galenic terms) of the body's complexions, as determined by the proper proportional mixture of the four primary qualities. The body itself and each and every one of its parts possesses its own "equality" proper to it. The particular proportions that constitute the best (i.e., most healthful) mixtures are specific to specific individuals, while at the same time, they are understood to change for each individual along with changes in age and environment. The complexions function, in Taddeo's words, as both the cause of composition (*causa compositionis*)

---

[51] Taddeo, *Tegni*, 6va: "nam medicina ratione teorice comprehenditur sub scientia speculativa naturali, et ratione practice comprehenditur sub mechanica scientia, sicut superius diximus, et hec est tota veritas."

[52] It is clear that Taddeo has read Ibn Ridwan's commentary on the *Tegni* with great care, referring to him often simply as "the commentator." In most cases, he approves of Ibn Ridwan's reading, although as is typical with his approach, he feels free to criticize him harshly at times, e.g., *Tegni*, 12ra.

and the instrument of operation (*instrumentum operationis*) for the body and its parts. Proper function (i.e., health) results from properly equalized complexional mixtures, while sickness or failure of function results from unbalanced mixtures.[53] The physician's determination of what constitutes proper proportional *aequalitas* or balance for the *complexio*, is fully relativized, judged solely insofar as it *works* toward supporting the proper function of the parts and whole of the organism.[54] The doctor must seek (through the aid of nature) not only to balance the particular complexions proper to particular parts, but also to reestablish "coequality" (*coaequalitas*) throughout the body; that is, to reestablish the balanced interaction of the body's myriad complexions to each other and to the whole.[55]

   In holding to this general scheme Taddeo is being true to the *Tegni*, but he also introduces new questions and distinctions in his concern to unify Galen's opinions with those of Aristotle, Avicenna, Ibn Ridwan, and others. With notable frequency Taddeo points out what appear at first to be genuine disagreements between Galen and these other authorities on points both medical and philosophical. In the great majority of these cases, however, he uses all the scholastic means at his disposal to reconcile seeming disparities and to show, in the end, that the disagreement is more apparent than real, more a matter of differing context and perspective than of substance. This way of proceeding is, of course, characteristic of scholasticism. But there is something about Taddeo's relentless attempt to reconcile authorities (and about very similar attempts at reconciliation performed by later scholastic medical writers, e.g., Peter of Abano, Turisanus, etc.) which brings to mind the very habit of balancing so central to the Galenic project, here extended from the treatment of human bodies to the treatment of textual bodies and bodies of thought.[56]

Continuity, the *neutrum*, and balance: reconciling Galen and Aristotle

One of Galen's central points in the *Tegni* – the existence of a neuter or "neither" state between the contrary states of health and sickness – clashed so directly with positions held by both Aristotle and Avicenna that it presented immense difficulties to the project of scholastic

---

[53] *Ibid.*, 17rb.   [54] Siraisi, *Taddeo Alderotti and his Pupils*, 160.

[55] Taddeo, *Tegni*, 10vb, for his discussion of the notion of "coequale": "Et notandum quod dicit Galenus coequale in organicis in quo notatur duplex aequalitas, scilicet membrorum in se et membrorum ad corpus totum."

[56] For a discussion of the history of the medical project of reconciliation, see Siraisi, *Taddeo Alderotti and his Pupils*, 186–202.

reconciliation.[57] Taddeo returns to the question of the *neutrum* again and again. His position is complicated. At the same time that he recognizes the philosophical problems presented by claims for the real existence of the *neutrum*, he also acknowledges the benefits this conception affords to the physician. His attempts to reconcile these positions are particularly germane here because they often involve, whether implicitly or explicitly, the question of balance.

Central to Aristotelian physics is the notion that all qualitative motion (all motion from hot to cold, wet to dry, white to black, etc.) involves motion between contraries. At the same time, as Taddeo clearly recognizes and records, Aristotle presents strong philosophical arguments against the possibility that the mid-point between any two contraries is a separable state or disposition with its own ontological status equal to that of the contraries themselves. Here Aristotle and Galen seem to be in profound disagreement. Galen (as we have seen) not only treats the *neutrum* as a real space, but he allows it its own heading in the *Tegni*, equal in importance to the headings for health and sickness. Although previous commentators, including Avicenna, had noted the discrepancy here between the positions of Aristotle and Galen, Taddeo cites Ibn Ridwan's conciliatory opinion that if the question be well understood, the discord disappears. Aristotle denied the existence of a *neutrum* as a separable disposition on perfectly legitimate philosophical grounds, while Galen accepted the *neutrum* as the space connecting the contraries on the defendable grounds of sense observation.[58] Judged according to intellectual/philosophical requirements (*ad iuditium intellectus*), as the philosopher must, the *neutrum* cannot be said to have a separable existence, but judged as the doctor must, according to sense (*ad iuditium sensibile*), it can.[59]

---

[57] On the implications of Galen's "neither" state (*neutrum*) for his modeling of balance, see the previous chapter. On philosophical questions raised by the presence of the "neither" or "neutral" state in Galen's vision of the body, see Joutsivuo, *Scholastic Tradition and Humanist Innovation*. For a study of the *neutrum* that centers on its reception history in scholastic commentaries, see Van der Lugt, "Neither Ill nor Healthy." Van der Lugt discusses Taddeo's understanding of the *neutrum* (25–6, 29) as well as a number of those positions that preceded his, including those found in Ibn Ridwan's commentary (18–25). Note that Van der Lugt often prefers to translate Galen's "*neuter*" as "the neutral" rather than as "neither." She recognizes, however (25), that in Taddeo's writing, the *neutrum* is primarily framed in negative terms, representing "neither" health nor sickness.

[58] Taddeo, *Tegni*, 5va: "De tertio dicit quod isti viri non discordant; siquis eos bene intelligat, quia quando Arist. ponit quod inter sanitatem et egritudinem non cadit medium ipse intelligit medium quod non participet et hoc est bene impossibile... sed quando Gal. ponit neutrum inter sanum et egrum ipse intelligit de medio quod participat extrema quoquo modo participationis."

[59] *Ibid.*, 6ra–b, where Taddeo contrasts these two modes of knowing.

One key to the solution of the *neutrum* lies in Galen's insistence, fully grasped and accepted by Ibn Ridwan and Taddeo, that the body as a systematic whole and in each of its operational parts is in *continuous* motion between health and sickness, across both continuous space and continuous time.[60] If one thinks as a doctor must, in terms of the actual functioning systems of the body, then it is impossible to conceive of motion between the contraries without recognizing that it must pass through a mid-point and a mid-range on the continuum.[61] Even, Taddeo writes, the complexion of the very rare body in perfect health (*corpus perfecte sanum*) is continually shifting around its state of balance because, as Galen teaches us (and Avicenna stressed), the body is composed of contrary elements, and these are always in opposition and tension. For this reason, the body and its parts must always be in flux – always either falling away from or approaching balance.[62]

In one of Taddeo's final discussions of this question, he follows Galen in noting that as the body moves from health to sickness, there must necessarily be a period, and a state, where the body is sickening but does not yet appear sick, and where the operation of the body is weakening but the operational failure is not yet apparent to the senses.[63] In short, even though as a time and a state the *neutrum*, with its fluid boundaries and its hazy and ambiguous signs, presents insurmountable problems in philosophical (Aristotelian) terms, it is (as Taddeo recognizes), a necessary construct for the doctor to *think* with.[64] Taddeo's discussions of the *neutrum* indicate that Galen accomplished with it just what I have argued he intended to accomplish.[65] It focused the attention of his readers on the reality of the body's continuous flux: it gave flesh to the underlying form of the continuum and motion along it; it undermined essentialist notions

[60] *Ibid.*, 15ra: "Et videtur quod extrema et coniunctio debeant esse ex tempore, quia huiusmodi coniunctio est quidam transitus sanitatis in egritudinem, et econverso, ut patet in convalescentibus et egrotativis." The importance he places on this point can be judged by its discussion at three separate places in his commentary: 6rb, 13rb–18vb, 29ra–33rb.

[61] *Ibid.*, 15va: "sed constat hoc corpus venire ad sanitatem nunc, quare transit per neutrum nunc, sed tale neutrum nunc necessario continuatur cum egro nunc a parte priori."

[62] *Ibid.*, 18rb: "et quamvis hoc sanum corpus [perfecte] dicatur variabile et permutabile sicut dicit Gal. infra de causis, tamen ista varitatio est generalis a communi natura corporis, scilicet in quantum corpus est compositum ex contrariis elementis, et hoc modo omne elementatum est variabile et corruptibile."

[63] Noted in Van der Lugt, "Neither Ill nor Healthy," 25.

[64] Taddeo, *Tegni*, 32rb: "Sic construe propter hoc quod talia corpora sunt ambigua, non habentia manifestos terminos, neque habentia facilem discretionem, hoc secundum genus lesionis istorum corporum participans neutro contrariorum; consistet dispositioni, idest adheret, quam scilicet dispositionem nos dicimus nominari neutram."

[65] See my discussion on this point in the previous chapter.

about knowable boundaries and perfections within the living body; it forced the doctor to match his conceptual apparatus to the unceasing rhythms of the body; and, as a result of all these, it deepened the sense of the body as a relational system in dynamic equilibrium.

Continuity, range, and degree: the latitude (*latitudo*)

In the process of giving intellectual shape to the *neutrum* and the qualitative motion along the continuum of health/sickness it represents, Taddeo made use of the word "latitude" (*latitudo*), a word and concept that in the Galenic tradition signified a graded range or continuum of value, divisible into degrees. It was made available to Taddeo through its appearance in the two extant Latin translations of the *Tegni*, as well as in both Ibn Ridwan's commentary and Avicenna's *Canon*. In Taddeo's hands, however, the latitude (which became, in the fourteenth century, a prime conceptual component of the "new model of equilibrium" in a wide range of discourses) gained considerable conceptual weight and clarity.[66]

Toward the beginning of Book II of the *Tegni*, the text reads: "And the whole latitude of health is divided into three parts."[67] As Taddeo begins his gloss, he appears annoyed by the carelessness of the wording here. He notes that rather than one latitude of health divided into three, there are actually three latitudes: one of health, one of sickness, and one of the *neutrum*, that together form the continuum of health/sickness.[68] He decides that he must simply go beyond the written text to divine Galen's "intent" in this passage.[69] One thing is clear throughout his discussion: he consistently links the latitude to the physics of continuous qualitative motion. It is not merely an approximative range, it is also a real distance on the qualitative continuum between health and sickness along which motion takes place. And as a real qualitative distance, it is conceptually divisible into degrees.[70] What does it mean, he asks, when Galen defines

---

[66] For the important role played by this conceptual instrument in Peter Olivi's model of equilibrium in economic exchange, see his discussion of a "latitude of just price" in Chapter 2, pp. 123–5; for the place it later assumed in fourteenth-century natural philosophy, see Chapter 8.

[67] Taddeo's discussion of the passage, "Et dividitur totius sanitatis latitudo in tres partes" begins 29ra.

[68] *Ibid.*, 29va: "Ad hanc questionem dico quod arbitror egritudinem et neutralitatem habere latitudinem sicut et sanitatem."

[69] Taddeo justifies this move by noting that in other of Galen's written works (e.g., *De complexionibus*, 2.4) Galen himself speaks of three latitudes rather than of a single latitude of health.

[70] Taddeo, *Tegni*, 31ra: "Latitudinem gradualem voco secundum quod magis et minus distat sanitas ab optima sanitate, inquantum optima sanitas comprehendit sub se sanitatem nunc."

health as a "just equality" or a "just medium"? For if the medium is taken to be a precise point of optimum equality, and even the healthiest bodies are ever in flux around this point, then no body can ever be said to be truly healthy.[71] Yet, clearly, there are healthy bodies, and the doctor must be able to distinguish between the healthy and the sick. Taddeo's initial solution to this set of problems follows Galen closely. The medium must be recognized as having two modes: in some cases and some applications it can be taken to be an indivisible mid-point, but in other cases, and specifically in the case of the living body, the medium can only be understood as a range or *latitude* and never as a precise point.[72]

Taddeo then responds to an imagined criticism of his position. A latitude, critics might say, can represent only a kind of ersatz medium, while a "true" medium must be an indivisible point representing "true" arithmetical equality. This might well be the opinion of someone whose model of equality was patterned on the balancing point on the mechanical scale, or the simple bisection of a line, or even the arithmetical division of a sum. It is an opinion that is perfectly congruent with a worldview based in fixed hierarchies and ontologies and centered in the philosophical investigation of perfections. It was an opinion that made perfect sense to Gratian and the early writers on the sin and illegality of usury.[73] But if this had at one time been the prevalent worldview in learned philosophical and theological culture, it was most certainly *not* the view of Galen, nor, by the later thirteenth century, of Galenists like Taddeo. Galen had shown in the *Tegni* (and other works) that the equality that is of primary concern to the *medicus*, the equality that it is the role of the physician to maintain or restore, the equality at the center of the *complexio*, is never representable by a single indivisible point but always by a mediating range or latitude divisible into degrees.[74]

Taddeo is very intent on defining the *latitudo* as a "true" medium (*vere medium*) in relation to its extremes – as "true" in its way, when defined in terms of practice and function, as the mid-point. He asserts that this is so even though the latitude contains degrees or parts that are demonstrably *not*

---

[71] *Ibid.*, 14va: "Sed non videtur possibile aliquid posse tenere vere medium inter duo extrema. Cum omne corpus et necessario sit semper in fluxu, et quidam est in fluxu nullo modo potest vere stare in medio. Preterea vere medium inter duo extrema non est nisi punctus, et esse in puncto nihil est apud medicum quia non est scibile." On this point, see Van der Lugt, "Neither Ill nor Healthy," 26.

[72] Taddeo, *Tegni*, 15ra: "Ad hec tria [objections above] una est solutio, et est quod duplex est vere medium, scilicet unum est cum latitudine, aliud indivisibile."

[73] As discussed in Chapter 1, this was the view expressed by Gratian and the authorities he cites in his question on usury in the *Decretum*.

[74] For the triumph of this recognition in the area of scholastic economic thought by the last quarter of the thirteenth century, see Chapters 1 and 2 above.

in the true middle of the extremes (*licet in se sint partes que non sunt vere in medio*).[75] This is a very important point to make, and the energy Taddeo expends to defend it indicates that it might well have been a difficult point for his audience to grasp. To make it, Taddeo interjects an elaborate illustrative example. If, he posits, there are twelve discrete bodies, such as twelve stones, placed evenly in a straight line, the four bodies in the middle of the line represent a "true medium" with respect to the first and last (twelfth) body, because these four, taken as a whole, which is to say, taken as a *latitude* (*tamen sunt cum latitudine inter se*), are equidistant from the beginning and end of the line. Moreover the latitude composed of the four stones represents a "true medium" even if none of the four bodies themselves are perfectly situated in the middle of the extremes.[76] While a modern audience might well expect to find an illustrative example like the twelve stones in a medical or scientific text, it is, in both its numeration and concretization of an abstract principle, quite unusual in the context of scholastic commentaries of the thirteenth century as well as in the context of this particular commentary of nearly three hundred folios. Its existence here is a good indication of just how important it was for Taddeo to establish the conceptual and mathematical framework in which the "true" medium sought by the *medicus* is at the same time a graded latitude rather than a point.

There are indications that Taddeo not only fully grasped the Galenic concept of the latitude but that the concept, once grasped, began actually to shape how he thought and viewed the world as a doctor.[77] As he saw it, the natural philosopher considers health only in terms of perfections: perfect balance, perfect equality; and perfect function. Everything that falls away from perfection would then, to the philosopher, fall into the category of sickness.[78] But this way of seeing, and these strict and static

---

[75] Taddeo, *Tegni*, 15ra: "Et dico quod medium habens latitudinem est vere medium quo ad extrema licet in se sint partes que non sunt vere in medio."

[76] *Ibid.*: "Sint enim. xii. corpora, scilicet lapides, vel alia corpora, posita secundum lineam rectam consequentia se. Dico quod quattuor que sunt vere in medio dicuntur vere medium respectu primi et duodecimi quia equaliter distant ab utrisque. Quia tamen quodlibet istorum per se sumptum non equaliter distat. Primum enim illorum. 4. distat a primo solum per tria et a duodecimo per. 6. Propter hoc quamvis illa quattuor corpora media sint secundum comparationem ad extrema: tamen sunt cum latitudine inter se. Sed si tollantur. 13. corpora posita consequenter, et tollatur unum corpus quod in medio est, istud est vere medium inter esse et dici cum sit unum solum corpus quod in medio est. Idest vere medium secundum se et secundum extrema ... quare dicitur vere medium secundum omnem modum sanissimi et egerrimi."

[77] Taddeo, *Tegni*, 33ra: "respondeo quod medicus considerat de ipsis aliter quam considerat naturalis et mathematicus."

[78] *Ibid.*, 33a: "Aliter vero dyalecticus vel naturalis accipit sanitatem et egritudinem fortasse nanque sanitatem vult solam contemperantiam et coequalitatem cum perfectissima operatione, et omne quod a tali natura labitur appelat egrum."

definitions, simply will not work for the practicing physician. "That is why," he continues,

Galen was intent to say that when the doctor speaks of coequality, he does not do so in terms of its perfection. And similarly, the doctor does not understand temperance to refer to a state of perfect equality or perfect temperance, as the words themselves might indicate, but he understands it instead to refer to a latitude that terminates at notable loss of physical function (*latitudo terminatur ad magnam lesionem operationum*). So that when Galen speaks of the words "equality" and "distemperament," he does not understand them in the way they might sound or signify [to the philosopher], but rather he allows them a certain magnitude.[79]

Taddeo's recognition here is clear. At this point, in the 1270s and 80s, the doctor and the philosopher have very different notions of how to view the world, and they possess correspondingly different notions of equality, equalization, the medium, and balance itself. Clearly, too, philosophy is at this time the dominant discourse, and medicine is in the position of simply trying to clear for itself a place at the learned table. In the century that follows, however, it is the model of equilibrium proper to Galenic medicine, constructed around latitudes, approximations, constant flux, and fully relativized perspectives, that comes to prevail in the most advanced speculation in multiple fields of scholastic thought, including the field of natural philosophy. There, in its new setting, it will transform the image of the natural world.[80]

The reception and comprehension of Galenic relativity

There is one pivotal aspect of the Galenic model of equilibrium that I have not yet specifically mentioned, even though it underlies all the concepts I have so far discussed: Galenic relativity. In the previous chapter I argued that it is the top-to-bottom relativity of Galen's vision of the working body that most characterizes it and sets it apart from the Aristotelian natural philosophy being practiced in the universities of the mid thirteenth century. By the early fourteenth century, however, the situation with respect to scholastic natural philosophy (and a host of other university disciplines) was changing, with newly relativized determinations being attached to all manner of questions and problems. The forms of scholastic speculation

---

[79] *Ibid.*: "Et hoc voluit dicere Gal. Cum dixit non secundum ipsam rerum naturam, cum enim dicat medicus coequalitatem. Et temperantium non intelligit coequalitatem et temperantium veraciter, ut haec vocabula sonant, sed cum latitudine quadam intellectuali, que latitudo terminatur ad magnam lesionem operationum. Et cum dicit in equalitatem et distemperantiam, non intelligit secundum quod haec vocabula sonant et significant, sed cum quadam magnitudine."

[80] The argument appears in Chapter 8 below.

that I identify most closely with "the new equilibrium" are invariably those which are organized around a profound relativization of position, function, and meaning. A question of potentially great importance both to intellectual history and to the history of balance, then, is when and to what degree did medieval thinkers begin to comprehend the richness and fullness of Galenic relativity? Taddeo Alderotti's leading role in the reception of Galen makes him an important source for the answer to these questions.

Taddeo's most direct discussion of relativity does not appear in his commentary on the *Tegni* but rather in his commentary on the *Isagoge of Johannitius* (the Latinized name of Hunayn Ibn Ishaq, the same scholar who translated the *Tegni* into Arabic).[81] This is somewhat puzzling, since relativity holds a much more central place in Galen's *Tegni* than it does in the very much shorter and more concise *Isagoge* ("Introduction"). In general, however, Taddeo used his later commentary on the *Isagoge* to ask and answer questions with a philosophical cast, as indicated by the great importance he affords Avicenna as an authority in this text.[82] He begins his discussion of relativity in the context of his philosophical analysis of the Galenic *complexio*, the cornerstone of Galenic medicine. After posing a series of questions, Taddeo arrives at the heart of the matter, his analysis of the *complexio equalis*, the equal complexion, the primary cause and sign of bodily balance and health. Taddeo follows Avicenna in defining the *complexio* as a "unity," a systematic whole comprised of a ceaselessly reproportionalizing mixture of the four primary qualities, working in opposition to each other.

He begins by noting that there are two forms of equality that this unity can assume: "*aequalitas quo ad pondus*" and "*aequalitas quo ad iustitiam*."[83] For the definition of *aequalitas ad pondus* he cites Avicenna: "equal *ad pondus* represents a [perfectly] equal quantity of the contrary qualities, no quality overpowering or being overpowered by another."[84] As we have seen, Galen and all his commentators recognized that this form of equality

[81] *In subtilissimum Joannitii Hagogarum libellum*, in *Thaddei Florentini Expositiones* (Venice: ad Iuntas, 1527), fols. 343r–400r. (This work can be consulted online at the *Gallica* website.)

[82] Siraisi (*Taddeo Alderotti and his Pupils*, 40) calls the commentary to the *Isagoge* "by far the most 'Aristotelian' and 'philosophical' of his works." Avicenna's writings are consulted on almost every point, and his judgments drive the discussion at least as much as do Galen's, despite the fact that the *Isagoge* was written specifically as a summary of the Galenic system, and Hunayn's text pre-dated Avicenna by more than a century.

[83] Taddeo, *In Joannitii libellum*, 346va: "complexio equalis est duplex; una est quo ad iustitiam, alia est quo ad pondus."

[84] *Ibid.*, 346va: "complexio equalis quo ad pondus est equalis quantitas qualitatum contrarium, equales non superantes neque superare."

was neither proper to, nor even found in, the complexions of the human body or, for that matter, in any living body. He then turns to the *aequalitas ad iustitiam* for which he again offers Avicenna's definition, which contains two parts. The complexion equal *ad iustitiam* is: (a) that which conforms to the requirements of the (human) species, and (b) that in which the quantities of the qualities conform to "the best and most equitable proportion and division."[85] From the beginning then, Taddeo's understanding of equality *ad iustitiam* is essentially relativized: it is that proportion (whatever it may be) among the four qualities which best promotes good function.

Once Taddeo has established the general outlines of *aequalitas ad iustitiam*, he is ready to launch into a deeper analysis of the term, accompanied by a similarly profound exploration of relativity. He notes first that Avicenna defines equality *ad iustitiam* through four modes of relation: in relation to a particular species; to particular parts of that species; to specific individuals within the species; to specific parts of those individuals.[86] He then analyzes each mode in turn, and each turns out to involve yet further levels of relativization applied to the process of equalization.[87] The human species, as a whole, possesses an equal complexion in relation to all other species. There are, however, parts of the human species (i.e., particular individuals) who possess a relatively "more equal complexion" than the standard for the species.[88] Moreover, for every individual within the species, equality of complexion is determined relative to age, with different qualitative proportions determined to be "equal" in relation to the differing needs and functions of the body at different ages. Then, he continues, equality must be considered relative to climate and ethnicity, with certain complexions being more proper, that is to say, more "equal," within certain *gens* (or peoples) than within others, and similarly more equal in certain climates than in others.[89] But even within each *gens* and each climate some individuals possess a "greater equality" of complexion

---

[85] *Ibid.*: "Item secundum Avicenna complexio equalis ad iustitiam est complexio in qua est de qualitatibus qualitatum elementorum ad mensuram quam debet habere humana *nam secundum meliorem proportionis et divisionis equitatem*" (my emphasis).

[86] *Ibid.*: "Notandum ergo quod complexio equalis ad iustitiam dicitur ab Avicenna 4 modis; nam aut dicitur equalis secundum speciem, aut secundum partem speciei, aut secundum individuum, aut secundum partem individui."

[87] Note the prevalence of the term "*aequalitas*" in the citations on this subject that follow.

[88] Taddeo, *In Joannitii libellum*, 346va: "Si vero comparetur species ad ea quae sunt intus ille ... dicitur esse aequalitas que reperitur in individuo speciei humane quod habet maiorem equalitatem quam sit possibilis in specie humana."

[89] *Ibid.*: "nam aut est ista aequalitas comparando gente unius climatis ad gentem alterius climatis ... dicimus quod sclavi habent equalitatem in suo climate per comparationem ad indos."

in relation to others.[90] And within each individual, even within those who possess an exceptionally equal complexion, there are certain stages in life when the equality is more and other stages where it is less.[91] Moreover, some bodily members within the individual body possess equality to a greater degree than other members. The heart, for example, is said to have a more equal complexion in comparison with the brain.[92] But even this is not the end of the matter, for the heart or any other organ or member, in comparison with itself, has at some times a greater and sometimes a lesser *aequalitas* of complexion.[93] In all, Taddeo elucidates eight separate "modes" of relativization over the course of this discussion.

The Latin phrases Taddeo uses to express relation for the most part derive from the verb "to compare" (*"comparatur," "per comparationem ad," "comparata ad,"* etc.). At the very conclusion of his discussion, however, he uses the phrase *"relatus ad,"* and he uses it interchangeably with the phrase *"per comparationem ad."*[94] Turning yet again to stress the labile characteristics of *"aequalitas ad iustitium"* he writes (following Galen's discussion in the *De complexionibus*):

Plato can be cold in relation to (*per comparationem ad*) the medium for the human species and yet hot in relation to (*relatus ad*) Martin, and similarly the dog is hot in relation to (*relatus ad*) humans and cold in relation to (*relatus ad*) the lion.[95]

What does it mean to say that equality is relative; that some individuals and some organs of the body are more equal than others; that the same individual and organ can be more equal at some time than at other times; that all equality must be judged relative to climate; that some climates are more equal than others, etc.? If we hold on to our modern metaphorical sense of "equality," we cannot grasp what Taddeo (and Galen before him) is saying, and we will not see its significance. The picture sharpens when we recognize (as I argue that we should) that the term *"aequalitas*

---

[90] *Ibid.*: "tunc est quintus modus, et hec est aequalitas quam habet individuum in qua vivum et sanum reperitur, et dicitur ista aequalitas per comparationem ad alia individua."

[91] *Ibid.*, 346vb: "aut comparatur ad seipsum in diversis suis dispositionibus, et hic est sextus modus, et talis aequalitas reperitur in individuo in tempore in quo est meliori dispositione."

[92] *Ibid.*: "et hoc modo dicitur quod cor habet equalem complexionem per comparationem ad cerebrum."

[93] *Ibid.*: "Et talis aequalitas reperitur in corde aut in quolibet alio membro quando est in meliori dispositione quam esse possit."

[94] *Ibid.*, 347ra: "Ad hoc dicendum est quod medium cum extremis non habent oppositionem contrariorum sed potius relativorum, nam extremum dicitur per comparationem ad medium et medium ad extremum in relativis." Again, 347rb.

[95] *Ibid.*, 347rb: "et hoc modo dicitur quod Plato cum sit frigidus per comparationem ad medium in genere hominis esset calidus relatus ad Martinum, similiter dicitur canis relatus ad hominem calidus, et relatus ad leonum frigidus."

ad iustitiam" was the way Galenists expressed what we today would call "systematic equilibrium," especially when they applied the term to the continuous reproportionalizing of the *complexio* as a systematic unity. They themselves could not use the word "equilibrium" in this way because its meaning had not yet expanded beyond its literal sense – two equal, balancing weights, on the model of the balancing scale. This restricted sense of the word is, as we have seen, proper only to the first form of equality, *aequalitas ad pondus*, and Galen, Avicenna, Taddeo, and all subsequent Galenists recognized that this first form was unfitting and inapplicable to the living body and to the complexion as a living unity.[96] For similar reasons, they could not use the word "balance," because the meaning of this word too – *bilancia* – had not yet expanded past its identification with the physical balance or scale and the simple arithmetical equality – *aequalitas ad pondus* – it implied. Lacking the possibility of using our words "equilibrium" or "balance," they used what word they had – *aequalitas* – which could expand to accommodate notions of proportionality and relativity when the qualifying phrase "*quo ad iustitiam*" (i.e., in the mode of justice) was appended to it. *Aequitas*, or the equality proper to legal judgments, maps beautifully onto Galenic *aequalitas ad iustitiam*; both imply the search for approximative solutions that have been proportionalized and relativized to fit the specifics of each particular case.[97]

Taddeo's capacity to grasp the relativity Galen invested into the concept of *aequalitas ad iustitiam* and then to accentuate it through his categorization of eight fully relativized modes within it, demonstrates how clearly he has comprehended its place in the systematic equalization envisioned by Galen. The answer, then, to the question I posed at the beginning of this chapter – when and to what degree did medieval thinkers begin to comprehend the full implications of Galenic relativity? – is that Taddeo, writing in the 1280s, is well on his way to doing so.

There are, however, limitations to Taddeo's comprehension. Galen's relativity extends from structure and definition to *act*: it exerts a continuous force within his system of thought; it underlies his rhetorical strategy; it shapes his representation of the workings of the body; and it drives the logic of both function and cure. Taddeo has clearly comprehended

---

[96] See the parallel development in usury theory (Chapter 1) and price theory (Chapter 2) over the course of the thirteenth century, with respect to the evolution of the "equality" required in exchange, from *aequalitas ad pondus* to *aequalitas ad iustitiam*.

[97] E.g., as cited earlier: Taddeo, *In Joannitii libellum*, 346va: "Item secundum Avicennam complexio equalis ad iustitiam est complexio in qua est de qualitatibus qualitatum elementorum ad mensuram quam debet habere humana *nam secundum meliorem proportionis et divisionis equitatem*" (my emphasis).

the taxonomy of Galenic relativity, but it exerts little force on his own speculation. It does not appear to be fully applied as a habit of thought and perception beyond those cases where it is clearly enunciated by Galen.[98] Since a highly developed sense of relativity is central to the full model of Galenic balance, and equally central to the modeling of the "new equilibrium," we turn now to see where and when this sense became more fully and vitally present.

The expansion of Galenic thought and equilibrium: Arnau de Vilanova's *Aphorismi de gradibus*

By the late thirteenth century, the medical writings of Avicenna and Averroes had entered the curriculum of university medicine alongside, and in some cases ahead of, those of Galen. Avicenna's encyclopedic presentation of Galen's work in the *Canon* offered students an exhaustive overview of his writings in systematized and regularized form. Averroes brought his authority as the preeminent interpreter of Aristotle to his reading of Galen, further integrating medicine into a scholastic culture now deeply Aristotelian. More than any other learned doctor of his time, Arnau de Vilanova (*c.* 1238–*c.* 1312) saw the dangers in this mediation of Galen's vision, and, in a larger sense, in the contemporary preference for abridgments and synthetic interpretations over Galen's thorny particularity.[99] Arnau responded by championing Galen and authentic Galenic texts over any and all of his commentators and interpreters, finding frequent occasions to criticize the opinions of Avicenna and Averroes in the process.[100]

Arnau's belief that Galen provided the best and truest guide to medical knowledge led him to translate previously untranslated texts by the master from Arabic into Latin, and to retranslate certain key writings and portions of writings that he considered particularly necessary to medical

---

[98] I find this particularly true in comparison to its application by leading medical writers of the following generation, as I discuss below.

[99] García Ballester, "The New Galen," section V. Siraisi (*Avicenna in Renaissance Italy*, 38) notes that Avicenna's "drastic condensation of Galenic material" resulted at times in the oversimplification of his positions.

[100] McVaugh, "Nature and Limits of Medical Certitude," 66. In those cases where Avicenna differs from Galen, Arnau often attributes the cause to Avicenna's failure to grasp the "subtlety and profundity" of Galen's discussion. For an example of this criticism, see Arnaldus de Villanova, *Commentum supra tractatum Galieni De malicia complexionis diverse*, ed. Luis García Ballester and Eustaquio Sanchez Salor, in *Arnaldi de Villanova Opera medica omnia*, vol. XV (Universitat de Barcelona, 1985), 191 ff. García Ballester notes ("New Galen," 78–80) that Rhazes was the one Arabic medical authority spared Arnau's criticism.

understanding.[101] These new texts, added to those already in circulation, brought to more than forty the number of authentic Galenic works in circulation by the beginning of the fourteenth century. Louis García Ballester has given the title "the new Galen" to this formidable collection of writings – "new" not only for its volume but for the expanded comprehension of the Galenic system that followed from its availability. In Arnau's position as a highly respected and influential teacher in the Medical Faculty at the University of Montpellier in the 1290s – arguably the leading medical school of its time – he saw to it that the reading of the "new Galen" moved to the center of his university's curriculum.[102]

The pivotal role that Arnau played in the advance of Galenism is only one reason for his appearance here. Equally important are the links his writings provide between the model of equilibrium as it was evolving in medical speculation toward the end of the thirteenth century and the "new model of equilibrium" as it was emerging in a host of disciplines in the first decades of the fourteenth century: from economic, political, and ethical thought to theology and natural philosophy.[103] Evidence for the existence of rich connections between medicine and other speculative areas appears continually in medical treatises, both Arabic and Latin, as scholastic physicians reinforced their commentaries with repeated references to Aristotle's *Physica, Metaphysica, De anima, De generatione, Ethica Nichomachea*, and even (as we will see) *Politica* and *(Pseudo-)Economica*, in addition to their references to his writings on logic, medicine, and other *naturalia*. In referencing Aristotle's writings, Arabic and scholastic *medici* could follow the path of Galen himself, who relied heavily on Aristotelian physical principles and referred often to Aristotelian texts. For these reasons, the proposition that theoretical medicine drew on other areas of scholastic thought in the elucidation of its principles is hardly

---

[101] García Ballester, "New Galen," 72–8.

[102] The revised medical curriculum, dated to 1309, required, in addition to the study of the *Tegni*, the study of Galen's *De complexionibus, De malicia complexionis diverse, De simiplici medicina, De morbo et accidenti, De crisi, De criticis diebus*, and *De ingenio sanitatis*. Records indicate that still other of Galen's writings were being read and lectured upon at this date. In this same period, and as part of this same return to Galen as the font of medical knowledge, Jean de Saint-Amand wrote an abbreviation of twenty-eight Galenic works that soon became a standard text in the medical schools at Paris and Oxford. On this development, see García Ballester, "New Galen," 67–70.

[103] Arnau's reputation rested as much on his theological writings as on his medical writings. For a study that focuses on the connection between Arnau's medical thought and his later theological speculations, see Joseph Ziegler, *Medicine and Religion c. 1300: The Case of Arnau de Vilanova* (Oxford University Press, 1998). On this same subject, see Michael McVaugh, "Moments of Inflection: The Careers of Arnau de Vilanova," in *Religion and Medicine in the Middle Ages*, ed. Peter Biller and Joseph Ziegler (Woodbridge: York Medieval Press, 2001), 47–67.

controversial. Much less recognized and appreciated are the ways in which even after Aristotle had come to dominate university education, writings in scholastic medicine informed innovative speculation in a range of non-medical subjects, including, importantly, political theory and natural philosophy.

Some of the strongest evidence in favor of this influence has been offered by the historian of medicine, Michael McVaugh, in the course of his analysis of the writings of Arnau de Vilanova, particularly Arnau's treatise on the measurement of pharmacological dosage, the *Aphorismi de gradibus*, or *Aphorisms on Measurement by Degree*.[104] In a masterful introduction to this work, McVaugh reveals the parallels between proto-scientific insights generated within medical discourse at the end of the thirteenth century and those that begin to appear in other scholastic disciplines in the same period.[105] The influence of Arnaldian insights and innovations on later pivotal developments in natural philosophy is of particular interest.[106] McVaugh does not consider the subject of balance or equalization in Arnau's thought directly, since up to now it has not been recognized as a separable subject in itself. Nevertheless, drawing from the text of the *Aphorismi de gradibus* and from McVaugh's introduction to it, I have isolated four ways in which Arnau's program attaches strikingly new potentialities to the imagination of balance and systematic equilibrium. These are: (1) Arnau's imagination of a comprehensive system of mathematization applicable to the quantification of qualities and qualitative intensities; (2) Arnau's thorough application of relativity to his understanding of qualities and qualitative action; (3) the centrality of proportions and proportionalization to Arnau's mathematical program of measurement and to his imagination and use of the latitude (*latitudo*) as a graded and numbered line scale to measure and proportion qualitative intensities; and (4) Arnau's resituation of qualitative effect and qualitative measurement, including the notion of degree itself, from an

---

[104] Arnaldus de Villanova, *Aphorismi de gradibus*, ed. Michael McVaugh, in *Arnaldi de Villanova Opera medica omnia*, vol. II (Granada-Barcelona: Seminarium Historiae Medicae Granatensis, 1975); Michael McVaugh, "Arnald of Villanova and Bradwardine's Law," *Isis* 58 (1967), 56–64.

[105] McVaugh, Introduction to *Aphorismi*, 89: "It is of great interest for the history of medieval science as a whole to discover that there are repeated parallels between the treatment of the general problem of qualitative change that Arnald advances here to justify his new pharmacy and the contemporary scientific developments within the very different context of European faculties of theology."

[106] *Ibid.*, 131: "there is striking evidence that scholars at Merton College, Oxford, appreciated the mathematical and philosophical implications of this new science [as imagined by Arnau] and attempted to apply its conclusions to their own concerns." This is the subject of McVaugh's article, "Arnald of Villanova and Bradwardine's Law."

arithmetical (additive) to a geometrical (multiplicative) scale. In what follows I discuss the implications of these four elements for the evolution of the new model of equilibrium by the last years of the thirteenth century.

Arnau's contributions to the new model of equilibrium

Element 1: Quantifying qualities and qualitative intensities within a comprehensive mathematical framework

The *Aphorismi de gradibus* reveals that Arnau was a leader in the area of systematic mathematization and quantification. He directed his mathematical schema primarily toward the quantification of qualities and qualitative intensities, a project which, although in clear opposition to the Aristotelian definition, came to dominate scholastic natural philosophy over the fourteenth century.[107] Aristotle had repeatedly denied that qualities were susceptible to division and hence to quantification, and this denial was generally upheld through the thirteenth century. No scholastic ever doubted the obvious: that qualities varied in their appearance within subjects, that this man was whiter than that one, that this bowl of water was hotter than that other. In order to follow Aristotle, however, thirteenth-century philosophers explained this variation in terms of the differing capacities of specific subjects to absorb or express unvarying and indivisible qualities. According to Aristotle, qualities like heat or whiteness were unitary and singular, always defined by their maximum degree or perfection.[108] At some point in the later thirteenth century, these universally held philosophical positions began to break down. The *Aphorismi de gradibus* represents the clearest early case of a unified

---

[107] On the crucial importance of the project to quantify qualities within scholastic theology and natural philosophy, see Sylla, "Medieval Quantifications of Qualities"; John Murdoch, "*Mathesis in philosophiam scholasticam introducta*: The Rise and Development of the Application of Mathematics in Fourteenth Century Philosophy and Theology," in *Arts libéraux et philosophie au Moyen Âge*, Actes du Quatrième Congrès International de Philosophie Médiévale (Montreal: Institut d'études médiévales, 1969), 215–46; John Murdoch, "*Subtilitates Anglicanae* in Fourteenth-Century Paris: John of Mirecourt and Peter Ceffons," in *Machaut's World: Science and Art in the Fourteenth Century*, ed. Madeleine Pelner Cosman and Bruce Chandler (New York Academy of Sciences, 1978), 51–86. For an overview of this project, with fuller bibliography, see Kaye, *Economy and Nature in the Fourteenth Century*, 2–4, 165–70. Gentile da Foligno's (d. 1348) later systematic and sophisticated treatment of the question of qualitative quantification in his commentary on Avicenna's *Canon* illustrates its continued importance, with continuing refinement, within the medical tradition. On this, see French, *Canonical Medicine*, 97–108.

[108] McVaugh provides a brief description of the Aristotelian position before Arnau, in the Introduction to *Aphorismi*, 90–2.

and logically ordered framework under which the qualitative intensities of various simple medicines and their compounds could be thoroughly quantified – graded, numbered, proportioned, measured, and compared.[109]

Connections between Arnau's quantification of pharmacological qualities and the question of equilibrium are profound and pervasive. In essence, Galenic pharmacology is directed toward equalization. Its goal is the restoration of proportional equality (i.e., health) to the body that has lost it, and its means is defined by the principle, "cure by contraries." The establishment of proportional equality, or in Galenic terms *aequalitas ad iustitiam*, lies at the very center of Arnau's logic and mathematics as well. He accepted the proposition that for every individual body and each of the myriad bodily organs and members, there exists an optimally balanced mixture of the four primary qualities. This qualitative mixture, or *complexio*, could vary from *aequalitas ad iustitiam* or *temperantia* (its optimally balanced mixture) to four degrees of increasing imbalance (*discrasia*). Working from the Galenic principle of cure by contrary, Arnau accepted that the doctor's task was to balance the degree of *discrasia* with an opposing medicine of the same degree toward the end of reestablishing complexional balance (*equa complexio*), the definition of health. To correct, for example, a *discrasia* cold in the third degree, the physician should prescribe a medicine hot in the third degree.

A generation before Arnau wrote the *Aphorismi*, Taddeo Alderotti asserted that physicians possessed no workable theory of medicinal action, and that there was no way for the doctor to know the qualitative degrees of medicines with any certainty. He specifically challenged any suggestion of certitude that Galen's use of numbers in the *Tegni* to quantify medicinal strength might have implied.[110] The qualitative degree of heat or cold possessed by any medicine could only, Taddeo maintained, be determined through trial and error and the observation of effects, guided by the physician's "artful conjecture." In writing this, Taddeo conveyed the *communis opinio* among medical writers of his time.[111] And yet, little more than two decades after Taddeo expressed his (generally shared) skepticism, Arnau produced a fully articulated scheme of standardized

---

[109] *Ibid.*, 75–86. At times Arnau appears to realize that his system works by quantifying the underlying quality of heat itself contained in the medicines; at times he claims that his quantification applies not to the quality itself but to its action upon the senses – its *quantitas virtutis*. On this see McVaugh, Introduction to *Aphorismi*, 54 and 91; Arnau, Aphorism 4, at 148: "Augmentum qualitatis fortificatio est virtutis."

[110] Taddeo, *Tegni*, 202vb–203va, commenting on Galen, *Tegni*, K 383, as discussed in the previous chapter.

[111] McVaugh, Introduction to *Aphorismi*, 24–8, 45; Michael McVaugh, "Quantified Medical Theory and Practice at Fourteenth-Century Montpellier," *Bulletin of the History of Medicine* 43 (1969), 397–412, at 402–3.

measurement for medicinal intensities, built upon the unquestioned use of numbered degrees. Indeed, Arnau maintains in the *Aphorismi de gradibus* that adequate knowledge concerning the effects of combining or compounding medicines can *only* be achieved through the use of numbered degrees within a mathematized framework.[112] Interesting to note, Arnau insisted upon the precision of mathematics in this case despite his clear recognition that medical knowledge can never escape the realm of estimation and probability and can never attain the certainty of philosophical knowledge.[113]

While moves in the direction of the quantification of qualities were taking place in the sphere of natural philosophy contemporary with Arnau's writing, the particular requirements of medicinal practice and art led Arnau to bring to his scheme what philosophers were not required to bring to theirs: a concern for constructing a *working system* of measurement, a system of measurement that could actually be practiced and employed by the working doctor.[114] The mathematical measuring scheme he envisions must, he writes, be able to represent how increases and decreases in the qualitative degrees of medicines are actually experienced by those who take them.[115] In short, Arnau recognized that the judgments of sense and experience must form the basis of any adequate theory of pharmacological balancing. Is the measuring system apt (*aptus*)? Is the imagined solution congruent or fitting (*conveniens, decens*) with both experience and the generalized *sense* of how things actually work in the world? These questions, which will come to occupy an important place

---

[112] Arnau, Aphorism 19, at 164: "quod augmentabile et diminubile non cognoscitur ab intellectu quantum ad diversitatem sue mensure nisi per racionem numerorum; igitur necesse est medico differenciam graduum considerare quantum ad numeros."

[113] Arnau, *Proemium, Aphorismi*, 145: "non potest habere noticiam nisi probabilem, que procedit per estimacionem appropinquantem veritati quantum possibile est racioni humane."

[114] McVaugh here makes two points: that Arnau clearly intended his system to be useful and to be used (Introduction to *Aphorismi*, 111), but that given the real difficulties in standardizing medicinal strengths and dosages in his day, he himself pulled back from putting it into use in his own practice (*ibid.*, 112, 121–2), relying more on the physician's traditional method of trial and error than on theoretical systematization.

[115] Arnau, Aphorism 22, at 174–5; Aphorism 21, at 168: "Et enim secundum diversitatem augmenti quod fit in qualitate diversificatur proporcionaliter eius impressio, cum omnis operacio sue virtuti proporcionetur." McVaugh (Introduction to *Aphorismi*, 110) finds great importance in Arnau's insistence on bringing his mathematics into line with human perception: "To modern eyes, one of the most impressive passages in the *Aphorismi* [Aphorism 22, 174–5] is that in which he argues that the geometric relationship of qualitative force to sensory effect is a general natural law that is evident in all cases of action upon the sense and is consequently valid for the particular case of pharmacy."

in the scientific speculations of the fourteenth century, are clearly present in Arnau's medical writings.[116]

Element 2: The relativization of qualities and qualitative action

Just as Arnau's plan to divide and quantify qualities ran counter to Aristotle's strict separation of quality and quantity as categories, so too his relativization of the qualities "hot" and "cold" (the qualities of greatest importance to Galenic medicine and pharmacology) ran counter to Aristotle's insistence that qualities be considered as absolute wholes and, in the case of hot and cold, absolute contraries. In his medical treatises and commentaries, Arnau demonstrates that he is fully determined to follow Galenic relativity in this area rather than adhere to Aristotelian principles. Arnau's sensitivity to relation and relativity is, in my judgment, far more developed than Taddeo Alderotti's and far more of a force in the formation of his positions.[117] I want to suggest, further, that in Arnau's program in the *Aphorismi*, we can see evidence that the Galenic physician's deep training in relativized thought and perception is now assisting the transference of relativized determinations beyond the body to the world surrounding it, which is to say, beyond the sphere of medicine itself.

According to Aristotle's absolutist definitions, a quality like heat will always exert the same effects in the same direction. While this principle may seem on the surface to accord with reason, by the end of the thirteenth century philosophers and physicians were coming to recognize that it did not square with experience. If heat is always presumed to have the same effect (i.e., of heating), why does adding a measure of lukewarm water to a measure of hot water have the effect of *cooling* the mixture rather than increasing it through addition? Why does adding one measure of

---

[116] While McVaugh stresses the integration of theory and practice in Arnau's *Aphorismi de gradibus*, he also notes the general failure of physicians after Arnau to continue in this direction. He speculates on the possible reasons for this failure in his "Quantified Medical Theory and Practice at Fourteenth-Century Montpellier," esp. 405.

[117] E.g., Arnau, Aphorism 2, at 147: "quod in temperamento complexionis non est omnimodo *aequalitas* predictarum qualitatum, sed tantum *aequalitas* proportionis vel iusticie que debetur complexionato secundum exigenciam sue speciei." Unfortunately, Arnau's commentary to Galen's *Tegni*, with all the openings to conceptions of relativity that this work provides, has not survived (McVaugh, Introduction to *Aphorismi*, 73), but many such openings appear in his other Galenic commentaries, e.g., *Commentum supra tractatum Galieni De malicia complexionis diverse*. Noteworthy throughout this commentary is the recognition of difference, diversity, and relativity with regard to complexional equality: e.g., *De malicia complexionis diverse*, 233: "quod mala complexio in carne differt a mala complexione in osse, et sic de aliis membris; et dictum fuit quod talis differencia complexionis est quoad gradum, quoniam non secundum eundem gradum sunt membra qualitatis alicuius susceptiva."

lukewarm water to a second measure of the same not lead to the increase of the degree of heat in the mixture?[118] Arnau used his precocious sense of relativity to answer these questions. After asserting that every substance contains some mixture of the qualities heat and cold, he argued that the action and effects of these two qualities in any mixture will be determined by their *relative* presence and strength. In McVaugh's words:

> In the *Aphorismi*, both hot and cold are retained as real entities, and both are required to establish the ratio that alone determines effective hotness and coldness. In such a system it becomes perfectly permissible to say (as Arnald does) that the less hot is the colder ... a medicine hot in the first degree cools still hotter medicines because it contains more coldness than they.[119]

Equally importantly, Arnau appears to have been the first medical writer to recognize that in order to conform his pharmacological system to experience and to render it "fitting," he had to incorporate within it a conceptual relationship between medicinal quantity and medicinal force. He did so by imagining that the *intensity* of a medicine's effects on the body could and should be considered in relation to the *extension* of its effects within the body.[120] As McVaugh writes: "Here for perhaps the first time in medical science, 'intensive' and 'extensive' are *bound together* in their logically complementary sense" (my emphasis).[121] Compounding two medicines of the same degree (just as compounding two measures of the lukewarm) will not, Arnau asserts, double the degree of a medicine's intensity. It will, however, double the *extension* of the medicine's effect within the subject, extending the medicine's power to balance and heal from one bodily organ to two, for example. The complexity of Arnau's imagination here, with its multiple layers of qualitative interchange and relation, has left Aristotle far behind. He has reimagined Aristotle's single-dimensioned scheme for qualitative action, where the hot can only heat and the cold can only cool, into a fully relativized working system in which the less hot can cool and the less cold can heat. At the same time, his imagination of a physical system in which intensity and extension are bound together in an integral and

---

[118] McVaugh outlines the general problem in Introduction to *Aphorismi*, 98–105.
[119] *Ibid.*, 103. McVaugh cites Aphorism 37 in support of this, but not surprisingly he finds (n. 33) Arnau's strongest statement of this principle in his commentary to Galen's *De malicia complexionis diverse*.
[120] McVaugh, Introduction to *Aphorismi*, 84–6, 95–8.
[121] *Ibid.*, 100–2, at 102. See also Arnau, Aphorism 34, at 193: "Verum enim est quod multiplicata quantitate complexionati, augetur complexio; non tamen secundum intensionem eius in gradu, sed secundum extensionem eius in subiecto proprio." Note, however, McVaugh's finding (104) that Arnau never advanced to the position that complexional intensity would, for example, be doubled if the affected subject were halved – an insight (as discussed in Chapter 8) that is pivotal to the new model of equilibrium as it was applied in fourteenth-century natural philosophy.

dynamic relationship – changes in the value of one tied inextricably and proportionally to changes in the value of the other within a relational field – proved to be an immensely important step in the history of scientific speculation and in the history of balance as well.[122]

From what has been said about the place of relativity in the Galenic system, it should be clear that the turning of Aristotelian definitions of qualities and qualitative action in the direction of a multilayered relativized system began with Galen himself. As McVaugh writes: "It was clear to the West that Galen accepted *the principle of qualitative relativity* (my emphasis), which made it even more necessary to reconcile philosophy and experience."[123] In support of this statement, McVaugh cites a passage from Galen's *De complexionibus* that bears repeating in part:

Dryness in the absolute sense ... belongs only to the elements, fire and earth ... Heat and cold should be understood in the same way: no other object is perfectly hot or cold, only the elements. Any other object that you encounter is a mixture of these, and is described as hot or cold not in this absolute sense, of something pure and unadulterated, but in the second sense, whereby it has in it more heat and less cold, or vice versa.[124]

When Arnau applies this principle broadly to the question of the quantification of qualities, we have yet another case where by the end of the thirteenth century Galenic relativity has jumped the bounds of medicine and is beginning to bend the way thinkers, both physicians and philosophers, perceive form and activity in nature at large.

Element 3: The centrality of proportions and proportionalization to measurement, and the imagination of the latitudo *as a graded and numbered line scale, divisible into degrees, to measure and proportion qualitative intensities*

Just as proportion and proportionalization are built into virtually every element of Galen's system, so it is central to Arnau's program in the

---

[122] I have in mind here the remarkable program of quantification put forward by Nicole Oresme in his *De configurationibus* (*c.* 1350) in which intensity and extension are brought together within a mathematically determinable relational system capable of geometric representation. I discuss this development in detail in Chapter 8. McVaugh raises the possibility of connections between Arnau's writings and other of Oresme's positions at a number of points in his Introduction to the *Aphorismi* (e.g., 95–6 and n. 12).

[123] McVaugh, Introduction to *Aphorismi*, 103, n. 32.

[124] *Ibid.*, citing *De complexionibus*, I.6, translated here by Singer in *Galen: Selected Works*, 216. McVaugh might have cited numerous other passages from the *De complexionibus* in support of this statement, e.g., I.3, K, I: 520; I.5, K, I: 535, K, I: 537–8; I.6, K, I: 540, K, I: 542, and more. Indeed, the whole of the *De complexionibus* is dedicated to criticizing absolutist understandings of qualities and qualitative action.

Aphorismi. Similarly, for Arnau as for Galen, the conception of a measuring continuum or latitude is nearly inseparable from the working out of proportionality. In the opening twelve aphorisms of his treatise, Arnau establishes that degrees (*gradus*) measure the "elevation" of a medicine's qualitative intensity over an imagined *qualitative distance*. To this distance, following Galen, he attaches the word "latitude" (*latitudo*).[125] Aphorism 17 of the *Aphorismi de gradibus* then reads: "All elevation and depression (*elevacio et depressio*) of effect or quality involving one degree with respect to another is by some genus of proportion."[126] The aphorism that follows asserts: "All such proportions are ordered by number."[127] The use of the terms *"elevacio"* and *"depressio"* here makes it clear that Arnau is imagining qualitative increase or decrease as a species of motion along an axis, echoing Galen, but going past him as well.[128] Then he imagines the existence of a continuous numbered line (*diametrum altitudinis*), beginning at the first degree of qualitative intensity and rising on a gradient to numerically higher and higher degrees.[129] As imagined by Arnau, all measurement along this numbered line or latitude is essentially relational and expressible in numerable proportions.[130]

---

[125] For Galen's multiform use of the conceptual latitude, see Chapter 3. Its continued uses by Avicenna and Taddeo Alderotti are discussed earlier in this chapter. For an argument that links the greatly expanding use of the conceptual *latitudo* in scholastic speculation to social, economic, and administrative developments beyond the schools, see my *Economy and Nature in the Fourteenth Century*, esp. 124–6, 167–70, 182–5, 192–4.

[126] Arnau, Aphorism 17, at 158: "Omnis elevacio et depressio virtutis vel qualitatis unius respectu alterius fit secundum aliquod genus proporcionis."

[127] *Ibid.*, Aphorism 18, at 159: "Omnis proporcio fit secundum numeri racionem." Notice that here and elsewhere Arnau is emphatic in asserting that the proportioned measurement of the intensity of any qualitative degree corresponds directly with the measurement of its "real" effects on the body. Aphorism 21, at 168: "Et enim secundum diversitatem augmenti quod fit in qualitate diversificatur proporcionaliter eius impressio, cum omnis operacio sue virtuti proporcionetur."

[128] On qualitative increase and decrease as local motion, McVaugh, Introduction to *Aphorismi*, 95 and Arnau, Aphorism 7, at 152: "Omne autem superius habet racionem elevati et inferius racionem depressi ... ideo attribuuntur eis nomina verbalia que important mocionem, scilicet elevatio et depressio."

[129] Arnau, Aphorism 13, at 155: "Gradus in complexionibus est elevacio qualitatis alicuius complexionalis supra temperamentum secundum distanciam integram." Again, Aphorism 9, at 152–3. In Aphorisms 14 to 16 he recognizes that the term "latitude," despite its association with breadth and horizontality, actually measures increase and decrease along a vertical axis. See the identical point made a half-century later by Nicole Oresme, and discussed in Chapter 8 below.

[130] *Ibid.*, Aphorism 37, at 200: "idem erit modus accipiendi proporciones, scilicet per numerum unius qualitatis relatum ad numerum alterius." He also states (Aphorism 13, at 155–6) that the degree of qualitative increase and decrease will differ for each and every bodily member: "que membra, cum sint valde varia et diversa, non in eisdem gradibus intensionis et remissionis exigunt predictas qualitates."

Particularly noteworthy is Arnau's consistent identification of the latitude of qualities with a *spatial magnitude* and spatial extension, functioning as a graded continuum – literally, a graded line – capable of representing the degree of qualitative intensity at any point.[131] As such, it is an essential element in what was conceived by Arnau as a practical system of measurement and relation. By tying the increase or decrease in the quality along this continuum directly to the increase or decrease in its sensible effects, Arnau was envisioning a *workable* system of measurement capable of directly reflecting human observation and experience.[132] Arnau's measuring latitude thus functions as a working tool that enables the physician to better perform his Galenic function of balancing toward the end of health. While Galen originated the use of the *latitudo* in medical thought and practice, Arnau has taken this element and stretched it, as he has other Galenic elements, transforming it into a working instrument of equalization. The measuring latitude, here imagined as a conceptual instrument directed toward pharmacological balancing, had a great future ahead of it.[133]

Element 4: The resituation of qualitative effect (and the notion of degree itself) from an arithmetical (additive) to a geometrical (multiplicative) scale

I will hold most of my discussion of this immensely important fourth area – the shift from an experiential world defined by arithmetical addition to one defined by geometric multiplication – until Chapter 8, when I consider the mathematical function derived by the theologian Thomas Bradwardine, some thirty years after the writing of the *Aphorismi de gradibus*.[134] But since the shift from arithmetic to geometry and from

---

[131] McVaugh, Introduction to *Aphorismi*, 95; Arnau, Aphorism 14, at 157: "Distancie cuiuslibet gradus integritas tanta est quanta est latitudo ipsius . . . quod distancia integra qualitatis a temperamento constituit gradum." See also Aphorism 7, at 152, Aphorism 13, at 155–6, Aphorism 31, at 184.

[132] E.g., Aphorism 15, at 157: "Latitudo cuiusque gradus tantum extenditur quanta est differencia manifeste impressionis."

[133] Retaining many of the characteristics Arnau imagined for it, it was to become the prime conceptual instrument of qualitative measurement and relation within the quantifying schemes of fourteenth-century theology and natural philosophy, as discussed further in Chapter 8.

[134] McVaugh was the first to recognize the connections between Arnau's writings and Bradwardine's mathematics. See the argument put forth in his "Bradwardine's Law," and Introduction to *Aphorismi*, 36. For the scientific implications of this shift in vision from an arithmetical to a geometrical scale, and some thoughts on the possible causes of this transformation, see my *Economy and Nature in the Fourteenth Century*, under the heading "Mathematics and the Geometry of Exchange," 211–20.

addition to multiplication is such a crucial element of the new model of equilibrium, I add a few words about it here.

Where the traditional scheme inherited from Galen held that each succeeding degree of a medicine's qualitative intensity represented a single unit step above the one below it, Arnau asserted that degrees ascend by "doubling" (*per augmentum dupli*).[135] In his scheme, if the temperate degree (a ratio of equality between heat and cold) is represented by 1, then the first degree is double this, or 2 units in intensity, measured by 2 units of length along the measuring latitude. The second degree then doubles to 4 units in intensity and length, the third degree multiplies to 8 units, and the fourth degree to 16 units. The general mathematical rule covering Arnaldian degrees holds that as the numbered degree of intensity increases arithmetically, the powers of the qualitative intensities increase geometrically.[136] Arnau found the skeleton of this mathematical scheme outlined in a short medical work by the ninth-century Iraqi philosopher and physician, Al-Kindi, but as McVaugh frequently shows, Arnau's system greatly surpassed Al-Kindi's in its comprehensiveness and its logical and conceptual coherence.[137] By adopting Al-Kindi's mathematical scheme Arnau was able to extend Galen's privileging of proportional/geometrical equality (*ad iustitiam*) over arithmetical equality (*ad pondus*) beyond Galen, beyond its restricted application to the body's complexional mixtures, to comprehend the entire field of qualitative change – indeed, to comprehend the entire field of activity in nature.

Between each degree, Arnau writes, there exists both a "proportional equality" and at the same time a "quantitative inequality" (*aequalitas proporcionis et inaequalitas quantitatis*). That is, the *effective* difference between degree 2 and degree 3 (for example) is proportionally "equal" to the *effective* difference between degree 3 and degree 4, even though the difference between the second and third degree measures 4 units along the latitude of qualities, while the difference between degrees 3 and 4 measures 8 units[138] Within his new measuring scheme, Arnau brings all increase in qualitative intensity, effect, and perception within a system determined by geometric multiplication.

---

[135] Arnau, Aphorism 19, at 159–64, for the scheme's outline.
[136] Arnau lays down his three basic rules in Aphorism 22, at 173: "Et una est hec, scilicet quod in ordine naturali numeri primum augmentum est dupli"; 2: "omnis *inaequalitas* cuiuscumque augmenti reducitur ad equalitatem mediante proporcione dupli"; 3: "in sola proporcione dupli naturaliter reperitur *aequalitas*."
[137] McVaugh, Introduction to *Aphorismi*, 57–60.
[138] The expansion of the scheme of proportional equalization is worked out primarily in Aphorisms 21 and 22, at 166–79.

McVaugh is very concerned to show that Arnau believed his principle of geometric multiplication or "doubling" attached to degrees was not merely a mathematical convenience (which he also thought it to be), but that it actually represented the way qualitative degrees were experienced and perceived by the human senses of sight, touch, taste, and smell. The only qualitative steps that are sensible, Arnau maintains, are those accomplished through doubling.[139] This recognition represents a sharp departure from the scheme of his master, Galen, and a break from all earlier scholastic determinations. And yet he clearly believed that his new system was *conveniens*, that it actually "fit" the world he experienced.[140] In short, he was registering both the activity he perceived and the underlying logic of this activity differently than had previous generations of thinkers.[141] A new sense of how the world works, orders itself, equalizes itself, and holds together is emerging here. Again the question: What might lie behind a reenvisioning of this magnitude, and why at this point in time?

Grounds for imagining a new model of equilibrium in the late thirteenth century

Connections between the models of equalization underlying Arnau's medical writings (particularly the *Aphorismi de gradibus*), and the writings of Peter Olivi (including the *Tractatus de emptionibus et venditionibus, de usuris, de restitutionibus* [*c.* 1295]) are both plentiful and profound. Both recognize, *contra* Aristotle, that opposite qualities (e.g., heat and cold) can coexist and interact in the same mixture; both conceive of qualitative action (e.g., heating and cooling) in the relativized terms of proportion and ratio; both adhere, in a general sense, to what McVaugh

---

[139] Arnau, Aphorism, 22, at 175: "Est autem in obiectis aliorum sensuum evidens ... necesse est ut potencia qua movere habet sensum illum ad minus dupletur in eo." He then extends this insight to the doctor's capacity to perceive distinctions between (and changes in) complexional degrees: "quod in situ temperamenti nullatenus alteret tactum et in primo gradu alteret manifeste, necesse est ut in primo gradu respectu temperamenti saltem dupletur."

[140] McVaugh, Introduction to *Aphorismi*, 110; Arnau, Aphorism 37 at 201: "Sed inter quascumque virtutes diversa est proporcio, necesse est ut diversus sit effectus mutue alteracionis vel accionis." See also Arnau, Aphorism 19, where he criticizes the standard opinion that degrees differ by the addition of a single unit: "cum tamen sensu probet esse plures."

[141] Anneliese Maier speaks of the imagination of a new "image du monde" in this period, based upon her sense of the changes that were occurring in early fourteenth-century natural philosophy, "La doctrine de Nicolas d'Oresme sur les 'configurationes intensionum,'" in Maier, *Ausgehendes Mittelalter*, 3 vols. (Rome: Edizione di storia e letteratura, 1964–77), vol. I, 335–52.

has called "the principle of qualitative relativity," first enunciated by Galen in contrast to Aristotle's position on the question.[142] At a still deeper level, McVaugh has speculated that Olivi may have communicated to Arnau the philosophical debates on the quantification of qualities that were then current in university culture, which Arnau may then have adapted and applied in the *Aphorismi*.[143]

From what we know of the biographies of Arnau and Olivi, it is quite possible that they knew each other and, more, that they actively exchanged ideas with one another.[144] Their residence in the city of Montpellier overlapped for considerable parts of the decade of the 1290s, Arnau as a professor in the Medical Faculty of the university, Olivi as a lector in theology from 1289 at the city's Franciscan *studium*.[145] (Both the *Aphorismi de gradibus* and the *Tractatus de emptionibus et venditionibus* were written during this period.) McVaugh found so many links between Arnau's thinking and Olivi's at the intersection of medicine and natural philosophy, that he was led to speculate that Arnau may, for a period, have attended Olivi's lectures at the *studium*.[146]

While direct intellectual contact between the two seems likely, I would add that Olivi's precocious exploration of the potentialities of systematic equilibrium in his economic thought indicates that if intellectual exchange between the two thinkers did occur, Olivi would have had as much to gain from Arnau's mastery of Galenic insight in the area of systematic equalization as Arnau gained from Olivi's familiarity with current philosophical debates on the quantification of qualities. The measuring *latitudo*, with all that it implies about the place of estimation and approximation in judgment, was developed in Galenic medical thought before its transference to other intellectual areas.[147] More generally, Olivi makes the point that due to the uncertainties involved in value estimation in the marketplace, the best that can be expected in the realm of exchange is an equality to which he gives the name "healthful," by which he means an equality that is proportional and

---

[142] McVaugh, Introduction to *Aphorismi*, 103, n. 32.   [143] *Ibid.*, 96.

[144] For the assumption of some level of acquaintanceship, see Ziegler, *Medicine and Religion*, esp. 23 and 70. The case for Olivi's direct influence on Arnau's theological writings is particularly strong.

[145] Juan Paniagua, "Maître Arnau de Vilanova: paradigme de la médecine universitaire médiévale," in *Studia Arnaldiana: Trabajos en torno a la obra Médica de Arnau de Vilanova, c. 1240–1311* (Barcelona: Fundación Uriach, 1994), 64–73.

[146] McVaugh, Introduction to *Aphorismi*, 96 and nn. 13–16; 105, n. 36.

[147] Olivi, *Tractatus*, 61: "Propter quod nulli proprio aut communi iuditio censeatur aut censeri debeat per enormi nec sic respectu nostri iuditii recedit a moderantia iusti pretii sub competenti latitudine mensurandi."

approximative rather than being precisely one to one.[148] These are distinctions that would be perfectly familiar to Arnau, and indeed to all Galenists.

If we are to understand the many insights shared between Olivi and Arnau and the parallel directions they followed in their intellectual innovations, we need to consider the social context of their intellectual exchange: the vibrant commercial cities of southern France, northeastern Spain, and northern Italy to which both Olivi and Arnau were attached throughout their lives, and particularly the city of Montpellier. As the medical historian Luis García Ballester notes, Arnau's presence in Montpellier "coincided with the period of the city's greatest economic growth."[149] In the two decades between 1280 and 1300 Montpellier was at its medieval height in economic, administrative, political, and demographic terms: one of the twenty or so largest cities in all of Europe.[150] The geographical area in which Olivi and Arnau lived and moved throughout their lives formed a precocious center of economic and administrative development in this period.[151] Olivi makes his concern with, and close observation of, the details of economic life crystal clear in his writings. While we have no such written evidence in the case of Arnau, we know that as a young man he married into a powerful merchant family and that he maintained connections to this family and its affairs throughout his life. We can also surmise that his long career as a physician to the wealthiest and most powerful in his society, including the papal court and the royalty of Aragon and Catalonia (for which he was very well remunerated), sensitized him to the larger economic currents in his day.[152] The paucity of surviving records from the university at Montpellier does not permit us to know whether Arnau was personally involved in the school's economic administration either as a student or as a teaching master, but evidence

---

[148]   *Ibid.*: "Licet autem exterior actio seu commutatio secundum veridicam extimationem sui pretii contineat aliquantulam inequalitatem … ymo potius benignam et concessoriam aut salutiferam equitatem et ideo quantum ad hoc tam divino quam humano iure robur obtinet firmitatis."

[149]   García Ballester, "Introduction," to *De malicia complexionis diverse*, 15. On commercial and administrative Montpellier in this period, see Kathryn Reyerson, *Business, Banking and Finance in Medieval Montpellier* (Toronto: Pontifical Institute of Mediaeval Studies, 1985).

[150]   Caille, "Urban Expansion in the Region of Languedoc from the Eleventh to the Fourteenth Century."

[151]   On the precocious development of administrative practices in the Midi in this period, see Jan Rogozinski, "The First French Archives," *French Historical Studies* 7 (1971), 111–16.

[152]   On the business of medicine in general in this period and with respect to Arnau's career in particular, see Michael McVaugh, *Medicine Before the Plague: Practitioners and their Patients in the Crown of Aragon, 1285–1345* (Cambridge University Press, 1993); Ziegler, *Medicine and Religion*, 23.

from other universities in this period indicates that such involvement was highly likely.[153]

I stress the importance of considering the social context shared by Olivi and Arnau because I want to argue that each of the elements I have highlighted in their modeling of equalization – (1) qualitative quantification, (2) thoroughgoing relativization, (3) proportional measurement and comparison by latitudes, and (4) the move toward geometrical multiplication – were congruent with, and may well have derived from, the structures and activities of the social world they inhabited and perceived. Arnau's recognition that multiplication or "doubling" provides the key to integrating qualitative change with human perception occurs in the same half-decade, and in the same social context, in which Olivi argued that money directed toward commerce contains within it a multiplying and superadded power that the merchants in his society commonly recognized and referred to as *capitale*.[154]

In constructing an argument that accepts and rationalizes the social "fact" of fructifying commercial capital in his urban environment, Olivi overturned deeply embedded scholastic fears concerning the multiplying powers of money. At the same time, he recognized that this multiplying power had to be integrated within a rational scheme of equalization, the *sine qua non* of licit exchange. In the end, this could only be accomplished by expanding the imagined potentialities of *aequalitas* and equalization far beyond their traditional bounds. And *capitale* was but one of the multiplying elements attached to monetized exchange that Olivi managed to rationalize within his new vision of exchange *aequalitas*. The merchant, he wrote, could licitly add not only the value of his time, labor, and expenses to the cost of the goods he brought to market, but also the qualitative value of his specialized training, skills, and knowledge; also the qualitative value of the dangers and hardships he faced in his journeys; also his need for a surplus large enough to sustain his necessary activities. Since the measuring continuum of money was, Olivi recognized, capable of quantifying even ephemeral *qualities*, both material and human, into the numerable terms of price, they could be integrated into his imagined grand equation of exchange.[155] But for this to happen, Olivi's equation

---

[153] William Courtenay, "The Registers of the University of Paris and the Statutes against the Scientia Occamica," *Vivarium* 29 (1991), 13–49; Kaye, *Economy and Nature in the Fourteenth Century*, 28–36. For the complex financial transactions involved in the foundation and maintenance of even a small college at the University of Paris in the early fourteenth century, see Astrik L. Gabriel, *Student Life in Ave Maria College, Mediaeval Paris* (University of Notre Dame Press, 1955), esp. 61–81.

[154] See Chapter 1 above, pp. 66–73.

[155] For the detailed exposition of these and other of Olivi's attempts to integrate principles of commercial multiplication into a rational model of equalization, see Chapter 2, pp. 121–3.

itself had to expand from a base in arithmetical addition to a new base in geometrical multiplication.

Arnau's thinking in terms of approximative ranges and measuring latitudes, and his integration of these elements into his equalizing program, also found their parallel in Olivi's economic speculation. Witness Olivi's conception of the legitimate equalizing range of price as a "fitting latitude" (*sub aliqua latitudine competenti*), numbered by the numerable continuum of money, and understood to expand and contract in direct relation to the changing degree of scarcity in the marketplace. Both thinkers envisioned their graded latitudes undergoing continuous expansion and contraction, since in both contexts (the Galenic body and the marketplace of the late thirteenth century) it functioned within a system of equalization perceived to be both highly sensitive and fully relational.[156] Arnau's continual assertion that the increase or decrease of qualitative intensity along this numbered continuum relates directly to the increase or decrease of the quality's *sensible* effects, underscores his intent to construct a *workable* system of measurement – workable because of its capacity to accurately reflect human observation and experience, which is to say, to reflect Arnau's own observation and experience.[157]

To both inhabit and imagine a world in which a numbered latitude of price, open to continual expansion and contraction, can be attached to every good and service in exchange, and even (as Olivi argued) to the personal qualities of the exchangers themselves, is to inhabit and imagine a world of ever-expanding, contracting, and intersecting lines. Within this environment, the older vision of a world composed of fixed points and perfections, where balance was represented by the precise and knowable balancing point between two equal weights, gave way to a vision of a fluid, interconnected "world of lines," which required a radically new model of how balance could be attained and maintained.[158] While arithmetic is adequate to describe the plan of a

---

[156] McVaugh, Introduction to *Aphorismi*, 95; Arnau, Aphorism 14, at 157: "Distancie cuiuslibet gradus integritas tanta est quanta est latitudo ipsius ... quod distancia integra qualitatis a temperamento constituit gradum." See also Aphorism 7, at 152; Aphorism 13, at 155–6; Aphorism 31, at 184.

[157] E.g., Aphorism 15, at 157: "Latitudo cuiusque gradus tantum extenditur quanta est differencia manifeste impressionis."

[158] On the emergence of a new "world of lines" in this period and further thoughts on the possible causes of its formation, see Kaye, *Economy and Nature in the Fourteenth Century*, under the heading "The Social Geometry of Monetized Society," 158–62. For Arnau's application of the latitude in a sphere other than medicine (with continued parallels to Olivi's latitude), see Ziegler, *Medicine and Religion*, 70.

universe thought to be composed of discrete points and contained perfections, it will not suffice for the measurement of a world of lines. For that, a new mathematics of multiplication must be imagined, new conceptual measuring scales must be found, a new fluid geometry capable of representing and measuring the ever-in-flux world of qualitative intensities must be invented.[159] And a new model of equalization must be imagined and applied to make sense of it all.

The monetized marketplace of Montpellier and other urban centers at the cusp of the fourteenth century provided the social context within which this re-visioning occurred. Within this marketplace, as Olivi understood it, economic value was relative value, shifting continually and systematically in relation to shifting common need and scarcity in the marketplace. Within this marketplace, the individual and his desire for unequal profit could be imagined to be subsumed and "equalized" within the overarching system of communal exchange.[160] By the end of the thirteenth century, I think it is fair to designate the *aequalitas* envisioned by Arnau, Olivi, and other forward-looking thinkers of the time with the modern term "systematic equilibrium." This term captures, as mere *aequalitas* cannot, the unprecedented conceptualization of a working systematic "unity" that orders itself and maintains itself in balance despite the essential imbalance of its component parts. "Equilibrium" captures the conceptualization of a self-equalizing system within which the identity and value of each component part shifts continually in relation to its position and function within the whole. "Equilibrium" captures the imagination of a relational field in which the single axis of intensity (*indigentia* for Olivi) is linked to a second axis of extension (*raritas* for Olivi) in the quantification of qualitative effect.

Just as in Arnau's scheme the doctor only senses that a new qualitative degree has been achieved when the intensity has doubled, even though the actual process of increase is additive, it is possible that the historian can only sense that a new model of equilibrium has come into being at a similar (if metaphorical) point of doubling, even though the historical process leading up to it has also been additive. If that is the case, it appears to me that Arnau's *Aphorismi de gradibus* and Olivi's *De emptionibus et venditionibus, de usuris, de restitutionibus*, taken together, represent such an elevation in qualitative degree.

---

[159] Note that, for Arnau, even the degree (*gradus*) is not imagined as a point. All degrees possess their own latitudes, and each degree represents the whole of its proper latitude; Arnau, Aphorism 20, at 165: "quia integritas gradus ... consistit in distancia vel a temperamento vel a vicino gradu."

[160] As outlined in Chapter 2.

Galen's *Tegni* in the fourteenth century: the *Plusquam commentum* of Turisanus

The concluding section of this chapter centers on the most important and influential commentary on Galen's *Tegni* written in the fourteenth century, the *Plusquam commentum* of Pietro Torregiano de Torregiani, also known as Turisanus (died *c.* 1320).[161] The *Plusquam* succeeded and for the most part supplanted the earlier commentary on the *Tegni* written by Turisanus' teacher at the University of Bologna, Taddeo Alderotti, and it maintained its authority well into the sixteenth century.[162] Where the previous section on Arnau's *Aphorismi de gradibus* centered on links between scholastic medicine and natural philosophy, this section centers on connections between scholastic medicine (the medical body) and scholastic political theory (the political body) around their shared ideal and goal of *aequalitas*. Particularly important in this respect are the connections between the medical writings of Turisanus and the political writings of Marsilius of Padua, a trained physician himself, and arguably the preeminent political theorist of the fourteenth century.

Turisanus grew up in a wealthy Florentine family. In the last decades of the thirteenth century, he went to Bologna to study medicine with Taddeo Alderotti. Later in life, between 1313 and 1319, he taught in the Faculty of Medicine at the University of Paris, at the same time that Marsilius of Padua was teaching there in the Faculty of Arts.[163] There is no surviving evidence of an acquaintanceship between the two, and proving that Marsilius (who had been educated in the Medical Faculty at the University of Padua, and who continued to practice as a doctor while at

---

[161] In what follows I cite from Pietro Torregiano de Torregiani (Turisanus), *Plusquam commentum in Parvam Galeni Artem, Turisani Florentini Medici Praestantissimi* (Venice: ad Iuntas, 1557). One advantage to using this uncolumned edition is that it can be easily consulted on the BIUM website. For a brief biography of Turisanus, see Siraisi, *Taddeo Alderotti and his Pupils*, 64–6. Siraisi discusses Turisanus' commentary and his contributions to medicine at several points throughout this work. She dates the *Plusquam* to the last years of his life, possibly *c.* 1315–20.

[162] The continuing influence of the *Plusquam*, Turisanus' only major work, is evidenced by its position as a required text in the medical school at Padua as late as the statutes of 1465 and 1495. On this, see Nancy Siraisi, "Music of the Pulse," in *Medicine and the Italian Universities, 1250–1600* (Leiden: Brill, 2001), 114–39 at 135, n. 36. Joutsivuo (*Concept of Neutrum*, 34) notes that it was still being systematically referred to into the seventeenth century. Equally telling are its eight printed editions up to 1557. On its continued importance, see also Ottosson, *Scholastic Medicine and Philosophy*, 49 (and n. 97), 179, 189.

[163] On Turisanus' studentship at Bologna and later career at Paris, see Siraisi, *Taddeo Alderotti and his Pupils*, 26–7, 64–6; Ottosson, *Commentaries on Galen's Tegni*, 44–50; Danielle Jacquart, *La médecine médiévale dans le cadre parisien, XIVe–XVe siècle* (Paris: Fayard, 1998), 148. On the presence of both Pietro d'Abano and Turisanus in Paris in this period, see O'Boyle, *Art of Medicine*, 34.

the University of Paris) knew Turisanus or was familiar with his writings is not essential to the argument I present here.[164] Nevertheless, there are so many overlapping areas in their biographies that imagining their acquaintanceship, both personal and intellectual, presents (in my judgment) no more risk than doubting it.[165]

The elements within the *Plusquam* that are germane to connections between medicine and political thought represent but a fragment of this large work. At 168 folios, the 1557 edition of the commentary dwarfs the text of the *Tegni*, which was generally presented in under 20. The *Plusquam commentum* earns its reputation of being "more than" a simple commentary by virtue of its consideration of questions and subjects not specifically covered in the *Tegni*, and by virtue of Turisanus' willingness to add his own thoughts and interpretations to those of Galen and the other authorities he cites.[166] Even more than his teacher Taddeo Alderotti, Turisanus seems intent on impressing the reader with his mastery of the Aristotelian corpus, pushing yet further the integration of scholastic medicine and philosophy.[167] To that end, he insists from the start that a thorough knowledge of logic is necessary for mastering the "scientific" (i.e., theoretical) aspects of medicine, and in the course of the commentary, he demonstrates wide knowledge of the philosophical and logical writings of Avicenna and Averroes alongside those of Aristotle.[168] Also from the start, Turisanus follows Galen and earlier medical commentators in recognizing that medicine is a "mechanical art" as well as a science.[169]

Near the beginning of his commentary (fol. 7r) Turisanus raises what had become by his time a pivotal point of distinction between Galen and Aristotle since it involved the definition of health itself. Galen had written

---

[164] Marsilius makes no direct reference either to Turisanus or to the *Plusquam*.

[165] On the difficulty of identifying relationships between scholars at the University of Paris in this period, whether personal or intellectual, see William Courtenay, "The University of Paris at the Time of Jean Buridan and Nicole Oresme," *Vivarium* 42 (2004), 3–17, esp. 8–11.

[166] Turisanus himself (1r) styles his work "Plus quam commentum." For examples of Turisanus' originality and willingness to reason beyond Galen and his medical contemporaries, see Chiara Crisciani, "History, Novelty, and Progress in Scholastic Medicine," *Osiris* 6 (1990), 118–39, at 126; Siraisi, "The Music of the Pulse," 135; Ottosson, *Commentaries on Galen's Tegni*, 46.

[167] It is Jacquart's judgment (*La médecine médiévale*, 374) that Turisanus' treatment of philosophical questions is more sophisticated and better structured than Taddeo's. That this may also have been the contemporary opinion is indicated by the subtitle added to the 1557 edition: "Opus non solum Medicis utile ac necessarium, verum etiam Philosophis valde accommodatum."

[168] The opening six folios, in particular, are replete with references to writings on logic.

[169] Turisanus, *Plusquam*, 8r: "Hoc ergo modo, secundum quod medicina est ars, est una ex mechanicis. Et hac consideratione Ari[stotle] et Aver[roes] in principio de Anima innuunt eam mechanicam."

in the *Tegni* that medicine was the knowledge (*scientia*) of health, of sickness, and of that "neither" state (*neutrum*) between health and sickness.[170] The problem presented to scholastic physicians by this definition was, as we have seen, that Aristotle had denied the existence of any state or disposition between health and sickness, allowing no room for Galen's "*neutrum*."[171] Avicenna, Ibn Ridwan, Taddeo Alderotti, Averroes, and virtually every thinker previously engaged in the attempt to reconcile Galen and Aristotle had all recognized the problem here, and they had partially resolved it by noting in some form the distinction between the requirements of art and the requirements of "science," as Aristotle defines it. Turisanus does the same. Aristotle, he writes, who adheres to the scientific requirement for exactitude, understands health in a "strict" sense as perfect equality, and sickness as any deviation whatsoever from equality. Following from this philosophical definition, Aristotle is correct to maintain that nothing, and certainly no recognizable state such as the *neutrum*, lies between equality and inequality, and for that reason, between health and sickness.[172] In contrast, Turisanus notes, Galen views health and sickness through the lens of sense experience and practice, as is proper to the art of medicine. He thus regards the *aequalitas* and *inaequalitas* associated with health and sickness more broadly (*largius*) than Aristotle. Rather than define them philosophically as perfections, the physician should regard them as approximate locations on a continuum separated by a "space" (*spatium intellectum*) – a space where to the senses the body *appears* to be neither demonstrably healthy nor sick.[173]

In order to comprehend the mixture of art and science that constitutes the theory and practice of medicine, Turisanus arrives at the category of

---

[170] *Ibid.*, 7r (citing the *Tegni, translatio antiqua*): "Medicina est scientia sanorum, aegrorum, et neutrorum." The *Plusquam* proceeds in the manner of text and gloss. First a small section from the text of the *Tegni* is presented, which is followed by a gloss that can range from a few paragraphs to a dozen folios. In the 1557 edition, the text of the *Tegni* is presented in two parallel translations, first a section from the *translatio antiqua*, followed by the humanist translation of Nicolai Leoniceni (Leonicenus) (1428–1524) of the same section. On the persistent controversy surrounding the *neutrum*, see Joutsivuo, *Concept of Neutrum, passim.*

[171] Turisanus, *Plusquam*, 8 r–v.

[172] *Ibid.*, 8v: "Nam arist. accipit sanitatem stricte, secundum quod est aequalitas calidi, frigidi, humidi, et sicci, aequalitas (dico) [sic] non absolute sed ad opus et secundum opus perficiendum egritudinem autem intelligit esse inaequalitatem eorundem, et secundum idem. Sed sicut inter aequale et inaequale non est medium, sic inter sanum et aegrum isto modo non est medium."

[173] *Ibid.*: "Gal. vero accipiens sanitatem et egritudinem largius, terminat eas ambas ad duo puncta, inter quae est spatium intellectum." For more on the doctor's measurement by latitudes rather than discrete points, see 136v.

"operative science" (*scientia operativa*) in contrast to the "speculative science" (*scientia speculativa*) proper to philosophy in general and Aristotelian natural philosophy in particular. Within all operative sciences, knowledge, while based in theory, is nevertheless directed toward practice (*ad opus*) and thus must remain open to the particularities of the individual case. It is here, under the heading "operative science" that Turisanus links the project of medicine to the fields of ethics, law, and politics.[174] It is also here that he joins together the major elements we have so far identified with both Galenic balance and the "new equilibrium."

Approximation based on sense experience, as opposed to the certainty provided by philosophical definition, is but one in a series of dividers separating art and "operative science" from "speculative science." Of equal importance is Turisanus' association of medicine, and the operative sciences in general, with relativized determinations, contrasting this relativity to the fixity and universality required by speculative science. He notes, for example, that while in philosophical terms "the good" can be assigned an essential definition, in the spheres of medicine, ethics, and politics, definitions of "the good" are determined "*ad opus*" and "*secundum quid*" (i.e., relative to changing conditions and requirements) rather than "*absolute*" and "*in se*."[175] In order to frame the crucial distinction between absolute and relative modes of determination in medical terms, he recasts them in the Galenic categories (from the *Tegni*) of "*simpliciter*" and "*ut nunc*": *simpliciter* holds absolutely and in itself; *ut nunc* holds only for this particular place, or this part, or this time, or this person, or in relation to this particular context.[176] Turisanus thus makes crystal clear that, in his mind, Galen's pivotal diagnostic category "*ut nunc*" is fully equivalent to the traditional philosophical markers of relativistic determinations, the terms *secundum quid* and *ad aliquid*.

---

[174] *Ibid.*, 10r: "Hinc ergo orta est divisio medicinae in theoricam et practicam: et similis divisio potest fieri in omnibus scientiis operativis, est nanque similiter in ethicis aliquod theoricum reperire, et aliquod practicum. Quod enim ibi dicitur, quod oportet politicum aliqualiter scire."

[175] *Ibid.*, 11b: "Multis ergo in locis distinguens Philosophus bonum et malum in simpliciter et secundum quid, vel in simpliciter et ad aliquid, vel in simpliciter et ut nunc, dicit illud esse simpliciter bonum, quod in se et absolute bonum est privatione omnis conditionis." This emphasis on relativity carries through the *Plusquam*: e.g., 128v: "Omne autem instrumentum oportet proportionari ei, cuius est instrumentum, et ad opus illius: quare oportet calorem naturalem habere temperamentum non absolutum, set relatum ad opera virtutum."

[176] *Ibid.*, 11b: "Non tale ergo simpliciter, contra divisum contra simpliciter tale, erit tale quo, vel secundum quid, vel secundum partem: et tale quando, seu ut nunc: vel tale ubi, vel in hoc loco: vel tale ad aliquid, sive comparatum, et huiusmodi." Joutsivuo discusses the Galenic distinction between *simpliciter* and *ut nunc* in *Concept of Neutrum*, 127–32.

The first concrete example he chooses to illustrate the opposition between considerations made *simpliciter* and *ut nunc* is instructive. It derives from Aristotle's discussion in *Nicomachean Ethics* III.1 of a ship's captain faced with the dilemma of what to do with his cargo when in the midst of a violent storm.[177] Where, speaking *simpliciter*, men seek to gain and hold on to their possessions rather than to destroy them, nevertheless, there are particular occasions (*ut nunc*) where as Turisanus notes, "throwing away [valuable] goods can be a voluntary act, as in the case of a storm at sea."[178] From the mid thirteenth century, the case of the ship's captain, with its roots in economic decision-making, appears often in both Roman law treatises and in Aristotelian commentaries to clarify the distinction between absolute and relative determinations.[179]

Notably, in many Aristotelian commentaries written before Turisanus completed the *Plusquam*, this very example was also applied to legal, moral, and economic discussions surrounding the sin of usury. While no one questioned the law of the Church which held usury to be in essence unjust, scholastics nevertheless posed the question: How can a contract entered into "voluntarily" by both lender and borrower be judged illicit? The answer hinged on whether the borrower's decision to engage in a usurious loan was truly (*simpliciter*) voluntary, or whether his will was conditioned by circumstance (*ut nunc*) and was thus in some sense coerced, like that of the ship's captain jettisoning his goods. The common decision, supported by Aristotle's example in *Ethics* III, held that some element of coercion was present in all usurious loans, thus rendering them unjust *in se*.

It is certainly possible Turisanus was unaware that the example he chose to illustrate a pivotal medical distinction was in continual use in medieval writings on ethics and, in particular, on the question of usury.[180] It is also possible he was unaware that his close contemporary and fellow student of Taddeo Alderotti's at Bologna, the medical writer and teacher Bartolomeo da Varignana (d. after 1320), wrote a commentary to the Pseudo-Aristotelian *Economics* in which his discussion of usury turned on the moral and economic questions raised by the ship captain's

---

[177] Aristotle, *Ethica Nicomachea*, III.1 [1110a4–19]. The place of this discussion in scholastic *economic* thought is given exhaustive treatment in Odd Langholm, *The Legacy of Scholasticism in Economic Thought* (Cambridge University Press, 1998), 17 and *passim*.

[178] Turisanus, *Plusquam*, 11v: "nam proiectio mercium est alicui eligibilis, ut in procellis periclitanti: et haec eadem est ut nunc eligibilis, ut stante procella."

[179] Langholm, *Legacy of Scholasticism*, 62–74; Wei, *Intellectual Culture*, 312–14.

[180] Langholm (*Legacy of Scholasticism*, 62–9) makes it clear, however, that the example was in common use from the mid thirteenth century.

conditioned decision (*ut nunc*) to jettison his cargo.[181] But what cannot be denied, and what is demonstrated by Turisanus' choosing of this example, is his easy linking of medicine with the realms of moral, legal, economic, and political thought. All are designated as "operative sciences"; all are directed toward practice and proper function (*ad opus*); all heavily depend on determinations *ut nunc*; all are joined through the mode of relativized judgment proper to them; and all are conceptualized around the forms of *aequalitas* that constitute their proper end.[182]

Turisanus on equality and balance

At this point, after having introduced and surveyed the field of relativity proper to the operative sciences, Turisanus is in a position to gloss Galen's opening words on equality in the *Tegni*: the healthy body *ut nunc* is that which at present possesses a well-tempered and proportionally equalized mixture (*est eucraton et coaequale*) considered not in terms of perfect temperament and equality but in terms of what is suitable (*propriam*) to it.[183] This definition is followed by a long commentary of roughly six thousand words that establishes many crucial points we have seen before. Turisanus presents these points with a clarity and logic that demonstrate just how fully the lessons of Galen's text have been comprehended by the early fourteenth century.[184] The Greek "*eucraton*," Turisanus explains, is equivalent to the Latin "well-complexioned" (*bene complexionatum*) or well-proportioned mixture.[185] All physicians agree that the absolutely equal complexion is never found in nature and is, indeed, inimical to life. Complexional equality and the equality proper to medicine as a whole is always proportional equality determined in relation to the specific requirements of form, species, and function.[186]

---

[181] Bartolomeo's interest in economic questions (an interest shared in good measure by many of Taddeo's students) is discussed in Nancy Siraisi, "The *libri morales* in the Faculty of Arts and Medicine at Bologna: Bartolomeo da Varignana and the Pseudo-Aristotelian *Economics*," *Manuscripta* 20 (1976), 105–17, reprinted in Siraisi, *Medicine and the Italian Universities*, 100–13, at 109–11. See also Siraisi, *Taddeo Alderotti and his Pupils*, 85–94.

[182] Turisanus, *Plusquam*, 11b: "Similiter quod est bonum in domo, non est necessarium esse ut nunc bonum in domo, cum possit esse semper bonum." And again, "et potare aquam frigidam est bonum ad febrem, et non simpliciter ... Adhuc est eiectio mercium in procellis, aut occisio matris tyranno cogente, et huiusmodi operationes (sicut dicit Philosophus tertio Ethic.) sunt simpliciter involuntariae, ut nunc aut voluntariae."

[183] *Ibid.*, 13r, from *Tegni*, K, I: 310, *translatio antiqua*: "Est autem et hoc, secundum tempus, quo sanum est eucraton et coaequale, non tamen secundum optimam eucrasiam et coaequalitatem, sed secundum propriam."

[184] *Ibid.*, 13r–19v.   [185] *Ibid.*, 13r.

[186] *Ibid.*: "Propter quod oportet scire, quod dupliciter dicuntur equari contraria in misto. Aut secundum aequalitatem rei, que est per similem mensuram quantitatis et virtutis: et

So far, Turisanus has followed Galen, but as he begins his elucidation of Galen's concept of the *latitudo*, he adds his own insights and in so doing takes the mathematics and logic of the divisible latitude considerably further than his teacher Taddeo.[187] The actual proportions that complexional equalities can assume, he writes, are infinite in number, but they all fall within a given range or latitude proper to the given species.[188] It is, furthermore, the infinitude of possible proportions that assures, in turn, the great diversity of living forms.[189] Turisanus has tied together two assumptions here: the infinitely divisible latitude as the site of a potentially infinite number of proportionally "equal" mixtures is joined to an expanded sense and appreciation of the richness and complexity of life. Both of these assumptions constitute elements of the new equilibrium.[190]

With Turisanus as with Galen, complexity and diversity were understood to exist not only between species but also within any given species, including man.[191] Within the range of proportional mixtures proper to the human species, for example, some produce a state of health, judged in terms of the production of better bodily form or function, while others fail to do so in various degrees.[192] Proper proportional *aequalitas* is

> hoc in nullo potest esse commisto ... Aut dicuntur aequari secundum aequalitatem proportionis ad quondam alterum, quod est generatione enim fit mistio, et ad ipsam ordinatur, sicut dixit: et hoc est possibile."

[187] To the extent that Turisanus' conception parallels Arnau's, it was likely not the result of textual transmission, since I have found no evidence that he read the *Aphorismi de gradibus*. See, for example, his discussion of pharmacological degree (136r–v), and his conclusion (164v) that the doctor must rely on his trained experience (*experimentum*) rather than any theory or fixed scheme in the determination of medicinal dosage.

[188] Turisanus, *Plusquam*, 14r: "Et haec *aequalitas* proportionis ... hoc autem infinitae est latitudinis: quod ostendit diversitas generatorum, in nullo quorum est eadem proportio calidi ad frigidum, et humidi ad siccum cum aliquo alio."

[189] *Ibid.*: "Sicut ergo res diversificantur in forma, ita oportet mistionem elementorum ad ipsas, et equationes eorum in misto esse sub altera et altera proportione complexiones quoque alteras et alteras esse."

[190] On the newly positive values associated with diversity in this period, and the links between this new value and commercial culture, see Katharine Park, "The Meanings of Natural Diversity: Marco Polo on the 'Division' of the World," in *Texts and Contexts in Ancient and Medieval Science*. ed. Edith Sylla and Michael McVaugh (Leiden: Brill, 1997), 134–47. See also Suzanne Conklin Akbari, "The Diversity of Mankind in *The Book of John Mandeville*," in *Eastward Bound: Travel and Travellers, 1050–1550*, ed. Rosamund Allen (Manchester University Press, 2004), 156–76. The place of these two elements within the new model is discussed in the following chapters on scholastic political thought and natural philosophy.

[191] Turisanus, *Plusquam*, 14r: "Aequatio vero contrariorum in complexione secundum proportionem ad formam humanam multae latitudinis est inter duas extremitates ... quam quidem humanam complexionem medici adhuc subdividunt in aequalem, et in inaequalem."

[192] E.g., *ibid.*: "Nam aequatio ista contrariorum in complexione secundum proportionem ad formam humanam potest esse taliter, ut in ea sit de elementorum quantitate et qualitate mensura, quam humana natura debet habere secundum meliorem proportionis et divisionis aequitatem, non solum ad formam, sed ad omne opus formae: et haec erit vicinissima aequalitati certae."

defined strictly in relation to proper form and function."[193] Turisanus
reminds us that those proportions that do produce signs of health
(i.e., possess excellence of form and function) are said by physicians
to possess "*aequalitas ad iustitiam*."[194] Then, immediately after introducing this often glossed term, he announces that the purpose of
his commentary is not merely to follow Galen's text but to digress
from it at times, since much lies hidden whose clarification and exposition would prove useful to readers.[195] In the digression that follows,
he proceeds, with an explicitness and articulation that had no precedent
up to this point, to link the principles governing the Galenic body to
those governing the spheres of political, ethical, and economic life
within the *civitas*.[196]

Parallels between equilibrium in the Galenic body and in the body politic

Earlier in this chapter, when discussing Avicenna's application of the term
"*iustitia*" to the proportional equality proper to the Galenic complexion,
I pointed out that his choice of terms closely reflected Aristotle's discussion of justice and forms of equalization in Book V of the *Nicomachean
Ethics*.[197] Thanks to the text of the *Plusquam*, we can now be certain of
this reflection.[198] Turisanus begins his digression by linking the Galenic
concept of proportional equality (*aequalitas proportionum*) to the political
and legal concept of justice (*iustitia*). Both, he writes, are relational
concepts in that both are judged relative to practical purpose, function,

---

[193] E.g., *ibid.*, 128v: "Omne autem instrumentum oportet proportionari ei, cuius est instrumentum, et ad opus illius: quare oportet calorem naturalem habere termperamentum
non absolutum, set relatum ad opera virtutum."

[194] E.g., *ibid.*, 14v: "Nam in specie hominis, canis, et formicae, et reliquorum est quoddam
complexio aequalis ad iustitiam, in qua secundum meliorem proportionem et divisionis
aequitatem *ad ipsum opus* rei proprium contraria sunt aequata, et ita secundum iustitiam"
(my emphasis).

[195] *Ibid.*: "non est intentionis nostre commentari solum, quod hic habetur, sed digredi,
ubicunque fuerit aliquid occultum de his, quae medico sunt utilia sciri."

[196] The existence and importance of this ideational connection was first noted by Nancy
Siraisi, *Taddeo Alderotti and his Pupils*, 75–7, 151: "One could argue too, as Turisanus
did, for parallels between Aristotle's concept of justice and Galen's complexion
theory, *both of which are based on the idea of balance, due proportion, and the mean*"
(my emphasis).

[197] See my discussion above of Avicenna's use of the term *iustitia* in the *Canon* to modify the
idea of *aequalitas*.

[198] Siraisi, *Taddeo Alderotti and his Pupils*, 75–7. Siraisi's comments here should be read in
concert with her essay, "The *libri morales* in the Faculty of Arts and Medicine at
Bologna," cited above.

and effect.[199] He then recognizes that "distributive equality" (which he labels *aequalitas in distributione)* is the form of justice that corresponds to the *aequalitas proportionum* proper to the complexion and to medicine as a whole.[200] There is no mistaking that Turisanus has taken this term and the form of equalization it represents from Aristotle's discussion of justice in *Ethica Nicomachea,* Book V, which I have described and discussed earlier.[201] On one level, Turisanus' equation of the medical *aequalitas ad iustitiam* with Aristotle's *iustitia distributiva* from the *Ethics* merely signals that the equality proper to the Galenic complexion was to be understood as relational, proportional, and approximative rather than absolute and discrete. He need not have specified, nor indeed stressed, the parallels between the model of balance/*aequalitas* applicable to the workings of the Galenic body and the model applicable to the systematic workings of political and economic life. But he did.[202]

When Turisanus first introduces Aristotle's two forms of justice/equality from the *Ethics,* he designates the first simply "*iustitia commutativa,*" but he chooses to designate the second, the one that he defines as proper to medical concerns, in much fuller terms: "equality in the distribution of money and honors and all other things of this kind" (*aequalitas in distributione pecuniarum, et honorum, et aliorum, quaecunque*). This fuller description does indeed capture Aristotle's intent, but even in the text of the *Ethics* the term *iustitia distributiva* appears without further qualification at a number of points, as it certainly could have here. It seems to be important to Turisanus to elucidate not only the components of *iustitia*

---

[199] Turisanus, *Plusquam,* 14r: "Dicamus igitur, interponentes aliquid de his, quo secundo Ethic. determinate sunt, videlicet quod iustitia est virtus perfecta non simpliciter, sed ad alterum, nam habens ipsam ad alterum potest virtute uti, non solum ad seipsum: haec autem est aequalitas quaedam proportionalis: proportionalitas autem est aequalitas proportionum."

[200] *Ibid.:* "alia vera est aequalitas in distributione pecuniarum, et honorum, et aliorum, quaeunque; partibilia sunt communicantibus urbanitatem: cui assimilatur iustitia, quo attenditur in complexione."

[201] Chapters 1 and 2 above.

[202] And he had precedent for doing so. On the links between medical and political concepts going back to Hippocrates and Plato, see Schubert, "Menschenbild und Normwandel in der klassischen Zeit." Pietro d'Abano, who was teaching at Paris between approximately 1295 and 1306, more than a decade before Turisanus arrived there, is another important source for the transference of models of balance/equalization between the medical body and the body politic in Turisanus' day. See, for example, his *Conciliator controversiarum, quae inter philosophos et medicos versantur* (Venice, ad Iuntas, 1565; reprint, Padua: Editrice Antenore, 1985), diff. 18, 27vb: "Sed complexio iustitialis dicta iustitae merito coaptatur, proprieque naturali: quaedam enim naturalis, altera positiva: et huiusmodi quidem distributiva, ut honores, et substantie, alia vero commutativa; ceu quae in particpatione invicem, 5 Ethico. Est autem iustitia virtus quaedam perfecta non simpliciter, sed ad alterum ... Et talis vere, ut apparebit, est complexio aequalis quo ad iustitiam." I consider the writings of Pietro d'Abano further in Chapter 6.

distributiva, but also its connection to the form of equalization active in civic life.

Moreover, in his use of *Ethics* V to underscore these connections, Turisanus constructs a paradigm of proportional distribution in the *civitas* that actually goes beyond Aristotle's in its modeling of systematic equilibrium. Aristotle employed two examples to illustrate the difficult point that proportional equality most often entails arithmetical *inequality.* The first was of a partnership in which an arithmetically unequal share in the profits is nevertheless "just" if the shares are proportional to unequal investment; the second was that of a central authority, the *civitas,* awarding the city's common goods to its individual citizens in proportion to how much they proved themselves worthy of reward through service and accomplishment. Since the quality of service and accomplishment is inherently unequal among citizens, the "just" proportional distribution of rewards must also be unequal.[203] When Turisanus repeats this lesson from the *Ethics,* he adopts a more de-centered framing. There is no head or representative of the city implied in his vision of civic distribution, no unified dispenser of rewards. There is, instead, only the systematic self-ordering and self-balancing of the *civitas* itself; only individual citizens interacting with each other in the political and economic sphere, each possessing his own talents, accomplishments, and relative degree of merit or "*dignitas,*" and each seeking and finding a distribution of rewards proportionate to his contributions and accomplishments.[204]

The determined multicenteredness of Turisanus' model of equalization comes out strongly in his detailed response to the notion, advanced by Aristotle and somewhat modified by Galen, that the body possesses one primary or "principal" part or "first instrument" (*primum instrumentum*), which has the leading role in ordering and proportioning the other, secondary, parts of the body.[205] Aristotle identified the heart as this principal part, the source of the body's vivifying heat and the vital directing center of the body's order and function. Galen countered with the idea of

---

[203] *Ethics,* V [1130b30–4], [1131a25–30].
[204] E.g., Turisanus, *Plusquam,* 14r: "Sicut ergo adinvicem se habent personae, quibus fit distributio, sic et illa, quae distribuuntur illis, oportet se habere: et permutatim, sicut una persona se habet ad illud, quod sibi distribuitur, sic et alteram ad id, quod sibi, oportet habere, ad hoc, ut sit iustum." And again, 14r: "Haec autem dignitas apud diversos diversa iudicatur: quidam enim dicunt eam virtutem, quidam nobilitatem, quidam divitias, quidam aliud, propter quod honor inter eos secundum dignitatem distribuendus est, ex quo fit, quod iustum est proportionale quoddam." And finally: 14r: "Sicut ergo cives se habent adinvicem in dignitate, ita se habent ad mensuram honoris: et quantum superat unus alium in dignitate, tantum per iustitiam stare debet in mensura honoris est."
[205] See below, Chapter 6, for Marsilius of Padua's "confused" (in my interpretation) positions on this point.

three principal parts, liver, heart, and brain (and a fourth, the testicles, in the *Tegni*), and when he gave precedence to one of these three, it was generally to the liver because of its nutritive function.[206] Scholastic *medici* came down on both sides, with some, like Pietro d'Abano, Turisanus' contemporary at Paris, favoring Aristotle in this matter as he did on most disputed matters.[207] Turisanus, at times, appears to argue on both sides of the question, but his strongest arguments support the Galenic position that every part depends on and mutually interacts with every other part, and that the order and equalization of the whole is a product of this mutual interaction.[208] If, he notes, a nerve is cut, the member will fail, and if an artery is cut, the flow of vivifying blood and heat will cease.[209] There are, he writes, seven parts that are most crucial to the body's function, each of them regulated by their interior complexions, but they all work together as a collectivity, so that none can be truly "primary" with regard to the others.[210] Moreover, the working of all of the body's parts, even those most crucial to its function, depends on the mutual interaction of each of their component *particulae*: the eye, for example, has its crystalline sphere, its tunic, and its humors, among other *particulae*, all of which must work together in order for the larger part to operate properly. What Turisanus provides, in short, is an argument against the idea of a unitary descending hierarchy and in favor of a drastically more complex multicentered "field" of intersecting and communicating functions and powers.[211]

Immediately following his discussion of the workings of *aequalitas in distributione pecuniarum, et honorum, et aliorum quaecumque* in the *civitas*,

---

[206] This point, too, is discussed more fully in Chapter 6.

[207] E.g., Pietro d'Abano, *Conciliator*, diff. 31, 51b; diff. 38, 62b–63a.

[208] Turisanus, *Plusquam*, 38r: "Et est cordi serviens praeparator pulmo, et lator arteria: cerebro autem praeparator est hepar, et alia membra circa nutrimentum operantia, et circa custodiam spiritus, sicut arterie, et lator eius nervus est: hepatis vero praeparator est stomachus et lator est vena: et testiculorum praeparator sunt membra."

[209] *Ibid.*: "per hoc prohibet fluxum vitae, quia rei instrumentaliter vivificantis quantum est a parte illius arteriae."

[210] *Ibid.*, 38v.

[211] Here, Turisanus' fertile conception of the role of the "spiritus" comes into play as a kind of universalizing connecting medium, facilitating fluid communication between each of the body's myriad parts. On the *spiritus*, see *Plusquam*, 39r: "Spiritus enim, qui est vehiculum virtutis ... sicut Solis radius totum mundum." Also, 151r; 167r: "Vocat autem spiritum vitalem, qui ex primo et principali membro consurgit in totum corpus sicut ex camino, per quem spiritum anima corpus vivificat influendo per ipsum omnes virtutes suas, sicut coelum per radios Solis et stellarum, ut supra ostendimus." Note that the *spiritus* itself relies on the healthy body for its circulation. For a discussion of this concept, see Jacquart, *La médecine médiévale*, 340–1. Note, too, that Jacquart suggests (374–5) that there are similarities between Turisanus' conception of the action of *spiritus* and certain physical conceptions later put forward by Nicole Oresme in the realm of natural philosophy.

Turisanus turns to describe its workings in the human body. With not a word separating the two spheres of application, he writes:

Similarly [to the way equalization works in the *civitas*] the qualities heat, cold, wetness and dryness found in the human complexion are mixed with respect to the work (*opus*) they must accomplish, toward which end each complexion acts either as an instrument or the disposition of an instrument: each one directed toward its proper function (*opus*), but one more [successfully] than the others.[212]

And if the reader could possibly have missed Turisanus' point, he then returns with another series of comments linking the Galenic body to the body politic through the process of equalization they share:

And just as among citizens there occurs strife and recriminations when those who are equal in dignity participate unequally in honors, or those who are unequal participate equally, just so in the complexion, when the proportioning [of its qualitative mixture] does not fit its proper function (*non convenit operi*), there arise weaknesses and illnesses, and the complexion is said to be "proportionally unequal" (*inaequalis ab iniustitia*).[213]

There are many inferences that can be drawn from Turisanus' framing of Galenic *aequalitas* here. I conclude this chapter by enumerating six of them: (1) that Turisanus envisions balance as the dynamic product of mutually competing forces and interests, whether it is the product of the continual "mutual interaction" of contrary qualities within the complexion (*ex actione ad invicem et passione contrariarum qualitatum*) or of the ceaseless competition between citizens for honor and wealth within the *civitas*; (2) that Turisanus has come to view both the living body and the political body as integrated systems of distribution and equalization in which the identity of each part is both fluid and essentially relational, determined with respect to its proper work or function (*ad opus*) within the systematic whole:[214] (3) that in Turisanus' understanding, the Galenic term "*aequalitas ad iustitiam*" has come to express much of what we today express through the term "systematic equilibrium"; (4) that by the early

---

[212] Turisanus, *Plusquam*, 14r–v: "Similiter calidum, frigidum, humidum, et siccum, quae sunt in complexione hominis, aliqualiter se habent ad opus eius, ad quod ipsa complexio aut est instrumentum, aut dispositio instrumenti: unumquodque enim ad opus confert, sed unum plus alio."

[213] *Ibid.*, 14v: "Et sicut inter cives, quando aequales in dignitate, inaequaliter; aut inequales aequaliter honore participant, fiunt pugne et accusationes, sic in complexione, quando non secundum quod convenit operi, fuerit facta complexio et aequatio, fiunt languores et morbi quae quidem complexio dicitur inaequalis ab iniustitia."

[214] *Ibid.*: "Est ergo opus illud, in quo comparantur, vel respectu cuius comparantur calidum, frigidum, siccum, humidum, quae sunt in complexione, sicut dignitas est id, in quo et respectu cuius comparantur cives: et mensura quantitatis de unoquoque in illa est, penes quam est iustum, quod distribuibile est ad illa."

fourteenth century, commentators had come to grasp the full implications of Galenic balance and had even begun to move beyond it in the direction of envisioning the workings of self-equalizing systems; (5) that by this same period, scholars were both sensing and asserting a clear connection between the equilibrium (*aequalitas ad iustitiam*) that underlay and ordered the living body and that which underlay and ordered the living city; and (6) that there are close and meaningful parallels between the modeling of the self-equalizing *civitas* that Turisanus presents in the *Plusquam commentum* and the justly famous modeling of the *civitas* found in the political writings of Marsilius of Padua, his near contemporary and fellow physician at the University of Paris, and perhaps the most important political theorist of the medieval period.[215] The ground of their joining, I contend, is their shared sense of the potentialities of balance.

I suggest, finally, that Turisanus' expansive sense of balance and its potentialities derived not only from his reading of authoritative texts and his learned practice as a physician, but also and importantly from his immersion in and observation of the great cities he inhabited throughout his life: Florence, Bologna, and Paris. The same, I maintain, can be said for each of the thinkers who shared in the new model of equilibrium and participated in its shaping. The three chapters that follow, which focus on political thought in general, and the city as a site of dynamic equalization in particular, offer further reasons for linking intellectual innovation to the experience of urban environments – political, economic, social, and institutional – via the sense and modeling of balance.

---

[215] Evidence in support of this last point will be presented in Chapter 6 below.

5 Evolving models of equalization in medieval political thought, c. 1250–1325

> [General opinion] holds that justice involves two factors – things, and the persons to whom things are assigned – and it considers that persons who are equal should have assigned to them equal things. But here there arises a question which must not be overlooked. Equals and unequals – yes; but equals and unequals in what? This is a question which raises difficulties, and involves us in philosophical speculation on politics.
> Aristotle, *Politics*, III.12

> The goodness of any part is considered in comparison with the whole; hence Augustine says that "unseemly is the part that harmonizes not with the whole." Since then every man is a part of the *civitas*, it is impossible that a man be good, unless he be well proportionate to the common good.
> Thomas Aquinas, *Summa theologica*, I, II, 92, 1, ad 3

> so that, when one series [of goods for sale] had been half-viewed, soon the impetus of desire (*impetus desiderii*) would hurry to another, and once the whole length [of the market hall] had been traversed, the unsated (*insatiatus*) desire for resuming enjoyment would lead to repeated inspections, going back to the beginning, not just once or twice but seemingly an infinite number of times (*quasi infinicies*).
> Jean de Jandun, *De laudibus Parisius* (*c.* 1323)

While the model of equilibrium is shaped and shared for the most part on the level of unworded sense, it is continually linked to a cluster of conscious and explicitly articulated concepts, many of which are centered on the analysis of order and processes of ordering. In the realm of medieval political thought, the concern for order extended to three primary areas, each of which involved assumptions concerning the ideal of balance and the means by which it could be attained and maintained: the order of justice, the order of rule and authority, and the order of individual to communal whole. In the thirteenth and fourteenth centuries these three areas were in large part subsumed under a single concept of remarkable power and importance – the ideal of the *bonum commune* or Common Good.[1] Due to

---

[1] I capitalize Common Good here and elsewhere in this chapter to underscore its privileged status within medieval political thought. See Chapters 1 and 2 for the role of the Common Good in shaping the model of equilibrium applied to economic exchange, particularly with respect to the writings of Peter Olivi.

the rich interplay of notions of order and equalization that underlay the much articulated concept of the Common Good, it can provide a valuable lens through which to view the emergence and impact of the new model of equilibrium within political thought after 1250.

In this and the following two chapters I will present evidence to support a series of propositions: that the concept of the Common Good in political thought was tied to models of equality and equalization (i.e., to the modeling of *aequalitas*) at every point; that the evolution of the Common Good between 1250 and 1350 was tied to the simultaneous evolution – and expansion – of this underlying model; and that the model's evolution was closely linked to the experience of particular political, social, and economic environments at every turn. Intellectual innovation of a degree and kind that took place between 1250 and 1350 involved a tangled back-and-forth between environment and insight, between text and experience. Almost without exception, leading scholastic thinkers in this period actively participated in vibrant self-governing institutions, serving university, Church, religious order and various forms of secular government in official capacities. I will argue that their continued involvement in institutional life, combined with their social, political, and economic experience of city life from their earliest student days, gave body to their conceptualization of the Common Good and shaped their sense of the new potentialities of equilibrium that underlay it.[2]

This present chapter is divided into two parts, each of which is preliminary to the two chapters on political thought that then follow. The first part considers the formulation of the Common Good as it appeared in the writings of two mid-thirteenth-century thinkers, Albertus Magnus (*c.* 1206–80) and Thomas Aquinas (*c.* 1225–74). Both gave extensive attention to the concept and its implications, and both were among the first to integrate Aristotle's influential writings on the subject into their

---

[2] There have been many works devoted to the communal form of self-government practiced within varying institutions of the thirteenth and fourteenth centuries. For the case of the University of Paris – home at some point to each of the thinkers considered in this chapter – see William Courtenay, *Teaching Careers at the University of Paris in the Thirteenth and Fourteenth Century* (University of Notre Dame Press, 1988); William Courtenay, *Parisian Scholars in the Early Fourteenth Century: A Social Portrait* (Cambridge University Press, 1999). For a rare attempt to imagine the psychological implications of being and feeling part of a collectivity (*universitas*) in this period including, specifically, the *universitas magistrorum* of the medieval university, see Pierre Michaud-Quantin, "La conscience d'être membre d'une *universitas*," in *Beiträge zum Berufsbewusstsein des mittelalterlichen Menschen* (Berlin: Walter de Gruyter, 1964), 1–13, esp. 11–13. See also Joseph Canning, "The Corporation in the Political Thought of the Italian Jurists of the Thirteenth and Fourteenth Centuries," *History of Political Thought* 1 (1980), 9–32.

formulations. While a modeling of *aequalitas* is central to the conceptual-ization of the Common Good in the thought of both, in neither does it take the form of the "new" equilibrium as we have seen it appear in the economic writings of Peter Olivi (Chapters 1 and 2), and the medical writings of Arnau de Vilanova and Turisanus (Chapter 4), and as it will later appear in the political thought of both Marsilius of Padua and Nicole Oresme (Chapters 6 and 7). For this reason I employ the writings of Albert and Thomas as a conceptual baseline for the story I tell, and I designate their underlying model of equalization the "old" model, against which I delineate the "new." I do so in the belief that the development of the concept of the Common Good between 1250 and 1350, and the evolution of the "new" model of equilibrium which came ever more to underlie and shape it, can be more clearly recognized and gauged when viewed against the earlier writings of Albert and Thomas.

Although in my story Albert and Thomas represent "old" models of equality and equalization, it should be clear that terms like "beginning point" and "end point" or "old model" and "new model" are entirely relative to choice of periodization. Viewed in relation to the writings of virtually any thinker who preceded them, many aspects of the model of balance represented by Albert and Thomas were "new" – even radically new – rather than "old."[3] This is especially true to the extent that both men absorbed Aristotelian teaching into their philosophical and theological systems and were among the first generation of scholastic thinkers to fully do so. The immense task they accomplished, synthesizing pagan Greek and Christian learning, points to the necessary "newness" of their sense of order and the potentialities of ordering compared to what had prevailed in medieval intellectual culture before them. More to the point, their rich sense of systematic wholeness, their committed assertion of the superiority of whole over part, and their concern to work out the relationship between part and whole in their conceptions of the Common Good, marks their sense of balance and its potentialities as strikingly new compared to what had come before.

The second part of this chapter turns from an analysis of texts to an analysis of contexts. If, as I argue, the evolution of the new model of equilibrium was tied to the experience of particular political, social, and economic environments at every turn, then the question becomes: what specific factors within these environments, and what specific perceptions relating to these factors, encouraged the incorporation of new elements into the model and guided its consequent reshaping? In Chapters 1 and 2

---

[3] Moreover, the evolution from "older" to "newer" models of equalization should never be taken to imply the motion from simpler to more complex forms.

above, I directed these questions to the environment of the monetized urban marketplace as it evolved over the twelfth and thirteenth centuries. In this chapter, I direct these same questions to the social environment of which the marketplace was but a part: the encompassing environment of the commercial city of the late thirteenth and fourteenth century.

From this chapter to the one that follows I will jump more than a half-century from the Common Good of Albert and Thomas to the Common Good as it was imagined and represented by Marsilius of Padua in his immensely important politico/religious treatise, *Defensor pacis* (1324). Chapter 6 devoted to Marsilius is then followed by a chapter devoted to the political thought of the Paris-trained natural philosopher, Nicole Oresme. By juxtaposing this present chapter with the chapters that follow, I hope not only to reveal the gulf that separated these later visions of political order from those of Albert and Thomas but to offer clues, as well, as to why this transformation took place and why it took the direction(s) that it did.

The primacy of the Common Good in the political thought of Albertus Magnus and Thomas Aquinas

The political ideal of the Common Good finds full expression in the idea, emphasized by Aristotle in his *Politics* and *Ethics*, that humans are by nature political, by nature a part of a political whole. Life within a political community is necessary not only for our survival but also for our learning of virtue and our perfection as humans; it is necessary not only so that we might live but so that we might live well. After the appearance of the first full Latin translations of Aristotle's *Ethics* (1250) and *Politics* (1260–5), this sentiment came to be enthusiastically cited and seconded by Christian scholastics.[4] In order to live the life of virtue, judged not only in ethical and philosophical terms but in theological and Christian terms as well, it was held that the individual must order his own good to the good of the whole political community. In cases where the individual good conflicts with that of the Common Good, the prevalent scholastic opinion came to be that the Common Good takes precedence. It was one thing for scholastic philosophers to read in Aristotle's *Politics*, "As worthwhile as it might be for one man to attain the good, it is finer and more

---

[4] On the dating of the Latin translations of the *Politics*, see Christophe Flüeler, "Die Rezeption der 'Politica' des Aristoteles," in *Das Publikum politischer Theorie im 14. Jahrhundert*, ed. Jürgen Miethke and Arnold Bühler (Munich: Oldenbourg, 1992), 127–38, at 128–9. For the first Latin translation of the *Ethics*, see D. A. Callus, "The Date of Grosseteste's Translations and Commentaries on the Pseudo-Dionysius and the *Nicomachean Ethics*," *Recherches de théologie ancienne et médiévale* 14 (1947), 186–210; F. M. Powicke, "Robert Grosseteste and the *Nicomachean Ethics*," *Proceedings of the British Academy* 16 (1930), 85–104.

divine (*melius et divinius*) to attain the good of whole peoples or political communities."[5] This is a perfectly congruous statement in the context of pagan philosophy. It was quite another, given the persistent focus of Christianity on the morality and destiny of the individual and the individual soul, for these same thinkers to enthusiastically and seemingly unproblematically embrace this notion.

Albertus Magnus and Thomas Aquinas, who were among the earliest Christian commentators on the newly translated *Ethics* and *Politics*, provide a clear indication of the power that the ideal had attained within scholastic thought by the 1260s. To take but three statements from the work of Thomas out of dozens that could be applied:

> The goodness of any part is considered in comparison with the whole; hence Augustine says that "unseemly is the part that harmonizes not with the whole." Since then every man is a part of the *civitas*, it is impossible that a man be good, unless he be well proportionate to the common good.[6]

> For since one man is a part of the community, each man, in everything that he is and has, belongs to the community; just as a part, in all that it is and has, belongs to the whole.[7]

> The common good of the many is more godlike (*divinius*) than the good of an individual. Wherefore it is a virtuous action for a man to endanger even his own life, either for the spiritual or for the temporal common good of his country (*pro bono communi reipublicae*).[8]

In the context of the time, these are large claims, and they have large implications, not least for questions concerning forms of order and *aequalitas*.

Long before the translations of Aristotle's *Ethics* and *Politics* into Latin in the mid thirteenth century, the ideal of the Common Good held a place in Latin Christian thought.[9] From its earliest expressions, it was always

---

[5] Aristotle, *Politics*, I.2 [1094b8–10].

[6] Thomas Aquinas, *Summa theologica* (henceforth, *ST*), I, II, 92, 1, ad 3. Since the Latin texts of Thomas' major works, including the *ST* are easily accessible on the web (e.g., at www.corpusthomisticum.org), I at times refrain from citing the Latin in the notes. I use throughout the Leonine edition of the *ST* (Rome, 1888–1906). For English translations of the *ST*, I use the revised translation by the English Dominican Fathers as my guide (New York: Blackfriars, 1964–81), for that too is easily accessed (www.newadvent.org), but at times I modify this translation.

[7] *ST*, I, II, 96, 4.   [8] *Ibid.*, II, II, 31, 3, ad 2.

[9] On this question, see M. S. Kempshall, *The Common Good in Late Medieval Political Thought* (Oxford: Clarendon Press, 1999), 15–16. Kempshall views the Latin translation of Aristotle's *Ethics* and *Politics* in the mid thirteenth century as the fourth great influence on the development of the ideal. The three that preceded it were Roman law, the Ciceronian tradition, and the Augustinian tradition. Kempshall's book, which represents the most comprehensive recent study of the Common Good, devotes its first four chapters to an analysis of the concept in the writings of Albertus Magnus and Thomas Aquinas.

more than a strictly "political" concept. The central problem of the relationship of the individual to his larger community, or, framed another way, of how the part is, can be, or should be ordered to and balanced against the whole, had profound metaphysical, theological, ethical, and even mathematical implications. Breadth of meaning and application characterized the ideal of the Common Good from its early treatments in the writings of St. Augustine and Pope Gregory the Great to those of Albertus Magnus and Thomas Aquinas. Thus Thomas could write in the *Summa contra gentiles*,

> a particular good is ordered to the common good as to an end; indeed, the being of a part depends on the being of the whole. So, also, the good of a nation is more godlike than the good of one man. Now, the highest good which is God is the common good, since the good of all things taken together depends on Him.[10]

Metaphysical and theological meanings continued to be attached to the ideal even when it was employed in fourteenth-century treatises that were specifically "political" in their intent, such as Marsilius of Padua's *Defensor pacis* or the commentary on Aristotle's *Politics* of Nicole Oresme.

From the twelfth through the fourteenth century, the practical/material roots of the *bonum commune* lay in the growth of innumerable self-governing bodies and institutions across Europe, from the great independent urban communes of northern Italy, to the chartered towns and cities developing north of the Alps, to the thousands of guilds, corporations, and confraternities flourishing in all corners of Latin Europe, to the university itself, the home of scholastic thought.[11] Well before the translation of the *Ethics* and the *Politics* into Latin, the ideology of the *bonum commune* was being shaped

See also David Luscombe, "City and Politics Before the Coming of the *Politics*: Some Illustrations," in *Church and City 1000–1500*, ed. David Abulafia, Michael Franklin, and Miri Rubin (Cambridge University Press, 1992), 41–55.

[10] Saint Thomas Aquinas, *Summa contra gentiles*, III, 17, 6. For the Latin text I use that edited by C. Pera (Turin: Marieti, 1961); for the English translation *Summa contra gentiles*, *Book III*, trans. Vernon J. Bourke (New York: Hanover House, 1955–7).

[11] Georges de Lagarde, "Individualisme et corporatisme au Moyen Âge," in *L'organisation corporative du Moyen Âge à la fin de l'Ancien Régime* (Louvain: Bibliothèque de l'Université, 1937), 1–59. Lagarde speaks (5) of "un vaste réseau de cellules collectives extrêmement diversifiées ... plus ou moins autonome." At the upper end of this hierarchy of autonomy were the cities, communes, and universities, which all had a role producing, in Lagarde's words, a "corporatist social philosophy." See also, Michaud-Quantin, "La conscience d'etre membre d'une *universitas*." On the shared structures of university and trade guild, see B. B. Price, "Paired in Ceremony: Academic Inception and Trade-Guild Reception," *History of Universities* 20 (2005), 1–37. For the great importance of lay religious confraternities in this period, André Vauchez, "*Ordo Fraternitatis*: Confraternities and Lay Piety in the Middle Ages," in André Vauchez, *The Laity in the Middle Ages: Religious Beliefs and Devotional Practices*, ed. Daniel Bornstein, trans. Margery Schneider (University of Notre Dame Press, 1993), 107–17; Lester Little, *Liberty, Charity, Fraternity: Lay Religious Confraternities at Bergamo in the Age of the Communes* (Bergamo: Lubrina, 1988).

to provide the Italian communes with a counterweight to the absolutist claims of both emperor and pope to dominion.[12] At the same time, the unquestionable military, economic, and political successes of self-governing cities like Venice, Florence, Genoa, Padua, and a score of others in northern Italy, lent weight to the *bonum commune* not only as an ideal but as a legitimate governing principle and a successful governing strategy.

To write on the Common Good is to confront a host of interpretive controversies concerning its origins and implications. Medieval proponents have been read as representing opposing "schools," whether monarchical or "democratic," naturalistic or theological, corporatist or individualist, realist or nominalist, Aristotelian, Ciceronian, Averroistic, or Augustinian, and more.[13] Those, however, who fully embraced or even confronted the concept of the Common Good shared something that transcended these divides – the recognition of the potential of a political collectivity to act, react, judge, govern, and institute virtue as a unified body. As we will see, the understanding of these potentialities changed dramatically between 1250 and 1350, but there remained considerable continuities as well.

Thinking with the concept of the Common Good involves the problematic of ordering at every turn. On an organic level, medieval thinkers considered whether a living body, such as the body politic, can survive without an organizing and directing head. On the level of practice they asked: By what means does a communal body balance the antagonistic forces within it? How does it arrive at those customs, laws, decisions, and judgments that serve it best? Can election work as a mechanism of self-governance and equity, and if so, how and why? On a philosophical level, thinkers speculated on how individual parts of the community could

[12] On the linkage of the ideal of the common good to the communal movement of the twelfth and thirteenth centuries, see Jeremy Catto, "Ideas and Experience in the Political Thought of Aquinas," *Past & Present* 71 (1976), 3–21 at 11. Catto suggests a number of legal precedents available from Roman and canon law for making claims for the superiority of the common good, e.g., *Codex* VI.51; XII.62.63; and *Decretum* II, 7, 1, 35. On the common good in legal texts, both Roman and canon, see Brian Tierney, *Foundation of the Conciliar Theory: The Contribution of the Medieval Canonists from Gratian to the Great Schism* (Cambridge University Press, 1955); Brian Tierney, *Religion, Law, and the Growth of Constitutional Thought* (Cambridge University Press, 1982); Jean Gaudemet, "Utilitas Publica," *Revue Historique de Droit Français et Étranger* 29 (1951), 465–99; Kempshall, *Common Good*, 14–15. For the broader question of how collectivities were defined and imagined in the medieval law, see Michaud-Quantin, *Universitas: expressions du mouvement communautaire dans le Moyen-Âge latin* (Paris: J. Vrin, 1970), esp. 111–27, 169–70, 201–31.

[13] For a discussion of these controversies, see Kempshall, *Common Good*, 3–10, 16–25; Ewart Lewis, "Organic Tendencies in Medieval Political Thought," *American Political Science Review* 32 (1938), 849–76; L. P. Fitzgerald, "St. Thomas Aquinas and the Two Powers," *Angelicum* 36 (1979), 515–56; Cary Nederman, "Nature, Sin and the Origins of Society: The Ciceronian Tradition in Medieval Political Thought," *Journal of the History of Ideas* 49 (1988), 3–26.

be ordered to and balanced against the needs and will of the communal whole; they questioned what forms, forces, and mechanisms are involved in such ordering and balancing, and they asked where the resultant order might stand in relation to contemporary ideals of equity and justice. I have found that each of these problems in ordering, indeed the problem of order itself in this period, rested on assumptions concerning the definition and bounds of balance/*aequalitas*, assumptions that (as we have already seen in relation to medical and economic thought) were themselves in the process of transformation over the course of the thirteenth century.

The Common Good and the model of equalization in the writings of Albertus Magnus

With all the legal, philosophical, and theological sources that Christian thinkers of the thirteenth century could and did draw upon in their construction of the ideal of the Common Good, it would still be difficult to exaggerate the influence that Aristotelian texts, particularly the *Nicomachean Ethics* and the *Politics*, had on this development.[14] Albertus Magnus was the first scholastic to comment on the full text of the *Nicomachean Ethics* (c. 1250), soon after it had been fully translated from the Greek into Latin by Robert Grosseteste.[15] More than a decade later, Albert wrote a second complete commentary on the *Ethics*.[16] In the period between the two versions, he had completed a commentary on Aristotle's *Metaphysics* and had gained access to the complete Latin translation of Aristotle's *Politics*. It has been conjectured that Albert wrote his second commentary on the *Ethics* in order to include within it insights gained

---

[14] Christoph Flüeler, *Rezeption und Interpretation der aristotelischen Politica im späten Mittelalter*, 2 vols. (Amsterdam: Grüner, 1992); Jean Dunbabin, "The Reception and Interpretation of Aristotle's Politics," in *The Cambridge History of Later Medieval Philosophy*, ed. N. Kretzman et al. (Cambridge University Press, 1982), 723–37.

[15] Albert's first commentary on the *Ethics* has been edited as volume XIV of the recent Cologne edition of his *Opera omnia: Alberti Magni super Ethica commentum et quaestiones*, ed. Wilhelm Kübel (Monasterii Westfalorum: Aschendorff, 1972). On the construction of this text see Auguste Pelzer, "Le cours inédit d'Albert le Grand sur la Morale à Nicomaque, recueilli et rédigé par saint Thomas d'Aquin," *Revue néoscolastique de philosophie* 24 (1922), 333–61, 479–520.

[16] Albert's second commentary, *Ethicorum libri decem*, is vol. VII of *Opera omnia*, ed. August Borgnet (Paris: Vivès, 1891). All citations to the *Ethica* in this chapter will be from the Borgnet edition. See Jean Dunabin, "The Two Commentaries of Albertus Magnus on the Nicomachean *Ethics*," *Recherches de théologie ancienne et médiévale* 30 (1963), 232–50. Dunbabin (at 245) dates this second commentary to 1267–8, and this dating is seconded by Kempshall (*Common Good*, 29). James Weisheipl, however, provides an earlier probable date of 1262–3, "Albert's Works on Natural Science in Probable Chronological Order," in *Albertus Magnus and the Sciences*, ed. James Weisheipl (Toronto: Pontifical Institute of Mediaeval Studies, 1980), Appendix I, 575.

from his close study of these two major texts.[17] The second *Ethics* commentary, dated to 1267–8, is the text upon which I focus my analysis because it presents his clearest and fullest treatment of the conception of the Common Good. That Albert's fullest treatment of what would seem to be a quintessentially political concept appears in his commentary on the *Ethics* speaks to the wealth of concerns – ethical, political, theological, metaphysical, physical – that were attached to this ideal in this period.

The first three chapters of Book I of Albert's commentary on the *Ethics* are concerned with arriving, step by step, at Aristotle's definitive statement (in the *Politics*) that attaining the Common Good of the *civitas* is "something greater and more complete" and, moreover, "finer and more divine" than attaining the good of a single man.[18] Arrive there Albert does, seemingly without hesitation or hedging. In Albert's words, repeated a half-dozen times with little variation at the conclusion of Book I, ch. 3: "Truly better and more divine (*melius vero et divinius*) is the good of a people (*genti*) and of a city (*civitati*) than the good of a single individual."[19] Immediately before making these statements, Albert found a way to illustrate their truth through the use of a geometrical figure, thus framing his philosophical/theological argument for the superiority of the Common Good as, quite literally, a geometrical proof. It is significant that the geometrical representation he chose for this purpose is based on the mechanical scale as an instrument of balance and equalization. In this way, Albert makes explicit the connections between his vision of the Common Good and his vision of the ideal of political and social balance.

He imagines a mechanical scale inscribed within a circle. The circle, in turn, with its center, radii, and circumference all specified, serves to translate into geometrical terms the working of the scale's arms. He writes:

The Greeks call the proportion that describes the relation between the individual good and the ultimate good, *reperim*.[20] *Reperim* refers to the arm of a mechanical

---

[17] Kempshall, *Common Good*, 33–6. The complete Latin text of the *Politica* that informed Albert's second commentary on the *Ethics* was translated by William Moerbeke, *c.* 1265. See *Aristotelis Politicorum Libri Octo cum vetusta translatione Guilelmi de Moerbeka*, ed. Franz Susemihl (Leipzig: Teubner, 1872).

[18] Aristotle, *Politics*, I.2 [1094b7–10], Kempshall, (*Common Good*, 28): "si enim et idem est uni et civitati, maiusque et perfectius quod civitatis videtur et suscipere et salvare, amabile quidem enim et uni soli, melius et divinius genti et civitatibus."

[19] Albert, *Ethica*, I.3.14, 49a: "Amabile quidem igitur est quod est uni soli bonum, melius vero et divinius est quod est bonum genti et civitati."

[20] *Ibid.*, I.3.14, 48b: "Et ideo Graeci dicunt hoc bonum sic proportionatum ad unum, operari ad bonum ultimum per modum *reperim*." I have searched without success to find evidence of the term "reperim" (or its meaning) in Greek or Latin. In the margin of the Borgnet edition opposite this word, the printed phrase "reperim quid sit?" appears.

balance (*brachium librae*) that holds the heavier weight. This arm moves quickly downward and away from the position of equilibrium (*brachium ab aequilibrio subito movetur*) in the direction of a right angle drawn at the center of the circle. The circle as a whole represents the rising and falling of both arms of the scale. The greater the weight of the heavier arm, the greater its descending along the quarter circle, and the closer its angle approaches a right angle. And this angle can be measured in terms of greater and lesser.[21]

Albert then uses this framing to demonstrate that the greater the angle (and the arc along the quarter circle), the closer the good is to the primary good (the Common Good); the lesser the angle (and the arc), the more distant it is. The intersection of geometry and the mechanical scale renders visual the comparison of the two goods (common and individual), making immediately apparent which is the more valuable of the two.[22]

Albert's translation of the relation between Common Good and individual good into a geometrical demonstration is tied to two other species of translation. In the largest sense, he assumes the possibility of translating political and ethical conditions into quasi-physical terms and representations. More specifically, he accepts the idea that a political and ethical quality (the good) can, for the purposes of demonstration, be translated into a physical quantity (weight), which can then be measured according to greater and lesser degree (*incrementum majus vel minus*). As M. S. Kempshall rightly notes in his discussion of this demonstration, "Albert is clearly presupposing that goodness can be identified with heaviness, the size of the angle at the centre with the proximity of the individual to the Common Good."[23] I emphasize the direction of Albert's set of "translations" because singly and together they facilitate the framing of political questions quite literally

---

[21] *Ibid.*, I.3.14, 48b: "Reperim autem brachium librae est, in quo est pondus praeponderans. Hoc enim brachium ab aequilibrio subito movetur ad angulum rectum descriptum in centro circuli, qui descripsit utrumque librae brachium ascendens et descendens, et secundum quantitatem quam brachium descendens describit in quarta circuli, quae sub centro, angulo recto ponderis est incrementum majus vel minus." Kempshall (*Common Good*, 31–2) not only comments on this passage and offers his reading of it, but he adds a geometrical illustration to clarify Albert's meaning. He notes that the geometric model described here had its origin in Eustratius of Nicaea's twelfth-century commentary on the *Ethics*, with which Albert was familiar, and that the drawing he presents had precursors in medieval commentaries on the *Ethics*, citing Paris, BNF, Nat. Lat. 10260 fol. 171r. I have modified Kempshall's translation of this passage.

[22] Albert, *Ethica*, I.3.14, 48b: "et sic bona tanto majus incrementum habent ad vitam, quanto fuerint primo bono propinquiora: et tanto minus incrementum habent ad vitam, quanto fuerint ab illa distantiora: et sic inter se dicuntur meliora."

[23] Kempshall, *Common Good*, 32

as questions of balance.[24] Yet for all the potential that Albert's model contains in its translation of abstract political qualities into measurable weights and distances, it is important to recognize that it is still based on the simplest and oldest form of the word "aequilibrium," the two arms of a mechanical scale designed to balance two equal weights. The model of the mechanical scale, while still thought by Albertus Magnus to be adequate to represent the balance of the Common Good, will be quite inadequate to represent the complex political equilibrium sensed by political thinkers of the fourteenth century, such as Marsilius of Padua and Nicole Oresme.[25]

Just as Albert's choice of the scale to represent the Common Good reveals that he is speaking for an "older" model of equalization, so too do the series of logical steps he takes to arrive at this figure. He begins his commentary with a discussion of the nature of the Good, which leads him to the question, "What is the highest good?"[26] After considering three aspects of the *summum bonum* – order (*in ordine*), comparison (*in comparatione*), and quantity (*in quantitate*) – he arrives at the conclusion that everything good finds its exemplar in God as first cause.[27] All things are good insofar as they imitate God and God "resonates" within them.[28] As he writes: "The accidental and temporary good is only such insofar as it reflects and is directed by and toward the simple and eternal good."[29] Albert's entire ordering plan follows from these premises: all causes and all good derive from a single unified cause and good, which is God, and therefore, all of human life, like all of existence, participates in a unified and unidirectional hierarchy. This unifying vision remains perfectly intact in every succeeding step that Albert takes, including those that lead from the notion of God as the source and cause of all good, to the assertion that the political Common Good is the highest human good.

---

[24] The framing of political questions in terms of weight and equilibrium will play an important role in Marsilius of Padua's *Defensor pacis*, and from there it continues through the seventeenth century and into the present in the inheritance of Hobbesian and Lockean political analysis, most familiar today in the ongoing discourse on "checks and balances" and "the balance of powers."

[25] We saw in previous chapters that the balance of the mechanical scale was similarly inadequate to express the new and complex sense of systematic equalization that came to underlie speculation in the area of scholastic economic and medical thought.

[26] Albert, *Ethica*, I.2.4, 21b.

[27] *Ibid.*, I.2.4, 22b: "et sic summum bonum est Deus. Quia licet Deus simpliciter sit, tamen omnes omnium bonitates primas formas exemplares in ipso habent, quas quantum imitantur, bona sunt: et quanto plus decidunt ab ipsis tanto plus malitiae permiscentur."

[28] *Ibid.*, I.2.4, 23b: "Et ideo pura bonitas est in summo bono quod est Deus vel idea boni, sicut dicit Plato. Alia autem bona sunt, quia quaedam imitationes et resonantiae sunt illius."

[29] *Ibid.*, I.3.6, 38b: "Bonum enim per accidens ut nunc, resonantia est boni simpliciter et semper, et non habet movere appetitum nisi in quantum est resonantia illius."

Albert credits Aristotle with having revealed the natural hierarchy of political association. He follows Aristotle in declaring that it is "unnatural" for individuals to live outside a political community, that the first community natural to all humans is the family household, and that the family community is, in turn, superseded in importance by the larger and more comprehensive political community (*polis*, *civitas*), which is itself, in Aristotelian terms, a "natural' community.[30] Only within the political community can men truly attain virtue and live well.[31] At this point in his exposition, Albert departs briefly from Aristotle to follow the lead of Cicero, when he states that the organization of individuals into communities is not an automatic or predetermined process but rather is accomplished through the free choice and free will of the participating citizens.[32] The idea that individuals freely will their participation and agreement in the political community then leads Albert to his discussion of law. He asserts (following Aristotle) that law functions as the fundamental ordering, connecting, and equalizing instrument within the *civitas*. Throughout his discussion, Albert's association of law with the attainment and maintenance of *aequalitas* is explicit. In its primary role as an instrument of equalization, law insures that judgments between members and groups within the community are based on the principle of equity (*secundum naturam aequi*).[33]

Albert's focus on the function of law underlies one of his basic principles: that communication (*communicatio*) is the essence of political life and essential for its perfection. Communication for Albert extends beyond the ties of speech and law. It includes, importantly, economic exchange. Since, he argues, the good of the soul is related to the good of the body, and there are many necessities that neither the individual nor the family can supply for themselves, economic exchange driven by human need (*indigentia*) is necessary for the good of both individual and community.[34] On the same model, the various human arts are instituted to satisfy needs

---

[30] Kempshall, *Common Good*, 49; Albert *Ethica*, I.3.1, 29b: "sic naturaliter est homo civile."

[31] Albert, *Ethica*, I.3.1, 29b–30a.

[32] *Ibid.*, I.3.1, 30a. For more on the Ciceronian strain in medieval political thought, see Nederman, "Nature, Sin and the Origins of Society."

[33] Albert, *Ethica*, I.3.1, 30a: "Aequum autem est dispositio civis ad civem, et iniquum corruptio ... Et si regit in casibus, virtus judicativa est, quae secundum leges et pacta et secundum naturam aequi omne determinat inter cives emergens." On the history of the association of the political community with "justitia communis" and "aequo jure," see Michaud-Quantin, *Universitas*, 113. As we will see in the following chapters, law is similarly represented as the principal instrument of communal equalization in the writings of Marsilius of Padua and Nicole Oresme.

[34] Albert, *Ethica*, I.3.2, 32b: "quod homo compositus est ex corpore et anima: et bonum hominis non est tantum bonum animae, sed etiam bonum corporis ad bonum animae relatum. Est enim corpus instrumentum animae."

that the individual cannot satisfy by himself.[35] Further still, human actions, human teachings, and human choices are all directed toward facilitating human communication in the direction of living well. In this way all social actions seek and are ordered toward the good.[36] While all social acts are directed, ultimately, to the Common Good, they are so not directly, but secondarily, as they pursue particular goods which are themselves good only insofar as they reflect the *primum bonum*.[37] The idea that every individual act (*omnis actus*), in itself, in its very nature, seeks and is ordered toward the good is essential here. It is a prime marker of the "old" model of equalization in which meaning and identity are inherent and fixed in intention and direction. It is also a point on which a representative of the "new" model of equilibrium, such as Marsilius of Padua, will differ profoundly from Albert.

Albert's close attention to the particulars of human existence leads him to acknowledge that there are some acts common to the *civitas* that are nevertheless difficult to imagine as being ordered to the good. The most prominent of these are acts directed toward personal economic acquisition. He recognizes the importance of production and exchange to the life of the *civitas*, and yet he finds it difficult to align the seeking of personal benefit through exchange with his general principle that "inferior ends are only desired insofar as they reflect the superior end."[38] His solution to this problem appears briefly here in Book I of the *Ethics*, but it is fully addressed only later in Book V in his commentary to Aristotle's discussion of justice and economic exchange. At this later point he cites with full agreement Aristotle's statement that the *civitas* is held together through exchange.[39] But then, in order to integrate the desire for personal gain into the Common Good, he asserts, with Aristotle, that what men are truly seeking in exchange is not their personal advantage but rather the establishment of an *equality*, and specifically, a *proportional equality*, in their exchanges.[40] The "*aequalitas proportionum*" sought by exchangers is

---

[35] *Ibid.*, I.3.2, 30a: "et cum multae sint indigentiae, varias oportet artes reperiri."

[36] *Ibid.*, I.3.2–5, 33a–37a: "quod omnis ars et omnis doctrina, similiter autem est omnis actus et electio bonum quoddam appetere videtur."

[37] *Ibid.*, 1.3.7, 39b–40a: "Omnia autem appetunt primum bonum, non secundum esse vel substantiam, sed secundum quod primum bonum ratio est movendi appetitum in omnibus bonum."

[38] *Ibid.*, I.3.11, 44b: "finis enim inferiorum non desideratur nisi propter finem superiorem."

[39] E.g., *ibid.*, V.2.9, 355b: "In contrafacere enim proportionale civitas commanere potest: civitas enim non commanet nisi indigentiae civium suppleantur: suppleri autem non possunt sine tali commutatione rei unius ad alteram."

[40] *Ibid.*, V.2.9, 356a: "Talis enim fluxus et refluxus gratiarum commanere facit civitatem; facit enim retributionem secundum proportionalitatem." Also, *ibid.*, V.2.9, 357a–b: "In talibus [commutatio] nihil prohibet opus unius melius esse in valore quam opus alterius, et magnam habere differentiam secundum labores et expensam. Commutatio autem

between the labor and expenses involved in the goods they produce and the labor and expenses involved in the production of the goods they receive in exchange. It is this mutual *search for equality* that forms the basis of economic exchange for Albert, and, to his mind, it is this alone that guarantees the place of exchange under the umbrella of both the good and the Common Good.[41]

Given his "older" sense of the potentialities of equalization, however, Albert is incapable of imagining (as Peter Olivi did) the production of exchange equality from willed inequalities, from each exchanger desiring to buy for less and sell for more. In Albert's imagination, equality must be built into each part, by nature, for the whole to be equalized. This is a crucial element of the "old" model of equalization. Thus in order for exchange to fulfill its function of binding together the *civitas*, each exchanger must be responsible for consciously seeking equality in every exchange, rather than seeking personal advantage. In Albert's view, one cannot arrive at the good through the evil; *one cannot arrive at balance through imbalance.*[42] There is no sense in Albert's writings that the multiplying of individual desires for advantage could possibly eventuate in the production of good, much less in a concept as exalted as the Common Good. In this, again, his understanding of the potentialities of equalization stands in stark contrast to the understanding of those thinkers, considered in the chapters that preceded and that follow this, who shared the model of the "new" equilibrium and who began to imagine how the massing of individual inequalities could conceivably result in the systematic balance of the whole.

For Albert, the Common Good of the political community mirrors the ultimate good of God. It is not that he cannot see the diversity in human acts, cannot recognize that some acts are better and directed higher than others, that some needs are purer and closer to the primary good.[43] But while some acts clearly are better and closer to God than others, ultimately all and everything that has real existence is aimed in the same unified and relentlessly unitary direction. Any act or desire that is not so ordered

---

non fit nisi in aequalitate proportionis." On the insistence within scholastic economic thought that equality be the end of the exchange process, see Chapters 1 and 2 above and my *Economy and Nature in the Fourteenth Century*, 58–133.

[41] Albert, in reference to *Ethica* V.2.7 [1133a14–16], 353a: "Artes enim illae destruerentur utique, nisi faciens qui per modum agentis se habet in contractu emptionis et venditionis, tantum et tale faceret, quantum et quale patiens passus est." Compare to Peter Olivi's position on the question in Chapter 2.

[42] Albert, *Ethica*, I.3.1, 30a: "Aequum autem est dispositio civis ad civem, et iniquum corruptio."

[43] *Ibid.*, I.3.9, 41a: "Meliora autem dico, quae fini ultimo hominis qui est felicitas, sunt propinquiora."

simply loses its ontological status and with it any claim to being a legitimate part of the *civitas*.[44]

This in itself makes possible a few general comments concerning the constituent elements of Albert's model of equalization, each of which will be challenged in succeeding decades, with the emergence of the new model of equilibrium. In Albert's model, the end of each particular act or desire is fixed in its very nature; the direction of each is inborn, determined by its imitation of or resonance with the ultimate good. Parts are ordered *in their very nature* to the whole; their identity and meaning are fixed in relation to their place within the whole. Order is pre-ordained, a*equalitas* is pre-ordained, built into God's eternal plan. It is impossible to arrive at equality through inequality; impossible to arrive at a balance of the whole through imbalanced parts. In marked contrast, the essence of the new equilibrium (as it has been outlined in our earlier chapters and as it will appear in those that follow) is that the whole (in this case the communal whole or *civitas*) is reconceived as a relativized system in equilibrium. Within this working system, the nature, identity, and purpose of individual parts can and does shift in relation to their position and function within the whole. As thinkers came to abandon Albert's belief in absolute and everlasting beginnings, end points, and directions in favor of a thoroughgoing relativity, it became possible for the first time both to imagine balance/*aequalitas* as the product of systematic activity and to integrate that product into the ratio of the Common Good.

The intertwined elements of Albert's model of equalization appear even more clearly drawn – and more distinct from the "new" equilibrium – when he considers in more concrete terms the implication of the political Common Good. In Albert's vision, the virtue and perfection of the political parts derive not merely from their being ordered within the political whole; they are literally "subsumed" and "subservient" to it in their particularity.[45] The example he uses is instructive: the victory of the army cannot be achieved unless all the components are directed toward the same end – infantry, cavalry, navy, artillery, and each of their human parts.[46] The political end is always one that must be aimed for, always

---

[44] *Ibid.*, I.3.10, 43a–b: "Si enim in operatione, humanum bonum impedientem seu adimentem, haec doctrina nullo modo civilis est. Vanum est quod nullum finem includit humani boni."

[45] *Ibid.*, I.3.10, 42b: "non perficitur sine virtutibus et potentiis multorum quae organice subserviunt."

[46] *Ibid.*: "Sicut enim victoria est in duce exercitus, quamvis expedite in ipso non nisi multa organice sibi subserviant ... et sic est in aliis multis facile considerare: ita facultas actus in uno quidem est, sed non perficitur sine virtutibus et potentiis multorum quae organice subserviant."

necessarily a *conscious* end, whether the goal derives from the ordering mind of the general, or the prince, or in the ordering intelligence of God. In essence, the governing ratio Albert imagines is a strict hierarchy of being, with inferior beings linked by necessity to superior and inferior bent to the order of the superior, all the way from the least in creation through the intermediate to the greatest and most comprehensive.[47]

In exploring the form of hierarchy that orders all of existence, something which he does again and again, Albert makes frequent use of the concept of relation. This is quite understandable given that to talk about hierarchy is to talk about the relationship of part to part within the whole. Since the evolution of relativistic thinking is central to the formation of the "new" equilibrium, Albert's thinking on relation once again provides a solid point of comparison between "older" models and "new." He writes:

> It is generally true that all things are ordered to the single ultimate good according to the relation they have to it (*secundum relationem quam habent*) in terms of being nearer or more remote. The more remote things are from the ultimate good, always the more obediently they are ordered to those things that are nearer.[48]

Relation, in this sense, and in the sense that Albert continually employs it when describing the hierarchy of the good, is clearly not a dynamic concept. It expresses a series of fixed relationships. Distances, one surmises, may expand or contract, but there is no possibility that what is now above will or could ever be below, that what is subservient now will or could ever be in command.[49] Relation here is tied to a world governed by an eternally fixed order and plan, with a single direction toward a single end. There is no sense whatsoever of relation as a *solvent* of hierarchy, or as *multidirectional*, or as a *transformative* principle that works counter to fixed notions of order and hierarchy. And yet as we have seen and will continue to see, all these other meanings of relation, so distant from Albert's that they seemingly derive from another conceptual world, will come to characterize the sense and application of relativity within the new equilibrium.

As with relation, so too with the concept of analogy, which in Albert's plan is the ordering principle that ties the whole system together.[50] As he

---

[47] *Ibid.*, I.3.11, 43b–44a: "Et cum semper sit superioris ordinare, inferioris autem ordinari ad formam et rationem superioris, quod inferiores aliquem superiorem ordinentur, necesse est. Facultates igitur quae dictae sunt, ad unam superiorem ordinantur, et superiori secundum rationem sui boni."

[48] *Ibid.*, I.3.11, 44b: "Regulariter enim verum est, quod quaecumque sunt ad unum bonum ultimum, secundum relationem quam habent illud bonum propinquius vel remotius ordinantur ad illud. Et ideo remotiores semper obedientes erunt his quae propinquius ordinantur."

[49] *Ibid.*, I.3.11, 44a: "et superior ordinans ad omnes inferiores retinet principatum."

[50] Kempshall, *Common Good*, 34–6.

writes: "all faculties are ordered to the one which is the operative good, and only with respect to this single good are all other things said, by analogy (*per analogiam*), to be good."[51] It is interesting that Albert characterizes his own use of analogy here as "*analogia simpliciter*" and recognizes the possibility of another form of analogy not based on a single hierarchical end point which he calls "*analogia secundum respectum ad illud.*"[52] In other of his works, particularly those on medicine and natural philosophy, he will make use of this other form of analogy and relation – fluid rather than fixed – to analyze with great skill and refinement the shifting powers of particular natural agents as they act within changing natural contexts. But not here; not in his elucidation of the metaphysical, ethical, and political order; not in his understanding of the forms of equality and equalization that underlie his conception of the Common Good.

In the concluding sections of the *Ethics*, Book I, ch. 3, after having constructed the metaphysical and physical grounds for the superiority of the Common Good, Albert turns to focus specifically on its political ramifications.[53] Here we get our first details concerning the life of the Greek *polis* and the Latin *civitas*, drawn from writers such as Aristotle and Cicero. Here we begin to see the *civitas* at work: imposing laws, fighting battles, disciplining its citizens. Since in the second part of this chapter and in the chapters that follow I link the concept of the "self-ordering city" to the emergence of the new model of equilibrium in political thought, it is important to note that Albert, too, has a vision of the city acting as an ordering agent. His *civitas* punishes and rewards; it establishes equality and just balance; it actively directs the lives of its citizens.[54] He offers as an example of this activity:

---

[51] Albert, *Ethica*, I.3.11, 44b: "quod omnes [facultates] ordinentur ad unam quae est operativa illius boni ad cujus respectum omnia alia per analogiam bona dicuntur." Also, *ibid.*, I.3.14, 48b: "Singulorum enim opera rationem boni non habent nisi per analogiam ad ultimum bonum." Kempshall (*Common Good*, 31) discusses the various possible senses of analogy in Albert.

[52] Albert, *Ethica*, I.3.11, 45b. This second, multicentered form, in which particular analogies work only within particular situations and sets of definitions, is tied to the species of logical arguments "secundum quid" or "ad aliquid," which Albert often employs in his analysis of the natural world and specifically in his writings on medicine. On this, see Nancy Siraisi, "The Medical Learning of Albertus Magnus," in *Albertus Magnus and the Sciences*, ed. James Weisheipl (Toronto: Pontifical Institute of Mediaeval Studies, 1980), 379–404. Here again, medicine, and particularly Galenic medicine, served as a source of relativistic determinations in this period.

[53] Again, Albert, *Ethica*, I.3.14, 49a: "Amabile quidem igitur est quod est uni soli bonum. Melius vero et divinius est quod est bonum genti et civitati."

[54] Kempshall writes (*Common Good*, 41): "This principle of ordering what is personal towards what is in common [in Albert] is the principle of right (*ius*) or justice."

If those of inferior ability happen to occupy positions of superior dignity, the inferior will be returned [by the ordering city] to their proper place. Similarly, if those in inferior positions exhibit superior virtues, they will be raised up.[55]

This statement, and others of similar bent, reveal that when Albert's city acts and orders, it does so to reinforce the hierarchy of meaning and identity that underlies all of God's creation. The city does not get to define what, in its terms, represents inferior and superior virtues because there is no sense that these might differ in any way over time or circumstance. There is no sense of the city creating its own forms of meaning and identity – forms that do not have their place in a divine, pre-ordained, and supra-historical plan. Indeed, he concludes his discussion of the city with the following thought: of all the spheres of human life, "the political sphere comes closest to being assimilated to God."[56] Once again, the contrast between Albert's vision of the city as orderer and the vision of those who followed him and reflected the new model of equilibrium – Jean de Jandun, Marsilius of Padua, and others – could not be clearer. For them, the city represented the relativized system par excellence. The meaning that it created and reinforced, the Common Good that defined its own good, derived essentially from its functioning logic and from its own particular necessities.

The Common Good and the model of equalization in the writings of Thomas Aquinas

Nothing I have written so far about Albert's conception of order and relation, and none of the ways in which I have situated Albert's position within the "old" model of equalization as opposed to the "new," would be out of place when posited about his illustrious student, Thomas Aquinas. To consider Thomas' positions on the Common Good in anything close to a comprehensive manner would take me far beyond the purposes of this chapter. His opinions touching on the Common Good are scattered widely throughout his writings. Taken together they form a truly grand conception, but there is, in the end, no systematic exposition, no single treatise dedicated to the thorough elucidation of the concept as a whole.[57]

---

[55] Albert, *Ethica*, I.3.13, 47b: "Civilis autem praeordinat quales disciplinas quilibet civium debet addiscere … Et si invenientur inhabiles in dignitatibus superioribus, ad inferiores retrudantur … et qui se idoneos exhibent de inferioribus, ad superiores exaltentur."

[56] *Ibid.*, I.3.14, 49b: "Propter quod dicit Eustratius, quod politicus maxime Deo assimilatur."

[57] There are still disagreements concerning the authenticity of what could be Thomas' most directed political writing, the *De regno*. Although many scholars consider Books I and II of *De regno* authentic, and a number base their conclusions about Thomas' political views

As a result, many studies have been dedicated to providing what Thomas did not – an integrated conception of his Common Good and its implications for his political thought.[58] Not surprisingly, there remain many points on which scholars disagree. In order to avoid wandering too far from the subject of equalization, I will consider only those aspects relating to Thomas' Common Good that touch on questions of order and hierarchy and, further still, only to a few selected points that add to or modify the components of equalization already observed in Albert's commentary on the *Ethics*.

As a place to begin, I offer a broad outline of Thomas' vision of hierarchy culled from recent works of interpretation on this question. God governs the cosmos which is ordered by his intelligence. The cosmos consists of a diversity of graded orders of lesser beings: angels, men, animals, vegetable life, inanimate things in descending order, but all are unified in that they possess a fixed relation to the whole and to every other order by virtue of the degree of being they possess. All things are good insofar as they possess being, and thus the descending order of being is also a descending order of value. Those higher in being and goodness possess all the perfections of those lower in the hierarchy. Each being in the hierarchy is subordinated to that which is above it. In return, that which is above rules and preserves that which is below. All of the graded orders of being (and each taken separately) are ordered by and toward the perfection of the whole. The whole cosmos is, in essence, a *societas perfecta*, created, balanced, and governed by God, the perfect being

upon it, I think the many doubts that have been expressed counsel caution. For this reason, in what follows I cite the *De regno* only in support of those positions that are also found in incontrovertibly authentic works.

[58] See, for example, Maurice De Wulf, "L'individu et le groupe dans la scolastique du XIIIe siècle," *Revue néoscolastique de philosophie* 22 (1920), 341–57; Jaime Vélez-Sáenz, *The Doctrine of the Common Good of Civil Society in the Works of St. Thomas Aquinas* (University of Notre Dame Press, 1951); R. A. Crofts, "The Common Good in the Political Theory of Thomas Aquinas," *The Thomist* 37 (1973), 155–73; Oscar Brown, *Natural Rectitude and Divine Law in Aquinas: An Approach to an Integral Interpretation of the Thomistic Doctrine of Law* (Toronto: Pontifical Institute of Mediaeval Studies, 1981); D. E. Luscombe, "Thomas Aquinas and Conceptions of Hierarchy in the Thirteenth Century," in *Thomas von Aquin: Werk und Wirkung im Licht neuerer Forschungen*, ed. Albert Zimmerman (Berlin: Walter de Gruyter, 1988), 261–77, esp. 269–75; John Finnis, "Public Good: The Specifically Political Common Good in Aquinas," in *Natural Law and Moral Inquiry: Ethics, Metaphysics and Politics in the Work of Germain Grisez*, ed. R. P. George (Washington, DC: Georgetown University Press, 1998), 174–210; Kempshall, *Common Good*, 76–129. The writings of Thomas Eschmann on this subject remain particularly useful: "A Thomistic Glossary on the Principle of the Pre-eminence of a Common Good," *Mediaeval Studies* 5 (1943), 123–65; "Bonum commune melius est quam bonum unius: Eine Studie über den Wertvorrang des Personalen bei Thomas von Aquin," *Mediaeval Studies* 6 (1944), 62–120; and "St. Thomas Aquinas on the Two Powers," *Mediaeval Studies* 20 (1958), 177–205.

and primary good.[59] The Common Good of the political community attains its superior position by virtue of its capacity to reflect more directly and communicate more widely the universal good of God.[60]

None of these elements would be out of place in the vision of order and equalization we have seen in Albert's commentary on the *Ethics*. Thomas, however, is even more inventive than Albert in his capacity to weave together numerous traditional forms of hierarchy in the construction of his own master hierarchy: neo-platonic emanation, Aristotelian teleology, a specifically Christian order of love (*ordo caritatis*), a hierarchy of virtue, and even a quasi-physical hierarchy of communication: the more something communicates its goodness (in this case the Common Good of the political community in comparison with the goodness of a single individual), the more divine (*divinius*) it is.[61] Thomas can layer hierarchy over hierarchy without creating dissonance because in his view each reflects the same divine order; each expands along a single axis in the same vertical direction; each employs the same form of relation and analogy to link parts within parts, part to part, and parts to whole. In each hierarchy, the principle of every act and motion is its proper end, and this end is ordained within its unchanging inborn nature.[62] Applying this structure to the political sphere permits Thomas to say:

As one man is a part of the household, so a household is a part of the *civitas*: and the *civitas* is a perfect community (*communitas perfecta*), as Aristotle says in the *Politics*. And therefore, as the good of one man is not the ultimate end, but is ordered to the Common Good (*ordinatur ad commune bonum*), so too the good of one household is ordered to the good of a single *civitas*, which is a perfect community.[63]

---

[59] Samuel Beer, "The Rule of the Wise and the Holy: Hierarchy in the Thomistic System," *Political Theory* 14 (1986), 391–422, at 394–5; Mark Murphy, "Consent, Custom, and the Common Good in Aquinas' Account of Political Authority,"*Review of Politics* 59 (1997), 323–50, at 324; Brian Tierney, "Hierarchy, Consent, and the 'Western Tradition,'"*Political Theory* 15 (1987), 646–52; Kempshall, *Common Good*, 79–83. Although Murphy agrees with Beer's overall description of Thomas' hierarchical plan, he disagrees with certain implications Beer draws from it, particularly that Thomas fully and completely extended this plan to his political thought and his conception of the Common Good. Brian Tierney expressed a similar criticism, but he also accepted Beer's general characterization of Thomistic hierarchy.

[60] Kempshall, *Common Good*, 79–82; *SCG*, III, 17, 6; III, 24, 1–8; *ST*, I, II, 90, 2.

[61] Kempshall, *Common Good*, 83, 97, and 103: "the order of goodness in the universe is defined as a hierarchy of perfection in which rank is dependent on degree of commonality." See *ST*, II, II, 31, ad 3 (cited above). Also *ST*, I, 108, 6, where Thomas cites Augustine on hierarchy (*De trinitate*, iii): "bodies are ruled in a certain order; the inferior by the superior; and all of them by the spiritual creature, and the bad spirit by the good spirit."

[62] E.g., *ST*, I, II, 9, 1: "The motion of the subject itself is due to some agent. And since every agent acts for an end ... the principle of this motion lies in the end."

[63] *Ibid.*, I, II, 90, 3, ad 3.

And when this scheme is further extended to law, the great ordering and equalizing principle of the *civitas*, it takes this form:

> the law denotes a kind of plan directing acts towards an end. Now wherever there are movers ordained to one another, the power of the second mover must be derived from the power of the first mover; since the second mover does not move except insofar as it is moved by the first. Wherefore we observe the same in all those who govern, so that the plan of government is derived by secondary governors from the governor in chief . . . Since then the eternal law is the plan of government in the Chief Governor, all the plans of government in the inferior governors must be derived from the eternal law.[64]

With all the attention and emphasis Thomas devotes to elucidating the cosmic order, and with all his general statements connecting this order to the Common Good of the political community, he pays notably little attention to the actual details of political life or to just how the correlation between each individual part and the communal whole works or should work in practice.[65]

One major component of the "old" model of equalization that was developed by Thomas with unmatched richness and comprehensiveness is the identification of order with an ordering intelligence or ordering mind. This identification, which holds without exception in both the supernatural and the natural world, lies at the foundation of Thomas' thought, as evidenced by its pride of place at the opening of the *Summa theologica*. Every demonstration Thomas presents there for the existence of God rests on the identification of cosmic order – the natural gradation of things from the highest to the least – with divine intelligence: "Therefore some intelligent being exists by whom all natural things are ordered to their proper end, and we call that being God."[66]

Thomas' argument identifying order with divine intelligence is yet more fully developed in his *Summa contra gentiles*, where he manages to tie it directly to his concept of the Common Good. In Part III, ch. 24 we find a multi-step proof: intellectual substance is the principal agent of the

---

[64] *Ibid.*, I, II, 93, 3.

[65] For a concise bibliography on the major schools of interpretation concerning Thomas' political views, which indicates the range of positions that have been maintained, see James Blythe, "The Mixed Constitution and the Distinction between Regal and Political Power in the Work of Thomas Aquinas," *Journal of the History of Ideas* 47 (1986), 547–65, at n. 1; Eschmann, "Two Powers," 201; Kempshall, *Common Good*, 88; Tierney, "Hierarchy, Consent, and the 'Western Tradition,'"; Charles Zuckerman, "The Relationship of Theories of Universals to Theories of Church Government in the Middle Ages: A Critique of Previous Views," *Journal of the History of Ideas* 36 (1975), 579–94.

[66] *ST*, I, 2, 3. Also *ST*, I, 5, 5: "whatever effects pre-exist in God, as in the first cause, must be in his intellection (*quod sint in ipso eius intelligere*), and all things must be in Him according to an intelligible mode (*secundum modum intelligibilem*)."

form and motion of lower bodies; the species of things preexist in and are directed by this intellectual substance; consequently, every working of nature is the work of an intelligent substance; thus even things which lack intelligence (e.g., even inanimate objects) seek the good with a natural appetite; and finally, "the more perfect and the higher a thing is in the scale of goodness (*eminentius in gradu bonitatis*), the more it has an appetite for a broader Common Good (*tanto appetitum boni communiorem habet*), and the farther from itself does it seek good and do good."[67]

I have given special attention to Thomas' indelible linking of order with an eternal governing intelligence directing everything to its "proper end," because it alone, in the absence of all the other components of the "old" model of equalization we have elucidated, would separate it sharply from the "new" model of equilibrium taking shape within scholastic thought in the later thirteenth century, with its recognition of the potentialities of systematic self-ordering and self-equalizing.

Armored by philosophical and scriptural authority, tightly woven and reinforced by strand after strand of argument, the structural logic of Albert's and Thomas' Common Good seems complete and virtually unassailable. And yet already in the 1280s and 90s, and gaining speed after the turn of the century, the logic underlying their modeling of order and equalization began to unravel. Mere decades after the mature political writings of Albert and Thomas, scholars such as Godfrey of Fontaines, Peter Olivi, and John of Paris were conceptualizing the Common Good in sharply different ways, able to see past the "old" model that had been so carefully constructed and protected because they shared in a new way of modeling the process of equalization, the key to the formulation of the ideal. It was, then, this new way of modeling equalization – derived from a new model of equilibrium being shaped within scholastic culture – that was continued and developed through the mid fourteenth century, coming eventually to underlie the monumental political speculations of the period, including the two works we will consider in later chapters, Marsilius of Padua's *Defensor pacis* (*c.* 1324), and Nicole Oresme's *De moneta* (*c.* 1356).

Environment and the formation of the Common Good

If the ideal of the Common Good was to be taken seriously, its logic had to account for and reflect in some fashion the political world to which it was being applied. A series of sharp political conflicts and crises occurred over the half-century separating Albert and Thomas from Marsilius of Padua

---

[67] *SCG*, III, 24, 1–8.

that posed new questions and raised new possibilities in the political sphere concerning what might constitute legitimate forms of government, legitimate models of ordering, and legitimate relationships between private good and the Common Good. Where, if anywhere, was the hierarchical plan that could order the conflicting claims to authority of the communes, the rising monarchies of France and England, the Empire, and the Papacy? Most work that has been done on the history of the concept of the Common Good in the later thirteenth and fourteenth centuries takes these momentous politico/religious disputes as their starting point: disputes within and among the communes; between communes and Papacy; between communes and Empire; between Empire and Papacy, between the French King Philip IV and the English King Edward I; between both kings and Pope Boniface VIII, between Pope John XXII and the Franciscan Order, etc.

Understanding the shifting political landscape in this period is surely necessary to a full understanding of the continuing debate about the Common Good. The many crises and confrontations provided an opportunity for polemicists and more dispassionate observers to pose the questions: Who can claim authority over whom? Can or should authority be shared or negotiated, and what can be done when faced with an authority that is manifestly unjust?[68] In my view, however, the crises themselves were less generative of a capacity to reimagine the potentialities of systematic order than were the more slowly building tectonic forces – social, economic, and political – whose movement and grinding realignment underlay the crises occurring at the historical surface. As the concept of the Common Good is tied to a model of equalization, shifting as the model shifts, so too, I believe, the model is tied far more closely – is far more sensitive – to environments than to events. For this reason, my search for the explanation of how the unidirectional model of Albert and Thomas could have shifted so dramatically in half a century, turns from a reading of texts to a reading of contexts; from an analysis of events to an analysis of environments.

The city as environment and site of equilibrium

It is my understanding that social environments exert a strong influence on the individual's inner "sense" of balance – the wordless anticipations

---

[68] Each of these questions is considered, for example, in John of Paris, *De potestate regia et papali* (*On Royal and Papal Power*), completed in 1302. For an insightful study of this work, see Janet Coleman, "The Intellectual Milieu of John of Paris," in *Das Publikum politischer Theorie im 14 Jahrhundert*, ed. Jürgen Miethke and Arnold Bühler (Munich: Oldenbourg, 1992), 173–206, at 175.

and assumptions concerning what balance can be and how it can be achieved and maintained. In earlier chapters I considered the environment of the monetized marketplace of the late thirteenth century, speculating on how the attempt – the perceived necessity – to integrate its dynamic and destabilizing elements into a legitimating "ratio" precipitated and shaped a new model of systematic equilibrium.[69] In addition to the monetized marketplace, there was, I believe, a social environment in this period that provided an even more enveloping (and hence influential) experience of balance than that of the marketplace – the commercial city itself, of which the marketplace was but one component. I turn now to consider how the day-to-day experience of life in the commercial city may have affected the modeling of balance, especially when that experience was filtered through the perception and intellection of minds trained in scholastic modes of thought. To the extent that the models of equalization proper to both social spaces – marketplace and city – overlapped, their capacity to reshape the sense of balance and its potentialities was multiplied, with multiplying effects on the content and direction of scholastic thought.

From the early political writings of Plato and Aristotle, through the writings of almost every major political theorist up to and including Albert and Thomas, it was the city (*polis*, *civitas*, *commune*) that represented the political universe in its fullest form. Many of the quotations from the writings of Albert and Thomas cited above simply equate the Common Good of the *civitas* with the Common Good of the political community.[70] The central place of the *civitas* within Aristotle's *Politics* and Cicero's *De officiis*, and the central place occupied by the *Politics* and the *De officiis* within medieval political discourse, almost guaranteed that this focus would continue through the fourteenth century, even as a new and larger political entity, the *regnum*, emerged as a possible rival, and even as the Empire maintained its theoretical supremacy through its association with *Romanitas* and Roman law.[71]

If at this time the *regnum* and the Christian Empire still remained somewhat amorphous as entities and concepts, too shapeless to be experienced as meaningful wholes, the city was real. Albert with his years in Cologne, Rome, and Paris; Thomas in Naples, Rome, Cologne, Perugia, and Paris; Marsilius in Padua and Paris, can stand here for virtually every

---

[69] See Chapters 1 and 2 above.

[70] E.g., *ST*, I, II, 92, 1, ad 3: "Since then every man is a part of the *civitas*, it is impossible that a man be good, unless he be well proportionate to the common good."

[71] Mario Grignaschi, "La définition du 'civis' dans la scolastique," *Recueils de la Société Jean Bodin* 24 (1966), 71–100.

major scholastic author on political questions in this period. All of them –
Giles of Rome, Peter of Auvergne, Ptolemy of Lucca, Henry of Ghent,
Godfrey of Fontaines, James of Viterbo, Peter of John Olivi, Duns Scotus,
John of Paris – spent the majority of their years as city dwellers, enmeshed
in vibrant and expanding urban environments, in the period between
1250 and 1325. That does not mean that they all drew the same political
lessons from their experiences of urban life. They did not. But their shared
experience of the living city imparted a particular character and direction
to political speculation in this period, one that, especially in the fourteenth
century, was linked to a growing sense of the potentialities of systematic
equality and equalization. This raises the question: What changes
occurred in the cityscape and the experience of the city in the half-century
separating the writings of Albert and Thomas from those of Marsilius of
Padua? And even more important for our purposes, what changes
occurred in the *perception* of the city as a systematic self-equalizing whole
over this half-century?

Raymond Cazelles, the eminent historian of Paris, has described the
steep trajectory of the city's expansion between the residency there of
Thomas and Albert in the 1260s and the residency of Marsilius there
from approximately 1310 to 1324. The expansion occurred on many
fronts: population, artisanal production, commercial wealth, bourgeois
influence, and municipal power.[72] He situates the "apogee" of this
urban expansion in the first decades of the fourteenth century, just at
the time that Marsilius was first arriving in Paris from his native
Padua.[73] This apogee followed upon more than a century of rapid
expansion in urban settlements and urban consciousness across Latin
Christendom.

Over the course of the thirteenth century, chronicles dedicated to the
life of the city became ever more prevalent, witnessing the emergence of a
profound sense of urban place and setting. This was true above all for the
self-governing communes of northern Italy, but it was also true for the
independent cities of the Low Countries and for "capital cities" like

---

[72] Raymond Cazelles, *Nouvelle histoire de Paris de la fin du règne de Philippe Auguste à la mort de Charles V, 1223–1380* (Paris: Hachette, 1994), 9 and *passim*. For a parallel assessment of the trajectory of urbanization in London and England at large, see Richard Britnell, "Commercialisation and Economic Development in England, 1000–1300," in *A Commercialising Economy: England 1086 to c. 1300*, ed. Richard Britnell and Bruce Campbell (Manchester University Press, 1995), 7–26.

[73] Cazelles, *Nouvelle histoire de Paris*, 215–17. On the vitality of the city of Paris in this period, see also Colin Jones, *Paris: Biography of a City* (New York: Viking Press, 2004), 62–70. For a biographical sketch of Marsilius, centering on his experiences in both Padua and Paris, see the following chapter.

London and Paris that accepted the overlordship of their king.[74] From the second half of the thirteenth century, in various chronicle sources, the city appears to come alive as a historical actor in itself.[75] Scenes from the life of the city abound: welcoming dignitaries, decorating itself in honor of its own festivals and religious holidays, recording elections and the transference of power, punishing wrongdoers, preparing for war, making war, and recovering from war. The richest examples of this literature appeared in the half-century between the political writings of Albert and Thomas and those of Marsilius, from chronicle sources such as the multi-volume *Chronica* of Giovanni Villani to literary sources like Dante's *Commedia*, both of which were being composed in the same decades as the composition of the *Defensor pacis*.

Another source of descriptive urban record that flourished in this period was the genre of *"laudes civium"* (Praises of the City).[76] The history of this genre in the medieval period stretches back to the twelfth century, but again the forms it assumed in the second half of the thirteenth century were like nothing that came before.[77] The great exemplar of this new form was Bonvesin da la Riva's "On the Great Things of the City of Milan" (*De magnalibus urbis Mediolani*), completed in 1288.[78] I will have occasion to speak of this work in greater detail below, but at this point I want only to mention one of its most fascinating and telling aspects (shared by other examples of the genre in this period): its fascination with numbers and numbering as a source of

---

[74] On this subject, George Holmes, "The Emergence of an Urban Ideology at Florence, 1250–1450," *Transactions of the Royal Historical Society*, 5th series, 23 (1973), 111–34; David Nicholas, "Medieval Urban Origins in Northern Continental Europe: State of Research and Some Tentative Conclusions," *Studies in Medieval and Renaissance History* 6 (1969), 55–114; Simon Roux, "L'habitat urbain au Moyen Âge: le quartier de l'Université à Paris," *Annales* 2 (1969), 1196–1219; Elisabeth Carpentier and Michel Le Mené, *La France du XIe siècle au XVe siècle: population, société, économie* (Paris: Presses Universitaires de France, 1996).

[75] I discuss the subject of the growing reflection of urban life in chronicle sources from the thirteenth to the fourteenth century in Kaye, "Monetary and Market Consciousness in Thirteenth and Fourteenth Century Europe." See also Antonia Gransden, *Historical Writing in England c.550 to c.1307* (Ithaca, NY: Cornell University Press, 1974); Christian Bec, "Sur l'historiographie marchande à Florence au XIVe siècle," in *La chronique et l'histoire au Moyen Âge*, ed. Daniel Poirion (Paris: La Sorbonne, 1982), 45–73; Chiara Frugoni, *A Distant City: Images of Urban Experience in the Medieval World*, trans.William McCuaig (Princeton University Press, 1991), esp. 86–8.

[76] Also styled "laudes urbium" and "laudes civitatis."

[77] J. K. Hyde, "Medieval Descriptions of Cities," *Bulletin of the John Rylands Library* 48 (1966), 308–40, at 327.

[78] Bonvesin da la Riva, *De magnalibus Mediolani. Meraviglie di Milano*, ed. and trans. Paolo Chiesa (Milan: Libri Scheiwiller, 1998).

description.[79] In Bonvesin's narrative, numbers tell the story of the city; numbers objectify the city's strength, growth, and wealth; numbers signify the city as the site, par excellence, of multiplication; and multiplication itself becomes a site of meaning.

From the many sources describing urban life in this period, I have chosen to focus on two: one is pictorial and one is a rather strange mixture of rhetorical styling and eyewitness account. Both sources are set in Paris in the decade before the completion of the *Defensor pacis* (1324), which is an important factor in my choosing them. Paris is the site where Marsilius composed his monumental treatise over many years while a master in the university's Faculty of Arts. Paris is also where, some decades later, Nicole Oresme spent his formative years, first as a student at university and then as a doctor of theology. Neither of the two sources I have chosen can be designated as "representative" of other extant sources from the period. The thirty street scenes of Paris found in the illuminated manuscript of *La vie de Saint Denys* (1317) have no equal. No other pictorial representation of Paris or any other city from the fourteenth century matches them singly, much less in series. The *De laudibus Parisius* (*On the Praises of Paris*) written in 1323 by Jean de Jandun, a close and longtime companion of Marsilius of Padua (and like Marsilius, a teaching master in the Paris Faculty of Arts), falls to some degree within the genre of "*laudes civium*," but, as we will see, its content and attitude also set it apart from other texts. While they are both *sui generis*, they can still reveal the contours of the commercial city that shaped Marsilius' sense of sociopolitical equilibrium. At the least, they provide evidence for how it was *possible* to see and sense the great commercial city of Paris at a time when it was home to the greatest university of its day.

The city as self-ordering system: *La vie de Saint Denys* manuscript

In 1317, a lavishly illuminated manuscript illustrating the life and martyrdom of St. Denis, the first bishop and patron saint of Paris, was presented to King Philip V of France by his chaplain, Gilles, Abbot of Saint-Denis.[80]

---

[79] A similar fascination with and use of numbers is apparent throughout Villani's *Chronica*, but they are especially prominent in his famous "*descriptio*" of Florence from 1336, Book 11, chs. 91–4.

[80] The manuscript rests today in the Bibliothèque Nationale in three parts, Ms. fr. 2090–2. The manuscript and its history is described in Henry Martin, *Légende de Saint Denis* (Paris: H. Champion, 1908); more recently in Virginia Wylie Egbert, *On the Bridges of Mediaeval Paris: A Record of Early Fourteenth-Century Life* (Princeton University Press, 1974). Egbert

The text was composed in Latin by a monk at the monastery of Saint-Denis, but as was increasingly common for works presented to the king and his court in this period, it contained portions translated into the vernacular.[81] It was originally composed in three parts: the first covering the life of the saint from his birth to his (apocryphal) meeting with St. Paul in Athens; the second covering his life from the time of his conversion to Christianity until his death in Paris on the hill that still commemorates his martyrdom (Montmartre), and the third an abridged history of France insofar as it intersected with the cult of the saint.[82] The third part has been lost for centuries. The two surviving parts contain seventy-seven large, beautifully drawn miniatures depicting the life of the saint. In the second part of the manuscript describing the saint's sojourn in Paris, twenty-nine of these miniatures are divided into an upper and lower register.[83] The upper registers depict scenes from the life of St. Denis and his two constant companions (and co-martyrs) St. Rusticus and St. Eleutherius; the lower registers depict street scenes from fourteenth-century Paris contemporary with the production of the manuscript. Both scenes, one above the other, are set in the same city space: the Île de la Cité and its two connecting bridges, the Grand Pont and the Petit Pont.[84]

In the first decades of the fourteenth century, the two main bridges of Paris were at the same time vibrant centers of commerce and exchange, covered over their length on both sides by shops and merchandise of all kinds.[85] Particularly prominent on the Grand Pont were the booths of the money-changers. In 1304 Philip IV, concerned that the money-changers of Paris lacked proper supervision, ordered them to move their shops to

provides black-and-white reproductions of each of the thirty contemporary scenes set on the bridges of Paris. Color reproductions of seven of the illuminated pages can be found in Cazelles, *Nouvelle histoire de Paris*, n.p., after p. 88. The *Légende de Saint Denis* contains fine reproductions of every image from the manuscript, and these, fortunately, are available in PDF format, courtesy of Google Books.

[81] Martin (*Légende*, 4), has determined that the French translation was an afterthought to the production of the manuscript, added sometime after the completion of the Latin text. For comments on the translation, *Légende*, 8–9.

[82] *Ibid.*, 3–4.

[83] A thirtieth miniature designed in this fashion represents the presentation of the manuscript by the Abbot Gilles to Philip V, and as such takes its place at the opening of the text (fol. 4).

[84] The view is always from the west. The Grand Pont, spanning the northern branch of the Seine and connecting the island to the Right Bank is pictured on the reader's left, the Petit Pont on the reader's right. They are represented as meeting each other at the western edge of the walled Île de la Cité, when in reality they spanned at different points of the island.

[85] In the scenes from *La vie de Saint Denys*, the bridge is depicted with shops on only one side, thus opening the scene to the viewer. This, like the representation of the two bridges meeting at the head of the Île de la Cité, was a product of artistic license.

the bridge and forbade them to operate anywhere else in the city.[86] The concentration of these moneyers amidst their scales and piles of coins, must have created quite a scene, especially considering the tumultuous state of French coinage in this period.[87] Fortunately we have the remarkable miniatures from *La vie de Saint Denys* to help us imagine it. While the identity of the illuminator is unknown, we do know a good deal about the artistic milieus of Parisian miniature painting and workshops in this period.[88] On the basis of this knowledge it is possible to conclude that the illuminator came from outside the monastery and produced his work in a lay workshop, most probably situated among the same Paris streets that provided the subject for his city scenes.[89]

Our first impressions of these scenes are of ceaseless circulation and communication (in Albert's terms). The actors, male and female, young and old, rich and poor, artisan, merchant, peasant, and beggar, move and pass across the bridges, their horizontal motion mirroring the ceaseless horizontal motion of the River Seine beneath them. The intersections take numerous forms: accidental passings, buying and selling, seeking and giving alms, window-shopping, entertaining, and observing entertainment. Virtually ever-present, both on the bridges themselves and on the river beneath, are images of the ceaseless hauling of goods to market in a dizzying variety of forms.

Notwithstanding all this activity, there is not a single sign of municipal oversight. Occasionally the face of a guard peeks out of a window in the towers of the walled city, but no one representing the city or government walks among the crowds and shops. No one – no intelligent entity whatsoever, whether human or institutional – appears to be in charge of ordering the life of the city. Activity appears to be ordered solely by the needs of the living corpus of the city itself, whether for grain, wine, meat, fish, labor, manufactured goods, transportation, entertainment, or money itself. Most of the figures are engaged in supplying these communal necessities, while at the same time they are satisfying their personal needs as well.

---

[86] Egbert, *Bridges*, 22; Cazelles, *Nouvelle histoire de Paris*, 104; Hercule Géraud, *Paris sous Philippe le Bel: d'après des documents originaux et notamment d'après un manuscrit contenant Le Rôle de la Taille imposé sur les habitants de Paris en 1292* (Paris: Crapelet, 1837), 376–9.

[87] Edouard Perroy, "À l'origine d'une économie contractée: les crises du XIVe siècle," *Annales ESC* 4 (1949), 167–82; Kaye, *Economy and Nature in the Fourteenth Century*, 19–21.

[88] See the discussions on this subject in Martin, *Légende*, 22–31, and Egbert, *Bridges*, 9–17. See also François Avril, *Manuscript Painting at the Court of France: The Fourteenth Century, 1310–1380*, trans. Ursule Molinaro (New York: George Braziller, 1978).

[89] Martin, *Légende*, 23.

A brief description of the activity taking place in three of these scenes can serve as a view into the whole. In the second of the miniatures depicting the saint after his arrival in Paris (Figure 1), he is shown preaching to the pagan inhabitants in the upper register, while beneath him (left to right) on the surface of the Grand Pont and the Petit Pont, a money-changer interacts with a customer carrying a written scroll; a goldsmith works at a table in his stall; a man on horseback heads toward the city carrying a hawk; a porter carries a sack over his shoulder; and a cutler in his shop, surrounded by his goods, appears to be bargaining with a customer. On the river flowing beneath the bridges five men in a boat consult a written scroll.

A later episode in the life of St. Denis, at the moment when he recognizes that he will be arrested and martyred (Figure 2), is enacted over an urban scene in which two horses pull five passengers in a carriage over the Grand Pont, while on the Petit Pont a woman offers a coin to a doctor who is holding up a urine flask to the light. Beneath them all, three boats filled with tuns of wine move along the river. In one of the boats a man drinks up part of the profits from a golden chalice, while in a second boat two men bargain with each other. In a third scene the pagan governor Sissinius confronts St. Denis over his having converted a nobleman to Christianity (Figure 3). Beneath them, two horses pull a cart laden with wheat, while a peasant approaches the city from the other side on the Petit Pont carrying a sheep over his shoulder, and two boats tied together and heaped high with melons are rowed to market. These three scenes, representative of the thirty such in the text, provide a vibrant picture of commercial Paris at the height of its prosperity c. 1315.

What is perhaps most striking about these images is their placement – the space they occupy on the manuscript page and within a manuscript devoted to the life of this third-century saint. The scenes of contemporary city life occupy the bottom register (roughly the bottom third) of pages whose top register is occupied by scenes of the ancient saint's life and miracles. The content and tone of the two registers are pointedly and inescapably different, and this contrast is further heightened by the artist's decision to forgo any formal or delineated division between the two. At times the crenellated towers of the "modern" city protrude into scenes from the ancient city of the saint; at other times scenes from the saint's life are enacted upon the paved roadway of the "modern" bridge, under which float commercial barges and pleasure boats. While this juxtaposition works to suggest the continuity of Paris as place, its overall effect is much more powerfully one of disjunction than of continuity.

1 Paris scene, *c.* 1315; Traffic on the Seine, showing the Grand Pont and the Petit Pont. *La vie de Saint Denys*, BNF ms. Français 2091, fol. 99r.

2 Paris scene, *c.* 1315; Traffic on the Seine, showing the Grand Pont and the Petit Pont. *La vie de Saint Denys*, BNF ms. Français 2091, fol. 125r.

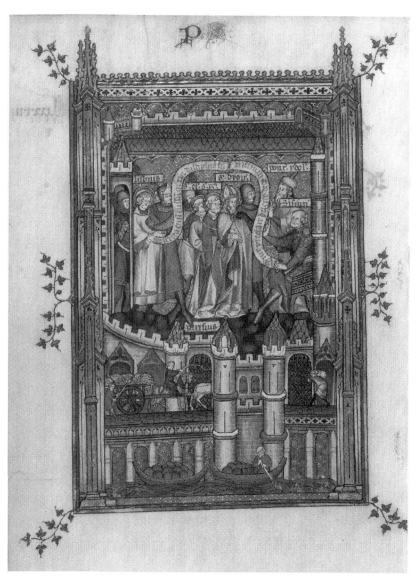

3 Paris scene, *c.* 1315; Traffic on the Seine, showing the Grand Pont and the Petit Pont. *La vie de Saint Denys*, BNF ms. Français 2092, fol. 6v.

Given their proximity on the page, it is telling that the artist chose not to indicate even a minimal degree of involvement or concern between ancient saint and the present-day city. The illustrator offers no evidence whatsoever that any of the religious figures in the upper register, including

St. Denis, the patron saint of Paris, is watching over the city, protecting or guiding it, concerned with it, or even aware of it in any way, despite the fact that the theme of saintly or divine oversight was standard in cityscapes of this period.[90] Conversely, there is no evidence that the present-day citizens have the slightest awareness of the suffering and martyrdom that saved their city and provided the roots for its history and prosperity. When in the midst of their martyrdom we see in the upper register the naked bleeding bodies of St. Denis, St. Rusticus, and St. Eleutherius as they are stabbed and scourged at the order of the pagan Prince Sissinius (Figure 4), in the lower register we see men carrying meat pies, a barber shaving a customer, a money-changer with his chin on his hands, and lower still (as if balancing the naked and bleeding figures above), a naked youth perched on the bow of a boat about to jump into the Seine for a swim. It is hard to imagine that this lack of recognition on the part of contemporary Parisians is entirely unfreighted by criticism. At the least it is striking. I take the utter lack of meaningful concern and interplay between the two registers as a sign that the illustrator intended to represent an essential disjunction between them. This is not an unusual stance for a monastic community to take in regard to the secular world of commerce and pleasure. At the same time, however, it appears that the painter, or his monastic advisor, is using the play between connection and separation to illustrate the defining character-istics of both spheres, spiritual city and secular city. In these contrasting characteristics we can, I think, perceive the outline of the new model of equilibrium.

The upper register representing the life of St. Denis is marked by *identity*: many figures are known by name from the role they played in the well-known story of the saint's life, and their identity is further under-scored by their names appearing above them in balloons in nearly every frame. This identity is perduring, attached to their faces, dress (e.g., St. Denis is always shown with his bishop's miter), and figures, and it follows them from scene to scene. The lower register of the "modern" city is marked by anonymity. No one is named because their particular identities and histories are irrelevant to the life of the city. Their identities, such as they are, are defined by their roles in, and their services to, the functioning whole of the city.[91] They are therefore represented by

---

[90] See, for example, the illustrations attached to Bonvesin da la Riva's *De magnalibus Mediolani* below.

[91] This point, with special reference to the manuscript illustrations of *La vie de Saint Denys*, is made in Michael Camille, "Signs of the City: Place, Power, and Public Fantasy in Medieval Paris," in *Medieval Practices of Space*, ed. Barbara Hanawalt and Michal Kobialka (Minneapolis: University of Minnesota Press, 2000), 1–36, at 20.

4 Paris scene, *c.* 1315; Traffic on the Seine, showing the Grand Pont and the Petit Pont. *La vie de Saint Denys*, BNF ms. Français 2092, fol. 10v.

function, whether as producers, consumers, buyers, sellers, or carters of every stripe. Given precedence in this representation is the nearly ubiquitous money-changer (represented in eleven of the thirty city scenes), whose shop is always depicted as the first on the Grand Pont (reading the horizontal motion from left to right), a clear recognition of his central role in the life of the city.

The upper register is concerned with capturing particular moments in the saint's life that carry with them a weight of fixed and particular *meaning*. The bands of text that extend from the mouths of the actors, recording their words in the *vita*, deepen the sense that every speech and action is invested with a meaning so timeless and so deep that their sound and effect still resonate after nearly a millennium – at least in the memory of the monks of Saint-Denis. In decided contrast, the moments represented in the lower register of the modern city are purely random. The time is a purely disencumbered present with no past or future, no resonance with any ancient text or truth. And indeed no texts or written signs of any kind appear in the lower register – with one notable exception – the single word *PARISIUS* that floats above the city in many of the illustrations.[92] This is the only sign we need. The city is a living whole, and all meaning within it derives from relation to the whole through the satisfaction of its needs.

The upper register represents a hieratic vision whose meaning depends upon the acceptance of a *world of fixed values*: Christ, the angels, St. Denis and his saintly companions, Christians newly converted from their pagan ways by the words of the saint, yet unconverted pagans, and persecutors. Everyone is graded by his fixed place in the great and well-known drama. In the lower register this hierocratic, vertically inte-grated vision has been utterly replaced by one we can fairly designate as "horizontal."[93] Both the unceasing human movement across the bridges and the unceasing movement of the great and unifying river beneath are pointedly horizontal. The horizontal plane, represented most clearly by the architecture of the bridges themselves, dominates the illustration of the city scene, just as the vertical axis of the elongated holy figures

---

[92] The sign "PARISIUS" is present in each of the six plates chosen here.

[93] For an exploration of the distinction between horizontal and vertical ordering that recognizes the privileging of the horizontal over the vertical in Chaucer's social vision, see Paul Strohm, *Social Chaucer* (Cambridge, MA: Harvard University Press, 1994), esp. 10–21. For an earlier statement of the significance of moving from vertical to horizontal forms of social ordering, see M.-D. Chenu, "The Evangelical Awakening," in *Nature, Man, and Society in the Twelfth Century: Essays on New Theological Perspectives in the Latin West*, ed. and trans. Jerome Taylor and Lester Little (University of Toronto Press, 1998), 239–69, at 265.

dominates the saintly scenes. Those social elements which could possibly indicate the presence of hierarchy in the city scene are completely absent. Notwithstanding all the figures moving back and forth across the bridges and over the waters, there is not one image of a commanding aristocrat, not one representative of the clergy, and not one officer of the municipal government of Paris. In short, there is no sign of hierarchical order or ordering whatsoever.

The base of fixed meanings and values upon which the hierocratic vision rests has been replaced by a world of fluid and relational values. There is here, certainly, distinction of craft, class, and gender, but none of these markers are placed within a fixed and recognizable hierarchy. Men on horseback share the bridge with carters and peasants, weavers and money-changers, ladies and drunkards. The shop proprietors are both male and female, as are the beggars. The intersections and exchanges of the anonymous actors as they cross the great bridges of Paris carry no essential meaning but are, rather, intentionally accidental, just as most intersections are in actuality in the streets of a city. If there is meaning here in the positioning of the actors, it is the relational meaning of buyer and seller, the "natural" and ever-shifting connection between those who have, those who supply, and those who need, all under the overarching sign of *PARISIUS*.

The stark contrast between a world infused with eternal meaning and a world of relativized meaning is illustrated in every scene but especially in Figure 5. In the upper register St. Denis (as usual named by text and distinguished by his bishop's miter) is preaching to the pagan inhabitants of Paris, and his words are having evident effect. A member of the audience reaches up and pulls down a golden idol from its niche, while others in the audience, including soldiers in their armor, hold their hands together in prayer. In the city below, under the sign of *PARISIUS* we see the usual everyday scenes of money-changing, commerce, manufacture, and carting, along with another form of city activity, begging, often pictured in these miniatures. In this case a woman with a baby on her back and a bowl in her hands is receiving alms from a female cutler in her shop.

I have already noted the frequent and prominent presence of the money-changer in these city scenes, who, when he is pictured (as he is in eleven of the scenes) is always pictured as occupying the first stall on the Grand Pont, reading naturally from left to right. Legal and moral writings at the time make it perfectly clear that money-changers were, as a group, distrusted, morally suspect, of questionable if not degraded status, and a target of theological criticism. And yet they were tolerated for purely functional reasons – their evident service to the economic life of the *civitas*.

5 Paris scene, *c.* 1315; Traffic on the Seine, showing the Grand Pont and the Petit Pont. *La vie de Saint Denys*, BNF ms. Français 2091, fol. 111r.

Indeed, their wealth brought them growing political power within a city increasingly dominated in this period by a bourgeois patriciate.[94] The prominent place of the money-changer in these scenes, in contrast to the absence of any trace of clergy or religious presence of any kind, crystallizes the impermeability, if not the sheer opposition, between the realm of eternal and inherent values above, where the degraded golden idols are being thrown down, and the realm of purely relativized and shifting values below, where value is determined solely by the current needs of the working city, symbolized by the money-changer's piles of golden coin.

The penultimate Paris street scene in the manuscript (Figure 6) can be seen to drive this point home. Here, in what is also the last representation that shows the saints intact, Denis, Eleutherius, and Rusticus, who will soon gladly give their lives for a heavenly ideal, stand upon the disembodied heads of their recently martyred Christian converts. The historic scene is set virtually on the roadway of the quotidian Petit Pont, and yet again there is no communication with the living city below, except, perhaps, in a way that is deeply problematic. In an aesthetic decision that raises all kinds of questions, the miniaturist (or his monastic advisor) has chosen to situate the three holy figures directly above the three great arches of the bridge below. The arches, in turn, surmount three large wooden water mills, their mechanisms lashed to the bridge's piers and their blades dipping into the moving Seine. Again, this is not a fanciful image. Mechanical mills were everywhere in the Paris of the fourteenth century, and the piers of the Seine bridges afforded a highly practical and much used siting for them.[95]

The linking of the three soon to be martyred saints above to the three mechanical mills below appears to be quite intentional. But what meanings might it convey? The wheel, and the mill-wheel in particular, carried many associations in this culture, representing everything from the vagaries of fortune to the torture of martyrs, to the miracle of the eucharist, to Christ himself: so many that it would be impossible to speak of meaning here in any simple sense. But given the consistent separation of the secular scenes in the lower registers from the spiritual associations of the upper,

---

[94] Cazelles (*Nouvelle histoire de Paris*, 103–5) notes how highly remunerative this questionable activity could be and how easily wealth was translated into political and social power within the city of Paris at this time. He cites, in particular, the story of the money changer, Guérin de Senlis, the grandfather of Étienne Marcel, who was moving quickly up the governmental ladder just at the time of the composition of *La vie de Saint Denys*. The growing power of a bourgeois governing elite in Paris in this period is a central theme in the historiography of the city.

[95] Egbert (*Bridges*, 80), remarks that in this period most of the flour for the city of Paris was ground in mills attached to piers of the Seine bridges.

6 Paris scene, *c.* 1315; Traffic on the Seine, showing the Grand Pont and the Petit Pont. *La vie de Saint Denys*, BNF ms. Français 2092, fol. 37v.

I offer the possibility that the mills here serve as an apt symbol for the power of the worldly city. Here the miraculous saving power of God and the inherent charismatic power of the saint are both linked to and contrasted with the mechanical, quasi-miraculous power of the mechanical mills. Just as the great moving wheels of the mills represent the essence of the wonder of the modern city, so the saints' power and willingness to be martyred represented the essence of wonder in their time. Again, juxtaposition and disjunction appear to be the message and the key; these two worlds function on entirely different principles. The sources of power and order in each are utterly distinct, and what is most unusual, they are, I suggest, clearly recognized and represented here as being so. Equally different are the models of equalization that underlie each.

Virtually every aspect of these urban scenes from 1317 can be observed to reflect the model of the "new" equilibrium as we have seen it take shape in previous chapters within medieval medical and economic thought. In moving from upper register to lower, from the early centuries to the early fourteenth century, we move from a vertically integrated world of fixed identities and fixed and timeless meanings, ordered by a hierarchical governing narrative authored by God, to an utterly fluid world of boats and barges, wheeled carts and passing fancies, as horizontal as the ceaseless motion of the ever-present river itself. Here, position, meaning, and identity are ever shifting; here values are relational, determined both by the needs of the city as a whole and by the needs of particular individuals at particular times; here connection and intersection are momentary and seemingly accidental. The fragmented moments and fragmented parts captured by the illustrator find whatever meaning they do possess only under the arch of the living city, and only under the sign of *PARISIUS*. The motions of the parts are ordered to the logic of the systematic whole rather than to or by any overarching ordering intelligence, whether divine or royal. The city, as systematic whole, orders itself. The city as working whole balances and equalizes itself. As distant as this new model of equilibrium is from ancient Christian models of order and balance represented in the upper register, it is at the same time strikingly distant from the equalizing order assumed and outlined mere generations earlier in the writings of St. Albert and St. Thomas.

The very juxtaposition yet separation of the two registers and realms carries a profound message about the potentialities of equalization. In the old model of equalization, organized around a graded hierarchy of identity, value, and meaning, there is a fixed and knowable top and bottom, a fixed and knowable beginning and end, both to the whole and to each of its parts. Motion is defined as the actualization of a unidirectional potential built into the very nature of each part of the whole. For humans, the motion of actualization, and hence of equalization, is upward. In Aquinas' vision, all humans, whether or not they are aware of it, came from God (the *exitus*) and are moving toward a return to God (the *redditus*), the actualization of their potential nature, their proper place within God's plan. This striving upward, this *anagoge*, is inscribed by God into every human nature and into the central plan of creation itself.

But where does *anagoge* appear on the streets of contemporary Paris? Is it possible that a world can exist without it, can even flourish without it? We see occasional indications that such a world is imperfect. We see a number of representations of beggars, both full-bodied and lacking limbs. But there is no overall sense of disease or dysfunction attached to the urban order – quite the opposite, actually. The moneyers and merchants work alongside the peasants and the artisans; all are clearly pursuing their own private aims, while all, at the same time, are evidently providing goods and services that serve the city as a whole and hence the Common Good. Overall, it is an image of plenty guaranteed by human labor, organized, somehow, and balanced, somehow, by the living city itself. *Anagoge* has been replaced by analogy; vertical striving has been replaced by horizontal exchange and interchange.

What historical weight can we put on these extraordinary images? That these images form a coherent set, that they possess a notable similarity in form and meaning, suggests that they were conceived as a whole, bound together by a unifying authorial intelligence and by a unifying sense of the logic of the urban present. Even recognizing that this set of images was unique for its time, at the very least (and this is of no small historical importance), we can say that they reveal a vision of the city and its logic that was *possible* and *available* to inhabitants of Paris in the first quarter of the fourteenth century. We turn now to examine a contemporary account of Paris, which mirrors this possibility and gives written form to the vision, organizing logic, and sense of urban equilibrium found of the images of *La vie de Saint Denys*.

The city as self-equalizing system: the *Tractatus de laudibus Parisius* of Jean de Jandun

In 1323, approximately six years after the manuscript, *La vie de Saint Denys*, was presented to King Philip V, another text appeared in which the city of Paris and its everyday existence took center stage: the *Tractatus de laudibus Parisius*. The author was Jean de Jandun (*c.* 1285–1328), master in the School of Arts at the University of Paris and close friend of his fellow master in arts, Marsilius of Padua.[96] There are, I believe, meaningful parallels between the text of the *De laudibus Parisius* and the visual text of *La vie de Saint Denys* – not least of which is the rather unexpected juxtaposition of exalted subjects with the close observation of mundane city life.[97] Since it is highly unlikely that Jean was familiar with the St. Denis manuscript, the echoes between the two texts speak to the existence of a shared sense of the city's dynamic environment, a sense of how its myriad parts worked together to maintain its vibrant life. The biography and intellectual trajectory of Jean de Jandun, living and teaching in the intellectual capital of Latin Christendom at the time of the writing of the *Defensor pacis*, makes him a particularly important witness to the self-equalizing potentialities of the city as a working whole.

Jean de Jandun was at the forefront of scholastic philosophy in his time. He was the author of an impressive number of Aristotelian commentaries and independent treatises, primarily in the area of epistemology and natural philosophy.[98] On the basis of his prolific output and the lasting importance of his writings, his biographer, Stuart MacClintock, has called him "perhaps the most important secular master [at Paris] between Siger of Brabant (d. *c.* 1284) and Jean Buridan (*c.* 1300–*c.* 1360)."[99] For reasons that will be explained below, Jean died an excommunicant, and this, no doubt, has not helped his reputation for orthodoxy over the centuries. He has long been associated with a position known as "Latin Averroism," which carries the implication that he preferred the truths of philosophy and natural reason over those of revelation and theology. Recent scholarship has tended to question the accuracy of this designation

---

[96] The Latin text of the *Tractatus* is edited, with facing page French translation in *Paris et ses historiens aux XIVe et XVe siècles*, ed. Antoine Le Roux de Lincy and L. M. Tisserand (Paris: Imprimerie impériale, 1867), 32–74, with introductory material 3–21. The two most comprehensive studies of Jean's life and works to date are Stuart MacClintock, *Perversity and Error: Studies on the "Averroist" John of Jandun* (Bloomington: Indiana University Press, 1956), and Ludwig Schmugge, *Johannes von Jandun (1285/9–1328): Untersuchungen zur Biographie und Sozialtheorie eines Lateinischen Averroisten*, Pariser Historische Studien V (Stuttgart: Anton Hiersemann, 1966).

[97] On this connection, see C. Serchuk, "Paris and the Rhetoric of Town Praise in the *Vie de St. Denis* Manuscript," *Journal of the Walters Art Gallery* 57 (1999), 35–47.

[98] A list of Jean's major works include *Sophisma de sensu agente* (1310), *Quaestiones libri Yconomice Aristotelis*, *Quaestiones super libros Physicorum* (1315), *Quaestiones de Anima*, *Quaestiones in duodecim libros Metaphysicae*, *Quaestiones super libros De caelo et mundo*, *Quaestiones in Parva Naturalia*, *De substantia orbis*, a redaction of Pietro d'Abano's exposition on the *Problemata*; and *De laudibus Parisius*, all written between 1310 and 1323. For MacClintock's attempted chronology of these works, see *Perversity and Error*, 117–29. For Schmugge's catalogue of Jean's works (with partial chronology), *Johannes von Jandun*, 128–31.

[99] MacClintock, *Perversity and Error*, 88.

and, in general, the charges of heterodoxy that have been leveled against Jean's positions.[100]

The text of the *De laudibus Parisius* is presented in the form of the ancient and well-known genre of "praises of the city" (*laudes civium*) but there are still many puzzles attached to it.[101] Some have speculated that its primary purpose was to gain the notice and protection of the French king, Charles IV.[102] This theory is supported by the almost obsequious tone of the *Prologue*, in which Jean declares that the glories of Paris redound to the "magnificent glories of the kings of France."[103] But if it were intended for the king and his court, one wonders why it was not written in the vernacular French, or at least partially translated into the vernacular, as was becoming the style for royal presentations in this period. And if it was meant to please the king and his aristocratic counselors, one also wonders why it would contain observational elements about the city that would be difficult for any figure of authority to take as reflecting praise. Another possibility that has been voiced is that the treatise was written to the Parisian university community.[104] This would explain its highly formal latinity and its choice of certain subjects, not least its two chapters devoted to praise of the university. But after these introductory chapters, not only the university but all of learned society is left far behind. The largest part of the remaining text contains descriptions of a cityscape that lie well outside normal university discourse. In short, taken as a whole this is a deeply puzzling text, not least concerning its purpose and its audience. I want to suggest, however, that when viewed through the lens of equality and balance, a fairly coherent message emerges: that the working city represents a strikingly new mode of being, acting, and ordering – or in

---

[100] Jean clearly expressed the opinion that Averroes was the greatest and truest expositor of Aristotle. On the other hand as both Schmugge (*Johannes von Jandun*, 46–63, 94) and Maclintock (*Perversity and Error, passim*) agree, labeling Jean an Averroist gains little toward explaining his philosophical positions and seriously underestimates both the originality and the orthodoxy of his philosophical views – at least until his split with the Papacy over the writing of the *Defensor pacis*.

[101] MacClintock suggests (*Perversity and Error*, 6, n. 35) that the *De laudibus* was written in the form of a "literary competition," a recognized part of the rhetorical tradition current at the Paris Faculty of Arts. Schmugge (*Johannes von Jandun*, 23) agrees that the work should likely be read as a "rhetorical exercise." As such, it would be open to a degree of irony and play, rendering the text all the more slippery.

[102] Schmugge, *Johannes von Jandun*, 24–5.

[103] Jean de Jandun, *Tractatus de laudibus Parisius* (henceforth *De laudibus*), with more praises added, 62–4.

[104] Erik Inglis, "Gothic Architecture and a Scholastic: Jean de Jandun's *Tractatus De laudibus Parisius* (1323)," *Gesta* 42 (2003), 63–85, at 64. Here consider also Schmugge's reading of it (noted above) as a rhetorical exercise directed toward his fellow university masters.

my terms, a new model of equilibrium – and that this new model profoundly confronts and confounds the old.

In Part II of the treatise, Jean moves abruptly through a series of descriptions, first of the Cathedral of Notre Dame and the Sainte-Chapelle, noting the sanctified worship that takes place there (ch. 1),[105] then of the king's palace and the administrative and legal labors performed there (ch. 2), and then, quite suddenly, to a long description of the central covered market of Paris, the Halls of Champeaux (*Hallas Campellorum*), the ancestor of Les Halles (ch. 3). The striking shift in registers – from cathedral to royal palace to marketplace – and the jarring juxtaposition of high and low brings to mind the illuminations of the St. Denis manuscript. So too do Jean's detailed descriptions of the artisanal products – fine cloth, furs, silks, ivory combs, gloves – found for sale in the market. The space he allows for his description of the grand market and its goods is approximately equal to the space he gives to the king's palace and to his combined description of Notre Dame and the Sainte-Chapelle. His decision to allow the marketplace equal space with structures of such immense symbolic importance is unprecedented and highly significant in itself.

Ch. 4 of Part II moves from describing the "almost infinite" number of artisanal goods for sale in the market to describing the artisanal class that makes them. Although Jean barely mentions the clergy of Paris in his encomium, and says nothing at all about the aristocracy per se, he spends an entire chapter on the Parisian artisanat and their crafts.[106] He lavishes attention on occupations and products that rarely if ever found their place in scholastic discourse: sculptors and painters, metalsmiths and weapons-makers, makers of clothes and ornaments, bakers, bookbinders, scribes, and more. Identity here, as in the St. Denis manuscript, is tied entirely to occupation. The workers are anonymous, devoid of individual identities, yet their numbers and the sheer weight of the goods they produce have gained them power and importance within the organizing form of the city. We see in Jean's description of these prosaic products the same breathless enthusiasm that we see in his description of the Sainte-Chapelle, but here instead of marveling at the beauty of cultic objects, he marvels at the profusion of trade goods directed toward the satisfaction of purely material needs.[107] Not the least of the lessons available to the reader of

---

[105] This section of the *De laudibus* has received the most interest from scholars due to its unusually rich and ordered visual description, combined with its hints of theoretical appreciation for artistic and architectural forms.

[106] Jean's striking choice of subjects again parallels the Parisian scenes in *La vie de Saint Denys*.

[107] *De laudibus*, 50: "que sagacimma factive rationis industria, ut lacune desideria compleantur."

the *De laudibus* is that objects – even the humblest of objects – can gain power and (social) meaning simply from their being multiplied and massed. This insight into the powers of multiplication, a characteristic element of the new model of equilibrium, finds no place in older models of equalization and is nowhere to be found in the thinking of Albert and Thomas.

From the opening of his chapter on the grand market of Paris and the shopping that takes place there, Jean uses terms expressive of the miraculous, the universal, and the infinite that would normally be applied to God and his wondrous creation. Here he finds goods of "inestimable value," including a "universe of the species of gems."[108] He notes that the sheer scope of the "genera and species" of goods on display dwarf his descriptive capacity.[109] Despite his expression of inadequacy in the face of such immense bounty, he proceeds to offer the reader some small idea of what can be found among the market's "innumerable" piles of goods.[110] He marvels at the beauty and delicacy of the cloths, skins, silks, and fine clothing, noting that many of the materials come from so far away that they lack Latin names. In the upper floor of the Hall, along an aisle of "miraculous length" he finds another universe of goods, these made to clothe every part of the human body from top to bottom: crowns and hats for the head, ivory combs for the hair, mirrors for the eyes, belts for the waist, etc. Here he speaks of "refulgent objects," in "infinite numbers" and he again apologizes for the inability of his words to match the wonders he sees.[111] The inflation of his language, here as elsewhere, results from his willful conflation of normally separated categories: worldly and heavenly, material and immaterial, the finite and the infinite. Throughout this chapter Jean represents the commercial city not only as a great engine of production, distribution, and consumption, but as an engine of fluid relation and categorical conflation as well. Lines that had once been clearly drawn, distinctions that had once been clearly made, ontological gradations that had once been clearly ordered, disappear within the functioning whole of the city.

---

[108] *Ibid.*: "sub inestimabilium preciosorum gazophilaciis permaximis, cunctas et universas jocalium species, in domo *Aule Campellorum* vocata, presentat."

[109] *Ibid.*: "Istorum autem generum singulas velle specialissimas species describere … propter impossibilia sibi querere insinuaret."

[110] *Ibid.*: "sub innumeris congieriebus et cumulis."

[111] *Ibid.*: "Sed, ut illa politorum corporum refulgentia creberrima, quorum secundum individua numerus infinitus complemento profunde et dearticulate narrationis obsistit." I presume Jean is well aware of the normal association of the adjective "refulgent" with the infusion of spiritual light.

Similar themes – the conflation of categories, the substitution of relation for hierarchy, the multiplication of prosaic parts serving as the source of the power and wonder of the whole – underlie Jean's ch. 4 on the artisans of Paris. His habit of conflation takes a specifically political tone in this chapter, when, on the basis of the economic importance of the producers of goods within the city, Jean concludes that "the full integrity of political association (*ultimata politice communicationis integritas*) cannot be achieved without the participation of the manual artisans."[112] This is a strong statement, especially in a treatise quite possibly directed toward the pleasure of the king and his court. Here, clearly, economic importance provides the argument for political importance; multicentered production provides the rationale for a multicentered political form. While Albert and Thomas had also recognized the importance of artisanal production to the *civitas*, this recognition lacked the weight necessary to alter their sense of the city's hierarchical order. Jean, however, valued the artisan's contribution to such an extent that it required integration into his vision of the urban order.[113]

As Jean moves to a loving description of artisanal products, we see his fascination with detail allied to his wonder at mass and abundance. We see multiplicity – to the point of innumerability – overwhelming his senses and his powers of description. He takes us, among other places, to the Grand Pont, scene of *La vie de Saint Denys* manuscript, where he records (recycling a scene first sketched in Boethius' *De musica*) that the metal-workers in gold and silver exist in such numbers that the sounds of their blows on their individual anvils resonate together as if to form a grand harmony.[114] It is hard to imagine a more apt metaphor drawn from artisanal life to illustrate the "miraculous" potentiality for dissonant parts to blend together into a consonant whole within the context of the living city. We are then introduced to the "wise makers" of "instruments of war" – saddles, swords, shields, bows, arrows, armor, and more – which reminds us that even if war and the defense of the city are still

---

[112] *Ibid.*, 52: "Dicamus igitur quod manuales artifices, sine quibus ultimata politice communicationis integritas non completur."

[113] For a description of the size and power of the Parisian artisanat in this period, with its more than three hundred recognized crafts, see Carpentier and Le Mené, *La France du XIe au XVe siècle*, esp. 298–301.

[114] *De laudibus*, 54: "supra Pontem vocatum Magnum, atque in ceteris, prout unicuique suppetit, pluribus locis, malleos super incudes, quasi armonice concurrentibus ictibus, faciunt resonare." For the literary source of this scene, see Boethius, *De musica*, ch. 10, where Pythagoras passes a blacksmith's workshop and is struck by the remarkable "consonance" of the massed hammer blows. On the sounds of medieval Paris at this time, see Emma Dillon, *The Sense of Sound: Musical Meaning in France, 1260–1330* (Oxford University Press, 2012).

associated with the aristocracy, they are all made possible by artisanal production.[115] But Jean's greatest wonder is reserved for the bakers of Paris. He cannot decide whether it is the "miraculous superiority" of their art or the superiority of their flour and water that is responsible for the "almost incommensurable goodness and delicacy" of Parisian bread compared to bread made elsewhere.[116] After raising this question he decides, in accord with his general tendency to blend rather than to discriminate, that he need not choose between the two: the end result is far better when these factors work together in concert.[117]

In comparison with chs. 3 and 4 on the goods and artisans of Paris, chs. 5–9 of the treatise, covering the health and morals of the citizenry, the Seine as the city's main artery, the physical site of the city, and the city's climate, are rather conventional. These subjects were often found within the genre of *laudes civium*, and Jean's treatment of these themes, with one notable exception, offers few surprising insights. These chapters do, however, share an important and telling characteristic: they focus on the *ideal of aequalitas* (what today we would call balance or equilibrium) and they identify the excellence of Paris with this ideal over and over again. When Jean praises the moral character of Parisians, he does so primarily for their general moderation (*moderatio*) and their equanimity (*mediocriter se habent ad irascendum*).[118] Repeatedly, the glory of the city's inhabitants is attributed to the fact that few abandon the medium (*relinquunt medium*) or depart from the middle way (*declinant a medio*).[119] In the matter of physical stature, Parisians are neither contemptibly diminutive nor grossly huge; their bodily members are neither coarsely brutish nor softly feminine but are rather of moderate form (*sed submediocris stature*).[120] Every ideal, from the characterological to the physical, is framed in terms of the balanced middle.

Without understanding the importance of this ideal it would be hard to understand why, in the short chapter he devotes to the River Seine, Jean singles out for praise its fittingly middling size (*magnitudinis congrua mediocritas*) and its moderate velocity (*velocitas moderata*) as those characteristics responsible for its success in conveying abundant riches from all over the world for the city's consumption.[121] And when in ch. 8 he writes on the climate and geographical situation of Paris, he speaks entirely in the language of equality. He ascribes the "miraculous" perfection and

---

[115] *De laudibus*, 52.
[116] *Ibid.*, 54: "quod vel ipsi mirabili artis prerogativa cunctis aliis sui generis dotati sunt, aut ipsorum materie utpote grana et aqua, in tantum meliores sunt ceteris, ut, ob hoc, panes quos faciunt quasi incommensurabilem suscipiant bonitatis et delicationis excessum."
[117] *Ibid.*, "Melius autem est si hec ambo concurrant."   [118] *Ibid.*   [119] *Ibid.*
[120] *Ibid.*, 56.   [121] *Ibid.*

plenitude of the city to its temperate geographical situation between zones of excessive cold and excessive heat, a geographical temperance, which, he explains, is perfectly suited to the tempered needs of the human body and spirit.[122] As a result of its physical situation the climate of Paris is neither too hot nor too cold, but presents, in his words, "a true third quality, which, through its beneficial proportional intermixture (*sub proportionalis commixtionis beneficio*) forms a medium between the two extremes."[123]

There is little that is exceptional about this language or this way of thinking throughout the whole of the medieval period.[124] There is a good deal of Aristotle here in the idealization of the mean, and there is a very good deal of Galen as well.[125] The discourse on the relationship between climate, geographical position, physical state, and character, all centered on the ideal of *aequalitas* and temperance, was to a large extent a standard medical discourse in this period, with nothing here that would have been out of place in a Galenic text.[126] Here the city is viewed as an organism, a "unity" made up of myriad moving parts in balance. The very ordinariness of this discourse is just the point. To imagine and picture the city (or the body, or economic exchange under the umbrella of the Common Good, or the polity, or the cosmos) in this period is to picture it in terms of proportional equalities and to imagine its dynamic forms of equalization. I would suggest that all the jarring juxtapositions, blendings, relational language and categorical conflations that we see in chs. 2, 3, and 4 of the *De laudibus* can be productively viewed as a product of this mode of imagination. In Jean's case, I would argue, the particular new forms that this imagination takes is a product of what happens when the lens of equality has been expanded beyond the passive and traditional elements of site, climate, and character, to cover the active (and by the early four- teenth century hard-to-ignore) dynamic urban elements of construction, production, and consumption. This expansion in itself had profound consequences: for in order to stretch the lens of *aequalitas* to cover these dynamic forms of city organization and growth, the understanding of equality and equalization themselves had to expand. But "expansion"

---

[122] *Ibid.*, 58.

[123] *Ibid.*, 60: "At vero qualitas tertia que in Gallia procreatur, sub proportionalis commix- tionis beneficio medians inter ista."

[124] See, for example, Bonvesin da la Riva's situation of Milan with regard to the ideal of equality (*De magnalibus*, 58), going so far as to derive the name of the city from this ideal: "ubi aeris est temperies ... inter duo flumina mirabilia equaliter inde distantia ... quoniam a sue ibi invento in medio tergo lanuto Mediolanum nomen accepit."

[125] Schmugge's suggestion (*Johannes von Jandun*, 6) that Jean's teacher at Paris may have been the Galenist physician, Pietro d'Abano is relevant here. For more on Pietro's influence as a teacher on Jean's companion, Marsilius of Padua, see the following chapter.

[126] The *locus classicus* of this form of description is Hippocrates' *On Airs, Waters, and Places*.

does not do full justice to the dynamism of the process. The modeling of equality and equalization involved a virtual leap from the realm of patient addition and subtraction to the realm of *exponential* multiplication. Jean indicates this in his breathless descriptions of city life that render him close to speechless: in the number, weight, and variety of the imports streaming in to feed the city; in the production and consumption of "innumerable" manufactured goods of "inestimable value"; in the "miraculous length" of the great covered marketplace; in the ever-growing number of the city's buildings, which he compares to the number of hairs on a head or stalks of grain in a large field;[127] and in the "almost infinite" expansion of desires that the city encourages and can apparently support.

The engine of urban shopping

When Jean describes the dynamic of urban shopping in chs. 3 and 4 of his treatise, he characterizes the passion behind it with the freighted phrase, "the impetus of desire" (*impetus desiderii*).[128] At the same time, he notes that artisanal production within the city is geared "to filling up the space created by desire" (*ut lacune desideria compleantur*).[129] To the modern ear this might sound like a defendable economic principle, but within both the Augustinian and the Aristotelian tradition, acquisitive desire was uniformly held to be fearful and dangerous.[130] Aristotle looked more favorably on the benefits of long-distance trade and exchange than did Augustine, but he did so squarely on the basis that it satisfied human *need* (*indigentia humana*), not human desire. In the Aristotelian scheme, economic need is bounded and can be satisfied, while economic desire (which he represents by the figure of Midas in his *Politics*) is boundless and therefore insatiable.[131] Desire drives men past any positive familial or social goal. Moreover, the notion of infinity that Jean attaches to the desire for goods is pure poison; it is the ultimate nullity, the ultimate in destructive potentiality. There is no possibility of integrating infinite desire into Aristotelian *Ethics*, nor for that matter into any model of Aristotelian, Albertian, or Thomistic *aequalitas*.[132]

---

127 *De laudibus*, 52.
128 *Ibid.*, 50: "ut, una serie semiplene prospecta, impetus desiderii mox festinet ad alterum."
129 *Ibid.*
130 It is important to note that in other of his writings Jean clearly recognizes this danger. On this see Schmugge, *Johannes von Jandun*, 61–3.
131 Aristotle, *Politics*, I.9. The boundlessness of desire also forms the basis of Aristotle's strong condemnation of usury in this same chapter.
132 St. Thomas, in his commentary to Aristotle's *Politics* I.9, underlines the distinction between "true" riches – those which are bounded and directed toward the satisfaction of human need and "natural" necessity – and "false" riches, which he associates with the infinite and the unnatural.

In Aristotle's view, shared by Albert and Thomas, a thing must possess the potentiality of balance *within its nature* in order for it to find balance within the whole. But as Aristotle notes at many points, the infinite possesses no limiting form and thus no such potentiality.[133] In the opinion of Albertus Magnus, nature itself abhors and avoids the infinite.[134] Jean de Jandun would have been well aware of Aristotle's distinctions between finite need and infinite desire in the economic realm, since they were much commented upon in the Latin tradition. Indeed, we have proof that he was aware of it.[135] Yet in Jean's presentation in the *De laudibus*, instead of leading inexorably to social or moral imbalance, desire is pictured as a productive force; it is the engine that drives the commercial city. As he presents it, the desire for the pleasure of seeing and possessing lies behind the appearance of the seemingly infinite numbers of "most beautiful" cloths and silks and crowns and ivory combs in the market setting he describes as "wondrous." It is hard to imagine that Jean would have been unaware of the reactions that his placing of desire at the center of the city's economic life might elicit in his scholastic readers.[136]

But Jean explicitly joins economic desire to the concept of infinity, flaunting rather than avoiding the dangerous implications of its boundlessness. He pictures the desire to shop as a nearly insatiable driving force:

so that, when one series [of goods for sale] had been half-viewed, the impetus of desire (*impetus desiderii*) would soon hurry to another, and once the whole length [of the market] had been traversed, the unsated (*insatiatus*) desire for resuming enjoyment would lead to repeated inspections, going back to the beginning, not

---

[133] E.g., Aristotle, *Ethics* II.6 [1106b 29–30]: "for evil belongs to the class of the unlimited, as the Pythagoreans conjectured, and good to that of the limited."

[134] Albert, *Ethica*, I.3.11, 45a: "Infinitum autem abhorret et ars et doctrina et actus et electio." Christian thinkers could "think with" infinity when attached to God and his attributes, but in the time of Albert and Thomas the boundary between divine and temporal held strongly at this point.

[135] Schmugge (*Johannes von Jandun*, 62, n. 92), cites this quintessentially Aristotelian position on economic exchange from Jean's *Quaestiones de bona fortuna* (81va–vb): "ad facilius permutandum et ad aequaliter in permutationibus conservandum. Omnia enim mensurat nummisma et fit aequaliter medium ad superabundantiam et defectum ... Divitiae naturales immediate et per se humanae indigentiae subveniunt et eam tollunt, artificiales vero numquam eam removant, nisi quantum in commutatione primarum."

[136] In the scheme of Albertus Magnus, for example, acts or arts that are aimed toward the satisfaction of purely personal or libidinous desires are essentially empty and vain. In this context he paraphrases Aristotle to powerful effect: "Just as a dead man is said not to be a man, so an evil art is not an art." For this discussion, see Albert, *Ethica*, I.3.10, 43a–I.3.11, 45a.

just once or twice but seemingly an infinite number of times (*quasi infinicies*), if reason were to believe itself.[137]

For Albert and Thomas this scene would be a recipe for social disaster. But not in Jean's picture. His shoppers go about with delight and joyful smiles on their faces.[138] There is wonder and intellectual surprise but no overt criticism in Jean's observation here, which concludes his chapter devoted to a description of the great market and its shoppers.

The vision Jean presents makes no sense in terms of textual authority, flaunting it in almost every particular. It makes sense only in terms of what he has actually seen and experienced. It should not work, but it does; it should not be possible, but it is. The city is not only capable of integrating forces like infinite desire and irrational pleasures into its functioning whole, but it prospers and grows mightily from them. It was traditional, as we have seen, to praise the city by associating it with the ideal of equality: the middle way is the natural way and the way of health. Here, however, Jean has had to imagine an entirely new species of equality and equalization, dynamic in its power to convert the essentially boundless, imbalanced, and unequal into a larger equality within the functioning whole.[139] The ideal of equalization remains constant, but its form and potentialities have been expanded almost beyond recognition within the social context of the commercial city.

A final illustration of the connection between the city and the expansion of equalization can be found in Jean's short ch. 7 on the victuals of Paris. The chapter begins with yet another declaration that merely to give name to the enormous variety of the city's foodstuffs is far beyond his powers. All he can say is that at any time of year Paris contains all manner of foods to satisfy both the hungry and those searching for delicacies (another danger sign in terms of Aristotelian *Ethics*). He concludes this chapter with the following words:

What appears marvelous, is that not infrequently it happens that the more people flock into Paris, the more exuberantly copious and copiously exuberant becomes the supply of victuals, instead [as one might suspect] of resulting in a proportional (*analogum*) scarcity and increase in price.[140]

---

[137] *De laudibus*, 50: "ut, una serie semiplene prospecta, impetus desiderii mox festinet ad alterum, et tota longitudine pertransita, insatiatus resumende oblectationis affectus, non solum semel neque bis, sed quasi infinicies, ad principium reflectendo, si ratio sibi crederet, inspectiones faceret iterare."

[138] *Ibid.*: "In illis foralibus locis, procedentium visibus tot et tales sponsalium jocunditatum ac festivatum celebrium varie decorationes arrident."

[139] We will see this recognition again in the political thought of Marsilius of Padua.

[140] *De laudibus*, 58: "Quod enim mirabile videtur, non nunquam visum est hoc accidere quod, quanto majores populorum turme inibi confluunt, tanto victualium exuberantior copia et copiosior exuberantia, preter analogum crementum caristie, presentatur ibidem."

This *is* marvelous. The city appears to be governed by a new form of equalization that transcends deeply rooted notions and expectations of how balance works; it transcends Aristotelian and even Galenic notions of the potentialities of balance – transcends, in modern terms, the rules of the zero sum game. The continual expansion of the city, the continual expansion of population, the continual multiplication of goods, without a corresponding deficit, defies our expectations of how balance works, and yet our eyes do not lie. It is the miracle of the loaves and fishes, although here performed not by divine power but by the new equilibrium of the living city, powered by boundless desire.

In older forms of equalization, including that which was dominant among Christian Aristotelians of the mid thirteenth century, order always implied the presence of an ordering intelligence. In the cosmos, this intelligence was equated with the mind of God; in the social world, most often with the guiding power of the Emperor or ruling prince – acting in accord with the ideal of "iustitia," which was itself identified with divine order. For Aquinas, cosmic order – even the ordering of brute objects in the physical world, or as he called it "the governance of things"– everywhere and always implies the existence of a divine ordering intelligence.[141] But a half-century later, that is no longer the case for the order (and equilibrium) Jean sees in the commercial city. In his vision, the marketplace, as well as the larger commercial city that comprehends it, orders itself – equalizes itself – independent of a single ordering intelligence, whether divine or secular.[142]

Surely only the rare few of the city's inhabitants at this time could see the city in these terms. From the evidence left by bourgeois *commerçants* in this period, they preferred to see themselves in quite traditional terms as serving God in their service of the Common Good, associating their profit and good fortune with God's blessing.[143] The capacity to see the city as a self-equalizing unity may have been limited to those who, like Jean, were trained in scholastic modes of thought, trained to see the operating logic behind appearances. But that does not make his observations any less revealing. As one who was deeply schooled in the works of St. Augustine, surely he recognized that the clerics in his audience would likely associate his dazzled shoppers with the mortal sin of idolatry, which Augustine had defined as the misdirection of spiritual desire and wonder to the object

[141] *ST*, I, 1, 2 ad 5, and his argument "ex gubernatione rerum" for the existence of God.
[142] For the development of this insight within scholastic economic thought both before and after Jean de Jandun, see Chapters 1 and 2 above and Kaye, *Economy and Nature in the Fourteenth Century*, chs. 3–5.
[143] Giacomo Todeschini, "Investigating the Origins of the Late Medieval Entrepreneur's Self Representation," *Impressa e storia* 35 (2007), 13–37.

world. At the very least the shoppers' unconscious desire and behavior would identify them with the category of *rudes*, imperfect Christians unworthy of inhabiting the Christian city.[144] And yet Jean expresses no open disdain for the commerce he describes, not even for the infinite and insatiable desire he locates as the engine of urban production and consumption.

It is possible that Jean's admiration for the productive and commercial juggernaut of the city is actually untouched by criticism, fear, and disdain, but I strongly doubt it. I think it more likely that he is playing a sophisticated game with his treatise, writing it in such a way that it would be read quite differently by different readers. Some will take him at his word and read it as a celebration of the commercial city; some will read past his words and see the yawning chasms of misplaced wonder and desire at every turn.[145] This possibility adds yet one more layer to this protean text, but it does not affect what from my view is its most important and interesting contribution: its brilliant recognition that the living city had – for better or for worse – given birth to a new kind of order, centered in a new sense of the potentialities of balance and a new model of systematic equilibrium.

An earlier vision of urban equalization: Bonvesin da la Riva's *De magnalibus Mediolani*

The "new" model of equilibrium that concerns us, the model that came to underlie striking innovations in scholastic speculation from the late thirteenth through the third quarter of the fourteenth century is, in addition to being a social product, the product of a highly developed intellectual culture. Its form was fully realized only in the thinking and writing of the very few – leading intellectuals at the forefront of their disciplines. It is by no means apparent in all scholastic writings from this period.

---

[144] Giacomo Todeschini, *I mercanti e il tempio: la società cristiana e il circolo virtuoso della ricchezza fra Medioevo ed Età Moderna* (Bologna, Il Mulino: 2002).

[145] Jean is very likely a good deal more conservative in his philosophical positions than is often assumed. Schmugge, *Johannes von Jandun*, cites many passages from Jean's writings on economic and political questions other than the *De laudibus*, that seem quite traditional (e.g., 62–3). Connections between Jean's thought and that of Albertus Magnus in the area of psychology and epistemology have also been noted. On this, see Katharine Park, "Albert's Influence on Late Medieval Psychology," in *Albertus Magnus and the Sciences: Commemorative Essays, 1980*, ed. James A. Weisheipl (Toronto: Pontifical Institute of Mediaeval Studies, 1980), 501–36, esp. 512–15. All of this raises the question whether Jean intended to stake out a radical position on the acceptable goals of human desire in the *De laudibus*, or whether he was playing with his audience's expectations.

Indeed, I have found that there is a direct connection between the capacity to recognize the new potentialities of balance in this period and the capacity to move to the forefront of this competitive intellectual culture. One way to illustrate the necessary role of a shaping intellectual culture in this production is to examine what happens when it is lacking. The writing of Bonvesin da la Riva offers such an example. Bonvesin completed his contribution to the genre of *laudes civium*, *De magnalibus Mediolani* (*On the Great Things of Milan*) in 1288, nearly half a century before Jean de Jandun wrote the *De laudibus Parisius*.[146] In its length, its immense appetite for facts and details, its reliance on actual administrative records for its story, and its near-obsessive concern to quantify aspects of city life in order to impress through the weight of numbers, Bonvesin's text represented a departure from all preceding works in the genre of *laudes civium* (praises of the city).[147]

Before examining the differences between the depictions of Paris in the *De laudibus Parisius* and *La vie de Saint Denys* on the one hand, and Bonvesin's descriptions of Milan on the other, it is well to consider their similarities. In all of these sources, we see a concerted focus on the productive capacities of the city. We see the careful depiction and description of artisanal products, the recognition of the sheer amount of commercial goods flowing into and out of the city, the association of the city with the function of satisfying the necessities of life, and the identification of the city with the process of equalization.[148] The very name of Milan, Mediolanum, derives, Bonvesin tells us, from its precise "equidistance" between two great rivers on a fertile plain known for its "temperate" air.[149] Like the later Paris sources, Bonvesin lends a rich visual quality to his description of city space: his city is shaped in a "perfect

---

[146] The English translations from this text are mine.

[147] Hyde, "Medieval Descriptions of Cities." In Hyde's words (at 328), Bonvesin exhibited "the kind of bourgeois mentality for which figures talk and for which statistics are a not inelegant form of praise." In the modern edition, Bonvesin's account occupies nearly seventy pages of text. For a brief biography of Bonvesin, who was a private teacher of grammar, see the introduction to *De magnalibus Mediolani*, 17–18.

[148] The full measure of Bonvesin's use of numbers to evoke the marvelous and invoke praise for his city is best appreciated by reading the text as a whole, but to take but a few examples: he notes the existence of 120 civil and canon lawyers, "who freely accept money for their litigation"; more than 1,500 notaries, 1,000 taverners, more than 440 butchers, 400 fishermen, 140 innkeepers, 80 smiths; and, not least, 6 principal trumpeters who celebrate public events and make a "terrible clamor" in battle.

[149] Bonvesin, *De magnalibus*, 58: "ubi aeris est temperies, quo fluunt undique humano usui necessaria, inter duo flumina mirabilia equaliter inde distantia … quoniam a sue ibi invento in medio tergo lanuto Mediolanum nomen accepit."

circle" with the palace situated "*in medio*," and with the positioning of the city's other major buildings described relative to each other and to the city's center.[150] His detailed description of the city's spaces leads him to a remarkable perspective image:

Whoever has the desire to see the overall form of the city and to judge the quality and quantity of its buildings should happily ascend to the top of the tower of the communal palace; there, wherever the eyes turn, he will be able to marvel at marvelous sights.[151]

Given the ways that Bonvesin's description of Milan anticipates the Paris sources, we might expect him to visualize the city's equalization in similar terms, imagining a form of equilibrium that confounds ancient categories and expectations, both religious and philosophical. But he does not. There is little or no recognition of self-ordering and self-equalizing around the requirements of production, consumption, and exchange in Bonvesin's city. Christ, the Blessed Virgin, St. Ambrose (Milan's patron saint and first bishop), the city's martyrs, and other holy men and holy women both ancient and contemporary have a real and continual ordering presence in his city.[152] When he does recognize that the city's order transcends customary notions of the potentialities of equalization – in its capacity for continual multi-plication and expansion and in its flirting with the infinite, for example – he explains it in supernatural rather than natural terms: life in Milan represents a foretaste of paradise.[153] Bonvesin concludes his treatise on Milan with a prayer to Christ, asking him to continue to lead its citizens in the path of righteousness and to bless the city so that its dignity might continue to increase. It is not surprising that in the illustrations accompanying the text of the *De magnalibus Mediolani*, Christ is pictured enthroned and with a scepter, watching closely over the contemporary city from outside and slightly above it.[154] As such, these sentiments indicate how far Bonvesin was from conceiving of his city as an

---

[150] *Ibid.*, 66: "In eius medio mirabile constat palatium."

[151] *Ibid.*, 70: "Si quem postremo civitatis formam et quantitatem videre delectat, super turrem curie comunis gratulanter ascendat; inde oculos circumquaque revolvens poterit miranda mirari."

[152] *Ibid.*, 84, praising the religious of Milan: "Quorum meritis et intercessionibus credimus hanc Deum civitatem a multis periculis liberasse." And 122: "Ecce igitur quam feconde divina providentia huic terre a principio hucusque providit."

[153] *Ibid.*, 72.

[154] *Ibid.*, n.p., before p. 49. The illustrations here are taken from Milan, Biblioteca Trivulziana, ms. 1438, 3r, 5r, 8v. The comparison of these illustrations to those of *La vie de Saint Denys* manuscript reveal the chasm between the two ways of viewing the city's governing logic.

organism capable of ordering itself in the absence of divine Intelligence and guidance.[155]

This lack of a sense of the capacities of self-ordering is found even in the realm of politics, despite the fact that Bonvesin was a strong proponent of republican government and a fierce critic of the recent takeover of his city by the forces of strong-man rule. In Bonvesin's Milan, the self-government associated with republicanism is pictured as subordinated to the governing power of Christ and the saints.[156] If it is true, as J. K. Hyde has written, that Bonvesin's minute attention to commercial foodstuffs and goods, and his application of precise numbers to his descriptions of the city's greatness, indicate a "bourgeois mentality," it is also true that in contrast to the Paris manuscripts, Bonvesin's image of the city is grounded in ancient verities. The city's shining virtue is its "nobility" not its acquisitive spirit; the city's greatness derives more from the "dignity" of its aristocrats and the continuing holy presence of its patron saint and martyrs than it does from the ingenuity of its merchants; its political order owes more to the governing grace of Christ than it does to the to and fro of republican politics (which he nowhere bothers to record). The deeply ingrained cultural habit of associating the existence of order with the controlling power of an overarching intelligent orderer (or ordering intelligence) is still intact. The old hierarchies remain firm in the way he chose to imagine and present his city's praises. In his imagination, vertical organization has not yet been replaced by horizontal ordering; hierarchy has not been replaced by a fluid relativity; enduring identity and meaning are still protected within the city's walls.[157] It is a case of old wine in the new bottle of the commercial *civitas*.

I do not mean to suggest that the vision of urban equilibrium evident in the St. Denis manuscript and the *De laudibus Parisius* supplants that of Bonvesin in the half-century separating their composition. For most observers it does not. Evidence suggests that Bonvesin's vision linking

---

[155] For a similar reliance on the intercession of the supernatural into the natural order of the city and its history in Villani's *Chronica*, see Louis Green, "Historical Interpretation in Fourteenth-Century Florentine Chronicles," *Journal of the History of Ideas* 28 (1967), 161–78, at 163.

[156] Bonvesin, *De magnalibus*, 166, where Mary, Jesus, and St. Ambrose, "nostri patroni et aliorum sanctorum ... incolentium interventu continuo, a tirranica sepissime rabie civitatem defendit."

[157] This is true not only of Bonvesin's account, but it is characteristic of the view found in contemporary Italian sources on the city, even though most of them were penned by representatives of the bourgeoisie. Hyde ("Medieval Descriptions of Cities," 388) notes the peculiarity of this seeming contradiction: "From the 12th century Italy was studded with virtually sovereign city-states, yet the ideology of the period was overwhelmingly imperialist and monarchical."

civic identity to religious identity, commercial success to religious devotion and hence to divine pleasure, and civic order to divine order persists for centuries, not least among the merchant elite.[158] Bonvesin is clearly not Jean de Jandun's equal as a thinker (very few were or are), nor did he have Jean's scholastic training or share in the intellectual culture of the university. These factors might help to explain his failure (and the failure of other writers of similar background) to follow through on exploring the logic of the self-equalizing city, especially since following this logic would almost certainly lead away from cherished verities. Jean de Jandun possessed the rare mind capable of seeing with analytic clarity the antagonisms between traditional models of order and equalization and the new model apparent in the dynamism of the commercial city, and he possessed as well the rare character bold enough to record his unsettling vision and to hold it up for others to see.

The gap separating Bonvesin's vision of the city from Jean's suggests that the emergence of a new model of equilibrium was not the simple product of urban experience, or market experience, or any conjunction of experiences in themselves. It emerged between 1250 and 1350 only through the intersection of social experience with a particular form of intellectual labor that was intense, rigorous, highly trained, and directed above all toward discerning the underlying order(s) in creation. What needs to be explained, therefore, is not the form of equalization that Bonvesin applied to Milan, but rather the emergence of the model of equilibrium that characterizes the Paris manuscripts. In the chapter that follows, I turn to examine Marsilius of Padua's monumental political treatise, *Defensor pacis*, whose publication was closely contemporary with the production of these works. Here we will see, in written and highly theorized form, a modeling of the city's equilibrium that mirrors and magnifies theirs in many ways. Then in the last chapter on political thought, which treats the political writings of Nicole Oresme, we will see that this extraordinary vision, although mirrored in the early political writings of Oresme, did not survive the fourteenth century.[159]

---

[158] Todeschini, *I mercanti e il tempio*; Todeschini, "Investigating the Origins of the Late Medieval Entrepreneur's Self Representation."

[159] I discuss this notable failure, its possible causes, and its historical implications, in Chapter 7 and again in the book's Conclusion.

6 The new model of equilibrium in medieval political thought, part 1: The *Defensor pacis* of Marsilius of Padua

Let us suppose with Aristotle in the first and fifth books of his *Politics*, chs. 2 and 3 respectively, that the city is like a kind of animate or animal nature. For an animal which is in a good condition with respect to its nature is composed of certain proportionate parts arranged in relation to each other (*componitur ex quibusdam proporcionatis partibus invicem ordinatis*), all communicating their actions between themselves and towards the whole (*suaque opera mutuo communicantibus et ad totum*); likewise too the city which is in a good condition (*bene disposita*) and established in accordance with reason is made up of certain such parts. A city and its parts would therefore seem to be in the same relation to tranquility as an animal and its parts is to health.   Marsilius of Padua, *Defensor pacis*, Discourse I (1324)

The active or productive causes [of tranquility or good disposition in the city or realm] are: the mutual interaction of the citizens (*conversatio mutua*) and the common exchange (*communicatio*) of their work, their mutual aid and help, and generally the power, unhindered from outside (*ab extrinseco non impedita*), to carry out both their own and the common tasks; and also their sharing in common conveniences and burdens in a measure appropriate to each (*secundum convenientem unicuique mensuram*).
      Marsilius of Padua, *Defensor pacis*, Discourse I (1324)

No study that jumps from the writings of Albertus Magnus and Thomas Aquinas in the 1260s to those of Marsilius of Padua in the mid 1320s can claim to provide even the bare bones of a history of political thought. Any such history would have to consider a number of important thinkers from the intervening decades: Giles of Rome, Peter of Auvergne, Henry of Ghent, Godfrey of Fontaines, James of Viterbo, Ptolemy of Lucca, Duns Scotus, and John of Paris among them. Furthermore, any study that wanted to provide a reasonably full view of the intellectual influences on Marsilius' political thought would have to pay close attention to a wealth of sources in Roman and canon law that were available to him and used by him.[1] And any study that seeks to provide enough "points" to suggest the arc of any important theoretical development over this period – whether of the Common Good, or of notions of consent and election or, more to the point, of the evolution of the model of balance/*aequalitas* underlying political thought, would again have to spend considerable time with a range of intermediate sources and thinkers.[2] Undertaking a proper analysis of these influences would, however, expand this study far beyond its central concern: to show how in little more than half a century the model of equalization underlying the political concept of the Common Good had been transformed into a true model of equilibrium.

In its current state, Marsilian studies are an exciting and contentious field. The details of Marsilius' life are meager, opening up all manner of speculation concerning the possible social and political influences on his religio/political program.[3] The interpretive difficulties presented by his major text, the *Defensor pacis*, are considerable, leading to a dizzying range of readings and characterizations, some of them quite clearly opposed to one another.[4] Among the more frequent and significant of these are: Marsilius as a "republican" and "proto-democrat," or Marsilius as a spokesman for imperial power; Marsilius as a pragmatist or as a utopian; as philosopher or rhetorician; as looking forward toward the modern "state" or backward toward the primitive Church; as motivated by the successes of communal politics in his native Padua, or by its failures; as conscious or unconscious of the intense reaction his treatise would provoke. Although Marsilius' political insights are often read as either surprisingly "modern" in themselves or as anticipating the modern, this position too has been forcefully contradicted. George Garnett has recently castigated what he sees as a plethora of anachronistic readings of the

---

[1] For Marsilius' knowledge of and reliance upon canon law writings, see Brian Tierney, *Religion, Law, and the Growth of Constitutional Thought* (Cambridge University Press, 1982), esp. 48–52; Brian Tierney, "Marsilius on Rights," *Journal of the History of Ideas* 52 (1991), 3–17.

[2] The contributions of a number of these thinkers (Peter of John Olivi, Henry of Ghent, Godfrey of Fontaines), while not considered in this chapter on political thought, are considered in Chapter 2 in relation to equalization in scholastic economic thought.

[3] For a recent bibliography of the major works on Marsilius' life, see Frank Godthardt, "The Philosopher as Political Actor – Marsilius of Padua at the Court of Ludwig the Bavarian: The Sources Revisited," in *The World of Marsilius of Padua*, ed. Gerson Moreno-Riaño (Turnhout: Brepols, 2006), 29–46, at 29, n. 1.

[4] It is common for writings on the *Defensor pacis* to begin with remarks on the exceptional diversity of extant interpretations. A number of the ongoing major debates are outlined in Cary Nederman, "Marsiglio of Padua Studies Today – and Tomorrow," in *The World of Marsilius of Padua*, ed. Moreno-Riaño, 11–25. A sense of the interpretive range can be gained by consulting the articles that grew out of the international convention on Marsilius held in Padua in 1980. These have been published in two consecutive issues of *Medioevo: rivista di storia della filosofia medievale* (1979, 1980).

Defensor pacis, writing: "They ['most modern historians'] have substituted their own modern words (and therefore thoughts) for Marsilius', in the mistaken belief that he somehow transcended his age."[5] I admit to belonging among those historians who see striking intimations of the modern in Marsilius' political thought. But I do not think that he transcended his age. Just the opposite. In my view, his seeming "modernity" resulted from his sharing (and helping to shape) a model of equilibrium that was one of the great intellectual products of his age. If anything, it is Marsilius' "age" – as represented by this shared model and the intellectual culture that produced it – that transcends certain modern assumptions, both historical and popular, as to what is properly "medieval."[6]

To reiterate, over the period 1250–1325 the new model of equilibrium was shaped and shared for the most part beneath the level of conscious thought and expression. I have found no evidence that any of the authors I consider was aware that the meaning of words such as *"aequalitas"* or *"temperamentum"* or *"medium"* were in the process of changing. No one appears to have been conscious that contrasting "models" of how equality might be attained or maintained were in play in his intellectual culture; no one appears conscious that he himself possessed or shared a particular "model" of equalization, and even less, if possible, that his thoughts were being directed by one. To apprehend the model underlying Marsilius' speculation, I have had to approach it indirectly, tracking its underlying presence within his consciously elaborated political positions. To do so, I focus on what he has to say concerning the potential of varied and at times discordant elements in the political sphere to nevertheless find balance (or "equilibrium" in our terms) within the workings of the

---

[5] George Garnett, *Marsilius of Padua and "the Truth of History"* (Oxford University Press, 2006), esp. 3–14. Garnett includes a number of historians and works under this critical umbrella, including Alan Gewirth, author of the first English translation of the work (indeed its first translation into any modern language), *Marsilius of Padua: The Defender of the Peace* (New York: Columbia University Press, 1956), as well as a major work of interpretation that remains influential to this day, *Marsilius of Padua and Medieval Political Philosophy* (New York: Columbia University Press, 1951); and, more recently, Cary Nederman, author of a number of articles cited below as well as *Community and Consent: The Secular Political Theory of Marsiglio of Padua's* Defensor Pacis (Lanham, MD: Rowman and Littlefield, 1994). (Henceforth I refer to the *Defensor pacis* in the notes as *DP*.)

[6] For the viability of Marsilius' political thought into the early modern and modern era, see Bettina Koch, "Marsilius and Hobbes on Religion and Papal Power: Some Observations on Similarities," in *The World of Marsilius of Padua*, ed. Moreno-Riaño, 189–209. Also, Antony Black, *Guilds and Society in European Political Thought from the Twelfth Century to the Present* (Ithaca, NY: Cornell University Press, 1984), 86: "one does not find another such earth-shaking yet well-tuned civil philosophy until Hobbes, who in fact shared much of Marsiglio's outlook." My sense is that a comparison of Marsilius and Hobbes on the level of their assumed models of equilibrium (rather than on the level of specific contents) would be highly productive.

systematic whole of the *civitas*. In short, I focus on his assumptions concerning the potentialities of equalization. My viewing point is thus intentionally narrow and necessarily partial. I do not hope to present a unified vision of the immensely rich text of the *Defensor pacis*. No one, to my view, has succeeded in tying up all its loose ends, and I do not intend to try. But I do hope to illustrate another way of reading it. If I steer clear of many of the concerns and lines of argument current in the Marsilian debate, it is because I am focusing on a theme that has so far received little attention: how Marsilius' assumptions concerning the potentialities of political balance and equalization may be seen as a key to this text.[7]

In what follows I will restrict my analysis almost entirely to Discourse I, the first of the three "discourses" (*dictiones*) that compose the treatise. This is the section in which Marsilius uses the instrument of reason to penetrate the logic of social and political organization within the *civitas*.[8] Discourse II is no less important to Marsilius' intent than Discourse I: indeed, it is arguably more so.[9] It is more than three times as long, and it contains Marsilius' fiercest criticisms of the "pretensions" of the Papacy in his day, as well as his boldest arguments, based heavily on scripture, for stripping it of its landed property and its coercive power. In it he frames his case for denying the primacy of St. Peter and hence denying the scriptural basis of papal authority. It is, moreover, almost certainly the portion that earned Marsilius his excommunication (in 1327, three years after its publication) and his title as an arch-heretic.[10] But because its arguments are based more on textual authority and supernatural revelation than on reasoned assumptions about the natural order (and of the place of equilibrium in that order), Discourse II is less suitable for my inquiry.[11]

---

[7] That is not to say that historians have entirely overlooked the pivotal importance of equalization to Marsilius' *DP*. One who shows considerable sensitivity to this aspect is Annabel Brett, the author of a fine new annotated English translation, *Marsilius of Padua: The Defender of the Peace* (Cambridge University Press, 2005). She notes for example (xxi): "[Marsilius'] solution to excesses of transitive actions is the restoration of the situation of balance or equality that existed prior to the excess committed: equalisation." All quotations from the *DP* in English that follow, with minor exceptions that are noted, are taken from Brett's recent translation. For the Latin text of the *DP*, I follow *The Defensor Pacis of Marsilius of Padua*, ed. C. W. Previté-Orton (Cambridge University Press, 1928).

[8] So Marsilius announces in *DP*, I.1.8.

[9] For this argument, see Garnett, *Truth of History*, 14–45.   [10] Ibid., 20 ff.

[11] I note also Gewirth's productive insight that only Discourse I has the Common Good of the *civitas* as its subject and context, while Discourse II takes the German/Christian Empire as subject and context. On this, see Gewirth, *Medieval Political Philosophy*, 253–6; Alan Gewirth, "Republicanism and Absolutism in the Thought of Marsilius of Padua," *Medioevo* 5 (1979), 23–48, at 47.

Less suitable too is the very short Discourse III, which consists of lapidary conclusions rather than reasoned arguments.

Background to the writing of the *Defensor pacis*: biographical and Galenic influences

Marsilius was born sometime between 1270 and 1290, a twenty-year range of possibility that indicates how little is known about his early years.[12] He was raised within the proudly independent self-governing commune of Padua at a time when the governing Grand Council (*Consiglio Maggiore*) numbered at some points 1,000 citizens out of an adult male population of approximately 11,000.[13] He spent his student years studying Galenic medicine at the University of Padua at a time when Padua was challenged only by Bologna and Montpellier as the preeminent center of medical education in Latin Christendom.[14] It is not known at what date he began to practice medicine, but a letter dated to the second decade of the fourteenth century continues to refer to him as "magistrum Marsilium physicum paduanum," and scattered references indicate that he remained a medical practitioner throughout his tumultuous life.[15]

---

[12] Most current historical estimates of his birthdate fall somewhere in the range 1275–85. He died in either 1342 or 1343.

[13] For a fine introduction to Paduan political and social life during the period of the independent commune, 1256–1311 (Marsilius' formative years), see J. K. Hyde, *Padua in the Age of Dante* (Manchester University Press, 1966). Hyde's description of the commune's political organization (e.g., the numbers of citizens serving in the *Consiglio Maggiore*) helps to shed light on Marsilius' confidence in the potential of communal self-order, just as Padua's growing political problems from the late thirteenth century may shed light on his doubts. For a similar emphasis on the importance of Paduan communal life to Marsilius' political vision, see Nicolai Rubinstein, "Marsilio e il pensiero politico italiano," *Medioevo* 5 (1979), 143–62. For a treatment that recognizes ambiguities in the political example offered by the Paduan commune, Jeannine Quillet, *La philosophie politique de Marsile de Padoue* (Paris: J. Vrin, 1970), 23–48. And for a discussion of the problems raised by associating Marsilius' political positions with his Paduan roots, see Gregorio Piaia, "The Shadow of Antenor: On the Relationship Between the *Defensor pacis* and the Institutions of the City of Padua," in *Politische Reflexion in der Welt des späten Mittelalters/Political Thought in the Age of Scholasticism*, ed. Martin Kaufhold (Leiden: Brill, 2004), 193–223.

[14] On medical education at the University of Padua in this period, see Nancy Siraisi, *Arts and Sciences at Padua: The Studium of Padua before 1350* (Toronto: Pontifical Institute of Mediaeval Studies, 1973). Siraisi emphasizes the degree to which the study of medicine at Padua was joined to the study of logic and natural philosophy. For the status of Galenism in the Italian universities in this period, see Siraisi, *Taddeo Alderotti and his Pupils*, and the discussion of Taddeo Alderotti in Chapter 4 above.

[15] Estimates for the dating of this letter, written by his friend, Alberto Mussato, have ranged from 1312 to 1324. On this, see C. Kenneth Brampton, "Marsiglio of Padua: Part I. Life," *English Historical Review* 37 (1922), 501–15 at 503; Piaia, "The Shadow of Antenor," 201; Carlo Dolcini, *Introduzione a Marsilio da Padova* (Rome: Laterza, 1995), 8–10.

In 1313, he appears in the records of the University of Paris as a *magister artium*, a teaching master in the Faculty of Arts, on the occasion of his having been elected Rector, the university's highest elective office, for a standard half-year term. He remained in Paris – the Paris contemporary with *La vie de Saint Denys* manuscript and the *De laudibus Parisius* – as an active member of the Parisian university community for much of the period between 1313 and his completion of the *Defensor pacis* in 1324.[16] We can be fairly certain that Marsilius continued to practice medicine during his residence in Paris, since a Parisian acquaintance of his (possibly his servant) witnessed that he had accompanied Marsilius on his visits to his patients within the city.[17] Sometime between 1324 and 1326 he departed Paris for the court of the recently excommunicated Emperor Ludwig of Bavaria, to live the rest of his life in exile, both from Paris and from the Roman Church.[18] In 1327, Pope John XXII excommunicated Marsilius, having declared heretical a number of assertions in the *Defensor pacis*.[19]

Marsilius was influenced by writings from many traditions: Aristotelian, Ciceronian, Augustinian, Averroist, Franciscan, Galenic, and more.[20] If we seek to measure the degree of influence on his thinking (in Discourse I) through his direct citations alone, then Aristotle, who is cited as the basis for

---

[16] Judging from the care and attention to logical order with which this grand treatise was constructed, Nederman (*Community and Consent*, 11) has suggested that its composition may have occupied nearly a decade (1314–24), the same decade in which Marsilius was known to have spent a good portion of his time in Paris. On Marsilius' years in Paris, see William Courtenay, "University Masters and Political Power: The Parisian Years of Marsilius of Padua," in *Politische Reflexion*, ed. Kaufhold, 209–23. Courtenay provides a strong argument for Marsilius having been in Paris and connected to the university for several years before his election as Rector in 1313, and for his having remained vitally connected to the university community through the period of the composition of the *DP*.

[17] On the Paris evidence, see Brampton, "Life," 515; and Garnett, *Truth of History*, 15.

[18] The traditional date of 1326 for his departure from Paris has recently been called into question. On this see Godthardt, "Philosopher as Political Actor," 34–9. For Marsilius' continued practice of medicine into his period of exile, see Alexander Aichele, "Heart and Soul of the State: Some Remarks Concerning Aristotelian Ontology and Medieval Theory of Medicine in Marsilius of Padua's *Defensor Pacis*," in *The World of Marsilius of Padua*, ed. Moreno-Riaño, 163–86, at 164.

[19] For the specific charges, see Garnett, *Truth of History*, 18–23. For a brief overview of the larger historical circumstances surrounding the writing of the *DP*, particularly the confrontation between Papacy and Empire, see Quillet, *Philosophie politique*, 11–16.

[20] The label "Averroist" has frequently been attached to Marsilius. In recent decades, however, there has been much questioning of the validity of this characterization. For a brief history of the controversy, weighted to the anti-Averroistic side, see Gregorio Piaia, *Marsilio e dintorni* (Padua: Antenore, 1999), 79–103. For an exploration of the question of Averroistic influences on Marsilius, see Quillet, *Philosophie politique*, 61–71; and Jeannine Quillet, "L'aristotélisme de Marsile de Padoue et ses rapports avec l'averroisme," *Medioevo* 5 (1979), 81–142; Mario Grignaschi, "Marsilio e le filosofie del Trecento," *Medioevo* 5 (1979), 201–22. For more on possible Averroistic leanings, see below under the discussion of Marsilius' close intellectual collaboration with Jean de Jandun.

virtually every major point that Marsilius puts forth, would be far and away the most important. According to this measure Cicero would be a distant second, and Galen, with his single citation, a yet more distant third. The list of serious readers of the *Defensor pacis* who see Aristotle (or Aristotle as read through the commentaries of Averroes) as its primary intellectual influence is long.[21] In recent decades, the argument has been made that the influence of Cicero on Marsilius' thought was far more pronounced than the mere number of citations would indicate, and further, that the naturalistic conception of human society that so influenced Marsilius owed as much to Latin authors – Cicero, Seneca, even St. Augustine – as it did to Aristotle.[22] I want to make a similar and perhaps even more emphatic argument for the influence of Galen and medieval Galenism on Discourse I.

I would not have seen evidence of Galenic thought in the *Defensor pacis* had I not studied Galen's writings for what they might reveal about the treatment of equalization and equilibrium in medieval medicine. But having become familiar with Galen's way of viewing both the human body and the physician's relation to the body, I have come to see strong evidence of his thought and his way of thinking throughout the *Defensor pacis*, most especially in the pivotal places where Marsilius bases his argument on assumptions concerning the potentialities of equalization within the political community. As I see it, there are three primary difficulties facing this claim: (1) the paucity of Galenic citations compared to the ever-present citations and quotations from Aristotle; (2) the problem of distinguishing characteristically Galenic positions both from genuinely Aristotelian positions and from positions that Marsilius supports through the citation of Aristotelian authority; (3) the possibility that other available non-Galenic models of the human body may have served as Marsilius' model of the body politic rather than the Galenic body.[23]

---

[21] For a bibliography of works that have investigated the influence of Aristotle and Averroist readings of Aristotle on the *DP*, see Cary Nederman, "Nature, Justice, and Duty in the *Defensor Pacis*: Marsiglio of Padua's Ciceronian Impulse," *Political Theory* 18 (1990), 615–37, at 615 and n. 3; Mario Grignaschi, "Le rôle de l'aristotélisme dans le *"Defensor Pacis"* de Marsile de Padoue," *Revue d'Histoire et de Philosophie Religieuse* 35 (1955), 301–40. For the English text of the *Politics*, I have followed *The Politics of Aristotle*, ed. and trans. Ernest Barker (Oxford University Press, 1958).

[22] Cary Nederman, "Nature, Sin and the Origins of Society," esp. 19–24; Nederman, "Marsiglio of Padua's Ciceronian Impulse."

[23] Separating Galenic insights from the Ciceronian would present its own set of problems since Galen and Cicero shared certain Stoic attitudes about nature and the natural, and they shared as well an experiential connection to the political and social life of the Roman metropolis, even if the city had expanded enormously by Galen's day. There is, however, no evidence that Galen was familiar with the writings of Cicero.

To take the third possibility first: non-Galenic representations of the workings of the body were certainly available to Marsilius, from both classical and medieval literature, but none came close to being as rich and as well articulated as Galen's. The famous and often repeated image of the joined human body/political body offered by John of Salisbury in the *Policraticus*, for example, a hierarchical structure of head, heart, feet, and hands representing the various "orders" in political society, bears about the same relation to the systematic complexity and coherence of the Galenic body as a stick figure does to Polyclitus' sculptured figures, whose proportions Galen so admired.[24] Just as Marsilius' political thought was unrivaled in its logical coherence and in the dynamic relationships of its working parts, so too was Galen's model of the working body. Existing images linking the segmented hierarchical body to the political body, like John of Salisbury's, may well have served older models of equalization, but not Marsilian equilibrium.

However, the second problem noted, of how to separate Galenic insights from those of Aristotle, is indeed a thorny one. Galen rightly claimed Aristotle as his philosophical guide in the realm of logic and philosophy, and he adopted much of Aristotelian physical theory. Furthermore, as is clearly seen in the writings of Taddeo Alderotti, Turisanus, and others discussed above, medieval Galenism developed within a scholastic culture that was heavily informed by Aristotelian logic and the whole of the Aristotelian corpus. How, then, can one be reasonably certain that one is dealing with an "authentic" Galenic insight in Marsilius' text? The answer, I suggest, lies in the depth, coherence, and distinctiveness of Galen's vision of the working body. Despite the many places where Galen relied on the authority of Aristotle, there remained weighty differences between their ways of viewing nature and natural activity.[25] Their theoretical disagreements (and the particular medical insights that flowed from them) were large enough to have been recognized, discussed, and argued by both Islamic and Christian scholars throughout the Middle Ages.[26]

At the cusp of the fourteenth century, Pietro d'Abano (*c.* 1255–1316), a formidable scholastic thinker trained both in Galenic medicine and

---

[24] John of Salisbury, *Policraticus*, ed. and trans. Cary Nederman (Cambridge University Press, 1990), 66–7. I discuss the legacy of John of Salisbury's image of the body and its metaphorical links to the political body again in greater detail in Chapter 7 below, with reference to Nicole Oresme's imagination of the political "body" in his *De moneta*. For Galen's admiration of Polyclitus' proportions, see Chapter 3 above, pp. 161, 175.

[25] See my discussion on this point throughout Chapter 3 and at its conclusion.

[26] I discuss these differences and their recognition at many points in Chapters 3 and 4 above, with respect to the writings of Ibn Ridwan, Avicenna, Taddeo Alderotti, and Turisanus.

Aristotelian philosophy, dedicated an entire treatise to isolating and reconciling discrepancies between the positions of the two masters. Titled Conciliator differentiarum philosophorum et praecipue medicorum, it was most often known simply as Conciliator.[27] Over its more than 500 double-columned pages (in the printed edition of 1565), Pietro considered hundreds of separate questions raised by his desire to bridge apparent differences or to decide between them. His own writings provide evidence for how deeply intertwined Galenic and Aristotelian insights had become within scholastic medicine. Like every Galenist in this period, Pietro identified the ideal state of health (defined as balance/aequalitas) with the ever-shifting relationship of the four oppositional qualities (heat, cold, wetness, and dryness), a theory that had its origin in the writings of Hippocrates and Aristotle. He identified the ideal of proportional aequalitas, which he termed "aequalitas ad iustitiam," directly with iustitia distributiva, that species of proportional equalization that Aristotle had identified and defined as "geometric" in Ethics V. Moreover, like Turisanus in the Plusquam commentum, Pietro argued that the process of equalization governing the Galenic complexio and the Galenic body was of the same type as that which Aristotle identified with the distribution of rewards within the civitas and with the "geometric" system of economic exchange that bound and ordered the political body.[28]

Nevertheless, there were indeed differences, some of them profound, between the approaches and determinations of Galen and Aristotle. Those that Pietro noted in the Conciliator ranged from the general to the particular (whether the nerves arise from the brain or the heart; whether there is one principal bodily member or several; whether the neutrum is a disposition or not, and hundreds more beside. Pietro frequently used these distinctions to point out crucial differences between the practical requirements of medicine as an art directed toward particular subjects and cures (associated with Galen) and the theoretical requirements of philosophy as a science directed toward universal determinations (associated with Aristotle). In those cases, however, where the positions of Galen and Aristotle were in clear opposition, Pietro most often sided with Aristotle,

---

[27] There are other extant forms of the title as well. The edition I am consulting is Conciliator controversiarum, quae inter philosophos et medicos versantur (Venice: ad Iuntas, 1565; reprint Padua: Antenore, 1985). The Conciliator was completed in 1303 and revised in 1310.

[28] E.g., Conciliator (1565), diff. 18, fol. 27d: "Sed complexio iustitialis dicta iustitiae merito coaptatur, proprieque naturali: quaedam enim naturalis, altera positiva: et huiusmodi quidem distributiva, ut honores, et substantiae alia vero commutativa: ceu quae in participatione invicem. 5. Ethico[rum] ... Et ipsa aequalis complexio non simpliciter, sed ad alterum, puta iustitia operationibus iustis relata." In Chapter 4 above I discuss the nearly identical opinion that appears in the writings of Turisanus, pp. 235–40.

even when the questions involved were essentially medical in nature. On the other hand, Pietro's assumptions concerning the potentialities of systematic equalization within the body are essentially Galenic. The immensely rich and logically articulated concept of the Galenic complexion, the representation *in nuce* of the Galenic model of equalization, had no parallel in Aristotle's medical thought, yet it provides the organizing center of Pietro's thinking, a testament to the process of Galenic reception that had occurred over the course of the thirteenth century.

In many ways Pietro d'Abano served as an intellectual model for Marsilius – arguably his most important living intellectual model. Like Marsilius, Pietro was born in the vicinity of Padua and began his training in Galenic medicine at the University of Padua, where he became a teaching master.[29] Like Marsilius, Pietro moved from the University of Padua to the University of Paris where he became an active member of the Paris faculty.[30] Like Marsilius, Pietro moved between the study of medicine, dominated by the theoretical principles of Galen, and the study of scholastic logic and philosophy, dominated by the writings of Aristotle.[31] And, like Marsilius, Pietro participated in the larger project of joining the intellectual culture of the northern Italian universities to the culture of the northern universities, Paris and Oxford in particular.[32] The parallels in their life experiences and intellectual trajectories are striking. So too are

[29] On Pietro's life and works, Eugenia Paschetto, *Pietro d'Abano, medico e filosofo* (Florence: E. Vallecchi, 1984), with his links to Marsilius at 53–4, 335; Siraisi, *Arts and Sciences at Padua*, esp, 58–62, 163. Joan Cadden explores the intersection of medicine and natural philosophy in Pietro's work in "'Nothing Natural is Shameful': Vestiges of a Debate about Sex and Science in a Group of Late-Medieval Manuscripts," *Speculum* 76 (2001), 66–89. The entirety of *Medioevo* 11 (1985) is dedicated to articles on Pietro. Those in this collection that are particularly germane to his connections with Marsilius include Paul Kristeller, "Umanesimo e Scolastica a Padova fino al Petrarca," 1–18; Marie-Thérèse D'Alverny, "Pietro d'Abano traducteur de Galien," 19–64; and Nancy Siraisi, "Pietro d'Abano and Taddeo Alderotti: Two Models of Medical Culture," 139–62. On the expanding concern in the late thirteenth century to make authentic Galenic writings the center of medical education, see Luis García Ballester, "Arnau de Vilanova (c. 1240–1311) y la reforma de los estudios médicos en Montpellier (1309): el Hipócrates latino y la introducción del nuevo Galeno," *Dynamis* 2 (1982), 97–158. For Pietro's contribution to this project, D'Alverny, "Pietro d'Abano traducteur de Galien," 26–41.

[30] Pietro moved from the University of Padua to the University of Paris in the last decade of the thirteenth century, and he returned to teach at Padua sometime between 1305 and 1307 after the orthodoxy of a number of his doctrines was questioned by the Paris Dominicans.

[31] Siraisi, "Pietro d'Abano and Taddeo Alderotti," 142–3, 150–4. Pietro received his Galenism both through authentic Galenic texts (which he could read in the Greek) and through the mediation of Arabic compilations, translated into Latin, such as the *Liber regius* of Haly Abbas and the *Canon* of Avicenna.

[32] Siraisi, *Medicine and the Italian Universities, 1250–1600*; Siraisi, "Pietro d'Abano and Taddeo Alderotti," 160–2; Dolcini, *Introduzione*, 12–13.

the parallels I have already noted between Marsilius and another well-known Italian Galenist at Paris, Turisanus (d. *c.* 1320), author of the influential *Plusquam* commentary on Galen's *Tegni* (*c.* 1315–20). Turisanus, like Marsilius, was educated in Galenic medicine in northern Italy (at the University of Bologna), and his residency at the University of Paris, from 1313 to 1319, overlapped with that of Marsilius.[33]

But where there are no surviving records linking Marsilius with Turisanus, and assertions of their personal and intellectual contact must remain conjectural, we have, in the case of Pietro, more than mere biographical parallels to evidence their long and close connection. Among the few things that scholars can generally agree upon concerning Marsilius' early life is that part of his student years at Padua were spent studying medicine under Pietro. Moreover, when Marsilius moved to Paris he joined an intellectual circle that Pietro had been part of there, which included other northern Italians trained in medicine, and in 1315 Marsilius returned to Padua to act as a witness on behalf of Pietro's profession of Catholic faith.[34] In short, Pietro d'Abano, the great mediator between Galenism and Aristotelianism, served as both mentor and friend to his fellow Paduan physician.[35]

I have taken this detour to introduce Pietro and his project of aligning Aristotle and Galen because I believe that the same project is central to the direction of the *Defensor pacis*. But if Galen's influence is at least as important as Aristotle's in this text, why does his name appear only once? There are many possible answers to this question. In Marsilius' time there was no *direct* association between Galen's writings and political thought. There are no surviving Galenic treatises on politics, and there are few comments in his vast surviving oeuvre that are overtly political in nature. Aristotle, on the other hand, wrote a surpassingly great treatise on the subject: a text that had been at the center of scholastic political thought since its translation from the Greek in 1260 and its early commentaries by Albert and (partially) by Thomas. Furthermore, theology, which is so essential to the anti-papal argument of the *Defensor pacis* and its call to action, had been integrated with Aristotelianism at Paris for more than a half-century when Marsilius composed his treatise. But nothing near

---

[33] On Turisanus' life, thought, and sojourn in Paris, see Siraisi, *Taddeo Alderotti and his Pupils*, and the concluding section to Chapter 4 above.

[34] Tiziani Presenti, "Per la tradizione del testamento di Pietro d'Abano," *Medioevo* 6 (1980), 533–42; Courtenay, "Parisian Years of Marsilius," 222; Quillet, *Philosophie politique*, 60–1.

[35] Rubinstein, "Marsilio e il pensiero politico italiano," 157 and n. 45. Pietro was well known in his day to be deeply schooled in and reliant on astrological reasoning. His reputation for orthodoxy suffered greatly because of it. In this area he appears to have had little or no influence on Marsilius' thought in the *DP*.

such integration had occurred between Christian theology and Galenic naturalism. And finally, Aristotelianism was by far the dominant intellectual mode in the Paris that Marsilius had adopted as his intellectual home and in whose environment he composed his treatise. Marsilius' use of the text of Aristotle's *Politics* to frame his argument at every point makes perfect sense; this is how an author, enunciating a radical program, and indeed a radical call to action against the great religious power of his age, might well use textual authority to support his project.[36] Moreover, Aristotle's thought can actually take Marsilius a good part of the way he wants to go. Since most historians of medieval political thought are far more schooled in Aristotle than they are in Galen, few are in a position to recognize that when Marsilius uses the words of Aristotle to support insights into the workings of political life that Aristotle never quite held, these insights turn out to have been heavily influenced by Galenic thought.

Given the central place of medicine in Marsilius' biography – his university studies in Galenic medicine, his connections to the work and person of Pietro d'Abano and other northern Italian *medici* at Paris (very possibly including Turisanus), his continued practice of medicine through the composition of the *Defensor pacis* – it is puzzling that there have not been more studies over the past half-century centered on possible Galenic influences on its construction.[37] Adding further to the puzzle, Alan Gewirth, in his excellent and influential study of Marsilius written

---

[36] For the argument that Marsilius' citations should be interpreted more as a component of his rhetorical strategy than as an accurate reflection of the sources of his thought, see Conal Condren, "Marsilius of Padua's Argument from Authority: A Survey of its Significance in the *Defensor Pacis*," *Political Theory* 5 (1977), 205–18.

[37] For articles devoted explicitly to this subject: G. Rosen, "The Historical Significance of some Medical References in the *Defensor Pacis* of Marsilio of Padua," *Sudhoffs Archiv für Geschichte der Medizin und der Naturwissenschaften* 37 (1953), 35–56; Aichele, "Heart and Soul of the State"; Takashi Shogimen, "Treating the Body Politic: Medical Metaphor of Political Rule in Late Medieval Europe and Tokugawa Japan," *Review of Politics* 70 (2008), 77–104. I received the most recent article on this subject, which is both thoughtful and wide-ranging, too late to include it in my study: Takashi Shogimen, "Medicine and the Body Politic in Marsilius of Padua's *Defensor Pacis*," in *A Companion to Marsilius of Padua*, ed. Gerson Moreno-Riaño and Cary Nederman (Leiden: Brill, 2012), 71–115. For the recognition of the weight of Marsilius' medical training (specifically the Galenic notion of bodily equalization) on the formation of his conception of original sin and salvation as "remedy" and "cure," see Floriano Cesar, "Divine and Human Writings in Marsilius of Padua's *Defensor Pacis*: Expressions of Truth," in *The World of Marsilius of Padua*, ed. Moreno-Riaño, 109–23, at 116–18. The one locus in the *DP* where Marsilius actually names Galen as an authority (the role of the *pars principans* or "ruling part," discussed below) has generated its share of biological/medical commentary, e.g., Joseph Canning, "Power and Powerlessness in the Political Thought of Marsilius of Padua," *ibid.*, 211–25, at 214–17.

more than a half-century ago, clearly recognized the "biological" leaning of Marsilius' political thought and analysis. He writes:

The Marsilian politics thus has its full basis not in ethics or theology but in biology: it is grounded in naturalistic necessity, the uniquely determinable economic and political conditions required for the fulfillment of biological needs ... The biological, therefore, is not merely the initial mainspring of the political realm, soon surmounted by ethical and theological values: it is rather the sufficient context which sets all the problems to whose solution politics is directly addressed, and which, moreover, also provides the essential criteria for the functioning and evaluation of political institutions.[38]

And yet Gewirth failed to underline the essential connection between this biological view and Marsilius' Galenic training.[39] I can only explain this by what I see as a general underappreciation (outside the sphere of the history of medicine) of the acuity and power of Galen's insights into the workings of nature, and a general absence of recognition that in some areas – above all in the dynamic balance of part to part and part to whole within the working system – Galen's scientific vision is not only quite distinct from Aristotle's, it represents a notable advance over it.[40] Once this has been recognized, it is a short step to seeing that these advances could well be applied to speculation in disciplines outside medicine, particularly those, like political thought, which are centered on attaining and maintaining a balance between competing elements within the *civitas*. As the *Plusquam commentum* of Turisanus demonstrates, Galenic commentators were making explicit connections between the system of proportional equalization governing the Galenic body and the system of proportional distribution governing the processes of ordering within

---

[38] Gewirth, *Medieval Political Philosophy*, 51. He continues with a very well made distinction between Marsilius' biological thought and earlier "organic" political theories: "for where they had moralized biology, Marsilius biologizes morals and politics."

[39] He does mention Marsilius' medical training as an influence (*ibid.*, 52), but in his view it is far less important than influences coming from Marsilius' "Averroist associations" and his particular reading of Aristotle's *Politics*. Gewirth never singles out Galen as a major influence on Marsilius' thought, and while there is an entry in his index under "biological basis of Marsilian politics," there is no entry for "Galen." And, finally, while noting the great discrepancy between Marsilius' overall argument and Aristotle's, he nevertheless maintains (*ibid.*, 211) that it is "Aristotelian physics which underlies Marsilius' doctrine."

[40] A notable exception is Annabel Brett who, in the notes to her recent translation of the *DP*, pays admirable attention to possible medical/Galenic influences on Marsilius' thought. In addition, her introduction points more clearly (e.g., *Marsilius of Padua*, xxi) than any previous work to the pivotal importance of "equalization" and balance to the entire argument of the *DP*. Given this combination, I would hope that the new translation alone spurs a deeper interest in the Galenic roots of Marsilian thought. A positive sign of this is the recognition of the need for studies on the implications of Marsilius' medical education in Cary Nederman's recent survey article, "Marsiglio of Padua Studies," 24.

the *civitas* in the very same period that Marsilius was composing the *Defensor pacis*.[41]

One last digression before turning to the text. As closely linked as Pietro d'Abano is with Marsilius, there is yet one figure even more closely associated with him: Jean de Jandun (d. 1328), the author of the *De laudibus Parisius*.[42] The few biographical details we possess for each tie them together as long-time friends and intellectual collaborators during the period that both were masters in the Faculty of Arts at the University of Paris.[43] In the preface to one of his writings, Jean refers to Marsilius as "*dilectissimum meum magistrum Marcillium.*"[44] In Marsilius' day, it was generally assumed that the *Defensor pacis*, completed in 1324 (one year before the *De laudibus Parisius*), had actually been written in collaboration with Jean.[45] Today the question remains

[41] See the concluding section of Chapter 4 above.

[42] Jean de Jandun was a close friend to Pietro d'Abano as well as to Marsilius. Given Jean's frequent identification as an "Averroist" philosopher in historical scholarship, Marsilius' long friendship and collaboration with Jean opens him up to similar claims of Averroistic leanings. On this, see Mieczyslaw Gogacz, "L'homme et la communauté dans le 'Defensor Pacis' de Marsile de Padoue," *Medioevo* 5 (1979), 189–200; Quillet, "L'aristotélisme de Marsile de Padoue." Although Jean was a great admirer of Averroes and considered him the finest interpreter of Aristotle's thought, recent scholarship has revealed just how unclear the label "Averroist" (often used pejoratively) is in a general sense, and how questionable it is when applied to the writings of Jean de Jandun. On this see MacClintock, *Perversity and Error*; also Schmugge, *Johannes von Jandun*. The question of Jean's "Averroism" is considered in greater detail in Chapter 5 above.

[43] Courtenay, "Parisian Years of Marsilius," 221; Quillet, *Philosophie politique*, 59–64; Schmugge, *Johannes von Jandun*, 26–38; MacClintock, *Perversity and Error*, 4–7. On links between Jean's formal scholastic writings and those of Marsilius, see Schmugge, *Johannes von Jandun*, 95–119; Quillet, "L'aristotélisme de Marsile de Padoue," esp. 124–42; Roberto Lambertini, "The Sophismata attributed to Marsilius of Padua," in *Sophisms in Medieval Logic and Grammar*, ed. Stephen Read (Dordrecht: Kluwer, 1993), 86–102.

[44] The phrase appears in the introduction to one of Jean's writings, a redaction (copy?) of Pietro d'Abano's commentary on the *Problemata* of Aristotle. Jean notes that he had been introduced to this work through Marsilius, who had presumably brought it with him from Padua. On this, see Schmugge, *Johannes von Jandun*, 27; Dolcini, *Introduzione*, 12. See also Zdzislaw Kukewicz, "Les *Problemata* de Pietro d'Abano et leur 'rédaction' par Jean de Jandun," *Medioevo* 10 (1984), 113–24.

[45] Noël Valois, "Jean de Jandun et Marsile de Padoue: auteurs du *Defensor pacis*," *Histoire littéraire de la France* 33 (1906), 528–623. Only Marsilius' name appears attached to the surviving manuscripts of the *DP*. Still, modern historians only seriously began to question the collaborative role of Jean in the writing of the *DP* with the publication of an article by Alan Gewirth that asserted fundamental differences in their ethical and political thinking: "John of Jandun and the *Defensor Pacis*," *Speculum* 23 (1948), 267–72. Even though denying co-authorship, Gewirth does not deny their close friendship or (272) that it is "highly probable that John contributed advice and assistance" to the writing of the *DP*. Among those who study the text today, there seems to be a roughly equal division between those who agree with Gewirth, e.g., Grignaschi, "Marsilio e le filosofie del Trecento,"

open.[46] In any case, both men were condemned and ultimately excommunicated for its publication in 1327. Both left (fled?) Paris together between 1324 and 1326 for the court of Emperor Ludwig of Bavaria, the prince to whom the *Defensor pacis* is dedicated and a committed opponent of the reigning Pope John XXII.[47] Both, while in exile, supported the Emperor in his struggle with the Papacy. We will never know for sure if Marsilius accompanied Jean on his visits to the great market at Champeaux (Les Halles), or if he shared Jean's amazement at the multiplication of riches and goods produced by the toiling anonymous of Paris, or shared Jean's insights into the productive powers of self-organizing commerce within the self-ordering city. But we do know that Marsilius walked the same streets as Jean, saw the same sights, and crossed over the same bridges illustrated in the manuscripts of *La vie de Saint Denys*.

I mention these connections at this point primarily to suggest this: if Galen's understanding of the animal body provided Marsilius with a way of understanding the possibilities of systematic self-equalization within the political body, it was not simply because the Paduan had read and internalized Galenic texts; it was because he had read and internalized them in a particular economic, social, and political environment in which they seemed vitally applicable to his own lived experience. When we consider that Galen gave shape to his remarkable vision of the co-equalizing body within the environment of late second-century Rome, we can understand more clearly why the Galenic vision might have "fit" so well, both with Marsilius' experience of urban Paris and with the model of equilibrium that was being shaped within Parisian scholastic culture at the very time that he was writing the *Defensor pacis*.[48]

---

esp. 211–18, and those who continue to assert their probable collaboration and the closeness of their thinking, e.g., Quillet, *Philosophie politique*, 59–70; Schmugge, *Johannes von Jandun*, 95–119.

[46] Although this was not Schmugge's intent, after reading his presentation of Jean's social and political views, I see little reflection of Jean's political ideas in the *DP*, beyond a focus on the ideal of the Common Good (*Johannes von Jandun*, 45, 102–3), which was hardly unique in his day. In all fairness, Schmugge himself recognizes points of disagreement between Jean's stated opinions and the *DP* (111, 118–19) and never claims to have demonstrated Jean's direct collaboration in its writing.

[47] Jürgen Miethke, "Marsilius und Ockham," *Medioevo* 6 (1980), 543–67, esp. 545–7.

[48] According to Raymond Cazelles, the eminent historian of medieval Paris (*Nouvelle histoire de Paris*, 9, 124), the first quarter of the fourteenth century represented the highpoint of a centuries-long process of urban and economic development in Paris, one that would not be attained again for centuries to come. The 1328 census has been read to indicate a population of 200,000. Even if this is an exaggerated figure it points to Paris as one of the greatest cities in Latin Christendom at that time. For a sketch of the demography and economy of Paris in this period, see Carpentier and Le Mené, *La France du XIe au XVe siècle*, 296–307.

Equilibrium, the body politic, and the Common Good in the *Defensor pacis*

In presenting the logic that underlies the first half of Discourse I of the *Defensor pacis*, I have chosen to follow the order of Marsilius' argument rather than to order his points to my own plan. Marsilius opens his great treatise by announcing the importance of its subject. The establishment of political tranquility and peace, he writes, is no less than "the greatest of all human goods."[49] In contrast to this grandeur, the compressed definition he provides for the true fruit of political peace, "the sufficiency of this life," appears rather surprisingly modest.[50] It is, however, characteristic of Marsilius, here and elsewhere, to have reduced the grand abstraction of the "Common Good" to its physical and (as Gewirth would have it) biological dimension – the physical presence of those things necessary to support and promote life for the individual.[51] While it is natural for individuals to desire to acquire these sufficiencies, and while individuals possess the natural capacity to do so, Marsilius maintains that they can only fully accomplish this goal in an ordered social and political setting. Hence, for Marsilius, humans are political not, as Aristotle has it, because it is in their very nature to be so, but because political life is their means to satisfying their natural desire for physical sufficiency.[52] Many modern commentators have noted and emphasized this distinction.

"Peace" is the name Marsilius gives to a political setting so ordered that individuals can obtain and maintain the sufficiencies of life.[53] From the outset, the simple word "peace," carries great weight for Marsilius and a great weight of meanings as well, many of them directly tied to what we today would call "balance" or "equilibrium." As Gewirth notes:

---

[49] *DP*, I.1.1. In what follows I adhere wherever possible to Annabel Brett's fine translation. For key terms and phrases I supply the Latin text, which I have generally taken from Previté-Orton's edition of the *DP*, cited earlier. Where noted, I cite the Latin text from *Marsilius von Padua: Defensor Pacis*, ed. Richard Scholz, in *Fontes Iuris Germanici Antiqui*, vol. I (Hanover: Hahnsche Buchhandlung, 1931).

[50] *DP*, I.1.1. One of the most insightful analyses I have seen on this point, and one that, while not specifically naming balance, nevertheless turns on its modeling, is Marjorie Reeves, "Marsilius of Padua and Dante Alighieri," in *Trends in Medieval Political Thought*, ed. Beryl Smalley (Oxford University Press, 1965), 86–104.

[51] Schmugge (*Johannes von Jandun*, 118–19) notes similarities between Marsilius' choice of "the sufficiencies of life" as the achievable end of political life and the value Jean de Jandun placed on the achievable secular ideal of *"felicitas politica."*

[52] This pivotal distinction, which breaks sharply with the commentary tradition on the *Ethics* and *Politics* established by Albert and Thomas, would be applicable as well to Jean de Jandun's city dwellers as represented in the *De laudibus Parisius*. Schmugge has shown, however, that in other of his writings, Jean asserts, along with Aristotle, that man is by nature a political animal. On this see Schmugge, *Johannes de Jandun*, 77, n. 175.

[53] *DP*, I.1.1.

Consequently the "good disposition of the state" by which Marsilius defines peace will primarily mean the stable equilibrium in which the state endures ... The Marsilian peace thus refers to political statics and dynamics, not to a theological cosmology: it is the peace of Padua's burghers, not that of her clergy.[54]

Central to Marsilius' understanding of "peace" is the concept of "concord," the agreement between individuals and groups to maintain mutual exchange to the point of achieving a tranquil order. In support he cites the words of Cicero: "We ought in this to follow nature as our leader, to contribute to the common stock the things that benefit everyone in common."[55] Through this use of Cicero, Marsilius establishes two important ideas: by serving the community we serve ourselves; and by serving ourselves we naturally serve the common utility (*communis utilitas*). Beneath this web of social and political agreement lies a sense of integration and cooperation that comes close to the Galenic concept of "health," the integrated balance (*coaequalitas*) of parts within the whole.[56]

"Tranquility," for Marsilius, is the physical manifestation of social integration and peace.[57] Its opposite is "discord" (*discordia*), which Marsilius again frames from the beginning in frankly physical/medical language: "Like sickness in an animal (*egritudo animalis*) *discordia* can be diagnosed (*dignoscitur*) as the indisposition of a civil regime."[58] Then, speaking in a tone reminiscent of a physician diagnosing a sick patient, Marsilius announces that the "singular and well-hidden cause" of the present disorder and intranquility in northern Italy (*regnum Italicum*) are certain "highly contagious" (*vehementer contagiosa*), "perverted opinions."[59] For the moment he refrains from explaining the precise nature of these poisonous falsehoods or who is spreading them, except to say that they are destroying the political structures and bonds of community that make the attainment of life's sufficiencies possible.[60]

In ch. 2, Marsilius uses Aristotle in his characteristic fashion: to establish a concept, or in this case an analogy, that is not quite Aristotelian.

---

[54] Gewirth, *Medieval Political Philosophy*, 96–8, at 98.
[55] *DP*, I.1.4, Cicero, *De officiis* I.22. On Marsilius' use of Cicero's authority here, see Nederman, "Nature, Justice, and Duty."
[56] As discussed in Chapters 3 and 4 above.   [57] *DP*, I.1.2.   [58] *Ibid.*, I.1.3.
[59] *Ibid.* On Marsilius' concern with the political health of northern Italy, and his choice of the phrase *regnum Italicum* to refer to this area of self-governing communes, including his native Padua, see Quillet, *Philosophie politique*, 75–7. On the status of the *regnum Italicum* and its links to the Aristotelian *"civitas"* and *"polis,"* see also Enrico Berti, "Il 'regnum' di Marsilio tra la 'polis' aristotelica e lo 'stato' moderno," *Medioevo* 5 (1979), 165–81. For Brett's thoughts on the problems of translating the term *"regnum,"* see her "Issues in Translating the *Defensor Pacis*," in *The World of Marsilius of Padua*, ed. Moreno-Riaño, 91–108, esp. 100–8.
[60] *DP*, I.1.4.

Here it is the analogy between the *civitas* and a living body – the political community as a living animal. In this case, as in so many others in the *Defensor pacis*, in the disjunctive space between what Aristotle has said and what Marsilius *uses* him to say, Galen and Galenic analysis appears.

Let us suppose with Aristotle in the first and fifth books of his *Politics*, chs. 2 and 3 respectively, that the city is like a kind of animate or animal nature. For an animal which is in a good condition with respect to its nature is composed of certain proportionate parts arranged in relation to each other (*componitur ex quibusdam proporcionatis partibus invicem ordinatis*), all communicating their actions between themselves and towards the whole (*suaque opera mutuo communicantibus et ad totum*); likewise too the city which is in a good condition (*bene disposita*) and established in accordance with reason is made up of certain such parts. A city and its parts would therefore seem to be in the same relation to tranquility as an animal and its parts is to health.[61]

Although Marsilius introduces his animal analogy by reference to Aristotelian authority, he has actually provided here a marvelously succinct description of the functioning Galenic body. In her footnote to this statement, Annabel Brett notes that while Aristotle does at times suggest a vague analogy between the parts of the *polis* and the parts of the human body, he never directly compares the *polis* to a living animal as Marsilius does here.[62] Moreover, where Aristotle's animal analogy is loose, Marsilius will, from this point on, lean heavily on it and draw many conclusions from it – not least about the forms of equalization proper to the "healthy" *civitas*.[63]

Once he has established this analogy, Marsilius can then move one level higher to associate the already established ideal states of peace and tranquility with the ideal medical state of health.

For they think that health (*sanitas*) is an animal's optimal condition according to nature, and likewise that tranquility is the optimal condition of a city established according to reason. Now health – as the more expert physicians say when they describe it – is that good condition of an animal, *in which each of its parts is enabled perfectly to perform the operations appropriate to its nature* (*secundum*

---

[61] *Ibid.*, I.2.3, ed. Previté-Orton, 8. Mieczyslaw Gogacz recognizes the new and crystallized form of equilibrium underlying this vision, but where I view the model as Galenic, he makes the case that it is essentially Averroistic. "L'homme et la communauté," 190. Galen, however, would be its ultimate source in the writings of Averroes, just as it is in the writings of Avicenna.

[62] *DP*, trans. Brett, 12, n. 4.

[63] Gewirth, after laying out the four major steps in Marsilius' argument writes: (*Medieval Political Philosophy*, 209): "It need hardly be pointed out that this striking argument contains glaring misinterpretations of Aristotle, particularly in transforming the hypothetical moral necessities of the *Politics* into absolute physical necessities." Cf. Aichele, "Heart and Soul," 177.

rationem et suam institutionem). If we follow this analogy, tranquility will then be that good condition of a city or realm, in which each of its parts is enabled perfectly to perform the operations appropriate to it according to reason and the way it has been established (my emphasis).[64]

At this point in her translation, Annabel Brett suggests in a note that since Galen defines health consistently and essentially as the *interior* quality of "good temperament" (i.e., proportionally equalized or balanced complexion), and since Avicenna's definition of health in the *Canon* is more centered on the proper *exterior* disposition and operation of bodily members, it is likely that Marsilius is here leaning on the authority of Avicenna rather than on Galen.[65] This is not necessarily so. While Galen does define health in terms of the maintenance of complexional balance, he also repeatedly states that the universal *sign* of health – the exterior sign of interior complexional balance – is, indeed, excellent function of the bodily members, singly and in concert, just as the sign of illness or imbalance is operational failure.[66] From what is known about university medical education in Padua and Paris in this period, it is fair to suggest that Marsilius was schooled in Avicenna's *Canon*. Since, however, his teacher at Padua was Pietro d'Abano, who learned Greek so that he could read Galen in the original, and who translated a number of Galenic works from Greek into Latin, it is also fair to suggest that Marsilius was thoroughly schooled in authentic Galenic texts, and he could well have made the statement above entirely from within the ambit of Galen's writings.[67]

Equilibrium of parts within the body politic

To underscore the importance of equality and equalization to the health of the *civitas*, Marsilius next introduces a theme that will be crucial to his entire argument: law as the instrument of equalization par excellence within the functioning organism of the *civitas*. Law is connected to the idea of equality and forms of equalization in many ways. Its deep

---

[64] *DP*, I.2.3, ed. Previté-Orton, "qua poterit unaquaeque suarum partium facere perfecte operationis convenientes sibi secundum rationem et suam institutionem."

[65] Although I question Brett's reading here, her translation (and hence her reading of the text as a whole) is exceptionally valuable for its general recognition of Marsilius' medical education and its possible influences on his political thought.

[66] One of many possible examples, Galen, *Tegni*, K, 314–15, *translatio arabica*, 179r: "A substantia quidem ipsa tunc, quando corpus est secundum meliorem formam. Nam ex signis eius est aequalitas membrorum eius partium similium, in calore, et frigore, humiditate, et siccitate; et aequalitas membrorum eius instrumentalium in quantitatibus partium, ex quibus sunt composita, et numero eorum, et forma cuiuslibet partium, et in loco, et forma instrumentalis totius, et loco eius."

[67] D'Alverny, "Pietro d'Abano traducteur de Galien," esp. 50–2.

associations to the ideal of justice ties it directly to the iconography of the balancing scale, and Marsilius explores the links between law and balance on many levels. In his introduction to the subject of law, when he discusses the earliest form it takes within political communities, Marsilius defines its form of equalization in the most basic biological terms as the "equalization of injury" (*aequalitas iniuria*), in the absence of which there would be perpetual strife.[68]

Following this, Marsilius provides a purely naturalistic account of the formation of the *civitas*. First comes the family, then the grouping of families within the village, then, with a gradual increase in population, comes the social and occupational differentiation that follows from the elaboration of arts and technique, and finally the development of law, which makes possible the formation of "the perfect community, we call the *civitas*."[69] Marsilius can rightly claim Aristotle as a source here, just as he claims Aristotle for his definition of the *civitas* as "a perfect community possessing every limit of self-sufficiency."[70] But, as usual, it is an Aristotle shaded toward Galen and the "new" equilibrium (and in this case, perhaps toward Cicero as well), which is to say, toward a more developed naturalism, a more fully realized relativity and structural dynamism, and a clearer vision of the potentialities of self-ordering within the systematic whole. It is, I posit, this shading and linkage with the new equilibrium that lends the arguments within the *Defensor pacis* their sometimes striking sense of "modernity."

To his description of the city as a natural product which makes possible the attainment of the "sufficiencies of life," Marsilius adds a crucial psychological component: human will and desire. This addition has the effect of moving his description of the working *civitas* beyond the merely biological. Will and desire are what motivate men to secure sufficiency and thus to form communities. But these very same forces lie at the root of social enmity and dispute. In this modeling of activity, I argue, we can clearly see the Galenic push and pull (once again, characteristic of the new model of equilibrium) that is built into the Marsilian system but that is absent from the earlier model of equalization that defined the Common Good for Albert and Thomas.

At this point Marsilius makes a very interesting move. Rather than persist in seeing will or desire in individualistic terms, he proposes that competing desires naturally organize themselves around competing

---

[68] *DP*, I.3.4.
[69] *Ibid.*, I.4.1. With the term *"perfecta communitas"* he is citing the Latin text of Aristotle, *Politics*, I.2.
[70] *Ibid.*: "omnem habens terminum per se sufficiencie," citing *Politics* I.1.

orders or functions within the *civitas*.[71] The crucial "part" of the *civitas* that concerns Marsilius and that most affects the whole of it, is thus not the individual citizen but the various orders and productive arts into which individuals group themselves, solely as a result of natural function and need.[72] Here again, we can clearly see the naturalistic model of the Galenic body, which is engaged in the continual balancing (*coaequalitas*) of the various organs, members and instrumental *parts* of the body, each to each and at the same time each to the whole, toward the production of good function.

Where in Albert's and Thomas' schema of the Common Good all parts are joined within a fixed hierarchical plan directed by a singular intelligence toward a singular determined end, in Marsilius' scheme the model is turned on its head. The functional parts of the Common Good that concern him have reference solely to natural human needs and activities, and it is the diversity of human need that directs the formation of the ordering structure of the *civitas*.[73] Once established, the well-governed *civitas* organizes and equalizes the relation of its ever-shifting functional parts through the imposition of law. Moreover, the city, as a living organism in the Galenic sense, must create its law, the principle and instrument of its equalization, from *within* itself. It cannot rely on order being imposed from above by an external governor or by a fixed and historically transcendent plan.

"Temperamentum" in the body of the *civitas*

In Aristotle's schema, the distinction between a rightly governed *civitas* and a perverted one is simple and clearly stated. Correct forms of government have constitutions ordered to the Common Good of the whole, whether they are ruled by the one (monarchy), the few (aristocracy), or the many (polity). Perverted governments are ordered toward the private good of a ruling part rather than the whole, whether the part is the individual ruler (tyranny), or the wealthy and powerful few (oligarchy), or the common people (democracy).[74] The term Aristotle uses to designate correctly ordered governments was properly rendered from the Greek as *rectae* or "right" in Moerbeke's Latin translation.[75] The term

---

[71] *Ibid.*, I.4.5.
[72] Cary Nederman has well labeled this aspect of Marsilius' thought "communal functionalism." On this, see Nederman, "Freedom, Community, and Function: Communitarian Lessons of Medieval Political Theory," *American Political Science Review* 86 (1992), 977–86.
[73] *DP*, I.4.3–5.   [74] Aristotle, *Politics*, III.7 [1279a17–22].
[75] Gewirth, *Defender of the Peace*, lxxxv.

that Marsilius chooses to designate these same correctly ordered forms, *bene temperatum* ("well tempered"), differs from that of both Aristotle and Moerbeke, as it once again bends the Aristotelian text in the direction of Galenic theoretical medicine.[76] The adjective "tempered" (*temperatus-a-um*) has a host of meanings: "appropriately proportioned," "appropriately mixed," "well balanced," "well functioning," and virtually all of them are linked to Galenic medical thought.[77] The Latin title given to Galen's major work on the proper balanced mixture of the primary qualities in the determination of health was sometimes *De temperamentis* and sometimes *De complexionibus*, indicating how closely identified the two terms were and how similar in tone and meaning.[78] As an adjective or verb, "to temper" or "tempered" contained within them the idea of *appropriate* or *good* balance: to temper a mixture was to equalize it, to balance it in order to maximize function.

Marsilius first introduces the term in reference to the individual's need to regulate his own actions and passions toward the end of "living well." When he does so, he explicitly links the ideal of good temperament to the notion of its being "well fitted" to its specific task (*bene id est in temperamento convenienti*).[79] Overall, the notion of "good fit" determined in terms of function (*ad opus*) is as important in Marsilius' scheme as it was in Galen's system and in that of his Latin commentators, such as Turisanus. It indicates that the balanced mixture is not a fixed proportion determined by an absolute standard (as it was in the writings of Albert and Thomas) but is instead fully relational and thus changeable, determined in relation to particular needs, conditions, and functions at particular times (as we have seen it described in the medical writings of Taddeo Alderotti, Arnau de Vilanova, and Turisanus).[80] To further underscore his determined translation of Galenic modes of analysis to political analysis, Marsilius recognizes that the maintenance of health in an organism (whether bodily or political) requires the maintenance of balance in two directions: the tempering of its ever-changing configuration of interior

---

[76] Gewirth notes that Moerbeke at times used the phrase "bene temperatae," to designate a *civitas* whose parts were "well mixed," but not in the decisive and categorical sense that Marsilius uses it here.

[77] Brett's footnote to Marsilius' first use of the term (*DP*, 24, n. 7) recognizes its roots in Galenic thought. Marsilius' choice of the term for the opposite "perverted" or "bad" forms of government, *vitiatum* (diseased), is similarly drawn from the medical lexicon.

[78] See Chapter 3 and 4 above.

[79] *DP*, I.5.3: "quod si debeat homo vivere et bene vivere, necesse est ut ipsius actiones fiant et bene fiant, nec solum actiones, verum etiam passiones, bene inquam, id est in temperamento convenienti."

[80] As Pietro d'Abano writes in *Conciliator* (1565), diff. 18, fol. 27d: "Et ipsa aequalis complexio non simpliciter, sed ad alterum, puta iustitia operationibus iustis relata."

elements and forces, and the tempering of influences coming from its ever-changing exterior environment. In essence, Marsilius envisions the political body having its own set of "non-natural" environmental factors impinging upon it.[81]

Up to this point I have followed the order of Marsilius' argument. From here on I want to focus on three particular instruments and processes of equalization that were of preeminent concern to the life of the *civitas* in Marsilius' scheme: (1) law and the "human legislator"; (2) election and common consent; (3) the principate. Perhaps because he truly intended his treatise to be taken as a blueprint for political action (as he announces at a number of points in his opening chapter), Marsilius is not content to treat law, election, and the principate as abstract political ideals. He is committed to exploring their logic and their working principles as instruments of social and political equalization. In his working out of these details we continue to see the influence of Galenic equalization, but we can discern a number of other contributing factors as well. Important among these were the insights Marsilius could draw from the rich contemporary discourse on political thought on such subjects as custom, consent, and community rights, whether written as commentary to Aristotle's *Politics* or as commentary to the political problems of the day. Of similar importance were the lessons Marsilius could draw from Roman and canon law writings on the status of self-governing corporate bodies and on the bounds (or lack thereof) on princely authority. Finally, there were lessons to be drawn from the deepening political conflicts and rapid changes in political environments, both north and south of the Alps, which greatly concerned Marsilius. Each of these factors has received attention in the burgeoning literature on Marsilius.

In addition to these I want to suggest another key influence, one that has not yet been recognized in the literature. Acting in concert with the Galenic model of equalization, there was a second model that had been taking shape within the scholastic culture of the northern universities, primarily at Paris and Oxford. I have already provided evidence for the shape and power of this "new" model in my earlier chapters on forms of equality and equilibrium in scholastic economic and medical thought.[82] In the previous chapter I pointed to its outline in the vision of the

---

[81] *DP*, I.5.4; I.5.6. Brett (*DP*, 25, n. 8) recognizes the similarities between Marsilius' list of exterior factors that must be tempered by the *civitas* and the Galenic "non-naturals" – those influences from the external environment that must be continually tempered (balanced) by the body for the maintenance of health. I discuss the Galenic concept of the "non-naturals" in Chapter 3, pp. 155–7.

[82] See also my article, "The (Re)Balance of Nature," and Kaye, *Economy and Nature in the Fourteenth Century*, chs. 5 and 7.

self-ordering and self-equalizing city in the manuscript of *La vie de Saint Denys* and Jean de Jandun's *De laudibus Parisius*. I want to argue that it is this new model of equilibrium, shared and shaped by the most creative thinkers writing at Oxford and Paris in Marsilius' day, that provides the key to how he molded together his intellectual influences with his social and political experiences into what he *felt* to be a working, "fitting" whole. Judging by the number of Marsilius' direct citations alone, Aristotle's *Ethics* and *Politics* would appear to be the primary sources informing this theoretical whole. But again and again, as we will see, positions Marsilius credits to these sources turn out to be positions he has taken a good way beyond them, particularly when they involve the subject of equalization.

The law as an instrument of civic equilibrium

In the view of Marsilius, law is the preeminent instrument of social and political equalization, the primary means of tempering the diversity of competing human functions, wills, and reasons within the *civitas*.[83] Law is the means "through which the excesses of such acts might be corrected and reduced to equality or due proportion (*et ad equalitatem aut proporcionem debitam reducantur*)."[84] As law is the instrument, so justice is its "tempered" product. When Marsilius speaks of the law he has a good deal more in mind than legislation and written law codes. In the pre-modern period, notions of custom, manners, ceremonial rules, and social conventions were often considered under the rubric of "law," and Marsilius' use of the term makes clear that this is his intent as well.[85] As such, the term "law" gives voice to the multiform and multicentered ways in which a community shapes and organizes itself through unwritten and anonymous activity as well as through written rules.

---

[83] *DP*, I.5.5.

[84] *Ibid.*, I.5.7. If this phrase has a familiar ring it may be because of its similarity to Aristotle's description (*Ethics*, V.3) of the role of the judge in restoring an equality that has been lost. Similar too is Aristotle's argument (*Ethics*, V.5) in which he describes the function of the instrument of money in reducing the naturally unequal values of goods to equality (via distributive justice) in economic exchange: *Roberti Grosseteste Lincolniensis, recensio recognita*, ed. R. A. Gauthier, in *Aristoteles Latinus*, vol. XXVI, 1–3, fasc. 4 (Leiden: Brill, 1973), 463 [1133a20–2]: "Propter quod omnia comparata oportet aliqualiter esse, quorum est commutacio; ad quod nummisma venit, et fit aliqualiter medium. Omnia enim mensurat, quare et superhabundanciam et defectum." On this, see Kaye, *Economy and Nature in the Fourteenth Century*, 45–6.

[85] For this broader definition of law applicable in Marsilius' day, see Constantin Fasolt, "Hermann Conring and the European History of Law," in *Politics and Reformations: Histories and Reformations*, ed. Christopher Ocker *et al.* (Leiden: Brill, 2007), 113–34, at 113–14.

It is, of course, a commonplace to associate law with justice and justice with balance, hence the ubiquitous use of the mechanical scale as law's iconographic representation. Aristotle, not surprisingly, centered his discussion of justice in *Ethics* V.3–5 around the search for equality and the forms of equalization that pertain to it. We have seen that Galen used both the word and the concept "justice" to define the forms of equalization that dominated his view of the working human body. The Latin translators of Galen then used the phrase "*aequalitas ad iustitiam*" to describe the particular species of proportional equality proper to bodily "complexion" (or *temperamentum*) – the physician's key to determining and restoring bodily health.[86] Moreover, both Turisanus and Pietro d'Abano drew an explicit connection between the medical ideal of "*aequalitas ad iustitiam*" and Aristotle's designation of *iustitia distributiva* as the proportional form of just equalization in the *civitas*. Just as the Galenic physician must constantly proportion his equalizing remedies to the rapidly changing circumstances of the body – circumstances often too particular and complex to find a place in medical textbooks – so Aristotle (and medieval legists) recognized that the judge must often go beyond the written law to do justice to the particularities of circumstance.[87] The links, then, between the theoretical underpinnings of maintaining (or restoring) balance in the body and establishing justice in the *civitas* were deep and abundantly recognized. It is not surprising, then, that both the Aristotelian and the Galenic sense of equalization were present and active in Marsilius' treatment of law and justice throughout the *Defensor pacis*. The mingling of these senses is quite apparent in his definition of law (above) as the instrument that reduces natural inequalities to "equality and proportion" toward the end of peace (which he has defined as civic health). And it is apparent, too, in Marsilius' statement that the art of medicine is "in some sense the governing art" of the arts of the *civitas*."[88]

Law and common consent in the best form(s) of government

As we have seen, when Marsilius comes to enunciate Aristotle's well-known and often-repeated distinction between the three "correct" forms of government (i.e., those that Aristotle defines as serving the Common

---

[86] Discussed in Chapters 3 and 4.
[87] See the discussion of *equitas* and *epieikeia* below in this chapter, where I discuss further the parallels Marsilius draws between the equalizing role of the judge and the equalizing task of the *medicus*.
[88] *DP*, I.5.6, ed. Previté-Orton, 17: "medicinalis practica, architectonica quodammodo ad plures [artes] predictarum."

Good: monarchy, aristocracy, and polity) and the three "corrupt" forms
(i.e., those that erode the Common Good: tyranny, oligarchy, and democracy), he shifts the terms from an Aristotelian to a Galenic register by
relabeling the good political forms "well-tempered" (*bene temperatum,
bene temperatae*), which is to say, proportionally balanced.[89] He then
uses the designation "well-tempered" consistently in the chapters that
follow when he refers to governments that promote tranquility by serving
the Common Good of the *civitas*. Marsilius' unmistakable shift in vocabulary perfectly suits his decision to equate the *civitas* with a living body
and political health with the Common Good. It serves, too, to bring into
still sharper focus his larger vision of the political whole and the constant
(and necessary) processes of equalization that enable it to function and
thus to promote tranquility. Galen, along with Aristotle, may even
be discernible in Marsilius' refusal to choose a "best" form among the
three tempered forms of government. Remedies, Galen insisted, are
relative rather than absolute and must be directed toward the condition
of the patient, the particular nature of the patient, and what the patient
can reasonably bear.[90] I hear echoes of both Aristotle and this central
therapeutic principle in Marsilius' words:

> perhaps a particular multitude, at some time or in some place, is not disposed
> to support the best form of principate, and therefore one should first attempt
> to lead it to the form of temperate principate that is the most suitable to it
> (*ad temperatorum sibi convenientiorem ipsam*).[91]

Of Aristotle's three "well-tempered" forms of government, the "polity" is
the one with the broadest base of rulership. Marsilius defines it as "a
tempered principate in which every citizen has some share in the principate or councillor function, in turn and according to his rank, means, and
condition."[92] Notice that for Marsilius, the term "principate" does not
imply rule by a prince but rather a legitimate form of political organization
that serves the common interest. Even a broad-based rulership can
constitute a principate. Similarly, even in a monarchy or aristocracy, the
notion of ruling *for* the common interest is inseparable from being ruled
by the common consent. While we may imagine medieval monarchy
as inimical to communal self-governing, Marsilius did not. He cannot

[89] *Ibid.*, I.8.3. Brett (*DP*, 41, n. 2) recognizes this shift away from an Aristotelian and toward
a medical vocabulary.
[90] Discussed in Chapter 3. In the following chapter, we will see that Nicole Oresme, when
describing the relativity proper to political judgments concerning the "best" form of
government, makes specific reference to Galen.
[91] *DP*, I.9.10, ed. Previté-Orton, 35.
[92] *Ibid.*, I.8.3: "Politia vero ... in quo civis quilibet participat aliqualiter principatu vel
consiliativo vicissim iuxta gradum et facultatem seu conditionem ipsius."

imagine a monarchy without it having been at some point actively "instituted" by the community.[93] Concerning every permutation of monarchy, he writes: "each shares more in the truly royal the more it is over willing subjects and in accordance with a law passed for the common advantage of those subjects."[94] And when he feels he must name the one mark which most clearly separates monarchies that are "tempered" from flawed principates, he declares that "it is the consent of subjects which in simple terms separates them – or at least more so."[95]

As important a role as the monarch might play as the head or executive of his *civitas*, Marsilius insists that his primary task is to serve the law and "to regulate the political or civil acts of men according to law."[96] Moreover, Marsilius viewed the law as a *common product of the community acting as a whole*, not the product of a single will or reason.[97] This is a critical point. From this it is clear that Marsilius' model of political equalization, even within the well-functioning monarchy, never devolves to the fixed and unidirectional hierarchy of earlier models, in which the ordering authority of the earthly king reflects the ordering authority of the king of heaven. In Marsilius' scheme, all forms of government are equally complex in their balancing of "bottom-up" with "top-down" principles; all forms assume that organized groups will develop around shared interests and functions at all layers of society; and all of these varied parts will actively participate in the balancing whole – as befits the model of the Galenic body and the "new" equilibrium.

The law for Marsilius is both thing and organism: he seeks both to define its essence and essential function within the *civitas* and to understand the logic of its growth and strength. In searching for definitions, he makes use of scripture, Aristotelian texts, and the tradition of written law itself, arriving at a dual conception: law as internal inclination and law as external stricture: "an ordinance concerning the just and beneficial and their opposites arrived at through political prudence, having coercive power."[98] Since law is something that every man experiences within himself, every man can and does participate in its formation. Since it is something that every man recognizes as necessary for the maintenance of social tranquility, every man willingly obeys its strictures. As he writes: "Included in this understanding of law are all those standards of things

---

[93] *Ibid.*, I.9.4.
[94] *Ibid.*, I.9.5: "consensu videlicet subditorum et lege ad ipsorum commune conferens instituta."
[95] *Ibid.* This is the dividing line between all "tempered" and "flawed" principates, but here it is attached specifically to the monarchical form.
[96] *Ibid.*, I.10.2.   [97] E.g., *ibid.*, I.11.3. Discussed further below.
[98] *Ibid.*, I.10.4. This is one of a number of definitions of law that he offers in this chapter.

just and advantageous in civil terms that have been instituted by human authority, such as customs, statutes, plebiscites, decretals, and all other things of this kind."[99] In short, the making of law within the *civitas* is an ongoing common enterprise, and Marsilius goes far to assert this. He counterposes the judge as an individual to the common law he serves: while judges can be corrupted by their personal affections and flaws, the law can never be because it has been made not with respect to person but "universally"(*universaliter*) with respect to the *civitas* as a totality.[100] While individuals are adept at discerning what serves their private needs, the law contains:

an almost complete definition of what is just and unjust, advantageous or harmful, in respect of any and every human civil act. But this cannot adequately come about through any single man, however resourceful.[101]

Rather, the law results from the accumulation of many co-articulated elements derived from varied sources over long periods; it is a supra-personal construct that forms itself, corrects itself, and perfects itself through communal deliberation and action over time.[102]

In support of this idea of law, Marsilius could cite a number of authorities: ancient authors of the Roman law, contemporary legists engaged in "growing" civil or Church law in his own day, and Aristotle's insights into the formation of the law, including his wonderful definition from the *Politics* that law is "intelligence without appetite."[103] But Marsilius goes beyond Aristotle in imagining how the functioning whole of the law is actually formed out of its disparate parts; how the law, the instrument of equalization par excellence, succeeds in balancing its own imperfect and imbalanced parts. His insights here are essentially grounded in questions of equilibrium, and Marsilius, both because of his personal sensitivity and the sensitivity of his Parisian intellectual culture to these questions, was in a position to see them and answer them with new sharpness and understanding. The phrase he chooses to describe the law – "a single eye composed of many eyes" (*oculus ex multis oculis*) – captures perfectly this new understanding:

what one man discovers or can know by himself, both in the science of what is just and beneficial in civil terms and in other sciences, is little or nothing. Going further, what men of one era observe is an imperfect thing in comparison with

---

[99] *Ibid.*, I.10.6.   [100] *Ibid.*, I.11.1.
[101] *Ibid.*, I.11.3. "Hoc autem nequit sic sufficienter fieri per unicum hominem quantum-cumque ingeniosum."
[102] *Ibid.*, I.11.3.
[103] *Politics*, III.16 [1287a32]. Marsilius, as Brett notes, also cites *Metaphysics*, II.1 [993b2–4] in relation to law as a common construct.

that which is observed as a result of many eras ... Therefore, the law is an eye composed of many eyes (*lex sit oculus ex multis oculis*), i.e., an understanding forged from the understanding of many, for the purpose of avoiding error with regard to civil judgments.[104]

Law, equilibrium, and the "human legislator"

This discussion leads Marsilius to one of his greatest contributions as a political theorist: his definition of the "efficient cause of human law," the "human legislator" (*legislator humanus*). Characteristically, he introduces his concept by citing the authority of Aristotle. And just as characteristically, it turns out that Aristotle's position can take him, at best, only part way on the path he travels.

Let us say, then, in accordance with both the truth and the counsel of Aristotle, Politics III chapter 6 that the "legislator," i.e., the primary and proper efficient cause of the law, is the people or the universal body of the citizens (*populum seu civium universitatem*) or else its prevailing part (*valentiorem partem*), when, by means of an election or will expressed in speech in a general assembly of the citizens, it commands or determines, subject to temporal penalty or punishment, that something should be done or omitted in respect of human civil acts.[105]

Marsilius' tone is one of unalloyed certainty. The analysis in terms of efficient cause follows the best "scientific" procedures of his time. Yet it is, I think, quite telling (and quite indicative of the power of the new model of equilibrium in this period) that the prime cause or "actor" here is not any individual but a collective body acting as a single whole. The source of law, the "human legislator," is the "collectivity of the citizens" working and deciding as one.[106] Alan Gewirth has argued that one essential difference between Thomas Aquinas' view of the community and Marsilius' is that Thomas visualized the common benefit as standing "over and above the private benefits of each individual, differing from the latter not only in number but in kind," while for Marsilius, "On the contrary, the common

---

[104] *DP*, I.11.3, ed. Previté-Orton, 44: "Cum igitur lex sit oculus ex multis oculis, id est comprehensio examinata ex multis comprehensoribus ad errorem evitandum circa civilia iudicia." I have slightly modified Brett's translation here.
[105] *Ibid.*, 49: "legislatorem seu causam legis effectivam primam et propriam esse populum seu civium universitatem aut eius valentiorem partem per suam electionem seu voluntatem in generali civium congregatione per sermonem expressam." In a footnote here (66, n. 3) Brett remarks that Aristotle does not actually discuss the efficient cause of law at this point in the *Politics*, nor does he arrive at a conclusion in any way as certain as Marsilius'. Rather, he raises the question of the benefits of having the multitude make the highest civic decisions through election.
[106] See the insightful analysis of the definition and role of the *legislator humanus* in Nederman, *Community and Consent*, 67–70.

benefit is *simply the sum* of these private benefits" (my emphasis).[107] This, I think, is a valid and valuable distinction, and it has the benefit of indicating the division between Thomas' model of equalization and Marsilius'. But I am not certain that "sum" does justice to Marsilius' sense of the dynamic joining of parts within the whole, whether considered in relation to the common benefit (*communis utilitas*) or to a concept such as the collectivity of the citizens (*universitas civium*). The idea of a sum does not convey Marsilius' care to show that the common whole is an active, self-regulating system (or organism) which must continually correct itself and equalize those individual parts that do not "fit" the plan as it is being arrived at by the whole. As the product of continual self-tempering, the formation of Marsilius' systematic whole necessarily involves the continual interaction and modification of parts as well as their simple addition.

At this point in his argument, Marsilius turns to explain the term "the prevailing part" (*valentior pars*), which he has just introduced as a critical component of the efficient cause of civic law:

I say "prevailing part" taking into consideration both the quantity and the quality of persons in the community (*considerata quantitate personarum et qualitate*) upon which the law is passed.[108]

In the first English translation of the *Defensor pacis*, Alan Gewirth translated "valentior pars" as "weightier part," and due in part to Gewirth's continued influence, this has more often than not become the accepted translation for this key Marsilian term.[109] Translated in this way, the term implies that those citizens who possess more of rank, ability, or position are the "weightier" citizens in qualitative terms, and therefore their influence on election and common consent would "weigh" or count for more than mere numbers would warrant. This interpretation might make sense from a modern perspective, but much less so from a Galenic point of view. Galen and Galenists specifically abandoned mere weight as the basis of equality (*aequalitas ad pondus*) in favor of a proportional equality determined relative to the proper end and operation of the whole (*aequalitas ad iustitiam*). The heart and the brain, for example, may be more important to the functioning of the body than any of the other organs, but that does

---

[107] Gewirth, *Medieval Political Philosophy*, 210.

[108] *DP*, I.12.3, ed. Previté-Orton, 49. I have made a minor adjustment to Brett's translation.

[109] See Gewirth, *Medieval Political Philosophy*, 181–93, where he explains his choice of "weightier" to translate "the complex variety of qualitative and quantitative features" in Marsilius' term "valentior." For a discussion of the term itself and its links to the more commonly found phrase "maior et sanior pars," see Quillet, *Philosophie politique*, 94–9.

not mean that they can go their own way or ignore the order and direction of the functioning whole.[110]

Gewirth recognized that adding the notion of "weight" to Marsilius' political equation through his choice of translation had a number of unintentional effects, some of them damaging. Most damaging of all was that it permitted the system to be read as less majoritarian, less the communal *product* of the *universitas civium*, and more open to the will of a powerful minority than Marsilius had intended.[111] In her recent translation of the *Defensor pacis* Annabel Brett avoids this problem with her decision to translate the term *valentior pars* as "prevailing part."[112] The notion of "prevailing" implies that the "*valentior pars*" may well be composed of the more honorable and educated, and it may possess more of the executive function of the *civitas*, but it must nevertheless support the prevailing decision or direction of the body as a whole.[113] As such, the term "prevailing part" echoes the Galenic turn of Marsilius' political community much more than does the term "weightier part." Self-ordering systems devise their own logic; the "prevailing part," even if qualitatively distinct, must conform to the logic of the whole.[114]

The human legislator, the efficient cause of law, is in essence the political community functioning as a systematic whole. In the case of legislation, once a law or set of laws has been passed, they are to be put before the assembled citizen body (*in universali civium congregatione*) for approval or rejection.[115] At that time any citizen can suggest additions, subtractions, or a complete repudiation, which would then be discussed and agreed upon by the whole.[116] Given the common process of the law's formulation and this open process of correction, Marsilius can castigate those elements of the population that, for whatever reason, find themselves "out of harmony with the common view," and he can specifically deny them the rationality that only the whole can embody.[117]

---

[110] Galen's vision is so fully relativized that all his qualitative judgments of parts are made in reference to their place and function within the whole. Aristotle's position is similar on this point in both his medical and non-medical writings (including the *Politics*). He consistently remarks that the good (or beauty) of the part is meaningless unless it be proportional to the whole, e.g., *Politics* [1281b10–15].

[111] Gewirth, *Medieval Political Philosophy*, 185–96; Gewirth, "Republicanism and Absolutism," 37–40.

[112] See Brett, *DP*, xxiii–xxiv for the reasoning behind her choice.

[113] For a contrasting interpretation of the phrase, see Quillet, *Philosophie politique*, 95–9.

[114] Gewirth (*Medieval Political Philosophy*, 189–90) recognized that this was Marsilius' intent, without recognizing its possible links to Galenic thought.

[115] *DP*, I.13.8.   [116] *Ibid*.

[117] *Ibid.*, I.12.5 (trans. Brett, 68): "things that are to the common advantage should not be impeded or neglected because of the irrational objection or opposition of these people."

The model of equalization underlying Marsilius' political imagination reveals itself in his view that laws derived in common and open congregation are fully rational even though they have been made without reference to the ordering mind or the governing Intelligence of God, in the sense that Albert or Thomas would have recognized and would have insisted upon. As I have argued earlier, this is a crucial component of the new model of equilibrium – perhaps its most crucial component and clearest marker – the component that most separates it from models of the past. The rational is determined from within the working system as a whole, not from any single part, and not in relation to an external ordering plan. Meaning and value are determined and defined relative to the functional needs of the whole. Even in a monarchy, the prince's first responsibility, Marsilius insists, is to serve the law of the community, to remain subservient to the law, and "to regulate the political or civil acts of men according to law."[118] The law is both the common *product* of the communal whole and at the same time the instrument employed by the community to maintain itself in equilibrium.

Election and common consent: the model of equilibrium in action

Aristotle's thoughts in the *Politics* on the subject of election, common judgment, and common participation in government are among his greatest contributions to political theory, remarkable for their clear sightedness and depth of insight. In Book III, ch. 10 he takes note of the fact that some people maintain the principle "that the multitude ought to be supreme rather than the few best." For Aristotle this position "though not free from difficulty seems to contain an element of truth." It raises for him a most difficult question that remains germane to this day: why should the many – inferior in education, knowledge, honor, and personal judgment – be capable of political judgments that are superior to those made by the few who possess these good qualities? His answer is tentative yet stunning in conception:

There is this to be said for the Many. Each of them by himself may not be of good quality; but when they all come together it is possible that they may surpass – collectively and as a body, although not individually – the quality of the few best ... In the same way, when there are many [who contribute to the process of

---

[118] *Ibid.*, I.10.2. And see also *ibid.*, I.12.5 (trans. Brett), 68: "The authority to pass or to institute laws belongs, therefore, solely to the universal body of the citizens or its prevailing part." Marsilius can legitimately cite words of Aristotle in support of his position that the king must remain "under the law."

deliberation], each can bring his share of goodness and moral prudence; and when all meet together the people may thus become something in the nature of a single person, who – as he has many feet, many hands, and many senses – may also have many qualities of character and intelligence.[119]

Aristotle makes no attempt to universalize this point or to prove it through logical deduction; indeed he immediately cites a number of situations in which it would be unlikely to hold. He supports it instead through analogy: the many, for example, are better judges of poetry and music than any one man, "for some appreciate one part, some another, and all together appreciate all."[120] As Aristotle continues to reason on this point, his doubts and hesitations remain on the surface. He seems to approve of Solon's decision to allow the many to elect to office, if not themselves to hold office, but his words in support of common election also indicate his qualms:

> When they all meet together, the people display a good enough gift of perception, and combined with the better class they are of service to the state (just as impure food [!], when it is mixed with pure, makes the whole concoction more nutritious than a small amount of the pure would be).[121]

In short, possibilities and doubts continue to alternate throughout Aristotle's exploration of the place of the many in the governing of the *civitas*.

Compare this to Marsilius. When he cites these words of Aristotle in support of common judgment and election, he neglects to indicate the uncertainties that accompanied them.[122] This cannot be due to the weaknesses of Moerbeke's Latin translation, since Nicole Oresme, using the same translation, fully recognizes Aristotle's hesitations here.[123] But rather than express any hesitation, Marsilius refers to the superiority of common assent and election as the "truth of Aristotle" (*secundum veritatem atque consilium Aristotelis*), which he fully accepts as his own

---

[119] *Politics* III.11 [1281a42–b3], trans. Barker, 123; *Aristotelis Politicorum Libri Octo cum Vetusta Translatione Guilelmi de Moerbeka*, ed. Franz Susemihl (Leipzig: Teubner, 1872), 191–2: "multos enim, quorum unusuisque est non studiosus vir, tamen contingit, cum convenerint, esse meliores illis, non ut singulum, sed ut simul omnes ... multis enim existentibus unumquemque partem habere virtutis et prudentiae, et fieri congregatorum quasi unum hominem."

[120] *Politics* III.11 [1281b9–10], trans. Barker, 123.

[121] *Ibid.* [1281b35–8], trans. Barker, 125; ed. Susemihl, 194: "sicut non purum alimentum cum puro totum facit utilius pauco."

[122] *DP*, I.12.3. In *ibid.*, I.13.4, on the same subject, he again asserts a certainty and comprehensiveness to Aristotle's position that does not appear in the original.

[123] E.g., *Maistre Nicole Oresme: Le livre de politiques d'Aristote*, ed. Albert Douglas Menut, *Transactions of the American Philosophical Society*, n.s. 60, pt. 6 (1970), 95a–97a, where at a number of points in his gloss Oresme concludes: "il dit *par aventure* et ne affirme pas ceste response." I discuss Oresme's position and its differences from that of Marsilius in the chapter that follows.

position, where Aristotle never could or did.[124] And Marsilius' position on the superiority of "common assent" assumes the direct participation in government of a far wider and far more diverse "public" than did Aristotle's.[125] To further underscore the certainty of his position, Marsilius frames it first in syllogistic terms and then in the mathematical terms of part and whole:

that to which the whole of that body tends, in both understanding and inclination, enjoys a more certain judgement of its truth and a more careful attention to its common utility (*communis utilitas*). For the greater number is more able than any one of its parts to notice a defect regarding a proposed law: since every whole – or at least every corporeal whole – is greater in mass and in strength than any part of it by itself (*omne totum corporeum maius sit mole atque virtute qualibet sui parte seorsum*).[126]

Here the truth of what has been or will be decided has no independent existence outside of the prevailing decision of the *universitas civium* via election.[127] The common decision on behalf of the Common Good is a relativistic decision, generated entirely from within the ever-changing conditions and permutations of the functioning whole acting as a whole.[128]

I have thus far spoken often of Galenic influences on Marsilius' model of equilibrium, but there is one large step in Marsilius' understanding of the potentialities of equalization, crucial to his vision of the Common Good, that follows a road not traveled by Galen. Marsilius insists on the one hand that every individual desires and pursues his own private benefit, which he defines as personal "sufficiency" or "the sufficient life." Indeed he refers to this desire as the "fundamental principle of everything we must demonstrate."[129] Yet, on the other hand, he insists that the will of all (or most) men is, and must be, directed toward the common benefit. This "double insistence" (as Gewirth phrases it) forms the basis of his argument that decisions made by the many who compose the *universitas civium* are necessarily superior to those made by the one or the few, no

---

[124] *DP*, I.12.3: "dicamus secundum veritatem atque consilium Aristotelis ... aut eius valentiorem partem per suam electionem seu voluntatem in generali civium congregatione per sermonem expressam."

[125] Nederman, *Community and Consent*, 64–6, citing in support *DP* I.13.4 and I.13.6.

[126] *DP*, I.12.5, ed. Previté-Orton, 51.

[127] For more on Marsilius' recognition of the relativity of law, see *DP*, I.14.4, where he again cites Aristotle yet moves beyond him in his position. On this, see also Gewirth, *Medieval Political Philosophy*, 214.

[128] *DP*, I.12.6. Moreover, the participation of the whole community through its consent guarantees an openness to the process of governing which, Marsilius asserts, encourages yet further respect for the law.

[129] *Ibid.*, I.4.2; II.8.9.

matter how distinguished the few may be.[130] The whole is not only superior to any of its parts (as Marsilius often states), the whole is capable of *transforming* its parts.

For Marsilius, in contrast to Aristotle, the individual is not driven to congregate in the *civitas* by his inner nature so much as by the lack or *imperfection* of his nature.[131] Alone or within the family unit he cannot supply the sufficiencies of life he desires and requires. He must remedy his imperfection and his essential "need" (*indigencia*), and he can do so only through association, communication, and exchange. In Marsilius' understanding, these activities are a product of self-interest, directed toward private bodily needs. Only secondarily are they moral and directed toward the benefit of the community.[132] Indeed, he recognizes that in their primary nature these self-interested parts can represent a great danger to the *civitas*.[133] In Marsilius' vision of the well-functioning political system, however, the very massing of competing private desires and functions within the aggregate whole creates a "tempered" product, the Common Good, when aided by the equalizing instrument of law and custom.[134] In effect, the multiplication of connections and associations within the systematic whole of the community *in itself* possesses the potential to transmute (temper/equalize/balance) the self-interested *nature* of its individual parts. In this vision, the *nature* of each individual part is likely *im*balanced in itself in the direction of self-interest, and yet, when massed together, and when counterposed within a system of law, these imbalances are transmuted into the systematic balance – the equilibrium – of the working totality; in political terms, the Common Good.

Marsilius does, at times, cite Cicero to the effect that it is natural for humans to congregate and thus to have concern for each other, and he employs a number of Aristotelian statements to support the proposition that mutual concern binds the *civitas*. But his complementary idea that

---

[130] Gewirth, *Medieval Political Philosophy*, 210–15, at 215. There have been many interpretations of Marsilius' intent here. Mario Grignaschi and others have seen in the collective will toward the common benefit a precursor of the social contract. Quillet (*Philosophie politique*, 79–80) disagrees, seeing the key to the formation of the "perfect community" in quantitative rather than qualitative terms, as the result of the aggregation and multiplication of citizens and the "differentiation of function" within the city that follows from it.

[131] This point is discussed in Nederman, "Ciceronian Tradition," 21–2.

[132] *DP*, I.4.3. On this point, see Francesco Gentile, "Marsilio e l'origine dell'ideologia," *Medioevo* 5 (1979), 293–301, at 294; Quillet, "L'aristotélisme de Marsile de Padoue," 84–7.

[133] On Marsilius' recognition of the potential dangers of self-interested actions, see Cary Nederman, "Community and Self-Interest: Marsiglio of Padua on Civil Life and Private Advantage," *Review of Politics* 65 (2003), 395–416, at 404–8; Quillet (*Philosophie politique*, 81) notes the constitutive role of the sheer multiplication of associations in the formation of the *congregatio perfecta*.

[134] *DP*, I.17.2 on the unifying whole.

individual natures can be reshaped and redefined within the workings of a naturalistic system is foreign to the core Aristotelian principle that individual natures perdure within the grand scheme of ordering Nature. It is certainly foreign to the way this principle was interpreted within the "old" model of equalization, associated with Albertus Magnus and Thomas Aquinas.[135] And while I often see Galen's shadow in the spaces separating Marsilius' understanding from Aristotle's, I do not see it here in Marsilius' conception of a systematic equilibrium capable of literally transforming individual natures within the workings of the whole.[136] In Galen's scheme, each part of the body is directed toward the good of the whole in its very nature. For this reason, if a part fails, the primary responsibility of the Galenic doctor is to aid Nature in its restorative activity. Marsilius' conception of transformative equilibrium is not, however, entirely original with him. By the time he wrote the *Defensor pacis*, the recognition of this potentiality was already emerging as a defining element in the new model of equilibrium being shaped and shared within university culture.

The earliest scholastic writings I have found containing the recognition that unbalanced parts can be balanced within the dynamic interchanges of the systematic whole date from the later thirteenth century and derive from the attempt by scholastic lawyers, theologians, and philosophers to comprehend the workings of monetized exchange. Speculation by Godfrey of Fontaines and Peter of John Olivi (discussed in Chapters 1 and 2 above) demonstrated an expanded awareness of the potentialities of exchange equilibrium, in which inequalities embedded in individual economic positions and decisions could nevertheless be equalized within the self-equalizing system of market exchange.[137] Students and scholars at the

---

[135] Quillet ("L'aristotélisme de Marsile," 86 ff.) examines the possible influence of Arabic texts (Al-Farabi, Averroes) to explain the differences between Aristotle and Marsilius on this point. For Albert, as discussed earlier, the good of each part is guided toward its proper end by the supreme Good. Each part is amenable to such guidance because its good end has been imbued in its nature by the same creating Good. Thomas literally cannot conceive of a *civitas* in which the committed pursuit of purely private advantage can lead to the Common Good. Indeed, he sees it as a recipe for political disaster. A statement of this position appears in *De regimine principum*, II, 3, the portion most likely authored by Thomas. See *On the Government of Rulers: De Regimine Principum*, trans. James Blythe (Philadelphia: University of Pennsylvania Press, 1997), 109–10. On the chasm between Thomas' view on this point and that of Marsilius, see Nederman, "Community and Self-Interest," 403–4.

[136] Each part of the Galenic body is directed toward the good of the whole in its very nature. For this reason, if a part fails, the primary responsibility of the Galenic doctor is to aid nature in its restorative activity.

[137] See Chapters 1 and 2 above for the following points concerning the effects of the model of equilibrium when applied to exchange in the *civitas*. We have also seen intimations of the market's capacity to transform exchange inequality into equality in Jean de Jandun's vision of commercial Paris.

universities of Paris or Oxford or Montpellier or Padua both observed and participated in this dynamic form of exchange equalization continually, whether as consumers or as administrators for their schools. In his *De laudibus Parisius*, the Parisian master and long-time friend of Marsilius, Jean de Jandun, could imagine the growth and prosperity of Paris somehow resting on the massing of its inhabitants' insatiable desire to gaze and possess; he could imagine dangerous, even poisonous, behaviors being turned to positive ends within and through the multiplication of cross-purposes that characterize the living city.[138] In a previous work I argued that the potentialities of transformative equilibrium, first recognized in scholastic speculations on economic equalization, were later projected onto nature, where they came to underlie the most adventurous and forward-looking speculations in scholastic natural philosophy.[139]

Marsilius was open to sharing in the Oxford/Paris model of equilibrium both through his immersion in the life of the city and his immersion in the intellectual life of the university at its center, as a master in the Faculty of Arts. But at the same time he was deeply influenced by the highly advanced Galenic model of equalization through his medical education at the University of Padua, an education that centered on training in the dynamics of bodily equalization. At the end of the first quarter of the fourteenth century, all of these influences intersected at Paris. In my view, the impressive and lasting power of Marsilius' political thought derives to a great extent from his linking together the rich assumptions concerning the potentialities of systematic equilibrium from each. By combining them he went further than any other medieval thinker toward embodying the full potentialities of the "new" equilibrium in his political thought. And by doing so he was able to invest his system with unparalleled explanatory power. And yet, after crafting this clear and careful presentation of the new potentialities of systematic equilibrium in the political sphere for more than half of Discourse I (through twelve of its nineteen chapters), suddenly this vision blurs, the focus changes (especially after ch. 15), and the new potentialities of balance that carried his thought appear to be challenged if not abandoned.

---

[138] Discussed in Chapter 5 above.

[139] Kaye, *Economy and Nature in the Fourteenth Century*, chs. 5–7, and see Chapter 8 below. This can be seen most clearly in the scientific thought of Jean Buridan and Nicole Oresme, who are also remarkable for the clarity of their recognition of the potentialities of transformative equilibrium in their economic speculations. For the importance of this insight to Oresme's political thought, see the following chapter.

The principate: the model challenged

It is not that reflections of the new model of equilibrium disappear entirely after ch. 13 of the *Defensor pacis*, with the introduction of the office of the prince or principate, or that positions established in the earlier chapters do not reappear, even at times with new emphasis, in the chapters that follow. But the continually reinforced logic of the early chapters is rather suddenly confronted by what seems to be a new logic, with its base no longer in communal authority but rather in the authority of the singular, and possibly the personal. In ch. 15 of Discourse I, Marsilius once again presents the *civitas* as a living body, "an animal whose parts are formed in accordance with nature,"[140] but now the analogy leads to lessons that point to the necessity for a "principal" or "leading" part with broad directing powers. It is this principal part that now acts as the "primary" cause of the *civitas*, rather than the mutual causal interdependence of parts. At the same time, where the first part of Discourse I explored the possibility of political communities taking shape around the satisfaction of their collective needs, the second part leans more heavily on the action of a particular inherent organizing "nature" that guides the community toward its proper ends.[141]

To speak first of the continuities: Marsilius continues to insist that all true principates, monarchies included, are elective, and that the power to "elect" belongs solely to the "legislator or universal body of the citizens" (*ad legislatorem seu civium universitatem*).[142] Similarly, in his words, "any correction of the principate or even its deposition (if that is necessary for the common advantage) likewise belongs to it [i.e., the universal body of the citizens]."[143] The law remains "universal in its causality,"[144] which implies that the principate, with all the instrumental and executive power Marsilius grants it, is still in some sense a co-power.[145] Marsilius continues to link the ideal of "tranquility" to the medical ideal of the "good disposition" of the component parts.[146] And finally, in his concluding summary of the "active or productive cause" of tranquility, he arrives at a crystalline description of the *civitas* as a self-regulating and self-equalizing body:

---

[140] *DP*, I.15.5.
[141] Gewirth, "Republicanism and Absolutism," 23 ff. recognizes the full force of this disjunction, but Quillet, *Philosophie politique*, 85–9, does not see a break in Marsilius' argument here. Contrasting positions on this point in the text form one of the primary dividing lines in the history of its interpretation.
[142] *Ibid.*, I.15.2.
[143] *Ibid.* I have altered the punctuation in this quotation. He makes a similar point concerning the correction of the prince, I.18.3.
[144] *Ibid.*, I.15.7.   [145] *Ibid.*, I.15.4.
[146] *Ibid.*, I.19.2, the concluding chapter of Discourse I.

These [its productive causes] are: the mutual interaction of the citizens (*conversatio mutua*) and the common exchange (*communicatio*) of their work, their mutual aid and help, and generally the power, unhindered from outside (*ab extrinseco non impedita*), to carry out both their own and the common tasks; and also their sharing in common conveniences and burdens in a measure appropriate to each (*secundum convenientem unicuique mensuram*).[147]

It is hard to imagine a clearer linking of the Marsilian political body to the new model of equilibrium, down to its recognition that the well-disposed *civitas* or realm orders itself from within itself, by means of the dynamic interchange of its functioning parts, without interference from outside.

While Marsilius succeeds, at times, in reconciling elements comprising the new model of equilibrium with the governing principle of "the principate," to my mind he also often fails. Where in the first part of Discourse I the "principate" stood for any governing principle of a well-ordered *civitas*, whatever its form, in the second part it appears more and more to be identified with an actual prince or ruling "part," which, in turn, comes more and more to resemble the princely powers of the reigning German Emperor.[148] Where in the first part of Discourse I Marsilius used the analogy between the *civitas* and the living body to emphasize the dynamic mutual tempering of parts within the whole, he now uses it, at times, to assert that there must be a "first" organic part, which has the primary role in causing, forming, and proportioning all the parts that follow from it.[149] Returning to his comparison of the *civitas* to the animate "body," he asserts a direct analogy between the principate as the necessary directing part of the *civitas* and the heart as the directing principal part of the body. In support of this point, he cites Aristotle's *Parts of Animals* and then, for the first time in the *Defensor pacis*, he cites by name a treatise of Galen's: *On the Construction of the Embryo*.[150] To my mind, however,

---

[147] *Ibid.*, ed. Previté-Orton, 100–1.

[148] In contrast to most contemporary monarchs, the German Emperor was elected to office, thus satisfying, in Marsilius' mind, the crucial requirement that "princes" be elected. The whole of the following chapter, Discourse I.16, is then devoted to demonstrating the superiority of elective over hereditary monarchies. There is considerable scholarly disagreement on whether or not there is a general break between the first and second parts of Discourse I in intent, argument, and tone. For two very different readings, see Gewirth, "Republicanism and Absolutism," who sees break here, and Quillet, *Philosophie politique*, 85–9, who does not. My reading tends closer to Gewirth's.

[149] *DP*, I.15.5.

[150] *Ibid.* Marsilius refers to this treatise by the rather idiosyncratic title, *De Zogonia*, but its more common title was *De foetuum formatione*. The treatise has been translated by Singer with the title *On the Construction of the Embryo*, in *Galen: Selected Works*, 177–201.

Marsilius' use of this particular work of Galen's in this particular context raises significant questions – questions that extend to the dominant governing role and identity he seems to have granted the ordering principate.

Questions and contradictions concerning the principate

It is true that Aristotle often argued for the heart as the principal member of the body – the source of the body's vivifying heat and the vital directing center of the body's order and function. Galen, however, questioned what he took to be Aristotle's over-assertion of the heart's primacy in the general case, articulating a tripartite system in which liver, brain, and heart, working together, shared in "leading" the body's processes. Moreover, he specifically questioned the heart's primacy in relation to the formation of the embryo.[151] Indeed, Galen's treatise *On the Construction of the Embryo* actually provides evidence *against* the argument that any single bodily part (whether the heart or any other organ) has causal primacy within the body analogous to what Marsilius appears to claim here for the principate.[152] On the basis of empirical evidence, Galen repeatedly argues *against* the claim that the heart is the first part of the body to appear in the embryo.[153] Moreover, he argues against what he sees as the oversimplified and unsupported position that all subsequent parts of the embryo are formed from the heart's action and at the heart's direction. And finally, he calls ignorant the claim that "the heart is in charge not only of

---

[151] In her translation and commentary on the *DP*, Quillet cites a number of passages from Pietro d'Abano's *Conciliator* that support the idea of the heart as the *"primum membrum"* and causative principal part. For this see *Marsile de Padoue: Le Défenseur de la paix*, trans. Jeannine Quillet (Paris: J. Vrin, 1968), 134 and n. 18. Pietro was, however, also part of a long and well-known tradition of Galenic commentary that recognized serious discrepancies between Aristotle and Galen specifically on the subject of the primacy of the heart in the embryo's formation. See, for example, Pietro d'Abano, *Conciliator* (1565), diff. 30, fol. 48a ff.; diff. 49, fol. 73a ff. Moreover, Pietro's position cannot be taken to represent Galen's on this question of the primacy of the heart. Indeed, Pietro was critical of Galen's position, siding, as was his habit, with Aristotle in this dispute. On this, see Michael McVaugh's "Introduction" to Galen, *Tractatus De intentione medicorum*, in *Arnaldi de Villanova Opera medica omnia*, vol. V.1, ed. Michael McVaugh (Barcelona: Seminarium Historiae Medicae Granatensis, 2000), esp. 148–54.

[152] See Brett's recognition (*DP*, 91, n. 4) of the disjunction between Galen's actual argument in this treatise and the argument that Marsilius uses to support it. The most careful analysis of this passage that I have seen to date has been offered by Aichele, "Heart and Soul," who finds much to puzzle about from the Aristotelian side of the equation but who in the end justifies Marsilius' use of Galen to support the analogy between the heart and the principate as leading parts.

[153] Galen, *Construction of the Embryo*, K, IV: 657, 658, 662, 667, 674, 677, 682, 683, 685, 686. The critique extends throughout this short treatise.

their formation but of their management, too."[154] Indeed, the model of development that he outlines in this work is one in which all the embryo's parts work together from the start, integrated in their complex interactions by the overarching "nature" (natura) or "soul" (anima) of the organism, through a process that he admits is beyond his knowing.[155]

For these reasons, I would argue that the model of bodily ordering that Galen presents in this treatise on the embryo differs significantly from the model that Marsilius was (apparently) deploying to support it. I would argue further that it points, instead, to a very different modeling of order than one based upon the assertion of the causal primacy of the principate. One could point, for example, to Galen's assertion that no part of the embryo can form without first the appearance of an undifferentiated "blood-like" nutritive medium (which itself has diffuse causal origins); or that after the appearance of this medium, the first structures to appear are myriad branching arteries and veins taking shape in multiple parts within it; or that after the primary organs of liver and heart finally make their appearance in the embryo (in that order), "the managing nature [within the body] is now at work in many parts simultaneously."[156] In short, this treatise supports a multicentered model of bodily ordering and proportioning on the model of the multicentered authority of the universitas civium Marsilius championed in the first part of Discourse I far more than it does a model based on the unitary ordering principle of the principate. What, then, did Marsilius intend when he cited this specific text of Galen's at this specific juncture? Was he signaling to knowledgeable readers that his arguments for the ordering primacy of the principate mixed together essentially immiscible models of order and equalization? I think it is possible that he was.

Beginning in ch. 15, Marsilius declares that the principate is not only the first among all other parts and causes, "it is more noble and more perfect (nobilior et perfectior) in its qualities and dispositions than the other parts of the animal."[157] It is the principate that has the authority to define and appoint to the offices of the civitas.[158] The principate rather than the living system as a whole now has the executive responsibility for ordering

---

[154] Ibid., K, IV: 677, trans. Singer, 189. For added and unmistakable emphasis, he concludes this treatise (at K, IV: 698, trans. Singer, 199) with yet another criticism of those who assert that the heart is the body's "first part" responsible for the construction of all subsequent parts.

[155] Ibid., K, IV: 696, trans. Singer, 198.

[156] Ibid., K, IV: 657–8, trans. Singer, 179; K, IV: 667, trans. Singer, 183–4.

[157] DP, I.15.5. "Haec siquidem pars, formata primum nobilior est et perfectior in suis qualitatibus et dispositionibus ceteris partibus animalis."

[158] Ibid., I.15.8; I.15.10.

and *equalizing* the functioning parts.[159] Although Marsilius has established that the law is derived from common consent and election, and
that the prince must serve the law, now the prince is given the primary
authority to "judge, command, and execute sentences," on behalf of the
law. It is now the prince ("whether he be one or many") who is responsible
for achieving the balance of justice (*equitas*).[160]

Without the prince the *civitas* cannot survive since it is through his
actions in enforcing the law that "everything will be brought back to
the appropriate equality or proportion (*ad convenientem aequalitatem aut
proportionum*)."[161] Ultimately, all parts of the *civitas* "are ordered for the
sake of and towards the prince as the first of them all."[162] In all these
statements, one thing is crystal clear: his description of the principate does
not conform to the "new" model of equilibrium. In its hierarchy of
nobility and perfection, its unitary principle of order and direction, and
its association of equalization with the conscious ordering decisions of the
prince, it is far closer to the earlier model of Albert and Thomas, and for
that matter to Aristotelian notions of order, teleology, and hierarchy, than
it is to Galenic equalization. But as I have already suggested, the lines
dividing the two logics of ordering are far from clear. At times, Marsilius
employs the term "principate" primarily to name the unifying principle
that allows the community to function as one, writing that it may be
composed of more than one man (aristocracy) or even many more

---

[159] *Ibid.*, I.15. 5: "Statuit enim in ea natura generans virtutem et instrumentum, per quae
partes animalis reliquae formantur ex convenienti materia, separantur, distinguuntur,
invicem ordinantur, in suis disposicionibus conservantur." Also *ibid.*, I.15.10. Marsilius
cites Aristotle as his authority for the biological logic that would require the principate to
"conserve" the equalizing order of the system, but Aristotle is not entirely consistent on
this point, and one presumes that Marsilius would have been aware of this.

[160] *Ibid.*, I.14.5; I.14.7. In support of this position, Marsilius cites Aristotle's notion of
epieikeia from the *Ethics*, which he identifies with the legal ideal of "*equitas*" (I.14.7).
On *epieikeia* and *equitas* as forms of equalization within the *civitas*, see Martin Stone,
"Aristotle's Doctrine of *Epieikeia* in 13th Century Ethics," *Documenti e studi sulla tradizione filosofica medievale* 27 (2006), 121–56. There are striking parallels here between
Marsilius' description of the judge's role and the role of the Galenic *medicus* who must
apply generalized theory to the infinite particularities of the individual body in his
attempt to return it to "*aequalitas ad iustitiam*."

[161] *DP*, I.15.11: "Cui vero illata fuerit iniuria curabitur emendam recipiendo, quo modo
reducentur omnia ad convenientem aequalitatem aut proportionum." See also *ibid.*,
I.15.6. Canning ("Power and Powerlessness," 213) assumes a necessary link between
Marsilius' biological naturalism and his arguments for the exercise of a singular regulating power by a ruling part. This link, however, does not hold within Galenic thought, nor,
despite Marsilius' citation of Aristotle as his primary authority for this opinion, does it
hold entirely for Aristotle, who contradicts this position at several points, e.g., *De motu
animalium* II.10 [730a30–3], a text that would likely have been familiar to Marsilius.

[162] *DP*, I.15.14: "quoniam propter principantem et ad ipsum tamquam omnium primum
ordinantur omnes pro statu praesentis saeculi."

(the polity) and still be considered a properly "tempered" principate.[163] At other times he directly correlates the unifying principate in the political realm with the unifying order of the Creator in the realm of all being. Even "the prince," whose authority and necessary leadership he supports, is hazy, sometimes described as if a singular person, at other times more as a unified office than a unified being.[164]

This confusion (which, I would argue, derives ultimately from his attempt to join together incompatible models of equalization) reaches its height in ch. 18, the penultimate chapter of Discourse I. Over a series of paragraphs, Marsilius first fully identifies the role of the prince in the *civitas* with the role of the heart, which (in Aristotelian terms) "regulates and measures, through its influence or action, the other parts of the animal in such a way that it is not itself regulated by them in any way and receives no influence from them either."[165] Here, the "*co-aequalitas*" that is the essence of the Galenic body, where every part of the body, even the principal parts, continually interact with each other in the production of systematic equality, is completely absent. In the very next paragraph, however, it returns. Marsilius has apparently recognized the dangerous implications of his metaphorical identification of the ordering prince and the ordering heart. If the prince, like the heart, is unregulated and beyond the influence of any part, by what means can he be checked or corrected should he violate the law or the public order, as princes have in the past? Marsilius' answer involves a return to the principle of the ordering *universitas civium*, a return to the active equalizing power of the "human legislator" that represents it, and, once again, a return to the principle of Galenic *co-aequalitas*.

For this reason, the prince is, in these [destructive] actions, rendered subject to measurement by something else that has the authority to measure or regulate him ... Now the judgement, command and execution of any arraignment of the prince for his demerit or transgression should take place through the legislator, or through a person or persons established for this purpose by the authority of the legislator.[166]

---

[163] E.g., *ibid.*, I.17.11 (trans. Brett, 120): "the numerical unity of a city or realm is ... a unity of order: not a unity simply speaking but a plurality of elements, called one or said to be one thing in number because they are spoken of in relation to something that is one in number, sc. the principate: towards which and for the sake of which they are ordered and governed." See also *ibid.*, I.17.2.

[164] Marsilius' position here may reflect contemporary thinking on the legal status and authority of corporations since, as Tierney notes ("Marsilius and Rights," 6), such thinking was marked by a "constant tension and interplay between the claims of individuals and those of the corporate whole."

[165] *DP*, I.18.2.

[166] *Ibid.*, I.18.3, ed. Previté-Orton, 97: "redditur principans mensurabilis ab aliquot habente auctoritatem mensurandi seu regulandi ipsum secundum legem."

It is clear that Marsilius hoped to join the multicentered principle of law and communal election to the unitary and hierarchical principle of the principate. Whether he recognized that this involved the yoking together of two quite different principles of ordering and equalization, and whether he foresaw the ongoing interpretive disagreements this yoking would give life to, Marsilius apparently decided that he needed the principate and its ordering principles to stand alongside the logic of the self-equalizing body.[167] There may well have been a strong practical element underlying this decision. In the religio/political environment of Marsilius' day, only the prince of all princes, the German Emperor Ludwig, had the where-withal to counter the Papacy's claims to fullness of power and coercive authority in the secular as well as the religious realm. Hence Marsilius' decision to dedicate the *Defensor pacis* to "you, most noble Ludwig, emperor of the Romans, as the minister of God who will give this work the ending it hopes for from outside."[168] Moreover, during Marsilius' lifetime, commune after commune of the *regnum Italicum* had collapsed as a result of internal strife and had devolved into the rule of a single man or family, including his own Padua, in large part because of their inability to "temper" the competing social forces within them. Even in their strong and prosperous days, most of the northern Italian communes had found it necessary to grant executive power to the office of "*podesta*," which functioned in many ways parallel to Marsilius' principate.

But if he bent to practical necessity in the authority he accords to the secular principate, he has also created a schism in his political theory. At the same time that he grants the secular prince responsibility for establishing equality and order in his realm, he continues to argue, in Discourse II, that the communal body of the Church can function, and

---

[167] One can see the coexistence of these two logics (the autonomous *civitas* and the supreme authority of the emperor) in the writings of the great Roman lawyer, Bartolus de Saxoferrato, Marsilius' near contemporary. On this, see Floriano Cesar, "Popular Autonomy and Imperial Power in Bartolus of Saxoferrato: An Intrinsic Connection," *Journal of the History of Ideas* 65 (2004), 369–81. For the editions of Bartolus' writings on which this work was based ("De tyranno," "De Guelphis et Gebellinis," and "De regimine civitatis"), see Diego Quaglioni, *Politica e diritto nel Trecento italiano* (Florence: Olschki, 1983). Condren ("Argument from Authority," 214) regards the logical and definitional inconsistencies within the *DP* as consistent with its polemical purpose: to undergird the critique of papal power using any and all arguments (even contradictory ones) that will serve. For a moderate restatement of this position that nevertheless credits the sophistication of Marsilius' theoretical program, see Gerson Moreno-Riaño, "Hierarchy, Ambiguity, and a *Via Media*," in *The World of Marsilius of Padua*, 249–69.

[168] *DP*, I.1.6. For evidence of Marsilius' involvement in Ghibelline politics in the decade before the writing of the *DP*, see Piaia, "Shadow of Antenor," 204–7; Quillet, *Philosophie politique*, 18–20.

indeed must function, without a religious leader who possesses anything like the authority he invests in the secular prince.[169] This is the essence of his case against the status quo of papal primacy and on behalf of an entirely different governing structure for the Church as a community of equals.[170] In the long Discourse II and the concluding Discourse III he relies heavily on a governing logic that is based upon communal ordering and equalization (through law and election) within the body of the Church – an equalization made actual both within "the community of the faithful" (*universitas fidelium*) and through the "common consent," and "general council" of the faithful. And yet, after hundreds of pages of arguments in this vein, at the conclusion of the *Defensor pacis* – in almost its concluding words – he declares that only the secular principate (i.e., Emperor Ludwig) can effect the drastic changes he has proposed in Church government, since only it (he) possesses the authority "to command the subject multitude," albeit with the consent of the subject multitude.[171]

Marsilius' ultimate reliance on the "outside" ordering principate to restore political "tranquility" can be taken as a sign of the limitations or weakness of the potential for systematic self-equalization that characterizes the new model of equilibrium. In the end, perhaps, Marsilius realized it could not take him as far as he wanted to go with his reforming plan. He appears to have believed that effective reform would only be accomplished through the coercive power of the Emperor. But I wonder which is more surprising. Is it that Marsilius bent his analysis to the political realities that faced him? Is it that he deferred to the only power that could possibly effect the solution to what he saw as the overriding problem of his day and the overriding threat to peace? Is it that he bestowed authority on the only power that could protect him or offer him exile should his bitter critique of the Papacy land him in danger? Or is it more surprising, and telling, given the actual power of the prince, whether embodied by Ludwig, or by the French king in Paris, or by the many new "princes" that had established their singular authority in the formerly self-governing communes of northern Italy – including, recently, his beloved Padua – that he could still maintain the right and power of the community as a living whole to temper and equalize *itself*, in the absence of rulers and princes, through the common instruments of custom, law, and election? Whatever the answer, it is the depth and detail of Marsilius' understanding of the potentialities of systematic self-ordering and self-equalization that has been my focus.

---

[169] E.g, *DP*, II.16, where Marsilius proves, by scripture, the equality of all the apostles in office and dignity (*de apostolorum equalitate in officio sive dignitate*), and *ibid.*, II.18, the argument against papal claims to primacy.

[170] E.g., *ibid.*, II,17.8–18; II.21.1–15.   [171] *Ibid.*, III.3.

The essential point, as I see it, is that the model of systematic equilibrium applied to the *civitas* that Marsilius imagines and outlines over the first half of *Discourse* I – a model of equilibrium that he locates at the center of his conception of the Common Good – was a model that had been literally unimaginable a half-century earlier. And with each stage in the remodeling of balance, the world and its workings are open to being reimagined anew.

7 The new model of equilibrium in medieval political thought, part 2: The writings of Nicole Oresme

> The state or kingdom, then, is like a human body and so Aristotle will have it in Book V of the *Politics*. As, therefore, the body is disordered when the humors flow too freely into one member of it (*quando humores excessive fluunt ad unum eius membrum*), so that that member is often thus inflamed and overgrown while the others are withered and shrunken, and the body's due proportions are destroyed and its life shortened; so also is a commonwealth or a kingdom when riches are unduly attracted (*attrahuntur ultra modum*) by one part of it [i.e., by the ruler].
>
> Nicole Oresme, *De moneta* (1356)

> No such debasement of the coinage is to be made except on behalf of the common utility (*pro utilitati communi*) on whose account money was invented and by which it is naturally ordered (*naturaliter ordinatur*).
>
> Nicole Oresme, *De moneta* (1356)

> In a well-ordered government those who are not inclined to virtue by their nature are assigned to perform work that is servile but necessary, such as cultivating the land or participating in business (*marcheander*) or working at a trade. And such men lack sufficient virtue because the lives they live are incompatible with it, and they are not as a result a true part of the city nor citizens in a well-ordered government. But the citizens are drawn from the three estates, that is to say, the men at arms, the men of council, and the men of the clergy.
>
> Nicole Oresme, *Le livre de politiques d'Aristote* (1374)

Nicole Oresme (*c.* 1320–82) was one of the great thinkers of his age, and it is with his writings that I conclude my chapters on the evolution of the model of equilibrium in political thought from the mid thirteenth through the mid fourteenth century. Placing Oresme at the conclusion of this process would normally imply (given the trajectory of my argument so far) that the form of equilibrium underlying his political thought and his conception of the Common Good represents the furthest stage of its development in the century-long process we have been following. Based on what I had previously read of his early political writing and of his exceptional contributions in the area of mathematics and natural philosophy, I had assumed and expected as much myself. But that is not what

345

I found. After a close reading of Oresme's last and most extensive political writings through the lens of balance, I now see him occupying a complicated and even contradictory place in the evolution of the "new" model in political thought. It appears to me that in his monumental translation and commentary to Aristotle's *Politics* (1372), written near the end of his life, he has decided to carefully and tightly close down the potentialities of communal self-ordering and self-equalizing that he had opened wide in his first great work in political economy, the *De moneta* (1356).

Up to this point I have organized my presentation around three questions: what changes occurred in the model of equilibrium underlying scholastic speculation between 1250 and 1350; what influences, both textual and historical, might lie behind these changes; and what were the effects of these changes on speculation in varying disciplines. There is a fourth question that I have not yet considered, although it is inherently linked to the first three. Given the social and intellectual ferment that generated the expansion of the potentialities of self-equalization at the root of the model's transformation between the 1280s and the 1350s, why did this expansion seemingly run out of steam and dissipate within scholastic discourse by the 1370s? Why did the circle of scholars at the University of Paris who reflected the last and furthest expansion of the "new" model in their speculations on economy and nature (what I loosely term "Buridan's Circle") all complete their long student years before the mid 1350s? What changes in the areas of urbanization and market development, occurring in the decades of the 1350s and 1360s, might have altered the direction of this formation? The cessation or even retreat of an evolutionary process is as significant and revealing as is its continuation and expansion. Given the known facts of Oresme's life and the history of the period in which Oresme lived, we can learn as much about the history of equilibrium from those elements in his later political thought that pulled back from the model's potentialities as we can from those elements in his early political thought that fulfilled and even expanded upon them.

Following first an analysis of Oresme's *De moneta* and then of his *Le livre de politiques*, I conclude this chapter with a sketch of the social and political environment that took shape over the decades separating these two texts. I will argue that the features of this shifting socioeconomic environment, and changes in the ways this environment was perceived by contemporaries, provide keys to understanding why his political positions and the potentialities he allowed to the Common Good diverge so sharply between these two works; or, put another way, why the models of equilibrium that undergird each of these works are so markedly different.

Background to the writing of the *De moneta*

We know relatively little about Oresme's early life. He was born in Normandy, *c.* 1320, to a family of slight means and status. In the 1330s he was enrolled as a student in the Arts Faculty of the University of Paris (likely as a scholarship student) at the prestigious College of Navarre, most probably incepting as a master of arts by 1341/2.[1] In 1348, university records list him as enrolled in the College of Navarre as one of the small number of graduates in arts accepted for doctoral study in theology at Paris. In 1356 he received his doctorate in theology and soon after was elected Grand Master of the College of Navarre, a position of great moral and administrative responsibility, which he held until 1362. Most of his epochal writings in mathematics and natural philosophy, as well as his first writings on ethical and political subjects, date from his time as a doctoral student and Grand Master at Navarre, with his most productive years coming between approximately 1350 and 1356.[2]

From early in his academic career Oresme gained and maintained very close ties to the French crown. It has long been suggested, although never proved, that Oresme had established an intimate connection with the young dauphin Charles (later to become King Charles V) in the early 1350s, whether as tutor or chaplain.[3] It is clear, however, that by the mid 1350s Oresme was a well-established member of the intellectual circle surrounding King Jean II, and he was almost certainly also serving as an advisor to the dauphin. Oresme continued in his role as counselor to the dauphin through the difficult years of Jean II's capture by the English and Charles' ascension to the throne (1356–64).[4] Following Charles' accession Oresme remained deeply and continually attached to him until the king's death in 1380, two years before his own.

The king repaid Oresme's long service and loyalty handsomely, supporting him as a patron and furthering his career within the Church. In 1363 Oresme was appointed as a canon in the King's Chapel

---

[1] William Courtenay, "The Early Career of Nicole Oresme," *Isis* 91 (2000), 542–8, at 543.

[2] For concise biographies of Oresme, see "Maistre Nicole Oresme: Le livre de politiques d'Aristote," ed. Albert Douglas Menut, *Transactions of the American Philosophical Society*, n.s. 60, pt. 6 (1970), 1–392, at 5–22; *Nicole Oresme: De proportionibus proportionum and Ad pauca respicientes*, ed. and trans. Edward Grant (Madison: University of Wisconsin Press, 1966), 3–10.

[3] *Politiques*, ed. Menut, 14, n. 11. Charles, born in 1338, would have been in his teens at this time.

[4] For speculation that in the mid 1350s Oresme may have given some support to Charles of Navarre, the enemy of the dauphin Charles, see John Bell Henneman, *Royal Taxation in Fourteenth-Century France: The Captivity and Ransom of John II, 1356–1370* (Philadelphia: American Philosophical Society, 1976), 22 and n. 74.

(the Sainte-Chapelle), where the two remained in close contact. Later Charles helped secure the important deanship of Rouen Cathedral for Oresme, which he held until he was appointed Bishop of Lisieux (Normandy) in 1377, again with the support of Charles.[5] In return, Oresme provided Charles with wise counsel and practical support over more than two decades of devoted service. Recognizing the long mutual dependence that existed between the wise king and his churchman, and the deep loyalty to the monarchy that this engendered in Oresme, is one key to understanding the tenor of his later political writings.

In the mid 1350s, when as a student at Paris Oresme had already established a close connection with the royal court, France was in near-continual crisis. The intermittent war with England, already two decades old, and marked by the disastrous defeat of the French army at Crécy in 1346, had destroyed royal finances. In the midst of the severe economic and political dislocation following Crécy came the catastrophic Black Death (1348–9), with repeated outbreaks of plague throughout Oresme's life. The disastrous demographic impact of the plague is well known, as are the agonizing personal responses of the survivors, which Oresme undoubtedly witnessed.[6] Along with its demographic effects, the plague exerted a powerful and continuing impact on the economy of Europe and on perceptions concerning the state of the social order. Sharp depopulation among rural laborers and high mortality among urban craft workers had destabilizing and long-term effects on prices and wages. These economic effects proved to be generally positive for manual workers, both craft and agricultural, while at the same time the aristocratic landlord class, who for the most part formed the circle of lay and clerical counselors that surrounded the French king, judged them to be highly detrimental, both to themselves and to the social order as a whole. Recent research has shown that the economic disruptions of the plague may have been less drastic than once thought (in both the French and the English case), but what is undeniable is the sharply fearful and defensive reactions on the part of the privileged classes

---

[5] For a study of Oresme's clerical career, see François Neveux, "Nicole Oresme et le clergé normand du XIVe siècle," in *Autour de Nicole Oresme: Actes du Colloque Oresme organisé à l'université de Paris XII*, ed. Jeannine Quillet (Paris: J. Vrin, 1990), 9–36.

[6] For a contemporary description of the impact of the Black Death on Paris, see Jean de Venette, *The Chronicle of Jean de Venette*, ed. Richard Newhall, trans. Jean Birdsall (New York: Columbia University Press, 1953), 48–51. See also Raymond Cazelles, "La stabilisation de la monnaie par la création du franc (décembre, 1360): blocage d'une société," *Traditio* 32 (1976), 293–311, at 294–6. For figures on the severe economic and demographic decline in France during Oresme's lifetime, see Harry Miskimin, "The Last Act of Charles V: The Background to the Revolts of 1382," *Speculum* 38 (1963), 433–42, esp. 434–6.

to these disruptions. The pervasive sense that the plague had turned the economic table upside down, in favor of the laboring classes and against the interests of society's "betters," elicited responses of fear and outrage lasting decades, accompanied by practical strategies to correct the social and economic "disorder" those of privilege perceived.[7]

As the costs of war and economic dislocation bankrupted the royal treasury, King Jean II, following in the footsteps of his royal predecessors, responded by adopting an economic policy of continual monetary debasement.[8] Although debasement had been employed as an instrument of royal economic policy from the early fourteenth century in France, between 1351 and 1360 the French coinage entered a stage of wild fluctuation, as coins were recalled and reminted, at times monthly.[9] Each time the royal mints issued a new coinage, the coins contained less and less gold or silver, and yet the value or "cours" of the coin, set by the king and his officials, was set ever higher than the precious metal content would warrant. This enabled the king to mint more coins from the same amount of precious metal (gained from recalling the previous coinage), while on each coin minted and reminted the king earned a percentage fee known as "monnayage."[10] The profits were considerable, and debasement was continually reemployed in this period of economic dislocation in large part because it proved to be so successful as a strategy for

---

[7] John Hatcher, "England in the Aftermath of the Black Death," *Past & Present* 144 (1994), 3–35, esp. 9–12. Hatcher notes, for example: "In direct contradiction to the statistical findings of historians, the chroniclers of the post-plague years wrote repeatedly and bitterly of the high cost of workmen, their arrogance, their over-indulgence in leisure and, of course, their contempt for the labour laws." See also W. M. Ormrod, "The Politics of Pestilence: Government in England after the Black Death," in *The Black Death in England*, ed. W. M. Ormrod and P. G. Lindley (Donington: Shaun Tyas, 2003), 147–81; Jim Bolton, "'The World Upside Down,' Plague as an Agent of Economic and Social Change," *ibid.*, 17–78; Mark Bailey, "Introduction," in *Town and Countryside in the Age of the Black Death: Essays in Honor of John Hatcher*, ed. Mark Bailey and Stephen Rigby (Turnhout: Brepols, 2012), xix–xxxv; James Davis, "Selling Food and Drink in the Aftermath of the Black Death," *ibid.*, 352–406, esp. 352–7; Robert Braid, "'Et non ultra': politiques royales du travail en Europe occidentale au XIVe siècle," *Bibliothèque de l'École des Chartes* 161 (2003), 437–91. The Black Death and its implications are discussed in more detail at the conclusion to this chapter.

[8] For a general discussion of the "scourge of debasement" in France, see Raymond Cazelles, "Quelques réflexions à propos des mutations de la monnaie royale française (1295–1360)," *Le moyen âge* 72 (1966), 83–103; Spufford, *Money and its Use*, 289–91; Henneman, *Royal Taxation*, esp. 7–9.

[9] For precise figures on the number and severity of the serial debasements, see Denis Menjot, "La politique monétaire de Nicolas Oresme," in *Nicolas Oresme: Tradition et innovation chez un intellectuel du XIVe siècle*, ed. P. Souffrin and A. P. Segonds (Paris: Les Belles Lettres, 1988), 179–93.

[10] Étienne Fournial, *Histoire monétaire de l'occident médiéval* (Paris: Fernand Nathan, 1970), esp. 115; Cazelles, "La stabilisation," 294 ff; Henneman, *Royal Taxation*, 7–8.

drawing wealth to the crown.[11] At the same time, however, it had strongly negative effects on the economy as a whole. It played havoc with all manner of contracts, record-keeping, and collections, whether of rents or debts.[12] The ever-weakening money had particularly negative consequences for the privileged class of rentiers and landlords who joined Oresme as counselors at court.[13]

The *De moneta* and the Common Good

In late 1355 or 1356, Oresme was asked for his thoughts on the subject of the monetary and fiscal crises crippling France. In response he wrote his first political work, the *De moneta*, which was, at the same time, the first treatise dedicated to the subject of monetary and minting policy in the history of Latin Christendom.[14] The work itself speaks to the openness of university culture in this period to the culture of the city, and specifically to its economic culture, since Oresme completed his first version of the treatise either while finishing his doctoral studies at Paris or as a newly incepted master in the Faculty of Theology.[15] His experiences of the dislocated finances of the realm, and his close observations of Parisian life and economy, find direct expression in the *De moneta*. But they are not unmediated. As a committed and self-professed Aristotelian, Oresme filtered his own observations of economic life through the lens of his deep reading of Aristotle. In every one of his writings throughout his career, including the *De moneta*, he demonstrated his comprehensive knowledge of the master's writings and principles. In the *De moneta*, Oresme drew primarily on Aristotle's discussion of trade and economic accumulation in Book I of the *Politics* as well as the brilliant analysis of money and economic exchange from Book V of the *Nicomachean Ethics*. While Oresme's debt to Aristotle in the *De moneta* is clear and often

---

[11] Cazelles, "Quelques réflexions," 83–103.
[12] Raymond Cazelles, *Société politique, noblesse et couronne sous Jean Le Bon et Charles V* (Geneva: Droz, 1982), 20.
[13] For the negative effects of debasement on landlords, see Cazelles, *Société politique*, 22; Cazelles, "La stabilisation," 294–300; Guy Bois, *The Crisis of Feudalism: Economy and Society in Eastern Normandy, c. 1300–1500* (Cambridge University Press, 1984), 219–20; Spufford, *Money and its Use*, 300. Note also Spufford's judgment on Oresme's critique of debasement (301): "On closer inspection Oresme turns out, therefore, not to be an idealistic, ivory-towered thinker, but a party man writing a tract for the times."
[14] The full title of this work is *Tractatus de origine et natura, iure et mutacionibus monetarum*. It has been edited with facing-page translation by Charles Johnson, in *The De moneta of Nicholas Oresme* (London: Nelson, 1956) (henceforth *De moneta*).
[15] I discuss the connections between university and marketplace in my *Economy and Nature in the Fourteenth Century*, ch. 1.

acknowledged,[16] there is one essential point on which he chose to depart sharply from the master. As much as any aspect of the text, this point reveals the presence of the new model of equilibrium in Oresme's perception and understanding of economic and political life.

Aristotle's words on money in the *Ethics* were (and still are) taken to imply that the value of money is rightfully decided, ordered, and imposed by the ruler who coins it and holds the right to impress his image upon it. Oresme expresses this opinion, but he does so only to refute it immediately, and, further, to base his entire thesis on its refutation.[17] In opposition, he argues that money is rightly the property of the *community as a whole*, and of the individuals who comprise the whole, not the private property of the king.[18] Only the community can decide the value of *its* money, and only the community can decide if, when, and for what purposes this value should be changed. There is, he argues further, only one legitimate reason for the community to change the value of its money: if its alteration will serve the Common Utility and Common Good of the community.

No such mixture [of base metal with gold or silver as occurs in debasement] is to be made except on behalf of the common utility (*pro utilitati communi*) on whose account money was invented and by which it is naturally ordered.[19]

The prevalence and centrality of this point throughout the *De moneta* renders Oresme's argument here one of the strongest cases made for the superiority of the Common Good over the private good of the ruler in the whole of the fourteenth century – the century in which this theme reached its height of expression. It is at the same time one of the strongest cases made for the new equilibrium in political life, which is to say, for the right and power of the community to order and equalize itself through the process of ordering and equalizing its own wealth.

But how does the community "order" its finances or decide on the value of its money? Oresme neither poses nor responds to this question explicitly. Everything he writes, however, points to the conclusion that under normal political circumstances, the community decides on the value of its money in the same way that it decides on the economic value of any good

---

[16] From the prologue (*De moneta*, 1): "quid secundum philosophiam Aristotilis principaliter michi videtur esse dicendum."

[17] *De moneta*, 10.

[18] *Ibid.*, 10–11: "Est igitur pecunia communitatis et singularum personarum."

[19] *Ibid.*, 8: "Rursum nulla talis mixtio facienda est, nisi dumtaxat pro utilitate communi, racione cuius moneta inventa est et ad quam naturaliter ordinatur" (my translation). This sentiment is repeated many times in different forms, but always with similar insistence, e.g., 36, 40.

or service. Just as he recognized that common need (*indigentia communis*) was the primary determinant of economic value, so he recognized that economic value is measured by a common aggregate price arrived at through free exchange in the marketplace.[20] His opinions on this matter mirror those of many scholastics of the late thirteenth and fourteenth century, including those held by Peter Olivi and by Oresme's great contemporary at the University of Paris, the arts master Jean Buridan.[21] The value of precious metals, just like the value of goods in the market-place, will, Oresme assumes, be determined by the price they are bought for in preparation for their minting.[22] When, for example, he considers the question of the proper ratio between gold and silver in a bimetallic currency, his answer rests on the notion of a common price. He assumes that the relative scarcity of the two metals will translate into a fairly stable relationship of proportional value:

gold of the same weight ought to excel silver by a definite proportion ... this proportion ought to follow the natural relation in value (*debet sequi naturalem habitudinem in preciositate*) of gold to silver, and a ratio should be fixed, not to be arbitrarily changed, nor justly varied except for a reasonable cause and an alter-ation arising from the material ... Thus, if it were notorious (*notabiliter*) that less gold was being found than before, it would have to be dearer as compared with silver, and would change in price and value.[23]

This is not a market in precious metals in the modern sense, where proportional values shift minute by minute. Oresme actually writes that "small" changes in availability should not be allowed to disturb the accepted value of the money or the proportion of gold to silver.[24] It is,

---

[20] He expresses this understanding in his gloss on Aristotle's discussion of money and exchange in *Ethics* V.5, with his statement that prices are determined "En compensant et considérant la necessité des choses *selon le commun cours* et la quantité de elles" (my emphasis). On this, see *Maistre Nicole Oresme: Le livre de éthiques d'Aristote*, ed. Albert Douglas Menut (New York: G. E. Stechert, 1940), 296. For the recognition of the economic principle that common need and common scarcity are the main determinants of price within scholastic thought of the fourteenth century, see my *Economy and Nature in the Fourteenth Century*, 116–32.

[21] John Buridan, *Quaestiones in decem libros ethicorum Aristotelis ad Nicomachum* (Oxford: H. Cripps, 1637), 431: "indigentia istius hominis vel illius non mensurat valorem com-mutabilium: sed indigentia communis eorum qui inter se commutare possunt." For the crystallization of this concept in Roman law and for Olivi's understanding on this point, see Chapter 2.

[22] Speaking of who should bear the cost for minting and how this cost should be determined, Oresme writes (*De moneta*, 11): "The most appropriate way of doing this is to distribute the expense [of minting] over the whole coinage by causing the material, such as gold, when it is bought to be coined or sold for coined money, to be bought for less money than it could be coined into."

[23] *Ibid.*, 15.

[24] *Ibid.*: "Si parum aut nichil mutatum sit in re, hoc eciam nullo modo potest licere principi."

however, a genuine market in the sense that the relative values of gold and silver are properly determined, proportioned, and at times corrected, on the basis of their scarcity. His is a complex and perhaps contradictory position. He recognizes that money (as precious metal) is valued in the same way that other goods are valued, and yet in order to properly perform its primary function as a measure of value, it should, he believes, remain as fixed and certain as possible.[25]

Even though Oresme consistently denies the king the right to debase the realm's coinage, enumerating all the social and economic ills that derive from such an action, in rare and restricted cases he recognizes that debasement might be a legitimate political act. In periods of monetary shortage brought on by political or military crisis, he allows the community, and *only* the community, to make the political decision to order and *revalue* the coinage for the benefit of the community alone.[26] He writes:

For in that case [crisis and shortage] it might raise the sum by an alteration of the coinage, nor would this be unnatural or like usury, because it would not be done by the prince but by the community to which the money belonged.[27]

He does not, however, go into any particulars on the political structures that would facilitate such a decision, except to assert that *if* the community does reach the conclusion to debase its coinage, it must do so free from the duress or influence of any private group or person, including that of the ruler.[28] And even should such a decision to manipulate the coinage arise, Oresme makes it clear that this can only be a temporary and rarely applied measure. He is deeply suspicious of any order imposed on economic life by a conscious orderer standing outside the system, even if that orderer be a well-intentioned king. In short, what we have in the *De moneta* is an expression of great faith in the self-ordering and equalizing capacities of the community, acting as an aggregate whole.

In saying this I need to reiterate that Oresme's ideal of "equality" differs considerably from the modern ideal. At one point he argues specifically against seeking "equality of possessions or power in all sections of the community," because it is unfitting (*non convenit nec consonant*) with the proper ordering of the *civitas*.[29] He encourages instead the institution of a "proportional and measured difference" (*ymo requiritur proporcionata*

---

[25] *Ibid.*, 13. He restates this position with great clarity in his later commentary on the *Ethics* of Aristotle, *Le livre de éthiques d'Aristote*, 297: "Les autres choses varient et muent leurs pris en divers temps ... [however] monnoie ne doit estre muee de son pris et de son cours fors tres peu souvent et en peu de cas pour le bien publique. Car c'est la mesure des choses de quoy l'en fait commutacion, et toute mesure doit estre certaine et durable. Et de ce ai je autre fois dit plus plainement en un *Traictié de Mutacions de Monnoies*."

[26] *De moneta*, 34–6, 39.   [27] *Ibid.*, 35.   [28] *Ibid.*, 40.   [29] *Ibid.*, 44.

inequalitas et commensurata) between the varied parts of the political whole (*omnes partes communitatis*).[30] In the musical metaphor he employs, too much sameness is as destructive as too much difference, since both destroy the "sweet melody of the kingdom's constitution."[31] The ideal of "proportional and measured difference" here is indistinguishable from what Galenists labeled "the proportionally balanced mixture" in their complexion theory. A well-proportioned mixture is what Oresme and all who shared in the "new" equilibrium in this period meant when they sought the ideal of "*aequalitas*." In its fluidity, its dynamism, its recognition that parts grow and shift and circulate continually within proportional bounds, Oresme's *aequalitas* is as different from that of Albert and Thomas as it is from our own.

Notably, however, Oresme argues in the *De moneta* that the greatest threat to this *aequalitas* comes not from the people who comprise the political body, but from the ruler whose "leading voice" is "overloud and out of tune" with that of the communal chorus.[32] Moreover, in Oresme's view, this danger does not merely result from the bad intentions of this or that particular prince; it is, rather, a *systematic* problem that can only be ameliorated through constant care and attention.

> But because the king's power commonly and easily tends to increase, the greatest care and constant watchfulness must be used, indeed extreme and supreme prudence is needed, to keep it from degenerating into tyranny, especially because of deceitful flatterers who have always, as Aristotle said, urged princes to be tyrants.[33]

Two attitudes here are of particular note and point to profound differences between the positions Oresme argues for in this work and those that appear in his later *Livre de politiques*: his general suspicion of the king's advisors, and his recognition that the responsibility for equalizing the working system of the political body cannot be left to the king or his counselors alone. Indeed, in the *De moneta*, the king and his counselors are regarded more as threats to the community's systematic *aequalitas* than as its guarantors. Responsibility for the maintenance of political *aequalitas* lies with the community as a whole: "For few things, as Aristotle says, should be left to the decision of a judge or a prince."[34]

---

[30] *Ibid.*   [31] *Ibid.*

[32] *Ibid.*: "Potissime vero ipse princeps, qui est in regno veluti tenor et vox principalis in cantu, si magnitudine excedat et a reliqua communitate discordat."

[33] *Ibid.*, 44–5: "Sed quoniam potestas regia communiter et leviter tendit in maius, ideo maxima cautela adhibenda est et pervigil custodia, ymo altissima et principalis prudencia requiritur ad eam preservandam, ne labatur ad tyrannidem, precipue propter adulatorum fallacias, qui semper principes ad tyranniam impulerunt, ut ait Aristotiles."

[34] *Ibid.*, 45: "Pauca enim, ut ait Aristotiles, sunt iudicis vel principis arbitrio reliquenda." Note the similarities here with the arguments in *Defensor pacis*, Discourse I.1–14, and its differences from the arguments in Discourse I.15–19.

Money and merchants as instruments of equalization in the *De moneta*

The *De moneta* opens with a précis of Aristotle's analysis of the origin of trade and money from Book I of the *Politics*. Oresme begins with the (Aristotelian) observation that economic inequality is a condition of human existence, and therefore so too is the resultant need to overcome or equalize inequalities through trade.[35] As Oresme tells the story, inequality existed at the time of the very first peopling of the earth by the sons of Adam. Some regions and groups possessed more than they needed of some commodities and little or none of others, while for another region and group the reverse was true. Men therefore began to trade by barter.

But as this exchange and transport of commodities gave rise to many inconveniences, men were subtle enough to devise the use of money to be the instrument for exchanging the natural riches (*instrumentum permutandi adinvicem naturales divicias*) which of themselves minister to human need.[36]

From these beginnings, coined money (*nummisma*) evolved into a tool of great service to the Common Good, one that was essential to the life of the civil community.[37]

Once Oresme has established the definition of money as the "instrument of exchange" (rather than a mere good in exchange) and as an "artificial invention" (rather than a natural product that can satisfy natural human needs), he expands on the implications of these definitions. Money, like all instruments, must be fit and "apt" for its purpose.[38] It must be easy to handle, light in weight, small in itself, yet capable of purchasing large quantities of natural riches.[39] The ancients discovered that the precious metals gold and silver were particularly suited to money's instrumental tasks: gold for interregional and large-scale trade, and the less valuable silver for purchasing smaller amounts and for "facilitating recompensation and equalization (*ad recompensaciones et equiparancias faciendas*)" between exchangers.[40] Another step in the evolution of money as instrument of equalization was taken when it was ordained that in order to counter doubt and suspicion it should be stamped with a design to indicate its quality and its "true weight."[41] Following Aristotle, Oresme maintains that not anyone can rightly do this; only the prince

---

[35] *De moneta*, 4, with reference to Aristotle, *Politics*, I.8–9.   [36] *Ibid.*.
[37] *Ibid.*, 5: "potest patere quod nummisma est valde utile bone communitati civili et rei publice usibus oportunum, ymo necessarium, ut probat Aristotiles quinto Ethicorum."
[38] *Ibid.*: "Et quoniam est instrumentum permutandi divicias naturales ... consequens fuit quod ad hoc tale instrumentum esset aptum."
[39] *Ibid.*   [40] *Ibid.*, 7.   [41] *Ibid.*, 9.

possesses this power. But after allowing this power to the prince, Oresme immediately qualifies it. Yes, the prince may stamp his personal image on the coin, but he does so solely as a service to the community in his office as "the most public person" (*persona magis publica*).[42] The weight and quality of the coinage can only be established:

by a public person (*persona publica*) or a group appointed by the community because money is, by its nature, devised and instituted for the Common Good (*instituta est et inventa pro bono communitatis*).[43]

Oresme then further deepens the connections between the Common Good, the community as actor, the instrument of money, and the "new" equilibrium, by defining money as a "balancing instrument" (*instrumentum equivalens*), one that is literally "owned" by the community as a whole, since its invention and proper use is directed toward the ordering and balancing of the community's natural wealth.[44] Once established, Oresme takes very seriously the notion of the whole community as owner, actor, and orderer of its wealth and its money. Since the community owns its money, it must incur the expense of its minting;[45] and if the community should decide that an alteration in the coinage would greatly benefit the Common Good, then it has the right to do so, recognizing the principle that such changes should be enacted only in cases of "evident necessity."[46] But woe to the private group or person – even the king! – who attempts to alter the weight or fineness of the coinage for his own private benefit. Oresme labels those who attempt to do this "criminals." It is highly significant that the crime he accuses them of committing is the sin of violating the *nature of the balance*.

For what is so criminal as to permit oppressors to sin against the very nature of the balance (*in ipsa trutine qualitate peccare*), so that the very symbol of justice is notoriously destroyed by fraud.[47]

Oresme extends the metaphor of balance yet further by suggesting the equation: the amount of profit the prince might draw from such a crime is precisely equal to the loss the community will suffer.[48]

---

[42] *Ibid.*, 10.   [43] *Ibid.*

[44] *Ibid.*: "Moneta siquidem est instrumentum equivalens permutandi divicias naturales ... Ipsa igitur est eorum possessio, quorum sunt huiusmodi divicie."

[45] Ibid., 11–12.   [46] *Ibid.*, 12; the discussion continues, 12–23.

[47] *Ibid.*, 20: "Quid enim tam nepharium, quam presumptoribus liceat eciam in ipsa trutine qualitate peccare, ut quod iusticie proprium datum, hoc per fraudes noscatur et corruptum." Here Oresme is quoting directly from the *Variae* of Cassiodorus. "*Trutina*" is a rather uncommon Latin word for the mechanical balance.

[48] *Ibid.*, 24: "quantum ibi princeps capit de lucro, tantum necesse est ipsam communitatem habere de dampno."

Oresme's condemnation (and the accompanying sense of criminality) directed at monetary mutation is repeated with similar heat for other economic sins against *aequalitas*. These include such practices as usury, money-changing, and even currency-trading, which was a fairly common, if generally condemned, banking practice in his day.[49] Indeed he seems deeply suspicious of banking itself.[50] In these condemnations and in his continual insistence that essential definitions (e.g., money as instrument, money as measure, money as balance) should set strict boundaries on its use, we can glimpse, even in this early work, Oresme's conservative side. I note this because his pioneering writing on money and minting, his insights into economic life, his recognition of the social benefits brought by merchants, his championing of the Common Good, his granting of certain unquestionable privileges and powers to the self-ordering community, and his willingness to condemn over-grasping kings and rulers in the harshest terms, even his own king, can lead to the underestimation of Oresme's conservative stances in the *De moneta*.

Oresme's warring impulses are evident in ch. 22 when he argues for the right of the community to make those changes in the coinage that he has categorically denied to the prince. In support, he claims that no other form of taxation is "more equal or proportional" (*magis equalis seu proporcionalis*) than debasement because those with more money, who can most afford to pay, will actually pay the most.[51] In this way, he writes, clerics and nobles who traditionally escape most royal taxation by privilege cannot escape the "taxation" of weakened money.[52] But immediately after outlining the potential social and political advantages of such leveling, he pulls back, offering even better reasons to be wary of monetary changes and of political changes in general.[53] Moreover, he says nothing at this point concerning the machinery of government that would permit the community to actually change the value of the coinage. At a later point in the treatise, he does, however, include a single phrase that could be taken to suggest a

---

[49] *Ibid.*, 27–30.

[50] *Ibid.*, 27, where among the three ways that money is used against its "natural purpose" (*in usu suo naturali*), he includes "custodiam vel mercanciam monetarum." He adds: "For there are certain vulgar crafts which defile the body, such as cleaning the sewers, and others which like this [i.e., banking], defile the soul." Oresme does, however, have highly positive things to say about merchants in the *De moneta* (33), which makes his near-complete failure to recognize their social contributions in his later commentary on the *Politics* all the more revealing of his deepening suspicion of bourgeois economic accumulation.

[51] *De moneta*, 36.   [52] *Ibid.*

[53] His general principle (following Aristotle) is that an ancient law should not be supplanted by a new one unless there is (12) "a notable difference in their excellence, because changes of this kind lessen the authority of the laws and the respect paid them."

legal or governmental form to structure such communal action. He writes that when the community has determined that an emergency of state requires the remedy of monetary debasement, "the community should be assembled, if there is the opportunity."[54] That is the end of it.

Perhaps he assumed that the existence of the political organ of the French Estates was sufficiently well known not to require comment, since they were active and powerful in this decade. But we can only guess at this.[55] In sharp contrast to the *Defensor pacis*, Oresme offers no mechanisms by which the community might act as a whole to remedy tyranny or to counter the economic predations of royal mismanagement. He openly prophesies that the king who sins against the nature of money (and hence against the Common Good) will not long survive; but it is, he implies, the impersonal workings of the political and economic *system* the king has disrupted that will bring his bad end, rather than any formal legal process. In making this point, he employs Aristotle's dictum, "Things contrary to nature most quickly decay." In other words, it is the action of the political community viewed as a self-regulating "natural" system rather than specific constitutional powers that will bring the tyrant – and his entire lineage – to a disastrous end.[56]

The self-equalizing body as metaphor in the *De moneta*

But if political mechanisms are lacking in the *De moneta*, metaphors are not. For Oresme, the dominant political metaphor is the human or animal body. While the use of the human body as metaphor for the body politic appears often in Greek, Latin, and earlier Christian writings, the projected shape and activity the body assumes in political writings of the fourteenth century, and the lessons that are drawn from it, can be as different from those of earlier centuries as the "new" equilibrium is different from older models of equalization.[57]

---

[54] *Ibid.*, 39: "ad hoc debet congregari communitas, si adsit facultas."

[55] He makes no mention whatsoever of the French Estates in his later extensive commentary on the *Politics* either, but in the case of the later work, his omission is surely intentional.

[56] *De moneta*, 42–8. The last two chapters of the *De moneta*, warning of the collapse awaiting tyrannous regimes is replete with passive verbs (e.g., "regnum perdicioni exponitur"), except when it is God who will punish directly. At one point (47), Oresme suggests that "the free hearts of Frenchmen" (*Francigenarum libera corda*) will likely not permit them willingly to become slaves to a tyrant, but again the details of how they might act in concert against the tyrant are missing.

[57] I made this point in my *Economy and Nature in the Fourteenth Century* with respect to the metaphors of the body employed by Oresme in the *De moneta*. I discuss the stark contrast between the metaphor of the segmented, hierarchical body and the immensely richer image of the body employed by Galen and scholastic Galenists in Chapter 4 above. For the

In the twelfth century, John of Salisbury illustrated the proper structure and workings of the political body through an image of the human body that is sometimes assumed to have prevailed throughout the medieval period.[58] In the fullest description John offers in his *Policraticus* (repeated with variations at many points), he writes:

> For a republic is, just as Plutarch declares, a sort of body ... The position of the head is occupied by the prince subject only to God and to those who act in His place on earth, inasmuch as in the human body the head is stimulated and ruled by the soul. The place of the heart is occupied by the senate ... The duties of the ears, eyes and mouth are claimed by the judges and governors of provinces. The hands coincide with officials and soldiers.

He then extends the metaphor by linking the causes of disease in the body to the causes of disease in the body politic:

> Treasurers and record keepers ... resemble the shape of the stomach and intestines; these, if they accumulate ... engender innumerable and incurable diseases so that their infection threatens to ruin the whole body. Furthermore, the feet coincide with the peasants perpetually bound to the soil.[59]

Authors writing in the tradition of John of Salisbury, both before and after the fourteenth century, often continued to use the image of the segmented hierarchical body to underscore their arguments for monarchy. Just as the human body requires a single ordering head to guide it, so the political body requires a single ruler (whether lay or religious) to organize and guide the less conscious lower parts into an ordered whole. After the Latin translation of Aristotle's *Politics* in the 1260s, Albert and Thomas found that they could fit the image of the segmented body crystallized by John of Salisbury to both hierarchical and monarchical purposes. They were encouraged in this by the many points in the *Politics* where Aristotle, too, draws a parallel between the functioning principles of the *civitas* and those of the human body, and where he links the science of politics

recognition of the new forms assumed by the political "body" of the fourteenth (and fifteenth) century, and in particular their touching on notions of equilibrium, see Cary Nederman, "Body Politics: The Diversification of Organic Metaphors in the Later Middle Ages," *Pensiero Politico Medievale* 2 (2004), 59–87; Cary Nederman, "The Living Body Politic: The Diversification of Organic Metaphors in Nicole Oresme and Christine de Pizan," in *Healing the Body Politic: The Political Thought of Christine de Pizan*, ed. Karen Green and Constant J. Mews (Turnhout: Brepols, 2005), 19–34.

[58] For a fine comparative study of metaphorical uses of the human body in political writings from the Latin era through the fourteenth century, see Tilman Struve, *Die Entwicklung der Organologischen Staatsauffassung im Mittelalter* (Stuttgart: Anton Hiersemann, 1978). With respect to John of Salisbury, see *ibid.*, 123–48.

[59] John of Salisbury, *Policraticus*, ed. and trans. Cary Nederman (Cambridge University Press, 1990), 66–7.

to the art of medicine.[60] At some points in his discussion, Aristotle's model of the body coincides more or less with John of Salisbury's in its segmentation and schematic hierarchy, but at other points it differs, sometimes considerably. One clear but rather minor difference is that Aristotle identified the heart, the source of vivifying heat, as the body's "leading" or "principal part," rather than the head. This in itself did not affect the overall lesson that both bodies were hierarchical in structure and function. At times Aristotle grants the heart full credit for directing the living functions of the body and for continually regulating its various parts. At other times, however, he envisions a less hierarchical and more de-centered model of the body's activity, which incorporates, in addition to a governing *telos* and "Nature," a greater sense of the body's potential for systematic self-organization through its maintenance of an "accustomed order."[61] This more organic and systematic modeling of the body is the one that Galen consistently adopted and then expanded upon in his many writings. It is, again, this primarily self-equalizing model that Marsilius of Padua worked from in Discourse I of the *Defensor pacis*, chs. 1–14, and then partially abandoned in chs. 15–19 when he made his case on behalf of the ordering authority of the principate.[62] But even at those points where Marsilius appears to accept the identification of the ruling principate with the ordering heart, his modeling of both the political body and the human body escapes, and indeed confounds, the simple segmented body conveyed by John of Salisbury in the *Policraticus*. So too does Oresme's modeling throughout the *De moneta*.[63]

The political body that Oresme gives shape to in the *De moneta* is capable of ordering itself, equalizing itself, and maintaining itself in dynamic balance through the mutual interaction of its varied parts. It does so not only in the absence of the controlling power of the prince, but, if necessary, in opposition to it. Oresme recognizes, however, that the communal body can maintain its internal equilibrium only so long as the

---

[60] For a discussion of Aristotle's use of bodily and medical metaphors in his *Politics*, see below in this chapter and Struve, *Organologischen Staatsauffassung*, 14–19. For Thomas' continuation of this linkage, *ibid.*, 149–64.

[61] Aristotle, *Movement of Animals [De motu animalium]*, X [703a30–7], trans. E. S. Forster (Cambridge, MA: Havard University Press, 1961), 475–7.

[62] See my previous discussion of this point in Chapter 6.

[63] An interesting mixture of bodily images occurs in *Politiques*, 209b, where Oresme first cites the *Policraticus* and states the applicability of John of Salisbury's model of the body politic (cited above) and then, in the same gloss, appends to it the Galenic model of the circulating humors in dynamic balance to capture the circulation of wealth within the commonwealth: "corps est mal disposé quant .i. des membres attrait a soy trop du nourrisssement et des humeurs; car par ce il est fait trop gran oultre proportion deue … Et tele policie est aussi comme .i. monstre et comme un corps malade."

ruler respects the fitting bounds of his authority, proportioned with respect to good function. In his image of the communal body in equilibrium, one can, I think, see a joining (or compounding) of the Aristotelian body, the Galenic body, and the Marsilian body. An illustration of this joining appears in Oresme's first statement of the argument (which occurs again at later points in the *De moneta*) that through the debasement of the coinage the king "draws" to himself the wealth and thus the "substance" properly belonging to the community.[64] The phrase Oresme employs, "to draw to itself" (*ad se trahere*), and the image of a systematic drawing or draining of substance, would be perfectly at home in a Galenic work to describe the faulty circulation of fluids or humors within the sick body. The second time Oresme uses the image of the king "drawing" the wealth from the community, he renders its bodily and medical implications crystal clear.

Among the many disadvantages arising from alteration of the coinage which affect the whole community is [that] ... the prince could draw to himself (*posset ad se trahere*) almost all the money of the community and unduly impoverish his subjects. And as some chronic sicknesses (*quedam egritudines cronice*) are more dangerous than others because they are less perceptible, so such an exaction is the more dangerous the less obvious it is.[65]

In employing this image, Oresme claims the authority of Aristotle. In Book V of the *Politics*, Aristotle lists "the disproportionate increase in any part of the state" as one of the prime causes of political instability and insurrection.[66] Aristotle then supports this point by suggesting a direct parallel between the causes of instability in the political body and the causes of debility in the animal body, directly equating, as was traditional, health and good function with the maintenance of proportional equality. Like the political body, the animal body, Aristotle writes, is composed of many members, and "every member ought to grow in proportion in order that symmetry be preserved."[67] Health is destroyed if one part grows beyond its proper size with respect to the other parts. And if the increase in the part is qualitative as well as quantitative,

---

[64] E.g., *De moneta* 22: "Rursum princeps per hunc modum potest ad se trahere populi substanciam indebite ... et multa alia inconveniencia sequerentur."

[65] *Ibid.*, 32.

[66] Aristotle, *Politics*, V.3 [1302b30–1]. The medical nature of this image is well preserved in Moerbeke's Latin translation used by Oresme, *Aristotelis Politicorum Libri Octo cum vetusta translatione Guilelmi de Moerbeka*, ed. Franz Susemihl (Leipzig: Teubner, 1872), 506: "Fiunt autem et propter excrescentiam quae praeter proportionem transmutationes politiarum."

[67] Aristotle, *Politics*, V.3 [1302b31–2, ed. Susemihl, 506: "Sicut enim corpus ex partibus componitur, et oportet augeri proportionaliter ut maneat commensuratio, si autem non, corrumpitur."

Aristotle concludes that there is even greater danger that the state will fail, just as any living body would fail under such circumstances.[68]

In Oresme's attempt to frighten the king who misuses the community's wealth (in effect to frighten *his* king, to whom this treatise is addressed) and to convince him that continued monetary mutations will bring his rule to a ruinous end, he takes this Aristotelian image of disproportionate growth and compounds it by adding a warning against the dangers of disequilibrious circulation that echoes Galen.[69] The result is powerful indeed:

The state or kingdom, then, is like a human body and so Aristotle will have it in Book V of the Politics. As, therefore, the body is disordered when the humors flow too freely into one member of it (*quando humores excessive fluunt ad unum eius membrum*), so that that member is often thus inflamed and overgrown while the others are withered and shrunken, and the body's due proportions are destroyed and its life shortened; so also is a commonwealth or a kingdom when riches are unduly attracted (*attrahuntur ultra modum*) by one part of it.[70]

The system of circulation (and equalization) that is thus out of balance produces yet more fearful images: the political body becomes "as it were a monster (*sicut unum monstrum*), like a man whose head is so large and heavy that the rest of his body is too weak to support it."[71] This is, of course, a body soon destined to die.[72] The only solution Oresme finds to such systematic imbalance is, "power regulated and limited by law and custom," which is to say, by a process of systematic ordering whose direction lies in and with the community as a whole.[73] In this his curative prescription parallels that offered by Marsilius of Padua. But note that where in Discourse I.15 of the *Defensor pacis*, Marsilius granted the prince

---

[68] *Ibid.*, 507: "sed et secundum quale crescat praeter proportionem, sic et civitas componitur ex partibus, quarum saepe latet aliqua excrescens, velut egenorum multitudo in demo-cratiis et politiis." Note that the example Aristotle gives of growing and dangerous qualitative disproportion is of the poor in a polity, where the example Oresme provides is the king himself.

[69] While Oresme does not explicitly mention Galen here or anywhere in the *De moneta*, references found in other of his works indicate that at some point in his intellectual career he became familiar with Galen's writings and their highly articulated modeling of system-atic self-equalization. In a single work (*De causis mirabilium*), Oresme refers to Galen's writings more than a half-dozen times and frequently to Avicenna's *Canon* as well. On this, see *Nicole Oresme and the Marvels of Nature: A Study of his* De causis mirabilium, ed. and trans. Bert Hansen (Toronto: Pontifical Institute of Mediaeval Studies, 1985). See below in this chapter for Oresme's explicit use of Galen and the image of the Galenic body in his later political writings.

[70] *De moneta*, 43. The notion of the four "humors" and their connection to proper bodily circulation and health derives from the Hippocratic/Galenic medical tradition and finds no place or mention in the writings of Aristotle.

[71] *Ibid.*, 44.   [72] *Ibid.*

[73] *Ibid.*, 45: "potencia legibus et consuetudinibus limitata vel regulata."

or principate the status of "principal part" (on the model of the heart within the body), with full authority to regulate, order, and proportion the lesser parts of the *civitas*, Oresme is concerned here precisely with the over-aggrandizement of the principal part in relation to the communal whole.[74] For Oresme, the principal part must itself be ordered to the communal whole by the communal whole.[75]

Equalization as a quasi-mechanical process in the *De moneta*

With the circulation of many authentic works of Galen and Galenic commentators by the mid fourteenth century, there were numerous medical/biological representations of the process of systematic equalization that were available to Oresme and other scholars of his day. But while these are clearly present in the *De moneta*, they appear to me to share place at some points in the text with representations whose equalizing form strikes me as being almost mechanical (quasi-mechanical). I do not think it accidental that Oresme applies this form to the activity of the realm's merchants. Rather than argue this point in the abstract, I offer some final images from the *De moneta* that seem to me to shade more to the mechanical than to the biological side of equilibrium, although the two ways of representing equilibrium reinforce each other at many points. In the metaphorical representations of imbalanced circulation so far discussed, it is liquid wealth or money as circulating coin that drains away from the whole as it is drawn to the ever-expanding ruling part. In two further images from the *De moneta*, Oresme has envisioned the economy so fully in terms of the "new" equilibrium, and he has allowed the economy such weight as a self-balancing system, that merchants and economic speculators – which is to say, living and calculating human subjects – are "drawn" along the arcs of the equalizing system alongside the coins they chase. Oresme writes:

Again, such alterations and debasements diminish the amount of gold and silver in the realm, since these metals, despite any embargo, are carried abroad, where they command a higher value. For men try to take their money to the places where they believe it to be worth most.[76]

---

[74] See the discussion on this point in Chapter 6.
[75] As noted in Chapter 6, this is one of the lessons I take from the opening chapters of the *Defensor pacis*.
[76] *De moneta*, 32: "Rursum aurum et argentum propter tales mutaciones et impeioraciones minorantur in regno, quia non obstante custodia deferuntur ad extra, ubi carius allocantur."

This insight is far from original to Oresme. Dozens of French royal *ordonnances* from the 1340s and 1350s recognize and condemn those "malicieux Changeurs & faux Marchands" who are exporting precious metals from the realm to take financial advantage of the weakening currency.[77] What is new here is Oresme's viewing of human economic activity as if it were a reflexive response to the imbalance of the realm's monetary system. Merchants and speculators are seen to be acting almost as animate balances in themselves, as they chase their advantage in response to economic openings and closings.[78] Implicit in such a statement is the understanding that the monetary economy of France does and *should* function as an equalizing system, just as the Galenic body does. But since the balance and health of the system has been lost, due to the king's policy of debasement, the equalization that *will* occur (that *must* occur by virtue of the iron logic of a quasi-mechanical system) will, necessarily, extend beyond the boundaries of the realm. In this scenario, equalization continues to occur through the exportation of coinage, but it does so to the detriment of the realm in which debasement takes place, and to the benefit both of external realms and of the merchant agents of equalization.

Oresme has no love for money-changers and speculators. At their worst they are sinners and criminals (he compares them to usurers), and at their best they are performing "vile" and "contemptible" business.[79] But he is not blaming them here. They are merely doing what they normally do and responding as they normally respond. They are moving elements within a larger system, and Oresme recognizes that it is the failure of the equalizing system as a whole that is the true problem.

If Oresme despises speculators, he has (at least in this early work) generally positive things to say about merchants, listing them, along with clerics, judges, soldiers, peasants, and artisans, among those "parts of the community occupied in affairs honorable or profitable to the whole republic."[80] They too, however, calculate in terms of profit and move inexorably in its direction, and so they too have been reduced in his thinking to quasi-automatic elements within the self-equalizing marketplace. He writes:

---

[77] E.g., *Ordonnances des roys de France de la troisième race*, vol. II, ed. E. de Laurière (Paris, 1729), 254 (1346), 286 (1347), 290 (1348); 309 (1349), 390 (1350), etc.

[78] This insight, which is clearly new with respect to its appearance in a scholastic work on economics, is one that had already found expression in the French royal *ordonnances* and was, apparently, already known to royal administrators. See, for example, *Ordonnances des roys de France de la troisième race*, vol. III, ed. D. Secousse (Paris, 1732), 655: "Et que l'on y prenoit et que l'on y donnoit les especes, non pour le prix qui avoit esté fixé par les Mandements, mais pour celuy qu'elles avoient réellement dans le commerce."

[79] *De moneta*, 27.

[80] *Ibid.*, 33: "occupate sunt in negociis honorabilibus aut utilibus toti rei publice."

Again, because of these [monetary] alterations, good merchandise or natural riches cease to be brought into the kingdom in which money is so changed, since merchants, other things being equal (*ceteribus paribus*), prefer to pass over to those places in which they receive sound and good money.[81]

The phrase *ceteris paribus* (all things being equal) attached to the activity of merchant subjects in the passage above is a phrase and framing device often used in Aristotelian natural philosophy to analyze activity in the natural or object world. Previously we saw that Oresme defined money as an "instrument of equalization "(*instrumentum equivalens*) or "balancing instrument," because of its central role in the grand equalizing system of exchange. Here we see that Oresme, by attaching the phrase *ceteribus paribus* to the activity of human agents in the economy, has, in effect, defined the merchant himself as an "*instrumentum equivalens*," reduced from subject to moving object along the arcs defined by the overarching system.

It is a striking image. But it is an image that is applicable as well to the carters and venders circulating ceaselessly on the Grand Pont, as pictured in the manuscript of *La vie de Saint Denys*. And it is an image equally applicable to the dazed and dazzled shoppers wandering from one pile of goods to another in the Paris of Jean de Jandun. In each case living individuals are represented as moving parts, ordered by a larger *something*, a larger systematic whole, much more comprehensive and powerful than they themselves. With his recognition of mercantile activity as pure action and reaction rather than as an aspect of conscious intent, Oresme's vision of systematic balance in the economic sphere also mirrors Marsilius of Padua's depiction of the naturalistic process of systematic equalization within the political sphere in the *Defensor pacis*; and it possesses strong parallels as well to Peter Olivi's analysis of merchant activity in the *Tractatus de emptionibus*. In my view, these images and positions all so resemble each other because they too, like the economic actors they present, were linked to and ordered by a larger *something* that they may never have recognized consciously; they themselves were "drawn" together through their common sensing of the potentialities of the new model of equilibrium.

Whether and to what extent a market economy existed in urban Europe between the mid thirteenth and mid fourteenth century is still an open question. Answers to it naturally vary with the definition of what constitutes a "true" market and the decision on where to draw boundaries of

---

[81] *Ibid.*: "Item propter istas mutaciones bona mercimonia seu divicie naturales de extraneis regnis cessant ad illud afferri, in quo moneta sic mutatur, quoniam mercatores *ceteris paribus* prediligunt ad ea loca transire, in quibus reperiunt monetam certam et bonam" (emphasis mine).

degree. But what cannot be denied is the existence of a vision of the economy as a vast equalizing system, capable of directing on a massive scale the motion of goods and beings caught up in it. I think it is justifiable to call this a vision of "market order" even if the phrase itself is anachronistic. Like many other aspects of the new equilibrium, its modeling attained particular definition and clarity over the first half of the fourteenth century. And then, at some point in the second half of the century, the "new" model faltered and failed, as other models emerged to take its place.

Equalization and the Common Good in Oresme's *Le livre de politiques d'Aristote*

In 1371, approximately fifteen years after writing the *De moneta* (and like the *De moneta*, at the request of his king, Charles V), Oresme began work on a grand project: to translate the entirety of Aristotle's *Politics* into French and to accompany the translation with a full and copious vernacular commentary. The resulting text, *Le livre de politiques d'Aristote* (hereafter, *Politiques*), completed by 1374, occupies more than 300 double-columned folios in each of the extant fourteenth-century manuscripts.[82] Oresme began his work on the *Politics* after carrying out a similarly ambitious and well-remunerated royal project of vernacular translation and commentary on Aristotle's *Nicomachean Ethics* (1370). After completing the *Politiques*, Oresme then produced two more works at his king's commission: a translation of the Pseudo-Aristotelian *Economics*, with commentary, and a final grand project of vernacular translation and commentary on Aristotle's *On the Heavens*. Beyond illustrating Oresme's brilliance as a thinker and commentator, these works are remarkable in many respects. They represent the first complete translations of any Aristotelian texts into any European vernacular. As such, each translation necessitated that Oresme coin hundreds of French words to convey the meanings of the Latin text, an impressive number of which are still in use today.[83] Their commission is evidence of the intellectual accomplishment and concern of Oresme's king,

---

[82] It occupies 375 double-columned quarto pages in its modern edition, *Maistre Nicole Oresme: Le livre de politiques d'Aristote*, ed. Menut. Oresme's vernacular translation is based on William Moerbeke's Latin translation (from the Greek) of the 1260s. For the English translation of the *Politics*, I use *The Politics of Aristotle*, ed. and trans. Ernest Barker (Oxford University Press, 1958); for the Moerbeke translation I use the Susemihl edition.

[83] Menut, "Introduction" to *Politiques*, 11. Menut's list of nearly one thousand words introduced into the French language by Oresme has been trimmed in half by Robert A. Taylor, "Les néologismes chez Nicole Oresme, traducteur du XIVe siècle," in *Actes du Xe Congrès International de Linguistique et Philologie Romanes*, vol. II, ed. Georges Straka (Paris: Librairie C. Klincksieck, 1965), 727–36.

Charles V ("Le sage"),[84] and they demonstrate the exalted place Oresme occupied in the esteem of his king after two decades of close and near-continual service.[85]

Like Albert, Thomas, and Marsilius before him, Oresme was profoundly influenced by his reading of Aristotle's *Politics*, and yet each drew different – sometimes very different – meanings and lessons from this protean text. All texts are open to multiple readings, but the range of readings the *Politics* received over the period 1250–1375, and the markedly different uses it was put to, also reflected the open-ended and at times seemingly contradictory lessons it conveyed. Rather than a unified treatise, the *Politics* as it has come down to us is a conflation of separate essays, probably written at different points in Aristotle's life, whose arrangement (whether by Aristotle or a later editor) is far from orderly.[86] William of Moerbeke's exceedingly literal and at times difficult to comprehend Latin translation, which remained the standard Latin version from the earliest commentaries of Albert and Thomas through those of Marsilius and Oresme (and into the fifteenth century), added further levels of obscurity and possibilities for debate. But uncertainty was not merely the result of textual history. Aristotle himself recognized that of all "sciences" the science of politics was particularly freighted by doubt and uncertainty.[87] To his great credit, he wrote the *Politics* in such a way as to convey rather than to obscure the difficulties in finding universally applicable judgments to cover the multitude of political particulars. Throughout the work he not only accepts and presents the immense variety of particular political states and solutions known to him, but he also adds to this a profound recognition of relativity in the political sphere. Constitutions, forms of authority, political structures, and even political ideals that prove effective and beneficial in one context (historical,

---

[84] In the *Songe du Vergier*, written in 1378, we find the following appreciation of King Charles at I, 132: "il lisoit ou faisoit lire chaque jour devant lui d'Ethiques, de Politiques ou d'Yconomiques ou d'autres moralite pour savoir qui appartient au government de tout Seigneur naturel." On the *Songe du Vergier* and its connections to the court of Charles V, see Jeannine Quillet, *La philosophie politique du Songe du Vergier (1378): Sources doctrinales* (Paris: J. Vrin, 1977). See also the somewhat later panegyric by Christine de Pizan (1404), *Le livre des fais et bonnes meurs du sage roy Charles V*, ed. Suzanne Solente (Paris: H. Champion, 1936). This work has been translated into English by Eric Hicks and Thérèse Moreau (Paris: Stock, 1997).

[85] In the document that records the commission of the translation of the *Ethics* and *Politics*, Charles refers to Oresme as his "dear friend": "Nous faisons translater a notre bien aimé le doyen de Rouen, maistre Nicole Oresme, deux livres lesquiex nous sont tres nécessaire."

[86] For a description of the problematic ordering of the text, see *The Politics of Aristotle*, trans. Barker, xxvii–xli.

[87] Oresme concludes the *De moneta* with the statement (44): "nam secundum Aristotilem, civilia negocia plerumque sunt dubia et incerta."

climatic, geographic, etc.) can fail badly when applied in another; and even the judgment of success and failure can change when applied from different perspectives.

It would be possible, then, for Marsilius and Oresme to cite the *Politics* in support of nearly every point they make, as they did, and yet, in the end, to differ profoundly in their political conclusions and assumptions. In my reading, when comparing Marsilius' civic vision outlined in Discourse I of the *Defensor pacis* (to I.14) and Oresme's *later* political vision, as outlined in his commentary on the *Politics*, profound disagreement was more often than not the case, despite certain surface similarities, which often derive from their shared use of the *Politics* as textual authority.[88] I find this disagreement not only in the particulars of their vision of the ideal (i.e., well-balanced or well-tempered) polity but, deeper still, in their sense of what constitutes the ideal itself of proper equality (*aequalitas, equitas*) and balance (*temperantia, justitia*) in political discourse – a question of great importance to both. Once again, their political assumptions about equality and equilibrium are revealed most clearly in the positions they take on the core questions we have been following: definitions of the Common Good; the proper role of the community of citizens in the function of government; the making of custom and the promulgation of law; and the community's potential for self-ordering and self-equalizing in the absence of an overarching orderer, whether in the form of an animate "head" or prince, or of an overarching ordering intelligence. As a result of applying the lens of balance to their writings, I have found not only profound differences between Oresme and Marsilius on these questions, but profound differences between Oresme's earlier positions on them in the *De moneta* and his later positions as voiced in his *Livre de politiques*.

Throughout Oresme's commentary on the *Politics*, I see evidence of a willful conservatism, a willful defense of the status quo as it applied to the monarchy of Charles V, and a determined resistance to the great potentialities of civic self-government opened up by Marsilius in Discourse I of the *Defensor pacis*.[89] There are exceptions to this characterization, and I will note some of them below, but overall I see a failure – what

---

[88] Cary Nederman, with whom I often find myself in agreement, presents a very different reading of the relationship between Oresme's later political writings and the insights embedded in the *Defensor pacis*. See, for example, his "A Heretic Hiding in Plain Sight. The Secret History of Marsiglio of Padua's *Defensor pacis* in the Thought of Nicole Oresme," in *Heresy in Transition: Transforming Ideas of Heresy in Medieval and Early Modern Europe*, ed. Ian Hunter, John Christian Laursen, and Cary Nederman (Aldershot: Ashgate, 2005), 71–88.

[89] In his attitudes toward Church government (as distinct from his attitudes toward French monarchical government), Oresme's championing of a moderate conciliarism did present a challenge to the status quo of Church practice. Even here, however, there are

I believe is an *intentional* failure on Oresme's part – to build on the rich sense of systematic self-ordering in the political and economic spheres that he explored with such insight in the *De moneta*. Most to the point, I see a conscious retreat on many fronts from the implications of the new model of equilibrium as applied to the political sphere. I specify here "as applied to the political sphere" because, as I will indicate in the concluding chapter of this work, while retreating from the possibilities of the new equilibrium in the political realm, Oresme continued to explore and even to expand upon them with brio and success in his writings on physics and natural philosophy.[90]

Any case for the core "conservatism" of the *Politiques* needs qualification. As noted in the previous section on Marsilius, the text of Aristotle's *Politics*, which Oresme follows closely, contains powerfully "progressive" elements in itself, especially when viewed in the context of the Latin Christian culture into which it was introduced in the second half of the thirteenth century. Aristotle's definition of man as a political animal,[91] his exaltation of citizenship and his encouragement of citizen participation in government,[92] his appreciation for diversity with respect to status and function within the *civitas*,[93] his assertion that all governments must function within and under the law,[94] his association of the political body and its viability with a complex vision of the human body and human health centered on the ideal of equality,[95] his identification of equality with proportionality,[96] and his assertion that the Common Good is of all goods the highest and "most divine,"[97] are among the most notable of these, and Oresme for the most part seconds them.

---

considerable differences between Oresme's moderate stance (which was well in line with what many others were thinking and writing in the decade of the 1370s) and Marsilius' uncompromising one. For more on Oresme's conciliarist positions, see below.

[90] In the chapter that follows this on the new model of equilibrium in scholastic natural philosophy, I use selections from Oresme's great vernacular commentary on Aristotle's *De caelo*, which he produced soon after completing his commentary on the *Politics*, to provide evidence for this claim. I suggest reasons for his retreat in the political sphere at the conclusion to this chapter.

[91] Oresme, *Politiques*, 48b.   [92] *Ibid.*, 115b, 134b–135a, 119b.

[93] *Ibid.*, 77a, 85a, 171b, 339b.

[94] *Ibid.*, 119b, 137a–138b, 145a, 158a, 243b. Note that Oresme shades this insistence by recognizing the limits of written law and the wide field in which no written law exists. In the multitude of cases not covered by existing laws, the king has the power to make law through his judgments made on behalf of "natural equity" and the good of the community. On this, see *ibid.*, 137a.

[95] *Ibid.*, 44a, 65a, 77a, 144b, 209b, 223a, 240b, 322a, 339b.

[96] *Ibid.*, 65a, 77a, 92a, 114a, 130b, 144b, 347b, 349b–358a. If anything, Oresme expands on this identification. Almost every time the Aristotelian text cites equality as an ideal, Oresme adds that by equality Aristotle intends proper proportionality.

[97] *Ibid.*, 45b, 78b, 109a, 114a, 127a–b, 208a.

There are other reforming elements in Aristotle's *Politics* that relate specifically to monarchies, and Oresme often seconds these as well. Among these: the king stands above everyone, but he must choose good men as his counselors, and having chosen them he must listen to their counsel;[98] the king should not appoint counselors based solely on their lineage but on their virtue;[99] the king sins (Oresme continues to maintain) if he draws the wealth of his people to himself through excessive exactions or through the mutation of the coinage.[100] These positions can be summed up in the statement, often repeated by Oresme, that the king's power is best when it is tempered and "moienne" – greater than that of any other in his realm, but not greater than all others together.[101] What Oresme never doubts or questions in the *Politiques*, however, is that monarchy is the best form of government. Where Aristotle at times expressed reservations about the monarchical form and placed it along-side aristocracy and popular polity as one of three "tempered" forms of government, Oresme holds monarchy far above the other two.[102] Monarchy is the only form he presents as capable of holding its "temper" and of maintaining its equilibrium or mean, and he consistently interprets the Aristotelian text as if it supported this reading.[103] Jeannine Quillet is well justified in characterizing the Oresme of the *Politiques* as "un idéologue d'une monarchie tempérée."[104]

One can go even further. Virtually every one of the hundreds of positions Oresme arrives at in glossing the *Politics* is favorable to his king and the status quo of the governance of his realm.[105] There is not a single mention of the English Parliament, or the Spanish Cortes, or the northern Italian communes, whether Florence, Milan, Venice, or the rest, nor even of the Assembly of the French Estates, either as examples of viable governmental forms other than the monarchical or, yet, as political elements that are potentially applicable to the tempering of monarchical form. The distance between Aristotle's inquiry in the *Politics*, which

---

[98] *Ibid.*, 329b–330a.   [99] *Ibid.*, 139b.

[100] *Ibid.*, 63b–64a (where he cites his *De moneta*), 208a, 209b, 247b–248a.

[101] *Ibid.*, 274b.

[102] For the most concentrated questioning of monarchical form, see Aristotle, *Politics*, III.10, V.10–11.

[103] For examples of this strained reading, see Oresme, *Politiques*, 240b, 149b, 152b–156b, 167a.

[104] Quillet, *Songe*, 187.

[105] In one or two cases Oresme recognizes that there may be governmental practices more ideal than those in place in France, as when he recognizes that, in the ideal case, election is a better way to select the best man as king than by succession. But even in these rare cases, he asserts that the practice in France, although perhaps not ideal, is still best when viewed in terms of the practical exigencies that France faces and that the science of politics must take into consideration. On this see Oresme, *Politiques*, 109a, 154a–156b.

was so open to and curious about the viability of different political forms, and Oresme's closed and airless discussion in the *Politiques*, could not be starker. Gone are Oresme's passionate calls for reform from the *De moneta*; gone are the warnings and threats to the royal house if it does not succeed in restraining itself; gone is the sense that the "community" must at times act on its own, whether to protect itself from its own king or to save the realm. Indeed, gone is the community itself as judge, actor, or orderer in any meaningful sense. All political action and judgment now centers on the prince and his counselors.

It is hard to imagine a historian more familiar with Oresme's writings and more impressed by Oresme's genius and creativity then Albert Douglas Menut. Menut either edited or shared in the editing (and translating) of each of Oresme's four monumental vernacular translations and commentaries: the *Ethics*, *Politics*, *Economics*, and *On the Heavens*. In the introduction to his edition of the *Politics* Menut makes the following judgment:

Admittedly, Oresme's contribution to the forward movement of political ideas suffers by comparison with that of such major figures as Marsilius and Ockham before him, or Nicholas of Cusa and Machiavelli after him. His contribution to medieval science was unquestionably of far greater importance than to behavioral wisdom.[106]

Although I would suggest that this statement does not fully take into account Oresme's contributions to political thought in the earlier *De moneta*, it seems apt when applied to the *Politics*.[107] This can be partially explained by the deference Oresme shows to the Aristotelian text. He is clearly determined to present the words and thoughts of Aristotle as clearly and directly as possible to his vernacular audience – an audience of laymen and French government servants with needs and competencies quite different from those of a university audience. Charles V had just such an audience of lay royal counselors in mind when he commissioned Oresme's translation. Still, given the copious gloss added by Oresme and his considerable digressions on diverse political topics, the mundane nature and overall lack of speculative adventurousness in the *Politics* commentary is notable, especially when compared to the

---

[106] Menut, "Introduction" to *Politiques*, 32.
[107] Susan Babbitt, the author of the most extensive treatment of Oresme's *Politiques*, expresses essential agreement with this judgment. See her *Oresme's Livre de Politiques and the France of Charles V* (Philadelphia: American Philosophical Society, 1985), at her preface (n.p.), and in her conclusion (147): "It is unlikely that a new Duhem will arise to champion Oresme the political writer, for in this field he was clearly neither an inspirer of later thinkers, as were the Constance conciliarists, nor a figure of originality, like Pierre Dubois."

intellectual animation of virtually all his other writings, including his other late vernacular commentaries. I would argue that the differences are similarly stark and revealing when the comparison is made between the *Politiques* and the dynamic vision of political equilibrium found earlier in the *De moneta* and in the *Defensor pacis* of Marsilius of Padua.

There is some disagreement on the distance between the *Politiques* and the *Defensor pacis*. Jeannine Quillet, whom we have already often cited for her work on the *Defensor pacis*, devoted a considerable portion of her book on the *Songe du Vergier* to a nuanced reading of Oresme's *Politiques*.[108] She recognizes a number of points on which Oresme disagreed with Marsilius, sometimes sharply. Oresme's frequent criticisms of mendicant poverty, his defense of "moderate" Church property, and his critique of the universalist claims of both Roman law and the Roman/German Empire, provide clear examples of such disagreement.[109] She recognizes too that Oresme was influenced in his reading of Aristotle by the earlier commentaries on the *Politics* by Albert and Thomas and by the particular situation he found himself in as a counselor for King Charles. Still, building on the incontrovertible evidence that Oresme was familiar with the *Defensor pacis*, she frequently notes and tries to show that important concepts in Oresme's commentary were "directly inspired" by it.[110] At several places in his commentary Oresme cites from it directly, records its general theme, and even makes note of the critical Marsilian concept of the "prevailing part" (*la plus vaillante partie*).[111] It is also clear that some of Oresme's contemporaries identified him with the Marsilian text. He was one of a small group of intellectuals accused of having prepared a French translation of the *Defensor pacis* (no longer extant), which, given Marsilius' excommunication and the papal condemnation of his writing, would have been a serious offense, especially if committed when Oresme occupied the

---

[108] Oresme figures at many points in Quillet's book on the *Songe du Vergier*, since he had frequently been credited with authoring it. After providing evidence to question this assertion, Quillet devotes a separate chapter (*Songe*, 123–38) to analyzing Oresme's political thought.

[109] For select examples of Oresmian positions contra mendicancy, see *Politiques*, 83a–84b, 307a–308b; in favor of the maintenance of Church property free from secular exactions, 144b, 311a–313b; against the claims of Roman law to precedence over all laws, 242b–244a; and against the presumptions of claims for the Empire, 289b–294b.

[110] Quillet, *Songe*, 127. Quillet draws parallels between the two texts in *Songe*, 125, 126, 128, 129, 132, 137. Cary Nederman's reading of the relationship between Oresme's *Politiques* and Marsilius' *Defensor pacis* parallels Quillet's on a number of points.

[111] Oresme, *Politiques*, 137a: "En un livre intitulé *Defensor pacis* ceste raison est alleguee a monstrer que lay humaines positives doivent estre faictes, promulguees, corrigees ou muees de l'auctorité et consentement de toute la communité ou de la plus vaillante partie." On this see Menut, "Introduction" to *Politiques*, 5–9; Quillet, *Songe*, 124; Nederman, "A Heretic Hiding in Plain Sight," *passim*.

office of dean of Rouen Cathedral. After a period of living under suspicion, Oresme denied the charge before an inquest of his fellow doctors of theology at the University of Paris (1375), and the affair ended there.[112]

Given the distinctions that Alan Gewirth and others have observed between the Marsilius of the composite *universitas civium* (Discourse I.1–14), and the Marsilius of the unitary *principate* (Discourse I.15–I.19), it makes quite a difference which aspects of Marsilius' thought one attempts to link to Oresme's positions in the *Politiques*. Quillet, who disagrees with Gewirth and who finds no appreciable disparity in Marsilius' positions over the course of the *Defensor pacis*, understands the differences between the two thinkers primarily as the difference between Marsilius as "théoricien de l'Empire," and Oresme as "théoricien du pouvoir royal."[113] While I find Quillet's linking of the Oresme in the *Politiques* to the Marsilius of the triumphant *principate* to be generally well founded, I find her attempt to join Oresme to such stimulating Marsilian notions as the *universitas civium* and the composite *human legislator* far less convincing or likely.[114] In short, I would argue that the linkage fails precisely at those points where the dynamism of the new model of equilibrium is most clearly present in the Marsilian text. It is, I believe, Oresme's failures at these points, his abandonment of the potentialities of the self-organizing and self-equalizing political community, that leave so many close readers of the *Politiques* with the sense of its relative conceptual dullness and conservatism.[115]

In relation to Oresme's treatment of balance/*aequalitas* in the *Politiques*, three questions present themselves at the outset: how does Oresme conceptualize the Common Good?; whom does he admit into (and exclude from) citizenship in the political community?; and what role in governance does he envision for the community as a whole? As we have seen, the idea and ideal of the Common Good dominated the *De moneta* of 1356. There it moves beyond the realm of intellectual abstraction to become a force and power in itself. It *drives* the argument of the whole. In Oresme's hands it is wielded like a club, ready to knock back anyone, including the king, whose private interests violate the public interests of the community as a whole. When we move from the *De moneta* to the *Politiques* (1374), the Common Good appears in a shrunken and weakened state. It continues to be referenced, and it continues to possess

---

[112] On this affair, see Menut, "Introduction" to *Politiques*, 5–9. I am led to wonder whether some of the deep divisions I see between Oresme's positions and Marsilius' more innovative and bold assertions do not owe something to his desire to actively separate himself from Marsilian insights in order to escape the taint of complicity.
[113] Quillet, *Songe*, 129.   [114] *Ibid.*, 126.
[115] Even Quillet accords with this judgment, *ibid.*, 167.

meaning, but it has been reduced from a dynamic force to a passive standard against which political actions are judged – the line that divides good government from bad.

This, indeed, corresponds to one of its meanings and uses within the Aristotelian text. Susan Babbit, who has dedicated an entire chapter in her study of the *Politiques* to an analysis of Oresme's conception of the Common Good, details the many places in which Oresme follows Aristotle in this axiomatic application,[116] noting as well a few places in which he modestly extends the concept.[117] But given the immense expansion of this concept over the course of the fourteenth century, and the expansion as well of the transformative powers associated with it,[118] Babbit's overall judgment that "Oresme showed himself an excellent pupil of Aristotle in the matter of the common good" is telling.[119] Even more telling is her apt conclusion: "The citizens, or rather subjects, in the *Livre de politiques* seem to be involved only passively in the common good. Promoting the benefit of the whole is a matter for the [king's] government."[120] In the *Politiques*, it is the king and his officers who get to define the Common Good, and they who get to decide what is good for the community.

Since, Oresme argues, the Common Good is the mark of good government, those who govern must hold and care for the public good before their own personal good. He labels those who can accept this responsibility of government (an acceptance which involves a renunciation of their private concerns), "public persons" (*personnes publiques*).[121] In this sense, not only the king's servants and counselors, but the king himself, are and must recognize themselves to be public rather than private persons.[122] Here we can see an opening for the Common Good – and the associated notion of the "public" – to possess an active power, capable of superseding the power of personal rule. Once again, however, Oresme adds a series of definitions that have the effect of closing down the potentialities he seemed to have opened. Only the very few, he argues, are capable of attaining the exalted status of "public" persons. The majority of men,

---

[116] Babbit's comments are found throughout ch. 4 of *Oresme's Livre*, "The Public State and the Common Good," 69–97.

[117] *Ibid.*, 93–4: "Thus for Oresme public utility justified abandoning some of the 'great caution' which Aristotle considered necessary in the changing of laws."

[118] E.g., the great weight and power it assumes in the writings of Peter Olivi (chs. 1 and 2) and in the *Defensor pacis* itself (ch. 6).

[119] Babbit, *Oresme's Livre*, 94.   [120] *Ibid.*, 97.

[121] Oresme, *Politiques*, 78b: "Item, verité est que les princes et les personnes publiques doivent plus curer du bien commun que du leur propre, car il sunt a ce ordenés et deputés."

[122] Babbit, *Oresme's Livre*, 84.

on the contrary, have care primarily for their own private good and sustenance and are thus incapable of the renunciation associated, by definition, with "public" status.[123]

Having asserted the intractable self-interestedness of the great majority, Oresme notably refrains from criticizing them on these grounds or from seeking to impose on them an ideal that he thinks they are unlikely to uphold. Rather, he recognizes that the great majority who pursue their private interests can, at the same time, also serve the Common Good, if only *indirectly*. These "private persons" (*personnes privées*), by nourishing their children, by feeding their animals, and by cultivating their lands, actually serve the Common Good in the best way they can.[124] In Oresme's casting of this situation, where "private" parts, driven by "private" goals nevertheless join together to serve the interest of the whole, we can, perhaps, see a sign of the new equilibrium. We can see as well a reflection of Marsilius' "double insistence" which holds, on the one hand, that each individual desires and pursues his own private benefit and personal "sufficiency," and, on the other hand, that at the same time all (or most) men direct their will toward the common benefit.[125]

But the differences in the two formulations are as telling as the similarities. Marsilius, too, frees individuals to pursue their private sufficiencies and recognizes that in doing so they serve the good of the whole. But in pursuing their private needs men do not give up their function as political actors. Far from it. For Marsilius, the pursuit of the private is a contributing element of the dynamics of political life in which imbalanced parts are turned to balance within a system of equalizing law and custom.[126] Marsilius' vision here is characteristically expansive and inclusive. In contrast, Oresme, as is his habit in the *Politiques*, takes a potentially expansive formulation and turns it to restrictive ends. Since, he argues, most men will never succeed in sublimating their private interests to the Common Good, most can never, and *should* never, participate in government. Moreover, in Oresme's modeling, we see a return to the older vision of the political "body," in which the various parts (head, hands, feet, etc.), while contributing to the good of the whole, are each

---

[123] Oresme, *Politiques*, 78b: "A ce je dit premierement que posé que l'en deust plus curer du bien commun, toutesvoies de fait le plus des gens curent plus du propre."

[124] *Ibid.*, 78b: "Et la cause est car par leur propres possessions il soustiennent leur vie et secuerent as necessités presentes … Mes les personnes privées doivent plus curer de leur bien propre et en ce faisant, il curent et font assés pour le bien commun, si comme en nourrissant leur enfans, leur bestes et en cultivant les terres, etc."

[125] Marsilius, *Defensor pacis*, I.4.2; I.4.3; II.8.9, discussed above, Chapter 6.

[126] *Ibid.*, I.17.2. On Marsilius' recognition of the potential dangers of self-interested actions, see Nederman, "Community and Self-Interest," 404–8.

tied to an unchanging hierarchy: hands will always be hands, heads always heads. Oresme has returned to the segmented metaphorical "body" of John of Salisbury, proper to an older model of equalization, and he has retreated far from the "co-equal" body envisioned by Galen and Marsilius, where position, status, and function are relativized within the functioning order of the whole.

Who is a citizen and what are his duties?

At the outset of his commentary, Oresme expresses agreement with the pivotal Aristotelian assertion that "man is by nature a civil being, ordered by nature to live in a civil community."[127] Also following Aristotle, at the beginning of his commentary to Book III, he reserves citizenship to "those who are capable of serving as a judge, with or without others, or who can exercise rulership alone or with another or others, or who can have a voice in the election of princes and judges or in public council."[128] He goes further to assert that some call this governing group of citizens "bourgeois," and in so doing he links this term to the concept of citizenship for what, in Quillet's judgment, is the first time in medieval political thought.[129] But he uses the term in a very restricted way. It does not refer to a general class within the *civitas*, and most definitely not (as we will see) to any elements actually engaged in commerce or banking or artisanal production. The term is purely an element in a circular definition: some call citizens "*bourgeois*" because they can perform the offices of citizens, serving as mayors and counselors and such.[130] Whatever opening the identification of citizenship with the term *bourgeois* may have permitted, it is, like many others, neglected here. Using the definitional distinction he has established between public and private persons, it is soon clear that only the very few "public persons" capable of putting the Common Good before their private interests (few among the aristocracy and much fewer among the city classes) will be admitted to the circle of citizen. In general, the great majority of Oresme's discussions about citizenship and governmental

---

[127] Oresme, *Politiques*, 7d: "que home est naturelement chose civile, ce est a dire qu'il est ordené de nature a vivre in communité civile."

[128] *Ibid.*, 115b: "Ce est a dire que celui que est citoien peut estre juge sans ou oveques autres ou qui peut estre prince seul ou oveques autre ou autres ou qui peut avoit voies en election de princes et de juges ou en conseil publique."

[129] *Ibid.*, 115b. On this point see Quillet, *Songe*, 126.

[130] Oresme, *Politiques*, 115b: "Et aucuns appellent telz citoiens bourgeois, car il pevent estre maires ou esquevins ou conseuls ou avoir aucunez honorabletées autrement nommees."

participation are dedicated to asserting its exclusivity and to demonstrating which social groups must be excluded.[131]

"In an extreme democracy," Oresme writes, supposedly following Aristotle, "the whole of the common people holds rulership. And this is a bad form of government."[132] Here Oresme conflates democracy (which in Aristotelian terms is a debased and untempered form of government not simply because the people rule but because they rule exclusively in their own interest) with the "polity," defined by common participation in government, which (again in Aristotelian terms) can be a legitimate and tempered form. On the basis of this reading he then declares that in a good government, "gens de artifice" can neither govern nor be citizens.[133] It is noteworthy that for textual support on this point, Oresme turns not to Aristotle but to the Bible.[134] In the end, however, he maintains that he is following Aristotle in maintaining this position of exclusion, never revealing that he has taken sometimes contradictory statements by Aristotle and made of them a general, fixed, and closed position. As with the exclusion of artisans from citizenship, so with the mass of those who cultivate the earth. In glossing Aristotle's statement that democracies work best when rural laborers outnumber those from inside the city [1319a], the best that Oresme can say about cultivators is that they are "less covetous, less envious, and less malicious then other kinds of popular multitudes."[135]

For the artisans, traders, and laborers of the city population, from leather-workers, butchers, cooks, and street cleaners, to brokers and middlemen of all sorts, to those who work for hire like clothmakers, dressmakers, and masons, he expresses only contempt: "they are low and dishonest ... covetous, malicious, and unjust."[136] They are incapable in Oresme's eyes of seeing past their private concerns and of being anything other than "private" persons, and so they are excluded by definition

---

[131] On this point, Babbitt, *Oresme's Livre*, 77–8.

[132] Oresme, *Politiques*, 122a–b: "Et entent par extreme democracie la pire que soit, et est quant tout le commun peuple tient le princey. Et est malvese policie."

[133] *Ibid.*, 122b: "Et par ce appert que telz gens de artifice en bonne policie ne doivent pas gouverner ne estre citoiens." He does allow, however (309a), that certain "gens de artifice," although properly excluded from citizenship, nevertheless possess the virtue and fortitude to serve as soldiers in defense of the city under the command of *chevaliers* who are citizens. He does not mention merchants acting in this capacity.

[134] *Ibid.*

[135] *Ibid.*, 264a: "moins conveteus et moins envieus et moins malicieus que les autres multitudes populaires."

[136] *Ibid.*: "car les bannauses sunt vilz et deshonnestes, et les autres selon leur office sunt communelement conveteus et maliciuz et iniustes."

from citizenship of any kind.[137] Even more than this, based in part on a statement by Aristotle, Oresme claims that the numbers of artisans, and presumably the massing of their productive capacity, do nothing in themselves to make the city "great."[138] Where once again Aristotle's statements in this area are nuanced and provisional, predicated on the relativist assumption that each city, like each individual, has a particular "work to do" and a particular limited size proper to that work, the lesson Oresme draws is unitary and final.[139]

But it is not only the lower strata of the city who labor in body that are excluded. Merchants, brokers, shopkeepers and, indeed, "all those who labor in solitude in the desire for personal profit and gain" are equally eliminated from the possibility of attaining virtue and thus from the status of "public" persons required for citizenship.[140] In excluding all those who pursue economic gain from citizenship, Oresme can again appear to be merely glossing Aristotle's position, but again he is picking from among Aristotle's often provisional and sometimes contradictory positions to fix on those that suit his understanding and his purpose.[141] Where Aristotle's goal of gauging the right "admixture of political elements" relative to a range of particular and ever-changing political histories and contexts requires that his method be inclusive and provisional, Oresme proceeds by rule and by elimination.[142] He does distinguish between those "negociants" who labor on behalf of the city and its citizens and those who are always occupied with their own affairs and their own profit, but the former are presumed to be rare. As a rule

---

[137] Ibid., 287b. The extent of this exclusion is expressed in lapidary form in the index of notable terms Oresme provides at the conclusion of his commentary (359a–369b), under the heading "Gent de mestier." Here five areas of exclusion for the artisanal class are noted: from the government of the city, from "honeur sacerdotal," from citizenship, from the possibility of virtue, and from serving as judges. No exceptions are noted.

[138] Ibid., 287b: "Si comme se en aucune cité est une tres grande multitude de menue gens, comme sunt gens de draperie ou de pluseurs autres mestiers, tele cité ne doit pas pour ce estre dicte grande."

[139] Aristotle, Politics, IV.12 [129b15–33]; VII.4 [1326a12–28].

[140] Oresme, Politiques, 305a: "Et les gens desuz diz, qui sunt continuelment occupés en labeur corporel ou en solitude et ardeur de gaignier, ne pourroient a teles chose soufissanment entendre [acquerir et excercer vertus morales], et donques il ne sunt pas citoiens en policie tres bonne." The comparison between his attitudes toward merchants and artisans here in the Politics and his attitudes two decades earlier in the De moneta, are striking. See De moneta, 33 and above.

[141] E.g., in Aristotle, Politics, VII.8 [1328b30–1329a2], the participation of these classes is not universally proscribed, only within the "best" and most ideal governments. In many forms of constitution Aristotle recognizes that their participation is proper, even beneficial.

[142] Ibid., IV.12 [1297a7–8].

he establishes a contradiction between the pursuit of profit through commerce or artisanal production and the pursuit of virtue necessary for citizenship.[143]

In a well-ordered government those who are not inclined to virtue by their nature are assigned to perform work that is servile but necessary, such as cultivating the land or participating in business (*marcheander*) or working at a trade. And such men lack sufficient virtue because the lives they live are incompatible with it, and they are not as a result a true part of the city nor citizens in a well-ordered government. But the citizens are drawn from the three estates, that is to say, the men at arms, the men of council, and the men of the clergy.[144]

From this it appears that the "bourgeois" he earlier identified as potential citizens are those selected members of the city patriciate, descendants of rich and powerful city families, who are no longer required to engage in the occupations that made their families rich in the first place.[145] The others still so occupied have been eliminated from citizenship. Step by step he uses the Aristotelian text to close down and cut off everything predicated on the potentialities of a self-ordering multitude, everything linked to the dynamism of the marketplace, everything smacking of the new equilibrium, and everything not consonant with the rule of King Charles and his circumscribed court.

Oresme on election in the *Livre de politiques*

But if Oresme makes continual use of those Aristotelian statements that argue for stringently limiting citizenship and governmental participation, how then is he to confront, as he must, Aristotle's striking position on the viability of popular election and massed popular judgment? How is he to respond to these well-known words of Aristotle:

---

[143] Oresme, *Politiques*, 305a: "Et par negotiation ne est pas a entendre la marchandise qui est pour garnir la cité et les citoiens, mes celle ou l'en est tousjours occupé pour soustenir sa vie et pour gaignier ... telz gens ne soient pas vertueus ne par consequent citoiens."

[144] *Ibid.*, 322a: "Et pour ce, en bonne policie, ceulz que ne sunt de leur nature enclins a vertu, l'en les doit deputer a oevres serviles et neccessaires comme sunt cultiver les terres et marcheander et ouvrer de mestier. Et telz gens ne sunt pas mont vertueus, car leur vie est subcontraire a vertu et ne sunt pas partie de cité ne citoiens en bonne policie."

[145] Where Oresme differs from Aristotle, here and elsewhere, is in his allowance that men born to the lower strata can, if possessed of innate virtue, raise themselves above their social origins. Since Oresme raised himself from an undistinguished family to become bishop of Lisieux and counselor to the king, he had good reasons to argue in support of this possibility.

There is this to be said of the Many. Each of them by himself may not be of a good quality; but when they all come together it is possible that they may surpass – collectively and as a body, although not individually – the quality of the few best.[146]

[And again]

Each individual may indeed be a worse judge than the experts; but all, when they meet together, are either better than the experts or at any rate no worse.[147]

As befits the importance of this argument and the difficulties it presents to him, Oresme pursues a many-sided strategy to defuse if not refute it. The elements employed in this strategy prove highly revealing of Oresme's reflex to close down all openings to the new equilibrium and of his genius for manipulating definitions and the Aristotelian text to support this purpose. At first he admits the general proposition, supported by Aristotle, that "many eyes see what one eye cannot."[148] He admits, along with Cicero, that "the multitude can at times possess virtues that the individuals comprising the multitude do not."[149] And he admits that a small number of men can never possess the quantity of virtue that reposes in the whole multitude."[150] But he warns that just as good can multiply in the multitude, so can evil. "From a multitude lacking reason, it is impossible to receive good counsel."[151] And when the multitude is made up for the most part of men without discretion or of perverse affections, it must never be allowed the authority to judge (*ne doit avoir nulle auctorité*).[152] Given these divided positions on the subject of the multitude, given his earlier stated position on the need to severely limit access to citizenship, how will he gloss Aristotle's statement that the many, taken together, are likely to be better judges and better able to elect and correct rulers than the virtuous few?

His first step is to insist on the partiality and provisionality of Aristotle's position. In other words, he does here, in relation to a text that he cannot digest, what he consistently neglects to do with aspects of the text he feels he can put to his own use: "But Aristotle does not speak here of royal rulership or government. And he does not allow this statement

---

[146] Aristotle, *Politics*, III.11 [1281b1–9], trans. Barker, 123. Oresme's translation here (136b) shows his understanding of this point. So too does Moerbeke's translation from the Greek, ed. Susemihl, 191: "multos enim, quorum unusquisque est non studiosus vir, tamen contingit, cum convenerint, esse meliores illis, non ut singulum, sed ut simil omnes."

[147] *Ibid.*, III.11 [1282a15–18], trans. Barker, 126; ed. Susemihl, 191–2 (cited in Chapter 6).

[148] Oresme, *Politiques*, 134a.   [149] *Ibid.*, 134b.   [150] *Ibid.*, 133b–134a.

[151] *Ibid.*, 134b: "de multitude qui ne est raisonnable ce est impossible que le conseil soit bon."

[152] *Ibid.*, 134b: "Quant la multitude est pur la plus grant partie de gens sans discretion ou de perverse affection, tele communité ne doit avoir nulle auctorité."

universal validity."[153] The next step is to magnify Aristotle's statement that the capacity for good judgment is only true of multitudes that are not "utterly degraded." In the Aristotelian text, such degradation appears as an exceptional case. In Oresme's recasting, the degraded multitude nearly *becomes the rule* in the secular sphere. Even should a multitude begin on good terms, it is likely that over time it will be dragged down in various ways to become a servile or "bestial" one.[154] It would, he argues, be perilous in the extreme to allow power and judgment to any multitude likely to suffer such degradation. Even if the multitude be not degraded in itself, by the very nature of its composition it is open to being deceived by demagogues and "false seducers."[155] Here the pessimism of Oresme's position in the *Politiques*, his sense that the world around him is tending toward dissolution and disorder rather than toward order, particularly with respect to the self-governing capacity of the multitude, is palpable, as is the sense of historical decline that generates and accompanies it.

It is at this point in the text that Oresme introduces, by name, the *Defensor pacis*. We have seen how Marsilius expanded every opening to communal self-ordering that Aristotle's discussion of election presented. How will Oresme use Marsilius here? As is his habit, rather than arguing with the text directly, he will *turn* it to his own purposes through the careful attachment and manipulation of limiting definitions. At first he seems to accept Marsilius' position that "positive human laws must be made, promulgated, corrected, or changed by the authority and consent of the whole community or of the most worthwhile part (*la plus vaillant partie*)."[156] But in the end all the weight will fall on the last part of this formula, Marsilius' ambiguous phrase *valentior pars*. We have seen that there remains to this day disagreement about the meaning Marsilius

---

[153] *Ibid.*, 136b: "Mes il ne parle pas ici de princey ou de policie royal. D'autre partie il ... ne afferme pas universalment."

[154] *Ibid.*, 136b: "nonobstant qu'elle ne fust pas bestial ne servile, si seroit ce grant peril, premierement car continuelment les personnes sunt transmuees, et viennent ou naissent gens nouveaux qui pevent estre moins bons que leur predecesseurs, et ainsi petit a petit la communité peut empirer et devenir servile ou comme bestial."

[155] *Ibid.*: "Item, il est possible que la multitude toute ensemble est raisonnable quant est de soy, et nientmoins elle peut estre deceue par aucuns faulx seducteurs et par emprendre malveses conclusions." Oresme is very concerned about the power and danger of demagogues. He mentions a number by name, including Jacques d'Artevelde (174b), but the one name one would clearly expect to find in this text – that of Étienne Marcel – is missing. This lack is especially notable since Oresme mentions the Jacquerie at one point (189a).

[156] *Ibid.*, 137a: "En un livre intitulé *Defensor pacis* ceste raison [i.e., Aristotle's discussion of election by the multitude] est alleguee a monstrer que lays humaines positives doivent estre faictes, promulguees, corrigees ou muees de l'auctorité et consentement de toute la communité ou de la plus vaillaint partie."

attached to this concept. But there is no doubt how Oresme will use it: to limit in every direction the ordering powers and prerogatives of a wider multitude. To do so, he translates the Marsilian term as *la plus vaillant partie* and then equates this "most worthwhile part" with the *"multitude raisonnable,"* a term he will henceforth apply continually throughout the commentary.[157] By definition, now, the authority of the "reasonable" multitude to elect and correct the ruler and to make the laws will be limited to those same few virtuous and "public" men to whom he had earlier allowed citizenship. They alone comprise the *"multitude raisonnable."* Once this definition is in place, he can continue to speak of the political authority of the multitude, while meaning almost precisely the opposite.

While Oresme strictly limits the "multitude" with respect to governance in the secular sphere, he refrains from doing so with respect to the governance of the Church. In writing of the Church he can assume that the clergy, by virtue of their office, possess the requisite virtue and reason to participate fully in governance. He makes the same assumption concerning the members of the faculty of the University of Paris.[158] In these restricted cases, all the parts of the whole are at the same time parts of the *"multitude raisonnable."* Here he can and does use Aristotelian and Marsilian notions about the responsibility of the multitude for election, correction, and the instituting of law without restrictive qualifications.[159] Indeed, it is in this context that he makes his most ringing statements in support of these positions.[160] With the papal claims to "fullness of power" (*plenitudo potestatis*) in the background, he writes that all who "govern according to their own will or govern in accordance with laws that they themselves have made without the proper council and consent of the multitude" do so against the Common Good and the nature of good

---

[157] *Ibid.*, 137b: "Et domination est deue *au plus vaillant* et par consequent, toute la multitude doit avoir domination sus la correction et election des princes. *Et est a entendre de multitude raisonnable, et encor non pas universelmen*t, si comme il est dit devant en glose" (my emphasis).

[158] *Ibid.*, 274a.

[159] It is not surprising, then, that Oresme raises the subject of the duties of the multitude in the governance of the Church just after the first glosses on Aristotle's position on election.

[160] It is also in the context of his long gloss on the government of the Church that Oresme makes his most expansive statement about who should comprise the governing multitude in a "policie royale" (i.e., a policy comparable to the Papacy). *Politiques*, 274a: "Meismement car toute ceste multitude de laquele le roy et son familier conseil sunt une petite partie scet miex considerer et ordener tout ce qui est bon pour la chose publique. Et aussi, ce que tous funt et appreuvent est plus ferme et plus estable, plus acceptable et plus aggreable a la communité, et donne moins de occasion de murmure ou de rebellion que se il estoient autrement."

government.[161] "Those," he continues, "who attribute to themselves full power and claim use of *plenitudine potestatis* as if they were not under the law" are acting as a tyrant.[162] The result of his application of Aristotelian principles to the governance of the Church is a well-developed case for conciliarism, more modest in its criticisms of papal prerogatives and its claims for conciliar power than those of Marsilius and later spokesmen, but potent nonetheless.[163] I add this discussion here because Oresme's support of conciliarism can be and has been taken as a sign of his positive attitudes toward communal self-government. While it might very well be taken thus in this restricted case, he carefully manipulates the dividing definition of the "reasonable multitude" in such a way as to prevent any seepage between his call for conciliar authority in the religious sphere and his strict limitation on broader community powers in the secular sphere of his king's government.[164] It appears that the very extremity of papal claims to power and authority over the course of the fourteenth century rendered it impossible for Oresme to reconcile them with the minimum require-ments of balanced or "tempered" government in the Aristotelian sense.

As Oresme limits the multitude capable of serving and judging the king, so, by and large, he restricts the capacity for judgment and correction even to those he admits to full citizenship. Even when the king unjustly treats an honorable man or violates the Common Good, thus presenting good cause for insurrection, Oresme argues against it, saying that in most cases its effects would be more damaging than helpful.[165] Moreover, as much as he has identified good government, including the good mon-archy, with the maintenance of the mean (*le moyen*), he permits the king to overstep it if he senses that his subjects are inclined to disobedience or

---

[161] *Ibid.*, 178b: "se aucuns governent selon leur volenté ou se il gouvernent selon lays lesqueles eulz meismes ont faictes sans le consentement de la multitude en leur faveur et a leur profit ou propre conferent et contre le bien publique."

[162] *Ibid.*, 178b: "ce est a dire que il se attribuent pleniere puissance, et qu il pevent user de *plenitudine potestatis*, sans ce que il soient soubz lay ... est contre la nature de toute bonne policie, et est principe de extreme olygarcie et de tirannie."

[163] Oresme's longest gloss on the subject of conciliarism comes at *ibid.* 159a–161b. Oresme recognizes a delicate line in his writings on conciliarism. Insofar as it is "natural," the government of the Church should conform to the norms of political science as enunci-ated by Aristotle, but insofar as it is governed by the Holy Spirit, it is above judgment based in natural reason.

[164] One of the rare times he refers explicitly to Charles V is when he suggests (*ibid.*, 161b) that he could play a positive role in aiding the conciliar effort and assuring that the government of the Church serve the interests of "le bien publique du peuple crestien."

[165] *Ibid.*, 204a: "sedition ne peut communelment estre mise a effect sans grans malz." His argument against sedition has many parts (203b–205a), utilizing spiritual authorities as well as natural (205a): "Or appert donques par raison et par Aristote et par la Sainte Escripture que sedition ne est pas lisible et pour queles causes." On this see Babbitt, *Oresme's Livre*, 84.

rebellion. In such cases, "it would be expedient, both for the ruler and for his people, for the king to increase his powers beyond moderation."[166] There is no sense whatever, here or elsewhere in the *Livre de politiques* that the king himself might bear responsibility for his subjects having become degraded or rebellious. The weakness of Oresme's position in this case – his failure to even mention the king's possible responsibility – is striking, especially when compared to his passionate denunciation of royal misuse of financial power in the *De moneta*. But analogous weaknesses and absences can be perceived in position after position in the *Politiques* when one looks beneath the surface of Oresme's well-arrayed rhetoric.[167]

Throughout his commentary Oresme prominently displays concepts that had been the carriers of the new equilibrium in political thought from the late thirteenth through the mid fourteenth century. Among these: the superiority of the Common Good; the privileges of citizenship; limitations on the singular exercise of power; the importance of the "middle" class in moderating the extremes of wealth and poverty; the restraining force of law (and the leading place of the multitude in its making and its changing); the prerogatives of the multitude in electing and correcting rulers; and the dynamic and productive intersection of private concerns and public benefits. But in every case Oresme has drained them of life, tamed them through the addition of qualifying definitions, and turned them to his own purpose: the ideological defense of monarchy. By doing so he systematically rejects the potentialities of the new model of equilibrium in the political sphere, not only in comparison with their place in the writings of Marsilius of Padua but in comparison with their place in his own *De moneta* of two decades earlier.

Behind Oresme's retreat from the new equilibrium

Sensitivity to the potentialities of the new model of equilibrium was never universal within scholastic culture. While it appears in the writings of the most adventurous and insightful thinkers working in widely different intellectual disciplines in the first half of the fourteenth century, there are also many works from this period that show little evidence of its presence. But with the *Politiques* we have something very different: an

---

[166] Oresme, *Politiques*, 244: "Je di donques que se le roy appercevoit que ses subjects s'enclinassent aucunement a desobeïsance ou a rebellion contre son gouvernement royal, il seroit expedient et pour lui et pour eulz que il enforçast et accreust sus eulz sa puissance oultre la moderation."

[167] Here Babbitt's judgment is germane (*Oresme's Livre*, 89): "On the whole, however, we do not see in Oresme's glosses a balance between the duties of the governors and the obligations of the citizens, a recognition of the mutual responsibilities of ruler and ruled."

author who had seen its potentialities (and continued to see them in his writings on natural philosophy) but who at some point decided that they were more dangerous than promising when applied to the political sphere and consequently turned them aside at every point where they might be applied politically. There is genius here, but it is a genius of deflection rather than invention. The question is why.

What changes occurred between the writing of the *De moneta* and the *Politiques* that might explain Oresme's retreat from the political implications of the new equilibrium? There are, first, the many influences that derive primarily from Oresme's personal history. Above all there is his long and close acquaintance with his king and the obvious respect and affection he felt for him.[168] Since the king's good graces facilitated Oresme's steep and steady advancement in his clerical career, one would also expect the accrual of a considerable debt of gratitude. Oresme's service to the king as a trusted counselor placed him within the limited circle whose singular political powers he defended throughout the *Politiques*. The enjoyment of such considerable personal privilege would be enough to turn many men's thoughts toward pleasing the agent of their good fortune. But I do not think this is what explains Oresme's stance. He is far too committed an intellectual, far too committed a seeker of truth to be swayed by personal interest alone. What then?

When Oresme wrote the *Politiques* in the early 1370s, he could find many legitimate reasons to identify the monarchical rule of King Charles with service to the Common Good. Charles' well-earned reputation for wisdom and prudence helped to cement the association of his person and his virtue with the good of the realm.[169] When Charles took over effective rule as dauphin in 1360 (soon after the writing of the *De moneta*) and then ascended the throne in 1364, France was near anarchy. It was bankrupted by war, mismanagement, and the cost of ransoming King Jean. It was helpless against the depredations of English armies and free companies and scarred by violent social upheaval, most notably the Jacquerie and the uprising of Étienne Marcel (1357–8). In the little more than a decade and a half of his effective rulership, Charles and his counselors managed to defuse all these threats to the realm through a series of adept military and political decisions. Oresme was but one of a multitude who were greatly impressed by the king's evident successes in governing. Moreover,

---

[168] An affection that was apparently returned, as Charles referred to Oresme as his "bien aimé" in the royal commission for the translation of the *Politiques*.

[169] On Charles as a patron of letters and the arts, see Jeannine Quillet, *Charles V, le roi lettré: essai sur la pensée politique d'un règne* (Paris: Librairie Académique Perrin, 1984). For a description of his impressive library, see Claire Sherman, *The Portraits of Charles V of France (1338–1380)* (New York University Press, 1969), 12–15.

Charles' consistent respect for higher learning, and his generous patron-
age of art and scholarship, earned him additional accolades from a wide
array of artists and intellectuals, including Oresme.[170] By the end of
the 1360s, the evident advantages of Charles' kingship had led many,
again including Oresme, to accede to his monarchical vision – a vision
that was highly jealous and protective of royal prerogatives. King Charles
welcomed good advice from his counselors, but he brooked no doubts
concerning who held the power of decision and rule. He never forgave the
insolence of the Estates-General of 1357, which in the *grande ordonnance*
presented demands for a series of reforms and claimed the unprecedented
privilege of calling itself to order on its own initiative. In response, Charles
eviscerated the general assembly as an institution of government over the
decades that followed.[171] Since Oresme failed to mention the Estates a
single time in his considerable glosses, we can only assume that he had
come to agree that Charles could better serve the Common Good without
their aid. In short, Oresme wrote the *Politiques* at a time when Charles
had proved that his vision of monarchical power could work for the benefit
of the whole.

It is possible that Charles' evident successes combined with the personal benefits Oresme derived from his position as counselor to the king
would have been sufficient in themselves to generate his determined
support for Charles' rule. But these factors alone cannot explain, to my
satisfaction, the collapse of Oresme's faith in the potentialities of the new
equilibrium as applied to the political community, which is evidenced
throughout the *Politiques*. Nor can they explain his later position that
political multitudes are far more likely to descend into bestiality over
time than to ascend to virtue. After all, Marsilius was able to hold on to
the richest implications of the new equilibrium even as he made the
judgment, for sound political reasons, to argue on behalf of the governing
prerogatives of the Emperor in his role as the "principal part" of the
political body. In contrast, Oresme's faith in the new equilibrium appears
to have collapsed at every point where it had formerly been maintained in
the *De moneta*, leading to his near-complete abandonment of the possibilities of systematic self-ordering vested in the community as a whole.
At every point he has replaced the potentialities of the self-ordering
multitude with the commanding will of the ordering ruler informed by

---

[170] As Babbitt notes (*Oresme's Livre*, 44), in this Charles followed the example of the
expanded claims to preeminence of his royal predecessors.

[171] Babbitt, *Oresme's Livre*, 44; Thomas Ertman, *Birth of the Leviathan: Building States and
Regimes in Medieval and Early Modern Europe* (Cambridge University Press, 1997), 85–6;
Quillet, *Charles V, le roi lettré*.

the small coterie of his advisors. When we compare the *De moneta* to the *Politiques*, we can see not only a change in particular political positions but a broader and deeper change occurring at the level of his basic assumptions – precisely the level at which, I argue, the model of equilibrium is shaped within intellectual cultures. In relation to the possibilities of communal action and systematic equalization, pessimism has replaced optimism, fear has replaced confidence, and, as a result, the possibilities that had been opened have been closed.

A change of this magnitude and on this level calls for further analysis. Cultural optimism and pessimism are undoubtedly ephemeral constructs, difficult to verify and impossible to quantify. For that reason historians are rightly wary of adding them to the mix of possible historical explanations. But there are, I would argue, some periods in which a sense of optimism or pessimism are so generally shared within a culture that to ignore them would be to ignore the elephant in the room. I believe the period between 1350 and 1375, covering the last half of Oresme's life, was one of these. Something happened in this period to undermine an earlier optimism and faith in the potentialities of the self-ordering and self-equalizing polity.

If we can understand the circumstances that derailed the new equilibrium in Oresme's thinking, we are in a better position to understand the circumstances that activated it in the first place. And Oresme's case was far from unique. His abandonment of the potentialities of the new equilibrium was mirrored in discipline after discipline within scholastic culture at large for generations following his, especially when viewed in terms of its acceptance and expansion over the first half of the fourteenth century. This wholesale abandonment indicates that something much deeper than purely personal considerations lay behind Oresme's re-visioning of political order and equalization in the *Politiques*. The wider we cast our net in our search for historical cause – beyond the experiences of a single person, or a single nation – the closer we are likely to come to understanding the retreat from the new equilibrium.

Few would disagree that the later fourteenth century was a difficult time, often characterized as a period of collapse and failure in many areas. I want to suggest that two broad areas of collapse were particularly implicated in the scholastic abandonment of the new equilibrium: loss of faith in the viability of communal self-government and loss of faith in the self-ordering and self-equalizing capacities of the marketplace. In regard to the first loss, for Oresme and those of his generation at the University of Paris, there were two evident failures of the political multitude that would likely have left a very deep impression: the Jacquerie and the bourgeois rebellion of Étienne Marcel. Both occurred over the period 1357–8, soon after the writing of the *De moneta*. The Jacquerie finds a mention in the *Politiques* in relation to Aristotle's position (seconded by Oresme) that all members of a polity neither can nor should be equal in an absolute sense.[172] The attempt to institute such an unnatural equality can, Oresme warns, only lead to trouble, which he illustrates with historical examples of serf rebellions like the Jacquerie.[173] In contrast to the Jacquerie, Oresme never once mentions the bourgeois uprising of Étienne Marcel, even though he continually trumpets the dangers of rule by the multitude and emphasizes its susceptibility to the domination of demogogues.[174]

Although Étienne's name is entirely absent from the *Politiques*, I would argue that he and his example exert a powerful presence throughout the text. As Provost of Paris and leader of the merchant opposition to royal rule, Étienne led the Estates-General of 1357 in compiling and ratifying the *grande ordonnance*, which issued scores of demands for royal and aristocratic reform, calling for severe limitations on the king's power. In support of bourgeois demands, Étienne led an angry crowd of supporters to march on the palace of the dauphin Charles in February 1358. He and his followers then forced their entry into the dauphin's quarters and there, in front of Charles, murdered two marshals of France in the royal retinue. In parting, Étienne and his followers insisted that Charles display the blue and red hood symbolic of bourgeois rebellion. We can only imagine the impact of these scenes on Oresme, who in 1358 was already a counselor and a close familiar of the dauphin. Although there is no evidence that Oresme was present at this scene, it is certainly possible, given both his position at court at this time and his position as Grand Master at the College of Navarre, situated across the river and part way up Mont-Sainte-Geneviève from the palace but within sight and sound of it. But of course Oresme would not have had to be physically present. These events (scandalous in many eyes) reverberated for decades and indeed centuries afterward in historical memory: how much more so in the mind of this intimate and devoted royal servant?[175]

I have noted that there was not a single mention of English or Spanish representative assemblies in Oresme's glosses to the *Politiques*. Equally note-worthy (especially given Aristotle's insatiable curiosity about contemporary

---

[172] Oresme, *Politiques*, 187a: "l'en doit savoir que ce ne est pas chose possible naturelment que toutes les gens d'une policie ou d'une communité soient equalz."

[173] *Ibid.*, 187a: "Et treuve l'en es hystoires que aucune fois les sers ont fait rebellion et guere contre leurs seigneurs. Et ce appeloient les anciens *bellum servile* – jacquerie."

[174] While not mentioning Étienne by name as a demagogue, he does single out Jacob van Artevelde in Flanders and "many others" that he identifies with the communes of Italy. On demagogues and "faulx seducteurs," *ibid.*, 136, 174b–175a: "Et tel demagoge fu en Flanders, un appelé Jaaques d'Artevele. Et es cités d'Ytalie ont esté pluseurs telz."

[175] The rebellion and the events in the city leading up to it, unfolding over months, are vividly described in *The Chronicle of Jean de Venette*, 66–79.

political forms and constitutions in the *Politics*), Oresme makes no mention of the communes of northern Italy, even though they represented the most extraordinary experiments in political order of the entire medieval period. Fifty years after the writing of the *Defensor pacis*, the Italian communes have nothing to teach Oresme except to the extent that they are indirectly implicated in his critique of the failures of democracies. This is perhaps not so surprising, considering the agonizing collapse of the republican ideal in commune after commune over this same half-century and the seemingly inexorable replacement of this ideal by the autocratic rule of powerful individuals and families. Given the extraordinary successes of these same self-governing communes in the previous century, and the support they provided for belief in the self-ordering capacity of political multitudes, it is understandable that their failure would, conversely, have severely undermined faith in this same capacity, for Oresme as for other observers of political life in his period.

But what is even more striking in the *Politiques* is the near-total absence of the city of Paris as an entity, whether economic, political, cultural, or otherwise.[176] Once Oresme has explained that for Aristotle *cité* is the equivalent of *civitas* or realm, Paris disappears as a subject, and his focus remains fixed on the *royaume*. It is hard to imagine another work on French politics or the French crown, whether written in the fourteenth century or any century after, in which Paris plays so little part. Its governance, its patriciate, its trade, its magnificent secular and religious buildings, its artisans and their products, its wealth and speed and creative energy, again have nothing to teach Oresme. It is almost as if he has banished Paris from his view, as if the political crimes of Étienne Marcel, the merchant guild, and the murderous Parisian multitude have nullified its existence as a political entity and example. But whatever the reasons behind this nullification, by banishing from consideration the city and its status as a self-ordering whole, Oresme effectively banished from consideration one of the primary engines of the new equilibrium. It is an engine we have seen at work at a number of points: in Oresme's earlier *De moneta*, in *La vie de Saint Denys* miniatures, in the commercial Paris of Jean de Jandun, in the *universitas civium* of Marsilius of Padua's *Defensor pacis*; in the Montpellier of Arnau de Vilanova and Peter Olivi. In the place of frank and even astonished admiration for the city's capacity to order and equalize itself, there is now fear and distrust of its tendency to verge into degradation and chaos if not controlled by a strong hand.

---

[176] I count ten fragmentary mentions of Paris in the whole of the *Politiques*, with no substance to any of them.

As the image of the self-ordering city disappears, so too the sensed potentialities for systematic equilibrium in other spheres disappear as well.

The second major area of collapse (after that of the city) most directly
implicated in the scholastic abandonment of the new equilibrium was the
evaporation of belief in the self-ordering and self-equalizing capacities of
the marketplace. Here the collapse was possibly even more profound and
long-lasting: here the effects were pan-European, sufficiently powerful to
affect not only the deeply rooted intellectual culture of the University of
Paris but the intellectual cultures of Oxford, Montpellier, Padua, and all
other universities as well. Equally pan-European was one of the primary
causes of this collapse in faith: the severe and long-lingering social, economic, and political effects of the Black Death. In the minds of privileged
witnesses, the plague and its lingering aftermath had the effect of radically
reordering – to great detriment – the economic relationships between
those who owned and those who labored. There has been a long and
still heated debate among economic historians over the extent to which
the laboring classes actually benefited in the generation following the first
outbreak of plague. The current view holds generally that their gains were
modest at best. What is not in debate, and what is revealed in numerous
contemporary accounts, is that the privileged classes *perceived* that their
own fortunes were being sorely damaged by the economic gains of those
who labored.[177]

The catastrophic mass mortality of the plague's first visitation (1348–50),
followed for generations by smaller outbreaks, led to a persistent scarcity
of agricultural and craft laborers and a consequent rise in the wages they
should have been able to command.[178] In this case, however, the aristocracy and the large landlords (which is to say those who saw themselves as
the "natural" betters and leaders of society and who presumed that they
were the proper beneficiaries of any well-ordered economic system) found
themselves in what they saw as an increasingly detrimental situation. They
soon came to perceive that they were on the losing end of the post-plague
market "order," or rather "disorder" as they came to view it. As John
Hatcher has written concerning the English case:

---

[177] For a survey of the debate and analysis of the response of the privileged classes, see
Hatcher, "England in the Aftermath of the Black Death," esp. 3–12. See also,
Samuel Cohn, "After the Black Death: Labour Legislation and Attitudes towards
Labour in Late-Medieval Western Europe," *Economic History Review* 60 (2007), 457–85,
for a pan-European study of legislative responses that comes to the same conclusion
concerning the perception of the propertied classes.

[178] For distraught accounts of the second through fifth visitation of the plague in England,
1361–93, see Rosemary Horrox, *The Black Death* (Manchester University Press, 1994),
85–92.

The survivors of the Great Plague of 1348–9 were in no doubt that the fortunes and demeanour of the lower orders had been transformed. In the experience of the upper strata of society, the trauma of successive waves of devastating pestilence was followed by the prolonged discomfort inflicted by obstreperous tenants and truculent workmen who, conscious of the prospects for betterment which the massive mortality had placed within their grasp, would not be coerced into placidly accepting their time-honoured subservient roles as the meek providers of ample rents and cheap labour.[179]

Responses on the part of the socially and economically privileged were remarkably swift. In England, already in June 1349, with the mortality of the plague still present, the government issued the Ordinance of Labourers, freezing wages at pre-plague levels and insisting that laborers accept any and all offers of employment at these levels.[180] The attempt was to undo or override the connection between increasing scarcity and need on the one hand and rising prices on the other – a connection that virtually everyone at the time recognized as characteristic of market order – whether they were renters or rentiers, producers for market or merchant middlemen, administrators of every stripe or, for that matter, Members of Parliament.[181] Aristotle had recognized the equation between human need and economic value in the *Ethics*, and he had even sought to represent it geometrically through his *figura* of exchange. Scholastic writers of the thirteenth and fourteenth centuries had refined the equation yet further through their identification of the relationship between scarcity (*raritas*), common need (*indigentia communis*), and common or market price.[182] The clear and general understanding of this systematic relationship is revealed in the text of the Ordinance of Labourers itself, which asserts that the government must intervene to see that labor scarcity does not translate into rising wages. And the 1349 Ordinance was only the beginning. The Statute of Labourers, issued by Parliament scarcely two years later, was far more detailed and draconian in its attempts to undo the "natural" economic relationship between scarce labor and the rising wages that the

---

[179] Hatcher, "England in the Aftermath of the Black Death," 10. See also A. C. Penn and Christopher Dyer, "Wages and Earnings in Late Medieval England: Evidence from the Enforcement of the Labour Laws," *Economic History Review* 43 (1990), 356–76; Ormrod, "The Politics of Pestilence"; Bolton, "The World Upside Down,"; David Stone, "The Black Death and its Immediate Aftermath: Crisis and Change in the Fenland Economy, 1346–1453," in *Town and Countryside in the Age of the Black Death*, ed. Bailey and Rigby, 213–44.

[180] Horrox, *Black Death*, 287–9.

[181] On this subject, see Chapter 2 above and Kaye, "Monetary and Market Consciousness in Thirteenth and Fourteenth Century Europe."

[182] For the level of sophistication that this understanding had achieved in scholastic thought by the late thirteenth century, see the sections dedicated to Peter Olivi in Chapters 1 and 2.

statute declared "outrageous."[183] Now, failure on the part of the laborers (with specific occupations listed by the dozen) to accept any employment offered at pre-plague wages was to be punished by imprisonment. The responsibility for the current economic disorder (as it was deemed by the powerful) was laid in part on the "malice" and "exceptional greed" of the laborers themselves for accepting wages they (presumably) knew to be beyond traditional bounds and thus beyond their due.

And the political reaction to the perceived evils of market disorder only increased over the 1360s and 70s (when Oresme was composing the *Politiques*) and into the 80s, as witnessed by the additions to the Statute of Labourers issued in 1388.[184] At this point all of official England – mayors, bailiffs, constables, seigneurial stewards, and justices of the peace – were enlisted in a project of social control of unprecedented scope. So intent had the authorities become on controlling the market forces whose effects they had come to fear, so conscious were they of the "great damage and loss to the lords as well as all the Commons" (i.e., to the landlords and landholders in Parliament), that every "employee" who traveled the roads of England, including pilgrims, was now required to carry "letters patent,"

and if any employee or labourer be found in any city or borough or elsewhere en route from another place and wandering about without such letters he shall be immediately taken by the said mayors, bailiffs, stewards or constables and put in the stocks and kept there until he has found surety to return to his employment.[185]

In short, social and economic control had become the overriding order of the day.

Over these same decades, in the France of Oresme, the failure of faith in the capacity of the economy to properly order itself, and the belief among the privileged classes that the post-plague economy was working to the detriment of aristocrats and landlords (those who, for the most, made up the circle of counselors around King Charles V), was comparable to that which was found in England, and so too was the consequent decision of the government to intervene in the matter of prices, wages, and social mobility.[186] If anything, the French royal *ordonnances* issued soon after the plague (that of February 1350, to take an early example) are even more determined in their attempt to bring wages and prices back into line with the levels they held "avant la mortalité."[187] An *ordonnance* of February 1351, addressed to the seneschal of Beaucaire, shows how the mechanism

---

[183] Horrox, *Black Death*, 312–16, at 312.   [184] *Ibid.*, 323–6.   [185] *Ibid.*, 323–4.

[186] Braid, "Politiques royales du travail en Europe occidentale," *passim*.

[187] An *ordonnance* issued in February 1350, begins with the insistence that all wandering poor must take up employment. It continues for almost thirty pages in its eighteenth-century edition, devoting scores of detailed paragraphs to regulating bakers, tavern-keepers,

of reordering was conceived. It commands the seneschal to deputize committees across his constituency, consisting of three "good men," chosen from among churchmen, nobles, and "others of authority," with the power, granted by the king, to force all sellers of food and merchandise to vend at a "fitting price" (*prix convenable*), which is to say at a "just and loyal price" (*juste et loyal prix*).[188] At the same time it gives these committees power to determine the "fitting" wages (*salaires et loüages competans*) for all laborers and workers.[189]

Note that in this and other cases what was "fitting" was now to be determined by custom, tradition, and fixed notions of proper status and station, and precisely *not* by the systematic self-equalizing produced within the marketplace – the process of equalization that Peter Olivi and others in an earlier period had invested with such great authority. In an *ordonnance* of 1354, we see that in the perception of the governing class, the economic disorder of the post-plague period, in which workers were demanding and receiving wages that coincided neither with custom nor with what was proper to their social "*estat*," was being linked to moral and societal disorders that were equally troubling. Workers, it claimed, were now earning more than they needed for simple sustenance; indeed, observers noted that workers now earned as much in two days as they used to earn in a week. To the privileged authors of the *ordonnance*, this new state of affairs transgressed "good custom and ancient observances" on a number of levels.[190] The *ordonnance* decries the fact that since laborers no longer had to work a full week to support themselves, they were now spending most of their time in the tavern, drinking and gambling. Equally shocking, they were now "demanding wines and meats other than was proper to their estate."[191] The solution was to punish

butchers, fisherman, carters, and dozens of other trades. A common solution to the problem of wages found in this *ordonnance* (*Ordonnances des roys de France*, vol. II, 368): "Toutes manieres de Boscherons et ouvriers és bois ... ne pourrant prendre et avoir pour leurs labeurs et journées que le tiers plus outre ce qu'on en souloit donner avant la mortalité, tant en tasche comme en journée, et non plus." The same *ordonnance* limits the profits of merchants and rentiers to 2 sous per 20, rewarding those who reported violations with one fifth of the assessed penalty.

[188] *Ibid.*, 489.   [189] *Ibid.*, 490.

[190] *Ibid.*, November 1354, 564: "contre les bonnes et aprouvée coutumes et observances anciennes ... pour le grant pris des journées qu'il ont accoutumes de prendre, qu il ne ouvriront la semaine que deux jours." On this, see Cohn, "After the Black Death," 480–1.

[191] *Ordonnances des roys de France*, vol. II, November 1354, 564: "demandent vins et viande autre que il ne appartient à leur estat." Such criticism continued throughout the 1350s and 60s. One of the striking effects of the dislocations of the plague was a general hardening of royal attitudes and policies toward the lower classes – peasants, workers, artisans – especially notable in contrast to the general concern for "le menu peuple" exhibited in royal social and economic policies over the first half of the century. On this see Cazelles, *Société politique*, 26–7.

laborers found drinking in taverns with a prison sentence of bread and water for three days. If they failed to find work after their imprisonment, it was the pillory for them. Laborers were forbidden to leave their present employment for better wages and were to be punished by fine or imprisonment if they refused to accept work at wages set by local committees.[192] At the same time, the *ordonnance* sought to give assurances that the government would protect honest workers by policing and limiting prices as well as wages. Again, a systematic extension of social and economic control, this time in the name of the king, had become the order of the day.[193]

In the case of France, the decade of the 1350s witnessed a series of economic, political, and social disasters that magnified the market and demographic dislocations of the plague: continuing war with England, the disastrous defeat at Poitiers, the capture of King Jean, the enormous ransom France was forced to pay to free its king, the widespread looting of English "free companies," the loss of whole districts to rebellion and anarchy, the murderous Jacquerie and its bloody aftermath, the rebellion of Étienne Marcel and its aftermath, all occurring while the legitimacy of the dauphin Charles was continually challenged and his authority questioned. Raymond Cazelles has described the period after Poitiers as one of "veritable disintegration."[194] In these years, Oresme wrote many of his most profound works in science and mathematics, while he continued as part of a group of "reformateurs" close to both king and dauphin, serving them as councillor and agent.

In the late 1350s the dauphin Charles began to reestablish royal control with a series of economic and political actions. Most important, both for the future of France and for the crown's eventual monopolization of economic and political power, were a series of taxes whose initial purpose was to pay the enormous ransom for King Jean (3 million écus) and to continue the war with England. These included a graduated tax on income, in which the rich were scheduled to pay considerably less in proportional terms than the working classes of the city, and a tax on salt

---

[192] *Ordonnances des roys de France*, vol. II, November 1354, 565: "par ainsi que aucun ne refuse aler ouvrer, pour le prix que seront mis sur les journées des Ouvriers."

[193] More than a century ago, the historian Charles Benoist commented on the program of economic control manifested by the post-plague *ordonnances*: "le prix des denrés et le maximum des salaires furent fixés dans des instructions aux baillis et aus sénéschaux; comme si le travail et la valeur etaient à la merci d'un droit regalien, et comme si l'on pouvait aller à l'encontre des lois naturelles, avec un règlement d'administration publique!" In *La politique du roi Charles V* (Paris: Cerf, 1886), 80.

[194] Cazelles, *Société politique*, 578. For the rapidly deteriorating economic condition of Paris over the second half of the fourteenth and first half of the fifteenth century, see Jones, *Biography of a City*, 62–95.

(*gabelle*), again particularly onerous to the lower classes.[195] These taxes and *aides*, proposed by Charles, were first granted by the Estates in 1357 on the theory that they would be in control of their renewal. But after the collapse of Étienne's rebellion and with it the program and reputation of the Estates themselves, Charles continued to collect them year after year on his own authority. Moreover, from 1358 he gained full control of the power to appoint and oversee the small army of assessors and collectors necessary to enforce payment.[196] From this point forward and for centuries to come, the Estates-General, having lost control of the governmental purse, lost their political relevance as well. Where in 1357 and 1358 they had exercised considerable political power and had served as a genuine counterweight to royal and aristocratic prerogative, Charles reduced them to a near nullity for the remaining twenty-five years of his reign, and a nullity they then remained for centuries.

In 1360, as part of the royal program to gain control of the finances of the realm, King Jean, seconded by the dauphin Charles, addressed the concern Oresme had so forcefully voiced in the *De moneta*: the continual debasement and weakening of the coinage. An *ordonnance* issued in December of that year noted the issue of a new "strong" coin, the "franc," at 96 percent silver and only 4 percent alloy.[197] This was far from the first revaluation of the French coinage in the fourteenth century – the last one had been attempted by King Jean in 1355. But where all the others had soon failed and given way to progressive weakenings, this one did not. After a half-century of monetary instability verging on anarchy, King Charles succeeded with the 1360 revaluation where no one else had. He held the money steady for the twenty years remaining of his reign, aided in doing so by the regular income produced by his basket of taxes.[198] This remarkable achievement gave proof that a wise king was capable of controlling the economy through sage decisions, force of will, and an army

---

[195] Henneman, *Royal Taxation*, 110–20; 226–72; Cazelles, *Société politique*, 512; Cazelles, "La stabilisation," 304–8.

[196] Benoist, *Politique du roi Charles V*, 63.

[197] *Ordonnances des roys de France*, vol. III, 433–42; Henneman, *Royal Taxation*, 117–20; Cazelles, "La stabilisation," 293, 301–3; Spufford, *Money and its Use*, 308.

[198] In addition to crediting King Charles, Cazelles (*Société politique*, 419) credits the group of "reformateurs," surrounding the king, within which he specifically includes Oresme, for the continued success of the revaluation. On the effect of Charles' taxes, see Philippe Contamine, "Lever l'impôt en terre de guerre: Rançons, appatis, souffrances de guerre dans la France des XIVe et XVe siècles," in *L'impôt au Moyen Âge*, ed. Philippe Contamine *et al.*, 3 vols. (Paris: Ministère de l'économie, des finances et de l'industrie, Comité pour l'histoire économique et financière de la France, 2002), vol. I, 11–39, esp. 35–9; Henneman, *Royal Taxation*, 276–9; Cazelles, *Société politique*, 511–12.

of royal administrators and tax collectors.[199] Increasingly, from 1360 on, economic order in France was identified with conscious governmental order under the direction of the king. In the economic as well as the political realm, order and "just" equalization were now to be established through the reasoned will of the prince. What chance did the faith in the promise of systematic self-ordering, which underlay the new model of equilibrium, have in this environment?

Under Charles' rule, taxation alone engineered an enormous transfer of wealth from the working classes of the towns and the countryside to the aristocratic class, but his "strong" money policy pushed this process even further.[200] Those who benefited from the continuing strong currency after 1360 were overwhelmingly the landlords and landowners, while those who lost were not only renters and debtors but all whose wellbeing depended on a vibrant and dynamic economy – especially the commercial classes of the towns.[201] Over the course of Charles' reign, the once vibrant economies and bourgeois communities of the French cities, including Paris, were gradually choked off by the king's economic policies.[202] In their place, and in place of the dynamism of the self-ordering marketplace, appeared a new "*engin*" of society – what Cazelles has called "the patrimonial monarchy," and which he described as "a global structure of relations: human, juridical, monetary, sociological, historical, linguistic and religious, all coordinated and organized hierarchically."[203] This is the essentially hierarchical and top-down model of social and political order that Oresme duly recorded and seconded in his commentary on the *Politics*.

---

[199] For a description of the administrative structure in place by the last years of King Charles, see Benoist, *Politique du roi Charles V*, 87–94. For the structure at the very end of the fourteenth century, see Roman Telliez, "Officiers et fermiers des aides devant la justice royale (fin du XIVe – début du XVe siècle," in *L'impôt au Moyen Âge*, ed. Philippe Contamine *et al.*, vol. III, 827–59.

[200] Cazelles, "La stabilisation," 294–6, 304–8; and Cazelles, *Société politique*, 570–5, where he makes the point that the transfer of wealth that occurred over Charles' reign had a determinative effect on the aggrandizement of the French aristocracy, and thus on French history for centuries following.

[201] Henneman, *Royal Taxation*, 303; Cazelles, *Société politique*, 511: "Cette stabilité qui favorise la situation de ceux qui perçoivent des revenus en monnaie de compte, c'est-à-dire surtout les possédants, les seigneurs fonciers laïques et ecclésiastiques, n'est pas conciliable avec une économie dynamique."

[202] Cazelles, *Société politique*, 565–7.

[203] *Ibid.*, 578: "Pour la première fois en France on rompt durablement avec le concept de la monarchie patrimoniale ... Cette notion nouvellement adoptée interdit désormais tout partage du royaume qui n'est plus la propriété d'un homme ou d'une famille, mais une structure globale de relations humaines, juridiques, monétaires, sociologiques, historiques, linguistiques et religieuses hiérarchisées et coordonnées."

This was Oresme's inheritance after 1356: a broken city and a broken marketplace. I want to argue that with the collapse of the city and marketplace as models of systematic self-ordering and self-equalization came the collapse of Oresme's faith in the potentialities of the new model of equilibrium. Thus the pervasive pessimism in the *Politiques*, leading to the closing off of possibilities and the clinging to the status quo; thus the trust placed in the ordering wisdom and power of the crown; thus the abandonment of the citizen multitude (a genuine citizen multitude rather than one effectively defined out of existence) and the communal body as a whole as the leading political and economic actor in the *civitas*; thus the radical reduction in the meaning and active power of the Common Good in his political scheme; and thus the breaks on so many levels between the assumptions underlying the *De moneta* and those underlying the *Politiques*.

There are, of course, aspects of the French response to the plague that are unique to France, and there are aspects of Oresme's response that are unique to his situation as well. But overall they conform to a larger pattern that continued well into the fifteenth century across Europe: from the repeated attempts to replace market order (or "disorder" as it was perceived) by governmental fiat or guild control, to the near-total collapse of self-governing communes in Italy and their replacement by strong-man rule, to the political quieting of the European bourgeoisie and the turning of this class from being dynamic agents of change (if not revolution) when in their ascendancy during the thirteenth and early fourteenth centuries, to becoming agents of political and economic reaction and control in the context of a generally contracting economy. By the late fourteenth century, with its socioeconomic sources in the self-governing city and self-equalizing marketplace blocked and withering, the new model of equilibrium was imagined and invoked less and less by thinkers to explain the workings of either society or nature. (In the sixteenth century the model begins to reemerge, and in the seventeenth century it has returned in force, but that is a story that remains to be told.) Given what I have argued is the centrality of the ideal of equality and equalization to virtually all medieval discourses, the intellectual effects of this retreat were as deep and as striking as had been the effects of its formation. I would argue as well that the retreat of this vision in the third quarter of the fourteenth century, in response to the historical reversals cited above, reveals as much concerning the dependence of models of equilibrium – and the history of balance itself – upon social, political, and economic contexts as did the remarkable flourishing of this vision from the late thirteenth through the mid fourteenth century.

8   The new model of equilibrium in scholastic natural philosophy, *c.* 1325–1375

Therefore, equal intensities are designated by equal lines, a double intensity by a double line, and always in the same way if one proceeds proportionally (*sic semper proportionaliter procedendo*). And this is to be understood universally (*universaliter intelligendum*) in regard to every intensity that is divisible in the imagination, whether it be an active or non-active quality, a sensible or non-sensible subject, object, or medium.   Nicole Oresme, *Tractatus de configurationibus qualitatum et motuum*

You should understand that exactness transcends the human mind . . . For if an imperceptible excess – even a part smaller than a thousandth – could destroy an equality and alter a ratio from rational to irrational (*equalitatem tollit et proportionem mutat de rationali ad irrationalem*), how will you be able to know a punctual [exact] ratio of motions or celestial magnitudes?
> Nicole Oresme, *Tractatus de commensurabilitate vel incommensurabilitate*
> *motuum celi*

Now the center [of magnitude] of the earth is not the center of the universe, rather, the center of the earth's weight (*gravitas*) is the center, because the earth occupies the center of the universe by reason of its weight not its magnitude. It balances itself (*equilibrat se*) at the center of the universe by virtue of its weight, as in the mechanical scale (*in statera*) equal weights balance equally (*equales equilibrant*) against each other, even if their magnitudes are not equal.
> Jean Buridan, *Questiones super tres libros Metheorum*

In 1328, Thomas Bradwardine, a fellow of Merton College, Oxford, published his *Tractatus de proportionibus velocitatum in motibus* (*Treatise on the Proportions of Velocities in Motions*). Its impact on the history of mathematics and science was immediate and profound. In the words of its modern editor and translator:

Bradwardine's *De proportionibus* is, indeed, one of the key works in the history of the development of modern science, having been the first to announce a general law of physics whose expression calls for anything more than the most rudimentary mathematics . . . [Within this treatise] what may be called a

398

logarithmic, exponential, or geometric function first came to be applied in the expression of a physical theory.[1]

In the many scholarly articles that have been written on this treatise since the 1940s, when Anneliese Maier first explored its argument and its significance, two questions have consistently come to the fore: what might explain the nature of its innovations, and what might explain its surprising "success" – its immediate, and near-universal acceptance and application by the leading natural philosophers, first at Oxford and then at Paris, in Bradwardine's lifetime and after?[2] I want to argue that the answer to both questions is linked to the presence of the new model of equilibrium in the thought of leading university scholars by the first quarter of the fourteenth century.

The source of the problem Bradwardine treats in the *De proportionibus* is Aristotle's suggestion in both the *Physica* and *De caelo* that the speed of an object is determined by the relationship between the forces (*potentiae*) acting to impel it and the resistances acting to retard it.[3] Although Aristotle never framed his rule as a mathematical formula, his solution was generally understood to imply that kV = F/R, where V is the speed, F is the motive force exerted on the moved body, and R is the resistance impeding motion. When, for example, motive power is doubled and resistance remains constant, Aristotle maintained that speed is doubled;

---

[1] *Thomas of Bradwardine: His Tractatus de Proportionibus; Its Significance for the Development of Mathematical Physics*, ed. and trans. H. Lamar Crosby (Madison: University of Wisconsin Press, 1955), 12.

[2] Anneliese Maier, "Der Funktionsbegriff in der Physik des 14. Jahrhunderts," in *Die Vorläufer Galileis* (Rome: Edizioni di Storia e Letteratura, 1949), 81–110. For portions of this article that have been translated into English, see Anneliese Maier, "The Concept of the Function in Fourteenth-Century Physics," in *On the Threshold of Exact Science: Selected Writings of Anneliese Maier on Late Medieval Natural Philosophy*, ed. and trans. Steven Sargent (Philadelphia: University of Pennsylvania Press, 1982), 61–75. For a recent article devoted to these two questions, Edith Sylla, "The Origin and Fate of Thomas Bradwardine's *De proportionibus velocitatum in motibus* in Relation to the History of Mathematics," in *Mechanics and Natural Philosophy before the Scientific Revolution*, ed. W. R. Laird and S. Roux (Dordrecht: Springer, 2008), 67–119. See also Marshall Clagett, "Some Novel Trends in the Science of the Fourteenth Century," in *Art, Science, and History in the Renaissance*, ed. Charles Singleton (Baltimore, MD: Johns Hopkins University Press, 1967), 275–303. For the claim that Bradwardine may have based elements of his mathematical approach on insights first published several years earlier by his fellow Oxford Calculator, Richard Kilvington, see Elzbieta Jung and Robert Podkonski, "Richard Kilvington on Proportions," in *Mathématiques et théorie du mouvement (XIVe–XVIe siècles)*, ed. Joël Biard and Sabine Rommevaux (Villeneuve d'Ascq: Septentrion, 2008), 81–101.

[3] The primary loci of Aristotle's discussion are *Physics* VII.5, IV.8; *De caelo* III.2. On the use of the word "speed" to translate *velocitas* in this context, see Jean Celeyrette, "Bradwardine's Rule: A Mathematical Law?" in *Mechanics and Natural Philosophy*, ed. Laird and Roux, 51–66, at 53, n. 9.

when motive power is constant and resistance is doubled, speed is halved, and so on.

A number of thinkers in the early Christian and Islamic centuries recognized that the rule as stated by Aristotle was inadequate, and they elaborated various interpretations to overcome its uncertainties and mathematical inconsistencies.[4] Bradwardine was fully aware of these earlier positions, devoting the entire second chapter of his treatise to an analysis and critique of four "erroneous theories" that had arisen to clarify Aristotle's position, and pointing out the logical and mathematical problems that each "solution" brought with it.[5] He expends particular care refuting the most common understanding, that $kV = F/R$.[6] Among the many problems he finds with it is that it involves an insurmountable mathematical difficulty. If, following this understanding, the value of the force falls below the value of the resistance, there should, according to Aristotle's explicit statement, be no movement, and yet as long as some force remains, however small, the ratio F/R will show a positive mathematical value.[7] To this difficulty, Bradwardine adds another: the formula fails to square with the way things actually work in the world. If one man can barely move a heavy object (R), two men (2F) exerting their force will, he writes, move the object far faster than twice the speed of the single man.[8]

Following his lengthy critique of previous theories, Bradwardine introduces his own solution, which he believes will erase all mathematical inconsistencies and be more consonant with experience:

Now that these fogs of ignorance, these winds of demonstration, have been put to flight, it remains for the light of knowledge and of truth to shine forth. For true knowledge proposes a fifth theory which states that the proportion of the speeds of motions varies in accordance with the proportion of the power of the mover to the power of the thing moved (*quod proportio velocitatum in motibus sequitur proportionem potentiae motoris ad potentiam rei motae*).[9]

Two things are clear: (1) Bradwardine's theory represents a logico/mathematical rethinking and reframing rather than a criticism of Aristotle's

---

[4] Marshall Clagett, "Aristotelian Mechanics and Bradwardine's Dynamic Law of Movement," in Clagett, *The Science of Mechanics in the Middle Ages* (Madison: University of Wisconsin Press, 1959), 421–44.

[5] Bradwardine, *Tractatus de proportionibus*, 86–111. Bradwardine is particularly attentive to the comments and doubts expressed by Averroes in his commentary to *Physics* IV.

[6] Bradwardine, *Tractatus de proportionibus*, ch. 2, part 3, 94–105, at 95: "this theory is seen to be founded in many passages of Aristotle's writings."

[7] Crosby, Introduction to Bradwardine, *Tractatus de proportionibus*, 35–6. For example, if resistance remains constant at 2, and the force declines from 3 to 1, the speed (F/R) would have the positive mathematical value of ½, even though no motion could occur.

[8] Bradwardine, *Tractatus de proportionibus*, 98–9.

[9] *Ibid.*, 110–11. Murdoch, "*Mathesis*," 226.

basic (mis)understanding that speed is determined by the relationship between force and resistance; (2) the difference between Bradwardine's "true" understanding and the earlier theories he now saw as erroneous, rests upon the way he has defined the term "proportion."[10] Rather than thinking in terms of comparisons between numbers, which are essentially discrete entities, Bradwardine sought to create a mathematics of proportion proper to his perception of the world as he saw it, a world composed of qualities and quantities undergoing continual and continuous expansion and contraction. Velocity, force, and resistance, were, for Bradwardine, all imagined as continuous quantities, better represented and analyzed by lines which were open to continuous increase and decrease, rather than by discrete numbers alone.[11] Hence, in the *De proportionibus*, Bradwardine engages in a conscious project to shift between arithmetical and geometrical registers.[12] This shift had multiple consequences.

Perhaps the most crucial and (as it proved) influential of these consequences is that Bradwardine came to imagine the relationship governing motion as one in which, in general, proportions are multiplied by proportions, and, in particular, the proportion of force/resistance is multiplied by itself. In modern terms, his framing of the mathematics of motion vaulted into the realm of exponents and powers.[13] His reframing of Aristotle's formula for motion in these terms resulted in the following general rule: velocities vary arithmetically as the ratios of forces to resistances vary geometrically (i.e., exponentially).[14] As Anneliese Maier explained:

[10] For the complications associated with medieval terminology related to proportions and ratios, see Sylla, "Origin and Fate," 67–9 and n. 1; A. G. Molland, "The Geometrical Background to the 'Merton School,'" *British Journal for the History of Science* 4 (1968), 108–25. Sylla notes that the definition of proportion employed here by Bradwardine is consistent with the definition found in Campanus of Novara's Latin edition of Euclid's *Elements*, Books V and VI.

[11] John Murdoch, "The Medieval Language of Proportions," in *Scientific Change: Historical Studies in the Intellectual, Social, and Technical Conditions for Scientific Discovery and Technical Invention, from Antiquity to the Present* (New York: Basic Books, 1963), 237–71, esp. 265–6; Bradwardine, *Tractatus de proportionibus*, 110–11. Jung and Podkonski ("Richard Kilvington on Proportions," 91) make this point with respect to Kilvington's earlier application of continuous proportions to continuous motion.

[12] Murdoch notes ("Medieval Language of Proportions," 270) that following Bradwardine, "In effect, number was being considered an element of geometry; the Greek distinction between the continuous and the discrete was beginning to undergo erosion."

[13] Crosby, Introduction to Bradwardine, *Tractatus de proportionibus*, 20 ff.; Murdoch, "Medieval Language of Proportions," 265–70.

[14] Clagett, "Aristotelian Mechanics and Bradwardine's Dynamic Law of Motion," 418. He refers elsewhere to this formulation as Bradwardine's "exponential law" in "Some Novel Trends," 284.

when Bradwardine speaks of doubling and trebling a proportion, he does not mean multiplication by two or three, as in the case of simple quantities. Instead, as he explains ... he means a twofold or threefold multiplication of the proportion by itself, which is the same as squaring it or raising it to the third power."[15]

Translating medieval into modern mathematical terms and notation, in Bradwardine's conceptual scheme, a twofold increase in velocity is accomplished by "doubling" (in modern terms squaring) the proportion of force/resistance; conversely, reducing the velocity in half is accomplished through taking the square root of the F/R proportion.[16] If, for example, an object is being moved with a power of 3 against a resistance of 1, doubling its velocity requires that the proportion be squared (i.e., raised to 9/1), rather than merely doubled (i.e., raised to 6/1). Tripling of speed requires that the proportion be cubed (i.e., raised to 27/1). Halving the speed requires a force equivalent to the square root of 3/1, and so on. Again translating medieval into modern mathematical notation, in place of $kV = F/R$, Bradwardine's rule held that $V^n = F/R$, or stated another way, $V = \log_n (F/R)$.[17] In short, in Bradwardine's new understanding, exponential roots and powers have become keys to the mathematical understanding of nature.

Marshall Clagett was one of the first historians of science after Anneliese Maier to recognize the crucial importance of Bradwardine's innovations in mathematical physics. Intrigued by Bradwardine's vault from an integer-based arithmetic to a roots- and powers-based "geometrical" treatment of proportions in the representation of natural activity, Clagett searched for possible textual precursors.[18] In his wide reading, the closest he came was a short treatise written by the great Muslim mathematician and philosopher, Al-Kindi (c. 800–70 CE), which had been translated into Latin in the twelfth century. In this work, Al-Kindi pegged the arithmetical ordering of degrees of intensity of compound medicines to a geometrical increase in their intensive force.[19] At roughly the same time, but unknown to Clagett, Michael McVaugh was coming to a parallel conclusion concerning the medical background to Bradwardine's understanding through his study of Arnau

---

[15] Maier, "The Concept of the Function," 72–3.

[16] Bradwardine, *Tractatus de proportionibus*, Theorem 2, 112–13.

[17] Crosby, Introduction to Bradwardine, *Tractatus de proportionibus*, 12–13; Murdoch, "*Mathesis*," 226; Maier, "Concept of the Function," 73.

[18] Bradwardine himself recognized that he was arguing for a specifically "geometric proportionality." His first theorem states (Crosby, Introduction to Bradwardine, *Tractatus de proportionibus*, 111): "Et hoc de geometrica proportionalitate intelligas." Sylla shows ("Origin and Fate," 92, 97) that Bradwardine's rule is associated with "geometric proportionality" throughout the fourteenth century.

[19] Clagett, *Science of Mechanics*, 439, n. 35.

de Vilanova's *Aphorismi de gradibus*.[20] McVaugh recognized that Arnau had read and utilized Al-Kindi's short treatise in the writing of this work, but he suggested that if Bradwardine and others at Oxford in the fourteenth century had indeed been influenced by a previous textual treatment of increase by geometrical progression, it was much more likely that medical writings from the University of Montpellier at the turn of the fourteenth century, and in particular the *Aphorismi de gradibus*, had been the manuscript source.[21]

McVaugh's evidence for this, based on numerous parallels between Arnau's mathematical scheme and Bradwardine's, as well as on the fact that an excellent manuscript of the *Aphorismi de gradibus* was held in the Merton College Library, persuaded Clagett, as it has historians of science to the present day.[22] McVaugh, however, had been admirably careful not to claim that he had provided "proof" of Arnau's influence, and I have no intention of making a further claim for his textual influence here. What I find more important is McVaugh's point that the *Aphorismi de gradibus* represented more than a new mathematical plan grounded in geometrical progression. It crystallized, in McVaugh's words, "a more general law of experience governing *all* sense impressions, a medieval hint at psychophysics" (McVaugh's emphasis).[23] In other words, for Arnau, the geometric "doubling" (squaring) of the ratios of intensities, which he posited behind every successive degree of pharmacological increase, actually represented the way that qualities (such as medicinal effects) were experienced and perceived by the body and its senses. Only those qualitative steps that represent a "doubling" (exponential) increase in intensity are, he believed, sensible to humans.[24]

McVaugh's recognition of the centrality of experience, "sense," and "fit" to Arnau's striking mathematical reformulation can, I believe, be applied equally to the case of Bradwardine and his followers. The innovations found in Bradwardine's physics are not (as all modern commentators note)

[20] For my discussion of the place of Arnau and his *Aphorismi de gradibus* in the evolution of the "new" model of equilibrium, see Chapter 4.
[21] McVaugh first published his findings in "Arnald of Villanova and Bradwardine's Law," *Isis* 58 (1967), 56–64.
[22] *Ibid.*, 59, 64; Clagett, "Some Novel Trends," 284.
[23] McVaugh, "Arnald of Villanova and Bradwardine's Law," 61–2. Discussed in Chapter 4 above, pp. 220–2.
[24] Arnaldus de Villanova, *Aphorismi de gradibus*, ed. and commentary Michael McVaugh, in *Arnaldi de Villanova Opera medica omnia*, vol. II (Granada-Barcelona: Seminarium Historiae Medicae Granatensis, 1975), Aphorism 22, 175: "Est autem in obiectis aliorum sensuum evidens ... necesse est ut potencia qua movere habet sensum illum ad minus dupletur in eo ... quod in situ temperamenti nullatenus alteret tactum et in primo gradu alteret manifeste, necesse est ut in primo gradu respectu temperamenti saltem dupletur."

the product of a rigorous empirical program. Rather, they derive from mathematical rules that "fit" his imagination of what was probable and possible in the environments he inhabited – environments in which an arithmetic based in discrete number had given way to a geometry of expanding, contracting, and intersecting lines, appropriate to a new "world of lines"; environments in which the process of multiplication was real and ever-present (as it was in the dynamic of commercial exchange and in the urban marketplace itself in this period); environments in which it had become *possible to think* in terms of the exponential increase and decrease of intensities and motions of all kinds, and in which such thinking now made good sense.

Systematic relation and equalization in Bradwardine's rule

One of the deepest links between the new model of equilibrium and Bradwardine's rule is that both are organized around the end of equalization. In Bradwardine's case, equalization takes the form of establishing a system of "functional dependence" among the variables of velocity, force, and resistance involved in motion, each capable of continuous and infinitely divisible expansion and contraction.[25] Changes to any of the variables automatically affect each of the others in a regular and mathematically definable manner. For this reason, the technical mathematical term "function" has been attached to Bradwardine's rule from the time that Anneliese Maier first analyzed it and recognized its significance. At the time Bradwardine wrote, neither the equals sign nor the form of the modern equation had yet been invented. Nevertheless, Maier saw fit to describe his mathematical "rule" as a "functional equation," and Marshall Clagett, normally wary of anachronism and careful with his nomenclature, speaks of it as a "mechanical equation."[26] Maier and later historians of science who continue to employ the term "function" with respect to the *De proportionibus* are well aware of the differences between scholastic understandings of mathematical functionality and modern understandings, but they recognize at the same time that Bradwardine's mathematical rule represented a large and crucial step in the direction of the modern function.[27]

---

[25] Maier, "Concept of the Function," 64.
[26] Maier, "Funktionsgleichung," in "Der Funktionsbegriff," 86; Clagett, Preface to the *Tractatus de Proportionibus*, vii.
[27] Maier, "Concept of the Function," 63; Sylla, "Origin and Fate," 68–9. For an argument questioning the application of terms like "law" and "function" to Bradwardine's rule,

In sum, Bradwardine's equation linking velocities, forces, and resistances represents in purified form a relational system in dynamic equilibrium: change one value and all other values change automatically in turn, according to a strict and knowable mathematical order. In its formal structure and working action, Bradwardine's function thus represents a model of equilibrium *in nuce*. As such it maps onto other such models in miniature examined in previous chapters: the dynamic equalization of Olivi's urban marketplace; the relational and proportional *aequalitas* of the Galenic complexion; the self-equalizing, geometrically proportioning *civitas* of Marsilius of Padua and Turisanus. As each of these previous intellectual constructions entered into intellectual culture, they "communicated" and reinforced the larger and more diffuse modeling of balance and its potentialities that they reflected. So too did Bradwardine's rule.

Historians of science have suggested a number of explanations for the surprising success of Bradwardine's rule. These include its mathematical "effectiveness," even "elegance," its improvement over previous explanations of the F/R relationship in observational terms, its provision of an instrument of analysis that could be used over a range of topics of interest within the medieval university, its application to continuous magnitudes, and, overall, its geometrical framing in an intellectual culture in which the infinitely divisible continuum was seen to be a key to the philosophical understanding of nature.[28] In addition to these factors, I want to suggest that the invention, acceptance, and rapid spread of Bradwardine's rule was tied as well to its close to perfect "fit" with the new model of equilibrium whose process of formation we have been following. The *De proportionibus* was composed within a half-decade of Marsilius of Padua's *Defensor pacis* (1324), and in the same generation as Turisanus' *Plusquam commentum* on Galen's *Tegni* (*c.* 1315). Judging by the evidence of these and other works, the *De proportionibus* was written at a time when the new model of equilibrium, and the greatly expanded sense of the potentialities of systematic equalization it carried, was already being shared and shaped at the highest levels of university culture.

see Celeyrette, "Bradwardine's Rule: A Mathematical Law?" 51–61. Celeyrette is, however, more accepting of these terms being applied to the expansion of the rule by Bradwardine's fellow Mertonians, John Dumbleton and Richard Swineshead.

[28] Sylla, "Origin and Fate," 78, 94; Anneliese Maier, "The Achievements of Late Scholastic Natural Philosophy," in *On the Threshold of Exact Science*, ed. Sargent, 143–70, at 156–7; John Murdoch, "Thomas Bradwardine: Mathematics and Continuity in the Fourteenth Century," in *Mathematics and its Application to Science and Natural Philosophy in the Middle Ages: Essays in Honor of Marshall Clagett*, ed. Edward Grant and John Murdoch (Cambridge University Press, 1987), 103–37, at 110: "Because the issue of the composition of continua is a central problem in [fourteenth-century] natural philosophy, it therefore follows that mathematics, and geometry in particular, should provide the basis for unraveling the truth relative to that problem."

In essence, Bradwardine's rule gave mathematical form and expression to the new model of equilibrium. Virtually all of the model's major elements find their place within it: the centering on the process of systematic equalization; the placing of its moving elements within a relativized field in dynamic equilibrium; the shift between arithmetical and geometrical registers; the jump to the exponential realm; the grounding in continuity and proportionality; the move away from fixed values and perfections toward representing and measuring motion and change; and the successful integration of formerly destabilizing and open-ended elements, such as infinite divisibility and exponential multiplication, into its philosophical/mathematical order. Bradwardine's rule accomplished the further task of tying all of these elements into a "functional" whole, one that "worked" mathematically, even if it was but loosely tied to empirical observation. Its remarkable success indicates that by the second quarter of the fourteenth century, it "worked" psychologically as well.

Bradwardine's rule and the latitude (*latitudo*) as a measure of intensities

The term "latitude" signifying a measuring continuum can, as we have seen, be traced back to Galenic writings. Its Latin form, *latitudo*, appeared in Gerard of Cremona's late twelfth-century translations of Galen's *Tegni* and Ibn Ridwan's commentary on the *Tegni* from Arabic source texts, as well as in his translation of Avicenna's *Canon of Medicine*.[29] In these early texts it signified an approximate range linking the healthy body to the sick body through the "neither" body. Each of these was itself viewed as a continuum within which the proportional balance of the four primary qualities that determined health and sickness could and did vary continually. In the late thirteenth century, both the conception and the use of the latitude rapidly expanded within a wide range of scholastic disciplines: medicine, natural philosophy, ethics, and (as we have seen) economic thought, as these discourses began to focus much more closely on questions touching on the measurement of motion and change.[30] In the field

---

[29] For discussions on this point, see Chapter 3 above.

[30] Duns Scotus and Henry of Ghent are among the philosophers and theologians who employ the concept of the latitude to signify an approximative, potentially numerable range of values. As noted in Chapter 2 above, Arnau's contemporary, Peter of John Olivi, applied it to the licit limit of price fluctuation in the marketplace through his conception of a "latitude of just price" (*latitudo iusti precii*). For an argument that links the expanding use of the *latitudo* as a conceptual measure of intensities in scholastic speculation to social, economic, and administrative developments in the area of measurement taking place in society both within and beyond the schools, see my *Economy and Nature in the Fourteenth Century*, esp. 124–6, 167–70, 182–5, 192–4.

of medicine, Taddeo Alderotti wrote of the latitude as if it were a real interval, divisible into degrees, defining a real distance along which the qualitative motion between health and sickness takes place.[31] In the following generation, Arnau de Vilanova imagined and employed the latitude as an instrument of proportionalization and relation as well as an instrument of measurement, as he made the conceptual leap from a mathematics of arithmetical addition to one of geometrical multiplication.[32] To reiterate: where the traditional scheme of pharmacological measurement held that each succeeding degree of a medicine's qualitative intensity represented a single unit step above the one below it, Arnau asserted that as degrees ascend arithmetically by single integers, the strength of the medicine (its qualitative intensity) increases geometrically by its square (*per augmentum dupli*).[33] It was the latitude's openness to infinite division and extension that allowed it to serve Arnau and others to come as a measure of geometric multiplication.[34] With all the links that exist and have been previously recognized between Arnau's mathematical scheme and Bradwardine's rule, there is, however, one link missing: the latitude itself.[35] The term never appears in the *De proportionibus*, even though Bradwardine's conception of proportions forming a continuous geometric progression would seem to invite its use.

The term does, however, appear, and frequently so, in the writings of Bradwardine's fellow logicians and natural philosophers at Merton College, Oxford, who soon came to recognize how well the measuring latitude fitted with the mathematics of Bradwardine's rule. John Dumbleton (*c.* 1310 – *c.* 1349), a fellow at Merton from 1338, and, like Bradwardine, a core member of that group of logicians and natural philosophers now commonly known as the "Oxford Calculators," dedicated a portion of his monumental *Summa logicae et philosophiae naturalis* to expanding the philosophical use of the latitude, with Bradwardine's

---

[31] Taddeo, *Tegni*, 31ra: "Latitudinem gradualem voco secundum quod magis et minus distat sanitas ab optima sanitate."

[32] Arnaldus de Villanova, *Aphorismi de gradibus*, Aphorism 37, at 200: "idem erit modus accipiendi proporciones, scilicet per numerum unius qualitatis relatum ad numerum alterius." For my argument linking the form and function of Arnau's latitude to the instrumental "shape" of money as measure in exchange, see Chapter 4 above, pp. 225–7.

[33] *Ibid.*, Aphorism 19, at 159–64. Note that Arnau's new scheme is constructed around the end of equalization, as were virtually all measuring schemes in scholastic medicine. Aphorism 22, 173: "omnis inequalitas cuiuscumque augmenti reducitur ad equalitatem mediante proporcione dupli"; "in sola proporcione dupli naturaliter reperitur equalitas."

[34] *Ibid.*, Aphorism 14, at 157: "Distancie cuiuslibet gradus integritas tanta est quanta est latitudo ipsius … quod distancia integra qualitatis a temperamento constituit gradum."

[35] McVaugh, "Arnald of Villanova and Bradwardine's Law"; *Aphorismi de gradibus*, 36. For my earlier discussion of this connection, see Chapter 4 above.

rule firmly in mind.[36] Dumbleton was not the first Mertonian to employ
the latitude, nor the first to link it to Bradwardine's "functional equation,"
but he took it in notable and, as it turned out, influential new directions.[37]
Of these directions, I restrict myself to those that served the project of
equalization.

From its earliest philosophical uses, even when it was still conceived
primarily as an approximative range with no representative dimension,
the latitude served the process of comparison.[38] Between its first
philosophical applications at the cusp of the fourteenth century and
the time of Dumbleton's *Summa*, the latitude had gained specificity
and tangibility to the point where it could, in Edith Sylla's description,
be physically identified as a "particular measure of the intensity of
a quality at a given point."[39] In concert with the expansion of geometrical thinking within fourteenth-century natural philosophy,
Dumbleton's latitude had evolved to where it could be represented
by a geometric line functioning as a measuring continuum: the greater
the intensity the longer the line, the lesser the shorter, with equal
intensities represented by equal latitudes.[40] Dumbleton was able
to employ his latitude in this fashion because he (as well as other
of the Merton Calculators) had begun to imagine the motion of
qualitative change (the increase and decrease in qualitative intensities)
as an additive process occurring over a real "qualitative space" or
"qualitative distance," which they envisioned as a linear magnitude.[41]
This cluster of conceptual innovations, shared by the Mertonians and

---

[36] Edith Sylla, *The Oxford Calculators and the Mathematics of Motion 1320–1350: Physics and the Measurement by Latitudes* (New York: Garland, 1991), 576–7; Sylla, "Origin and Fate," 92–4.

[37] Dumbleton's innovations are outlined in Sylla, *Oxford Calculators and the Mathematics of Motion*, 308–427.

[38] See for example, Edith Sylla's discussion of its early philosophical use to determine the mid-point or medium between two qualitative contraries in the writing of Walter Burley: "Medieval Concepts of the Latitude of Forms: The Oxford Calculators," *Archives d'histoire doctrinale et littéraire du Moyen Âge* 40 (1973), 223–83, esp. 236–8; Sylla, *Oxford Calculators and the Mathematics of Motion*, 345.

[39] Sylla, *Oxford Calculators and the Mathematics of Motion*, 345, 378: "What was primarily conceptual ... thus became physical also." The same can be said of its treatment by Dumbleton's fellow Calculator, Richard Swineshead. On this, see Marshall Clagett, "Richard Swineshead and Late Medieval Physics: The Intension and Remission of Qualities," *Osiris* 9 (1950), 131–61, at 139–40.

[40] Sylla, *Oxford Calculators and the Mathematics of Motion*, 385–6: "Both latitudes and degrees are homogeneous as distance in Euclidean space is homogeneous ... a latitude is imagined as similar to a geometric line, where any part of the line is similar to any other part."

[41] *Ibid.*, 397: "Unde si nominaremus spatium in quo est motus alterationis 'spatium qualitativum' ... sicut dicimus spatium in quo est motus localis 'distantiam quantitativam.'"

subsequently conveyed to the scholars at Paris, provides one of the clearest illustrations of the evolution of a new image of the world in this period – a world of lines in continual expansion and contraction.[42] By the mid fourteenth century, the dominant paradigm in natural philosophy held that all motion involves the linear traversal of space, whether that distance be qualitative (as in alteration) or quantitative (as in local motion).[43]

The more truly geometrical the latitude became, the more apt it became as an instrument of comparison and relation and thus as an instrument of equalization. In a passage from his advanced introduction to geometry (*Geometria speculativa*), Bradwardine underlined the connection between relation and equalization. The properties that geometers demonstrate about magnitudes are, he wrote, "almost all relative (*omnes relative*), like equality, inequality, regularity, irregularity, commensurability, incommensurability, the same and different."[44] Equality is the first geometrical relation Bradwardine lists because it is by far the most prevalent relation considered in Euclid's *Elements*. In the standard works on geometry from Euclid through the medieval period (including Bradwardine's *Geometria speculativa*), equalities are the first things students are taught to look for and work with.[45] When Dumbleton was writing, which coincided with the most innovative and productive period for the Merton Calculators, logicians and natural philosophers who were thinking and working in geometrical terms, thought and worked continually with equalities. They did so at the same time that they were developing the latitude as a conceptual instrument. Dumbleton's *Summa* provides two lucid examples of this fusion.

---

[42] *Ibid.*, 387–97, 570: "nulla qualitas intenditur nec remittitur per adquisitionem sed subiectum qualitatis intenditur et remittitur per adquisitionem et deperditionem realem qualitatum." For these comments of Dumbleton's, see also E. A. Moody, "The Rise of Mechanism in 14th Century Natural Philosophy: Translations of Texts on the Causal and Mathematical Analysis of Motion by John Buridan (ca. 1300–1358) and John Dumbleton (fl. 1328–1340)" (typescript, Columbia University Library, New York, 1950), 34–6.

[43] Sylla, *Oxford Calculators and the Mathematics of Motion*, 397; Sylla, "Medieval Concepts of the Latitude of Forms," 263: "Dumbleton's conception of a latitude is also more quantitative ... because his view of the latitude of quality makes it exactly analogous to distance in space. Thus the latitude of quality is a homogeneous continuum on which the only differences are differences in length, a longer segment of latitude starting from zero degree corresponding to a greater degree."

[44] Thomas Bradwardine, *Geometria speculativa*, ed. and trans. A. George Molland (Stuttgart: Steiner, 1989), 20–1: "Passiones autem quas de magnitudinibus demonstramus sunt omnes relative, sicut equalitas, inequalitas, regularitas irregularitas, commensurabilitas, incommensurabilitas, idem et diversum."

[45] See for example, Bradwardine's list of "prime and immediate propositions," *ibid.*, 24–5.

Equalization and early formulations of the Merton "mean speed theorem"

The first example illustrates the link between the Euclidean method of working with equalities and the use of latitudes to measure, relate, and equalize qualitative intensities. Dumbleton begins his discussion on the quantification of qualities with the proposition that, "The precise and essential cause of increase in an intensible and remissible quality [i.e., a quality capable of continuous increase and/or decrease] is the distance or latitude in which there occurs genuine motion in quality."[46] Based on this, he arrives at a relation of equality: "All qualities in the same species, whether they be uniform or non-uniform, are necessarily equally intense in their natures, as long as they contain equal latitudes – i.e., equal qualitative distances."[47] This is followed by a further linking of the latitude to a relation of equality: "From these things this conclusion is evident, that every quality in the same species, which has the same latitude, is of equal intension." Having established these points, Dumbleton is in a position to artic-ulate a mathematical theorem that had only recently been discovered by his fellow Mertonians and that is often judged to be among the most important and "fruitful" mathematical achievements of the fourteenth century: the so-called "Merton mean speed theorem."[48] Dumbleton framed the theorem in the following words: "Every finite latitude [of motion] beginning at rest and uniformly acquired, will correspond to its mean degree."[49] His fellow Calculator, Richard Swineshead, expressed the theorem in a slightly different way: "every latitude of motion uniformly acquired or lost corresponds to its middle

[46] Sylla *Oxford Calculators and the Mathematics of Motion*, 571: "Causa precisa et essentialis intensionis in qualitate intensibili et remissibili est distantia sive latitudo in qua fit motus verus in qualitate."

[47] *Ibid.*, 570: "Tertia dicit [the position Dumbleton holds] quod omnes qualitates in eadem specie sive fuerint uniformes sive difformes equales latitudines continentes, id est distantias qualitativas, equeintensas necessario in suis naturis consistere."

[48] The adjective is Clagett's, *Science of Mechanics*, 267. On the history of this theorem, see Edith Sylla, "The Oxford Calculators' Middle Degree Theorem in Context," *Early Science and Medicine* 15 (2010), 338–70. For an edition and translation of Dumbleton's treatment of the mean speed theorem in the *Summa logica*, with commentary, see Clagett, *Science of Mechanics in the Middle Ages*, 305–25. Clagett also includes editions and trans-lations of treatments by the Calculators William Heytebury (270–89) and Richard Swineshead (290–304). See also James Weisheipl, "The Place of Dumbleton and the Merton School," *Isis* 50 (1959), 439–54, at 453.

[49] Clagett, *Science of Mechanics*, 324–5: "Sed cum omnis latitudo incipiens a quiete et unifor-miter adquisita suo medio gradui correspondet." See also Sylla, *Oxford Calculators and the Mathematics of Motion*, 579.

degree."[50] Here again, we find equalization – in this case what can truly be labeled "dynamic equalization" – at the core of this mathematical innovation.

In modern terms, the mean speed theorem holds that the velocity of a uniformly accelerated motion, measured from its starting point to its maximum value, is equal to its value at the mid-point of the accelerated motion.[51] There is, characteristically, a balancing or mid-point in this equalizing imagination, but here, rather than being fixed and stable (as older models of equalization would have required), the balancing mid-point moves continually with respect to the increase of the total latitude. Here as elsewhere, the process of equalization and the goal of *aequalitas* are more than vague abstractions: they provide the conceptual framework for the theorem; they underpin the dynamic relationship between each of the elements that comprise the systematic whole; and their presence tests and confirms the logic and mathematics of the general rule. In performing these functions, the requirement for *aequalitas* within fourteenth-century natural philosophy functions much like conservation laws function in modern science. One thing is clear: with the formulation of the mean speed theorem more than two and a half centuries before Galileo employed it as a foundational element of his physics, Dumbleton and his fellow Calculators captured the dynamic potentialities of equalization in a way that had never before been imagined.[52]

The Calculator's latitude as a graded measuring line

Dumbleton's second application of the latitude to the project of equalization is similarly striking. Like all the leading natural philosophers of his period, he was won over by the explanatory power of Bradwardine's rule. He dedicated a section of his *Summa* to the task of explicating further Bradwardine's functional equation of velocity, force, and resistance. To do so, he employed the latitude as an instrument of representation and measurement, reasoning that since velocity, force, and resistance are all continuous qualities, the entity that represents and measures them must

---

[50] Clagett's translation, *Science of Mechanics*, 290, 298: "omnis latitudo motus uniformiter acquisita vel deperdita suo gradui medio correspondet."

[51] Weisheipl, "Dumbleton and the Merton School," 453. For Galileo's statement and use of the rule in the formation of his mathematical physics, see Galileo Galilei, *The Two New Sciences*, Third Day, Theorem 1, Proposition 1, in Clagett, *Science of Mechanics*, 409–14. It has been demonstrated that Galileo was familiar with the Mertonians' formulation of this theorem.

[52] The implications of the mean speed theorem and its links to the new model of equilibrium are discussed again later in this chapter.

be continuous as well.[53] On this basis, Dumbleton takes the step of depicting and employing the latitude as a geometric line capable of continuous expansion and contraction and, therefore, capable of representing and quantifying all manner of changing intensities, including the exponentially "doubling" proportions that Bradwardine's rule posits.[54] Indeed, Dumbleton imagines Bradwardine's continuous geometric proportions as constituting a latitude in itself, beginning with the proportion of equality and extending to ever greater proportions of inequality. The physical reality that Dumbleton allows the latitude of proportions finds clear expression in its actually being drawn in the margins of manuscripts of the *Summa*. It appears as an inked line on which the proportions 1:1, 2:1, 4:1, 8:1, and 16:1 are drawn equal distances apart.[55]

But there is more. Dumbleton has also imagined the latitude of velocity as a line on which varying velocities can be represented, with equal parts of the latitude corresponding to equal differences of velocity. This latitude of velocity, too, finds graphic representation in the manuscript's margins as a drawn line, divided into numbered sections.[56] Moreover, this second line is then drawn parallel and in relation to the line representing the latitude of proportions. In this way the two lines/latitudes are brought into visual as well as conceptual relation, providing a striking illustration of Dumbleton's statement that "to equal latitudes of proportions correspond equal latitudes of motion."[57] The juxtaposition of the two drawn lines also provides a concrete rendering of the assertion at the heart of Bradwardine's rule: a velocity that is arithmetically doubled or tripled corresponds to a proportion that is geometrically "doubled" or "tripled," i.e, squared or cubed.

With respect to this visible presentation of paired latitudes, Edith Sylla has written:

It seems very likely that the drawing of parallel lines and labeling of them to represent Bradwardine's function was not only an illustration but a practical tool. One could manipulate the variables and determine the results using the parallel lines more easily than by calculation. Thus the parallel scales or latitudes could function like a log table or a slide rule in simplifying mathematical operations.[58]

---

[53] Sylla, *Oxford Calculators and the Mathematics of Motion*, 402.
[54] Sylla, "Medieval Concepts of the Latitude of Forms," 263.
[55] Sylla, *Oxford Calculators and the Mathematics of Motion*, 402; Sylla, "Medieval Concepts of the Latitude of Forms," 265.
[56] Sylla, *Oxford Calculators and the Mathematics of Motion*, 403.
[57] Celeyrette, "Bradwardine's Rule: A Mathematical Law?" 60: "Equali latitudini proportionis correspondet equalis latitudo motus."
[58] Sylla, *Oxford Calculators and the Mathematics of Motion*, 407; Sylla, "Medieval Concepts of the Latitude of Forms," 266.

In regard to this statement, I have suggested elsewhere that the merchant's abacus and the numbered scale of "money of account," which were in common use as measuring and equalizing scales in economic exchange, were the medieval functional equivalents of the slide rule Sylla refers to above. They could well have provided the practical models for Dumbleton's conception of how equalizing latitudes might actually "work" in tandem as well as for their appearance as drawn and manipulable lines in the margins of the *Summa*. But whatever the practical models behind this construction may have been, Dumbleton's verbal descriptions of his paired latitudes, together with the marginal drawings that visually represented them, present us with both a fluid, fully integrated relational system and an equalizing "mechanism" in one, with exponential increase and decrease added to the mix. As such, it presents a lucid and graphic instantiation of the new model of equilibrium at work in a world of ever-expanding, contracting, and intersecting lines.

The transmission of ideas and insights from Oxford to Paris: the latitude as imagined by Nicole Oresme

The speculation of Bradwardine, Dumbleton, and other of the Oxford Calculators, in addition to that of William of Ockham, all of which contributed to what historians of science have termed the "new physics" of the fourteenth century, began filtering into the intellectual culture of the University of Paris in the 1330s.[59] It was not until the 1340s that the full implications of these innovations were being absorbed at Paris to the point that scholars not only routinely referenced the writings of the Calculators but began to build upon them.[60] Of these Parisian inheritors, the scholar who built the most impressive intellectual structures upon the earlier labors was Nicole Oresme. In the process, he created works

---

[59] Edith Sylla, "The Transmission of the New Physics of the Fourteenth Century from England to the Continent," in *La nouvelle physique du XIVe siècle*, ed. Stefano Caroti and Pierre Souffrin (Florence: Olschki, 1997), 65–110. Sylla notes (75–92) the importance of the reception of Ockham and his "minimalist ontologies" at Paris to the later reception of the writings of the Calculators. Cf. William Courtenay, "The Debate over Ockham's Physical Theories at Paris," in *La nouvelle physique*, 45–63.

[60] William Courtenay, "Arts and Theology at Paris, 1326–1340," in *Nicolas d'Autrécourt et la faculté des arts de Paris (1317–1340)*, ed. Stefano Caroti and Christophe Grellard (Cesena: Stilgraf Editrice, 2006), 15–63. For the continuation of the influence of the Calculator tradition at Paris into the later fourteenth century, see Jean Celeyrette and Edmond Mazet, "Le mouvement du point de vue de la cause et le mouvement du point de vue de l'effet dans le *Traité des rapports* d'Albert de Saxe," *Revue d'histoire des sciences* 56 (2003), 419–37.

of remarkable invention and scope, universally recognized today as landmarks in the history of mathematics and science.

Many of the critical components of the measuring *latitudo*, as it was imagined by Dumbleton and later Calculators, appear again in the writings of Oresme. Among these are: its widespread use as a measuring continuum in the intellectual project to quantify qualities and qualitative change; its capacity to represent (and measure) increases and decreases in qualitative intensities; its linkage to notions of "qualitative distance" and "qualitative space"; its potential to be infinitely divided and extended; its openness to proportional and numerable division and gradation; its identification with the geometric line; its association, specifically, with a line that can be physically drawn and utilized in the process of representation, calculation, and explication; and, perhaps above all, its use as an instrument of proportionalization and relation. Every one of these elements facilitated the application of the latitude to the intellectual project of equalization, a project shared by multiple disciplines within university culture of the fourteenth century. But it was Oresme's joining of these elements into a coherent and cohesive unity that signaled the compelling presence of the new model of equilibrium. Oresme not only adopted earlier uses of the latitude and earlier schemes of measurement and equalization by means of graded continua, he consistently refined and expanded upon them. Indeed, so many and so profound were his insights in this area, that a thorough consideration of them is beyond the scope of this chapter. Here I limit my discussion to several of his most important contributions, some of which are now commonly recognized as milestones in the history of mathematical and scientific thought.

For all that Oresme owed to the pioneering work of the Oxford Calculators, he also clearly recognized the weaknesses and limitations of their latitude as an instrument through which to measure and quantify qualitative change. While the Calculator's expandable, contractible, and numerable line/latitude can be applied to the increase (intension) or decrease (remission) of any qualitative intensity, Oresme recognized that it can say nothing about the quantitative *extension* of a quality within a given subject. In the Calculator's scheme, for example, two white squares of different sizes, which possess the same intensity of whiteness (or heat, or any other quality), or the same degree of increase or decrease of whiteness or any other quality, will be designated by the same latitude of intensity, even though the larger square will contain proportionally more whiteness than the smaller. The single scale represented by the Calculator's latitude was, Oresme saw, incapable of measuring or representing the crucial quantitative element of extension. He did more, however, than merely recognize this limitation. In a work of striking originality, he devised a dual-coordinate geometrical system to correct it.

There is substantial agreement among historians of science that Oresme wrote his *Treatise on the Configurations of Qualities and Motions* (*Tractatus de configurationibus qualitatum et motuum*) at some time in the 1350s, while he was attached to the College of Navarre at the University of Paris, either as a fellow (before 1356) or as its Grand Master (1356–62).[61] If, as Marshall Clagett, the editor and translator of this work, finds "inherently probable," the treatise was composed between 1351 and 1355, then the *De configurationibus* (along with virtually all of Oresme's major mathematical and scientific works in Latin), would have been composed at roughly the same time that he composed his *De moneta* (*c.* 1355–6).[62] Just as his pioneering analysis of money and minting reveals the clear imprint of the new model of equilibrium on his social and economic thought, so too do his most innovative speculations in the sphere of physical and mathematical thought. Nowhere is this imprint more apparent than in the systems of measurement and representation he invented and applied in his *De configurationibus*.

Systematic relation and equilibrium in Oresme's *De configurationibus*

The opening words to the *De configurationibus* are so revealing of how Oresme sensed and imagined the world he inhabited that they bear citing in some length.[63]

Every measurable thing except numbers is imagined in the manner of continuous quantity. Therefore, for the mensuration of such a thing (*pro eius mensuratione*), it is necessary that points, lines, and surfaces, or their properties be imagined ... For

---

[61] *Nicole Oresme and the Medieval Geometry of Qualities and Motions: A Treatise on the Uniformity and Difformity of Intensities known as Tractatus de configurationibus qualitatum et motuum*, ed. and trans. Marshall Clagett (Madison: University of Wisconsin Press, 1968), 14, 122–33.

[62] On the socioeconomic background to the writing of the *De moneta*, including a brief biography of Oresme, see Chapter 7 above. Clagett, in his magisterial edition and translation of the *De configurationibus*, speculates in his Introduction (141) that it was "written about the same time" as the *De moneta*.

[63] I cited these opening words previously in *Economy and Nature in the Fourteenth Century*, 202, where I read them as a reflection, in part, of the culture-wide use of the instrument of money (in form a graded and numbered continuum or line) to measure the continual increase and decrease of economic value in the marketplace. I also read the shared scholastic project to "quantify qualities," seen here in the opening chapters of the *De configurationibus*, as a reflection, in part, of the remarkable and often remarked upon capacity of money to quantify qualitative values in market exchange. I see my present analysis as complementary to my earlier reading.

whatever ratio is found to exist between intensity and intensity, in relating intensities of the same kind, a similar ratio is found to exist between line and line and
vice versa ... Therefore, the measure of intensities can be fittingly imagined as the
measure of lines, since an intensity could be imagined as being infinitely increased
in the same way as a line.[64]

Here, expressed with unparalleled clarity, is the vision of a world composed of ever-increasing and decreasing qualitative intensities open to
mathematical representation and analysis.[65] To an extraordinary degree,
but befitting his self-identification as a geometer, Oresme proposes
that this phenomenal world can be "imagined" (potest ymaginari) as a
dynamically fluid environment of expanding and contracting lines –
what I have called a "world of lines."[66] "Since," he writes, "the quantity
or ratio of lines is better known and is more readily conceived by us," their
imagination and use "naturally helps and leads to the knowledge of
any intensity."[67]

As careful as Oresme is to provide verbal descriptions of his scheme in
the De configurationibus, he is also intent, from the first, to illustrate its
elements with actual drawn figures representing the lines and "surfaces"
that he imagines. He does so reasoning that his plan to quantify qualities
will be more "quickly and perfectly understood when it is explained by
a visible example."[68] Toward this end, dozens of geometrical figures –
rectangles, triangles, parallelograms, semicircles, and a host of other
shapes – appear throughout the text to illustrate and drive home its
major points. As Oresme opens the phenomenal world ever further to

---

[64] De configurationibus, I.i, 164–7. This and all following translations from the De
configurationibus are Clagett's, except where noted. Given the availability of this
translation, I have chosen not to offer the Latin in full in the notes. Where the
Latin phrasing is particularly revealing of Oresme's intent, I include it within the
body of the quotation.

[65] In his short prologue (Proemium, 158–9), Oresme announces his intent to relay his
thoughts on quantification "clearly" (clare tradere) in contrast to earlier discussions
which he judges to have been presented in a confused and obscure manner. Most likely
he is referring here to the treatment of quantification in the expositions of the Oxford
Calculators.

[66] The crucial role of imagination and the use of imaginary cases in the natural philosophy of
the fourteenth century has long been a subject of interest to historians of science. For a
recent treatment of this question, see Elzbieta Jung-Palczewska, "From Oxonian Sources
to Parisian Rebellion: Attempts to Overcome Aristotelianism in Fourteenth-Century
Physics," in Bilan et perspectives des études médiévales, ed. J. Hamesse (Turnhout:
Brepols, 2004), 435–49, esp. 444–5.

[67] De configurationibus, I.i: 166–7. On the "representational" and "symbolic character" of
geometry in Oresme's hands, see Amos Funkenstein, Theology and the Scientific
Imagination from the Middle Ages to the Seventeenth Century (Princeton University Press,
1986), esp. 310.

[68] De configurationibus, I.iv, 174–5.

geometrical representation and analysis, so he expands the intellectual project of proportionalization and equalization.

Therefore, equal intensities are designated by equal lines, a double intensity by a double line, and always in the same way if one proceeds proportionally (*sic semper proportionaliter procedendo*). And this is to be understood universally (*universaliter intelligendum*) in regard to every intensity that is divisible in the imagination, whether it be an active or non-active quality, a sensible or non-sensible subject, object, or medium.[69]

At this point, still in the opening chapters of Book I, Oresme offers an observation that carried important implications. Where the Calculators and those who preceded him labeled the measure of qualitative increase and decrease the "latitude" of a quality, it should, he writes, more properly be called the "longitude" of a quality, because changes in intensity are more easily imagined as occurring along a vertical axis.[70] Since, however, he recognizes that philosophy is a common project, and since intensities are now commonly designated as "latitudes" (due to earlier representations in scholastic medicine and natural philosophy) he will, he informs us, keep to the "common way" (*volo sequi modum communem*) by continuing to refer to the line of intensity as a latitude.[71] But even as he seems to assent to the "common way," he introduces a most uncommon new element, one that provides the basis for crucial innovation in the area of qualitative mensuration. He imagines a system involving not one line measure but two, not a single measuring coordinate but dual coordinates, both of them bound together within a relational field.[72]

Oresme drives this pivotal point home in an introductory chapter that he himself titles "On the quantity of qualities" (*De quantitate qualitatum*). Here he asserts that if the quantity of any quality is to be properly represented and prepared for comparison, it must take into consideration *both* intensity (as did the Calculators) *and* extension, and so must incorporate

[69] *Ibid.*, I.i, 166–7.
[70] *Ibid.*, I.ii, 168–71. Compare to Arnau de Vilanova's conceptual *diametrum altitudinis*, noted above in Chapter 4: *Aphorismi de gradibus*, Aphorism 13, 155: "Gradus in complexionibus est elevacio qualitatis alicuius complexionalis supra temperamentum secundum distanciam integram." Aphorisms 14 to 16 continue to take note of the fact that the term "latitude," despite its association with breadth and horizontality, more properly measures increase and decrease along a vertical axis.
[71] *De configurationibus*, I.ii–I.iii, 168–73.
[72] There has been much debate on the question of whether Oresme's imagination of dual perpendicular lines to represent intensity and extension corresponds to a "true" graphing system. For Clagett's measured judgment that we have here a "start toward the coordinate approach," see his Introduction to *De configurationibus*, 34. On the significant differences between Oresme's application of the latitude within his system of dual coordinates and the latitude of the early Calculators, see Sylla, "Medieval Concepts of the Latitude of Forms," esp. 278; Sylla, "Medieval Quantification of Qualities," esp. 27–8.

both a latitudinal *and* a longitudinal dimension. He imagines the two axes of latitude and longitude (i.e., of intensity and extension) as intersecting lines: a horizontal base line to represent the extension of the subject in which the quality is found, and a vertical line drawn perpendicular to the base to represent the intensity of the quality at any point in the extended subject. Bound together within a relational system, these axes form a measurable "surface" or surface area, which now, in its totality, can be taken to properly represent the quantity of any given quality, as opposed to the single measuring line of the Calculator's latitude.[73] In Oresme's words:

Any linear quality can be designated by every plane figure which is imagined as standing perpendicularly on the linear [extension of the] quality and which is proportional in altitude to the quality in intensity.[74]

While Oresme explores the full scope of this scheme in the text of the *De configurationibus*, in a somewhat earlier work, his *Questions on Aristotle's On Generation and Corruption*, he showed how richly he had begun to think in terms of a fully systematic relativity applied to natural activity. Put another way, he showed how he had come to imagine the workings of nature in terms of a fully systematic and dynamic equilibrium. He writes:

quality is to be imagined to have two dimensions: longitude according to the extension of the subject and latitude according to intensity of degree ... Therefore, if by imagination the whole were placed in one half of the subject, it would be twice as intense as before ... And in the same way, if the whole quality were placed in a third part, it would be triply intense; and if in a fourth part, quadruply intense, and so on without end. Therefore, if the whole were placed in a point, it would be infinitely intense.[75]

In the background to this concept, one can see the habit of thinking in terms of establishing and maintaining equalities. Here a change to variable 1 automatically entails a proportional change in variable 2, to the end of maintaining a continuously proportional equality within the integrated system. As was his habit, Oresme extended his foundational principles to their furthest conclusions here, when he writes that were the extension of a

---

[73] *De configurationibus*, I.iv, 172–7. Anneliese Maier judged Oresme's linking of intensive and extensive magnitudes as his "most original contribution" to the discourse on quantification. On this see Maier, *Ausgehendes Mittelalter: Gesammelte Aufsätze zur Geistesgeschichte des 14. Jahrhunderts*, 3 vols. (Rome: Edizioni di Storia e Letteratura, 1964–77), vol. I, 335–52, at 338.

[74] *De configurationibus*, I.vii, 180–1.

[75] Nicole Oresme, *Questions on the Generation and Corruption*, quoted in Introduction to *De configurationibus*, 63 and n. 18.

quality to be infinitely reduced to a point, the intensity of the whole would necessarily be increased to infinity.[76] The terms "systematic equilibrium" and "dynamic equilibrium" can be clearly and "most fittingly" (*convenientissime*) applied to this imagination, to use an expression that Oresme himself often employs. The vision of the potentialities of equilibrium within a relational field, announced verbally in his *Questions on Aristotle's Generation and Corruption*, holds throughout the later text of the *De configurationibus*, leading Oresme to ever more refined insights into the potentialities of relation and equalization.[77]

Representing relation and equalization through geometric figures

The first example Oresme presents of qualitative quantification through figuration is that of a quality that increases regularly within a subject, either over time or over the subject's linear extension in space.[78] Following the language of the Calculators, these qualities are said to be "uniformly difform." One subset of uniformly difform qualities includes those in which the quality either begins its regular increase or ends its regular decrease at the zero degree. A primary example he offers is that of a motion that begins at rest (no degree of velocity) and whose velocity (conceived as a quality by both the Calculators and Oresme) increases uniformly over the course of the motion. Since in his configurational scheme the vertical lines representing qualitative intensity increase in proportion to the increasing velocity over time (which is represented by the extended base line), the quantity of velocity at any point in time can, he maintains, be "most fittingly" represented (*convenientissime designatur*) by a right triangle and the surface area it encloses.[79] This is so because right triangles, too, begin or end at no degree and rise or decline uniformly in altitude.

Not only can uniformly difform qualities of any kind be represented by right triangles, and not only can they be "quantified" for purposes of comparison, equalization, and proportionalization by the areas they

---

[76] Sylla ("Medieval Quantification of Qualities," 27) recognizes the importance of this point to Oresme's logic of systematic relation.

[77] See, for example, his elaboration of this argument in *De configurationibus*, III.v, 404–7.

[78] In Clagett's words (Introduction to *De configurationibus*, 15): "Thus the base line of such figures is the subject when we are talking about linear qualities or the time when we are talking about velocities, and the perpendiculars raised on the base line represent the intensities of the quality from point to point in the subject or represent the velocity from instant to instant in the motion."

[79] *De configurationibus*, I.vii, 182–3.

enclose, but, Oresme argues, uniformly difform qualities can be represented *only* by right triangles and by no other figure.[80] After establishing this point, he adds an essential qualification:

There is this proviso, however: if some quality is designated by one triangle, another quality of similar but double intensity must be designated by a triangle that is twice as high, and similarly for proportionally greater [intensities].[81]

Oresme's point here is that the quantification he envisions for his configurations is both purely proportional and purely relational. Indeed, his system of quantification through configurations represents a perfect marriage of proportionalization and relativity, governed by the dynamic of equalization. Absolute measurement is out of the question. He has no instruments to measure the intensities of any of the qualities he discusses, whether whiteness, heat, velocity, or any other. And so it is hardly surprising that over the course of this entire treatise on quantification, Oresme never actually measures anything. The lines that are chosen to represent intensities can initially be of any length whatsoever because there is no meaning attached to length itself. Nor, for that matter, is there any meaning attached to the quantifying surface area itself, as it has been determined by the intersection of latitudes and longitudes.[82] In Oresme's understanding, meaning – scientific and mathematical meaning – comes only through comparison, proportionalization, and the mental and mathematical act of relation. One can only speak of quantities and their increase and decrease in relative terms.[83] Nevertheless, Oresme makes it quite clear that he believes the system of quantification he has designed can actually work, can actually advance the project of natural philosophy. If it does so, however, it is only within the parameters he has defined. The persistent absence of observable and verifiable measurements in the natural philosophy of this period, and the absence of the recognition that the project of natural philosophy even requires them, means that the parameters within which scholastics like Oresme judged the success of their speculations differ in major respects from those of later science.

---

[80] *Ibid.*, I.viii, 184–7.   [81] *Ibid.*, 186–7.

[82] Clagett finds this essential relativity of measurement one of the most important points to stress concerning the Treatise. See his Introduction, 15, 18–19, 23, 48, 121.

[83] *De configurationibus*, I.vi, 178–9: "Indeed, no linear quality is imagined or designated by any figure except the ones which the ratio of the intensities at any points of that quality is as the ratio of the lines erected perpendicularly in those same points and terminating in the summit of the imagined figure." This same essential grounding in proportionality and relativity appears in each of the disciplines examined in previous chapters.

The fruits of Oresme's project combining systematic relation with systematic equalization

Perhaps the greatest proof that Oresme's grand scheme of quantification through configurations can, indeed, be said to work, is the celebrated use he makes of it to "prove" the so-called Merton mean speed
theorem. In the early chapters of Book I of the *De configurationibus*, soon
after his argument for the suitability of right triangles to represent
uniformly difform qualities (those that increase or decrease uniformly
in intensity), Oresme introduces the case of qualities that are uniform
and remain unchanged in intensity, whether it be the case of a velocity
that is uniform and constant in a motion over time, or of a qualitative
intensity that is uniform throughout its extension in a subject. In these
cases, where subjects are, for example, uniformly hot or white (or any
other quality), the (imagined) vertical lines of intensity are necessarily
of equal length over the whole of the subject's horizontal extension.
Thus, when the horizontal and vertical lines representing qualitative
extension and intension are considered in their totality, the quantity
of such a uniform quality will, he argues, be represented by a rectangle
and only by a rectangle.[84] After demonstrating this proposition with
a drawn rectangular figure, he sums up his argument to this point:
"And so every uniform quality is imagined by a rectangle and every
quality uniformly difform terminated at no degree is imaginable by a
right triangle."[85]

Oresme is well aware that these two modes of increase/decrease and
these two neat geometrical figures represent only a small portion of
possible modes and figures. His scheme, which recognizes that intensity
(or velocity) can change from instant to instant in time, or from point to
point in a moving subject, requires him to recognize scores of complex
qualitative possibilities and figures. Indeed, one of the extraordinary
aspects of Oresme's claims for his quantifying scheme is that it can
comprehend a phenomenal world of dizzying complexity and diversity.
He outlines, for example, four types of "simple difform difformity" and
a further sixty-two species of "composite difformity." These, then, lead
him to state:

In a similar way, some [particular quality] can be figured by means of a segment of
a sphere or of a cylinder, and we can proceed thus through the infinite modes and
variations dependent upon the kinds of uniformity and difformity [already]
posited ... Further, one quality of the body – say its hotness – can be figured

---

[84] *Ibid.*, I.x ("On quadrangular quality"), 188–91.   [85] *Ibid.*, I.xi, 190–1.

in one way, while another quality of the same body, such as its whiteness, can be figured in another way, and perhaps another of its qualities – possibly its sweetness – can be figured in a still different way, and similarly for other [qualities].[86]

Throughout the *De configurationibus* Oresme recognizes that he lives in a world of open-ended possibility and open-ended multiplication. Yet at the same time he appears serene in his belief that by applying the principles of relation, proportionalization, equalization and geometric figuration he can provide a logico-mathematical scheme sufficient to bring intellectual order to this immense diversity.

In the specific case of his geometrical representation and "proof" of the Merton mean speed theorem, however, Oresme can ignore this multiplicity. All that he requires are his previous demonstrations that the right triangle provides the "fitting" configuration to represent uniformly difform qualities and the rectangle does the same for uniform qualities. He takes up his proof in Book III, toward the conclusion of his treatise, preparing the ground for it with the following pronouncement:

The universal rule is this, that the measure or ratio of any two linear or surface qualities or velocities is as that of the figures by which they are comparatively and mutually imagined ... Therefore, in order to have measures and ratios of qualities and velocities one must have recourse to geometry.[87]

Following this, he restates his foundational principle, that qualitative extension and intension are bound together within a relational system, so that as one factor increases the other automatically decreases proportionally.[88]

With these points reaffirmed, Oresme is prepared to state a proposition that defines the relationship between all uniformly difform qualities "figured" by right triangles and all uniform qualities "figured" by rectangles, in such a way as to frame the mean speed theorem in purely geometrical terms. In his words:

Every quality, if it is uniformly difform, is of the same quantity as would be the quality of the same or equal subject that is uniform according to the degree of the middle point of the same subject (*secundum gradum puncti medii eiusdem subiecti*).[89]

As was his habit, he then translates this rule into a series of geometrical figures. For the uniformly difform quality terminated at no degree, he

---

[86] *Ibid.*, I.xviii, 210–11.
[87] *Ibid.*, III.v, 404–5. Clagett discusses Oresme's proof of this rule and its afterlife in scientific thought at many points in his Introduction, 46–7, 67–8, 71–3, 103–11.
[88] *Ibid.*, III.v, 404–7.   [89] *Ibid.*, III.vii, 408–9.

describes (and then draws) a right triangle, ABC, with AB as the base, BC as the hypotenuse, and CA as the height. He then specifies that the middle point (*punctus medius*) of the base or subject line AB (i.e, the mid-point of the quality's extension at any given moment) be represented by "D." According to the rules for qualitative figuration he has already established, the intensity or degree (*gradus*) of the quality at D is represented by a vertical line drawn perpendicular to the subject base line, in this case intersecting the hypotenuse BC at E.

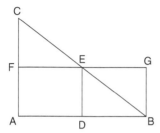

Once line DE is drawn, it becomes visibly clear that just as D represents the mid-point of the quality's base-line extension, so E represents the mid-point of the quality's uniformly difform intension (i.e, the mid-point of the hypotenuse). Oresme then solidifies this visual key by drawing rectangle ABGF, which represents what the quantification of the quality would have been had it remained uniform (rather than uniformly increasing) at intensity DE. He can then prove, with the aid of Euclid, that the surface area represented by triangle ABC (i.e., the quantification of the uniformly changing quality) is precisely equal to the area of rectangle ABGF (i.e., the quantification of the quality that is uniform at the middle degree).[90] QED. Oresme then takes his argument yet one step further:

> Now one should speak of velocity in completely the same fashion as linear quality, so long as the middle instant of the time measuring a velocity of this kind (*instans medium temporis velocitatem huiusmodi mensurantis*) is taken in place of the middle point [of the subject].[91]

In short, by placing intension and extension in systematic relation, and by imagining them as lines open to continual increase and decrease,

[90] An earlier and somewhat leaner proof of the theorem by means of these same configurations appears in Oresme's *Quaestiones super geometriam Euclidis*, ed. H. L. L. Busard (Leiden: Brill, 1961), 26–8, 36–8.
[91] *De configurationibus*, III.vii, 410–11.

Oresme has succeeded in devising a geometrical way to represent the ever-vanishing "middle instant" of any uniformly varying velocity.[92]

This is quite an accomplishment. The point here is not merely that Oresme is grounding his proof in the language of relation; not merely that he is working with equalities, congruences, and fit; and not merely that he is searching for and working with mid-points and balancing points. All of these were central to Euclid's program in the *Elements* and to the whole of the geometrical tradition up to the fourteenth century. What is extraordinary is that Oresme is applying these principles to entities that are undergoing continual expansion and contraction, rather than to static entities and static geometrical forms. The older model of the mechanical scale balancing two equal weights around a fixed point has been left far behind. The balancing points of the "middle degree" and the "middle instant" are in continual motion, ever shifting in relation to the increase or decrease of the "lines" of intensity and extension that define them. Once again, as we have seen before in the writings of other thinkers from other disciplines who were influenced by the new model of equilibrium, equality and balance serve here not merely as ideals but as dynamic regulators, as the core principles that make possible a rule-based philosophy and a mathematics of change. The timelessness and fixity of earlier geometrical models that made possible the application of generalized axioms and rules have here been replaced by a new basis for dependability and predictability: the imagination of a relational field in systematic equilibrium.

On the history of this imagination

Given that the project to quantify qualities dominated theology and natural philosophy for almost a half-century before Oresme wrote the *De configurationibus*, the modern reader might well be surprised that his decision to apply both intension and extension to qualitative measurement was new, even strikingly new, in the context of scholastic thought of the 1340s and 50s. It might seem reasonable that linking the two "dimensions" would occur "naturally" to anyone who had measured land or cloth, or to anyone who had considered both excellence (intension) and volume (extension) in determining the monetary value of a good for sale – which is to say to almost anyone at all, not excluding theologians

---

[92] For the conclusion that Oresme's representation of a "middle degree" of velocity is equivalent to representing "instantaneous speed" (in its modern understanding), see Pierre Souffrin, "La quantification du mouvement chez les scholastiques: la vitesse instantanée chez Nicole Oresme," in *Autour de Nicole Oresme*, ed. Jeannine Quillet (Paris: J. Vrin, 1990), 63–83, esp. 78–83.

and philosophers. I have, indeed, made the argument that by the mid fourteenth century scholastic schemes of quantification, and particularly those imagined by Oresme, show many signs of having been borrowed from (or influenced by) practical models of measurement in everyday use, even if the highly technical language in which these scholastic schemes are framed has generally masked this borrowing.[93]

But this borrowing can in no way be taken as a sufficient explanation for Oresme's solutions in the *De configurationibus*. It does not explain why the conceptualization of a relational system involving two variables proved so slow to emerge in philosophical discourse, so slow to be consciously elaborated before Oresme. It most certainly cannot explain the failure of Oresme's solution to be either widely adopted or carried further after his death in the 1380s, a failure that lasted through the fifteenth century. On the contrary, there is strong textual evidence that Oresme's scheme was far from a "natural" development and far from a predictable extension of previous philosophical thinking on the subject. There were many elements in his scheme that signaled a break from the philosophical past: not only the imagination of the two variables of intensity and extension as necessary components of proper quantification; not only the imagination of lines and areas to represent the interplay of these components; but even more, the automatic nature of the proportional interchange between the two variables that lay at the heart of Oresme's overall conception of systematic equilibrium. The measure of Oresme's awareness of the iron logic of this interchange is revealed in his speculation (already noted) that once a mathematical relation has been established between the two axes of measurement, any increase or decrease in one (even infinite increase or decrease) will necessarily entail a proportional increase or decrease in the other. These foundational elements had lain beyond imagination before the second quarter of the fourteenth century. They had to *become* thinkable, and they became so only with the emergence of a new sense of the potentialities of balance within which they made sense.

In his Introduction to the *De configurationibus*, Marshall Clagett sought to locate possible precursors to and inheritors of Oresme's scheme of quantification.[94] It is noteworthy that the most "fruitful line" of influence that Clagett was able to identify came from Galenic medical theory in the area of pharmacological measurement – the legacy of the profound exploration of equality and dynamic equalization with respect to attaining

[93] Kaye, *Economy and Nature in the Fourteenth Century*, esp. ch. 6, 163–99; cf. Souffrin, "La quantification du mouvement," 66, 73.
[94] Clagett's section on "The Configuration Doctrine in Historical Perspective," Introduction to *De configurationibus*, 50–121.

and maintaining bodily balance (health) by Galen and the thirteenth-century Galenists. The system of measuring pharmacological intensities by degrees ranging along a spatially conceived "latitude," found in Arnau de Vilanova's *Aphorismi de gradibus* of the 1290s, represented (as Michael McVaugh argued and Clagett agreed) a significant early step in the philosophical and mathematical project to quantify qualities to which Oresme was heir.[95] In the first quarter of the fourteenth century, innovation in the area of quantification appears to have passed from the realm of medical speculation to the logicians, mathematicians, and natural philosophers at Oxford University, including Thomas Bradwardine and John Dumbleton.[96] As Clagett is careful to note, however, even in the case of these earlier Oxford Calculators, quantification remained "unilinear," centered on the single "latitude" of qualitative intensity. This persistence, in itself, speaks to the strength and weight of previous unilinear medical and philosophical models for determining order, value, and equality.[97]

Only in the 1340s, with the writings of the later Calculator Richard Swineshead, does Clagett see the halting beginnings of a "dual coordinate" system of quantification.[98] In his *Liber calculationum*, Swineshead begins to explore the logic of how extension and intension might be conceived as lines integrated into a relational system.[99] At around the same time, Jean Buridan, master of arts at the University of Paris, also shows evidence of thinking in terms of integrating extension and intension, conceived as lines and areas, in the project of quantification.[100] But the writings on this subject by Swineshead and Buridan represent mere fragments of thought. Nothing that Clagett found, and nothing that has been discovered since by historians of science in their search for textual influences on Oresme's thought, comes even close to approaching the beautifully conceived and elaborated scheme worked out with such confidence and care in the *De configurationibus*.

---

[95] See my discussion of Arnau's scheme (in Chapter 4 above). To a notable degree, both Arnau and Oresme appear to have experienced their social and physical environments as worlds composed of ever increasing and decreasing qualitative values imagined as lines in continual expansion and contraction.

[96] McVaugh, "Arnald of Villanova and Bradwardine's Law"; Clagett, Introduction to *De configurationibus*, 56–7, notes 12–13.

[97] I discuss the older unilinear model in Chapter 5 above.

[98] Clagett, Introduction to *De configurationibus*, 58–61.

[99] For an edition and English translation of pertinent sections of Swineshead's *Liber Calculationum*, see Clagett, *Science of Mechanics*, 290–304.

[100] *Questiones super octo phisicorum libros Aristotelis* (1509), 15v, cited and translated by Clagett, Introduction to *De configurationibus*, 61–2.

It is clear that what Oresme drew on from the philosophical tradition that preceded him was not a set of particular insights or techniques that he then manipulated or combined or tweaked in order to arrive at new conclusions. From the evidence of his fully formed modeling of systematic equilibrium in the *De configurationibus*, I would argue, rather, that he inherited both an evolving sense of the potentialities of balance and an evolving mathematical modeling of this sense, to which he was exceptionally sensitive, and on which he succeeded in conferring ever more coherent and elegant form. This evolving sense and modeling was conveyed, in part, through texts that had been written over the previous half-century in many and varied disciplines, including the philosophical writings of the Calculators and the medical writings of Galen and scholastic Galenists.[101] But again I want to make the case that the sense and modeling of balance were being shaped and conveyed as well through the particular environments – social, economic, political, institutional, and technological, as well as textual – that Oresme inhabited, analyzed, and navigated with such evident success through the 1350s.[102] The history of the reception and afterlife of Oresme's doctrine of configurations can, I believe, offer evidence in support of this case.

The afterlife of Oresme's configurations

One might expect that Oresme's immensely insightful, beautifully elaborated, and mathematically rigorous text would have produced an efflorescence of commentaries, leading either to a steady advance in the logic and mathematics of the measuring latitude, or in the application of dual-coordinate configurations to the representation and analysis of motion, or in the area of the quantification of qualities through the application of geometrical figures, or, more generally, in the imagination and modeling of dynamic equilibrium. But nothing of the sort happened – for *centuries*. And this despite the great head of steam that had built over the first half of the fourteenth century behind each one of these directions and behind the modeling of the new equilibrium as a whole.

Without going into all of its details, the story Clagett tells of its reception is a story of rapid and nearly uniform decline.[103] People clearly read his text, and one can find reflections of it in other texts soon after its original appearance. But in the years and decades that followed, only a very few scholars appear to have meaningfully grasped any of its novel principles, whether the principles underlying its

---

[101] For evidence of Oresme's familiarity with Galenic writings, see Chapter 7 above.
[102] I discuss Oresme's sensitivity to his "technological environment" below in this chapter.
[103] Clagett, Introduction to *De configurationibus*, 73–111.

beautiful geometric proof of the mean speed theorem, or its basic "advance" in thinking about quantification in terms of intension and extension represented as latitudes and longitudes, or, still less, its expansive vision of the potentialities of balance – its profound understanding that these coordinates were bound together within a relational system in dynamic equilibrium. No one in the generations that followed had whatever it might have taken to actually add to or build upon the foundation Oresme so clearly established on every page of his text.[104] Indeed, not until the seventeenth century, in the writings of Descartes and Galileo, were the possibilities inherent in Oresme's configurations fully realized and surpassed.[105]

This failure raises many historical questions. Those who followed Oresme were in full possession not only of all the writings that might have stimulated his sense of the expanded potentialities of balance, but they possessed as well, in a single beautifully clear and argued text, Oresme's unsurpassed and mathematically rigorous modeling of dynamic equilibrium. If the history of balance is conveyed primarily through texts, it is hard to see what could possibly explain the fact that scholars following Oresme not only failed to build upon the De configurationibus but for the most part failed to grasp its argument and its implications. The body of texts remained, so they cannot be the cause of this failure. But something else, some non-textual element or set of elements crucial to the history of balance would have to have changed to explain this discontinuity. Here I suggest that the same "environmental" factors – economic, social, political, institutional – that I associated earlier with the collapse of the new model of equilibrium in the realm of political thought were similarly at work in its collapse in the realm of natural philosophy, and, indeed, within all scholastic discourses from the 1360s onward.[106]

---

[104] Clagett describes (Introduction, 85) the single most important, influential, and widely copied treatise based on the doctrine of configurations, the *Tractatus de latitudinibus formarum* (c. 1390), as "indeed but a pale reflection of the *De configurationibus*." He did, however, discover (101) a single later manuscript of the *De configurationibus* that contains "halting – but certainly significant" mathematical refinements.

[105] I discuss this point further in the Conclusion. Two articles dedicated to this subject (and written by historians of mathematics) appear in *Nicolas Oresme: Tradition et innovation chez un intellectuel du XIVe siècle*, ed. Pierre Souffrin and A. P. Segonds (Paris: Les Belles Lettres, 1998): A. P. Youskevitch, "La place de Nicole Oresme dans le développement des sciences mathématiques," 115–24; and Pierre Souffrin and J. P. Weiss, "Le traité des configurations des qualités et des mouvements: remarques sur quelques problèmes d'interprétation et de traduction," 125–44.

[106] See Chapter 7 above for discontinuities with respect to the modeling of balance in Oresme's political thought between the 1350s and the 1370s. I discuss the parallel discontinuities that were manifest over this period in scholastic economic thought, medicinal theory, and natural philosophy in the Conclusion.

Integrating approximation, probability, and mathematical irrationality into the balance of the cosmos

Another area in which Oresme arrived at brilliant, highly original, and potentially productive conclusions and propositions, which were then for the most part either ignored by natural philosophers in the generations that followed or lay beyond their comprehension, was in the area of mathematical incommensurability and irrationality.[107] The starting point for his two major treatises on this were questions that had been raised by the writings of the Oxford Calculators, in particular Thomas Bradwardine's treatment of mathematical incommensurability in his *Tractatus de proportionibus*.[108] In the opening page of this treatise, Bradwardine claims that in addition to those proportions that relate numbers to numbers or relate quantities that can be denominated by numbers, there is a "second order" of proportions comprising those that are called "irrational" because they cannot be immediately denominated by a number. Bradwardine makes this statement without preamble and without any recognition that assuming and working with irrational ratios might raise mathematical or philosophical objections among his readers.

Philosophical problems posed by the existence of "irrational" magnitudes were, however, of long standing.[109] For those who identified with the Pythagorean tradition and who believed that the cosmos was ruled and ordered by number, or for those who believed that God created the universe according to "number, weight, and measure," the idea that

---

[107] Oresme's major writings on the subject of incommensurability, all written before 1360, have been edited and translated by Edward Grant, who also provided indispensable introductions and commentaries to the texts: *De proportionibus proportionum and Ad pauca respicientes* (Madison: University of Wisconsin Press, 1966) (hereafter, *De proportionibus proportionum*), and *Nicole Oresme and the Kinematics of Circular Motion: Tractatus de commensurabilitate vel incommensurabilitate motuum celi* (Madison: University of Wisconsin Press, 1971) (hereafter, *De commensurabilitate*). On the historical discontinuities that these works represent, Grant notes (*De commensurabilitate*, 125), "the intense interest and fascination which he [Oresme] had for this subject seem to have died with him."

[108] Yet another notable "discontinuity" is that Oresme's treatment of Bradwardine's work represented, in Grant's judgment (*De proportionibus proportionum*, 24), "the last significant development of [Bradwardine's] function." For a brief summary of later treatments of Bradwardine's function, see Sylla, "Origin and Fate," esp. 78–9. The later analysis of incommensurability and irrationality with respect to the relationship of the diagonal and side of a square by Blasius of Parma (*c.* 1345–1416) represents a partial exception to the rule of discontinuity. On this see Sabine Rommevaux, "L'irrationalité de la diagonale et du côté d'un même carré dans les *Questions* de Biaise de Parme sur le *Traité des rapports* de Bradwardine," *Revue d'histoire des sciences* 56 (2003), 401–18.

[109] Molland, "The Geometrical Background to the 'Merton School,'" esp. 119.

natural numbers did not underlie and could not serve as a measure of every relationship in nature and the cosmos was deeply disconcerting. Oresme, for one, was fully aware that this attitude was current in his own culture. He represented it through the figure of "Arithmetic" in a remarkable imaginary debate he staged between personified Arithmetic and Geometry before the judgment of Apollo. He placed this dream debate at the conclusion of his *Treatise on the Commensurability or Incommensurability of Celestial Motions* (*Tractatus de commensurabilitate vel incommensurabilitate motuum celi*), his second and final major work on the subject of mathematical incommensurability and irrationality. In the debate, "Arithmetic," who speaks first, identifies "reason and harmony" with mathematical rationality. In doing so she cites Boethius as her authority for claiming that "everything that proceeded from the very origin of things was formed in reference to numbers."[110] Based on this belief, she looks upon mathematical irrationality with a contempt verging on disgust, identifying it with "imperfection, deprivation, and deformity" among other utterly negative connotations. Then she adds:

It seems unworthy and unreasonable that the divine mind should connect the celestial motions, which organize and regulate the other corporeal motions, in such a haphazard relationship, when indeed, it ought to arrange them rationally and according to a rule.[111]

Arithmetic is clearly incapable of integrating mathematical incommensurability into her worldview. But as we have seen, both Bradwardine and Oresme self-identified with Geometry, and what proves monstrous in the realm of arithmetic is simply business as usual to the geometer. As far back as the fifth century BCE, geometers had discovered that the relationship between the diagonal of a square and its side cannot be measured by a number, and that therefore the two line lengths are mathematically incommensurable. If the side of the square is designated by the number 1, the length of the diagonal will be the square root of 2, an "irrational" number because it approaches but never achieves finality and numerical form. No doubt Bradwardine, who centered his mathematics on the logic of the continuum, was claiming a kind of superiority for geometry when he claimed that it could incorporate irrational relationships into its analysis and provide them with the "rationality" and "rule" they are denied in number-based arithmetic.

---

[110] *De commensurabilitate*, 292–3.
[111] *Ibid.*, 288–9. "Arithmetic" cites numerous ancient and medieval authorities to support her claim that she represents the proper and accepted way of seeing the world, which is being threatened by "Geometry."

And no doubt Oresme, too, saw this as a great advantage to geometry and the geometrical worldview, especially since he, like Bradwardine, was heir to the late thirteenth-century vision of the world as a "world of lines." In the dream debate Oresme stages between Arithmetic and Geometry, he has Geometry give verbal expression to this sense of superiority:

We say that in numbers there is no measure and no ratio that is not included within our magnitudes; but along with these there can be discovered in continuous quantities an infinite number of other [ratios and measures], none of which is found among numbers. Therefore, we have what it has, and much more, so that we are the first-born [of Mathematics].[112]

What is new in the geometry of the fourteenth century is that neither Bradwardine nor Oresme confine their acceptance of mathematical irrationality to line segments or geometrical figures. Instead, they feel free to project it into the physical structure and activity of the cosmos.[113] As we saw earlier, Bradwardine, befitting his preoccupation with questions of relation and proportionality, is less concerned with rules pertaining to numbers than he is with rules pertaining to ratios themselves. And since he conceived of the increase and decrease of velocity, force, and resistance as continuous and thus properly represented by infinitely divisible "latitudes," he can imagine a "second order" of proportions involving these values that must themselves be infinitely divisible. Moreover, Bradwardine's great "advance" (perceived as an advance by his contemporaries) was to raise the level of his investigation from the realm of natural numbers to the realm of exponents and powers in his project to relate the ratios involved in the analysis of motion.[114] And while some of these "ratios of ratios" are numerically commensurable, others will be inescapably incommensurable. Edward Grant clearly illustrates this distinction: "a ratio of ratios (*proportio proportionum*) is said to be rational when the two ratios are commensurable, i.e., related by a rational exponent; or as Oresme would also express it, when the smaller ratio is a part or parts of the greater. But a ratio of ratios is irrational when . . . related

---

[112] *Ibid.*, 312–13. For an earlier statement of this position by Oresme, see his *Quaestiones super geometriam Euclidis*, q. 9, 22–3, 101.

[113] Both Bradwardine and Oresme, however, identify ratios with continuous quantities. E.g., *De proportionibus proportionum*, 158–9: "Any ratio is a continuous quantity in the sense that it is divisible into infinity just like a continuous quantity." See also Grant, Introduction, 36. In citing from Grant's edition of the *De proportionibus proportionum*, I have replaced his references to book and line number with page numbers from his text.

[114] E.g., Grant, Introduction to *De proportionibus proportionum*, 21: "The mathematical basis of Bradwardine's function is the application of geometric proportionality to ratios of force and resistance producing motion."

by an irrational exponent."[115] In the example Grant provides, 8/1 is said to be commensurable to 2/1 not because (in the arithmetical sense) 8 is a multiple of 2 but because (in the geometrical sense) the two ratios are connected through a rational exponent, $8/1 = (2/1)^{3/1}$.[116] Such a "rational" relationship would clearly not obtain in all cases. Oresme follows Bradwardine's move into the exponential realm and then goes far beyond him in his exploration and understanding of its logic. In doing so he demonstrates how fully the dynamic of geometric multiplication has been integrated into the new model of equilibrium by the mid fourteenth century. I limit my discussion here to those insights that most clearly reveal the shape and scope of the new model and its influence on Oresme's thinking.

Oresme took the possibilities inherent in the recognition of ratios related through irrational exponents further than anyone before him (or for that matter, for centuries after him). He makes this clear in his Proposition 10 of the *De proportionibus proportionum*, when after having carefully provided the mathematical foundation for working with irrational ratios, he comes to a significant conclusion:

It is probable (*verisimile est*) that [any] two proposed unknown ratios are incommensurable because if many unknown ratios are proposed it is most probable (*verisimillimum est*) that any [one proposed] would be incommensurable to any other.[117]

Expressing Proposition 10 in modern terms, any two ratios (A and B) can be related such that $A^n = B$. When this is done, it is most likely (*verisimillium est*) that n will be irrational, i.e., not an integer or a ratio.[118] Oresme is fully conscious of the far-reaching implications of Proposition

---

[115] *Ibid.*, 38. As Clagett explains ("Some Novel Trends," 285, n. 23): "In the ratio of ratio's vocabulary, when one ratio is said to be a certain ratio of another, the "certain ratio" is the exponent to which the second ratio is to be raised, rather than the arithmetic ratio in which the two compared ratios stand."

[116] Grant, Introduction to *De proportionibus proportionum*, 38.

[117] *De proportionibus proportionum*, 246–7: "Decima conclusio. Propositis duabus proportionibus ignotis verisimile est eas incommensurabiles esse; quod si multe proponantur ignote verisimillimum est aliquam alicui incommensurabilem fore." Grant has been questioned by some historians for substituting the English word "probable" for Oresme's consistent use of the Latin "verisimile," and in this way overstating the probabilistic element in Oresme's speculation. See, for example, H. Hugonnard-Roche, "Modalité et argumentation chez Nicole Oresme," in *Nicolas Oresme: tradition et innovation*, ed. P. Souffrin and A. P. Segonds (Paris: Les Belles Lettres, 1988), 145–63, esp. 158–62. These scholars have reason to call for a more literal rendering of "verisimile," but in my view Grant's translation captures the overall sense and direction of Oresme's argument.

[118] Murdoch, "*Mathesis*," 231; Michael Mahoney, "Mathematics," in *Science in the Middle Ages*, ed. David Lindberg (University of Chicago Press, 1978), 145–78, at 166–9.

10, and he seems to be extremely pleased and excited by the possibilities it creates. Just before citing the proposition, he writes: "Indeed, you will admire it [Proposition 10] even more as you reflect more deeply upon it and the things which follow from it."[119]

Oresme well knew that this proposition, stated as a general rule, would be perceived as shocking if not repugnant to those who continued to identify with the arithmetical worldview, expressed so forcefully by personified Arithmetic. But rather than hold back, he carried the logic of this proposition to even more shocking and destabilizing conclusions. He did so by marrying it to Bradwardine's rule, which had mathematized the physics of motion in the form of what in modern terms would be described as an exponential function relating forces, resistances, and velocities represented as ratios.[120] This permitted him to state:

When two velocities have been proposed whose ratio is unknown, it is probable (*verisimile est*) that their ratio is irrational and that these velocities are incommensurable.[121]

Going still further, he maintains that just as the ratio of any two unknown velocities is likely irrational, so too are the ratios of any two unknown distances, or any two unknown times, or, indeed, "any two things whatever acquirable [or traversable] by a continuous motion."[122]

Having established these propositions, Oresme then makes his boldest and most potentially controversial move, extending irrationality into the very fabric of the heavens and thus into the very structure of creation.

From all the things which have been said, this proposition also follows: When two motions of celestial bodies have been proposed, it is probable (*verisimile est*) that they would be incommensurable, and most probable (*verisimillimum est*) that any celestial motion would be incommensurable to the motion of any other; and if the opposite of this were true, it could not be known.[123]

Although personified Arithmetic, as Oresme represented her, was horrified by the implications of his mathematical discoveries, he himself was not. Far from finding his discovery a sign of "imperfection, deprivation, and deformity" he writes: "Now that I have declared that any celestial motion might be incommensurable to any other celestial motion, many very beautiful propositions that I arranged at another time follow,

---

[119] *De proportionibus proportionum*, 246–7. Oresme offers mathematical demonstrations to support this general conclusion in the pages that follow.

[120] Oresme makes this link between mathematical and physical ratios explicit in the opening suppositions of *De proportionibus proportionum*, ch. 4, 262 ff. Grant comments (Introduction, 51): "Oresme, in sharp contrast [to Aristotle], places the physical in direct dependence on the mathematical possibilities." See also Sylla, "Origin and Fate," 98.

[121] *De proportionibus proportionum*, 302–3.   [122] *Ibid.*   [123] *Ibid.*, 304–5.

and I intend to demonstrate them."[124] Rather than seeing indeterminate and irrational magnitudes as a threat to the divine order of nature and creation, Oresme "naturalized" them, integrating them into a coherent view of the order of the universe, to the extent that he could find them beautiful. He was able to do so, I suggest, because he had inherited and now inhabited the expanded sense of balance and its potentialities contained within and carried by the new model of equilibrium. Put another way, he was able to feel "at home" with their destabilizing potential because a home for them had already been prepared within both the textual environments he inherited and the socioeconomic environments he and his fellow scholars inhabited, dating from the last quarter of the thirteenth century.[125]

Oresme took a number of the "beautiful propositions" that followed from his naturalization of mathematical incommensurability and attached them specifically to one of his long-term intellectual projects: his uncompromising critique of astrological determinism.[126] Building on the logic of Proposition 10, he attacked astrology's naïve belief in the numerical exactitude of celestial motions, times, and conjunctions. This important element of Oresme's thought has received considerable attention and discussion over the previous decades.[127] The single point I want to make here is that when we look at the foundation of his critique of astrology, and, for that matter, when we examine the root assumptions

---

[124] *Ibid.* Grant surmises that "arranged at another time" refers to their appearance in the brief and incomplete work, *Ad pauca respicientes*, which, he further surmises, was later corrected and expanded (following its appearance at the conclusion of the *De proportionibus proportionum*) to produce the *De commensurabilitate*. For a summary of his argument, see *De commensurabilitate*, 75, n. 113.

[125] In an earlier work I linked Oresme's easy acceptance of mathematical irrationality and incommensurability to the capacity of the instrument of money, functioning as a common measuring continuum, to overcome value incommensurability in the marketplace of his day. On this, see Kaye, *Economy and Nature in the Fourteenth Century*, 222–3. I see my earlier analysis as commensurate with my present discussion.

[126] For an early use by Oresme of celestial incommensurability as the basis for a critique of astrology, see his *Quaestiones super geometriam Euclidis*, q. 9, 25: "et ex hoc sequitur quod iudicia astrologorum sunt valde incerta."

[127] G. W. Coopland, *Nicole Oresme and the Astronomers: A Study of His "Livre de divinacions"* (Cambridge, MA: Harvard University Press, 1952); Max Lejbowicz, "Chronologie des écrits anti-astrologiques de Nicole Oresme: étude sur un cas de scepticisme dans la deuxième moitié du XIVe siècle," in *Autour de Nicole Oresme*, ed. Quillet, 119–76. Oresme's "Quaestio contra divinitores horoscopios" has been edited by Stefano Caroti, *Archives d'histoire doctrinale et littéraire du Moyen Âge* 51 (1976), 201–310. For Oresme's critique of astrology at the court of Charles V as detrimental to the Common Good, see Joan Cadden, "Charles V, Nicole Oresme, and Christine de Pizan: Unities and Uses of Knowledge in Fourteenth-Century France," in *Texts and Contexts in Ancient and Medieval Science*, ed. Edith Sylla and Michael McVaugh (Leiden: Brill, 1997), 208–44, esp. 223–30.

that make possible his larger position on mathematical incommensurability, we can see the central role played by his recognition and full acceptance of estimation, approximation, and probabilistic thinking as legitimate ways of knowing – indeed, as the *only* ways we humans can ever "know" the universe. In Edward Grant's judgment, "By extending [the possibility of] mathematical incommensurability to all ratios of continuous quantities Oresme has, in effect, made inexactitude and imprecision an essential aspect of mathematical physics and astronomy."[128]

Oresme's probabilism can be found in various forms throughout his writings, but perhaps nowhere is his consciousness of its centrality to his epistemology expressed more clearly than in the epic debate between Arithmetic and Geometry under the judgment of Apollo. The god Apollo speaks:

You should understand that exactness transcends the human mind … For if an imperceptible excess – even a part smaller than a thousandth – could destroy an equality and alter a ratio from rational to irrational (*equalitatem tollit et proportionem mutat de rationali ad irrationalem*), how will you be able to know a punctual [exact] ratio of motions or celestial magnitudes?[129]

This is a lesson that "Geometry," speaking for Oresme, already knows well. When it is her turn to respond to Apollo's question she remains true to her principles. She freely admits that she cannot claim certainty for her arguments: all she can do is show that the positions maintained by her opponent Arithmetic are "less probable" than her own (*minus probabilem opinor*).[130]

Balance versus harmony in the new model of equilibrium

Given the many points at which ideas of balance and harmony can overlap, and indeed *have* overlapped, within models of equalization over the centuries, the question arises: Is balance the same as harmony? The simple answer is "not always," but since the degree of overlap and intersection between these two "ideas" varies considerably from one model of equalization to another, the question is better posed of specific models, with their links to particular historical periods and environments, rather than

---

[128] Grant, Introduction to *De proportionibus proportionum*, 82.
[129] *De commensurabilitate*, 284–5. Note Oresme's linking of estimation and approximation to the project of equalization. Note, too, the echoes here of the words of Galen, Taddeo Alderotti, Arnau de Villanova, Turisanus, Peter Olivi, and other shapers of the new model of equilibrium cited in earlier chapters.
[130] *Ibid.*, 310–11.

in the abstract. No doubt, within the arithmetical worldview that Arithmetic speaks for, the sense of what constitutes proper balance is closely intertwined, if not identified, with the idea of harmony. This was a view, Oresme recognizes, that preceded his own but that was still held by many within his intellectual culture. But there is equally no doubt that for Oresme (as represented by personified Geometry) the new sense of balance that accepts into itself the reality of mathematical irrationality and incommensurability differs *fundamentally* from traditional ideas and constructs of harmony.[131] Indeed, I want to make the case that one of the primary distinguishing characteristics of the "new" model of equilibrium – and one of the clearest signs of its break with the past – is the *distance* it has gained from traditional conceptions of harmony. The best way to illustrate this is through the words Arithmetic and Geometry speak on this question.

Arithmetic cites a long list of pagan, Islamic, and Christian authorities to support her position that "everything that proceeded from the very origin of things was formed in reference to numbers."[132] Resting on this firm foundation, she can assert that "the most potent primary, incorruptible elements of the world, and their motions, reflect a numerical relationship."[133] Indeed, Arithmetic asserts that God himself, creator and ruler of the universe, "arranges all things pleasantly [and agreeably], that is, harmonically (*disponit omnia suaviter, scilicet armonice*)."[134] She extends this principle both outward, into the divine plan of the cosmos, and inward, into the human mind: "Thus, an irrational ratio is neither suitable nor relatable to the understanding, for which reason the ancients said that the mind conforms to a certain numerical and harmonic plan (*quadam numerali et armonica ratione*)."[135] On this basis she excoriates the "disproportion," "deformity," "baseness," and "privation," introduced by the notion of mathematical irrationality. In a characteristic diatribe she declares:

> every such [irrational] ratio is discordant and strange in [its] harmony (*in armonica dissonans*) and, consequently, foreign to every consonance (*omni consonantia aliena*), so that it seems more appropriate to the wild lamentations of miserable hell than to celestial motions that unite, with marvelous control, the musical melodies soothing a great world.[136]

---

[131] One of the elements that distinguishes harmony from balance in this period is that one can legitimately speak of "conceptions" or "ideas" of harmony because it had long been the subject of direct analysis and discussion. In contrast, balance was never an "idea" in this period, never problematized or discussed in itself, even as it was intimately attached to voiced conceptions of order and equalization.

[132] *De commensurabilitate*, 294–5.   [133] *Ibid.*   [134] *Ibid.*, 296–7.   [135] *Ibid.*, 292–3.

[136] *Ibid.*, 296–7. After making this comment, Arithmetic begins a long and detailed discussion of musical harmony (297–307) that references traditional opinions, both pagan and Christian, on the subject.

There is no discordance in Arithmetic's argument. In her view, the existence of mathematical incommensurability is utterly inconsistent with the traditional notions of harmony she speaks for. And when such "shameful irregularity" is projected into the order of the heavens themselves, its effect is truly monstrous:

> to deprive us of divine goodness, diminish the perfection of the world, destroy the beauty of the heavens, bring harm to mankind, cause ignorance, and detract from the beauty of the whole universe of beings.[137]

How is Geometry to defend herself against this onslaught, especially when she herself can find no ancient authorities to cite in her defense, while Arithmetic can legitimately cite the writings of Plato, Cicero, Seneca, Boethius, Macrobius, John of Salisbury, and (pointedly) Aristotle and Averroes in her defense? How could Geometry defend against the argument that her placing of mathematical irrationality into the order of nature and the cosmos was inimical to the very essence of harmony and its precise mathematical underpinnings? How could she break not only with the authority of Aristotle and the philosophers on this point but with Christian authority as well? Given the profound and longstanding associations between harmony and the divine, associations that were deeply engrained in both pagan and Christian cosmology, it hardly seems possible that Oresme could have supported the idea of a God not identified with harmony or of a cosmos not ordered by harmony – in *some* form.

The dating of both the *De proportionibus proportionum* and the *De commensurabilitate* (the scene of the epic debate) remains uncertain. But whether these works date to the late 1340s or, as is most probable, to between 1351 and 1362, or possibly even later to 1370, they were written by a committed Christian theologian and churchman who remained determinedly and self-consciously orthodox in his religious beliefs throughout his life.[138] Geometry, speaking for Oresme the orthodox theologian, could not deny the existence of harmony in God's creation. Her strategy turned, instead, on her radical reimagination of what divine

---

[137] *Ibid.*, 288–9.
[138] Grant provides this possible range of dates in his Introduction to *De commensurabilitate*, 4–5 and *De proportionibus proportionum*, 12–14. As noted in Chapter 7, by the late 1340s Oresme was a doctoral student in theology at the University of Paris. After obtaining his doctorate in 1356, he then embarked on a long and successful career in the Church that ended with his elevation as bishop of Lisieux in Normandy, a position he retained from 1377 until his death in 1382. With respect to his orthodoxy, it is noteworthy that in his *Prologue* to the *De commensurabilitate* Oresme wrote (175): "I did not release this little book without first submitting it for correction to the Fellows and Masters of the most sacred University of Paris."

harmony might actually look like when projected onto the workings of the cosmos. Here, as elsewhere, Geometry follows Oresme, who had written earlier in the *De proportionibus proportionum*: "As I shall declare afterward, harmony comes from incommensurable motions."[139] When he later came to write the *De commensurabilitate*, he was well aware that this position would be attacked and condemned by those of his contemporaries who either still viewed the world through the eyes of Arithmetic or who believed that Aristotle's vision of the order of the universe was unchallengeable. Yet despite the opposition he foresaw on both philosophical and doctrinal grounds, he pushed ahead. This, in itself, gives us some feeling for the weight and impulsion that lay behind Oresme's new sense and modeling of balance – a weight and impulsion that appear to have simply evaporated in the decades following the writing of these treatises.

Balance versus harmony continued: Oresme's recognition of the new model of equilibrium

Beginning with the writings of Pierre Duhem in the early decades of the twentieth century, and continuing to the present day, Oresme has been justly celebrated for his profound and multiple contributions to the history of mathematics and science. In this concluding section on his treatment of mathematical incommensurability, I would like to draw attention to an equally notable aspect of his thought: the remarkable extent to which he appears to have been *conscious* of its implications.[140] In the clashing worldviews of Arithmetic and Geometry, Oresme reveals his awareness of the chasm between older, previously authoritative visions of cosmic order and equalization and his own. In doing so, he defines, with unsurpassed prescience, clarity, and fullness, the shape and organizing logic of the new model of equilibrium.

The physical world Oresme inhabits is a world so truly in flux that the human mind can never fully comprehend it. Yet he remains at peace with it and within it.[141] In the *De proportionibus proportionum* he had argued:

---

[139]   *De proportionibus proportionum*, 304–5.

[140]   As I argued in the previous chapter, this consciousness extended to his political speculation as well, as evidenced by his deft reworking, reframing, and (ultimately) undermining of the implications of the ideal of the Common Good.

[141]   This is true at least through the 1350s, the decade in which he most probably composed the *De proportionibus proportionum* and the *De commensurabilitate*, along with the *De configurationibus* and the *De moneta*. In the previous chapter I suggested that in the decades following, he became considerably less tolerant of the flux and uncertainty that he perceived in the social, economic, and political world around him (if not the physical world), and considerably more concerned with controlling it.

"In any instant (*in quolibet instanti*) it is necessary that celestial bodies be so related that in any moment (*in quolibet instanti*) there will be a configuration (*constellatio*) such that there never was a similar one before, nor will there be one after in all eternity."[142] He is well aware that his picture of cosmic order is neither neat nor pretty in a conventional sense; he recognizes that conclusions flowing from it contradict the expectations and assumptions of both astrologers and most Aristotelians. Yet he is not only unwilling to abandon it, he forcefully asserts that when properly considered it reveals not "deformity," "baseness," and "privation," but rather a greater and higher beauty that is truly worthy of God:

> it seems more delightful and perfect – and also more appropriate to the deity – that the same event should not be repeated so often, but that [on the contrary] new and dissimilar configurations (*constellationes*) should emerge from previous ones and always produce different effects.[143]

At the foundation of Oresme's claim to a higher beauty for his picture of the universe is the extraordinary value he allows to both diversity (*diversitas*) and novelty (*novitas*).[144] At the opening of her oration, Geometry argues that the heavens would be not less but rather more splendid and more beautiful if there were a mixture of irrationality and regularity in their motions (*irrationalitate et regularitate commixtis*) because in this way "the regularity would be varied by the irrationality" (*regularitas irrationalitate varietur*).[145] Soon after, Geometry declares that "a subtle man perceives the beauty in much diversity (*in multa variatione pulchritudinem percipiat*), while an ignorant man, *who fails to consider the whole* (*non advertens totum*), sees it as merely confused" (my emphasis).[146] But of course, it is not only human perception that is of concern to both Geometry and Oresme. In the next sentence she declares that "the infinite plan of God distinctly recognizes this diversity which, put in its proper place, is pleasing to the divine sight and makes the celestial revolutions more beautiful (*efficit pulchriores*)."[147]

Where Arithmetic sees irregularity, uncertainty, diversity, and category mixing as inimical to harmony and as openings for confusion, Geometry embraces them. In embracing them, Oresme not only reimagines the bounds of Pythagorean harmony, he moves far beyond the bounds of

---

[142] *De proportionibus proportionum*, 306–7; restated in *Ad pauca*, 422–3.
[143] *De commensurabilitate*, 316–17.
[144] *Ibid.*: "et novitas plus delectat." On the newly positive value granted to both "diversity" and "novelty" in the fourteenth century, and its connection to the successes and values of commercial culture, see Park, "The Meanings of Natural Diversity."
[145] *De commensurabilitate*, 310–11.
[146] *Ibid.*, 312–13; I have slightly altered the translation.
[147] *Ibid.* This sentiment is repeated in various contexts and forms throughout the oration.

Aristotelian conceptions of natural order as well. The "order of the whole" that Oresme describes looks much more like the approximative "working order" underlying the Galenic body than it does the definitional order underlying Aristotle's physical universe. It looks much more like the systematic equilibrium that Peter Olivi imagined to make sense of the dynamic of market exchange, grounded in the acceptance of approximation, aggregation, multiplication, and probability, than it does the model of equalizing exchange imagined by Aristotle in the *Ethics* and then taken up by Thomas Aquinas and other thinkers of his generation.

A universe composed of incommensurable velocities and distances related by irrational ratios should not hold together in the old scheme of things, but it does. Parts that are irrational (imbalanced) in themselves should not be able to be linked together to form a rational (balanced) whole, but they do. The elements in the new model do not fit together in terms that make sense within traditional models of balance and equalization based on knowable and numerable points, and yet they *work*. Indeed, the dazzling fluidity and complexity of the working system through which the systematic whole (whether the Galenic body, or the Olivian marketplace, or the Marsilian *civitas*, or the Oresmian cosmos) maintains itself in proportional *aequalitas* and balance can actually present a new vision of beauty and divinity – to some eyes at any rate.

One of the great defining elements of the new model of equilibrium is the imagination that the dynamic interaction of imbalanced parts can work together to produce the balance of the whole. We have seen the dawning of this recognition in each of the preceding chapters as the new model took shape in discourse after discourse from the late thirteenth to the mid fourteenth century. Oresme recognized this element, and the radical departure that it represented, more fully and consciously than any thinker before him. It finds crystalline expression in his descriptive phrase "regular inequality," which appears in the opening paragraph of the *Prologue* to the *De commensurabilitate*. Here he presents his vision of the "machine of the world" as it is regulated by God (*mundi machina sub deo regitur*): "a brilliant diversity of motions [moving] effortlessly with a certain regular inequality (*diversitatem motuum regulari quadam inequalitate*)."[148] Then, in the opening paragraphs of the great dream debate, he has Geometry speak in praise of a universe in which irrationality and regularity are combined together (*irrationalitate et regularitate commixtis*), thereby conferring on plain regularity the aesthetic benefits

[148] *Ibid.*, 172–3.

of variety (*regularitas irrationalitate varietur*), to the end that "the heavens would glitter with even greater splendor."[149]

But Oresme's most prescient statement of this principle comes at the conclusion of a highly technical mathematical demonstration of a case of "regular irregularity" in the body of the *De commensurabilitate*."[150] All of a sudden, in the midst of a long (and wholly original) series of mathematical propositions and corollaries, there is a rupture in tone, as his intellectual excitement breaks through to the surface:

> In the description of these angles and from the multiplication of such points, a diligent mind can consider the wonderful way in which some things arise from the incommensurability and regularity of motions, so that I could utter such [expressions] as "rational irrationality" (*rationalis irrationalitas*), "regular non-uniformity" (*regularis difformitas*), "uniform disparity" (*uniformis disparitas*), "harmonious discord" (*concors discordia*). *Thus by means of the greatest inequality, which departs from every equality, the most just and established order is preserved* (my emphasis).[151]

Here, for once, in each of its brilliantly conceived pairings and in its breathtaking concluding sentence, the shaping logic of the new model of equilibrium finds full conscious expression.

Arithmetic is right: Geometry's point of view *is* dangerous and destabilizing; it *does* violate authority and accepted wisdom; it does overturn the accepted aesthetics of order and traditional notions of harmony; it does confound an older *sense* of what balance is and how it can be achieved. But in his exploration of the implications of mathematical incommensurability and irrationality, Oresme is doing even more than pointing toward a daring new way of imagining the cosmos and its workings. He is posing and answering questions crucial to the future of science. Does or must the universe conform to human ideas of rightness and perfection? Does or must its workings make sense in human terms?[152] Or must the investigator take the world on its own terms and work with them as they are, strange as they may appear, and disturbing as they may be to deep-seated and strongly held conceptions of right order?

---

[149] *Ibid.*, 310–11.   [150] *Ibid.*, Proof of Part II, Proposition 4, 252–7.

[151] *Ibid.*, 256–7: "Et cum summa inequalitate que ab omni equalitate degenerat equissima atque ratissima ordinatio perseverat." See *De commensurabilitate*, 46, for Grant's comment and judgment on this statement.

[152] He has Arithmetic speak for this view at many points, e.g., when she demands of Geometry (294–5): "For if someone should construct a material clock (*horologium materiale*) would he not make all the motions and wheels as nearly commensurable as possible? How much more [then] ought we to think [in this way] about that architect who, it is said, has made all things in number, weight, and measure?"

Oresme's answer to these questions represents a giant step in the history of science. Through the figure of Geometry he argues, in essence, that science can only begin to make sense of the world when it gives up the expectation that the world must make sense in human terms. This is yet another legacy of the new model of equilibrium, yet another reason why we sense the presence of "modern" ways of thinking and seeing in the writings that most clearly reflect it. "Rational irrationality," "harmonious discord," *aequalitas* as a systematic product emerging out of the greatest inequality, a balanced whole produced from imbalanced parts: who would have thought this possible? Who could have thought this rational in any sense, much less beautiful? No one before the model's emergence in the last decades of the thirteenth century.[153]

The new model of equilibrium applied to the workings of nature: Jean Buridan's geological speculations

As evidence for the existence of a new *sense* of the balance of nature, given form and weight through the emergence and elaboration of a new model of equilibrium in university culture of the mid fourteenth century, I offer Jean Buridan's remarkable set of speculations in the area of terrestrial physics that we today would term "geology."[154] Buridan (*c.* 1295–1361) received his master of arts degree at the University of Paris in the mid 1320s, and he spent the remainder of his life teaching in the Faculty of Arts there while writing voluminously.[155] For the most part, his writings grew out of his university lectures. With the books of Aristotle dominating the arts curriculum at Paris in the fourteenth century, Buridan wrote commentaries on almost every major Aristotelian work, with some

---

[153] Consider, for example, the play of inequality/equality, imbalance/balance, irrationality/rationality in Peter Olivi's conception of *capitale*, discussed in Chapter 1 above.

[154] I have written previously on this subject in Kaye, "The (Re)Balance of Nature."

[155] Estimates for the date of Buridan's birth range from 1292 to 1300. For major studies of Buridan's life and work, see Jack Zupko, *John Buridan: Portrait of a 14th-Century Arts Master* (University of Notre Dame Press, 2002); Bernd Michael, *Johannes Buridan: Studien zu seinem Leben, seinem Werken, und zur Rezeption seiner Theorien im Europa des späten Mittelalters*, 2 vols. (Freie Universität Berlin, 1985); Edmond Faral, *Jean Buridan: maître ès arts de l'Université de Paris*, Histoire littéraire de la France XXXVIII (Paris: Imprimerie nationale, 1950), 462–605. For an appreciation of Buridan as natural philosopher, see Edward Grant, "Scientific Thought in Fourteenth-Century Paris: Jean Buridan and Nicole Oresme," in *Machaut's World: Science and Art in the Fourteenth Century*, ed. Madeleine Pelner Cosman and Bruce Chandler (New York Academy of Sciences, 1978), 105–24. For a discussion that centers on Buridan's integration into the economic and social life of his time, see William Courtenay, "Philosophy's Reward: The Ecclesiastical Income of Jean Buridan," *Recherches de théologie et philosophie médiévale* 68 (2001), 163–9; also, Kaye, *Economy and Nature in the Fourteenth Century*, 29–32.

reworked and rewritten several times over his teaching years. Among these commentaries is a set of questions on the (Pseudo-)Physiognomy of Aristotle. I single out this text because it provides evidence that Buridan studied the writings of Galen – at the minimum the Ars medica (or Tegni) and Ibn Ridwan's commentary – as well as those of Aristotle.[156] In his commentaries, Buridan did much more than merely explicate the thoughts and intentions of the master: he used them to reframe and reconceptualize field after field of study, from logic to the natural sciences, to metaphysics, ethics, and politics. Indeed, there is a quality in Buridan's approach and thinking that strikes readers today as being surprisingly "modern," in part due to its capacity to pose new questions and place them within new conceptual frameworks.[157] During his lifetime, he enjoyed an excellent reputation within the university, and was elected to its highest office, Rector, in 1328 and again in 1340. After his death, his philosophical reputation remained exceptionally high, with his writings on many subjects continuing to occupy a central place in the curricula of European universities well into the sixteenth century.

Buridan's relation to Oresme at Paris has long been a question of interest to historians. The idea that Buridan had been Oresme's teacher at the University of Paris had wide circulation through much of the twentieth century. It has recently been suggested that this is not only unlikely but impossible, given the institutional structures in effect at the university in the fourteenth century.[158] Even the existence of a hazier scholarly "circle" surrounding Buridan at Paris, which would have included Oresme, has recently been challenged.[159] Still, there is no denying the many parallels in their speculations on nature and the many meaningful similarities in their approach and thinking (although there are certainly differences as well).[160] This has led to the generally accepted

---

[156] Manuscripts of these questions were first described by Lynn Thorndike, "Buridan's Questions on the Physiognomy Ascribed to Aristotle," Speculum 18 (1943), 99–103. See also Joseph Ziegler, "Philosophers and Physicians on the Scientific Validity of Latin Physiognomy, 1200–1500," Early Science and Medicine 12 (2007), 285–312, esp. 291–6.

[157] Gyula Klima, John Buridan (Oxford University Press, 2009), 4–6 at 6: "if the mark of modernity in intellectual history is the capability to bring about a 'paradigm-shift' in the sense of re-conceptualizing the problems of an entire field, as it arguably is, then Buridan was indeed a very modern thinker in this sense." The same can be and has been said of other thinkers I have linked to the new model of equilibrium, especially Peter Olivi, Marsilius of Padua, and Oresme.

[158] Courtenay, "The University of Paris at the Time of Jean Buridan and Nicole Oresme"; Courtenay, "Arts and Theology at Paris, 1326–1340," 21.

[159] J. M. M. H. Thijssen, "The Buridan School Reassessed: John Buridan and Albert of Saxony," Vivarium 42 (2004), 18–43.

[160] These parallels extend to the speculations on nature considered below in this chapter, which, I contend, have their roots in their more general sharing in the new model of

opinion that there was communication on some level between the two, at the least through texts and most probably through personal contact as well.[161] As is the case with Oresme, there are many categories under which Buridan's thought can be and has been considered: as a nominalist inheritor and continuator of Ockham, as a logician and supposition theorist, as a philosopher of language, and many more.[162] Once again, however, in order to keep my course set on balance, I steer clear of categories of interpretation that have traditionally been applied to Buridan by historians of medieval philosophy and science.

The earth in equilibrium

Buridan pursued his geological speculations primarily in two works: his commentary on Aristotle's *De caelo et mundo*, Book II, chs. 7 and 22,[163] and his commentary on Aristotle's *Meteorologica*, Book I, chs. 20 and 21.[164] At the beginning of Book II of the *De caelo*, Aristotle raises the question whether the heavens can be said to have a proper right and a proper left.[165] In his discussion, Aristotle posits that someone on the other side of the earth from us would see the left and right of the heavens in a way

equilibrium. For one important area of disagreement between the two thinkers (regarding the status of mathematics), see J. M. M. H. Thijssen, "Buridan on Mathematics," *Vivarium* 23 (1985), 55–78; Jean Celeyrette, "Le statut des mathématiques dans la physique d'Oresme," *Oriens–Occidens. Sciences, mathématiques et philosophie de l'Antiquité à l'Âge classique* 3 (2000), 91–113.

[161] William Courtenay, "The Early Career of Nicole Oresme," *Isis* 92 (2000), 542–8. Courtenay suggests (548, n. 20) that although Oresme was certainly not an official student of Buridan's, he "may have attended Buridan's lectures, was certainly familiar with his writings, and knew him personally as a fellow master in the arts faculty at Paris."

[162] The range of articles in the collection *The Metaphysics and Natural Philosophy of John Buridan*, ed. J. M. M. H. Thijssen and Jack Zupko (Leiden: Brill, 2000), provide some idea of the breadth of Buridan's interests and influences.

[163] Buridan's questions and commentary on Aristotle's *De caelo* can be found in two modern editions: *Iohannis Buridani Quaestiones super libris quattuor de caelo et mundo*, ed. Ernest A. Moody (Cambridge, MA: Medieval Academy of America, 1942), and *Joannis Buridani Expositio et Quaestiones in Aristotelis* De caelo, ed. Benoît Patar (Louvain: Éditions Peeters, 1996) (abbreviated hereafter as *Quaest. De caelo*). I cite the Patar edition in the notes that follow. *Quaest. De caelo*, Book II, q. 7 has been partially translated by Grant in his *A Source Book in Medieval Science*, 621–4. *Quaest. De caelo* II.22, has been partially translated by Clagett and appears in his *Science of Mechanics*, 594–9. I use the Clagett translation (which followed the Moody edition) where it is consonant with the Patar edition cited in the notes.

[164] This work has been edited by Sylvie Bages, *Les Questiones super tres libros Metheorum Aristotelis de Jean Buridan: étude suivie de l'édition du livre I* (thesis, École de Chartes, Paris, 1986). Book I, qq. 20 and 21, occupy pages 288–316. I follow Patar's conclusion that Buridan's commentary on the *De caelo* precedes his commentary on the *Meteorologica*. The particular dating (the *De caelo* to 1328–30, and the *Meteorologica* to 1352) is less certain. On this, see Patar, Introduction, *Quaest. De caelo*, 19, 116–17.

[165] Aristotle, *De caelo*, II.2.

opposite to how we see it. At this point, obviously intrigued by Aristotle's suggestion, Buridan raises a question that Aristotle had not specifically considered: whether dry and habitable land might exist on the opposite side of the earth from which a person could actually view the heavens. This, in turn, raised a more universal question: "*Utrum tota terra sit habitabilis*" – "Whether the whole earth is habitable."[166] The long and many-layered answer that Buridan then provided appears out of place at this point in his commentary, since it bears no direct relation to the text of the *De caelo*. We know, however, thanks to the research of Pierre Duhem, that Buridan's question, along with some of the physical and mathematical presuppositions that underlie his response, stretched back to the first Greek commentaries on Aristotle, were picked up and carried further in a number of Arabic works, and found their way into Latin commentaries in the decades immediately preceding Buridan's treatment.[167]

Buridan recognizes at the opening of his question that it is commonly said (*communiter dicitur*) that one quarter of the earth's surface presently lies above water and is habitable. He then raises a question Aristotle had never considered: why would any one quarter of the earth be more likely to remain above water and habitable than any other quarter? That, in turn, leads to yet further questions, some of which had been asked before over the centuries. He sets up the problem as follows: given the spherical nature of the earth, given that according to Aristotelian physics all earth falls naturally to the earth's center, given the great abundance of water with respect to land, and assuming along with Aristotle (as Buridan clearly does) that the universe is eternal (*si mundus fuerit perpetuus, ut ponit Aristoteles*), why in the fullness of time should any portion of land whatsoever remain habitable above the water?[168]

---

[166] *Quaest. De caelo*, Book II, q. 7, ed. Patar, 410–17. On this *quaestio*, see Ernest A. Moody, "John Buridan on the Habitability of the Earth," *Speculum* 16 (1941), 415–25; Bernard Ribémont, "Mais où est donc le centre de la terre," in *Terres médiévales*, ed. Bernard Ribémont (Paris: Éditions Klincksieck, 1993), 261–76; Edward Grant, *Planets, Stars, and Orbs: The Medieval Cosmos, 1200–1687* (Cambridge University Press, 1994), esp. 622–9.

[167] Pierre Duhem, *Le système du monde: histoire des doctrines cosmologiques de Platon à Copernic*, vol. IX (Paris: Hermann, 1958), 79–323. Duhem's remarkable study, completed in the first decade and a half of the twentieth century, but remaining in manuscript until 1958, is still the best and most thorough treatment of the history of geological speculation from the ancient world through the fourteenth century, with special attention given to Buridan's place in that history.

[168] *Quaest. De caelo*, II.7, ed. Patar, 410. Duhem (*Système*, vol. IX, 79–170) considers the history of this observation, esp. 102, 120–2.

Systematic equilibrium imagined through infinite time

In answer to this question Buridan first suggests that the waters have not yet covered the whole of the earth due to the unevenness of the earth's surface and the existence of mountainous heights that are insurmountable by water. But after offering this possibility, he immediately argues against it, and his reasons for doing so are enlightening:

> For at all times, many of the higher parts of the mountains descend to the valleys, and no parts, or few ascend; thus, through an infinite time (*et sic ab infinito tempore*) these mountains ought to be wholly consumed and reduced to a sphere [beneath the waters].[169]

There are a number of startling assumptions here. Buridan's physical world – the world on which he bases his physical speculations – is eternal, with no beginning and no end. His sense of time, inherited from Aristotle, is vastly distant from the biblical period of six thousand years or so that medieval Christians are assumed to have believed in implicitly.[170] Buridan consistently applies his concept of an eternal universe to his speculations on nature despite fierce resistance in his day to philosophical arguments that deny the biblical account of the creation of the world in time and *ex nihilo*, and despite the resulting intellectual project engaged in by numerous medieval thinkers, including good Aristotelians, to construct logical arguments against an eternal world. Clearly, the infinite extension of Buridan's timeframe in his speculations on natural activity (which he shared with a number of Aristotelian natural philosophers) makes possible a considerably deeper exploration of the logic of natural systems than one based on a window of six thousand years. It also makes possible, and may well even require, a considerably deeper exploration of the logic of systematic equilibrium. Even the slightest imbalance would result in destruction, if continued over infinite time.

In an earth that has existed for six thousand years or so, Buridan's observation "that at all times, many of the higher parts of the earth are carried by the waters down into the sea,"[171] might well go no further. But since he is thinking in Aristotelian time, he reasons that if this process of

---

[169] *Quaest. De caelo*, II.7, ed. Patar, 410: "quia omni tempore partes superiores ex montibus descendunt multae ad valles, et nullae vel paucae ascendunt; et sic ab infinito tempore illi montes deberent esse toti consumpti et reducti ad planitiem."

[170] Buridan is far from alone in this sense of an eternal universe. He shares it and its unproblematized application to physical speculations with many fellow Aristotelians, dating back to the later twelfth century, and it appears as an a priori assumption in numerous other of his physical speculations.

[171] *Quaest. De caelo*, II.7, ed. Patar, 410: "omni tempore multae partes istius terrae altioris portantur cum fluviis in profundum maris."

erosion is continuous over eternity, then every mountain, and indeed all dry land, should eventually be washed into the sea. Moreover, if the world really is eternal, then all the earth that was once above the waters has *already* been washed into the sea. Given his observations and his assumptions about systematic order, it is the continued existence of any dry land whatsoever that needs to be explained. He writes: "Through an infinite time, then, it would seem that the whole depth of the sea ought to be filled with the earth, thus consuming the [portion of] earth that was elevated . . . Therefore, nothing ought to remain habitable."[172]

The systematic whole in dynamic equilibrium

As Buridan proceeds, he comes to ask not only how any land at all could remain above the waters, but how, given an eternal process, and given that every portion of dry land will eventually be washed into the sea by erosion, the *proportion* of dry land to sea could nevertheless remain *eternally constant* at one-quarter to three-quarters, as he proposes that it has over the eons. Through what natural processes are the mountains and heights that gradually disappear into the sea replaced by, or, as he comes to imagine it, perfectly balanced by, the growth of dry land and mountains at some other location on the sphere of the earth? For in an eternal universe, where erosion is perpetual, such a continuous, perfectly proportioned and balanced replacement is necessary to explain the continued existence of a fixed proportion of dry land into the present.

To answer this question, indeed to *ask* this question, Buridan imagines the whole of earthly nature as an interconnected physical system in dynamic equilibrium.[173] He then invents an elaborate physical explanation, which, as he writes, "seems probable to me and by means of which all appearances could be perpetually saved."[174] He imagines the earth and its surround as a grand, integrated, moving whole, whose workings are governed entirely by geometrical and physical principles: heat and cold cause evaporation and condensation, which in turn differentially rarify and condense earth and water, which in turn causes the earth above the

---

[172] Grant, *Source Book*, 621–2; *Quaest. De caelo*, II.7, ed. Patar, 411: "Ideo videtur quod ab infinito tempore tota profunditas maris deberet esse repleta terra, et haec elevatio terrae deberet esse consumpta; et sic aqua naturaliter deberet totam terram circumdare, nec deberent esse aliquae elevationes discoopertae."

[173] Duhem frames his entire discussion of Buridan's geology around the concept of equilibrium, entitling his section on the subject in *Système*, vol. IX: "L'équilibre de la terre et des mers."

[174] *Quaest. De caelo*, II.7, ed. Patar, 416: "quae videtur mihi probabilis, et per quam perpetuo salvarentur omnia apparentia."

waters to be lighter than the earth below, which results in a slight, eternally shifting variation between the center of the earth's weight (*centrum gravitatis*) and its center of magnitude (*centrum magnitudinis*).[175] This perpetual shifting of the two centers around each other results in a continual interchange of the relatively light with the relatively heavy.[176] As a consequence, some parts of earth are continually being raised above the circle of the waters, as other parts, in balanced and equal measure, are being carried beneath it.[177]

Indebtedness to and separation from Aristotelian nature

Like virtually every natural philosopher of his period, Buridan was a committed Aristotelian, and in constructing this speculation he relied on a number of Aristotelian first principles: the spherical earth; the natural tendency of the element earth to fall in a straight line toward the center of the universe; the heaviness of earth relative to water; the association of heat with rarification; the position of the earth itself at the center of the spherical universe; and the assumption of the eternity of the world. In the construction of his natural system in which there is an eternal balanced interchange between dry land and the waters of the deep, Buridan could draw on the profound sense of conservation built into the whole of Aristotle's physical thought and enunciated with particular clarity in the *De generatione et corruptione*. Finally, in the realm of what can be called geology, Buridan had the example of Aristotle's *Meteorologica*, which assumes at many loci the process of geological displacement. At one

---

[175] Duhem traces the long history of the idea that there might exist a disjunction between the earth's *centrum gravitatis* and its *centrum magnitudinis*, going back to Alexander of Aphrodisias (*Système*, vol. IX, 81), and he illustrates the sharpening of this speculation in the writings of two of Buridan's younger contemporaries at Paris, Nicole Oresme and Albert of Saxony (*Système*, vol. IX, 202–18). For Oresme's early speculations on the matter, see Garrett Droppers, "The *Quaestiones de Spera* of Nicholas Oresme: Latin Text with English Translation" (PhD thesis, University of Wisconsin, Madison, 1966), 65 ff.

[176] *Quaest. De caelo*, II.7, ed. Patar, 416: "Et ita apparet quod aliud est centrum magnitudinis terrae, et aliud est centrum gravitatis eius, nam centrum gravitatis est ubi tanta est gravitas ex una parte sicut ex altera, et hoc non est in medio magnitudinis, ut dictum est."

[177] *Quaest. De caelo*, II.7, ed. Patar, 416: "Modum ultra, quia terra per suam gravitatem tendit ad medium mundi, ideo centrum gravitatis terrae sit in centro mundi, et non centrum suae magnitudinis, propter quod terra ex una parte est elevata supra aquam, et ex alia parte est tota sub aqua." Buridan's assertion of the disjunction of the earth's two centers and his speculations on the geological implications of this disjunction are more fully developed in his commentary on the *Meteorologica*, Book I, q. 21, conclusions 2 and 3, ed. Bages, 308–9.

point in this work Aristotle employs his observations on the slow progressive building up of the Nile delta to note: "It is true that many places are now dry, that formerly were covered with water. But the opposite is true too: for if they look they will find that there are many places where the sea has invaded the land."[178] Clearly, the textual weight of Aristotle, and the sense of systematic conservation and equalization internalized through the committed study of Aristotle, are evident at many points in Buridan's geological speculations.

At the same time, however, Buridan is moving here in a speculative direction not taken by Aristotle, and he is seeing possibilities and potentialities in both nature and what can fairly be called natural equilibrium that neither Aristotle nor the thirteenth-century Latin commentators on Aristotle were capable of seeing. Indeed, following the logic of the new equilibrium, Buridan arrives at questions and conclusions that fly in the face of foundational principles of Aristotelian physics. We can easily superimpose the form of the mechanical balance on Buridan's geological model: as one particle of dry earth falls beneath the waters in one part of the sphere of the earth, another particle, of equal measure, rises above the waters at another place; as one mountain slowly disintegrates and falls, an equal weight of earth slowly rises to form a mountain somewhere else. But Buridan's model employs not the single equality of the mechanical scale, not one active balance, but rather a near infinity of risings and fallings, covering the whole of the shifting earth over all eternity.

Buridan's model of natural interchange encompasses every particle and portion of the vast globe, from the minute specks of earth he observes being carried down to the sea by mountain streams, to the formation of the mountains themselves; from the part of the earth he can see, to the opposite side of the earth he can only imagine; from the infinite past, through the present, to the infinite future. The whole model is driven by a slight but perpetual incongruence (inequality) between the earth's center of gravity and its center of magnitude. And yet, through it all, a perfectly proportioned equality, which one would have to call a "dynamic" equality, the generalized *product* of a dynamic equilibrium, is maintained within the whole of the functioning system over all eternity. The equalization at the heart of this model is fully systematic: the meaning of each part is determined relative to its shifting place within the working whole.

---

[178] Aristotle, *Meteorologica*, Book I, q. 14. This whole question is a marvel of observation and reasoning, much of which would have been instructive for Buridan.

Sensing the potentialities of dynamic equilibrium

In his discussion of the physical play of the earth's two separate centers, one of weight and one of magnitude, and the physical implications that follow, Buridan never uses the terms "equilibrium," but he does make explicit use of the mechanical scale (*statera*) and the "balance" it represents as a descriptive image at one point in his commentaries to both the *De caelo* and the *Meteorologica*. When he does so, however, he employs the balance of the scale to clarify one essential element of his argument rather than to characterize his vision as a whole. In the *Meteorologica* he writes:

Now the center [of magnitude] of the earth is not the center of the universe, rather, the center of the earth's weight (*gravitas*) is the center, because the earth occupies the center of the universe by reason of its weight not its magnitude. It balances itself (*equilibrat se*) at the center of the universe by virtue of its weight, as in the mechanical scale (*in statera*) equal weights balance equally (*equales equilibrant*) against each other, even if their magnitudes are not equal.[179]

In the *De caelo*, he provides an example of this principle: "If on a set of scales (*in statera*) a stone is placed on one scale and wool is placed [balanced] on another, the wool will be of much greater magnitude than the stone."[180]

Here the image of the mechanical balance serves to underscore the point that within the functioning system imagined by Buridan weight and weight alone is the moving force. Measurement by the scale ignores magnitudes, forms, species, and particular natures of every sort, even though they are clearly present in the substances being weighed. Apart from their weight, the particular natures of the elements in balance are irrelevant to the functioning of the system. In the case of geological interchange, the particles of earth and water have no influence on each other beyond what can be explained by their relative weights and densities.[181] This careful reductionism points to an important aspect of the new model of equilibrium: at the same time that it represents a

---

[179] *Questiones super tres libros Metheorum*, I.21, ed. Bages, 309: "Sed centrum terre non est centrum mundi; ymmo centrum eius gravitatis est centrum mundi quia terra non ratione sue magnitudinis sed ratione sue gravitatis tenet locum medium mundi. Ideo secundum suam gravitatem equilibrat se ad centrum mundi sicut in statera gravitates equales equilibrant se adinvicem, licet magnitudines non sint equales."

[180] *Quaest. De caelo*, II.22, ed. Patar, 500–8, at 506: "si in statera ex una parte ponatur lapis et ex alia parte lana, lana erit valde maioris magnitudinis" (my translation).

[181] In *De generatione et corruptione*, II.4, Aristotle had assumed the possibility of "reciprocal transformation" or actual "conversion" between the elements of earth and water, but this possibility is excluded by Buridan in the modeling of his working system.

globalization of vision and an increase in the complexity of the functioning system, it also works by *ignoring* the individual natures of the component parts in its strict limitation and isolation of the active factors and causal agents involved in systematic balance.[182]

Aside from this particular application of the image of the mechanical scale, Buridan does not explicitly attach the concept of equilibrium to the immensity of his imaginative construction.[183] He never hints that his vision of equalization or equilibrium is different from Aristotle's or from any that came before him. Equality is equality and equalization is equalization. He never seeks to communicate his model of equalization in itself. Indeed, he is almost certainly unaware that he has one, and even less aware (if possible) that his thoughts are being organized and directed by one. The very depth and scope of the model, and the lack of an established vocabulary or discourse through which to express or distinguish it, obscured its recognition, even from its creators and continuators.[184]

Is Buridan's model of balance "mechanical"?

Ever since the work of the great historian of science, Pierre Duhem, in the early twentieth century, the adjective "mechanical" has continued to be applied to aspects of Buridan's thought and to that of other fourteenth-century natural philosophers as well.[185] Ernest Moody, the first modern editor of *De caelo* II.7, called Buridan's framing of the problem here a "strictly mechanical explanation of a geological problem."[186] More recently, Patrick Gautier Dalché has credited Buridan with having

---

[182] We have witnessed this process of de-individuation at many points in the preceding chapters. See the illustrations of city life from the manuscript of *La vie de Saint Denys* discussed in Chapter 5 above.

[183] For a later geological argument, clearly based on Buridan's, in which the modeling of geological replacement is directly compared to the workings of the mechanical scale, see Lynn Thorndike, *A History of Magic and Experimental Science* (New York: Columbia University Press, 1934), vol. III, 568–84, esp. 580. New research has established Thorndike's anonymous author as the Augustinian Jacques Legrand. On this see E. Beltran, "Jacques Legrand OESA: sa vie et son œuvre," *Augustiniana* 24 (1974), 387–414, at 395; Patrick Dalché, "L'influence de Jean Buridan: l'habitabilité de la terre selon Dominicus de Clavisio," in *Comprendre et maîtriser la nature au Moyen Âge: Mélanges d'histoire des sciences offerts à Guy Beaujouan* (Geneva: Droz, 1994), 101–15, esp. 101.

[184] The immense and all-inclusive scope of his model is well represented in *Questiones super tres libros Metheorum*, I.21, Conclusion 10, ed. Bages, 314: "possibile est quod in terra que nunc est discooperta generabuntur de novo montes alti versus orientem et corrumpentur aliqui magni ad occidentem, ex quibus contingit fluvios augeri et multiplicari ad orientem et deficere vel diminui ad occidentem et e contrario, et quod mare redundet ex fluviis ibi accedentibus."

[185] Duhem, *Système*, vol. IX, 202.

[186] Moody, "John Buridan on the Habitability of the Earth," 420.

constructed "un modèle mécanique grandiose des changements de la surface terrestre."[187] Even with the recognition that Buridan's physical thought is a long way from the self-conscious mechanical philosophy of the seventeenth and eighteenth centuries, and even recognizing that there remain clear residues of pre-mechanical principles and assumptions within his and other of the most innovative physical speculations of this period,[188] it is still possible to sense that actual mechanical devices are being used as models of form and activity in a number of his (and Oresme's) most intriguing speculations on nature from this period.

It was in the fourteenth century that the mechanical clock first assumed its striking physical presence in the town squares of Europe – including the Paris of Buridan and Oresme. The clock as a metaphor for the workings of the heavenly spheres finds its first meaningful "scientific" expression in the cosmological speculations of Oresme.[189] Moreover, in Buridan's Paris, the great center of innovative natural philosophy in his day, mechanical mills, impressive in their size, were whirling, grinding, pounding, and sawing away in every quarter of the city. We have seen visual evidence of this in the great mill-wheels lashed to the piers of the bridges of Paris depicted in the miniatures from *La vie de Saint Denys*.[190] Buridan clearly paid close attention to the form and functioning principles of the mechanical mill (among other mechanical devices), and he makes a number of references to them in his speculations on nature's form and function.[191] For these reasons, I would agree that arguments applying the descriptor "mechanical" to Buridan's thought convey a certain sense of

---

[187] Dalché, "L'influence de Jean Buridan," 108.

[188] The argument against framing the thought of Buridan and Oresme as mechanical is made particularly well by Marshall Clagett, "Nicole Oresme and Medieval Scientific Thought," *Proceedings of the American Philosophical Society* 108 (1964), 298–310, esp. 300–2.

[189] For a concise summary of the relationship between Oresme and Buridan at the University of Paris, see Courtenay, "The Early Career of Nicole Oresme," esp. 548, n. 20. For Oresme's scientific use of the clock metaphor, see, for example, his commentary to Aristotle's *De caelo*, II.2, in *Le livre du ciel et du monde*, ed. and trans. Albert Menut and Alexander Denomy (Madison: University of Wisconsin Press, 1968), 288–9. Clagett ("Nicole Oresme and Medieval Scientific Thought," 300–2) notes the distinction between a truly "mechanical" solution to the motion of the spheres and that offered here by Oresme. Not surprisingly, though, the clock metaphor underlies a number of Oresme's most important and forward-looking speculations.

[190] See Chapter 5, Figure 6, p. 280.

[191] See, for example, the place that the observation of millworks plays in Buridan's striking speculations on *impetus* as an explanation for the acceleration of falling bodies: *Acutissimi philosophi reverendi Magistri Johannis Buridani subtillissime questiones super octo phisicorum libros Aristotelis* (Paris, 1509; reprint, Frankfurt: Minerva, 1964), Book VIII, q. 12, fols. 120rb–121rb. This question has been translated into English by Clagett, *Science of Mechanics*, 532–8.

what Buridan is after and achieves.[192] They also establish a clear marker separating Buridan's thought from that which came before it, while suggesting a direct link between his thought and the science to come in the seventeenth century.

But Buridan never uses the word "mechanical," nor, I think, would he have recognized its meaning and its implications as assumed by modern interpreters. My sense is that the intellectual leap implied by the movement from non-mechanical to mechanical thinking obscures the fine gradations between Buridan's vision of equilibrium in nature and those that both preceded and followed his. Moreover, and to my mind most importantly, the mental image connected with the adjective "mechanical" tends to obscure the numerous other developments and post-Aristotelian elements, all of them critical to Buridan's imagination, that combined to produce the particular model of systematic equilibrium he applied to natural activity. In his vision of geological interchange, for example, there is no privileged position within what has become a purely relational system; there is no imagined hierarchical order, no set top, bottom, or medium. There is no essential meaning attached to the individual part itself: the same particle of earth will one day form part of habitable earth and another lie buried in the watery deep. The idea that the system orders itself through "natural" principles and requires nothing outside of itself to function and to balance itself over infinite time is crucial. But given the heterogeneous mix of geometrical, physical, and a priori principles that lie behind Buridan's explanation, I would argue that the terms "self-ordering" and "self-equalizing" almost surely describe his model more closely than does the term "mechanical."

Another crucial element that "mechanical" misses is Buridan's denial of essential meaning to physical space and geographical place. His consistent relativization of space and place, quite extraordinary in the context of his culture, is made explicit in his commentary on the *De meteorologica*. There he speculates that given the progressive loss of land into the sea at one edge of the mass of dry land, and the concurrent building up of dry land from the sea at the opposite edge, it is possible that the same city (without naming any particular city) can, over an immense time, move from being the most eastern of cities to the most western of cities, as its position shifts in relation to the shifting mass of dry land and sea.[193] And as this shift occurs, the medium meridian of the land mass

---

[192] I myself have used the terms "mechanical" and more often "proto-mechanical" to describe certain aspects of the thought of Buridan and Oresme in the past.

[193] *Questiones super tres libros Metheorum*, I.21, ed. Bages, 316: "Tertia decima conclusio est quod eamdem civitatem possibile est fieri magis orientalem quam ante esset vel magis

(*medium meridianum terre*) will shift as well in relationship to the fixed stars.[194] Unspoken, yet clearly present in this scheme, is the conclusion that over infinite time all cities and all places will eventually be swallowed by the sea, as new ones arise on newly formed and habitable land.[195] All the parts and particles of the earth which are now above the water, including, by extension, the parts that make up his Paris, his native Picardy, and (one would have to conclude) even the holy city of Jerusalem, will one day disappear beneath the depths. The individual *res*, whether particle of earth or city or continent, is subsumed in the balancing whole. The meaning held by any individual point changes continually as it moves along the intersecting arcs of the continuous process.[196] All has been relativized. The site of meaning has become the totalizing system and the equilibrium that governs it. Equilibrium has become the tail that wags the dog.

In all of these elements and in their combination we have, I suggest, a stark departure from an Aristotelian framework, in which the concept of Nature as an overarching process exists alongside an insistence that each of its parts possesses its own inherent nature and its own proper end.[197] In the Aristotelian system it is the irreducible "nature" of the part that determines its place within the whole, connecting and ordering it within the larger functioning system of a purposeful Nature. Notions of hierarchy, ontological grading, individuated purpose, and meaningful place are central to Aristotelian thought, and these aspects were fastened upon by scholastic thinkers of the thirteenth century because of their central importance within other authoritative sources of medieval culture, both philosophical and religious. But meaning, purpose, and place find little or no space within Buridan's model of geological equilibrium: it is, instead, governed by geometrical and physical necessity, driven by its own internal logic, and held together by a new sense of the possibilities and potentialities of balance.

---

occidentalem, quia magis orientalis dicitur civitas ex eo quod est propinquior magno mari versus orientem, etc. Fiet autem propinquior si mare ex illo latere augetur et remotior si diminuatur."

[194] *Ibid.*: "Unde, secundum quod magnum mare circuit ipsam terram, oportet mutare medium meridianum terre habitabilis in ordine ad celum ymaginatum quiescens."

[195] In a number of sections of his commentary on *Meteorologica*, I.20, Buridan closely observes the changing coastline of the Mediterranean, noting the building up of certain delta islands and the erosion of other parts of the coast into the sea.

[196] The term "point" here (and always for Buridan), is intended to signify a position on a continuum rather than a real entity in itself. For a recent summary of Buridan's arguments against the real existence of points, see Jean Celeyrette, "La problématique du point chez Jean Buridan," *Vivarium* 42 (2004), 86–108. On the place of geometry in Buridan's thought, see Thijssen, "Buridan on Mathematics," 55–78.

[197] There is a similarly radical departure from any physics grounded in notions of microcosm/macrocosm.

The on/off switch of mechanical/non-mechanical is, in my opinion, inadequate to mark the subtle directions, continuities, and discontinuities in the development of thought in general and models of equalization in particular. It most certainly cannot do justice to the elements and arguments within Buridan's presentation that carry clear traces of pre-mechanical principles.[198] But since models of equalization are shared within virtually all cultures in virtually all time periods, I suggest instead that a focus on elucidating these models – paying close attention to the nature of their elements, their organizing logic, and their overarching form – has the potential to serve as a mode of analysis and comparison flexible enough to do justice to a history of ideas.

Speculative fruits of the new model of equilibrium

In Book II, question 22 of his commentary on Aristotle's *De caelo*, Buridan continues the geological speculation he began in II, 7. The question he poses is "whether the earth remains fixed and motionless at the center of the universe."[199] He should not have to ask this question. Aristotle asserted and demonstrated throughout his writings that the earth lay fixed and motionless at the very center of a spherical universe. Moreover, the Bible was interpreted to be in full agreement with the Aristotelian position on this point. To question the fixity of the earth, then, was to question a principle that was a pillar of scriptural interpretation and foundational to Aristotelian astronomical and physical thought. And yet this is the path that Buridan follows. Again, however, even as he turns to argue with Aristotle, he grounds his argument in Aristotelian physical principles that he clearly accepts. This raises the question: what might have been pushing or pulling him in the directions he takes?

If one accepts Aristotle's dictum that all weight moves naturally to the center point of the spherical universe, then the center of the earth's weight or gravity, the *medium mundi*, must lie at the absolute center of the universe. This being the case, for the earth itself (*tota terra*) to remain fixed and motionless there, Buridan recognizes that the earth's center of magnitude (*centrum magnitudinis*) must correspond precisely to its center of gravity (*centrum gravitatis*). This was not a problem for Aristotle, but it has become one for Buridan, because, as we have seen, he has based his

---

[198] I discuss several of these pre-mechanical elements in Kaye, "The (Re)Balance of Nature," 103–5.

[199] *Quaest. De caelo*, II.22, ed. Patar, 500–8: "Utrum terra semper quiescat in medio mundi." This question has been translated by Clagett and appears in his *Science of Mechanics*, 594–9.

whole model of geological interchange on the assumption of a perpetual disjunction between the earth's two centers.[200] If the geological process he described in his earlier question is not merely speculative but actually *probable*, as Buridan maintained that it is, then as mountains continually sink at one place on the sphere of the earth and rise at another, the weight of the earth must continually shift around its center, however small this weight shift might be in relation to the overall weight of the earth, and however small the resulting magnitude of the shift might be in relation to the earth's overall size.[201] Buridan writes:

And by this another doubt is solved, that is, whether the earth is sometimes moved according to its whole in a straight line. And we can answer in the affirmative ... [As the weight of the earth shifts due to the perpetual interchange of dry land and water] that which has newly become the center of gravity is moved so that it will coincide with the center of the universe, and that point which was the center of gravity before ascends and recedes.[202]

In short, in Buridan's scheme, *tota terra*, the whole earth, is constantly undergoing minute rectilinear motions about the center of the universe as the surface of the earth is systematically transformed and its weight shifts accordingly. The whole of the earth is envisioned as a working system in equilibrium. Here, the model of dynamic equilibrium has been worked out so exquisitely, and has been accorded such great intellectual weight, that it has become capable of moving the earth itself – and this despite the enormous counterweight of both scriptural and Aristotelian authority. The lesson is clear: wherever the model is applied, its effects are transformative.

From an equilibrium of weight to an equilibrium of perspective

Geology was only one of the areas and questions to which Buridan applied the new model of equilibrium with startling effect. I conclude this chapter

---

[200] *Quaest. De caelo*, II.7, ed. Patar, 416, restated in II.22, ed. Patar, 505–6.

[201] For a similar, considerably earlier speculation on this possibility, albeit one lacking much of the logical scaffolding Buridan here provides, see Al-Biruni, *The Determination of the Coordinates of Positions for the Correction of Distances between Cities*, ed. and trans. Jamil Ali (American University of Beirut, 1967), 17. Here, I would argue, is a case where the comparison of the physical speculations of these two thinkers, so distant in time and culture, in terms of the particular form of their underlying models of equalization, could be more historically revealing than a comparison based only on the similarities and differences of their particular insights.

[202] *Quaest. De caelo*, II.22, ed. Patar, 507: "Et per hoc solvitur alia dubitatio, scilicet utrum terra aliquando moveatur secundum se totam motu recto. Et possumus dicere quod sic ... illud quod de novo factum est medium gravitatis movetur ut sit medium mundi, et illud quod ante erat medium gravitatis, ascendit et recedit."

with a short visit to another of these areas: Buridan's (and later Oresme's) arguments on behalf of the possible daily *rotation* of the earth. Due to the landmark status of these speculations in the history of science, much scholarly attention has been paid to them, and even their cursory treatment is beyond the scope of this chapter. Fortunately, while their arguments are richly detailed, they are also quite concise, and interested readers can easily consult them.[203] I conclude with brief selections from these speculations because they provide one of the clearest windows into the impact of the new model of equilibrium on medieval thought, and they illustrate the model's prefiguring of "modern" ways of seeing and thinking with particular clarity.

Buridan's arguments for the possible diurnal rotation of the earth appear within the very same question, "whether the earth remains fixed and motionless at the center of the universe" (*De caelo* II.22), in which he imagined the earth perpetually balancing itself around the center of the universe through minute rectilinear motions. Proximity alone suggests that the same model of equalization serves as the ground of each. In the case of the earth's possible rotation, however, relative perspective substitutes for relative weight as the activating element. In both cases, Buridan's speculations on the earth's motion seem to contradict the evidence of the senses. As everyone can see, the sun and the stars appear to revolve daily around the earth; and as everyone can sense, the earth appears (at most times) to be utterly stable – the very definition of stability. Moreover, in the case of the earth's rotation, just as with the earth's rectilinear motion, Buridan is raising a possibility that flies in the face of authority as well as the evidence of the senses. The traditional position from Aristotle through Ptolemy and right up to his own day maintained that the earth's appearance of fixity reflected indubitable reality. Over the ages, an immense weight of meaning, both philosophical and religious, had become attached to the earth's central resting place, circled by the sun and the heavenly spheres. Buridan, however, was able to resist this weight and to strike a different path.[204]

---

[203] *Ibid.*, 500–5; Oresme, *Le livre du ciel et du monde*, II.25, 519–39. Menut provides a facing-page English translation of Oresme's French text. Clagett presents partial English translations of both (with commentary) in *Science of Mechanics*, 600–9. Grant reprinted Clagett's translations in his *A Source Book in Medieval Science*, 500–15.

[204] Both Buridan and Oresme, however, taking their cue from the text of Aristotle (*De caelo* II.13 [293b30–2]) begin their comments by noting that others before them have speculated on the possibility of a rotating earth. Buridan simply notes that before him "many have held it probable" (*multi tenuerunt tamquam probabile*) (ed. Patar, 501), and he gives responsibility for a number of his strongest arguments to unnamed "others." Oresme also speaks of "others" (*aucuns*) who have preceded him in his arguments, offering the names of both Plato and Heraclides of Pontus (ed. Menut, 520–1). It appears to be quite

At the opening of II.22, he asserts that the question of the earth's fixity, far from being settled, is actually a difficult one.[205] He then puts forward a series of arguments to show that the apparent circular motion of the sun as it rises and sets daily could also be explained by assuming that it is the earth itself that is revolving daily, while the sun and the heavenly spheres remain fixed in place. One key to Buridan's capacity to imagine the possibility of a rotating earth is his highly developed capacity to think and see in relative terms. He, and others who shared in the new model of equilibrium, are able to literally play with the possibilities of relativity.[206] But what gives this capacity its exceptional conceptual power – in this case, the power to move the earth – is its link to a vision of *systematic* activity. The product of this linkage is a coherent and impelling logic of *systematic relation*, intimately coupled to the logic of systematic equalization. By the second quarter of the fourteenth century, thinkers were capable of imagining the universe itself as a relational field. They were able to imagine the cosmos as a working system with no privileged point of viewing, no absolute directions, and no single unifying axis.[207] Thus Buridan recognized that he could connect the fact that we imagine the earth to be fixed in place while the heavens move around us to the example (*exemplum*) of two ships, one moving and one at rest. It is possible, he writes, for someone on a moving ship to nevertheless imagine (*imaginatur*) that he is at rest. Moreover, should someone on a moving ship see a second ship that truly (*secundum veritatem*) is at rest, it will appear to him (*apparebit sibi*) that not his but the other ship is moving.[208] "This is so," he explains, "because his eye would be completely in the same relationship to the other ship regardless of whether his own ship is at rest and the other moved, or the contrary situation prevailed."[209]

On the strength of his ship exemplum, Buridan then speculates that even if it were the earth that rotated daily while the sun was at rest, we would still imagine (*imaginemur*) that we were the ones at rest and the sun

important to both to assert that they are not the first to imagine this possibility, but the treatments by Buridan and (particularly) Oresme, are far fuller and more carefully constructed than any they had inherited.

[205] *Quaest. De caelo*, II.22, ed. Patar, 501: "Ista quaestio non est facilis."

[206] I made this argument earlier in *Economy and Nature in the Fourteenth Century*, 240–5. Here I linked their comfort with relativized determinations to the lessons conveyed by the triumph of relativity in the marketplace with respect to the determination of price and value. Once again, the earlier argument is consonant and complementary to this present one.

[207] Thijssen, "Buridan and Mathematics," 68: "there is no concept of an *unum transcendentale* in the works of Buridan."

[208] *Quaest. De caelo*, II.22, ed. Patar, 501.

[209] *Ibid.*: "quia omnino taliter se habebit oculus ad illam aliam navem, si propria navis quiescat et alia moveatur, sicut se haberet, si fieret e converse." Clagett's translation, *Science of Mechanics*, 595.

was rising and setting around us.[210] Indeed, he argues that even if the earth were rotating while the heavens remained at rest, "all the celestial phenomena [not just the rising and setting sun] would appear to us just as they now appear."[211] He then accompanies this statement with a series of brilliant arguments both in favor and opposed to the proposition of a rotating earth.[212] He actually solves one of the most difficult doubts attached to the earth's motion: why if it is moving are we not continually buffeted by the resulting wind? In response, he posits "that the earth, the water, and the air in the lower region are moved simultaneously with diurnal motion. Consequently there is no air resisting us."[213] After a series of similarly strong arguments against traditional objections, he comes, however, to an objection (posed by Ptolemy) that he cannot answer: why, if the earth is really rotating from west to east at great speed, does an arrow shot in the air come back to the same spot from which it was launched rather than some distance to the west? Having failed to offer an explanation, he rather suddenly drops this line of speculation and turns to the question of the earth's rectilinear motion around the center of the universe (discussed earlier), apparently satisfied with having shown that the question of the earth's possible rotation is a real and difficult one.

Following Buridan's formulation of these arguments (c. 1330), they appear again, expanded and highly refined, in Nicole Oresme's *Le livre du ciel et du monde*, his vernacular French commentary on and translation of Aristotle's *De caelo*, written toward the end of his life (1377).[214] Before turning to the speculations of Oresme, I offer a point to consider. Given the vitality of this branch of speculation and the powerful trajectory of the argument between the writings of Buridan and Oresme, one might well expect its continued development and refinement in the decades following 1377. But something very different happens. Rather than continuing development there is a sharp break, a break that is as meaningful for the history of balance (and consequently for the history of ideas) as is

---

[210] *Quaest. De caelo*, II.22, ed. Patar, 501.

[211] *Ibid.*, 502: "Et indubitanter verum est quod, si esset ita sicut ista positio ponit, omnia in caelo apparerent nobis sicut nunc apparent."

[212] *Ibid.*, 502–5.

[213] *Ibid.*, 504: "Sed isti respondet, quod terra et aqua et aer in inferior regione moventur simul illo motu diurno, ideo, non est aer nobis resistens." Notice that he credits this argument to others (*isti*).

[214] Oresme, *Le livre du ciel et du monde*, II.25, 519–39. Oresme's commentary on Aristotle's *De caelo* (completed 1377) was the third in his series of vernacular French commentaries on (and translations of) complete treatises of Aristotle, commissioned by Charles V. It is the rare work by Oresme in the area of mathematics and natural philosophy known to have been composed after his great period of invention, which ended c. 1362.

the continuous flow of insights that preceded Oresme's arguments and to some degree supported them. After 1377, the extraordinary possibilities opened up by the speculations of Buridan and Oresme close down and are taken no further for considerably more than a century.[215] The texts are there, the potent insights are there on parchment and paper, but no one, apparently, either sees their potential or builds upon them. Indeed, it is almost two centuries before they are fully appreciated. When they are finally taken up and expanded upon, they appear in strikingly similar form in a work that at last does justice to their forward-looking implications: the *De revolutionibus orbium coelestium* of Nicolaus Copernicus (1543), Book I, ch. 8.[216]

When Oresme approached the question of the possible rotation of the earth in his commentary to the *De caelo*, Book II, question 25, he took up Buridan's demonstrations of relative perspective and relative motion and then took them considerably further, fashioning them into evident principles.[217] Employing the same exemplum of the two ships to illustrate the possibility of the earth's diurnal motion, Oresme writes: "Now, I take as a fact that local motion can be perceived only if we can see that one body assumes a different position relative to another body (*autrement ou resgart d'autre corps*)."[218] On this basis, he argues that if today the sphere of the heavens revolved while the earth remained still, and if tomorrow it was the earth that revolved while the heavens were fixed in place, "we should not be able to sense or perceive this change, and everything would appear exactly the same both today and tomorrow with

---

[215] Indeed, as Clagett has noted (*Science of Mechanics*, 585–7, n. 8), Albert of Saxony, a scholar at Paris somewhat younger than Oresme, but often associated with his thought in the realm of natural philosophy, explicitly rejected Oresme's arguments for the possibility of a rotating earth.

[216] For the sake of comparison, Clagett (*Science of Mechanics*, 600–15) places Copernicus' arguments for diurnal rotation immediately following those of Buridan and Oresme. The similarities are indubitable and have long been remarked, even as the line of textual inheritance remains obscure.

[217] Oresme's basic argument in the *Livre du ciel et du monde* (1377), which was grounded in the logic of relative perspective and motion, first appeared almost two decades earlier in his *Quaestiones de sphaera*, written while he was still at the University of Paris, which is to say sometime between 1349 and 1361. On this, see Droppers, "The *Quaestiones de Spera* of Nicholas Oresme." This edition also contains (q. 3, 65–71) Oresme's first speculations on the implications of the disjunction between the earth's center of gravity and its center of magnitude.

[218] Oresme, *Livre du ciel et du monde*, 522–3: "Item, je suppose que movement [local ne] peut estre sensiblement apparceu fors en tant comme l'en apparçoit un corps soy avoir autrement ou resgart d'autre corps." All English translations from the *Livre du ciel et du monde* are Menut's. Further in the argument (522–3), Oresme underscores this point: "we do not perceive motion unless we notice that one body is in the process of assuming a different position relative to another."

respect to this mutation."[219] He then follows this startling statement, grounded in a fully relativized perspectival system, with others equally startling and revealing. Where in the end Buridan found no way to explain why an arrow shot into the air should fall at the spot from where it was launched, Oresme did. He writes: "one might say that the arrow shot upward is moved toward the east very rapidly with the air through which it passes, along with the whole mass of the lower portion of the world (*aveques toute la masse de la basse partie du monde*)."[220] With respect to Oresme's solution to this problem and to the elaborate series of examples he devised to illustrate it, Marshall Clagett observed: "Buridan hinted at, and Oresme rather specifically outlined, the concept of a closed mechanical system, wherein, due to the relativity of the perception of motion, the observer describes all movements as if they were part of his system only."[221] What is clear is that, for Oresme, vision is relative to perspective and perspective is relative to the system within which it is embedded.

The sheer transformative power of the new model of equilibrium – the realms of thought and vision that were opened to those that shared in it – is revealed in one last "imagination" that Oresme presents in support of the earth's possible rotation. He writes:

> Thus it is apparent that one cannot demonstrate by any experience whatever that the heavens move with diurnal motion; whatever the fact may be, assuming that the heavens move and the earth does not or that the earth moves and the heavens do not, *to an eye in the heavens which could see the earth clearly*, it would appear to move; if the eye were on the earth, the heavens would appear to move. Nor would the vision of this eye be deceived, for it can sense or see nothing but the movement itself (my emphasis).[222]

There are many remarkable facets to this conclusion. First among them, perhaps, is Oresme's capacity to project a disembodied eye into the heavens and then to visualize what that eye (unfreighted by the weight of meanings attached to an earth-centered perspective) would see when it looked back on the earth. Something has provided Oresme's eye with the power needed to escape the gravity of an earth-bound perspective. Here I think we see the impact of the new model of equilibrium that Oresme both shared and shaped, and here we have evidence of the power it and other such models possess. Within the systematic whole of the cosmos as

---

[219] *Ibid.*, 522–3: "nous ne pourrions apparcevoir en rien cest mutacion, mes tout sembleroit estre en une maniere huy et demain quant a ce."

[220] *Ibid.*, 524–5. My translation.

[221] In the words of Clagett (*Science of Mechanics*, 587).

[222] Oresme, *Livre du ciel et du monde*, 536–7: "se un ouyl estoit ou ciel et il voit clerement la terre, elle sembleroit meue, et se le ouyl estoit en terre, le ciel sembleroit meu. Et le voiement n'est pas pour ce deceu, car il ne sent ou voit fors que movement est."

Oresme perceives it, neither the earthly nor the heavenly eye is granted precedence. In his conception of systematic activity, all is relativized, even as relativity itself is systematized and integrated into the new equilibrium.

Oresme's fully realized "imagination" here completes the curve that began with Bradwardine's rule and carried through each of the speculative "advances" considered in this chapter. Dumbleton's exploration of the measuring "latitude" and his use of it to frame the Merton "mean speed" rule; Oresme's invention of a system of geometrical configurations to represent the automatic relation between extension and intension in the quantification of qualities; Oresme's exploration of proportionality and mathematical incommensurability at the level of exponential powers; Buridan's geological speculations in which the whole of the earth is governed by systematic equilibrium; the sustained arguments on the earth's possible rotation in which the cosmos itself is reimagined as a relational field in equilibrium: each of these can be viewed and appreciated as an isolated insight. I have tried, however, to show that there is something beneath the level of insight that links them all; something that impels them all in a similar and similarly innovative direction; something that invests them all with great speculative power; and something that connects them all to similarly innovative and potent speculations in disciplines far removed from natural philosophy. This unworded "something" is their sharing in a radically new sense of balance and its potentialities, a sense that was as much a product of social environment as it was of textual inheritance. When this diffuse sense was then shaped into a coherent and cohesive model of equilibrium within the vibrant intellectual culture of the medieval university, it gained the power to transform the image of the world and to move the earth in the process. In sum, the new sense of the potentialities of balance at play within scholastic natural philosophy through much of the fourteenth century was more than a mere detail in the story of scientific development: to a considerable degree, it was the story.

Conclusion

The history of balance is not the history of an idea. Ideas are verbalized, communicated directly, problematized, debated, and considered as subjects in themselves. None of this was true of balance. And yet the core questions I pose and seek to answer through the lens of the history of balance are situated squarely in the tradition of the history of ideas. How does the inconceivable become conceivable? How do thoughts once unthinkable become thinkable? How do new images of the world and its workings take shape within intellectual cultures, and what conditions might underlie and inform this process? In the specific case of the emergence of the "new model of equilibrium," where multiple thinkers contributed to the process of invention over generations, I ask further: what is common to the insights and perceptions these thinkers shared?; what shaped the particular constellation of elements and ideas around which their speculation centered?; what gave this constellation its transformative power and potential?; and what was unique about the speculation its formation made possible? I have responded to these questions within the restricted analytical framework of the history of balance because although balance in this period was never an idea in itself, it functioned as the fertile and indispensable *ground* of ideas. As such, it provides a key to answering each of the crucial questions above – a key that has so far gone for the most part unrecognized.

As I approach the end of this lengthy book, I am aware of how much I have left unsaid about the history of balance in this period. In my original plan, I had intended to include additional thinkers and writings in each of the areas I covered: in the area of medical thought, Gentile da Foligno (d. 1348) and his extraordinary commentary on Avicenna's *Canon*; in the area of economic thought, the continuation of Peter of John Olivi's insights in the writings of Geraldus Odonis and other Franciscan authors of the fourteenth century, along with Jean Buridan's speculations on price, value, and the dynamics of exchange; in the area of political and religio-political thought, the works of John of Paris and Ptolemy of Lucca that preceded Marsilius of Padua, and the writings of the Conciliarists that succeeded him; in the area of natural philosophy, the speculations of Nicholas of Autrecourt on epistemology and perspective, and (among other texts) the collection of scholastic commentaries on Aristotle's *De generatione et corruptione*, which itself centers on processes of equalization in nature. First among the ranks of the missing is William of Ockham. He is not entirely absent from this study, but even a cursory analysis of the model of equalization that underlies his new and influential speculations in the areas of logic, epistemology, political thought, and natural philosophy, would, I soon came to realize, require a book in itself and be beyond my powers. I would consider this book a success if it could inspire the study of Ockham on these terms.

Clearly, the role that balance plays as the ground of thought neither begins nor ends with the medieval period. By providing the outlines of what a history of balance can look like; by suggesting how to recognize the cluster of interlocking elements and assumptions that cohere within models of equalization; and by indicating the power these models exercise in the realm of thought, my hope is that readers will be able to extend the analytical focus on balance to thinkers, disciplines, periods, and cultures other than those I have treated here. As my sensitivity to balance has grown, I find that I cannot read the great thinkers of the seventeenth and eighteenth centuries – Galileo, Descartes, Spinoza, Bacon, Pascal, Locke, Hume – without seeing and sensing their profound grounding in models of equalization – models, moreover, that possess many of the elements that constituted the "new" model of equilibrium. I would like to suggest, further, that the link between intellectual invention and the ever-evolving sense of balance (tied to ever-evolving social, political, economic, and technological environments) continues right into the present day of chaos theory and string theory. Readers expert in the intellectual history of later (or earlier) times can be the judge of whether such parallels drawn across cultures and periods – with respect to the remodeling of balance and its intellectual effects – seem apt, or fruitful, or historically significant, or not.

Since the matters I present in the first four chapters of this book make claims, raise questions, and call for conclusions that differ somewhat from those presented in the final four chapters, I have divided my concluding comments into two parts. Part 1 is directed to the main subjects I treat in Chapters 1–4: the intertwining of textual and contextual factors that underlay the emergence and continuing evolution of the new model of equilibrium through the first half of the fourteenth century. Part 2 introduces the subject of *discontinuity* in the history of balance, particularly with regard to my assessment of the model's dissolution in the last quarter of the fourteenth century. Here I examine both the evidence for and the nature of this dissolution, considering which of the model's defining elements fail, what might explain this failure, and what effects this failure had on the history of balance and the history of ideas.

Part 1: The intersection of texts and contexts in the history of balance

If one judges Galenic medicine in terms of its contributions to medical practice, there is certainly room for criticism. But as a system of thought devised to capture the moving, integrated, and working system of the body, it is a brilliant achievement. Within it, complexity and uncertainty were embraced; positive attitudes toward empiricism and a modified experimentalism were forged; the relationship between theory and practice in scientific investigation was both theorized and to a degree effected; and an appreciation for the role of estimation and conjecture in the formation of scientific knowledge was established. The indomitable resistance of the Galenic medical tradition to the allure of the ideal, the absolute, and the fixed, and its parallel commitment to an epistemology built on relativity, indeterminacy, and probability, represent an extraordinary intellectual accomplishment. This is especially true given the high value placed on universal, unchanging, and transcendent truths within the same intellectual culture in which scholastic medicine developed. With the gradual but steady appearance of authentic Galenic texts from the later twelfth into the fourteenth century, the intellectual system of Galenic medicine was *available* to all scholastics seeking to uncover and understand the working principles of systematic activity in nature and society. After the mid thirteenth century, it would, of course, have represented a complementary intellectual model for most scholars, secondary to the model of Aristotelian nature that came to so dominate university education. Nevertheless, given that Galen consciously incorporated many elements of Aristotle's philosophy into his medical theory, there were broad grounds of agreement between the two bodies of thought.

There is no question that medicine was below, even many degrees below, Aristotelian philosophy in the accepted ontology of knowledge in this period. The same epistemological elements within medicine that to modern eyes look to be moving toward a more "modern" scientific outlook – its empiricism, probabilism, instrumentalism, and modified experimentalism – were generally perceived as inferior ways of knowing within scholastic university culture. To counter this negativity, medical writers sought to associate themselves and their discipline with the superior discipline of philosophy whenever possible. Hence their continued claim that medicine is a science (in the Aristotelian sense) as well as an art, dependent on the universal "first principles" provided by Aristotelian physics. Hence, too, their continual citations of the more purely philosophical works of Aristotle (and many others) along with his writings on *naturalia* and physics. But this dynamic worked both ways. Just as *medici* were eager to cite philosophers on every possible occasion, so, after the mid thirteenth century, university philosophers and theologians would be unlikely to cite medical authorities or medical texts as witnesses to or for their *philosophical* determinations (as opposed to those determinations that touched directly on medical questions as well).[1] Indeed, direct citations of contemporary works of any kind were rare within this literature. Partly for this reason, I suggest that the importance of medicine for the history of ideas in the fourteenth century, and in particular for the history of natural philosophy during this brilliant phase of its development, has been greatly underestimated.

There is clear evidence that a number of the major figures in the elaboration of the new model of equilibrium were knowledgeable in Galenic medicine. I have discussed the intellectual connections between Peter of John Olivi and the *medicus* Arnau de Vilanova at Montpellier in the 1290s.[2] Michael McVaugh has found evidence that Arnau's *Aphorismi de gradibus*, with its mathematical scheme for quantifying qualitative intensities, was read at Merton College, Oxford, just at the time when similar mathematical schemes were being developed there in the sphere of natural philosophy.[3] The case for Marsilius of Padua, who was actually trained in Galenic medicine at the University of Padua, is clear.[4] And Nicole Oresme, who advanced the new model of equilibrium at many points and from many directions, cites Galen directly, both in his writings on natural philosophy and in his commentary on Aristotle's *Politics*.[5] But there are so many connections between the Galenic model of bodily equalization and the

---

[1] Jordan, "The Disappearance of Galen in Thirteenth-Century Philosophy and Theology." For evidence against the "disappearance" of Galen with respect to the numerous writings on philosophical and theological questions that touched *directly* on medical questions, see Maaike van der Lugt, *Le ver, le démon et la Vierge: les théories médiévales de la génération extraordinaire. Une étude sur les rapports entre théologie, philosophie naturelle et médecine* (Paris: Les Belles Lettres, 2004); Joseph Ziegler, "*Ut dicunt medici*: Medical Knowledge and Theological Debates in the Second Half of the Thirteenth Century," *Bulletin of the History of Medicine* 73 (1999), 208–37.

[2] See Chapter 4 above.

[3] See Chapter 8 for McVaugh's case on behalf of Arnaldian influence on the Oxford Calculators.

[4] I discuss Marsilius' education in Galenic medicine and his considerable debt to Galenic thought in his modeling of political equilibrium in Chapter 6.

[5] See Chapter 7 for discussion on this point. In Chapter 8 I offer evidence that Jean Buridan, Oresme's older contemporary at Paris and an equally important contributor to the new model of equilibrium, was also a close reader of Galen, particularly of Galen's *Tegni*.

"new equilibrium" as it appears in the most advanced university speculation in numerous non-medical spheres, that I presume a much wider readership of scholastic medicine than public citations alone would indicate. If this is indeed the case, could the reading and proliferation of Galenic texts alone have prepared the way for the new equilibrium?

Communication of the model of equilibrium through texts

On the yes side, consider how thoroughly woven together are the major components of the Galenic system: relativity, proportionality, probability, approximation, continuity, continuous qualitative motion, the *neutrum*, the "latitude of health," the numerable degree, division and distribution in terms of fit and function, the positive stance toward difference and diversity – all (and more) are intertwined around the central concept of the complexion (*complexio*), and the central ideal and requirement of balance, defined as continual proportional equalization (*aequalitas ad iustitiam*). When a cluster of concepts links together to form a web of meaning of such complexity and reflectivity, it becomes, I have argued, more than a collection of elements. It becomes a self-reflecting whole, a "unity" that possesses a sensible as well as an intellectual presence and conveys a characteristic "feel" and "sense" of form and motion.[6] As the unity takes on these quasi-sensual qualities, it becomes, in my definition, a "model," capable of exerting influence in the sphere of sensing as well as in the sphere of knowing.

Given the riches of the Galenic model of equalization, and the availability of these riches even in works as short and accessible as Galen's *Tegni* or Avicenna's introductory chapters to the *Canon*, I think it is worthwhile to imagine what the effects might have been when one of the Oxford Calculators, or a Buridan, or an Oresme, or any one of a score of other fourteenth-century contributors to the "new" model of equilibrium, came to the reading of a text in scholastic medicine. They would almost certainly have done so after having received intense training in Aristotelian logic and philosophy, and likely after having engaged with the Aristotelian system as commentators in their own right. My sense is that the intellectual effect of reading Galen and/or Galenists (including the often-read Arabic commentators and the Latin continuators) could well have been profound at this stage of their preparation, capable, in itself, of opening up new avenues of thought and new ways of conceptualizing the working logic of systematic equalization.

---

[6] Discussed in Chapters 3 and 4.

Those who read Galen with care would have been exposed to a vision of how balance might be achieved and maintained in nature that was expanded and elaborated beyond anything available in Aristotle's writings. If I am right in thinking that the transformation of the model of equalization, and the consequent emergence of a shared model of equilibrium, was central to the opening up of conceptual possibilities in virtually every field of scholastic speculation (given the centrality of the ideal of balance/*aequalitas* to virtually every field of medieval discourse), then the impetus toward this transformation would likely have come from writings in that area – medicine – which most fully theorized and elaborated the modeling of *aequalitas*.

Communication of the model of equilibrium from beyond the text

Despite the evidentiary advantages of reading intellectual innovation as a process of textual absorption and combination, or as the product of ideas being passed along from text to text and thinker to thinker, I do not think this view is adequate to explain a shift in the modeling of balance (and hence in intellectual innovation) of a kind that occurred between 1250 and 1360. And yet the counter-view – that texts alone, no matter their depth and brilliance, are insufficient in themselves to generate new models of equalization (and the new ideas and ways of seeing that follow from them) – has its own difficulties. To assume that intellectual change of this magnitude requires the compounding of texts with lived environments is to assume as well the existence of modes of communication that in themselves leave little or no visible or palpable evidence: modes which can only be deduced from their effects – the traces they leave in the language, imagery, and organizing logic of the text itself.

Looking back at Arnau's *Aphorismi de gradibus*, for example, we can see how deeply indebted it was to Galen's writing and Galenic equalization in particular. But there is something in it – in him – pulling and stretching his conceptualization of qualitative intensity and degree beyond anything he read in Galen. It may well have been a short and introductory text by Al-Kindi that opened his eyes to the possibility of moving from arithmetical addition to geometrical multiplication in the measurement of qualitative degree, but it was Arnau who saw the promise in this neglected text; he who saw that such a move "fitted" the dynamic of his own environment, experience, and perception. Again, while Arnau clearly relied on Galenic texts for the base concept of the measuring latitude, there was something beyond the text that led him to expand and stretch what he had inherited into the imagination of a world composed of myriad latitudes attached to myriad qualities in perpetual expansion and contraction – the imagination of what I have called a "world of lines." And the same point made here about Arnau can be made about each of the thinkers considered in this book. Even in the rare cases where this or that idea can be clearly traced back to an earlier text, the question still remains why the thinker opened up to these particular insights and possibilities out of the countless available, and why he ignored or actively closed down to others. Here again, the concept of "fit" is crucial, with the understanding that the sense of "fit" is always linked to experience and environment.

There is no denying the intellectual power of Galen's mind and Galen's texts. But the very reception of the Galenic model of equalization from the mid thirteenth century was shaped by profound changes in the reception environment: intellectual and ideational, of course, but here again, institutional, social, political, and economic as well. The reading of Galen or any set of texts takes place in personal contexts that can greatly affect the meaning drawn from them, greatly affect the judgment of which insights seem more productive or "apt" and thus more true. Taddeo Alderotti, like Galen before him, recognized not only that this kind of insight selection occurred, but that it *should* occur. The philosopher, he wrote, rejects the existence of the *neutrum* on philosophical grounds, but the *medicus* does and should accept it as "true" because it is true to his living and working experience.[7] Experience not only exerts a pull on the choice of which models, particular insights, or solutions are chosen out of all that are available, but once they are chosen, it has the power to bend these too in the further direction of conformance to experiential "fit." Even given the sensual and intellectual weight I attach to the Galenic model of equalization, the stepped history of its reception between 1250 and 1350 indicates that at every stage its comprehension depended upon its being experienced by thinkers as *conveniens ad opus*, as congruent with their sense of how things actually worked in the world they inhabited, which included their economic, social, and material environments.

In Chapters 1 and 2 I offered an explanation for the emergence of the new model of equilibrium based in the experience and understanding of the dynamic of market exchange. In Chapters 3 and 4 I offered an explanation based in the comprehension and transmission of Galenic texts. In Chapters 5–7 I offered an explanation based on the experience of life within the vital, self-ordering city of the late thirteenth and fourteenth centuries. What I discovered, in the process of writing these chapters, is that after the mid thirteenth century, all three of these areas – the urban marketplace, the Galenic body, and the working *civitas* – came to be

---

[7] Discussed in Chapter 4, pp. 200–5.

viewed in strikingly similar terms as self-ordering and self-equalizing systematic wholes.[8] All three came to be described as systems in which order and equalization, rather than being imposed by any single over-arching power or intellect (as was the case in earlier medieval models of equalization) was instead envisioned as the working aggregate *product* of the functioning system itself. This shift had immense implications for the history of ideas. From the last quarter of the thirteenth century, one can see a growing recognition that the proper analysis of all three areas (and others beside) required the exercise of the same intellectual tools: relativization, proportionalization, estimation, and approximation, all to the end of imagining a working system capable, through its own internal logic of activity, of producing systematic balance out of the free play of its intersecting and interacting parts.

In Galen's case, the shape and complexity of his total vision of the functioning body was constructed over decades of residence in late second-century Rome at a time when the immense city lay at the heart of a vast Empire, and the Empire itself (held together by the *media* of law, administration, and commerce) was reaching its furthest stage of connectivity and communication. The deep links between environment and ideation in the formation of his model of bodily equalization come to the surface at points in his writings.[9] In the opening to Book IV of his *De usu partium*, for example, at the point where he is describing the interrelation-ship of the organs of nutrition, Galen likens the esophagus to the "main thoroughfare" through the city; the stomach to a "central storehouse" for the city; the work of the stomach to the work of the city officers who sift the city's grain and clean it of its impurities; and the veins that carry purified nourishment to the liver are likened to the many routes followed by the city's porters carrying grain to the public bakery.[10] He then caps off his metaphorical excursion by praising those *medici* through the ages who had the wisdom to "liken the governance of an animal to that of a city."[11]

---

[8] In the fourteenth century, the body, the city, and the marketplace were joined by a fourth systematic whole in dynamic equilibrium: nature itself.

[9] Temkin, "Metaphors of Human Biology."

[10] Galen, *De usu partium*, IV.1, IV.2, in *Opera omnia*, ed. C. G. Kühn, vol. III (Leipzig, 1821–33), 266–8; Galen, *On the Usefulness of the Parts of the Body*, ed. and trans. Margaret Tallmadge May (Ithaca, NY: Cornell University Press 1968), 204–5. Kühn, translating from the Greek text, provides the Latin term *"promptuarius"* for the stomach, which has the meaning of both a central storehouse and a public center of distribution. He continues (267–8): "quemadmodum baiuli in civitatibus repurgatum in promptuario frumentum in aliquam commune civitatis deferunt officinam ... venae ipsae deferunt ad aliquem concoctionis locum commune totius animalis, quem hepar nominamus."

[11] *De usu partium*, IV.2, trans. May, 205.

In short, the joinings and parallels between the social/political body and the medical body around the shared ideal of *aequalitas*, which we find elaborated in scholastic commentaries on Galen from the late thirteenth century, were there from the beginning. Recognizing that multiple environments – social, economic, political, technological, spatial, and textual – interact in the process of both the invention and the reception of models of equalization makes for an admittedly complicated way of approaching intellectual innovation. It is certainly far more complicated than assuming that ideas travel from text to text and thinker to thinker. But such complication may simply be necessary if the goal is to come closer to understanding how new ideas, new ways of seeing, and new images of the world take shape.

Part 2: The dissolution of the "new" model of equilibrium and its intellectual effects

The "new" model of equilibrium was by no means the only model available in its time; nor did it ever fully replace earlier models, except in the minds of a small group of committed scholars. Its interest, therefore, lies not in its cultural dominance but in the range of conceptual innovations and openings that followed in its wake. Although there was a genuine and recognizable trajectory to the evolution of the new model between approximately 1280 and 1360, after the 1360s it slows down considerably, and by the end of the 1370s its creative period has effectively come to an end in each of the discourses I have followed, whether in the area of economic, medical, political, or scientific thought. Those speculations from the 1360s and 70s in which the new model is still discernible are almost invariably the product of a refined circle of thinkers who had been university students in the 1340s and 50s, when, in my view, the social and intellectual factors that drove and supported its formation were still active. While I believe, therefore, that the notion of "progressive evolution" can justly be applied to the model of equilibrium as it took shape within scholastic culture between 1280 and 1360, my argument is limited to a particular intellectual culture over a particular period of time. I have no intention of making general statements in support of the continuous evolution of medieval thought over its many centuries, nor, by any means, of arguing for the persistence of medieval ideas into the present. To do so would be to detach thought from its particular social and historical contexts, which would go squarely against my intent and my view of intellectual development. Indeed, I hope to bring new attention to the *discontinuities* in scholastic thought after the mid fourteenth century, in the belief that these discontinuities are as historically meaningful and revealing as the continuities I have traced.

Evidence for the model's dissolution

First a clarification. I do not mean to imply that after the mid fourteenth century there was a decrease in intellectual creativity or innovation per se. Actually, if innovation is associated with intellectual curiosity, or with freer speculation on a larger constellation of subjects, or with the criticism of authorities and authoritative positions of the past, or with the expansion of social groupings engaged in intellectual production (particularly its extension to the artisanat), or with the multiplication of centers of intellectual production outside the university, or with the deeper grounding of thought in empirical observation and experience, then there was no loss of creativity and innovation in the centuries following the dissolution of the new model of equilibrium.[12]

Over the century or more following the dissolution of the "new" model and the emergence (in the sixteenth century) of a yet "newer" model, with something approaching the coherence, cohesion, and level of sharing among intellectual innovators that the earlier model had enjoyed, the concern for attaining and maintaining balance/*aequalitas* never ceased to be a central concern. What changed was the shared sense of what *aequalitas* was and could be, and, consequently, of how it could be attained and maintained. One of the characteristics of this intervening period is that rather than one single model of equalization emerging to take the place of the "new" model, there appeared instead a plethora of competing models. Many of these models returned to positing the necessary intervention of a primary ordering and equalizing power, either from above or from within; others identified order and equality with adherence to a preexisting plan, reinscribing hierarchies of various sorts; others fitted equalization to the form of macrocosm/ microcosm, following this scheme through with astounding detail; others moved away from naturalism toward supernaturalism in their explanations; many moved away from a belief in open and public knowledge toward a belief in the power of private knowledge, looking for the key to truth in secret texts and secret codes knowable only to the select few. With all this variety, there was no loss of intellectual vitality. Indeed, the very diversity of models that ensued when the university ceased to be the center and arbiter of speculation may actually have had vivifying effects on thought.

My point is not to denigrate the intellectual accomplishments of the period that followed the dissolution of the "new" model of equilibrium. My point is rather to observe that from the last quarter of the fourteenth

---

[12] For an overview of artisanal culture and its positive contributions to intellectual production in this era, see Pamela Smith, *The Body of the Artisan: Art and Experience in the Scientific Revolution* (University of Chicago Press, 2004).

century, a particularly rich and productive form of invention associated with this model disappears from scholastic thought, and with it a particularly incisive and "forward-looking" type of speculation that had borne great fruit in a wide range of disciplines and discourses. Among the greatest strengths of this model was that it made possible a form of naturalistic explanation that did not require the existence or intervention of an intelligence or ordering power existing above or outside the sphere that it governed. It made possible explanations based on the assumption that the working systems underlying the world of nature and society are capable of ordering themselves and organizing themselves in ways that assure the production of an aggregate *aequalitas* – an *aequalitas* sufficient to satisfy the requirements not only of reason and law, but even (as Olivi maintained) of Christian charity. It certified the idea that valid knowledge was public knowledge, open to all who were capable of employing the universal instruments of logic and mathematics. At its height, the new model made possible a form of invention whose promise attracted the best and the brightest minds of the medieval university. And then it failed.

There are, I recognize, risks attached to arguing from absence, but the failure of the new model raises questions that are as historically significant, and as vital to the history of ideas, as those that surround its emergence. Following the model's failure in the area of natural philosophy, for example, scholars at university seem for the most part unable to recognize the great potential contained in the speculations that had been built over the first three-quarters of the fourteenth century, or even to fully comprehend them, much less to expand upon them. This subsequent failure is particularly evident regarding the brilliant earlier speculations of Nicole Oresme, despite his having dedicated entire treatises to their clear and careful elaboration.[13] We know, however, that Oresme's insights and philosophical approach to nature did not remain forever unfathomable or unsurpassable. When, in the 1960s Marshall Clagett argued for their reappearance, more than two centuries later, in the thinking and writings of Galileo, he joined a tradition in the history of science that stretched back to the writings of Pierre Duhem in the first quarter of the twentieth century and continues into the present. And Oresme is not a singular case. Historians of science have noted numerous anticipations of insights associated with Galileo and early modern science in the natural philosophy produced at Oxford and Paris in the first half of the fourteenth century.[14]

[13] I discuss this failure at many points in Chapter 8.
[14] For an assessment of these links, see, for example, the series of studies in William A. Wallace, *Prelude to Galileo: Essays on Medieval and Sixteenth-Century Sources of Galileo's Thought*, ed. Robert Cohen (Dordrecht: Reidel, 1981).

In almost every case, however, the story these connections tell is one of *discontinuity* rather than the continuity one might expect if textual transmission and the reading of texts were the primary engines of intellectual innovation. With few exceptions, there is a speculative break after the 1370s, after which these early anticipations lie dormant and mostly unrealized for a period lasting from generations to *centuries*.

A similar pattern is evident in each of the areas I have covered in this book. With regard to writings on economic subjects, Peter Olivi's insights from the 1290s into the multiplying powers of merchant *capital* and the dynamic process of price formation in the urban marketplace remained unsurpassed into the sixteenth century. Notable contributions on particular points continued to be made through the fourteenth century, with Buridan's commentaries on Aristotle's analysis of exchange in the *Nicomachean Ethics* and Geraldus Odonis' *Treatise on Contracts* (*De contractibus*) of particular interest. But Buridan's analysis was sparser and more diffuse than Olivi's, even if it does reflect the dynamism of the new model of equilibrium.[15] And Odonis' *De contractibus* (c. 1315–17), while it integrated new insights and approaches into its systematic treatment, was indebted to Olivi's *Tractatus* for the majority of its most astute points, with lesser borrowings from the economic insights of Duns Scotus.[16] Odd Langholm, who spent decades uncovering and commenting upon scholastic economic writings, made note of this falling off: "The near total gap in original source material of interest to economics, which characterizes the second half of the fourteenth century, speaks eloquently to the sensitivity of intellectual effort to material conditions."[17] Indeed, in the opinion of the recent editors of Odonis' *De contractibus*, it would be "another two centuries" before the level and comprehensiveness of the economic insights contained in Odonis' treatise were surpassed.[18] A gap of this length in the systematic analysis of economic exchange calls for study and explanation.

In the area of medicine, the situation is more complex, but a similar theme emerges. There is no diminishment in the literature of medicine per se after the mid fourteenth century; the focus of medical theory remains on the Galenic complexion as a site of proportional equalization, and there are new developments in the fifteenth and sixteenth century that

---

[15] Kaye, *Economy and Nature in the Fourteenth Century*, 132–7, 142–52.

[16] Ceccarelli and Piron, "Gerald Odonis' Economic Treatise." This article contains a partial edition of Odonis' treatise preceded by an introduction that details Odonis' frequent and profound borrowings from Olivi's *Tractatus*.

[17] Langholm, *Economics in the Medieval Schools*, 16. Rather than being devoid of original material, I suggest that economic writings after the mid fourteenth century lacked precisely the systematic, universalizing vision I associate with the new model of equilibrium.

[18] Ceccarelli and Piron, "Odonis' Economic Treatise," 193.

undoubtedly served to strengthen the discipline as a whole.[19] A deepening of empirical investigation and observation in many areas is perhaps first among these, but there were also technical advances in surgery, anatomy, and public health, and theoretical advances in the area of the etiology of disease. Not surprisingly, the advent of printing after the mid fifteenth century accelerated these developments by greatly expanding the capacity to share observations and techniques through both words and the mechanical reproduction of finely drawn illustrations. I think it can be argued, however, that no period in the history of pre-modern medicine saw the same degree and quality of growth in the area of medical *theory* than the period between 1280 and 1350.[20] These years witnessed the appearance of the monumental commentaries by Taddeo Alderotti, Arnau de Vilanova, Pietro d'Abano, Turisanus, and Gentile da Foligno. It was this period that saw unprecedented advances in the comprehension and elaboration of the Galenic modeling of the body. In this period – the period of the "new equilibrium" – the systematic conception of bodily form and function around the goal of equalization reached its height, as did the theorization, in purely naturalistic terms, of the *complexio* as the primary site of systematic equilibrium.[21] In the medical sphere, evidence of rupture appears more in the realm of invention than application.

In the area of political thought, I see evidence of a similar trajectory. The question of continuity/discontinuity in political thought has been the subject of long and at times tendentious debate, carried on by many voices.[22] Were I to add my voice, I would avoid the standard terms and

---

[19] For an outline of these advances, see Nancy Siraisi, "Medicine, 1450–1620, and the History of Science," *Isis* 103 (2012), 491–514.

[20] Nancy Siraisi, "Some Current Trends in the Study of Renaissance Medicine," *Renaissance Quarterly* 37 (1984), 585–600, at 587–8: "Whatever the significance attached to the impact on medicine of such later factors as the Black Death, the revival of Greek learning, or the invention of printing, it is clear that by the early fourteenth century important aspects of medicine had already acquired a shape they would retain until at least the late sixteenth century, and in some respects and some areas well beyond. These aspects included the organization and methodology of academic medical instruction, the structure of the medical profession, and large areas of the content of medical learning."

[21] French, *Gentile da Foligno and Scholasticism*, 3, 11, 91–7. Unfortunately, I found I could not include the impressive speculations of Gentile da Foligno in this study. French's verdict on Gentile's model of complexional equalization, which he considers the "high-point of scholastic medicine," is instructive (140): "The physical logic of their [the complexions'] actions built up more elaborate propositions, and the treatment was ideally syllogistic. There was a necessity about the whole: Gentile, through a doctrine of 'resis-tances' and 'co-alteration,' explained how parts came to be complexioned in a way that permitted and indeed demanded their action."

[22] For a judicious overview and analysis of this debate, see Cary Nederman, "Empire and the Historiography of European Political Thought: Marsiglio of Padua, Nicholas of Cusa, and the Medieval/Modern Divide," *Journal of the History of Ideas* 66 (2005), 1–15.

questions of the debate – whether and to what extent there was continuity between "medieval" and "early modern" or "modern" political ideas – because they seem to me unworkably large and diffuse, and because they themselves often rest on political terms that are protean and thus almost endlessly debatable.[23] I would suggest, instead, what I see as a more manageable and demonstrable marker of continuity/discontinuity in political theory: the presence or absence of analogous models of equalization. Thinkers who shared in the new model of equilibrium and contributed to its evolution between 1280 and 1360 would include (among others) Godfrey of Fontaines, John of Paris, and Ptolemy of Lucca on the early side, Marsilius of Padua and William of Ockham at its center and possibly its apogee, and the Oresme of the *De moneta* on its later side. Clear continuities can, I think, be shown to exist between the vision of these earlier thinkers regarding the potentialities of systematic *civic* equalization (through law, custom, election, the play of competing interests, and communal self-government) and those that appear again in certain political writings from (once again) the later sixteenth and seventeenth centuries. On the other hand, there appear to me to be equally clear discontinuities, on these same lines, between the earlier thinkers who shared in the new model and those from the intervening period who appear to have lost faith in it, including the Oresme of the *Le livre de politiques d'Aristote*.[24]

Failing faith in the potentialities of systematic equilibrium: the transformation of attemprance/temperantia

The "dissolution" of the new model followed from the failure of several of the elements that were most crucial to it and that most distinguished it from all previous models that it replaced. Chief among these was a failure of faith in the potential of systematic self-ordering and self-equalizing: a failure in the assumption that the process of interior self-ordering can, in itself, replace the ordering power of an intervening or overarching intelligence. A retreat from public into private knowledge accompanied this failure, as did the replacement of a thoroughgoing relativity with a renewed reading of "natural" hierarchies into structures and orders of

---

[23] The opinion of Nederman, *ibid.*, 14.

[24] For Oresme's "retreat" from the model in his political thought, see Chapter 7. I note that in my reading of the *Politiques*, the new model of equilibrium is still present, as it was in all of his writings. But in the case of his political thought, it survives in hollowed-out form, and it serves primarily as a foil. He references the model continually through the general terms and categories he employs, but at the same time he continually abandons or negates it through the particular lessons he draws from the text, having recognized its political dangers.

all kinds. With regard to the possibilities of systematic equalization, doubt replaced confidence. Psychological and emotional states described by binaries such as confidence and doubt, optimism and pessimism, pushing out and pulling back, the feeling that powers are expanding or declining, or the apprehension of a prevailing order or a prevailing disorder in the world, are, no doubt, hard to pin down, especially when applied beyond individuals to whole intellectual cultures. Historians are therefore rightfully hesitant to offer them as historical explanations. And yet, if I am right in suggesting that experience is linked to intellection through the medium of the "sense" of balance (and the models of equality and equalization that follow from it), and if "experience" is inseparable from the sentiment and perceptions that accompany and shape it, then psychological and emotional states must be allowed a place in the history of ideas.

Consider what happened to the pivotal concept and image of *attemprance* in Anglo-French culture between the first and last quarter of the fourteenth century. Between 1280 and 1360, *attemprance* was identified with *temperamentum*, the balanced product of a systematic mixing and blending together of potentially antagonistic elements. In the medical speculation of scholastic Galenists, the four primary "qualities" or "powers" strove against each other to produce and continually reproduce a tempered *aequalitas* (or *temperamentum*) in each of the myriad complexions within the body, while at the same time the various organs and members of the body equalized each other through their continual interactions, thus maintaining a dynamic balance within the body as a whole. In the economic thought of Peter Olivi (and others), exchangers desiring to buy for less and sell for more nevertheless succeeded in establishing a "common" aggregate price through the process of "free" (*libere*) bargaining, a price then accepted as representing the legitimate bounds of exchange equalization. In the political speculation of Marsilius of Padua (and others), the *civitas* was imagined to "temper" its "contrary elements" with their "contrary actions and passions" through a process of mutual communication, mutual contribution to a shared law (defined as "an eye composed of many eyes"), and mutual commitment to the shared goal of communal health and good function. In the geological speculations of Buridan, the whole of the earth perpetually maintained itself in balance (*equilibrat se*) through the contrary natural actions of earth and water, heat and cold. And in the natural philosophy of Nicole Oresme (and others) the cosmos itself could be imagined as being governed by the principle of "harmonious discord" (*concors discordia*), through which "by means of the greatest inequality, which departs from every equality, the most just and established order is preserved."

Then, in the last quarter of the fourteenth century, the image of *attemprance* changes dramatically: from its previous identification with the free and dynamic mixing and balancing of parts, to its new identification with the most strenuous control and self-restraint. The literary historians, Carolyn Collette and Nancy Mason Bradbury, have been particularly attentive to this change.[25] They have noted that before the late fourteenth century, the virtue of *temperantia*, expressed by the Anglo-French word *attemprance* (from the Latin *temperare*: to divide or duly apportion), was figurally represented by images of intermixing. Most often, a female personification is pictured holding either a mixing pitcher or two vessels she is about to pour together.[26] They then note the occurrence of a sharp break:

an important development in the semiotics of *attemprance*, from an earlier sense of "co-mingling, mixing, tempering extremes," to a new set of referents characteristic of late fourteenth- and early fifteenth-century Anglo-French literature . . . its new figuration involves images of checking, holding back, or restraining.[27]

This new figuration is reflected in semantic change as well. According to the *Middle English Dictionary*, the verb form of "to temper" takes on the meaning "to restrain," as the noun form takes the meaning of "a restraining force."[28] Collette has traced the intellectual effects of this transformation not only on Anglo-French literature of the late fourteenth and fifteenth century (with special reference to Chaucer) but on political discourse in the period as well, including the political writings of Christine de Pizan and Oresme's *Le livre de politiques*.[29]

A parallel shift in the iconography and semantics of *temperantia* in this period has long been noted by historians.[30] Émile Mâle, writing more than a century ago, may well have been the first to draw attention to a series of

---

[25] Carolyn Collette, "Aristotle, Translation and the Mean: Shaping the Vernacular in Late Medieval Anglo-French Culture," in *Language and Culture in Medieval Britain: The French of England c.1100–c.1500*, ed. Jocelyn Wogan-Browne *et al.* (Woodbridge: York Medieval Press, 2009), 373–85; Nancy Mason Bradbury and Carolyn Collette, "Changing Times: The Mechanical Clock in Late Medieval Literature," *Chaucer Review* 43 (2009), 351–75.

[26] Bradbury and Collette, "Changing Times," 361–2.   [27] *Ibid.*

[28] *Ibid.*, 365. See the online Middle English Dictionary under "tempen" and "temperer."

[29] Bradbury and Collette, "Changing Times," 360–5; Collette, "Aristotle, Translation, and the Mean," 378–85, at 379. In my own reading of Chaucer, I have sensed his play with and against the bounds of restraint through his exploration of transgression. I have also noted the absence of a unifying model of equalization, replaced by the mixture, or perhaps the play, of competing and at times antagonistic models. This is in line with Collette and Bradbury's argument that Chaucer's definition of *attemprance* is highly unstable.

[30] Charity Cannon Willard, "Christine de Pisan's 'Clock of Temperance,'" *L'Esprit Créateur* 2 (1962), 149–54; Lynn White Jr., "The Iconography of *Temperantia* and the Virtuousness of Technology," in *Action and Conviction in Early Modern Europe: Essays in Memory of E. H. Harbison*, ed. Theodore Rabb and Jerrold E. Siegel (Princeton University Press, 1969), 197–219.

illustrations from the mid fifteenth century representing the personified virtue, Temperantia, in her new guise, standing on a windmill and carrying a large clock on her head.[31] The historian of medieval technology, Lynn White Jr., examined these images with great care. He noted the newly central place that Temperantia had assumed within the circle of the seven virtues over the first half of the fifteenth century, signaling her move from the margins to a now dominant position among them, even with respect to Justitia, who now stands to the side holding her set of scales.[32] But as strange as the windmill and clock might be as symbolic representations of Temperantia, they are not, I think, what led Mâle to "recoil" (in White's words) from these images.[33] That is more likely to have been the well-defined brace and bit now attached by straps to the female Temperantia's mouth and head.[34] Once this image has been seen, it is hard to forget. Moreover, once this image appeared, far from being rejected for its strangeness or its "disconcerting lack of taste" (as Mâle had judged), it was picked up and developed by other illuminators over the course of the fifteenth century.[35] In these later images, Temperantia remains linked to the clock and the windmill, but now her hands, rather than holding vessels to be mixed, or holding anything for that matter, are pictured as bound to the same black straps that fasten the bit between her teeth and the bridle around her head.[36]

I have intentionally detached the above scholarly observations on the changing iconography of *temperantia* from their original connection to the iconography of the mechanical clock, as important as that iconography might be. I think it highly unlikely that the spread of clock technology could itself have brought about this image of Temperantia bound and bridled. Indeed, representations of the clock and the mechanical mill have taken many forms, and their "virtues" have been appreciated and presented in many ways. The clock must certainly regulate itself, even "restrain" itself mechanically, in order to function, but with its scores of intersecting gears and physically interacting parts, with the striking of part against part, not to mention its striking of the hours, with its marvelous mechanical order, the clock (and the mill, for that matter) could just as well represent a naturalistic model of multiplying power, gained through

---

[31] White, "Iconography of *Temperantia*," 213. The earliest of these representations discussed and reproduced by White dates to 1450: Bodleian Library, MS Laud, 570, fol. 16r.
[32] *Ibid.*, 215.   [33] *Ibid.*, 213.
[34] *Ibid.*, 215. This image (figure 13) appears in a lavishly illuminated volume of Oresme's *Le livre de ethiques d'Aristote*, Rouen, Bibliothèque Municipale, ms. 927.
[35] White, "Iconography of *Temperantia*," 213.
[36] *Ibid.*, 214. BN fr. 9186, fol. 304r (figure 12), dated to *c.* 1470.

advances in systematic ordering and organization.[37] Associating the clock entirely with enforced restraint is a highly determined choice, with its basis in history rather than in necessity or nature.[38] Here is where the weight of feeling and sentiment plays a part.[39]

Thus the question remains: why did the image of Temperantia change so radically in and after the last quarter of the fourteenth century? Why was she now associated with the bit and bridle, and why was it seen as a positive attribute of this most powerful virtue that her hands were tied to the reins that restrained her? My sense is that the answer to this question will go a long way toward answering the central question I have posed: why, given the great head of steam that built behind the new model of equilibrium within university culture from the end of the thirteenth century, did it dissipate and fail in the last quarter of the fourteenth century? If, as I have argued, the experience and perception of concrete instantiations of equilibrium within lived social environments was one of the engines of the new model, these experiences and perceptions must have changed, and changed profoundly, between the first and last quarter of the century.

It would be a mistake to overestimate or overstate the peaceful and constructive nature of the decades between 1250 and 1350. Among other persistent problems, they were marked by constant political turmoil in the Italian communes, war and famine north of the Alps, and deeply disturbing religious controversies that affected all of Latin Christendom. Still, the dislocations that followed the first outbreak of the plague in 1347–50, and that continued as the outbreaks of plague continued throughout the second half of the fourteenth century and on through the fifteenth century, were of a different order of magnitude. I am aware that the plague has been used as a historical *deus ex machina* to explain all kinds of historical effects, and I am wary of doing the same. I recognize that even today historians disagree about both its short-term and long-term social, political, and economic impact; or, rather, the effects they find in their focused studies often fail to

---

[37] I note that Dante, for example, emphasizes the dynamic and percussive aspects of the water clock (*orologio*), the forerunner of the mechanical clock, speaking of its geared wheels as "drawing and urging" each other on in *Paradiso* 10: "che l'una parte e l'altra tira e urge, / tin tin sonando con sì dolce nota, / che 'l ben disposto spirto d'amor turge."

[38] Bradbury and Collette, "Changing Times," 361. Similarly, from the early fifteenth century, *Attemprance* is often represented as a female figure reaching in and adjusting (regulating) the wheels of a clock, in near-perfect negation of what was most marvelous about the mechanism.

[39] For evidence of the degree to which restraint and control become the legal and political order of the day, see, for example, "Additions to the Parliamentary Statute of Labourers, 1388," in Horrox, *The Black Death*, 323–6.

fall into a neat pattern.[40] I agree with those who deny to the plague any singular effect across Europe or across multiple generations or social classes.[41] My sense is that its cultural effects, though real, are subtler and more varied than they are often pictured, especially if they are to be taken as generalized responses.[42] Nevertheless, its catastrophic nature is undeniable; the secondary dislocations that followed in its wake – social, economic, political, *and* emotional – were real, even if they took somewhat different forms in different localities, different periods, and (perhaps most significant in terms of its intellectual effects) different social strata.[43] This last factor might help to explain why the retreat and restraint that colored the more traditional sources of intellectual culture, whether in the university, the literate bureaucracy, or the aristocratic court, seem not to have affected the intellectual contributions of the urban artisanat. Their enthusiastic offerings to learned culture increased enormously over the course of the fifteenth century, grounded as they were more in practice, technique, and empirical observation than in traditional sources of theory.

In the concluding section of Chapter 7 I considered in some detail the dislocations of the post-plague decades and their effects on the history of balance. There my focus was on the particular case of Nicole Oresme's sharp retreat from the new model of equilibrium in his later commentary on Aristotle's *Politics* (1374), when he had been so fully in tune with the model in his *De moneta* of two decades earlier (1356). Oresme's position was clearly singular in many ways, but many of the sharply altered environments he inhabited after mid-century were shared by other university scholars in this period.[44] To conclude this section on the dissolution of the "new' model of equilibrium, I offer a review of these sharp "environmental" changes, along with a review of their implications for the modeling of balance.[45]

[40] See, for example, Mark Bailey's comment that "debate will continue to rage over the exact consequences of the Black Death" in his Introduction to a recent collection of articles on the subject, in *Town and Countryside in the Age of the Black Death*, xxiv–xxv.
[41] Samuel Cohn, Jr., *The Black Death Transformed: Disease and Culture in Early Renaissance Europe* (London: Arnold, 2002).
[42] For a judicious treatment of the question of the impact of the plague on artistic production, see Phillip Lindley, "The Black Death and English Art: A Debate and Some Assumptions," in *The Black Death in England*, ed. W. M. Ormrod and P. G. Lindley (Donington: Shaun Tyas, 2003), 125–46, which concludes (146): "even the most cataclysmic of disasters seldom stands in a simple relationship to artistic change . . . But what is unequivocal is that the Black Death did have a dramatic effect on cultural production in England."
[43] See Chapter 7 for discussions on this point.
[44] I discuss these changes in some depth at the conclusion to Chapter 7.
[45] My decision to conclude with an explanation of the model's dissolution risks the charge (undoubtedly deserved) that I overgeneralize and simplify the sociopolitical situation after 1375. But for the history of balance, the end or abandonment of a model is as meaningful as its emergence, and it therefore calls for at least some consideration, however preliminary.

Over the reign of King Charles V (1364–80), the once vibrant economies and bourgeois communities of the French cities, including that of
Paris, were gradually choked off by royal economic policies. In their place,
and in place of the dynamism of the self-ordering urban marketplace,
appeared a new "*engin*" of society – what Raymond Cazelles has called
"the patrimonial monarchy."[46] It was this essentially hierarchical and top-
down model of social and political order that Oresme duly recorded and
seconded in his commentary on the *Politics*. There are, clearly, many
parallels between the shift to a top-down social and political order that
Cazelles describes for France and its cities and the shift that occurred in
many other governing structures in Europe over the course of the fourteenth century, especially in those great cities of northern Italy in which
the order of the commune gave way to the order of the aristocratic court.

One area in which the catastrophic visitation of the Black Death in
Europe made its deep mark was the marketplace, especially the market in
labor. As I have noted, the privileged classes of both France and England
responded sharply to their perception that the economic effects of the
plague benefited the laboring classes to the detriment of the landlords and
those who constituted society's "betters."[47] Those in power passed law
after law over the second half of the fourteenth century in an attempt to
"restore order" to an economy now thought to be profoundly disordered.
They attempted to undo the effects of supply and demand on labor prices
by fiat, setting and enforcing strict limits on both wages and prices at the
pre-plague level. In short, the common view from the top (a view that
Oresme came more and more to share) was that the establishment of a
"common price" in the marketplace could no longer be trusted as a guide to
"just" prices and wages. Both the free movement of laborers and the free
movement of wages had to be restrained, and the full force of the government's legal and administrative machinery was put to this task.[48]

In France, in the decade following the plague, severe social, economic,
and political dislocations led to the 1358 revolt of Étienne Marcel and the
Parisian bourgeois against the king, his counselors, and his son the dauphin (Oresme's patron). Following the shocking violence of the Parisian
city classes against the representatives of royal order, in which the dauphin's chief counselors were murdered in front of his eyes (scenes that
were reenacted in the cities of England, Italy, and Flanders in the 1370s

---

[46] Cazelles, *Société politique*, 578, as discussed in Chapter 7, pp. 392–6.
[47] I discuss these perceptions and their consequences in Chapter 7.
[48] For evidence of just how far this was taken, see Horrox, *The Black Death*, esp. 312–26. For
an important pan-European study of legislative responses to post-plague market "disorder," motivated by elites who perceived it as favoring the laboring classes, see Cohn,
"After the Black Death."

and 80s), and in the wake of the long and bloody aftermath to the revolt, Oresme inherited what now, I suggest, appeared to him to be a broken city and a broken political community – a sad complement to the perception of a broken and disordered market that remained in the wake of the plague. I suggest that with the collapse of these three environments, each of which had embodied the potentialities of systematic self-order and self-equalization, and each of which had provided concrete evidence of its viability and productivity, came the collapse of faith in this power.[49] Thus the pervasive pessimism and fear in Oresme's later *Politiques*; thus the closing off of possibilities and the clinging to the governmental status quo; thus the near-complete trust he now placed in the ordering wisdom and power of the crown; thus the abandonment of the citizen multitude (a genuine citizen multitude rather than one effectively defined out of existence) and of the community itself as the leading political and economic actor in the *civitas*; thus the near-total absence of the city of Paris from his political calculations; thus the radical reduction in the meaning and scope of the Common Good in his political scheme; thus the emphasis on the necessity for *restraint* from above; and thus the breaks on so many levels between the assumptions underlying his earlier *De moneta* and those underlying the *Politiques*.

There are, certainly, aspects of the French response to the plague that are unique to France, and there are aspects of Oresme's response that are unique to his situation as well. But overall, as I argued earlier, they conform to a larger pattern that continued well into the fifteenth century across Europe: from the repeated attempts to replace market order (or "disorder" as it came to be perceived by the landlord class after the economic dislocations of the Black Death) by governmental fiat or guild control, to the near-total collapse of self-governing communes in Italy and their replacement by strong-man rule,[50] to the political quieting of the European bourgeoisie and the turning of this class from being dynamic agents of change (if not revolution) when in their ascendancy in the thirteenth and early fourteenth centuries, to becoming agents of political and economic reaction in the context of a generally contracting economy.

By the late fourteenth century, with its socioeconomic sources in the self-governing city and self-equalizing urban marketplace blocked and withering, the new model of equilibrium was imagined and invoked less and less by thinkers to explain the workings of either society or nature.

---

[49] I provide further details in support of this argument in the concluding section of Chapter 7.

[50] Witness Oresme's failure in the *Politiques* (as discussed in Chapter 7) to even mention the Italian communes as a viable form of political life.

To "temper" was no longer to freely mix but to restrain, and restraint now became both the guarantor of order in society and the preeminent social ideal, pushing even Justice to the side. Given the centrality of the ideal of balance/*aequalitas* to virtually all medieval discourses, the intellectual effects of the model's retreat in the last quarter of the fourteenth century were profound – as deep and wide-ranging as had been the effects of its emergence a century earlier.

Bibliography

PRIMARY SOURCES

Albertus Magnus, *Alberti Magni super Ethica commentum et quaestiones*, ed. Wilhelm Kübel, vol. XIV of *Opera omnia*. Monasterii Westfalorum: Aschendorff, 1972.

Commentarius in IV sententiarum (Dist. I–XXII), ed. A. Borgnet, vol. XXIX of *Opera omnia*. Paris: Vivès, 1894.

Ethicorum libri decem, ed. A. Borgnet, vol. VII of *Opera omnia*. Paris: Vivès, 1891.

Al-Biruni, *The Determination of the Coordinates of Positions for the Correction of Distances between Cities*, ed. and trans. Jamil Ali. American University of Beirut, 1967.

Alexander Lombard, *Un traité de morale économique au XIVe siècle: le "Tractatus de usuris" de maître Alexandre d'Alexandrie*, ed. A.-M. Hamelin. Analecta medievalia Namurcensia XIV. Louvain: Nauwelaerts, 1962.

Anonymous, *La vie de Saint Denys*. Paris, Bibliothèque Nationale Française, ms. Français 2090–2.

Aquinas, Thomas, *On the Government of Rulers: De regimine Principum*, trans. James Blythe. Philadelphia: University of Pennsylvania Press.

Quaestiones disputatae De malo, vol. XXIII of *Opera omnia*, Rome: Commissio Leonina, 1982.

Sancti Thomae de Aquino Sententia libri ethicorum, vol. XLVII of *Opera omnia*. Rome: Commissio Leonina, 1969.

Sancti Thomae de Aquino Summa theologica, vols. II–XII of *Opera omnia*. Rome: Commissio Leonina, 1888–1906.

Summa contra Gentiles, ed. C. Pera. Turin: Marieti, 1961.

Summa contra Gentiles, Book III, trans. Vernon J. Bourke. New York: Hanover House, 1955–7.

Summa theologica: Latin Text and English Translation, Introductions, Notes, Appendices, and Glossaries. 61 vols. New York: Blackfriars, 1964–81.

Aristotle, *Aristotelis Politicorum Libri Octo cum vetusta translatione Guilelmi de Moerbeka*, ed. Franz Susemihl. Leipzig: Teubner, 1872.

De generatione et corruptione, trans. C. J. F. Williams. Oxford University Press, 1982.

Ethica Nicomachea: translatio Roberti Grosseteste Lincolniensis, recensio recognita, ed. R. A. Gauthier, in *Aristotles Latinus*, vol. XXVI, 1–3, fasc. 4. Leiden: Brill, 1973.

Meteorologica, trans. H. D. P. Lee. Cambridge, MA: Harvard University Press, 1952.

Movement of Animals [De motu animalium], trans. E. S. Forster. Loeb Classical Library. Cambridge, MA: Harvard University Press, 1961.

Nicomachean Ethics, trans. W. D. Ross, in *The Basic Works of Aristotle*, ed. Richard McKeon. New York: Random House, 1941.

Parts of Animals [De partibus animalium], trans. A. L. Peck. Loeb Classical Library. Cambridge, MA: Harvard University Press, 1961.

The Politics of Aristotle, ed. and trans. Ernest Barker. Oxford University Press, 1958.

Arnaldus de Villanova, *Aphorismi de gradibus*, ed. Michael R. McVaugh in *Arnaldi de Villanova Opera medica omnia*, vol. II. Granada-Barcelona: Seminarium Historiae Medicae Granatensis, 1975.

Commentum supra tractatum Galieni De malicia complexionis diverse, ed. Luis García Ballester and Eustaquio Sanchez Salor in *Arnaldi de Villanova Opera medica omnia*, vol. XV. Universitat de Barcelona, 1985.

Avicenna, *Canon. Avicennae Arabum medicorum principis. Ex Gerardi Cremonensis versione*. Venice: apud Iuntas, 1608.

Liber Canonis Avicenne revisus et ab omni errore mendaque purgatus ... Venice, 1507.

Bonvesin da la Riva, *De magnalibus Mediolani. Meraviglie di Milano*, ed. and trans. Paolo Chiesa. Milan: Libri Scheiwiller, 1998.

Bradwardine, Thomas, *Geometria speculativa*, ed. and trans. A. George Molland. Stuttgart: Steiner, 1989.

Thomas of Bradwardine: His Tractatus de Proportionibus; Its Significance for the Development of Mathematical Physics, ed. and trans. H. Lamar Crosby, Jr. Madison: University of Wisconsin Press, 1955.

Buridan, Jean, *Acutissimi philosophi reverendi Magistri Johannis Buridani subtillissime questiones super octo phisicorum libros Aristotelis*. Paris, 1509; reprint Frankfurt: Minerva, 1964.

Iohannis Buridani Quaestiones super libris quattuor de caelo et mundo, ed. Ernest A. Moody. Cambridge, MA: Mediaeval Academy of America, 1942.

Joannis Buridani Expositio et Quaestiones in Aristotelis De Caelo, ed. Benoît Patar. Louvain: Éditions Peeters, 1996.

Quaestiones in decem libros ethicorum Aristotelis ad Nicomachum. Oxford: H. Cripps, 1637.

"Les Questiones super tres libros Metheorum Aristotelis de Jean Buridan: Études suivie de l'édition du livre I," ed. Sylvie Bages. Thesis, École de Chartes, Paris, 1986.

Christine de Pizan, *Le livre des fais et bonnes meurs du sage roy Charles V*, ed. Suzanne Solente. Paris: H. Champion, 1936.

Codex Iustinianus, ed. Paul Krueger, in *Corpus iuris civilis*, vol. II. Berlin: Weidmanns, 1954.

Decretales Gregorii IX, ed. A. Friedberg, in *Corpus iuris canonici*, vol. II. Graz: Akademische Druck- u. Verlaganstalt, 1959.

Digesta, ed. Theodore Mommsen, in *Corpus iuris civilis*, vol. I. Berlin: Weidmanns, 1954.

Galen, *Ars medica* (or *Tegni*) in *Opera omnia*, vol. I, fols. 10ra–15vb. Venice: Philippus Pincius, 1490.

The Art of Medicine, in *Galen: Selected Works*, trans. P. N. Singer. Oxford University Press, 1997.

"The Best Doctor is Also a Philosopher," in *Galen: Selected Works*, trans. P. N. Singer. Oxford University Press, 1997.

Claudii Galeni pergameni De usu partium corporis humani, Nicolao Regio Calabro Interprete. Paris: Simonis Colinaei, 1528.

De elementis secundum Hippocratem. English translation: *On the Elements According to Hippocrates*, ed. and trans. Phillip de Lacy. Berlin: Akademie Verlag, 1996.

De foetuum formatione, in *Galeni omnia quae extant opera*, vol. II. Venice: ad Iuntas, 1565.

De optimo medico cognoscendo. English translation from the Arabic: Galen: *On Examinations by Which the Best Physicians Are Recognized*, ed. and trans. Albert Iskandar. Berlin: Akademie Verlag, 1988.

De placitis Hippocratis et Platonis. English translation: *On the Doctrines of Hippocrates and Plato*, ed. and trans. Phillip de Lacy, 3 vols. Berlin: Akademie Verlag, 1978–84.

De usu partium, in *Opera omnia*, vol. III, ed. K. G. Kühn, 22 vols. Leipzig: Teubner, 1821–33.

Galeni Ars medica, in *Opera omnia*, vol. I, ed. K. G. Kühn, 22 vols. Leipzig: Teubner, 1821–33.

Galenus Latinus: Burgundio of Pisa's Translation of Galen's Peri Kraseion "De complexionibus," ed. Richard Durling. Berlin: Walter de Gruyter, 1976.

Galien, vol. II: *Exhortation à l'étude de la médecine: Art médical*, ed. and trans. Véronique Boudon. Paris: Les Belles Lettres, 2000.

Liber Tegni, in *Ars medicinae*, Harley MS. 3140, 7v–21r.

Liber Tegni, in *Articella nuperrime impressa cum quamplurimis tractatibus pristine impressioni superadditis*, fols. 107v–135v. London: Jacob Myt, 1519.

Liber Tegni, in *Articella seu Opus artis medicinae*, ed. Gregorius Vulpe and Franciscus Argilagnes. Venice: B. Locatelli, 1493.

"On Mixtures," in *Galen: Selected Works*, ed. and trans. P. N. Singer. Oxford University Press, 1997.

On the Construction of the Embryo, in *Galen: Selected Works*, trans. P. N. Singer. Oxford University Press, 1997.

On the Usefulness of the Parts of the Body [De usu partium corporis humani], ed. and trans. Margaret Tallmadge May. Ithaca, NY: Cornell University Press, 1968.

Gentile da Foligno, *Primus Avicenne canonis cum argutissima Gentilis expositione*. Pavia: Jacob de Burgofranco, 1510.

Giles of Lessines, *De usuris in communi, et De usurarum in contractibus*, ed. S. E. Fretté, as part of Thomas Aquinas, *Opera omnia*, vol. XXVIII. Paris: Vivès, 1889.

Girolami, Remigio, *De bono communi*, in *"Remigio Girolami's De bono communi,"* ed. L. Minio-Paluello, *Italian Studies* 11 (1956), 56–71.

Godfrey of Fontaines, *Godefroid de Fontaines, Quodlibet III*, ed. M. De Wulf, in *Les philosophes belges*, vol. II. Louvain: Institut supérieur de philosophie, 1904.

Godefroid de Fontaines, Quodlibet V, ed. M. De Wulf and J. Hoffman, in *Les philosophes belges*, vol. III. Louvain: Institut supérieur de philosophie, 1914.

Gratian, *Decretum*, in *Corpus iuris canonici*, ed. A. Friedberg, vol. I. Graz: Akademische Druck- u. Verlagsanstalt, 1959.

Gregory of Rimini, *Tractatus subtilissimi doctoris Gregorii de Arimino: De Imprestantiis Venetorum. Et de Usura*. Regio Emilia: Ludovici de Mazalis, 1508.

Henry of Ghent, *Henrici de Gandavo: Quodlibet I*, ed. Raymond Macken, in *Opera omnia*, vol. V. Leuven University Press, 1983.

Hostiensis, *Summa aurea*. Venice, 1574; reprint Turin: Bottega d'Erasmo, 1963.

Ibn Ridwan, *Hali Filii Rodbon in Parvam Galeni Artem Commentatio*, in *Plusquam commentum in Parvam Galieni Artem, Turisani Florentini Medici Praestantissimi*. Venice: ad Iuntas, 1557, fols. 175r–217r.

Innocent IV, *Super Libros Quinque Decretalium*. Frankfurt, 1570, reprint Minerva, 1968.

Jean de Jandun, *Tractatus de laudibus Parisius*, in *Paris et ses historiens aux XIVe et XVe siècles*, ed. Antoine Le Roux de Lincy and L. M. Tisserand. Paris: Imprimerie impériale, 1867, 32–74.

Jean de Venette, *The Chronicle of Jean de Venette*, ed. Richard Newhall, trans. Jean Birdsall. New York: Columbia University Press, 1953.

John of Salisbury, *Policraticus*, ed. and trans. Cary Nederman. Cambridge University Press, 1990.

Marsilius of Padua, *The Defensor Pacis of Marsilius of Padua*, ed. C. W. Previté-Orton. Cambridge University Press, 1928 (Latin edition).

Marsilius of Padua: The Defender of the Peace, trans. Annabel Brett. Cambridge University Press, 2005.

Marsilius of Padua: The Defender of the Peace, trans. Alan Gewirth. New York: Columbia University Press, 1956.

Marsile de Padoue: Le Defenseur de la paix, trans. Jeannine Quillet. Paris: J. Vrin, 1968.

Marsilius von Padua: Defensor Pacis, ed. Richard Scholz, in *Fontes Iuris Germanici Antiqui*, vol. I. Hanover: Hahnsche Buchhandlung, 1931.

Olivi, Peter of John, *Quodlibet I*, in "Gli scritti sul capitale et sull'interesse di Fra Pietro di Giovanni Olivi: Fonti per la storia del pensiero economico medioevale," ed. Amleto Spicciani, *Studi francescani* 73 (1976), 289–325.

Tractatus de emptionibus et venditionibus, de usuris, de restitutionibus, in *Un trattato di economia politica francescana: il "De emptionibus et venditionibus, de usuris, de restitutionibus" di Pietro di Giovanni Olivi*, ed. Giacomo Todeschini. Rome: Istituto storico italiano per il medio evo, studi storici, 1980.

Ordonnances des roys de France de la troisième race: recueillies par ordre chronologique, avec des renvoys des unes aux autres, des sommaires, des observations sur le texte: vol. II, ed. Eusèbe de Laurière; vol. III, ed. Denis-François Secousse. Paris: Imprimerie royale, 1729, 1732.

Oresme, Nicole, *De causis mirabilium*, in *Nicole Oresme and the Marvels of Nature: A Study of his De Causis Mirabilium*, ed. and trans. Bert Hansen. Toronto: Pontifical Institute of Mediaeval Studies, 1985.

De proportionibus proportionum and *Ad pauca respicientes*, ed. and trans. Edward Grant. Madison: University of Wisconsin Press, 1966.

Le livre du ciel et du monde, ed. and trans. Albert Menut and Alexander Denomy. Madison: University of Wisconsin Press, 1968.

Maistre Nicole Oresme: Le livre de éthiques d'Aristote, ed. Albert Douglas Menut. New York: G. E. Stechert, 1940.

"Maistre Nicole Oresme: Le livre de politiques d'Aristote," ed. Albert Douglas Menut, *Transactions of the American Philosophical Society*, n.s. 60, pt. 6 (1970), 1–392.

Nicole Oresme and the Kinematics of Circular Motion: Tractatus de commensurabilitate vel incommensurabilitate motuum celi, ed. and trans. Edward Grant. Madison: University of Wisconsin Press, 1971.

Nicole Oresme and the Medieval Geometry of Qualities and Motions: A Treatise on the Uniformity and Difformity of Intensities known as Tractatus de configurationibus qualitatum et motuum, ed. and trans. Marshall Clagett. Madison: University of Wisconsin Press, 1968.

"Quaestio contra divinitores horoscopios," ed. Stefano Caroti, *Archives d'histoire doctrinale et littéraire du Moyen Âge* 51 (1976), 201–310.

Quaestiones super geometriam Euclidis, ed. H. L. L. Busard. Leiden: Brill, 1961.

Tractatus de origine et natura, iure et mutacionibus monetarum, in *The De Moneta of Nicholas Oresme*, ed. and trans. Charles Johnson. London: Thomas Nelson and Sons, 1956.

Pegolotti, Francesco di Balduccio, *La pratica della mercatura*, ed. Allen Evans. Cambridge, MA: Medieval Academy of America, 1936.

Pietro d'Abano, *Conciliator controversiarum, quae inter philosophos et medicos versantur*. Venice: ad Iuntas, 1565; reprint, Padua: Editrice Antenore, 1985.

Pietro Torregiano de Torregiani (Turisanus), *Plus quam commentum in Parvam Galeni Artem, Turisani Florentini Medici Praestantissimi*. Venice: ad Iuntas, 1557.

Taddeo Alderotti, *In subtilissimum Joannitii Hagogarum libellum*, in *Thaddei Florentini Expositiones*, fols. 343r–400r. Venice: ad Iuntas, 1527.

Micratechne Galeni, in *Thaddei Florentini Medicorum sua tempestate principis in C. Gal. Micratechnen Commentarii*. Naples, 1522.

Thomas of Chobham, *Summa confessorum*, ed. F. Broomfield. Analecta Mediaevalia Namurcensia XXV. Louvain: Nauwelaerts, 1968.

Zibaldone da Canal, in *Merchant Culture in Fourteenth Century Venice*, ed. and trans. John Dotson. Binghamton, NY: Medieval and Renaissance Texts and Studies, 1994.

SECONDARY SOURCES

Aichele, Alexander, "Heart and Soul of the State: Some Remarks Concerning Aristotelian Ontology and Medieval Theory of Medicine in Marsilius of Padua's *Defensor Pacis*," in *The World of Marsilius of Padua*, ed. Gerson Moreno-Riaño. Turnhout: Brepols, 2006, 163–86.

Akbari, Suzanne Conklin, "The Diversity of Mankind in *The Book of John Mandeville*," in *Eastward Bound: Travel and Travellers, 1050–1550*, ed. Rosamund Allen. Manchester University Press, 156–76.

Armstrong, Lawrin, "The Politics of Usury in Trecento Florence: The *Questio de monte* of Francesco da Empoli," *Mediaeval Studies* 61 (1999), 1–44.

Usury and Public Debt in Early Renaissance Florence: Lorenzo Ridolfi on the Monte Comune. Toronto: Pontifical Institute of Mediaeval Studies, 2003.

Avril, François, *Manuscript Painting at the Court of France: The Fourteenth Century, 1310–1380*, trans. Ursule Molinaro. New York: George Braziller, 1978.

Babbitt, Susan, *Oresme's Livre de Politiques and the France of Charles V.* Philadelphia: American Philosophical Society, 1985.

Baeck, Louis, *The Mediterranean Tradition in Economic Thought.* New York: Routledge, 1994.

Bailey, Mark, "Introduction," in *Town and Countryside in the Age of the Black Death: Essays in Honour of John Hatcher*, ed. Mark Bailey and Stephen Rigby. Turnhout: Brepols, 2012, xxiv–xxv.

Baldwin, John W., *Masters, Princes, and Merchants: The Social Views of Peter the Chanter and His Circle.* 2 vols. Princeton University Press, 1970.

"The Medieval Theories of the Just Price: Romanists, Canonists, and Theologians in the Twelfth and Thirteenth Centuries," *Transactions of the American Philosophical Society*, n.s. 49, no. 4 (1959), 1–92.

Barnes, Jonathan, "Galen and the Utility of Logic," in "Galen und das hellenistische Erbe," ed. J. Kollesch and D. Nickel, special issue of *Sudhoffs Archiv* 32 (1993), 33–52.

"Galen on Logic and Therapy," in *Galen's Method of Healing*, ed. F. Kudlien and R. J. Durling. Leiden: Brill, 1991, 50–102.

Bec, Christian, "Sur l'historiographie marchande à Florence au XIVe siècle," in *La chronique et l'histoire au Moyen Âge*, ed. Daniel Poirion. Paris: La Sorbonne, 1982, 45–73.

Beer, Samuel, "The Rule of the Wise and the Holy: Hierarchy in the Thomistic System," *Political Theory* 14 (1986), 391–422.

Beltran, Evencio, "Jacques Legrand OESA: sa vie et son œuvre," *Augustiniana* 24 (1974), 132–60, 387–414.

Benoist, Charles, *La politique du roi Charles V.* Paris: Cerf, 1886.

Bernd, Michael, *Johannes Buridan: Studien zu seinem Leben, seinem Werken, und zur Rezeption seiner Theorien im Europa des späten Mittelalters*, 2 vols. Freie Universität Berlin, 1985.

Berti, Enrico, "Il 'regnum' di Marsilio tra la 'polis' aristotelica e lo 'stato' moderno," *Medioevo* 5 (1979), 165–81.

Black, Antony, *Guilds and Society in European Political Thought from the Twelfth Century to the Present.* Ithaca, NY: Cornell University Press, 1984.

Blythe, James, "The Mixed Constitution and the Distinction between Regal and Political Power in the Work of Thomas Aquinas," *Journal of the History of Ideas* 47 (1986), 547–65.

Bois, Guy, *The Crisis of Feudalism: Economy and Society in Eastern Normandy, c. 1300–1500.* Cambridge University Press, 1984.

Bolton, Jim, "'The World Upside Down': Plague as an Agent of Economic and Social Change," in *The Black Death in England*, ed. W. M. Ormrod and P. G. Lindley. Donington: Shaun Tyas, 2003, 17–78.

Bouchard, Constance, *Holy Entrepreneurs: Cistercians, Knights and Economic Exchange in Twelfth-Century Burgundy.* Ithaca, NY: Cornell University Press, 1991.

Boudon, Véronique, "L'*Ars medica* de Galien est-il un traité authentique?" *Revue des Études Grecques* 109 (1996), 111–56.

"Art, science, et conjecture," in *Galien et la philosophie*. Geneva: Fondation Hardt, 2003, 269–305.

"La *Translatio antiqua* de *L'Art médical* de Galien," in *Storia e ecdotica dei testi medici greci*, ed. Antonio Garzya and Jacques Jouanna. Naples: M. D'Auria, 1996, 43–55.

Bowersock, G. W., *Greek Sophists in the Roman Empire*. Oxford: Clarendon Press, 1969.

Bradbury, Nancy Mason and Carolyn Collette, "Changing Times: The Mechanical Clock in Late Medieval Literature," *Chaucer Review* 43 (2009), 351–75.

Braid, Robert, "'*Et non ultra*': politiques royales du travail en Europe occidentale au XIVe siècle," *Bibliothèque de l'École des Chartes* 161 (2003), 437–91.

Brampton, C. Kenneth, "Marsiglio of Padua: Part I. Life," *English Historical Review* 37 (1922), 501–15.

Brett, Annabel S., "Issues in Translating the Defensor Pacis," in *The World of Marsilius of Padua*, ed. Gerson Moreno-Riaño. Turnhout: Brepols, 2006, 91–108.

Britnell, Richard H., "Commercialisation and Economic Development in England, 1000–1300," in *A Commercialising Economy: England 1086 to c.1300*, ed. Richard H. Britnell and Bruce Campbell. Manchester University Press, 1995, 7–26.

The Commercialisation of English Society, 1000–1500. Cambridge University Press, 1993.

Brown, Oscar, *Natural Rectitude and Divine Law in Aquinas: An Approach to an Integral Interpretation of the Thomistic Doctrine of Law*. Toronto: Pontifical Institute of Mediaeval Studies, 1981.

Burr, David, *Olivi and Franciscan Poverty: The Origins of the Usus Pauper Controversy*. Philadelphia: University of Pennsylvania Press, 1989.

"The Persecution of Peter Olivi," *Transactions of the American Philosophical Society*, n.s. 66, no. 5 (1976), 1–98.

Cadden, Joan, "Charles V, Nicole Oresme, and Christine de Pizan: Unities and Uses of Knowledge in Fourteenth-Century France," in *Texts and Contexts in Ancient and Medieval Science*, ed. Edith Sylla and Michael McVaugh. Leiden: Brill, 1997, 208–44.

"'Nothing Natural is Shameful': Vestiges of a Debate about Sex and Science in a Group of Late-Medieval Manuscripts," *Speculum* 76 (2001), 66–89.

Cahn, Kenneth, "The Roman and Frankish Roots of the Just Price of Canon Law," *Studies in Medieval and Renaissance History* 6 (1969), 3–52.

Caille, Jacqueline, "Urban Expansion in the Region of Languedoc from the Eleventh to the Fourteenth Century: The Example of Narbonne and Montpellier," in *Urban and Rural Communities in Medieval France: Provence and Languedoc, 1000–1500*, ed. Kathryn Reyerson and J. Drendell. Leiden: Brill, 1998, 51–72.

Callus, D. A., "The Date of Grosseteste's Translations and Commentaries on the Pseudo-Dionysius and the Nichomachean Ethics," *Recherches de théologie ancienne et médiévale* 14 (1947), 186–210.

Camille, Michael, "Signs of the City: Place, Power, and Public Fantasy in Medieval Paris," in *Medieval Practices of Space*, ed. Barbara Hanawalt and Michal Kobialka. Minneapolis: University of Minnesota Press, 2000, 1–36.

Canning, Joseph, "The Corporation in the Political Thought of the Italian Jurists of the Thirteenth and Fourteenth Centuries," *History of Political Thought* 1 (1980), 9–32.

"Power and Powerlessness in the Political Thought of Marsilius of Padua," in *The World of Marsilius of Padua*, ed. Gerson Moreno-Riaño. Turnhout: Brepols, 2006, 211–25.

Capitani, Ovidio, "Il 'De peccato usure' di Remigio de Girolami," *Studi Medievali* 6, 3rd series (1965), 537–662.

"Sulla questione dell'usura nel Medio Evo," in *L'Etica economica*, ed. Ovidio Capitani. Bologna: Il Mulino, 1974.

Carpentier, Elisabeth and Michel Le Mené, *La France du XIe siècle au XVe siècle: population, société, économie*. Paris: Presses Universitaires de France, 1996.

Caroti, Stefano and Pierre Souffrin (eds.), *La nouvelle physique du XIVe siècle*. Florence: Olschki, 1997.

Catto, Jeremy, "Ideas and Experience in the Political Thought of Aquinas," *Past & Present* 71 (1976), 3–21.

Cazelles, Raymond, *Nouvelle histoire de Paris de la fin du règne de Philippe Auguste à la mort de Charles V, 1223–1380*. Paris: Diffusion Hachette, 1994.

"Quelques réflexions à propos des mutations de la monnaie royale française (1295–1360)," *Le Moyen Âge* 72 (1966), 83–103.

Société politique, noblesse et couronne sous Jean le Bon et Charles V. Geneva: Droz, 1982.

"La stabilisation de la monnaie par la création du franc (décembre, 1360): blocage d'une société," *Traditio* 32 (1976), 293–311.

Ceccarelli, Giovanni, *Il gioco e il peccato: economia e rischio nel tardo medioevo*. Bologna: Il Mulino, 2003.

"Le jeu comme contrat et le *risicum* chez Olivi," in *Pierre de Jean Olivi (1248–1298): pensée scolastique, diffidence spirituelle et société*, ed. Alain Boureau and Sylvain Piron. Paris: J. Vrin, 1999, 239–50.

"The Price of Risk-Taking: Marine Insurance and Probability Calculus in the Late Middle Ages," *Journ@l Electronique d'Histoire des Probabilités et de la Statistique* 3.1 (2007), article 3.

"Risky Business: Theological and Canonical Thought on Insurance from the Thirteenth to the Seventeenth Century," *Journal of Medieval and Early Modern Studies* 31 (2001), 607–58.

Ceccarelli, Giovanni and Sylvain Piron, "Gerald Odonis' Economics Treatise," *Vivarium* 47 (2009), 164–204.

Celeyrette, Jean, "Bradwardine's Rule: A Mathematical Law?" in *Mechanics and Natural Philosophy before the Scientific Revolution*, ed. Walter Roy Laird and Sophie Roux. Dordrecht: Springer, 2008, 51–66.

"La problématique du point chez Jean Buridan," *Vivarium* 42 (2004), 86–108.

"Le statut des mathématiques dans la physique d'Oresme," *Oriens–Occidens. Sciences, mathématiques, et philosophie de l'Antiquité à l'Âge classique* 3 (2000), 91–113.

Celeyrette, Jean and Edmond Mazet, "Le mouvement du point de vue de la cause et le mouvement du point de vue de l'effet dans le *Traité des rapports* d'Albert de Saxe," *Revue d'Histoire des Sciences* 56 (2003), 419–37.

Cesar, Floriano, "Divine and Human Writings in Marsilius of Padua's *Defensor Pacis*: Expressions of Truth," in *The World of Marsilius of Padua*, ed. Gerson Moreno-Riaño. Turnhout: Brepols, 2006, 109–23.

"Popular Autonomy and Imperial Power in Bartolus of Saxoferrato: An Intrinsic Connection," *Journal of the History of Ideas* 65 (2004), 369–81.

Chandelier, Joël, "La réception du Canon d'Avicenne: médecine arabe et milieu universitaire en Italie avant la peste noire." PhD thesis, École Pratique des Hautes Études, Paris, 2007.

Chenu, M.-D., "The Evangelical Awakening," in *Nature, Man, and Society in the Twelfth Century: Essays on New Theological Perspectives in the Latin West*, ed. and trans. Jerome Taylor and Lester Little. University of Toronto Press, 1998, 239–69.

Clagett, Marshall, "Aristotelian Mechanics and Bradwardine's Dynamic Law of Movement," in *The Science of Mechanics in the Middle Ages*, ed. Marshall Clagett. Madison: University of Wisconsin Press, 1959, 421–44.

"Nicole Oresme and Medieval Scientific Thought," *Proceedings of the American Philosophical Society* 108 (1964), 298–309.

"Richard Swineshead and Late Medieval Physics: The Intension and Remission of Qualities," *Osiris* 9 (1950), 131–61.

"Some Novel Trends in the Science of the Fourteenth Century," in *Art, Science, and History in the Renaissance*, ed. Charles Singleton. Baltimore, MD: Johns Hopkins University Press, 1967, 275–303.

Cohn, Samuel K., "After the Black Death: Labour Legislation and Attitudes towards Labour in Late-Medieval Western Europe," *Economic History Review* 60 (2007), 457–85.

The Black Death Transformed: Disease and Culture in Early Renaissance Europe. London: Arnold, 2002.

Coleman, Janet, "The Intellectual Milieu of John of Paris," in *Das Publikum politischer Theorie im 14. Jahrhundert*, ed. Jürgen Miethke and Arnold Bühler. Munich: Oldenbourg, 1992, 173–206.

Collette, Carolyn, "Aristotle, Translation and the Mean: Shaping the Vernacular in Late Medieval Anglo-French Culture," in *Language and Culture in Medieval Britain: The French of England c.1100 – c.1500*, ed. Jocelyn Wogan-Browne *et al.* Woodbridge: York Medieval Press, 2009, 373–85.

Condren, Conal, "Marsilius of Padua's Argument from Authority: A Survey of its Significance in the *Defensor Pacis*," *Political Theory* 5 (1977), 205–18.

Contamine, Philippe, "Lever l'impôt en terre de guerre: rançons, appatis, souffrances de guerre dans la France des XIVe et XVe siècles," in *L'impôt au Moyen Âge: l'impôt public et le prélèvement seigneurial fin XIIe–début XVIe siècle*, ed. Philippe Contamine *et al.*, vol. I. Paris: Ministère de l'économie, des finances et de l'industrie, Comité pour l'histoire économique et financière de la France, 2002, 11–39.

Coopland, G. W., *Nicole Oresme and the Astronomers: A Study of His "Livre de divinacions."* Cambridge, MA: Harvard University Press, 1952.

Courtenay, William, "Arts and Theology at Paris, 1326–1340," in *Nicolas d'Autrécourt et la faculté des arts de Paris (1317–1340)*, ed. Stefano Caroti and Christophe Grellard. Cesena: Stilgraf Editrice, 2006, 15–63.

"The Debate over Ockham's Physical Theories at Paris," in *La nouvelle physique du XIVe siècle*, ed. Stefano Caroti and Pierre Souffrin. Florence: Olschki, 1997, 45–63.

"The Early Career of Nicole Oresme," *Isis* 91 (2000), 542–8.

Parisian Scholars in the Early Fourteenth Century: A Social Portrait. Cambridge University Press, 1999.

"Philosophy's Reward: The Ecclesiastical Income of Jean Buridan," *Recherches de théologie et philosophie médiévales* 68 (2001), 163–9.

"The Registers of the University of Paris and the Statutes against the Scientia Occamica," *Vivarium* 29 (1991), 13–49.

Teaching Careers at the University of Paris in the Thirteenth and Fourteenth Century. University of Notre Dame Press, 1988.

"University Master and Political Power: The Parisian Years of Marsilius of Padua," in *Politische Reflexion in der Welt des späten Mittelalters/Political Thought in the Age of Scholasticism*, ed. Martin Kaufhold. Leiden: Brill, 2004, 209–23.

"The University of Paris at the Time of Jean Buridan and Nicole Oresme," *Vivarium* 42 (2004), 3–17.

Crisciani, Chiara, "History, Novelty, and Progress in Scholastic Medicine," *Osiris* 6 (1990), 118–39.

Crofts, R. A., "The Common Good in the Political Theory of Thomas Aquinas," *The Thomist* 37 (1973), 155–73.

Dalché, Patrick, "L'influence de Jean Buridan: l'habitabilité de la terre selon Dominicus de Clavisio," in *Comprendre et maîtriser la nature au Moyen Âge: Mélanges d'histoire des sciences offerts à Guy Beaujouan.* Geneva: Droz, 1994, 101–15.

D'Alverny, Marie-Thérèse, "Pietro d'Abano traducteur de Galien," *Medioevo* 11 (1985), 19–64.

Daston, Lorraine J., "Attention and the Values of Nature in the Enlightenment," in *The Moral Authority of Nature*, ed. Lorraine Daston and Fernando Vidal. University of Chicago Press, 2003, 100–26.

Classical Probability in the Enlightenment. Princeton University Press, 1988.

"The Domestication of Risk: Mathematical Probability and Insurance 1650–1830," in *Ideas in History: The Probabilistic Revolution*, ed. Lorenz Krüger, Lorraine Daston, and Michael Heidelberger, vol. I. Cambridge, MA: MIT Press, 1987, 237–60.

"Fitting Numbers to the World: The Case of Probability Theory," in *History and Philosophy of Modern Mathematics*, ed. William Aspray and Philip Kitcher. Minneapolis: University of Minnesota Press, 1988, 221–37.

Davis, James, "Selling Food and Drink in the Aftermath of the Black Death," in *Town and Countryside in the Age of the Black Death: Essays in Honour of John Hatcher*, ed. Mark Bailey and Stephen Rigby. Turnhout: Brepols, 2012, 352–406.

De Roover, Raymond, "The Concept of the Just Price: Theory and Practice," *Journal of Economic History* 18 (1958), 418–34.

La pensée économique des scolastiques: doctrines et methodes. Montreal: Institut d'Études Médiévales, 1971.

San Bernardino of Siena and Sant'Antonino of Florence: The Two Great Economic Thinkers of the Middle Ages. Boston: Kress Library of Business and Economics, 1967.

De Wulf, Maurice, "L'individu et le groupe dans la scolastique du XIIIe siècle," *Revue Néoscolastique de Philosophie* 22 (1920), 341–57.

Dillon, Emma, *The Sense of Sound: Musical Meaning in France, 1260–1330*. Oxford University Press, 2012.

Dolcini, Carlo, *Introduzione a Marsilio da Padova*. Rome and Bari: Laterza, 1995.

Droppers, Garrett, "The *Questiones de Spera* of Nicole Oresme: Latin Text with English Translation, Commentary and Variants," PhD thesis, University of Wisconsin, Madison, 1966.

Du Cange, Charles, *Glossarium mediae et infimae latinitatis*, 10 vols. Graz: Akademische Druck- u. Verlaganstalt, 1954.

Duhem, Pierre, *Études sur Léonard de Vinci*, vol. III. Paris: Hermann, 1913.

Le système du monde: histoire des doctrines cosmologiques de Platon à Copernic, vol. IX. Paris: Hermann, 1958.

Dunbabin, Jean, "The Reception and Interpretation of Aristotle's Politics," in *The Cambridge History of Later Medieval Philosophy*, ed. Norman Kretzman *et al*. Cambridge University Press, 1982, 723–37.

"The Two Commentaries of Albertus Magnus on the Nicomachean Ethics," *Recherche de théologie ancienne et médiévale* 30 (1963), 232–50.

Durling, Richard, "Corrigenda and Addenda to Diels' Galenica," *Traditio* 23 (1967), 461–76.

"Lectiones Galenicae *Techne iatrike*," *Classical Philology* 63 (1968), 56–76.

Egbert, Virginia Wylie, *On the Bridges of Mediaeval Paris: A Record of Early Fourteenth-Century Life*. Princeton University Press, 1974.

Eijk, Philip van der, "Galen's Use of the Concept of 'Qualified Experience' in his Dietetic and Pharmacological Works," in *Galen on Pharmacology: Philosophy, History, and Medicine*, ed. Armelle Debru. Leiden: Brill, 1997, 35–57.

Ertman, Thomas, *Birth of the Leviathan: Building States and Regimes in Medieval and Early Modern Europe*. Cambridge University Press, 1997.

Eschmann, Thomas, "Bonum commune melius est quam bonum unius: Eine Studie uber den Wertvorrang des Personalen bei Thomas von Aquin," *Mediaeval Studies* 6 (1944), 62–120.

"St. Thomas Aquinas on the Two Powers," *Mediaeval Studies* 20 (1958), 177–205.

"A Thomistic Glossary on the Principle of the Pre-eminence of a Common Good," *Mediaeval Studies* 5 (1943), 123–65.

Evangelisti, Paolo, "Contract and Theft: Two Legal Principles Fundamental to the *civilitas* and *res publica* in the Political Writings of Francesc Eiximenis, Franciscan Friar," *Franciscan Studies* 67 (2009), 405–26.

Faral, Edmond, *Jean Buridan: maître ès arts de l'Université de Paris*. Histoire littéraire de la France XXXVIII. Paris: Imprimerie nationale, 1950.

Fasolt, Constantin, "Herman Conring and the European History of Law," in *Politics and Reformations: Histories and Reformations*, ed. Christopher Ocker *et al*. Leiden: Brill, 2007.

Fichtner, Gerhard, *Corpus Galenicum: Verzeichnis der galenischen und pseudogalenischen Schriften*. Tübingen: Institut für Geschichte der Medizin, 1989.

Finley, M. I., "Aristotle and Economic Analysis," in *Articles on Aristotle,* vol. II: *Ethics and Politics,* ed. Jonathan Barnes, Malcolm Schofield, and Richard Sorabji. London: Duckworth, 1977.

Finnis, John, "Public Good: The Specifically Political Common Good in Aquinas," in *Natural Law and Moral Inquiry: Ethics, Metaphysics and Politics in the Work of Germain Grisez,* ed. R. P. George. Washington, DC: Georgetown University Press, 1988, 174–210.

Fitzgerald, L. P., "St. Thomas Aquinas and the Two Powers," *Angelicum* 36 (1979), 515–56.

Flüeler, Christophe, "Die Rezeption der 'Politica' des Aristoteles," in *Das Publikum politischer Theorie im 14. Jahrhundert,* ed. Jürgen Miethke and Arnold Bühler. Munich: Oldenbourg, 1992, 127–38.

Rezeption und Interpretation der aristotelischen Politica im späten Mittelalter, 2 vols. Amsterdam: Grüner, 1992.

Fournial, Étienne, *Histoire monétaire de l'occident médiéval.* Paris: Fernand Nathan, 1970.

Les villes et l'économie d'échange en Forez aux XIIIe et XIVe siècles. Paris: Les Presses du Palais Royal, 1967.

Franklin, James, "The Ancient Legal Sources of Seventeenth Century Probability," in *The Use of Antiquity: The Scientific Revolution and the Classical Tradition,* ed. Stephen Gaukroger. Dordrecht and Boston: Springer, 1991, 123–44.

The Science of Conjecture: Evidence and Probability Before Pascal. Baltimore, MD: Johns Hopkins University Press, 2001.

Frede, Michael, "Introduction," in *Three Treatises on the Nature of Science,* ed. and trans. Richard Walzer and Michael Frede. Indianapolis: Hackett, 1985.

"On Galen's Epistemology," in *Galen: Problems and Prospects,* ed. Vivian Nutton. London: Wellcome Institute, 1981, 65–86.

French, Roger, *Canonical Medicine: Gentile da Foligno and Scholasticism.* Leiden: Brill, 2001.

Frugoni, Chiara, *A Distant City: Images of Urban Experience in the Medieval World,* trans. William McCuaig. Princeton University Press, 1991.

Funkenstein, Amos, *Theology and the Scientific Imagination from the Middle Ages to the Seventeenth Century.* Princeton University Press, 1986.

Gabriel, Astrik L., *Student Life in Ave Maria College, Mediaeval Paris.* University of Notre Dame Press, 1955.

Gallagher, Clarence, *Canon Law and the Christian Community: The Role of Law in the Church According to the* Summa aurea *of Cardinal Hostiensis.* Analecta Gregoriana CCVIII. Rome: Università Gregoriana, 1978.

García Ballester, Luis, "Arnau de Vilanova (c. 1240–1311) y la reforma de los estudios médicos en Montpellier (1309): el Hipocratés latino y la introducción del nuevo Galeno," *Dynamis* 2 (1982), 97–158.

"*Artifex factivus sanitatus*: Health and Medical Care in Medieval Latin Galenism," in *Knowledge and the Scholarly Medical Traditions,* ed. Donald Bates. Cambridge University Press, 1995, 127–50.

"Galen as a Medical Practitioner: Problems in Diagnosis," in *Galen: Problems and Prospects,* ed. Vivian Nutton. London: Wellcome Institute, 1981, 13–46.

Galeno en la sociedad y en la ciencia de su tiempo. Madrid: Ediciones Guadarrama, 1972.

"Introduction," in *Arnaldi de Villanova Opera medica omnia*, ed. Luis García Ballester, vol. XV. Barcelona: Universitat de Barcelona, 1985.

"The New Galen: A Challenge to Latin Galenism in Thirteenth-Century Montpellier," in *Text and Tradition: Studies in Ancient Medicine and its Transmission*, ed. Klaus-Dietrich Fischer *et al*. Leiden: Brill, 1998, 55–83; reprinted in *Galen and Galenism: Theory and Medical Practice from Antiquity to the European Renaissance*, ed. Luis García Ballester and Jon Arrizabalaga. Aldershot: Ashgate, 2002.

"On the Origin of the 'Six Non-Natural Things' in Galen," in "Galen und das hellenistische Erbe," ed. J. Kollesch and D. Nickel, special issue of *Sudhoffs Archiv* 32 (1993), 105–15.

"Soul and Body: Disease of the Soul and Disease of the Body in Galen's Medical Thought," in *Le opere psicologiche di Galeno*, ed. Paola Manuli and Mario Vegetti. Naples: Bibliopolis, 1988, 117–52.

Garnett, George, *Marsilius of Padua and "the Truth of History."* Oxford University Press, 2006.

Gaudemet, Jean, "Utilitas Publica," *Revue Historique de Droit Français et Étranger* 29 (1951), 465–99.

Gauthier, René Antoine, "La date du commentaire de Saint Thomas sur l'Éthique à Nicomaque," *Recherches de théologie ancienne et médiévale* 18 (1951), 66–105.

Gauthier, René Antoine and Jean Yves Jolif, *L'Éthique à Nichomaque: introduction, traduction et commentaire*, 2 vols., 2nd edn. Louvain: Publications Universitaires; Paris: Béatrice-Nauwelaerts, 1970.

Gentile, Francesco, "Marsilio e l'origine dell'ideologia," *Medioevo* 5 (1979), 293–301.

Géraud, Hercule, *Paris sous Philippe-le-Bel: d'après des documents originaux et notamment d'après un manuscrit contenant Le Rôle de la Taille imposé sur les habitants de Paris en 1292.* Paris: Crapelet, 1837.

Gewirth, Alan, "John of Jandun and the *Defensor Pacis*," *Speculum* 23 (1948), 267–72.

Marsilius of Padua and Medieval Political Philosophy. New York: Columbia University Press, 1951.

"Republicanism and Absolutism in the Thought of Marsilius of Padua," *Medioevo* 5 (1979), 23–48.

Godthardt, Frank, "The Philosopher as Political Actor – Marsilius of Padua at the Court of Ludwig the Bavarian: The Sources Revisited," in *The World of Marsilius of Padua*, ed. Gerson Moreno-Riaño. Turnhout: Brepols, 2006, 29–46.

Gogacz, Mieczyslaw, "L'homme et la communauté dans le 'Defensor Pacis' de Marsile de Padoue," *Medioevo* 5 (1979), 189–200.

Gordon, Barry, "Aristotle and the Development of Value Theory," *Quarterly Journal of Economics* 78 (1964), 115–28.

Economic Analysis before Adam Smith. New York: Barnes and Noble, 1975.

Gouron, André, "Some Aspects of the Medieval Teaching of Roman Law," in *Learning Institutionalized: Teaching in the Medieval University*, ed. John Van Engen. University of Notre Dame Press, 2000, 161–76.

Gransden, Antonia, *Historical Writing in England c. 550 to c. 1307*. Ithaca, NY: Cornell University Press, 1974.

Grant, Edward, *Planets, Stars, and Orbs: The Medieval Cosmos, 1200–1687*. Cambridge University Press, 1994.

"Scientific Thought in Fourteenth-Century Paris: Jean Buridan and Nicole Oresme," in *Machaut's World: Science and Art in the Fourteenth Century*, ed. Madeleine Pelner Cosman and Bruce Chandler. New York Academy of Sciences, 1978, 105–24.

A Source Book in Medieval Science. Cambridge, MA: Harvard University Press, 1974.

Green, Louis, "Historical Interpretation in Fourteenth-Century Florentine Chronicles," *Journal of the History of Ideas* 28 (1967), 161–78.

Grignaschi, Mario, "La définition du 'civis' dans la scolastique," *Recueils de la Société Jean Bodin* 24 (1966), 71–100.

"Marsilio e le filosofie del Trecento," *Medioevo* 5 (1979), 201–22.

"Le rôle de l'aristotélisme dans le *Defensor pacis* de Marsile de Padoue," *Revue d'Histoire et de Philosophie Religieuse* 35 (1955), 301–40.

Grossi, Paolo, *L'ordine giuridico medievale*. Rome: Laterza, 1995.

Gruner, O. Cameron, *A Treatise on the Canon of Medicine of Avicenna Incorporating a Translation of the First Book*. London: Luzac, 1930.

Gutas, Dimitri, "Medical Theory and Scientific Method in the Age of Avicenna," in *Before and After Avicenna*, ed. David Reisman. Leiden: Brill, 2003, 145–62.

Hagenauer, Selma, *Das "justum pretium" bei Thomas von Aquino: ein Beitrag zur Geschichte der Objectiven Werttheorie*. Vierteljahrschrift fur Sozial- und Wirtschaftgeschichte XXIV. Stuttgart: W. Kohlhammer, 1931.

Hankinson, R. J. "Causation in Galen," in *Galien et la philosophie: huit exposés suivis de discussions*, ed. Jonathan Barnes, Jacques Jouanna, and Vincent Barras. Geneva: Fondation Hardt, 2003, 31–72.

"Galen and the Logic of Relations," in *Aristotle in Late Antiquity*, ed. Lawrence Schrenk. Washington, DC: Catholic University Press, 1994, 57–75.

"The Man and his Work," "Epistemology," "Philosophy of Nature," in *Cambridge Companion to Galen*, ed. R. J. Hankinson. Cambridge University Press, 2008, 1–33, 157–83, 210–41.

Hatcher, John, "England in the Aftermath of the Black Death," *Past & Present* 144 (1994), 3–35.

Henneman, John Bell, *Royal Taxation in Fourteenth-Century France: The Captivity, and Ransom of John II, 1356–1370*. Philadelphia: American Philosophical Society, 1976.

Holmes, George, "The Emergence of an Urban Ideology at Florence, 1250–1450," *Transactions of the Royal Historical Society*, 5th series, 23 (1973), 111–34.

Hon, Giora and Bernard Goldstein, *From Summetria to Symmetry: The Making of a Revolutionary Scientific Concept*. New York: Springer, 2010.

Horrox, Rosemary, *The Black Death*. Manchester University Press, 1994.

Hugonnard-Roche, H., "Modalité et argumentation chez Nicole Oresme," in *Nicolas Oresme: tradition et innovation* ed. Pierre Souffrin and A. P. Segonds. Paris: Les Belles Lettres, 1998, 145–63.

Hyde, J. K., "Medieval Descriptions of Cities," *Bulletin of the John Rylands Library* 48 (1966), 308–40.

Padua in the Age of Dante. Manchester University Press, 1966.

Ibanès, Jean, *La doctrine de l'Église et les réalités économiques au XIIIe siècle*. Paris: Presses Universitaires de France, 1967.

Inglis, Erik, "Gothic Architecture and a Scholastic: Jean de Jandun's *Tractatus de laudibus Parisius* (1323)," *Gesta* 42 (2003), 63–85.

Jacquart, Danielle, *La médecine médiévale dans le cadre parisien, XIVe–XVe siècle*. Paris: Fayard, 1998.

"Medical Scholasticism," in *Western Medical Thought*, ed. Mirko Grmek *et al.* Cambridge, MA: Harvard University Press, 1998, 197–240.

Le milieu médical en France du XIIe au XVe siècle. Geneva: Droz, 1981.

"L'œuvre de Jean de Saint-Amand et les méthodes d'enseignement à la Faculté de médecine de Paris à la fin du XIIIe siècle," in *Manuels, programmes de cours et techniques d'enseignement dans les universités médiévales*, ed. Jacqueline Hamesse. Louvain: Institut d'études médiévales de l'Université catholique de Louvain, 1994, 257–75.

"La réception du canon d'Avicenne: comparaison entre Montpellier et Paris au XIIIe et XIVe siècles," in *Histoire de l'École médicale de Montpellier, Actes du 110e Congrès national des sociétés savantes*. Paris: Éditions du CTHS, 1985.

Jacquart, Danielle and Françoise Micheau, *La médecine arabe et l'occident médiéval*. Paris: Éditions Maisonneuve et Larose, 1990.

Jones, Colin, *Paris: Biography of a City*. New York: Viking Press, 2004.

Jordan, Mark, "The Disappearance of Galen in Thirteenth-Century Philosophy and Theology," in *Mensch und Natur im Mittelatler*. Miscellanea Medievalia XXI, no. 2. Berlin and New York: Walter de Gruyter, 1992, 703–17.

Jouanna, Jacques, comments on "Menschenbild und Normwandel in der klassischen Zeit," in *Médecine et morale dans l'antiquité*, ed. Hellmut Flashar. Geneva: Fondation Hardt, 1977, 121–55.

Joutsivuo, Timo, *Scholastic Tradition and Humanist Innovation: The Concept of Neutrum in Renaissance Medicine*. Helsinki: Academia Scientiarum Fennica, 1999.

Jung, Elzbieta and Robert Podkonski, "Richard Kilvington on Proportions," in *Mathématiques et théorie du mouvement (XIVe–XVIe siècles)*, ed. Joël Biard and Sabine Rommevaux. Villeneuve-d'Ascq: Presses Universitaires du Septentrion, 2008, 81–101.

Jung-Palczewska, Elzbieta, "From Oxonian Sources to Parisian Rebellion: Attempts to Overcome Aristotelianism in Fourteenth-Century Physics," in *Bilan et perspectives des études médiévales*, ed. J. Hamesse. Turnhout: Brepols, 2004, 435–49.

Kaluza, Zénon, "Les cours communs sur *L'Éthique à Nicomaque* à l'université de Paris," in *"Ad Ingenii Acuitionem": Studies in Honour of Alfonso Maierù*, ed. Stefano Caroti, Ruedi Imbach, Zénon Kaluza, *et al.* Louvain-la-Neuve: Collège Cardinal Mercier, 2006.

Karabatzaki, Helen, "Stoicism and Galen's Medical Thought," in *Philosophy and Medicine*, ed. K. J. Boudoris. Athens: Ionia Publications, 1998, 95–113.

Kaye, Joel, "Changing Definitions of Money, Nature, and Equality, c. 1140–1270, Reflected in Thomas Aquinas' Questions on Usury," in *Credito e usura fra teologia, diritto, e amministratione*, ed. Diego Quaglioni, Giacomo Todeschini, and Gian Maria Varanini. École Française de Rome, 2005, 25–55.

Economy and Nature in the Fourteenth Century: Money, Market Exchange, and the Emergence of Scientific Thought. Cambridge University Press, 1998.

"Monetary and Market Consciousness in Thirteenth and Fourteenth Century Europe," in *Ancient and Medieval Economic Ideas and Concepts of Social Justice*, ed. S. Todd Lowry and Barry Gordon. Leiden: Brill, 1998, 371–404.

"The (Re)Balance of Nature, 1250–1350," in *Engaging with Nature: Essays on the Natural World in Medieval and Early Modern Europe*, ed. Barbara Hanawalt and Lisa J. Kiser. University of Notre Dame Press, 2008, 85–113.

Kempshall, M. S., *The Common Good in Late Medieval Thought*. Oxford: Clarendon Press, 1999.

Kirshner, Julius, "Storm over the *Monte Comune*: Genesis of the Moral Controversy over the Public Debt of Florence," *Archivum Fratrum Praedicatorum* 53 (1983), 219–76.

"*Ubi est ille?* Franco Sacchetti on the *Monte Comune* of Florence," *Speculum* 59 (1984), 556–84.

Kirshner, Julius and Kimberly Lo Prete, "Peter John Olivi's Treatises on Contracts of Sale, Usury and Restitution: Minorite Economics or Minor Works?" *Quaderni Fiorentini* 13 (1984), 233–86.

Klima, Gyula, *John Buridan*. Oxford University Press, 2009.

Koch, Bettina, "Marsilius and Hobbes on Religion and Papal Power: Some Observations on Similarities," in *The World of Marsilius of Padua*, ed. Gerson Moreno-Riaño. Turnhout: Brepols, 2006, 189–209.

Kollesch, Jutta, "Anschauungen von den *archai* in der *Ars medica* und die Seelenlehre Galens," in *Le opere psicologiche di Galeno*, ed. Paola Manuli and Mario Vegetti. Naples: Bibliopolis, 1988, 215–30.

Kristeller, Paul Oskar, "Bartholomeus, Musandinus and Maurus of Salerno and Other Early Commentators of the 'Articella', with a Tentative List of Texts and Manuscripts," *Italia medioevale e umanistica* 19 (1976), 57–87.

"The School of Salerno," *Bulletin of the History of Medicine* 17 (1945), 138–94.

"Umanesimo e scolastica a Padova fino al Petrarca," *Medioevo* 11 (1985), 1–18.

Kukewicz, Zdzislaw, "*Les Problemata* de Pietro d'Abano et leur 'rédaction' par Jean de Jandun," *Medioevo* 10 (1984), 113–24.

Lagarde, Georges de, "Individualisme et corporatisme au moyen âge," in *L'organisation corporative du Moyen Âge à la fin de l'Ancien Régime*. Recueil de travaux publiés par les membres des conférences d'histoire et de philologie, 2nd series. Louvain: Bibliothèque de l'Université, 1937, 1–59.

"La philosophie sociale d'Henri de Gand et de Godefroid de Fontaines," in *L'organisation corporative du Moyen Âge à la fin de l'Ancien Régime*. Louvain: Bibliothèque de l'Université, 1937, 55–134.

Lambertini, Roberto, "The Sophismata attributed to Marsilius of Padua," in *Sophisms in Medieval Logic and Grammar*, ed. Stephen Read. Dordrecht: Kluwer, 1993, 86–102.

Langholm, Odd, *The Aristotelian Analysis of Usury*. Bergen: Universitetsforlaget, 1984.

"Buridan on Economic Value," *History of Political Economy* 38 (2006), 269–89.

Economics in the Medieval Schools: Wealth, Exchange, Value, Money, and Usury According to the Paris Theological Tradition. Leiden: Brill, 1992.

The Legacy of Scholasticism in Economic Thought. Cambridge University Press, 1998.

Price and Value in the Aristotelian Tradition: A Study in Scholastic Economic Sources. Bergen: Universitetsforlaget, 1979.

"Scholastic Economics," in *Pre-Classical Economic Thought,* ed. S. Todd Lowry. Boston: Kluwer, 1987, 122–3.

Le Bras, Gabriel, "L'usure," in *Dictionnaire de théologie catholique,* vol. XV. Paris: Letouzey et Ane, 1950.

Lejbowicz, Max, "Chronologie des écrits anti-astrologiques de Nicole Oresme: étude sur un cas de scepticisme dans la deuxième moitié du XIVe siècle," in *Autour de Nicole Oresme: Actes du colloque Oresme organisé à l'université de Paris XII,* ed. Jeannine Quillet. Paris: J. Vrin, 1990, 119–76.

Lewis, Ewart, "Organic Tendencies in Medieval Political Thought," *American Political Science Review* 32 (1938), 849–76.

Lindley, Phillip, "The Black Death and English Art: A Debate and Some Assumptions," in *The Black Death in England,* ed. W. M. Ormrod and P. G. Lindley. Donington: Shaun Tyas, 2003, 125–46.

Little, Lester, *Liberty, Charity, Fraternity: Lay Religious Confraternities at Bergamo in the Age of the Communes.* Bergamo: Lubrina, 1988.

Lloyd, G. E. R., "Galen on Hellenistics and Hippocrateans: Contemporary Battles and Past Authorities," in "Galen und das hellenistische Erbe," ed. J. Kollesch and D. Nickel, special issue of *Sudhoffs Archiv* 32 (1993), 125–43.

Lopez, Robert S., *The Commercial Revolution of the Middle Ages, 950–1350.* Englewood Cliffs, NJ: Prentice Hall, 1971.

Lopez, Robert S. and Irving Raymond (eds.), *Medieval Trade in the Mediterranean World: Illustrative Documents.* New York: Columbia University Press, 1955.

Lowry, S. Todd, "Aristotle's Mathematical Analysis of Exchange," *History of Political Economy* 1 (1969), 44–66.

Luscombe, David E., "City and Politics before the Coming of the *Politics*: Some Illustrations," in *Church and City, 1000–1500: Essays in Honour of Christopher Brooke,* ed. David Abulafia, Michael Franklin, and Miri Rubin. Cambridge University Press, 1992, 41–55.

"Thomas Aquinas and Conceptions of Hierarchy in the Thirteenth Century," in *Thomas von Aquin: Werk und Wirkung im Licht neuerer Forschungen,* ed. Albert Zimmermann. Miscellanea Medievalia XIX. Berlin: Walter de Gruyter, 1988, 261–77.

MacClintock, Stuart, *Perversity and Error: Studies on the "Averroist" John of Jandun.* Bloomington: Indiana University Press, 1956.

McGovern, John, "The Rise of New Economic Attitudes: Economic Humanism, Economic Nationalism during the Later Middle Ages and the Renaissance, A.D. 1200–1550," *Traditio* 26 (1970), 217–53.

McLaughlin, T. P., "The Teaching of the Canonists on Usury (XII, XIII and XIV Centuries)," *Mediaeval Studies* 1 (1939), 81–147.

McVaugh, Michael, "Arnald of Villanova and Bradwardine's Law," *Isis* 58 (1967), 56–64.

"Introduction" to Galen, *Tractatus De intentione medicorum,* in *Arnaldi de Villanova Opera Medica Omnia,* vol. V.1, ed. Michael McVaugh. Granada-Barcelona: Seminarium Historiae Medicae Granatensis, 2000.

Medicine Before the Plague: Practitioners and their Patients in the Crown of Aragon, 1285–1345. Cambridge University Press, 1993.

"Moments of Inflection: The Careers of Arnau de Vilanova," in *Religion and Medicine in the Middle Ages*, ed. Peter Biller and Joseph Ziegler. Woodbridge: York Medieval Press, 2001, 47–67.

"The Nature and Limits of Medical Certitude at Early Fourteenth-Century Montpellier," *Osiris* 6 (1990), 62–84.

"Quantified Medical Theory and Practice at Fourteenth-Century Montpellier," *Bulletin of the History of Medicine* 43 (1969), 397–412.

Mahoney, Michael, "Mathematics," in *Science in the Middle Ages*, ed. David C. Lindberg. University of Chicago Press, 1978, 145–78.

Maier, Anneliese, "The Achievements of Late Scholastic Natural Philosophy," in *On the Threshold of Exact Science: Selected Writings of Anneliese Maier on Late Medieval Natural Philosophy*, ed. and trans. Steven Sargent. Philadelphia: University of Pennsylvania Press, 1982, 143–70.

Ausgehendes Mittelalter: Gesammelte Aufsätze zur Geistesgeschichte des 14. Jahrhunderts, 3 vols. Rome: Edizioni di Storia e Letteratura, 1964–77.

"The Concept of the Function in Fourteenth-Century Physics," in *On the Threshold of Exact Science: Selected Writings of Anneliese Maier on Late Medieval Natural Philosophy*, ed. and trans. Steven Sargent. Philadelphia: University of Pennsylvania Press, 1982, 61–75.

"La doctrine de Nicolas d'Oresme sur les 'configurationes intensionum,'" in *Ausgehendes Mittelalter: Gesammelte Aufsätze zur Geistesgeschichte des 14. Jahrhunderts*, 3 vols. Rome: Edizioni di Storia e Letteratura, 1964–77, vol. I, 335–52.

"Der Funktionsbegriff in der Physik des 14. Jahrhunderts," in *Die Vorläufer Galileis*. Rome: Edizioni di Storia e Letteratura, 1949, 81–110.

Manuli, Paola, "Galen and Stoicism," in "Galen und das hellenistische Erbe," ed. J. Kollesch and D. Nickel, special issue of *Sudhoffs Archiv* 32 (1993), 53–61.

Marmursztejn, Elsa, *L'autorité des Maîtres: scolastique, normes et societé au XIIIe siècle*. Paris: Les Belles Lettres, 2007.

Martin, Henry, *Légende de Saint Denis: reproduction des miniatures du manuscrit original présenté en 1317 au roi Philippe le Long*. Paris: H. Champion, 1908.

Mayhew, Nicholas, "Modelling Medieval Monetisation," in *A Commercialising Economy: England 1086 to c.1300*, ed. Richard H. Britnell and Bruce Campbell. Manchester University Press, 1995, 55–77.

Menjot, Denis, "La politique monétaire de Nicolas Oresme," in *Nicolas Oresme: tradition et innovation*, ed. Pierre Souffrin and A. P. Segonds. Paris: Les Belles Lettres, 1998, 179–93.

Michaud-Quantin, Pierre, "La conscience d'être membre d'une *universitas*," in *Beiträge zum Berufsbewusstsein des mittelalterlichen Menschen*, Miscellanea Mediaevalia III. Berlin: Walter de Gruyter, 1964, 1–13.

Universitas: expressions du movement communautaire dans le Moyen-Âge latin. Paris: J. Vrin, 1970.

Miethke, Jürgen, "Marsilius und Ockham," *Medioevo* 6 (1980), 543–67.

Miskimin, Harry, "The Last Act of Charles V: The Background to the Revolts of 1382," *Speculum* 38 (1963), 433–42.

Money, Prices, and Foreign Exchange in Fourteenth-Century France. New Haven, CT: Yale University Press, 1963.

Molland, A. G., "The Geometrical Background to the 'Merton School,'" *British Journal for the History of Science* 4 (1968), 108–25.

Moody, Ernest A., "John Buridan on the Habitability of the Earth," *Speculum* 16 (1941), 415–24.

The Rise of Mechanism in 14th Century Natural Philosophy: Translations of Texts on the Causal and Mathematical Analysis of Motion by John Buridan (ca. 1300–1358) and John Dumbleton (fl. 1328–1340). New York: typescript, 1950.

Moraux, Paul, "Galien comme philosophe: la philosophie de la nature," in *Galen: Problems and Prospects*, ed. Vivian Nutton. London: Wellcome Institute, 1981, 87–116.

Moreno-Riaño, Gerson, "Hierarchy, Ambiguity and a Via Media," in *The World of Marsilius of Padua*, ed. Gerson Moreno-Riaño.Turnhout: Brepols, 2006, 249–69.

Morison, Ben, "Logic" and "Language," in *The Cambridge Companion to Galen*, ed. R. J. Hankinson. Cambridge University Press, 2008, 66–115, 116–56.

Mortarino, Marzia, *Galeno: sulle facoltà naturali.* Milan: Mondadori, 1996.

Munro, John, "The Medieval Origins of the Financial Revolution: Usury, Rentes, and Negotiability," *International History Review* 25 (2003), 505–56.

Murdoch, John, "*Mathesis in philosophiam scholasticam introducta*: The Rise and Development of the Application of Mathematics in Fourteenth Century Philosophy and Theology," in *Arts libéraux et philosophie au moyen âge*, Actes du Quatrième Congrès International de Philosophie Médiévale. Montreal: Institut d'études médiévales, 1969, 215–46.

"The Medieval Language of Proportions," in *Scientific Change: Historical Studies in the Intellectual, Social and Technical Conditions for Scientific Discovery and Technical Invention, from Antiquity to the Present.* New York: Basic Books, 1963, 237–71.

"*Subtilitates Anglicanae* in Fourteenth-Century Paris: John of Mirecourt and Peter Ceffons," in *Machaut's World: Science and Art in the Fourteenth Century*, ed. Madeleine Pelner Cosman and Bruce Chandler. New York Academy of Sciences, 1978, 51–86.

"Thomas Bradwardine: Mathematics and Continuity in the Fourteenth Century," in *Mathematics and its Application to Science and Natural Philosophy in the Middle Ages: Essays in Honor of Marshall Clagett*, ed. Edward Grant and John Murdoch. Cambridge University Press, 1987, 103–37.

Murphy, Mark, "Consent, Custom and the Common Good in Aquinas' Account of Political Authority," *Review of Politics* 59 (1997), 323–50.

Nederman, Cary J., *Community and Consent: The Secular Political Theory of Marsiglio of Padua's Defensor Pacis.* Lanham, MD: Rowman & Littlefield, 1994.

"Community and Self-Interest: Marsiglio of Padua on Civil Life and Private Advantage," *Review of Politics* 65 (2003), 395–416.

"Empire and the Historiography of European Political Thought: Marsiglio of Padua, Nicholas of Cusa, and the Medieval/Modern Divide," *Journal of the History of Ideas* 66 (2005), 1–15.

"Freedom, Community, and Function: Communitarian Lessons of Medieval Political Theory," *American Political Science Review* 86 (1992), 977–86.

"Healing the Body Politic: The Diversification of Organic Metaphors in Nicole Oresme and Christine de Pizan," in *Healing the Body Politic: The Political Thought of Christine de Pizan*, ed. Karen Green and Constant J. Mews. Turnhout: Brepols, 2005, 19–34.

"A Heretic Hiding in Plain Sight: The Secret History of Marsiglio of Padua's *Defensor Pacis* in the Thought of Nicole Oresme," in *Heresy in Transition: Transforming Ideas of Heresy in Medieval and Early Modern Europe*, ed. Ian Hunter, John Christian Laurson, and Cary Nederman. Aldershot: Ashgate, 2005, 71–88.

"The Living Body Politic: The Diversification of Organic Metaphors in the Later Middle Ages," *Pensiero Politico Medievale* 2 (2004), 59–87.

"Marsiliglio of Padua Studies Today – and Tomorrow," in *The World of Marsilius of Padua*, ed. Gerson Moreno-Riaño. Turnhout: Brepols, 2006, 11–15.

"Nature, Justice, and Duty in the *Defensor pacis*: Marsiglio of Padua's Ciceronian Impulse," *Political Theory* 18 (1990), 615–37.

"Nature, Sin and the Origins of Society: The Ciceronian Tradition in Medieval Political Thought," *Journal of the History of Ideas* 49 (1988), 3–26.

Neveux, François, "Nicole Oresme et le clergé normand du XIVe siècle," in *Autour de Nicole Oresme: Actes du colloque Oresme organisé à l'université de Paris XII*, ed. Jeannine Quillet. Paris: J. Vrin, 1990, 9–36.

Nicholas, David, "Medieval Urban Origins in Northern Continental Europe: State of Research and some Tentative Conclusions," *Studies in Medieval and Renaissance History* 6 (1969), 55–114.

Noonan, John, *The Scholastic Analysis of Usury*. Cambridge, MA: Harvard University Press, 1957.

Nutton, Vivian, "The Chronology of Galen's Early Career," *Classical Quarterly* 23 (1973), 158–71.

"Galen and Egypt," in "Galen und das hellenistische Erbe," ed. J. Kollesch and D. Nickel, special issue of *Sudhoffs Archiv* 32 (1993), 11–31.

"Galen and Medical Autobiography," *Proceedings of the Cambridge Philological Society* 198 (1972), 50–62.

"Galen in the Eyes of his Contemporaries," *Bulletin of the History of Medicine* 58 (1984), 315–24.

O'Boyle, Cornelius, *The Art of Medicine: Medical Teaching at the University of Paris, 1250–1400*. Leiden: Brill, 1998.

"Discussions on the Nature of Medicine at the University of Paris, ca. 1300," in *Learning Institutionalized: Teaching in the Medieval University*, ed. John Van Engen. University of Notre Dame Press, 2000, 197–228.

Ormrod, W. M., "The Politics of Pestilence: Government in England after the Black Death," in *The Black Death in England*, ed. W. M. Ormrod and P. G. Lindley. Donington: Shaun Tyas, 2003, 147–81.

Ottosson, Per-Gunnar, *Scholastic Medicine and Philosophy: A Study of Commentaries on Galen's Tegni (ca. 1300–1450)*. Naples: Bibliopolis, 1984.

Pacetti, D., "Un trattato sulle usure e le restituzioni di Pietro di Giovanni Olivi falsamente attribuito a fr. Gerardo da Siena," *Archivum Franciscanum historicum* 46 (1953), 448–57.

Palmieri-Darlon, N., "Sur les traces d'une ancienne traduction de l'*Ars medica*," *Latomus* 56 (1997), 504–11.

Paniagua, Juan, "Maître Arnau de Vilanova: paradigme de la médecine universitaire médiévale," in *Studia Arnaldiana: Trabajos en torno a la obra Médica de Arnau de Vilanova, c. 1240–1311*. Barcelona: Fundación Uriach, 1994, 64–73.

Park, Katharine, "Albert's Influence on Late Medieval Psychology," in *Albertus Magnus and the Sciences: Commemorative Essays, 1980*, ed. James A. Weisheipl. Toronto: Pontifical Institute of Mediaeval Studies, 1980, 501–36.

"The Meanings of Natural Diversity: Marco Polo on the 'Division' of the World," in *Texts and Contexts in Ancient and Medieval Science*, ed. Edith Sylla and Michael McVaugh. Leiden: Brill, 1997, 134–47.

Paschetto, Eugenia, *Pietro d'Abano, medico e filosofo*. Florence: E. Vallecchi, 1984.

Pelzer, Auguste, "Le cours inédit d'Albert le Grand sur la Morale à Nicomaque, recueilli et rédigé par Saint Thomas d'Aquin," *Revue néoscholastique de philosophie* 24 (1922), 333–361, 479–520.

Penella, R. J. and T. S. Hall, "Galen's 'On the Best Constitution of Our Body': Introduction, Translation, and Notes," *Bulletin of the History of Medicine* 47 (1973), 282–96.

Penn, A. C. and Christopher Dyer, "Wages and Earnings in Late Medieval England: Evidence from the Enforcement of the Labour Laws," *Economic History Review* 43 (1990), 356–76.

Perroy, Édouard, "A l'origine d'une économie contractée: les crises du XIVe siècle" *Annales. Histoire, Sciences Sociales* 4, no. 2 (1949), 167–82.

Piaia, Gregorio, *Marsilio e dintorni*. Padua: Editrice Antenore, 1999.

"The Shadow of Antenor: On the Relationship between the *Defensor pacis* and the Institutions of the City of Padua," in *Politische Reflexion in der Welt des späten Mittelalters/Political Thought in the Age of Scholasticism*, ed. Martin Kaufhold. Leiden: Brill, 2004, 193–223.

Pigeaud, Jackie, "Les problèmes de la création chez Galien," in "Galen und das hellenistische Erbe," ed. J. Kollesch and D. Nickel, special issue of *Sudhoffs Archiv* 32 (1993), 87–103.

Piron, Sylvain, "Censures et condamnation de Pierre de Jean Olivi: enquête dans les marges du Vatican," *Mélanges de l'École française de Rome – Moyen Âge* 118 (2006), 313–73.

"The Formation of Olivi's Intellectual Project," *Oliviana* 1 (2003) (online journal).

"Marchands et confesseurs: le Traité des contrats d'Olivi dans son contexte (Narbonne, fin XIIIe–début XIVe siècle)," in *L'Argent au Moyen Âge*. Paris: Publications de la Sorbonne, 1998.

"Le traitement de l'incertitude commerciale dans la scolastique médiévale," *Journ@l Electronique d'Histoire des Probabilités et de la Statistique* 3.1 (2007), article 2.

Postan, Michael, *The Medieval Economy and Society: An Economic History of Britain 1100–1500*. Berkeley: University of California Press, 1972.

Powicke, F. M., "Robert Grosseteste and the *Nichomachean Ethics*," *Proceedings of the British Academy* 16 (1930), 85–104.

Presenti, Tiziani, "Per la tradizione del testamento di Pietro d'Abano," *Medioevo* 6 (1980), 533–42.

Price, B. B., "Paired in Ceremony: Academic Inception and Trade-Guild Reception," *History of Universities* 20 (2005), 1–37.

Quaglioni, Diego, *Politica e diritto nel Trecento italiano*. Florence: Olschki, 1983.

Quillet, Jeannine, "L'aristotélisme de Marsile de Padoue et ses rapports avec l'averroisme," *Medioevo* 5 (1979), 81–142.

Charles V, le roi lettré: essai sur la pensée politique d'un règne. Paris: Librairie Académique Perrin, 1984.

La philosophie politique de Marsile de Padoue. Paris: J. Vrin, 1970.

La philosophie politique du Songe du Vergier (1378). Paris: J. Vrin, 1977.

Reeves, Marjorie, "Marsilius of Padua and Dante Alighieri," in *Trends in Medieval Political Thought*, ed. Beryl Smalley. Oxford University Press, 1965, 86–104.

Renouard, Yves, "Le rôle des hommes d'affaires italiens dans la Méditerranée au Moyen Âge," in *Études d'histoire médiévale*, 2 vols. Paris: SEVPEN, 1968, 405–18.

Reyerson, Kathryn, *The Art of the Deal: Intermediaries of Trade in Medieval Montpellier*. Leiden: Brill, 2002.

Business, Banking and Finance in Medieval Montpellier. Toronto: Pontifical Institute of Mediaeval Studies, 1985.

Reyerson, Kathryn and Debra A. Salata (eds. and trans.) *Medieval Notaries and their Acts: The 1327–1328 Register of Jean Holanie*. Kalamazoo, MI: Medieval Institute Publications, 2004.

Ribémont, Bernard, "Mais où est donc le centre de la terre," in *Terres médiévales*, ed. Bernard Ribémont. Paris: Éditions Klincksieck, 1993, 261–76.

Rogozinski, Jan, "The First French Archives," *French Historical Studies* 7 (1971), 111–16.

Rommevaux, Sabine, "L'irrationalité de la diagonale et du côté d'un même carré dans les *Questions* de Biaise de Parme sur le *Traité des rapports* de Bradwardine," *Revue d'histoire des sciences* 56 (2003), 410–18.

Rosen, G., "The Historical Significance of some Medical References in the *Defensor Pacis* of Marsilio of Padua," *Sudhoffs Archiv für Geschichte der Medizin und der Naturwissenschaften* 37 (1953), 35–56.

Roux, Simon, "L'habitat urbain au Moyen Âge: le quartier de l'Université à Paris," *Annales* 2 (1969), 1196–1219.

Rubinstein, Nicolai, "Marsilio e il pensiero politico italiano," *Medioevo* 5 (1979), 143–62.

Sarton, George, *Galen of Pergamon*. Lawrence: University of Kansas Press, 1954.

Schmugge, Ludwig, *Johannes von Jandun (1285/9–1328). Untersuchungen zur Biographie und Sozialtheorie eines Lateinischen Averroisten*, in *Pariser Historische Studien*, vol. V. Stuttgart: Anton Hiersemann, 1966.

Schubert, Charlotte, "Menschenbild und Normwandel in der klassischen Zeit," in *Médecine et morale dans l'antiquité*, ed. Hellmut Flashar *et al.* Geneva: Fondation Hardt, 1997, 121–55.

Serchuk, Camille, "Paris and the Rhetoric of Town Praise in the *Vie de St. Denis* Manuscript," *Journal of the Walters Art Gallery* 57 (1999), 35–47.

Sherman, Claire Richter, *The Portraits of Charles V of France (1338–1380)*. New York University Press, 1969.

Shogimen, Takashi, "Treating the Body Politic: Medical Metaphor of Political Rule in Late Medieval Europe and Tokugawa Japan," *Review of Politics* 70 (2008), 77–104.

Singer, P. N., "Aspects of Galen's Platonism," in *Galeno: obra, pensamiento e influencia*, ed. J. A. López Férez. Madrid: Universidad Nacional de Educación a Distancia, 1991, 41–55.

Siraisi, Nancy, *Arts and Sciences at Padua: The Studium of Padua before 1350*. Toronto: Pontifical Institute of Mediaeval Studies, 1973.

Avicenna in Renaissance Italy: The Canon and Medical Teaching in Italian Universities after 1500. Princeton University Press, 1987.

"The *libri morales* in the Faculty of Arts and Medicine at Bologna: Bartolomeo da Varignana and the Pseudo-Aristotelian Economics," *Manuscripta* 20 (1976), 105–17; reprinted in *Medicine and the Italian Universities, 1250–1600*, ed. Nancy Siraisi. Leiden: Brill, 2001, 100–13.

"The Medical Learning of Albertus Magnus," in *Albertus Magnus and the Sciences: Commemorative Essays, 1980*, ed. James A. Weisheipl. Toronto: Pontifical Institute of Mediaeval Studies, 1980, 379–404.

"Medicine, 1450–1620, and the History of Science," *Isis* 103 (2012), 491–514.

Medieval and Early Renaissance Medicine: An Introduction to Knowledge and Practice. University of Chicago Press, 1990.

"Music of the Pulse," in *Medicine and the Italian Universities, 1250–1600*, ed. Nancy Siraisi. Leiden: Brill, 2001, 114–39.

"Pietro d'Abano and Taddeo Alderotti: Two Models of Medical Culture," *Medioevo* 11 (1985), 139–62.

"Some Current Trends in the Study of Renaissance Medicine," *Renaissance Quarterly* 37 (1984), 585–600.

Taddeo Alderotti and his Pupils: Two Generations of Italian Medical Learning. Princeton University Press, 1981.

"Vesalius and the Reading of Galen's Teleology," *Renaissance Quarterly* 50 (1997), 1–37.

Smith, Pamela, *The Body of the Artisan: Art and Experience in the Scientific Revolution*. University of Chicago Press, 2004.

Soudek, Joseph, "Aristotle's Theory of Exchange: An Inquiry into the Origin of Economic Analysis," *Proceedings of the American Philosophical Society* 96 (1952), 45–75.

Souffrin, Pierre, "Oresme, Buridan, et le mouvement de rotation diurne de la terre ou des cieux," in *Terres médiévales*, ed. Bernard Ribémont. Paris: Éditions Klincksieck, 1993, 277–99.

"La quantification du mouvement chez les scholastiques: la vitesse instantanée chez Nicole Oresme," in *Autour de Nicole Oresme: Actes du colloque Oresme organisé à l'université de Paris XII*, ed. Jeannine Quillet. Paris: J. Vrin, 1990, 63–83.

Souffrin, Pierre and J. P. Weiss, "Le traité des configurations des qualités et des mouvements: remarques sur quelques problèmes d'interprétation et de traduction," in *Nicolas Oresme: Tradition et innovation*, ed. Pierre Souffrin and A. P. Segonds. Paris: Les Belles Lettres, 125–44.

Spicciani, Amleto, *Capitale e interesse tra mercatura e povertà nei teologi e canonisti dei secoli VIII–XV*. Rome: Jouvence, 1990.

La mercatura e la formazione del prezzo nella riflessione teologica medioevale. Rome: Accademia dei Lincei, 1977.

"Pietro di Giovanni Olivi: indigatore della razionalità economica medioevale," in *Usure, compere e vendite: la scienza economica del XIII secolo, Pietro di Giovanni Olivi*, ed. Amleto Spicciani, P. Vian, and G. Andenna. Milan: Europía, 1998.

Spufford, Peter, *Money and its Use in Medieval Europe*. Cambridge University Press, 1988.

Staden, Heinrich von, "Galen and the 'Second Sophistic,'" in *Aristotle and After*, ed. Richard Sorabji. University of London Institute of Classical Studies, 1997, 33–54.

Herophilus: The Art of Medicine in Early Alexandria. Cambridge University Press, 1989.

"Inefficacy, Error and Failure: Galen on dokima pharmaka aprakta," in *Galen on Pharmacology: Philosophy, History, and Medicine*, ed. Armelle Debru. Leiden: Brill, 1997, 59–83.

"Science as Text, Science as History: Galen on Metaphor," in *Ancient Medicine in its Socio-Cultural Context*, ed. P. J. van der Eijk, H. F. Horstmannshoff, and P. H. Schrijvers, vol. II. Amsterdam: Rodopi, 1995, 499–518.

Stone, David, "The Black Death and its Immediate Aftermath: Crisis and Change in the Fenland Economy, 1346–1453," in *Town and Countryside in the Age of the Black Death: Essays in Honour of John Hatcher*, ed. Mark Bailey and Stephen Rigby. Turnhout: Brepols, 2012, 213–44.

Stone, Martin, "Aristotle's Doctrine of Epieikeia in 13th Century Ethics," *Documenti e studi sulla tradizione filosofica medievale* 27 (2006), 121–56.

Strohm, Paul, *Social Chaucer*. Cambridge, MA: Harvard University Press, 1994.

Strohmaier, Gotthard, "Galen in Arabic: Prospects and Projects," in *Galen: Problems and Prospects*, ed. Vivian Nutton. London: Wellcome Institute, 1981, 187–96.

Struve, Tilman, *Die Entwicklung der Organologischen Staatsauffassung in Mittelalter*. Stuttgart: Anton Hiersemann, 1978.

Sylla, Edith, "Business Ethics, Commercial Mathematics, and the Origins of Mathematical Probability," in *Oeconomies in the Age of Newton*, ed. Margaret Schabas and Neil de Marchi, History of Political Economy XXXV. Durham, NC: Duke University Press, 2003.

"Medieval Concepts of the Latitude of Forms: The Oxford Calculators," *Archives d'histoire doctrinale et littéraire du Moyen Âge* 40 (1973), 223–83.

"Medieval Quantification of Qualities: The 'Merton School,'" *Archive for History of Exact Sciences* 8 (1971), 7–39.

"The Origin and Fate of Thomas Bradwardine's *De proportionibus velocitatum in motibus* in Relation to the History of Mathematics," in *Mechanics and Natural Philosophy before the Scientific Revolution*, ed. Walter Roy Laird and Sophie Roux. Dordrecht: Springer, 2008, 67–119.

The Oxford Calculators and the Mathematics of Motion 1320–1350: Physics and the Measurement by Latitudes. New York: Garland, 1991.

"The Oxford Calculators' Middle Degree Theorem in Context," *Early Science and Medicine* 15 (2010), 338–70.

"The Transmission of the New Physics of the Fourteenth Century from England to the Continent," in *La nouvelle physique du XIVe siècle*, ed. Stefano Caroti and Pierre Souffrin. Florence: Olschki, 1997, 65–110.

Taylor, Robert A., "Les néologismes chez Nicole Oresme, traducteur du XIVe siècle," in *Actes du Xe Congrès international de linguistique et philologie romanes*, ed. Georges Straka, vol. II, pt. 4. Paris: Librairie C. Klincksieck, 1965.

Telliez, Roman, "Officiers et fermiers des aides devant la justice royale (fin du XIVe – début du XVe siècle," in *L'impôt au Moyen Âge: l'impôt public et le prélèvement seigneurial fin XIIe–début XVIe siècle*, ed. Philippe Contamine *et al.*, vol. III. Paris: Ministère de l'économie, des finances et de l'industrie, Comité pour l'histoire économique et financière de la France, 2002, 827–59.

Temkin, Owsei, "Galenicals and Galenism in the History of Medicine," in *The Impact of Antibiotics on Medicine and Society*, ed. Iago Galdston. New York: International Universities Press, 1958, 18–37.

Galenism: Rise and Decline of a Medical Philosophy. Ithaca, NY: Cornell University Press, 1973.

"Metaphors of Human Biology," in *The Double Face of Janus and Other Essays in the History of Medicine*, ed. Owsei Temkin. Baltimore, MD: Johns Hopkins University Press, 1977, 271–83.

Thijssen, J. M. M. H., "Buridan on Mathematics," *Vivarium* 23 (1985), 55–78.

"The Buridan School Reassessed: John Buridan and Albert of Saxony," *Vivarium* 42 (2004), 18–43.

Thijssen, J. M. M. H. and Jack Zupko (eds.), *The Metaphysics and Natural Philosophy of John Buridan.* Leiden: Brill, 2000.

Thorndike, Lynn, "Buridan's Questions on the Physiognomy Ascribed to Aristotle," *Speculum* 18 (1943), 99–103.

A History of Magic and Experimental Science, vol. III. New York: Columbia University Press, 1934.

Thorndike, Lynn and Pearl Kibre, *A Catalogue of Incipits of Mediaeval Scientific Writings in Latin.* Cambridge, MA: Medieval Academy of America, 1963.

Tieleman, Teun, "Methodology," in *The Cambridge Companion to Galen*, ed. R. J. Hankinson. Cambridge University Press, 2008, 49–65.

Tierney, Brian, *Foundation of the Conciliar Theory: The Contribution of the Medieval Canonists from Gratian to the Great Schism.* Cambridge University Press, 1955.

"Hierarchy, Consent, and the 'Western Tradition,'" *Political Theory* 15 (1987), 646–52.

"Marsilius on Rights," *Journal of the History of Ideas* 52 (1991), 3–17.

Religion, Law, and the Growth of Constitutional Thought. Cambridge University Press, 1982.

Todeschini, Giacomo, "Eccezioni e usura nel Duecento: osservazioni sulla cultura economica medievale come realtà non dottrinaria," *Quaderni storici* 131 (2009), 443–60.

"'Ecclesia' e mercato nei linguaggi dottrinali di Tommaso d'Aquino," *Quaderni storici* 105 (2000), 585–621.

Franciscan Wealth: From Voluntary Poverty to Market Society, trans. Donatella Melucci. Saint Bonaventure, NY: Franciscan Institute, 2009.

"Investigating the Origins of the Late Medieval Entrepreneur's Self Representation," *Impresa e storia* 35 (2007), 13–37.

I mercanti e il tempio: la società cristiana e il circolo virtuoso della ricchezza fra Medioevo ed Età Moderna. Bologna: Il Mulino, 2002.

"'Oeconomica francescana' I: Proposte di una nuova lettura delle fonti dell'etica economica medievale," *Rivista di storia e letteratura religiosa* 12 (1976), 15–77.

"'Oeconomica francescana' II: Pietro di Giovanni Olivi come fonte per la storia dell'etica-economica medievale," *Rivista di storia e letteratura religiosa* 13 (1977), 461–94.

"Olivi e il *mercator* cristiano," in *Pierre de Jean Olivi (1248–1298): pensée scolastique, dissidence spirituelle et societé*, ed. Alain Boureau and Sylvain Piron. Paris: J. Vrin, 1999.

"Participer au bien commun: la notion franciscaine d'appartenance à la civitas," in *De Bono Communi: discours et pratique du Bien Commun dans les villes d'Europe occidentale (XIIIe–XVIe siècles)*, ed. Elodie Lecuppre-Desjardins and Anne-Laure Van Bruaene. Turnhout: Brepols, 2010, 225–35.

Il prezzo della salvezza: lessici medievale del pensiero economico. Rome: La Nuova Italia Scientifica, 1994.

"La riflessione etica sulle attività economiche," in *Economie urbane ed etica economica nell'Italia medievale*, ed. Roberto Greci. Rome: Laterza, 2005.

Torrell, Jean-Pierre, *Saint Thomas Aquinas: The Person and his Work*, trans. Robert Royal, vol. I. Washington, DC: Catholic University of America Press, 2005.

Touwaide, Alain, "La thérapeutique médicamenteuse de Dioscoride à Galien: du pharmaco-centrisme au médico-centrisme," in *Galen on Pharmacology: Philosophy, History, and Medicine*, ed. Armelle Debru. Leiden: Brill, 1997, 255–82.

Valois, Noël, "Jean de Jandun et Marsile de Padoue: auteurs du *Defensor Pacis*," *Histoire littéraire de la France* 33 (1906), 528–623.

Van der Lugt, Maaike, *Le ver, le démon et la Vierge: les théories médiévales de la génération extraordinaire. Une étude sur les rapports entre théologie, philosophie naturelle et médecine*. Paris: Les Belles Lettres, 2004.

"Neither Ill nor Healthy: The Intermediate State between Health and Disease in Medieval Medicine," *Quaderni storici* 136 (2011), 13–46.

Vauchez, André, "'Ordo Fraternitatis': Confraternities and Lay Piety in the Middle Ages," in *The Laity in the Middle Ages: Religious Beliefs and Devotional Practices*, ed. Daniel Bornstein, trans. Margery Schneider. University of Notre Dame Press, 1993, 107–17.

Vélez-Sáenz, Jaime, *The Doctrine of the Common Good of Civil Society in the Works of St. Thomas Aquinas*. University of Notre Dame Press, 1951.

Veraja, Fabiano, *Le origini della controversia teologica sul contratto di censo nel XIII secolo*. Rome: Edizioni di Storia e Letteratura, 1960.

Wallace, William A., *Prelude to Galileo: Essays on Medieval and Sixteenth-Century Sources of Galileo's Thought*, ed. Roger Cohen. Dordrecht: Reidel, 1981.

Wei, Ian, *Intellectual Culture in Medieval Paris: Theologians and the University c. 1100–1330*. Cambridge University Press, 2012.

Weisheipl, James A., "Albert's Works on Natural Science in Probable Chronological Order," in *Albertus Magnus and the Sciences: Commemorative Essays, 1980*, ed. James A. Weisheipl. Toronto: Pontifical Institute of Mediaeval Studies, 1980, Appendix I.

Friar Thomas d'Aquino: His Life, Thought, and Works. Washington, DC: Catholic University of America Press, 1983.

"The Place of Dumbleton and the Merton School," *Isis* 50 (1959), 439–54.

White, Lynn, Jr., "The Iconography of *Temperantia* and the Virtuousness of Technology," in *Action and Conviction in Early Modern Europe: Essays in Memory of E. H. Harbison*, ed. Theodore Rabb and Jerrold E. Siegel. Princeton University Press, 1969, 197–219.

Wilkie, J. S. and G. E. R. Lloyd, "The Arabic Version of Galen's *Ars Parva*," *Journal of Hellenic Studies* 101 (1981), 145–8.

Willard, Charity Cannon, "Christine de Pisan's 'Clock of Temperance,'" *L'Esprit Créateur* 2 (1962), 149–54.

Wippel, John F., *The Metaphysical Thought of Godfrey of Fontaines: A Study in Late Thirteenth-Century Philosophy*. Washington, DC: Catholic University of America Press, 1981.

Wittreck, Fabian, *Geld als Instrument der Gerechtigkeit: Die Geldrechtslehre des Hl. Thomas von Aquin in ihrem interkulturellen Kontext*. Paderborn: Ferdinand Schöningh, 2002.

Wolter, Alan B., *John Duns Scotus' Political and Economic Philosophy*. St. Bonaventure, NY: Franciscan Institute Publications, 2001.

Youskevitch, A. P., "La place de Nicole Oresme dans le développement des sciences mathématiques," in *Nicolas Oresme: tradition et innovation*, ed. Pierre Souffrin and A. P. Segonds. Paris: Les Belles Lettres, 1998, 115–24.

Ziegler, Joseph, *Medicine and Religion c. 1300: The Case of Arnau de Vilanova*. Oxford University Press, 1998.

"Philosophers and Physicians on the Scientific Validity of Latin Physiognomy, 1200–1500," *Early Science and Medicine* 12 (2007), 285–312.

"*Ut Dicunt Medici*: Medical Knowledge and Theological Debates in the Second Half of the Thirteenth Century," *Bulletin of the History of Medicine* 73 (1999), 208–37.

Zuckerman, Charles, "The Relationship of Theories of Universals to Theories of Church Government in the Middle Ages: A Critique of Previous Views," *Journal of the History of Ideas* 36 (1975), 579–94.

Zupko, Jack, *John Buridan: Portrait of a Fourteenth-Century Arts Master*. University of Notre Dame Press, 2002.

Index

Marsilius of Padua (cont.)
  conception of the "human legislator,"
    327–9
  Defensor pacis, 299–343
  emphasis on good fit and function,
    319–21
  influence of Galenic model of
    equalization, 303–5, 309–12, 315–17,
    319–21
  law as instrument of equalization, 322–3
  new model of equilibrium applied to
    election, 330–5
  new model of equilibrium applied to law
    and authority, 323–30
  ordering of parts within the political body,
    318–19
  relativity applied to political "health,"
    319–21
Merton mean speed theorem
  and the new model of equilibrium, 410–11,
    421–4
  framed geometrically by Oresme, 421–4
models of equality and equalization
  as medium between environment and
    intellection, 14–15, 19, 468–70
  assessing the Galenic model, 179–82
  characteristics of, 4–5, 11, 18–19,
    189–92, 467
  components of the "older" model, 254–6,
    259–62
  formative influences on, 12–17, 222–7
  links to the model of justice, 235–40
  Thomistic model, 258–62
money
  as instrument of equalization (Aristotle),
    45–7, 91–3
  as instrument of equalization (Oresme),
    355–7
money-changers, 268, 270, 274, 277
multiplication
  and merchant profit, 121–2
  and the seminal nature of capital, 66–9
  and the urban marketplace, 285–8
  in mathematics and natural philosophy,
    402–7, 431–4
  integrated into economic *aequalitas*,
    118–23
  progression by "doubling" introduced
    into medical thought, 218–22,
    402–3
  progression by "doubling" introduced
    into physical thought, 400–4

Naviganti (1237)
  and usury theory, 35

neutrum
  relation to balance in Galen's thought,
    141–4, 153
  relation to balance in Taddeo Alderotti,
    198–202
  relation to balance in Turisanus, 229–30
new model of equilibrium
  a list of distinguishing elements, 5–11
  and Bradwardine's "rule," 404–6
  and Jean de Jandun's "impetus of desire,"
    291–2
  and Oresme's geometry of qualities,
    413–24
  and the Common Good in Oresme's
    De moneta, 350–4
  and the Merton mean-speed theorem,
    410–11, 421–4
  applied to both medical body and political
    body, 235–40
  applied to economic thought (Olivi),
    70–5, 106–27
  applied to election and the Common
    Good (Marsilius), 330–5
  applied to law and political order
    (Marsilius), 323–30
  applied to mathematical thought
    (Bradwardine), 404–6
  applied to political thought (Marsilius),
    317–19, 325–8
  applied to the motion of the earth,
    455–6
  applied to the political body (Oresme's
    De moneta), 358–66
  applied to the rotation of the earth,
    456–62
  applied to the workings of nature
    (Buridan), 442–55
  applied to the workings of the cosmos
    (Oresme), 429–42, 459–62
  cessation and retreat in multiple
    disciplines, 345–6, 473–84
  cessation and retreat in natural
    philosophy, 427–8, 473–4
  cessation and retreat in Oresme's
    Politiques, 368–76, 384–97
  contrast with the "old" model, 243,
    254–7, 258–62, 294–8, 383–4,
    476–80
  contrasts to harmony, 11, 435–41
  distinguished from mechanical order,
    451–4
  emergence in economic thought, 222–7
  emergence in medical thought, 213–27
  represented in art, 281–2
  represented in literature, 282–94

17098595R00292

Printed in Great Britain
by Amazon